Contesting the Saudi State

The terms Wahhabi or Salafi are seen as interchangeable and frequently misunderstood by outsiders. However, as Madawi Al-Rasheed explains in a fascinating exploration of Saudi Arabia in the twenty-first century, even Saudis do not agree on their meaning. Under the influence of mass education, printing, new communication technology, and global media, they are forming their own conclusions and debating religion and politics in traditional and novel venues, often violating official taboos and the conservative values of Saudi society. Drawing on classical religious sources, contemporary readings and interviews, Al-Rasheed presents an ethnography of consent and contest, exploring the fluidity of the boundaries between the religious and political. Bridging the gap between text and context, the author also examines how states and citizens manipulate religious discourse for purely political ends, and how this manipulation generates unpredictable reactions whose control escapes those who initiated them.

MADAWI AL-RASHEED is Professor of Anthropology of Religion at King's College, University of London. She specialises in Saudi history, society, politics and religion. Her recent publications include *A History of Saudi Arabia* (2002) and *Transnational Connections and the Arab Gulf* (2005).

Cambridge Middle East Studies 25

Cambridge Middle East Studies has been established to publish books on the nineteenth- and twentieth-century Middle East and North Africa. The aim of the series is to provide new and original interpretations of aspects of Middle Eastern societies and their histories. To achieve disciplinary diversity, books will be solicited from authors writing in a wide range of fields including history, sociology, anthropology, political science, and political economy. The emphasis will be on producing books offering an original approach along theoretical and empirical lines. The series is intended for students and academics, but the more accessible and wide-ranging studies will also appeal to the interested general reader.

A list of books in the series can be found after the index.

Contesting the Saudi State

Islamic Voices from a New Generation

Madawi Al-Rasheed

University of London

CAMBRIDGE
UNIVERSITY PRESS

CAMBRIDGE UNIVERSITY PRESS

Cambridge, New York, Melbourne, Madrid, Cape Town, Singapore, São Paulo

Cambridge University Press
The Edinburgh Building, Cambridge CB2 2RU, UK

Published in the United States of America by Cambridge University Press,
New York

www.cambridge.org
Information on this title: www.cambridge.org/9780521858366

First published 2007

Printed in the United Kingdom at the University Press, Cambridge

A catalogue record for this publication is available from the British Library

ISBN-13 978-0-521-85836-6 hardback

A prince is always compelled to injure those who have made him the new ruler, subjecting them to the troops and imposing the endless other hardships which his new conquest entails   Niccolo Machiavelli *The Prince*

Contents

Glossary

ahfad al-sahaba	grandsons of the companions of the Prophet
ahl al-dhimma	people of the book, Christians and Jews
ahl al-hadith	those who interpret the Prophetic tradition literally
ahl al-hall wa 'l-ʿaqd	decision makers (lit. 'people who loose and tie')
ahl al-qibla	people who face Mecca for prayer
ahl al-sunna wa 'l-jamaʿa	Sunnis (lit. 'people of the tradition of the Prophet and community')
ahl al-tawhid	people of monotheism
aimat al-daʿwa al-najdiyya	Najdi religious scholars
amir (pl. *umara*)	ruler, prince
amr bi 'l-maʿruf wa 'l-nahy ʿan al-munkar	promotion of virtue and prohibition of vice
ʿaqida	creed
asl	principle
baghi (pl. *bughat*)	usurper
baraʾ	dissociation from infidels
bayʿa	oath of allegiance
bidʿa	innovation, heresy
bilad al-haramayn	the Land of the Two Holy Mosques
daʿif	weak
daʿiyya (f. *daʿiyyat*; pl. *duʿat*)	preacher
daʿwa	religious call, mission
dawla	state
dawlat al-tawhid	monotheist polity
dhal	one who has gone astray
dhalal	debauchery, obscurity
duʿat al-islah	reformers
fajir	sinful, despotic
fard ʿayn	an obligation incumbent upon every Muslim

fard kifaya	an obligation performed by a sufficient number of Muslims
fasiq	debauched
fatwa	religious opinion issued by *shari'a* expert
al-fi'a al-dhalla	the group that has gone astray
fiqh	Islamic jurisprudence
fitna	strife, dissent
Hadith	tradition, saying of the Prophet
hajr al-mubta'di'	ostracisation of innovators
hakim	ruler
hakimiyya	sovereignty
haraki	politicised activist
haram	forbidden
harb 'ala al-kuffar	a battle against the infidels
hayat al-amr bi'l-ma 'ruf wa 'l-nahy 'an al-munkar	Committee for the Promotion of Virtue and Prohibition of Vice
hijra	migration
hizb al-ghulat	radicals
hizbiyya	adherence to party politics
hizb al-wulat	loyalists
'ibada (pl. *'ibadat*)	Islamic rituals, worship
ijtihad	applying reason to reach a religious ruling
'ilm	knowledge
'ilmani (pl. *'ilmaniyyun*)	secular, secularist
imama	state, leadership of the Muslim state
inkar al-munkar	disavowing the abominable
iqamat al-hadd (pl. *iqamat al-hudud*)	punishment
islah	reform
islahi (f. *islahiyya*; pl. *islahiyyin, islahiyyat*)	reformer
jahil	one who is ignorant
jahiliyya	the age of ignorance
ja'ir	despot
jami'at al-'ulama	association of *'ulama*
jazirat al-'arab/jazira al-'arabiyya	the Arabian Peninsula
jihad	exertion, struggle for the way of God
kafir (pl. *kafirun*)	unbeliever, blasphemous
khawarij al-'asr	contemporary Kharijites
al-khitab al-dini	religious discourse
khuruj bi 'l-sayf	violent rebellion

khuruj siyasi	political rebellion
khuruj ʿala wali al-amr/ *khuruj ʿala al-hakim*	rebellion against the ruler
kitab	book
kufr	unbelief, blasphemy
kufr bawwah/kufran *bawahan*	obvious blasphemy
maʿasi	minor sins
madhhab (pl. *madhahib*)	school of jurisprudence
majlis	meeting, council, study circle
majlis al-hiwar al-watani	National Dialogue Forum
majlis al-shura	consultative council
maʿruf	that which is known in *shariʿa*
maslaha	interest, public good
muʿahadin	infidels enjoying a protected contractual relationship with Muslims
muʿamalat jaʾiza	permissible relations
mufti	jurisconsult, highest religious authority
al-muhajirun	the Muslims who migrated from Mecca with the Prophet
mujahidun	Jihadis
munafiq (pl. *munafiqun*)	hypocrite
munkar	evil
murabitun ʿala al-thugur	'tied to the fortresses'
mushrik (pl. *mushrikun*)	polytheists, blasphemers
mutʿa	temporary marriage
mutawaʿ (pl. *mutawaʾa*)	religious specialist
muthaqaf	intellectual associated with acquiring Western knowledge
muwahhidun	monotheists
naqidh lil islam (pl. *nawaqidh al-Islam*)	that which removes a Muslim from the religious community and Islam
nidham	legislation
nidham kufr	a blasphemous regime
nifaq	hypocrisy
nukhba	elite
al-nukhba al-fikriyya	intellectual elite
qadi	judge
qaʿidun	those left behind (lit. 'sitting')
qiyas	deduction by analogy
raʿiyya	subjects
al-sahabiyyat	early female companions

sahwa	awakening
al-salaf al-salih	pious ancestors
shabab	youth
shari'a	Islamic legal codes and rules
sheikh	tribal leader, religious scholar, notable
shirk	blasphemy, heresy, polytheism
shubuhat (sg. *shubuha*)	misguided opinions
shura	consultation
sunna	tradition of the Prophet (words and deeds)
sura	Quranic verse
taghut (pl. *tawaghit*)	despot, idol
tajdid al-khitab al-dini	renewing religious discourse
takfir	excommunication
takfir al-mu'ayan	the excommunication of an individual
takfir al-mujtama'	the excommunication of an entire society
takfir al-'umum	mass excommunication
taraju'at	going back on previous opinions, repentance
taraju'at qasriyya	forced repentance
tariqa (pl. *turuq*)	Sufi way
tawba	repentance
tawhid	doctrine of the oneness of God
tawwali	subservience through loyalty
tawwali al-kuffar	subservience to infidels
tayar	movement, trend
tayar al-haraki	organised Islamist movement
tazkiyya	an approval certificate
'ulama (sg. *'alim*)	religious scholar, scientist
'ulama al-sultan	the religious establishment
umami	global
umma	the Muslim community
wala'	association, loyalty
al-wala' wa 'l-bara'	association with Muslims and dissociation from infidels
wali al-amr (pl. *wulat al-amr*)	ruler, the one who is in charge of affairs
wasat (n. *wasatiyya*)	centrist
watan	homeland
wataniyya	citizenship
zaffat al-shahid	celebration of a martyr
zakat	Islamic tax

Foreign words and phrases

ʿashʿash fiha al-shaytan	the abode of Satan
ʿahd	oath
ahfad al-sahaba	grandsons of the companions of the Prophet
ʿahirat al-rum	'Roman prostitutes' (Pejoratively American female soldiers on Saudi soil)
ahkam	rules
ahl al-dhalal	those who have gone astray
ahl al-dhimma	people of the book, Christians and Jews
ahl al-fiqh	people of jurisprudence
ahl al-hadith	those who interpret the Prophetic tradition literally
ahl al-hall wa 'l-ʿaqd	decision makers (lit. 'people who loose and tie')
ahl al-qibla	people who face Mecca for prayer
ahl-al-sulban	Christians (lit. 'people of the cross')
ahl al-sunna wa 'l-jamaʿa	Sunnis (lit. 'people of the tradition of the Prophet and community')
ahl al-tawhid	people of monotheism
ahzab siyasiyya	political parties
ʾaima	religious scholars
aimat al-daʿwa al-najdiyya	Najdi religious scholars
ajnabi	foreigner
ʿajuz	old
akhtar ghaltha	more harsh
aman	peace
amir (pl *umara*)	ruler, prince
ʿamm	public
amr bi 'l-maʿruf wa 'l-nahy ʿan al-munkar	promotion of virtue and prohibition of vice
ansab	genealogies
al-ansar	supporters of the early Muslim immigrants in Madina
ʿaqida	creed
ʿaql	reason
aqwal al-sahaba	sayings of the Prophet's companions
ʿaris	bridegroom
ʿarus	bride
asl	principle
ʾasr	captivity

al-awliya	pious men
ayam al-dhalal	days of obscurity
azma	crisis
bagdha'	hatred
baghi (pl. *bughat*)	usurper
bara'	dissociation from infidels
bay'a	oath of allegiance
bayn dhuhrani al-mushrikin	living among polytheists
bid'a	innovation, heresy
bilad al-haramayn	the Land of the Two Holy Mosques
burqa'	veil that allows only the eyes to appear
da'if	weak
da'iyya (f. *da'iyyat*; pl. *du'at*)	preacher
da'wa	religious call, mission
dawla	state
dawlat al-tawhid	monotheist polity
dayuuth	pimp
dhal	one who has gone astray
dhalal	debauchery, obscurity
dhikr	devotional recitation
diya	blood money
du'at al-islah	reformers
fajir	sinful, despotic
faqih (pl. *fuqaha'*)	jurist, jurisprudent
fard 'ayn	an obligation incumbent upon every Muslim
fard kifaya	an obligation performed by a sufficient number of Muslims
faridha	duty, obligation
fasad	corruption
fasiq	debauched
fatwa (pl. *fatawa*)	religious opinion issued by *shari'a* expert
al-fi'a al-dhalla	the group that has gone astray
fida'iyyin	soldiers, comrades
fikr shadh	perverse thought
fiqh	Islamic jurisprudence
fiqh al-halal wa 'l-haram	jurisprudence of the permissible and the forbidden
fiqh al-'ibadat	jurisprudence of worship
al-firqa al-dhalla	those who have gone astray
fitna	strife, dissent
fitra	instinct, nature

gafwa	sleep
ghadh al-basar	lowering the gaze
ghazu	raid
ghulat	religious extremists
ghulu	radicalism
ghutra	white headcover
hadith	tradition, saying of the Prophet
hafadhat Quran	people who memorised the Quran
hajj	pilgrimage
hajr al-mubtadi'	ostracisation of innovators
hakim	ruler
hakimiyya	sovereignty
hakim ja'ir	a despotic ruler
hakim kafir	a blasphemous ruler
al-hakim al-munafiq	the hypocrite ruler
haraki	politicised activist
haram	forbidden
harb 'ala al-kuffar	a battle against the infidels
harbi	aggressive
hasad	envy
hayat al-amr bi'l-ma'ruf wa 'l-nahy 'an al-munkar	Committee for the Promotion of Virtue and Prohibition of Vice
hayba	aura, authority
hijab	veil
hijra	migration
himla salibiyya	a crusade
hisba	accountability
hizb al-ghulat	radicals
hizbiyya	adherence to party politics
hizb al-wulat	loyalists
hudud	punishments
hukam al-riyadh	(pejoratively) the rulers of Riyadh
al-hukm al-jabri	coercive rule
hurra	free woman
'ibada (pl. *'ibadat*)	Islamic rituals, worship
iftar	breakfast
ijma'	consensus
ijtihad	applying reason to reach a religious ruling
'ilm	knowledge
'ilmani (pl. *'ilmaniyyun*)	secular, secularist
iltizam	commitment to the tradition
imama	state, leadership of the Muslim state

inhizamiyyat al-umma	the defeatist attitude of the *umma*
inkar al-munkar	disavowing the abominable
iqamat al-hadd (pl. *iqamat al-hudud*)	punishment
islah	reform
islahi (f. *islahiyya*; pl. *islahiyyin, islahiyyat*)	reformer
islah al-mawruth al-ijtima'i	reform of social heritage
isti'ana	assistance
istila	seizure of power by force
istirahat al-muharib	a temporary period of rest
itisal	communication
jadwal zamani	timetable
jahil	one who is ignorant
jahiliyya	the age of ignorance
ja'ir	despot
ja'iz	permissible
jami'at al-'ulama	association of *'ulama'*
jariyya	a female slave
jazirat al-'arab, jazirat al-arabiyya	the Arabian Peninsula
jihad	exertion, struggle for the way of God
jihad 'amali	practical *jihad*
jihad daf'i	defensive *jihad*
jihad hadari	civilisational struggle
jihad madani	a civil *jihad*
jihad nadhari	theoretical *jihad*
jihad qitali	military struggle
jihad talab	offensive *jihad*
junun al-'adhama	grandiose madness
kaffara	compensation in money or deeds
kafir (pl. *kafirun*)	unbeliever, blasphemous
kahanut	clergy
al-kalima	'the word'
khal'	forcing a ruler to leave office
al-khassa	an elite minority
khawarij al-'asr	contemporary Kharijites
al-khitab al-dini	religious discourse
khubth	filth
khuruj 'aqa'idi	religious rebellion
khuruj bi al-sayf	violent rebellion
khuruj siyasi	political rebellion

khuruj ʿala wali al-amr/ khuruj ʿala al-hakim	rebellion against the ruler
kitab	book
al-kitab wa 'l-sunna	the book and the deeds of the Prophet
kitman	concealing God's message as revealed in the Quran
kufr	unbelief, blasphemy
kufr bawwah/kufran bawahan	obvious blasphemy
maʿahid	institutes
maʿasi	minor sins
madhhab (pl. *madhahib*)	school of jurisprudence
madrasa	school
mafahim	understanding
mahram	male guardian
maharim	forbidden women (close relatives such as mother, sister etc.)
majlis	meeting, council, study circle
majlis al-hiwar al-watani	National Dialogue Forum
majlis nuwab	a parliament
majlis al-shura	consultative council
maqasid al-shariʿa	the objectives of *shariʿa*
maʿruf	that which is known in *shariʿa*
mashaykh al-haydh	'the sheikhs of menstruation'
maʿsiyya	sins
maslaha	interest, public good
mawada	affection
al-mawruth al-ijtimaʿi	inherited social tradition
millat al-kufr	the religion of blasphemy
mithaq	treaty
muʿahadin	infidels enjoying a protected contractual relationship with Muslims
muʿamalat jaʾiza	permissible relationship
al-muʾawal	interpreted religious discourse
mubdiʿun	innovators
mubiqat	grave sins
mufakir Islami	a Muslim thinker
mufaraqat al-hayat	leaving life
mufti	jurisconsult, highest religious authority
al-muhajirun	the Muslims who migrated from Mecca with the Prophet
mujahidun	Jihadis
mujtahid	scholar entitled to give individual opinions

mukataba	writing (to the ruler)
mukhalafat	errors
mulhid	atheist
mulk	kingship
munafiq (pl. *munafiqun*)	hypocrite
munathirun	armchair theoreticians
al-munazal	revealed religious discourse
munkar	evil
muqalid	follower of a previous generation of scholars
murabitun ʿala al-thugur	'tied to the battlefield'
murtadd	apostate
mushʿawithun	charlatans
mushrik (pl. *mushrikun*)	polytheists, blasphemers
al-mustabid al-ʿadil	a just despot
mustahab	desirable
mustawtanat	(colonial) settlements
mutʿa	temporary marriage
mutadayin	religious, observant
mutawa (pl. *mutawaʿa*)	religious specialist
mutawwaʿin	low-ranking Wahhabi preachers
muthaqaf	intellectual associated with acquiring Western knowledge
muwahhidun	monotheists
muwalat	an affectionate relationship with infidels
najs	impure, polluting
naqidh lil islam (pl. *nawaqidh al-Islam*)	that which removes a Muslim from the religious community and Islam
naql	tradition
nashid	songs
nasiha	advice
nidham	new legislation
nidham kufr	a blasphemous regime
nifaq	hypocrisy
nifaq ʿamali	practical hypocrisy
nifaq ʿaqadi	'creed' hypocrisy
niʿma	grace
nukhba	elite
al-nukhba al-fikriyya	intellectual elite
qadi	judge
qahr	coercion
qaʿidun	those left behind (lit. 'sitting')

qawi	strong
qiyas	deduction by analogy
quburi	grave-worshipper
al-quwa al-mutadharira	those who are hurt by reform
rafidha	rejectionists
rahat	crowd
ra'iyya	subjects
rijal din	clergy
sabb	insult
sad al-thara'i'	prohibition of acts that might violate the law (lit. 'blocking the means')
al-sahabiyyat	early Muslim women
sahwa	awakening
al-salaf al-salih	pious ancestors
al-sha'b	the people
shabab	youth
shabab al-sahwa	the youth of the awakening
al-shahada	the Muslim declaration of faith
al-sha'n al-'am	public affairs
shari'a	Islamic legal codes and rules
sheikh	tribal leader, religious scholar, notable
shirk	blasphemy, heresy, polytheism
shirk asghar	'the minor association', a lesser blasphemy
shirk akbar	'the great association', a major blasphemy
shirk jadid	new blasphemy
shubuhat (sg. *shubuha*)	misguided opinions
shura	consultation
sunna	tradition of the Prophet (words and deeds)
sura	Quranic verse
ta'asub	fanaticism
taghut (pl. *tawaghit*)	despot, idol
tahkim al-shar'	application of *shari'a*
ta'iyyin	the appointment of a successor by the current ruler (hereditary rule)
tajdid al-khitab al-dini	renewing religious discourse
takfir	excommunication
takfir al-mu'ayan	the excommunication of an individual
takfir al-mujtama'	the excommunication of an entire society
takfir al-'umum	mass excommunication
tamasuh	touching
tanbih	to alert
taraf fikri	intellectual luxury

taraju'at	going back on previous opinions, repentance
taraju'at qasriyya	forced repentance
tarasubat wa tarakumat ijtima'iyya	social norms
tari'	temporary, accidental
tariqa (pl. *turuq*)	Sufi way
tarikh	history
tashabuh bi 'l-kuffar	imitating infidels
al-tatarus bi 'l-nisa	using women as human shields in time of combat
tatbiqat	application
ta'til faridhat al-jihad	suspending the obligation of *jihad*
tawba	repentance
tawhid	doctrine of the oneness of God
ta'wil	interpretation
tawwali	subservience through loyalty
tawwali al-kuffar	subservience to infidels
tayar	movement
tayar al-haraki	organised Islamist movement
tazkiyat al-hakim	praising the ruler
tazkiyya	an approval certificate
thaqafat al-jihad	a culture of *jihad*
thawb	male robes
thulathi al-takfir	trinity of excommunication
tughyan	oppression, despotism
turath	heritage
'ulama (sing. *'alim*)	religious scholar, scientist
'ulama al-sultan	the religious establishment
uli al-amr	those charged with authority
'ulum shari'yya	religious knowledge
'umala	traitors
umami	global
umma	Muslim community
al-umma al-muntasira	'the victorious party'
'umra	minor pilgrimage
al-'unsor al-da'if	the weak element
'unsoriyya	racist
'uqal	head-rope
'uyub	faults, shameful behaviour
wala'	association, loyalty
al-wala' wa 'l-bara'	association with Muslims and dissociation from infidels

wali al-amr (pl. *wulat al-amr*)	ruler, the one who is in charge of affairs
warathat al-anbiya'	heirs of the Prophets
wasat (n. *wasatiyya*)	centrist
watan	homeland
wataniyya	citizenship
wilaya ʿama	high leadership
yahsum al-khiyar	a final resolution
zaffa	wedding celebration
zaffat al-shahid	celebration of a martyr
zakat	Islamic tax
zawaj al-misyar	'visiting marriage', a marriage without formal obligations
ziyara	visit

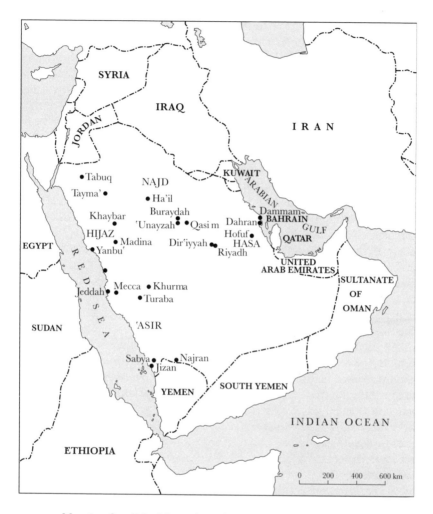

Map 1.   Saudi Arabia, main regions and cities.

Source: F. Clements, *Saudi Arabia,World Bibliographical Series* (Oxford: Clio Press, 1979; reprinted 1988). Courtesy of Clio Press.

Introduction: debating religion and politics in the twenty-first century

This book is an ethnography of consent and contestation. It is about contemporary Saudis who debate politics and religion. Outsiders often refer to Saudis as Wahhabis or Salafis, but in the twenty-first century Saudis themselves no longer agree on the meaning of these terms and many do not accept their validity. Most Saudis believe that there is no separation between religion and politics at the level of public discourse. Yet the majority agree that in practice there is a separation between the professed religious rhetoric of the state, on the one hand, and the reality of political practice, on the other. Calls for the reformation of state and society always invoke religion and politics together in a single framework. This book focuses on what I call Wahhabi religio-political discourse, the sum total of interpretations that draw on religion to comprehend, justify, sanction or challenge politics. This discourse is rooted in the Wahhabi tradition and the intellectual heritage of its *'ulama*. Wahhabi interpretations are the dominant intellectual reference point.

Some scholars claim that authoritarianism generates conceptual impotence. Others argue that authoritarian rule produces development outcomes that are either very good or very bad. In the Saudi case, authoritarianism has generated consenting subjects, incomplete projects, diverted journeys, betrayal and opportunism – but not intellectual impotence. Saudi authoritarianism has led to consent and confrontation at the same time. The regime, together with a mushrooming religious bureaucracy, created a world that insisted on complete submission to political authority while preaching total submission to God. Rather than being paralysed by impotence, the Saudis have produced a complex intellectual tapestry, woven by debating subjects, some of whom consent while others confront. Against the background of authoritarianism, vibrant diversity, pluralism and debate has arisen. There is also blind and indiscriminate violence. Violence is committed by a state that demands complete surrender to its will and by a minority that challenges this surrender. Both the state and its subjects are engaged in perpetual cycle of real and symbolic violence. The majority of ordinary Saudis are either

1

spectators or active participants in volatile debates about religion, politics and society.

Wahhabiyya and Salafiyya

Wahhabiyya is a label imposed on people who would rather call themselves simply Muslims. In the past, so-called Wahhabis preferred to be known as *al-muwahhidun* or *ahl al-tawhid* (monotheists), but today this appellation is rather archaic. Many *al-muwahhidun* would probably prefer to be known as Salafiyyun. In this book, I will retain the name Wahhabiyya to refer to the Saudi variant of Salafiyya, thus applying the Arab saying that 'a known error is better than an unknown correctness' ('khata shai' ahsan min sawab majhul'). My justification for retaining the name Wahhabiyya is based on the assumption that there is a body of religious knowledge that has common intellectual ancestry, without assuming that this factor gives the discourse rigid unity or coherence.

In this study, Wahhabiyya is considered a fragmented but hegemonic religious discourse. It is distinguished from other Sunni Muslim religious discourses by its own specific interpretations and interpreters. Wahhabiyya is simply a religious worldview that can promote both consent and contestation, depending on the context in which its teachings and texts are interpreted. This book tries to bridge the gap between text and context. Politically, Wahhabiyya can be both quietist and revolutionary, as will be shown here.

In its early eighteenth-century phase, Wahhabiyya[1] proved to be conducive to political centralisation, and did contribute to the formation of the first Saudi–Wahhabi emirate (1744–1818).[2] The historical alliance between sheikh Muhammad ibn Abd al-Wahhab and Muhammad ibn Saud led to the formation of the first Saudi state. This state expanded in Arabia under the pretext of purifying faith from innovation and applying Islamic law. Wahhabi enthusiasm and military expansion led to the Egyptian invasion of Arabia, under the patronage of the Ottoman sultan, early in the nineteenth century. While the political leadership, mainly the Al-Saud, were temporarily removed from the Arabian scene, the Wahhabi movement remained alive, although it avoided direct confrontation with the Ottoman empire after the Egyptian invasion. However, it seems that Wahhabis learned a serious lesson from the Egyptian annihilation of their power base in Deriyyah in 1818: they learned to be pragmatic. Wahhabis survived afterwards because they supported political power, which meant moderating religious zeal. Since then, Wahhabi scholars have accepted a subservient position. They lived in the shadow of the sultan. While this history does not concern us here, it is important to remember its contours because it continues to affect the way religion and politics coexist in Saudi Arabia in the twenty-first century.

Salafiyya is a methodology that invokes the literal interpretation of religious texts, and the return to the early tradition of the pious companions of the Prophet. It must be said that there is no consensus among Sunni Muslims on who the pious ancestors (*al-salaf al-salih*) were, although the majority of scholars would probably identify them as including the first generation that accompanied the Prophet. Other Sunnis might stretch the *salaf* to include three generations after the Prophet. For some contemporary advocates, Salafiyya dates back to the works of medieval scholars who called for literal interpretations of religious texts. Some contemporary Islamists argue that Salafiyya is rooted in medieval theology, especially the early calls to return to the Quran and Sunna (tradition of the Prophet), associated with Ahmad ibn Hanbal (780–855), Ibn Taymiyya (1268–1328) and their followers.

As a descriptor, Salafiyya is a modern term, dating back to the late nineteenth-century Islamic reformist movements, especially the one associated with Azharite Muhammad Abduh (1849–1905) and the activist Jamal al-Din al-Afghani (1839–97). The Saudi Wahhabi Salafiyya does not have much in common with this modernist Salafiyya. Muhammad Abduh preached a reformist–modernist Salafiyya while Wahhabiyya was a revivalist Salafi movement, concerned mainly with the purification of religious practice and the application of *shari'a*. Modernist Salafiyya grew as a result of the encounter with the West and as the result of a quest for advancement. The Wahhabi Salafiyya emerged in central Arabia prior to this encounter, although Western powers were beginning to encircle Arabia in the eighteenth century. Its main objective was the purification of faith and worship. The eighteenth-century Wahhabi Salafi tradition had a more limited objective than that propagated by modernist Salafis. When contemporary Wahhabis invoke *al-salaf al-salih*, one is led to believe that Sheikh Muhammad ibn Abd al-Wahhab could be counted among them, but not many Sunni Muslims would agree.

In the twenty-first century, those who call themselves Salafis are engaged in fierce debate among themselves to define who is a Salafi and who is not. As there is no agreement over the meaning of Salafiyya or who is a Salafi, I am inclined to consider it an elastic identity that is invoked to convey a meaning or several meanings. In the West today, Salafiyya represents extreme radicalism, intolerance, backwardness and violence. In Western media and even scholarly work, Salafis are portrayed as 'fundamentalists' and potential terrorists. Yet for others outside the West, Salafiyya represents authentic, unmediated Islam. For those people, Salafiyya means worshipping God according to the Quran and the tradition of the Prophet, transmitted by those who were his contemporaries, without the mediation of later generations.[3] According to advocates of Salafiyya, the movement empowers the ordinary worshipper, who is no longer dependent on a wide circle of interpreters. A Salafi can be actively involved in interpretation himself, provided that he has a basic standard of knowledge and literacy. Modernity encouraged and perpetuated Salafiyya. Literacy and mass communication favour its survival in contemporary Muslim society. Salafiyya and modernity are inseparable.

Eighteenth-century Wahhabiyya was the main impetus behind political centralisation in Arabia. Without Wahhabiyya, there would have been no Al-Saud and no Kingdom of Saudi Arabia. However, in the twenty-first century, Wahhabiyya continues to support the power it created and defended. In its official version, Wahhabiyya is the discourse of power legitimisation. From its early eighteenth-century history, it developed religious interpretations to legitimise political power which led to deep grounding in authoritarianism, and even despotism, within Islam. Wahhabiyya sanctioned a regime that claims to rule according to Islam but in reality in the twenty first century retains only Islamic rhetoric and external trappings. The latter include public beheadings, excluding women from the public sphere, closing shops for prayers as well as other orchestrated and dramatised displays of religiosity. The exclusion and confinement of women have become a symbol for the piety of the Saudi state. Islam is consequently reduced to this dimension. In reality the regime operates according to personalised political gains rather than religious dogma or national interest.

Under state control Wahhabi interpreters – for example, *'ulama*, intellectuals and activists – gradually developed into a class of *noblesse d'état*. Although Saudi *'ulama* appear to enjoy more power, financial resources, prestige and privileges than their counterparts elsewhere in the Muslim world, it must be emphasised that the modern state has pushed them towards a ceremonial role. This does not rule out influence and control: unlike their counterparts in other Arab countries, Wahhabi scholars have considerable control over the social sphere. However, like other official religious scholars in the Arab world, Wahhabis lost control over policy and politics to royalty and state bureaucrats and technocrats – the political sphere is beyond Wahhabi control. In order to survive in a changing world, interpreters of Wahhabiyya accepted this reality, which had serious consequences. The Saudi state is not a Wahhabi state, as claimed by amateur observers. State policy is determined by a coterie of individuals who do not have Wahhabiyya as their reference paradigm, but who use it as a convenient device to cloak their personal political activities. Outside observers often do not distinguish between the 'Wahhabised' social sphere and Saudi politics.

Like the political regime it supports and sanctions, Wahhabiyya is authoritarian. It does not tolerate difference in opinion, and fears any theological debate which may result in questioning either its own monopoly over religious interpretation or the legitimacy of the political power it supports. It abides by the maxim of *hajr al-mubta'di*, an old principle grounded in religious texts that calls for the ostracisation of innovators, defined as those who do not share Wahhabi teachings. Wahhabis ostracise the 'other', especially the Muslim other. They shun their adversaries for fear of contaminating or shaking their own beliefs. Yet Wahhabiyya is constantly engaged in vigorous preaching (*d'awa*), both inside and outside Saudi Arabia. This, however, is different from debate with the other, who does not share Wahhabi interpretations. Official Wahhabiyya is religiously dogmatic, socially conservative and politically acquiescent.

Saudi Arabia may have a single dominant official religious discourse, commonly referred to as Salafi Wahhabiyya, but in the shadow of this discourse there are people who are engaged in challenging, redefining, destroying and reinterpreting it. Today in Saudi Arabia, as elsewhere in the world, there is no monopoly over religious knowledge, thanks to new communication technology, literacy and printing. A religious tradition such as the Wahhabiyya was based on the interpretation of a closed circle of scholars, who trace their intellectual genealogy to the interpretations of Muhammad ibn Abd al-Wahhab. Today, Wahhabiyya itself is not produced and reproduced only by this closed circle; it is both asserted and challenged by people who are brought up on its teachings but who may belong to regions in Saudi Arabia outside that of its earlier advocates. *'Ulama*, intellectuals and laymen are engaged in a fierce debate that not only touches upon religious matters but spills over to politics, history and society. Yet in the twenty-first century Wahhabiyya remains the main intellectual background against which both consent and confrontation are understood, assessed and measured.

Given the historical marginality of central Arabia where Wahhabiyya originated in the eighteenth century, the movement would most probably have shared the fate of other eighteenth- and nineteenth-century revivalist movements in the Muslim world:[4] it would have gone down in historical imagination as a nuisance to the Ottoman Empire in one of its most far-flung, insignificant territories. However, the Saudi regime hoped that the combination of *da'wa* (call) and *dawla* (state), together with a changing regional Arab power context would shift the centre from Egypt to Saudi Arabia in the second half of the twentieth century.[5] This granted Wahhabiyya a hegemonic status unmatched by its early humble eighteenth-century intellectual credentials. The small size of the Saudi population and its limited development at the time militated against

Saudi Arabia replacing Egypt but it became more influential. Since the 1970s, oil wealth has allowed this religious tradition greater visibility – not only in Saudi Arabia, but also abroad.

Wahhabiyya's historical alliance with an absolutist monarchical state under the leadership of the dynastic Al-Saud family, which became extremely rich as a result of oil revenues, allowed the movement greater visibility while at the same time bestowing legitimacy on the political leadership. Oil wealth brought to Saudi Arabia mass education, printing, communication technology, and easy travel and movement: all facilitated the consolidation of Wahhabiyya. Hence Najdi Wahhabiyya became prematurely transnationalised under the patronage of the Saudi regime. The religious treatises and epistles of its founding fathers and its latter advocates travelled to all continents. Oil wealth allowed the Saudi regime to be recognised as a major international player, but Wahhabiyya granted it Islamic legitimacy among Muslims, not only in Saudi Arabia, but also worldwide. This legitimacy derived from the claim that the Saudi state is a monotheist state that upholds *shari'a* and Islamic values, in addition to being the protector of the most sacred Islamic shrines, although it only assumed that role in the late 1920s.

Wahhabi discourse generated consent among people who were not naturally predisposed to submit to the political authority that carried its banner. Wahhabiyya not only facilitated conquest but ensured consent after battle. From the very beginning, the Saudi–Wahhabi project was centred on accusing the people of Arabia of being polytheists whose religion needed to be purified and corrected. This required them to submit to the political will of the Al-Saud. Rebelling against the Saudis was no longer a political act but a sin, a violation of the principles of monotheism. Therefore, obeying rulers became a religious duty, part and parcel of worshipping God. This consenting Wahhabi religio-political discourse is today contested from within.

It is ironic that the forces that consolidated the consenting Wahhabi religio-political discourse are also responsible for its contestation. Under state control, Wahhabi discourse mutated and fragmented in an attempt to escape the straitjacket imposed by political power. Furthermore, communication technology, mass education and printing, while allowing the consolidation of this discourse, also led to confrontation with Wahhabiyya. The oil wealth that consolidated Wahhabiyya generated challenging voices. Schisms within Wahhabiyya characterise its religio-political discourse at the turn of the twenty-first century. While the world fears Wahhabiyya, Wahhabiyya itself fears the schisms within its own rank and file. While the Western world condemns Wahhabiyya, Wahhabiyya itself condemns its own people, especially when those people challenge it from within.

Wahhabiyya in the eyes of others

As a religious movement that was tied up with a political project, Wahhabiyyya was always a contested tradition within the Sunni world of Islam. *Ulama* in the immediate vicinity of the centre of Wahhabiyya,[6] together with those in Mecca and Madina,[7] devoted considerable energy to refuting its claims and interpretations. Some local Najdi *ulama* referred to it as 'the fifth *madhhab*', which Sunni *ulama* in Istanbul, Mecca, Cairo, Damascus and Baghdad[8] denounced in long treatises that circulated across the Ottoman Empire.[9] Wahhabiyya regarded Islam in these lands as corrupted, and even as closer to polytheism than to monotheism. It was only natural for those Muslims to defend their religious practices and tradition.

Non-Sunni Muslims – for example, Shi'is, Ismailis, Zaydis and others – immediately felt the greater danger of Wahhabi teaching, which denounced their traditions as contemporary forms of innovation, and even blasphemy.[10] Non-Sunni *ulama* rejected what they regarded as bigoted and uncompromising radicalism associated with the call of Muhammad ibn Abd al-Wahhab. Intellectual battles between Wahhabi advocates and their critics have continued throughout the last 250 years. While on the surface these conflicts were grounded in religion, they nevertheless reflected political concerns. To understand the various responses to Wahhabiyya, one must situate the polemic in the context of competition and rivalry between various power centres and regional groups in the pre-modern world of Islam – mainly Cairo, Damascus, Baghdad and Arabia. The debates between Wahhabis and other Muslims continue until the present day.

For many decades, Western academic wisdom on Wahhabiyya accepted the old Philby–Rentz[11] thesis, which regarded the movement as an authentic revivalist Unitarian Muslim tradition. It was agreed that Wahhabiyya can be rather excessive and rigorous but in no way constitutes a threat to the West, as long as its advocates remained under the control of the Al-Saud. Wahhabiyya even proved to be capable of rendering great services to the Western project of defeating communism in the context of the Cold War and the liberation of Afghanistan. For decades, Western governments whose nationals worked and benefited from Saudi oil had faith in the ability of the Al-Saud to keep the so-called Wahhabis under control by ensuring minimal contact between the expatriate Western minority and Saudi society. For this purpose, the regime confined the Western expatriate elite to luxurious residential compounds while Saudis built high walls around their abodes to 'protect' themselves against the influx of 'infidels'. They also clung to a mixture of religious and social tradition that favoured not only exclusion of the other but also its demonisation. This was neither a sign of an inherent xenophobia nor a national characteristic. It was a defensive reaction to the sudden inundation of 'aliens' with whom there were no common cultural or linguistic grounds. This was clearly reflected in the residential segregation that most Saudi cities experienced since the 1970s.

In the twentieth century, the expatriate Western residential compounds in major Saudi cities constituted a porous boundary, a physical and moral ghetto that a small minority of Saudi locals admired as a refuge from their own restrictive traditions. Such Saudis considered these compounds an escape from rigid morality, excessive prohibitions and surveillance. Other Saudis condemned this segregated physical space, the ghetto that came to symbolise foreign domination, moral bankruptcy, debauchery, corruption and sin. Most, however, tried to ignore the existence of what they regarded a necessary physical evil in the midst of a vast land of piety. Western residential compounds became oases in a Muslim conservative desert. As such they were and still are contested and dangerous 'liminal' spaces. Recently a very small minority endeavoured to eliminate these compounds physically, depicting them as colonial settlements (*mustawtanat*). It is not without significance that the residential expatriate compound was the prime target during the wave of violence that swept Saudi Arabia in 2003.

Common Western wisdom regarded Wahhabis as enigmatic puritans who were best left to their own devices. In the past many Western scholars celebrated the stabilising effect of Wahhabiyya at the level of politics but resented its excessive social conservatism. They would have preferred a socially lax Wahhabiyya that allowed them greater access to Saudi society or more freedoms in this society but guaranteed the stability of the political regime that is seen by many as a 'friend'. But social conservatism and political acquiescence are inseparable in a context such as Saudi Arabia. Nothing annoyed Westerners in Saudi Arabia more than the social aspects of Wahhabiyya – for example, its uncompromising views on sex segregation, the ban on alcohol and women driving, public beheadings and other 'idiosyncrasies', which they did not encounter elsewhere in the Muslim world. For years the West was happy to live with this social conservatism. Westerners recognised that there is often a little price to be paid for untaxed income, lavish financial contracts, weapon purchases, commissions, investment and an ongoing flow of oil at reasonable prices. For the Western world, Saudi Arabia has a double significance, as it remains both a prime producer of important energy and an avid consumer of Western goods.

After the events of 11 September 2001, Wahhabiyya and terrorism became connected in the minds of many Westerners. The attack on New

York and the Pentagon, in which fifteen of the nineteen hijackers were Saudis, changed many things, one of which was Western perceptions of Wahhabiyya. Its Western critics suddenly became louder. The movement and its supporters were accused of generating terrorism, intolerance and hatred towards the West. Wahhabi discourse was suddenly held responsible for delaying the emancipation of Saudi women, abuse of human rights and discrimination against religious Muslim minorities – for example, Saudi Shi'is, Ismailis and Sufis, long-forgotten groups whose plight nobody had until then bothered to highlight in the West. Moreover, the movement was accused of providing the religious justification for denouncing Jews and Christians and promoting a culture of confrontation with the West in general. Suddenly Wahhabiyya moved from being the 'puritanical' Unitarian movement that had created a glorious empire, according to ARAMCO American historian George Rentz, to being the discourse of hatred, intolerance and terrorism.

The events of 11 September brought about new dimensions in the controversy surrounding Wahhabiyya. The West, through its academic community, media specialists and think-tank consultants, became an active agent in the debate about Wahhabiyya. While not all this debate is based on scholarly assessment aimed at understanding contemporary Saudi–Wahhabi religious discourse,[12] serious effort was put into identifying the origins of terrorism, with the result that the Wahhabis were directly accused of promoting religiously motivated and sanctioned violence.[13] Despite official Saudi attempts to dissociate their state religion from the atrocities of 11 September, such accusations against Wahhabiyya continued to flourish. These were given substance and credibility by Saudi political activists, both inside the country and abroad, some of whom had a vested interest in demonising Wahhabiyya.[14] The war on Iraq in 2003 contributed to the further demonisation of Wahhabiyya, especially after it transpired that Saudis were active participants in the *jihad* against Americans as part of the Iraqi resistance. Almost all observers assumed that those Saudis were acting in the name of Wahhabiyya, after being indoctrinated in its teachings in Saudi schools. In those commentators' minds, by the age of eighteen Saudi men are fully prepared to launch *jihad* against 'infidels'. Saudi males suddenly became suspect potential terrorists; there were calls for their eyes to be screened and kept on record, along with their fingerprints. If not Wahhabis, they are assumed to be Salafi fanatics. In the minds of many outsiders, Wahhabiyya and Salafiyya are synonymous, both standing for fanaticism and violence.

In response to the events of 11 September, the Saudi regime quickly encouraged academic studies in English, in addition to religious publications,[15] to restore its own image and that of the Wahhabiyya in the

Western English-speaking world.[16] Conferences sponsored by Saudi embassies were held in Washington, London and Paris to improve the standing of Saudi Arabia and the Wahhabi tradition. The country opened the once almost impenetrable borders for Western researchers, graduate students, journalists and other visitors to scrutinise local society. Books in English appeared, presenting Wahhabiyya as a peaceful tradition that encourages dialogue with the other and respects women's rights and minorities. For example, a defense of Wahhabiyya, under the patronage of Saudi princes and research centres was written by Natana DeLong-Bas. In this book, the author contests negative images of Wahhabiyya and absolves it from any responsibility for twenty-first-century terrorism.[17] The Saudi regime insisted that it was a victim rather than an incubator of terrorism. Sponsored publications absolved Wahhabiyya from any responsibility for the atrocities of 11 September. These propaganda publications lay the blame on modern imported Islamist movements and ideologies such as the Egyptian Muslim Brotherhood and militant Jihadi movements.[18] While evaluating Western accusations is beyond the scope of this study, it is important to emphasise that, despite Saudi efforts, Wahhabiyya became in Western popular imagination a model of the uncompromising and radical religious interpretation that inspires violence. Many Muslims, including Saudis, share this view.

These negative accounts ignore a long history of Western–Saudi harmony. Scholars in the West overlook the fact that the Al-Saud were more than happy to seek military and financial help from so-called infidels as early as 1915, and even to pursue a policy that was subservient to imperial powers. Saudi–British relations prove that the Saudi leadership was capable of making compromises, or even turning a blind eye to intimate relations with a foreign power, defined in Wahhabi world view as a *kafir* state. Most Western accounts of official Wahhabiyya do not make distinctions between the movement's religious intolerance of other Muslims, on the one hand, and its acceptance of Western influence in Saudi Arabia, on the other. They fail to highlight that political acquiescence and subservience to political authority is an important characteristic of the domesticated tradition that grew in the shadow of Saudi kings.[19] When Ibn Saud clashed with the Ikhwan fighters in the 1920s, it was assumed that this resulted from their objections to his relations with 'infidel' Britain. In fact the conflict with the Ikhwan was more to do with the marginalisation of the tribal population and the failure of its leadership to secure a place in the new Saudi polity, after its military contribution to the Al-Saud project. The Ikhwan rebellion was not simply a rebellion against Ibn Saud's subservience to Britain. It was a last cry against Ibn Saud's Machiavillian policy that required eliminating those who brought him to power.

Wahhabi social conservatism is often held responsible for terrorism directed against the West. Wahhabiyya can be an idiom of resistance to foreign domination, but it can equally be a discourse that enforces obedience to political authority. Official Wahhabiyya has no problem with princes making alliances with 'infidels' – Christians, and even Jews. After all, the Prophet himself sought refuge for his followers with Christians in Abyssinia and Jews in Madina. Some Wahhabis believe that their contemporary Imam, the Saudi king, follows these glorious political examples of ancient political wisdom. After all, the Imam knows best what is in the people's interest and the public good. Wahhabis would rather not interfere as long as they continue to control the domestic social sphere, which must be kept uncontaminated by signs of blasphemy – for example, worshipping trees, visiting tombs and seeking knowledge from charlatans and sorcerers posing as holy men. Purifying Arabia from these signs of *shirk* (blasphemy) is more important than formulating a Muslim foreign policy. They are happy to leave the latter to the *wali al-amr*, the Custodian of the Two Holy Mosques.

Western accusations of Wahhabiyya remain controversial, as they fall short of explaining political development inside Saudi Arabia – let alone world terrorism, international relations and current affairs. The accusers assume that there is one Wahhabiyya, that can potentially breed violence and confrontation. The reality is that there are several brands within this Salafi movement.[20] At one end there is the extremely subservient and pragmatic tradition associated with official Wahhabiyya, described in the first chapter, while at the opposite end there is the revolutionary brand that is often associated with Jihadi groups. All groups are socially conservative, although the pragmatism of official Wahhabiya may lead to some flexibility even in social matters: it would not be a surprise if Wahhabi scholars issued a *fatwa* in support of women driving in the near future. The main difference between various Wahhabi–Salafi trends relates to their political discourse and strategies regarding resistance, relations with the ruler and non-Muslims and political activism.

Reducing world terrorism to the influence of Wahhabiyya is a misguided approach that attributes more influence, power and organisational potential to this movement than it is actually capable of generating. Moreover, such an oversimplification ignores aggressive American intervention in the Muslim world and the US misguided foreign policy. It also overlooks the fact that for decades the USA was the strongest supporter of many regimes seen by their subjects as oppressive and authoritarian. It goes without saying that fighting terrorism requires more than changing the Saudi religious education curriculum. Western accusations are founded on the assumption that there is a single Wahhabiyya–Salafiyya that embodies a radical call for violence against the West; in fact, histori-cally most Wahhabi violence was directed against other Muslims.

It is doubtful whether the masterminds of the attacks on New York, mainly Osama bin Laden and his aides, can be easily described as Wahhabis. While they would most probably accept being called Salafis, they may well feel that the label Wahhabi does not reflect the global message of al-Qa'ida. It is certain that Bin Laden does not subscribe to the official Wahhabi religio-political discourse described in the first chapter of this book. This discourse is but one strand within the spectrum of interpretations that constitute Salafiyya. Bin Laden may be selective when it comes to formulating a revolutionary worldview based on partic-ular interpretations of religious texts. He seems to adopt a post-modern mix-and-match approach to theorise and justify violence against the West and its 'local Muslim agents'. This approach certainly incorporates the idiom of leftist revolutionary and nationalist struggles that swept the world in the twentieth century.[21] If one is to edit his speeches and cut out religious references, his rhetoric cannot be very clearly distinguished from early revolutionary slogans that drew on Western rather than Islamic intellectual traditions. Bin Laden does not call upon all workers of the world to break their chains: he calls upon all Muslims to do so. He does not reject Western capitalism: he calls for an alternative Islamic capitalist mode of production. But there is a strong mystical Islamic dimension to Bin Laden that is not well captured by statements likening him to early leftist, nationalist revolutionaries or contemporary anti-globalisation and environmentalist militants.[22]

This book is not about Wahhabiyya as a theological body of religious knowledge produced over 250 years, nor is it an exposition of the main teachings of the movement. I am not concerned here with Wahhabi debate on God and his names and adjectives, or with definitions of poly-theism, or salvation by faith and deeds. I do not deal with Wahhabi debates on *naql* (tradition) and *'aql* (reason). I overlook Wahhabi theolog-ical positions on Sufism and other Sunni schools and sects in Islam. I only consider these aspects as long as they are relevant to the political debate that is continuing in Saudi Arabia.

The focus of the book

This book examines Wahhabiyya in the twenty-first century as a con-tested intellectual, religious and political field, which is currently appro-priated by several actors. My aim is to capture the ongoing public debate. Like other Muslims, Saudis are engaged in debating religion, which touches upon politics. According to Dale Eickelman, 'the combination of

mass education and mass communications is transforming this world . . .
the faithful . . . are examining and debating the fundamentals of Muslim
belief and practice in ways that their less self-conscious predecessors
would never have imagined'.[23] However, Muslims have always debated
religion and politics. What is new is the speed of the debate and the circles
in which it revolves. Its contemporary manifestations are characterised by
the participation of a wider circle. Today, regardless of their level of education, all Muslims – including Saudis – can engage in this debate, both as
recipients and participants. They do not even need to be literate: religious
cassettes and television screens bridge the gap between the literates and
the illiterates of the Muslim world. New media, especially satellite television, have contributed to the consolidation of an audio-visual rather than
a literate culture. The religious cassette is more powerful than several
printed books. The revolutionary religious Jihadi *nashid* (songs and
recitations) is more inspiring than volumes of ancient theological texts.

There is a darker side to this ongoing debate. Since the 1990s, political
violence has shattered the myth about Saudi Arabia as a secure country.
In 2003, the situation deteriorated. Suicide attacks on residential compounds occupied mainly by non-Saudis, skirmishes amounting to battles
between security forces and al-Qa'ida members, the assassination of
public figures in remote towns and the unfolding of plots to assassinate
members of the royal family all point to the escalation of the battle
between the state and sections of society. More than at any other time,
Saudi society is polarised over religious interpretation and political aspirations. Without ignoring the impact of rapid social and economic
change, the polarisation is primarily a product of the widening gap
between professed symbols and reality. The ongoing debate, together
with increased violence, simply indicates that Saudi Arabia is undergoing
a transformation rather than a reformation. The latter is a term deeply
rooted in European history with no applicability in a context such as
Saudi Arabia. Surveying the religious scene, one is struck by the absence
of a Saudi Luther. This is not surprising. Despite regime attempts to cir-
cumvent and control religious interpretation, there has never been a pope
in Saudi Arabia. Without a pope there will never be a Luther.

The televised repentance of the 'misguided' *'ulama*, especially Jihadi
ideologues, invokes the image of repenting witches. Similarly, the *taraju'at*
(those going back on previous opinions) find their way to the local and
international press. This is a phenomenon in which individuals who are in
the process of changing their convictions, renouncing violence or developing new worldviews pose in front of television cameras, playing the role
of sages, and narrating their intellectual journey and its hazards. By the
age of thirty, many such men have experimented with various religious

interpretations and acted in accordance with them. A number of individuals move from 'radicalism' to the so-called middle path (*wasatiyya*), or even to a new religiosity, searching for a humanist Islam.[24] Such individuals claim to have abandoned Ibn Taymiyya and Muhammad ibn Abd al-Wahhab in favour of Locke and Voltaire. Those who move in this direction are celebrated in local and international media as people who have abandoned misguided thoughts in favour of true moderate Islam. Other Saudis condemn them as heretics who sin by promoting a rather unusual interpretation of Islam. Many Saudis move in the opposite direction. We only know about those when they blow themselves up or die in shoot-outs with security forces.

Official Saudi discourse highlights reasons for radicalism and terrorism, and celebrates the conversion of specific individuals to more moderate views. As this book will show, some 'conversions' and 'confessions' are expressed in less conventional ways, mainly in internet discussion boards and, obviously, violence. These confessions tend to be in the opposite direction, from moderate Islamism to radicalism, if we can invoke such problematic classifications with ease. Saudi discourse is characterised by shifting boundaries rather than clear-cut intellectual paradigms.

In capturing the contours of Saudi religio-political debate, this book tries to identify what is being debated (the main contested social, religious and political areas); who claims to have the authority and knowledge to contribute to the debate (state actors, *'ulama*, intellectuals and laymen) and where the debate takes place (public forums, the press and the internet).

Given that religious discourse permeates all aspects of public debate, it is very difficult to draw the boundaries between the religious, the political and the social. Public debate revolves around key questions relating to the nature of the state and its relationship with religion. More and more Saudis are questioning whether their state is an Islamic state, something which had been taken for granted for most of the twentieth century – at least in public forums. Some are concerned with 'theorising' the nature of the rightful Islamic government and the nature of the *bay'a* (the oath of allegiance) to the legitimate ruler, another question ignored by an earlier generation of *'ulama* and intellectuals. Who selects the leader of the Muslim community? Is it a small circle of *ahl al-hall wa 'l-'aqd* (lit. 'people who loose and tie': selected and appointed decision makers), or every adult male member of the community? Are women eligible to select the ruler and give *bay'a*? Or is this a theoretical question in the absence of mechanisms allowing men to choose the ruler? These issues are no longer the territory of *al-nukhba*, a small circle of the educated, articulate and outspoken intelligentsia who engage in *taraf fikri* (intellectual luxuries), but are now urgent matters attracting the attention of a wide circle of men and women. Furthermore, relations with the outside world, mainly the USA, and the Saudi role in the world are central in public debate.

The ongoing public debate in the twenty-first century is no longer the one that dominated the second half of the twentieth century. Previously Saudis discussed how to modernise while remaining faithful to the authentic Islamic tradition. Today, the debate moves on to more complex and focused questions relating to increasing political participation, social justice, the rights of women and minorities, freedom of speech, an independent judiciary and other urgent issues which many Saudis feel are neither properly addressed nor fully applied by the current regime. These concerns have emerged from the bottom up rather than as a result of royal patronage or outside pressure. Saudi society debated these matters before 11 September and before a royal decree established the *majlis al-hiwar al-watani* (National Dialogue Forum) in 2003. This confined and state-controlled space does not move beyond being a public-relations exercise envisaged to absorb public frustration and anger over the political paralysis of the top leadership since the 1990s and the less than satisfactory reforms of King Abdullah.

At the religious level, for the first time the debate centres on how Saudi religious discourse deals with the 'Muslim other', who today is not far away but is in the midst of the country. State-appointed religious scholars, independent and dissident *ulama* and ordinary Saudis are all engaged in a reflection on the status of other Muslims in their own country. A minority among them questions interpretations which demonised the other – for example, Sufis, Shi'is, Ismailis and followers of other *madhahib* (Hanafis, Shafi'is, Malikis). Some Saudis go as far as questioning the merit of the office of grand mufti (jurisconsult), considering it an invention, a *bid'a* (innovation), circumscribing religious interpretation and creating *kahanut* (clergy). Others debate the benefits of the state-appointed Committee for the Promotion of Virtue and Prohibition of Vice, *hayat al-amr bi'l-ma'ruf wa 'l-nahy 'an al-munkar*. They criticise its restriction to the guarding of public morality while ignoring corruption and deviation among the higher echelons of the political princely elite. Some argue that the meaning of *hisba* (accountability) in Islam must be wider than controlling the wearing of the *hijab* in the public sphere by women or the flirtation of *shabab* (youth). Yet a small minority of Saudis would prefer to abolish the institution altogether.

An integral part of public debate is the question of the status of women. A distinction is beginning to emerge between the *shari'a* position on gender issues and what is referred to as *tarasubat wa tarakumat ijtima'iyya* (social norms). Some Saudis call for a clear distinction between what

Islam allows women to do and what social norms dictate. For the first time Saudis are making a public distinction between the religious field and social tradition. In short, today they no longer shy away from discussing important religious principles and interpretations, to the extent that some are openly reconsidering the heritage of Muhammad ibn Abd al-Wahhab, whose message has held hegemonic status for almost 250 years.

This book addresses the question of who is entitled to lead the debate and formulate opinions about the above-mentioned political and religious issues. It identifies an emerging intellectual elite, *al-nukhba al-fikriyya*, consisting of *ulama* and judges, intellectuals, professionals, dissidents, writers close to the centre of power and others who are outside the political patronage networks. While the book gives substantial space to those who articulate a vision embedded in speech, text and other media, considerable attention is paid to a novel field, that of the internet discussion boards, opposition media networks and the discourse of ordinary Saudis. Because of continuous state censorship, oppression of dissidents and the imprisonment and torture of those who offer alternative visions, radical public calls for the reformation of religion and politics increasingly take place behind the scenes and are partially dependent on people who write using pseudonyms. While the state builds and consolidates its own media empire, dissident voices are successful in establishing alternative media forums, thus challenging the official political and religious narrative. Similarly, print and electronic publications have proved to be effective means for the dissemination of alternative views and an entry into the debate, which hitherto may have seemed elitist and exclusive.

The book gives special attention to the internet, which has become the battleground of groups that are struggling to reinterpret religious concepts, challenge established religious scholars, undermine religious authority and thwart state politics. At the same time, internet discussion boards are used to consolidate and spread official religious interpretations. Although the Saudi regime succeeded in establishing tight censorship of this novel communication channel,[25] Saudis with sufficient financial resources purchase computer programs that allow them to avoid censorship. More recently, radio channels broadcasting from London (previously Islah Radio and now Debate Radio and Tajdid Radio) have become accessible media outlets, as they can be listened to on satellite television and the internet. The interactive style, together with the topics discussed – especially criticism of the government and the traditional religious establishment – make such channels popular among Saudis searching for outlets to express forbidden alternative opinions. The discussions captured in this book draw on these sources, in addition to lengthy interviews and correspondence with Saudis.

Today debating religion and politics is no longer the monopoly of a small circle of privileged individuals. Several groups are formulating the agenda, participating in the debate and struggling to control the outcome. These include the state, the traditional religious establishment, dissident *'ulama*, Islamist intellectuals, liberal activists and ordinary Saudis. The picture is complicated further by external pressure and the exposure of Saudi Arabia to outside scrutiny after 11 September. In order to understand the debate described here, the role of the USA (administration, media and scholarly community) must be taken into account to assess the extent to which global pressure influences local religio-political debates and outcomes.

The chapters

It is important to avoid easy classifications of those who are engaged in the debate in a world dominated by multiple interpretations. Fluidity of discourse, shifting boundaries and the ease with which people switch from one position to another militate against clear-cut categories. Classifications such as moderate, traditional, secular, liberal, centrist, radical, Salafi and Sufi reflect the attempts of those who classify to fix sometimes illusory boundaries rather than the way Saudis identify themselves.[26] In their quest to define for policy makers 'who is friend and who is foe', analysts propose typologies often more accurately reflecting the power of word-processing programs than the reality of the diverse Muslim tradition in the twenty-first century. We can recall that Sufis, who are currently hailed as among the greatest pacifists of all times, can be extremely revolutionary, anti-Western and even radical. Those who are classified as traditional, preaching vigorous commitment to Islamic rituals, can easily inflame the imagination of young Muslims who are united by common faith and worship.

It must be said that after fourteen centuries of its existence, neither Muslim governments nor colonial powers have been able to control religious debate within Islam. Throughout Muslim history scholars and others had to live with religious diversity and a general inability to control religious interpretation. In fact, the more they tried to control religious interpretation, the more such interpretations proliferated. As a world religion with a sacred text that is constantly interpreted in specific contexts, Islam, its interpreters and their interpretations can never be successfully controlled or pointed in a particular direction.

In order to promote the kind of Islam desired by Western governments, the context in which the interpretation of texts takes place must be the right one. While texts can be easily censored, modified, altered, shortened and expanded, their interpretations remain firmly grounded in specific contexts. In addition, while mosque preachers, religious teachers and instructors can be imprisoned, eliminated or rehabilitated and taught new interpretations, their new preaching will have limited impact if the right context is simply not there.

Unfortunately the Muslim world in general and Saudi Arabia in particular does not find itself at the moment in a context that favours the promotion and internalisation of the discourse that celebrates peace, tolerance and harmony, as desired by the West, repressive governments in the region and the majority of Muslims. In fact, both the West and such governments created contexts in which these desired interpretations are impossible to emerge. A combination of factors, agents and powerful media images combined to consolidate a social and political context in which uncompromising interpretations increasingly find resonance. In the twenty-first century, Saudis resent their political vulnerability against a background of economic prosperity, dependence on the West against a rhetoric of sovereignty and pride, political impotence against rhetoric that glorifies their historical role in spreading Islam and their inability to translate wealth into real power. There is tension between globalised deterritorialised religious identity, based on belief in common Islamic values and celebrated in the idiom of the unity of the Muslim *umma*, and underdeveloped nationalist sentiments. National identities are undermined by localised regional, tribal and sectarian belonging. In the modern world of Saudi Arabia, globalised and localised identities are articulated at the expense of national belonging.

Notwithstanding the fluidity of the religio-political debate and the ability of those who are engaged in it to cross boundaries and change positions, presenting the debate in a book imposes its own rules. Writing about this ongoing debate requires the author to organise the material in chapters, which immediately imposes a classification and a way of organising the data. I chose to present the data in six chapters, each capturing a glimpse of the main features and concerns of a specific trend. However, it must be kept in mind that each chapter refers to arguments and interpretations promoted by groups who escape easy classification. One of the main themes is to show that people can frequently switch allegiance and change direction. Another theme is to show that interpretations grounded in one particular trend (or chapter) can be used and interpreted to mean anything but what was initially intended. A religious scholar can easily situate himself in the discourse of official *ʿulama*, then move to a Sahwi position, but later end up as a Jihadi ideologue. He can easily do that while invoking the same religious texts as the official religious establishment. The journey in the opposite direction is equally possible.

The first chapter deals with the religio-political discourse of those who may or may not be employed by the state but who all endorse interpretations that promote consent and obedience to rulers. Such scholars and laymen draw on the Wahhabi tradition and its early disciples. They are referred to as official *'ulama* because they not only legitimise power but also condemn attempts to challenge this power. The chapter discusses the genealogy and geography of this discourse. It traces its development and describes its objectives, mainly the consolidation of consenting subjects, people who leave politics to those who know better. This chapter challenges the view that the Saudi state of today is an Islamic Wahhabi state. It argues that there is a clear distinction between the Islamised public social sphere and politics. Politics is disenchanted in Saudi Arabia. It is no longer anchored in Islam as claimed by the leadership

Against this disenchantment, some Saudis have struggled for the past three decades to re-enchant politics, the subject of chapter 2. The so-called Sahwis represent an attempt to contest the status quo, namely the disenchantment of the world of politics and power. Regardless of their party affiliation, Sahwis represented a plea to Islamise politics after the regime departed from what they regarded as Islamic principles. The story of Sahwa (*sahwa*: awakening) is well documented but its later development is not so well known. Chapter 2 captures the debate within Sahwa after 11 September when this so-called awakening came under pressure from the regime and other sections of Saudi society to reconsider its early positions.

Chapter 3 traces the transnationalisation of Saudi religio-political discourse as it travelled under regime sponsorship to places such as Afghanistan and London. I argue that this discourse prematurely moved from obvious localism to transnationalism with unintended consequences for the Saudi regime. In Afghanistan, Wahhabiyya freed itself from its status as parasitic discourse that had grown in the shadow of the sultan. Regardless of how strong or efficient the sponsors of transnational flows were, the outcome escaped their control. Sometimes it seemed that the more the Saudi regime spent on spreading its religious discourse, the more promoters and recipients of this discourse resisted Saudi hegemony and asserted their own autonomy. Some propagators of Saudi religious flows proved to be autonomous agents once they found themselves beyond the reach of Saudi authoritarianism. The transnationalised consenting Wahhabi tradition generated serious contestation of the Islamic credentials of the Saudi regime itself. In Afghanistan and London, competing with heavy Saudi spending on religious flows, there appeared the most revolutionary rhetoric that not only challenged the Saudi regime but also accused it of blasphemy.

Chapter 4 analyses Jihadi discourse as presented by dissident ʿulama, activists and laymen. I argue that far from being an imported Islamist ideology, Jihadism is a local tradition that resonates with cultural, religious and political contexts. It invokes shared meanings and symbols. *Jihad* is not only about archaic words and religious interpretations. Neither is it a quest for the 'Talibanisation' of Saudi Arabia, as claimed by Saudi princes addressing Western audiences. In the twenty-first century, Jihadism is a performance that captures the imagination of many Saudi men and women who are not necessarily poor, alienated and downtrodden. It invokes meanings which are at the heart of the Wahhabi tradition. Its discourse flourishes because there is a political and social context which makes it resonate with people.

Through the life of one Saudi, chapter 5 traces the personal journey of a young Jihadi man called Lewis and his navigation of a very difficult and complex religio-political field. An analysis of his words and autobiography allows us to see the world through his own eyes. It also allows us to comprehend why an educated Saudi invokes Islam to articulate a desire to change the world. Having spent years acquiring a Western education, Lewis returns to reassert his Arabian and Muslim identity. While he definitely has multiple identities, he celebrates only one.

The final chapter examines the Saudi quest for the unmediated word of God. The quest is a product of modernity rather than archaic and obscurantist inclinations. To worship God without mediators is an idiom that inspires many Saudis to challenge political hierarchies and religious monopolies. Furthermore, to worship God without mediators is the ultimate outcome of modernity that empowers man to seek direct relationship with the divine, a relationship that is not 'corrupted' or 'violated' by the intervention of another human. Mass education and literacy allow this to happen. This quest threatens to erode the pillars of authoritarian rule: history, theology and politics.

The book depends on a mixture of methodologies. I consulted classical works by the early generation of *aimat al-daʿwa al-najdiyya* (Najdi religious scholars) from Muhammad ibn Abd al-Wahhab to Abdulaziz Ibn Baz. I have supplemented classical texts with an analysis of public lectures, mosque sermons and media statements. To capture the growing debate, especially that which is still unacceptable in public, I consulted many internet websites and discussion boards. Finally, I have interviewed many Saudis; some I came to know very well, while others will remain virtual. I exchanged e-mails with strangers and even spoke to them on the phone without knowing their real identity. I initiated contacts with some, while a few contacted me directly. They knew me but I will probably never know their real names. They opened up and presented a rich tapestry of arguments, evidence and analysis of their own. They were great conversationalists, open discussants and daring voices, once they found themselves outside the restrictions of official religion and politics. I will always remember their anonymous voices and aliases. As far as I was concerned, guessing the symbolic significance of their *noms de plume* proved to be one of the most challenging but intellectually rewarding experiences.

This book is written neither to glorify Wahhabiyya nor to condemn it. There are hundreds of books that seek to do both. My objective is to capture contemporary debate about religion and politics. I have an advantage as a result of my presence outside Saudi Arabia, which grants me the freedom to subject Wahhabiyya, its advocates and adversaries to serious scrutiny, drawing on interpretive and analytical tools – an impossible academic endeavour in Saudi Arabia itself. I examine Wahhabiyya as a religious discourse produced by people rather than as a sacred tradition. I have not come across an impartial sociological or anthropological study of religion and religious practice or a scholarly work on contemporary ʿulama or the royal family conducted by a Saudi researcher.[27] If such studies exist, they tend to glorify the ʿulama's role without critical evaluation. There are several chronicles and biographies of famous ʿulama and umara (princes). But these are a different kind of work. Scholarly investigation of the umara and ʿulama remains taboo. To study religion and politics from a social scientific perspective, without demonstrating the umara and ʿulama's contribution to Islam and Muslims, violates the taboo. To study both and conclude that they mystify the world, legitimise authoritarian rule, sanction despotism and produce both consenting and rebellious subjects amounts to blasphemy. To capture the ongoing Saudi debate that contests official religious discourse amounts to privileging the despised and dangerous other. I have violated the taboo with a clear conscience. As a result of this academic exercise, my faith is solid and is in fact stronger. I continue to retain one aspect of Wahhabiyya, namely worshipping God without mediators but I strongly reject its claim that obeying the Al-Saud rulers and Wahhabi ʿulama is part of obeying God and the Prophet.

Saudis inside the country debate Wahhabiyya. Those who go 'too far' are usually imprisoned and subjected to restrictions and harassment. Daring arguments are often veiled under pseudonyms and anonymous internet discussion boards. This book is an attempt to unveil the debate. The unveiling proved to me that it is easy to explain why people rebel but much harder to explain why they consent. This book is an attempt to address both.

1   Consenting subjects: official Wahhabi religio-political discourse

> O ye who believe Obey Allah, and obey the Messenger, and those
> charged with authority among you. If ye differ in anything among your-
> selves, refer to God and His Messenger, if ye
>   Do believe in Allah and the Last Day: that is best, and most suitable
> for final determination.   Quran, Sura al-nisa, verse 59

Eighteenth- and nineteenth-century Wahhabi chronicles claimed
that the message of Muhammad ibn Abd al-Wahhab (1703–92) in
Deriyyah aimed to revive religion by returning to the Quran, Sunna and
the tradition of the pious ancestors. While the sheikh and his followers
never accepted the label Wahhabis, they considered themselves to be *ahl
al-sunna wa 'l-jama'a* (people of tradition and community), or *ahl
al-tawhid* (*al-muwahhidun*: the people of monotheism). In contemporary
scholarship, they represent one of the Salafi trends within Sunni Islam.[1]
The return to the tradition of the pious ancestors was meant to
remove religious innovations, and apply the *shari'a* at a time when
the population of Arabia was believed to have degenerated into blasphemy, corrupt religious practices and laxity. This allegedly took place
mainly under Ottoman rule,[2] whose religious traditions, particularly
Sufism, incorporated interpretations and practices considered outside
the realm of true Islam. The rhetoric of the return to the pious ancestors and the sacred text, in addition to rejecting *madhahib* (schools
of jurisprudence), allows Wahhabiyya to be counted as a Salafi movement.

Wahhabiyya painted an image of Arabia as the land of blasphemy and
savagery. The myth that Arabian society was blasphemous prior to the
rise of Wahhabiyya is taken for granted by many Saudi and Western
scholars without any serious attempt to revisit what has become a 'divine
wisdom' initially propagated by the supporters of Wahhabiyya, and later
on by outside commentators. In a recent assessment of the evolution of
Wahhabiyya, the blasphemy of other Muslims is taken for granted as a
historical fact without any serious attempt to question the validity and

accuracy of this assumption.[3] Like the Saudi royal family, Wahhabi descriptions of the past are sacrosanct.

Throughout the twentieth century, many – but not all – Saudis regarded the Salafi–Wahhabi movement as a solution to heterodoxy, religious laxity, saint veneration, immorality and superstition. Wahhabiyya claimed to safeguard the souls of its followers against the misguided Islam of others, such as other Sunnis, Shi'is, Sufis, Zaydis, Ismailis and grave-worshippers (known as *quburis*).[4] It was also regarded as a shield against subsequent 'corrupting' Western influences, undesirable social behaviour and immoral and unacceptable alien ideas such as secularism, nationalism, communism and liberalism. Wahhabiyya promised liberation from heterodox religious worship and folk Islam, the Islam practised by either a *jahil* (ignorant), or *dhal* (one who has gone astray). So-called misguided Muslims who deviated in their creed and worship from the right path were seen as practising a corrupted religion, often dominated by *mush'awithun* (charlatans) parading as holy men, witches, sorcerers and mystics. Such 'corrupted' Islam is centred on excessive ritual and festivity, punctuated by tomb visiting, intercession and mediation. Saudis viewed the religious practices dominant among Sunnis in other Arab countries as impure and corrupted. Wahhabiyya condemned all these folk practices as innovations and privileged the literal interpretation of sacred texts, the Quran and the Sunna, and called for an unmediated relationship with the divine, required by *tawhid*, the oneness of God. In religious discourse, the *umma* consists of sinners who need to be reprimanded and brought back to the true path.

Wahhabi demonisation of Arabian society in both past and present stems from the movement's desire to control and gain legitimacy. Wahhabi legitimacy today rests on a myth that was perpetuated by generations of Wahhabi writers, historians, religious scholars and laymen, as well as royalty. The myth claims that Muslims in Arabia were and are blasphemous, and their salvation is entirely dependent on the message of Muhammad ibn Abd al-Wahhab and the political power that endorsed his message, the Al-Saud family. The Wahhabi narrative of the past undermines the seventh-century message of the Prophet Muhammad. If one is to believe this narrative, one must accept that the Prophet's message had virtually no lasting influence. The teachings of Muhammad ibn Abd al-Wahhab were therefore needed to correct corruption and ignorance that had crept into the religion. If Wahhabiyya and the Al-Saud were accomplices in the salvation of Arabian society, then they must be obeyed, revered and sanctified. Saudi–Wahhabi efforts at mystifying the past have resulted in the disappearance of sources that might have challenged the myth about the alleged blasphemy in Arabia in the pre-Wahhabi era. Even if tomb visiting, saint veneration or tree worship was practised in Arabian society, it cannot be taken for granted that all members of that society indulged in such practices. It is possible that they only existed among a minority of the population. However, such myths have continued to dominate the historiography of the movement, often written by its own 'ulama.[5] This demonisation of Arabian society continued in the twentieth century in order to justify the establishment of the modern Saudi state.[6]

The war against the so-called blasphemous religious practices that survived despite the sacred message of the Prophet Muhammad in the seventh century and a later wave of religious revivalism and purification in the eighteenth century by Muhammad ibn Abd al-Wahhab was always in need of a political authority.[7] In Wahhabi discourse, an executive power is needed to protect faith from corruption, uphold the Salafi tradition and punish transgressors. Only a strong and pious state can practise the fundamental Islamic obligation of *amr bi 'l-ma'ruf wa 'l-nahy 'an al-munkar* (the promotion of virtue and prohibition of vice).[8]

It is important, however, to emphasise that describing the Wahhabi movement as a puritan tradition does not necessarily imply austerity or asceticism. While the ecology of the area where Wahhabiyya originated was austere in the past, the advocates of the movement were partly driven by a desire to amass wealth and treasures from the conquered territories, to compensate for the poverty of their homeland. Wahhabi historians celebrated the collection of booty from the conquered territories with a strong sense of pleasure and satisfaction as they described the newly acquired treasures that were brought first to Deriyyah and later Riyadh. The conquests did not only mean the spread of monotheism, as claimed, but also the seizure of camels, horses, weapons and coins.[9]

Muhammad ibn Abd al-Wahhab considered it a characteristic of the people in the age of ignorance to 'worship God through prohibiting the permissible', implying that excessive austerity does not make one closer to the divine.[10] Oil wealth and consumerism enabled Wahhabi 'ulama, the ruling group and Saudi society in general to indulge in a great degree of material consumption and the fulfilment of all worldly desires, within the limits prescribed in the holy book and the tradition of the Prophet – at least in public. The *da'wa* (call) was from the very beginning a project to create an Islamised personality, society and state, according to Wahhabi criteria. An Islamised personality is not necessarily one that abstains from worldly pleasures, as often mistakenly projected in some outside accounts of the movement. In fact, it indulges itself fully in all permissible pleasures, according to Islamic tradition in general, and the Wahhabi variant in particular. An Islamised personality also enjoys the gains that accrue to it as a result of God's *ni'ma* (grace). In the past this grace had come from conquering new territories and looting its population, whereas in modern times oil became the main source. Wahhabis may be seen as excessive in resorting to the principle of *sad al-thara'i'* ('blocking the means') – for example, when they continue to prohibit certain practices in order to prevent possible sins (for example the ban on women driving), yet they do not and cannot forbid pleasures that are divinely permitted.[11] However, a group of religious scholars is always needed to define and regulate the permissible, while the state ensures that the prohibited does not become permissible, at least in theory.

In the twentieth century a state was born, under the pretext of fighting religious innovations, to protect the realm and ensure its purity against the return of such innovations. With excessive coercion, Wahhabiyya was extremely successful in eradicating most but not all so-called religious innovations in the Arabian Peninsula. With the establishment of the modern Saudi state, Wahhabiyya became a hegemonic discourse supported, protected and promoted by political authority. However, although Wahhabi *'ulama* and preachers were convinced that the state reflected Wahhabi teachings, this was an illusion. Wahhabi scholars controlled nothing but religious praxis and the social sphere, while royalty and a group of technocrats with modern educations were in full control of politics, the economy, foreign relations and defence matters.[12] The state needed Wahhabi *'ulama* to control the social sphere in such a way as to ensure compliance. The appearance of an Islamised social sphere was mistakenly taken to represent an Islamic polity.

Under state control, there were in fact multiple interpretations within the hegemonic Wahhabi discourse. While the state strove to contain Wahhabi discourse through its institutionalisation, alternative interpretations and marginal but challenging Wahhabi voices continued to appear throughout the twentieth century. These voices articulated alternative visions, which occasionally resulted in violence, as the history of Salafi dissidence in the country demonstrated.[13] State control of Wahhabiyya was directly proportionate to the violence that erupted. The proliferation of state-financed and controlled religious institutions, ministries and hierarchies generated co-opted and independent scholars; the first enforced loyalty to the state while the second remained a potential threat. Through its substantial wealth, the state patronised circles of religious knowledge. The state created co-opted networks but some remained outside the circle of royal patronage. As relations between royalty and religious notables were personalised, there were bound to be certain individuals outside the circle.

Who has corrupted the teachings of Muhammad ibn Abd al-Wahhab and the chain of scholars known as *aimat al-da'wa al-najdiyya*, the *imams* of the Najdi call? Who has remained faithful to these teachings? These are central questions that accompanied the institutionalisation of Wahhabiyya in the second half of the twentieth century and the search for answers continues in the twenty-first century. The question for Wahhabis was not the legitimacy of their previous claims about Arabian society and its alleged blasphemy, but about the degree to which contemporary royalty, Wahhabi *ulama* and laymen have remained faithful to the message of the founder. Because of censorship and heavy sanctions against dissident voices, both religious and political, violence accompanied the process of state subjugation of Wahhabiyya, which began to fragment into several strands. Today debating the movement does not take place among a small and limited group of *ulama*. A wide circle of people discuss controversial religious matters, thanks to mass education and media. Violence in the twenty-first century is yet another episode of alternative Wahhabi interpretations erupting, this time not only in Saudi Arabia, but also worldwide, especially among groups that claim ideological and organisational connections with the original Wahhabiyya.

Under Saudi control, Wahhabiyya became a religious discourse used by political authority against society and a weapon wielded by society against this authority. Its interpretations are neither representative of the Sunni tradition nor a culmination of consensus among the people known as *ahl al-sunna wa 'l-jama'a*. It is, in fact, a hybrid tradition that matured under royal authority. While it draws on well-known Hanbali sources without becoming a monolithic tradition, Wahhabiyya is a product of the historical and political context of growing in the 'shadow of the Saudi sultan'. It is a religious discourse that evolved in response to the concerns of political authority. As such, it was subject to schisms, dissent, transformation and mutation.

In the twenty-first century official Wahhabiyya is a discourse of consent. It propagates religious interpretations that require subservience to political authority. This chapter traces the contours of Wahhabi religiopolitical discourse, especially that related to the mystification of the world for the purpose of consolidating the state and perpetuating obedience to rulers. To understand the Wahhabi contribution to state formation and its later perpetuation of a tradition of total subservience to power, the narrative in this chapter moves from the original sources (mainly the writings of Muhammad ibn Abd al-Wahhab) to the contemporary invocations of the Wahhabi tradition.[14] It demonstrates how the establishment of the current Saudi state, together with the forces of modernity, contributed to two outcomes as far as Wahhabiyya is concerned. Both the state and the forces of modernity led both to the consolidation of a consenting Wahhabi discourse and the contestation of this discourse. Under the banner of the contemporary Saudi state, Wahhabiyya developed this double discourse. It is important to begin by introducing the interpreters of Wahhabiyya.

Genealogies and geographies of people of knowledge

Like any religious discourse, Wahhabiyya is dependent on the so-called 'people of knowledge', who claim to articulate its message, uphold its tradition and guard its spirit. Wahhabiyya depended both on people of knowledge and on the protection of political power, without which it was at the risk of disintegrating and vanishing. As it lacked the power of persuasion in the early decades of the eighteenth century, it needed the sword. Yet this sword had to be Islamised to be effective.

From the eighteenth century Wahhabi discourse was developed and defended by those locally known as *aimat al-da'wa al-najdiyya*, 'religious notables' who were closely associated with central Arabia, the geographical region known as Najd. To be more precise, the early advocates of Wahhabiyya were drawn from southern Najd, mainly the small towns, oases and villages to the south and south-west of Riyadh.[15] Their opponents in Najd referred to Wahhabiyya as the 'new religion of al-Aridh', a reference to the region where it originated. Yet in the minds of outsiders, Najd and Wahhabiyya are mistakenly considered inseparable. Similarly, Wahhabiyya and the sedentary Banu Tamim, the tribe to which the Al-Shaykh family of Muhammad ibn Abd al-Wahhab and substantial sections of the sedentary population of Arabia belonged, are closely interrelated in the imagination and historiography of the region.[16] From Muhammad ibn Abd al-Wahhab Al-Shaykh to present Saudi mufti Abdulaziz Al-Shaykh, one can count at least fifteen al-Shaykh scholars who occupied very important posts in the religious hierarchy. In 2005 both the mufti and the minister of religious affairs belonged to Al-Shaykh. The highest religious authority had always been occupied by an Al-Shaykh, although *mufti* Abdulaziz ibn Baz (1912–99) was an exception. However, although the so-called *aima* (religious scholars) belonging to the Al-Shaykh family were prominent and had a near monopoly on high religious posts, other Najdi families were among those who preserved and developed the Wahhabi tradition.[17]

While the socio-economic background of the *aima* in the eighteenth and nineteenth centuries is well documented,[18] we need merely say here that the genealogy of the Wahhabi religious tradition was historically anchored in the sedentary families of southern Najd, with very limited infiltration from families from other provinces in the Arabian Peninsula, other tribal groups or the Muslim world in general. The so-called *'ulama* of Najd who were counted as part of *aimat al-da'wa al-najdiyya* included members from families such as al-Bassam, al-Bulayhid, al-Angari, al-Sayf, al-Mutawa, al-Atiq, al-Fawzan and others.[19] Members of these families and their descendants became the state religious notables. Today scholars belonging to these families represent a contemporary *noblesse d'état* who delivered to the state vast numbers of docile subjects. They were the intellectual instruments of political domination par excellence.[20] Wahhabiyya remained a regional religious tradition kept alive by the sedentary southern Najdi religious families for over two hundred years.

In the second half of the twentieth century, and specifically in the later decades, advocates of Wahhabi–Salafi discourse began to be drawn from a wider circle of people belonging to families and regions recently converted to Wahhabiyya as a result of their incorporation in the Saudi realm in 1932. Bligh argues that since the 1940, there has been a decline in the number of *'ulama* belonging to Al-Shaykh because they were less polygamous than royalty, and several members of the family chose non-religious careers.[21] It is also possible that the Al-Saud wanted to widen the circle of religious experts to weaken the monopoly of Al-Shaykh over religious discourse. The state itself opened the *noblesse d'état* to a wide circle as it established its hegemony over newly conquered territories that needed to internalise the consenting discourse. Widening the circle was also a strategy to counter reliance on one kinship solidarity group. Furthermore, it is perhaps easier to dominate religious scholars who belong to less prominent families than those belonging to well-established religious lineages. This 'opening up' of the religious circle both geographically and genealogically was also a product of Wahhabi proselytising beyond the limited geography of southern Najd, Qasim and its environs.

State control over religious discourse manifested itself clearly after the termination of the Ikhwan rebellion in 1927 when Wahhabiyya was institutionalised and Ibn Saud declared that only a number of named religious scholars were entitled to give religious opinion and issue *fatwa*s. This circle became the nucleus of the *noblesse d'état*. Scholars who were not approved by the Riyadh *'ulama* were not allowed to preach or interpret texts. The approved were Abdullah ibn Abd al-Latif Al-Shaykh, Saad ibn Atiq, Muhammad ibn Abd al-Latif al-Shaykh, Abdullah al-Angari, Abdullah ibn Sulaym, and Abdulrahman ibn Salim, a coterie that included the most loyal *'ulama*.[22] This royal decision, supported by other loyal Riyadh-based *'ulama*, together with later bureaucratisation and further institutionalisation, set the scene not only for the emergence of schisms within Wahhabiyya but also for its later contestation in the twentieth century.

With the establishment of the modern state in 1932, both the genealogies and geographies of religion were stretched beyond Najd and its religious families. The Najdi *imams*, although initially a very small group, travelled from Riyadh to preach and apply the *shari'a* in distant lands – for example, in the Hijaz, Asir, and the Northern and Eastern provinces. A Salafi tradition existed in the Hijaz before the new conquest; it was not, however, the only religious tradition or even the dominant one, but coexisted with other Islamic schools and Sufi *turuq* (sg. *tariqa*). With the expansion of the modern state, the situation changed. Wahhabi interpretations dominated the religious field while other discourses and practices went underground.

While some scholars left the capital, other people came to Riyadh to seek religious knowledge directly from the *aima*, mainly the al-Shaykh scholars and their intimate circle of disciples. Famous *aima* served as important transmitters of religious knowledge, while their intellectual genealogies anchored their discourse in the tradition of the early scholars. Migration to and emigration from Riyadh were two parallel movements that widened the circle of recruits and ensured the traditional transmission of religious knowledge to a new generation at a time when there were no formal religious educational institutions in the country. Both masters and disciples[23] continued to be drawn mainly from the sedentary communities of the Arabian Peninsula. In the pre-oil period, their livelihood depended on a combination of agriculture, trade and very simple cottage industries. In the new state after 1932, traditional religious education guaranteed social mobility both from the geographical periphery and from the margins of society to the centre of religious learning and political power. Religious education offered the prospect of employment as preacher, judge and mosque *imam* in territories that had been recently incorporated into the realm and had to be initiated into the new religio-political tradition. Migration to Riyadh in pursuit of religious knowledge was also a move to prosperity from the poverty-stricken peripheral regions in the pre-oil period. Riyadh became the religious centre par excellence, the seat of the *noblesse d'état*, at the expense of the historically and religiously more important centres, Mecca and Madina. The establishment of the Saudi state marginalised these individual centres of religious learning, as its conquests were religious as well as military and territorial. The state sent its own people of knowledge, emissaries whose aim was to 'Saudise' and 'Wahhabise' newly conquered territories, thus ensuring their political subjugation and loyalty. New disciples turned up in Riyadh to be closer not only to the pillars of religious knowledge but also to political power. Religious indoctrination was a solid foundation for political subservience. It promised domesticated and acquiescent subjects.

The biographies of two important *aima* members of the religious *noblesse d'état*, who played a central role in the consolidation of Wahhabi discourse in the twentieth century are revealing, as they reflect the changing geographies and genealogies of religion under the auspices of the modern state. The first is the biography of Sheikh Muhammad ibn Ibrahim ibn Abd al-Latif Al-Shaykh (1311–86/1890–1969), a descendant of the Al-Shaykh family, the religious nobility of the Najdi mission, who for a long time maintained a historical monopoly over the highest religious posts in the kingdom in return for an undisputed loyalty to the Al-Saud.[24] The second biography is that of Sheikh Abdulaziz ibn Baz, who was outside that religious nobility but managed to become the highest religious authority as mufti until his death in 1999. Both sheikhs were Najdis, however: the first represented the monopoly of the closed circle of al-Shaykh, whereas the second embodied the opening up of the closed circle, which began to include in its rank and file people drawn from other less prominent families both inside and outside southern Najd.

Sheikh Muhammad ibn Ibrahim served the Saudi state between 1932 and 1969, occupying about eighteen posts, assisted by brothers, sons and cousins. He was born in Riyadh in 1311 (1890). He learnt the Quran at the age of ten and became blind at the age of sixteen. His father, Sheikh Ibrahim, was the *qadi* of Riyadh. In addition to his father and uncles, his mentors were the famous *'ulama* of Riyadh, for example Saad ibn Atiq, Hamad ibn Faris, and Abdullah ibn Rashid.[25] He is described as having grown up in a wealthy household, which freed him from poverty. In addition, he grew up in Riyadh, described as 'the capital where students take refuge to study and work. They lived in an atmosphere that encourages competition for religious excellence.'[26] According to his biographers, he benefited from the fact that 'Najdi ulama enjoyed a distinguished status among both the authority and the people'.[27] For thirty years (1340–70AH) 'he listened to readers of the Quran with attention, until God opened the chests of the earth [a reference to oil], then Riyadh became a centre attracting *ulama* from different parts of the world'.[28]

Muhammad ibn Ibrahim is described as someone who

witnessed the changes that swept Saudi Arabia, especially the rejection of all things old, people began to see pious men as backward. People abandoned religious knowledge (*'ulum shari'yya*) in favour of foreign languages, and natural sciences. The Sheikh warned against this sudden change, which was a direct reflection of modernisation arriving in Saudi Arabia. He advised *wulat al-amr* to open *al-ma'ahid al-'ilmiyya* [colleges that teach Arabic and *shari'a*]. The *'ulama* lured students with gifts and rewards. The Sheikh was responsible for the colleges.[29]

Muhammad ibn Ibrahim was behind establishing the Islamic University in Madina, whose purpose was to train students from all over the Muslim world and enhance the call to religion. In its early days, the university recruited 75 per cent of its students from the Muslim world and

25 per cent from Saudi Arabia. He was also responsible for the education of girls through his appointed aide, Nasir al-Rashid. His biographer lists sixty-seven famous scholars and judges who trained with him, among them Abdulaziz ibn Baz, Abdullah ibn Humaid, Salih al-Shaykh, Abdullah ibn Jibrin, Abdullah al-Masari, Hamad ibn Jasir and Salih al-Lohaydan, the core of the *noblesse d'état* that dominated the Saudi religious field in the second half of the twentieth century.[30]

Sheikh Muhammad ibn Ibrahim's famous epistle, *Risalat tahkim al-qawanin*, in which he denounced secular labour legislation, is held in esteem among his followers and contemporary Salafis, especially those who lament the *ʿulama*'s loss of freedom and independence.[31] In this epistle, the sheikh announced that it is a great blasphemy to introduce new legislation because 'the *shariʿa* is the source of all legislation'.[32] Today he is regarded by several Jihadi ideologues as one of the *ʿulama* who was most faithful to the original message of Muhammad ibn Abd al-Wahhab. This perhaps prompted contemporary Jihadi Sheikh Nasir al-Fahad to write a biography of this *ʿalim*. According to this biography, Sheikh Muhammad ibn Ibrahim married six times, and at the time of his death he had three wives. His responsibilities included leading prayers, preaching and teaching in his mosque, as well as more advanced posts such as chief of justice, mufti, head of the founding council of Rabitat al-Alam al-Islami and director of the Islamic University. As a religious authority, his legacy survived in his disciples, among them Sheikh Abdulaziz ibn Baz. His lessons also attracted royalty. It was reported that Prince Muhammad ibn Abdulaziz ibn Saud (a son of Ibn Saud) and Prince Musaid ibn Abdurahman ibn Saud (brother of Ibn Saud) were regular visitors to his study circle. Scholars from the Muslim world were known to have visited him and benefited from his knowledge, for example Sheikhs Ahmad Shakir, Muhammad Hamid al-Faqi, and Muhammad al-Shanqiti.[33]

Sheikh Muhammad ibn Ibrahim's study circle attracted those who sought religious knowledge and training. In the age prior to mass education, it was the centre par excellence. He was a descendant of the famous Al-Shaykh family, which made him the model of the revered Wahhabi *ʿalim*. Genealogy guaranteed Muhammad ibn Ibrahim a special status in the eyes of his disciples. He lived through that transitional period in which the monopoly of his family began to be broken down as a result of the transformation of the circle of knowledge. It was a twilight zone, when Saudi Arabia was beginning to gradually shed its past without being yet firmly anchored in the new age. New disciples outside the traditional religious families began to be incorporated into the circle of religious scholars. After Ibn Ibrahim's death, King Faysal announced the establishment of a seventeen-member Council of Senior Ulama in 1971. This was the beginning of the institutionalisation of Wahhabiyya, although its subjugation to political authority dates back to the 1920s.[34]

One disciple of the sheikh was the famous Abdulaziz ibn Baz (1912–99). Ibn Baz succeeded Muhammad ibn Ibrahim as one of the most influential non-Al-Shaykh Wahhabi scholars since the 1970s. The biography of Sheikh Ibn Baz demonstrates the expansion of the circle of *aimat al-da'wa al-najdiyya* beyond the well-known al-Shaykh. According to his biography, Ibn Baz's family originally came from Madina to Deriyyah. Later the family moved to Hawtat Bani Tamim. He grew up in Riyadh and never left it except for the pilgrimage. He belonged to a family whose members practised trade and agriculture and which produced several religious scholars.[35] Like his mentor, Sheikh Ibn Baz became blind later in life. Nevertheless he has memorised the Quran at an early age, helped by the Riyadh *'ulama* and readers. He occupied the post of judge in several towns before he returned to Riyadh and became member of the Council of Senior Ulama and later the mufti of Saudi Arabia in 1993, a post that had remained vacant after the death of Ibn Ibrahim in 1969.

It is at the hands of sheikhs such as Ibn Baz, together with sheikhs Muhammad al-Uthaymin, Abd al-Muhsin al-Obaykan, Salih al-Fawzan, the current mufti Abdulaziz Al-Shaykh and many others that the Wahhabi tradition underwent a transformation beyond genealogy and geography. Under their guidance Wahhabiyya ceased to be a religious revivalist Salafi movement and became an apologetic institutionalised religious discourse intimately tied to political authority. Ibn Baz and other members of the Council of Senior Ulama provided the intellectual input, namely the religious discourse which confirmed the servitude of religion to the state. Ibn Baz's inability to engage with the politics of the modern world and the superficiality of his religious opinions and interpretations contributed to the trivialisation of the Wahhabi message. Ibn Baz, however, is perhaps more famous for several controversial opinions, one of which was the *fatwa* justifying the invitation of foreign troops to Saudi Arabia during the 1990–1 Gulf War and his 1993 *fatwa* legitimising peace with Israel.[36] These religious opinions confirmed official Wahhabiyya in its role as a state religion and the official people of knowledge as subservient 'clergy'.

In order to survive as traditional religious notables in an age where the state began to be dominated by technocrats who were mainly educated abroad, the official Wahhabi *'ulama*, under the religious leadership of Ibn Baz, ceased to be independent mediators between government and governed; they confined themselves to being guardians of public morality.

This amounted to enforcing the appearance of a highly Islamised public sphere, represented by the number of mosques in cities, minarets calling for prayers, predominance of religious education, segregation of the sexes, government spending on proselytising inside the country and abroad, and other related matters of appearance. Official Wahhabi *ulama* abandoned their role as loosely organised religious intellectuals who guard the sacred tradition, interpret it to the public and mediate between state and society. This mediating role was what Saudis expected from them. With state co-optation they developed into a class in its own right and with its own interests. The majority of them confirmed political decisions by providing a religious seal of approval for policy matters.[37] Official *ulama* sanctioned authoritarian rule and anchored it in religious interpretations.

Official Wahhabi *ulama* turned to defensive conservatism as they encountered the drastic changes that swept the country in the second half of the twentieth century. They continued to discipline society, in some instances a practice amounting to coercion, while state politics – mainly foreign relations, defence and the economy – remained beyond their reach and religious rulings. Although the Council of Senior Ulama was meant to provide general guidance on all aspects of policy and decisions taken by the state, it became a legitimisation umbrella. In order to remain in control of the only space left for them, the social public sphere, official *ulama* glorified the state that guaranteed them such monopoly. They promised the state acquiescent and subservient subjects, despite a strong tradition calling for subservience only to God, expressed clearly in *tawhid*, as explained in the undisputed message of Muhammad ibn Abd al-Wahhab.

Throughout the twentieth century, senior *ulama* belonged to the al-Shaykh family and other well-known Najdi groups. As a commoner of a humble origin, Sheikh Ibn Baz was an exception. Other non-Najdi Saudi *ulama* entered the intellectual field together with other Arab and Muslim interpreters of the tradition. A recent survey of *du'at* (preachers) in Riyadh lists sixty-nine sheikhs from various regions and tribal groups. Sheikh Abdulaziz ibn Abdullah al-Shaykh occupies the first position on the list, followed by sheikhs belonging to known Najdi religious families (for example al-Bassam, al-Barak, al-Awdah, al-Lohaydan, al-Obaykan, al-Fawzan, al-Zamil) together with others who are newly recruited disciples (al-Ghamdi, al-Qahtani, al-Asmari, al-Yami, al-Zahrani). The new disciples belong to tribes in the west and south-west of the country, historically outside Saudi–Wahhabi domination. The list is meant to identify those sheikhs who are considered as authorities in Wahhabi religious discourse. Listing them in a Wahhabi website automatically grants them *tazkiyya* (an approval certificate). Visitors to the web page are encouraged to invite these *aima* to give lectures in mosques, consult them and attend their lectures in centres where they normally preach.[38]

Today, it is slightly inaccurate to claim that Wahhabiyya represents Najdi discourse, because those who participate in its articulation are no longer exclusively drawn from this region. As mentioned before, from the very beginning Wahhabiyya was the religious discourse of the area south and south west of Riyadh rather than Najd as a whole. However, despite the hybridity of the scholars who are intellectually loyal to the Wahhabiyya today and their geographical diversity, the tradition retained some important core characteristics, reflecting its original message and homeland.

Consolidating the state: mystification of the world

Twentieth-century official Wahhabi scholars used three mechanisms to consolidate the political realm. *Hijra* (migration), *takfir* (excommunication) and *jihad* (struggle in the way of God) are religious concepts that were conducive to domesticating the population and ensuring total control over the public sphere. It is ironic that these old concepts that consolidated the state are currently used to denounce it and even destroy it.

Hijra

Hijra is a boundary-drawing mechanism that requires an individual to migrate to the realm of the pious state, established by Wahhabi efforts: the Saudi state.[39] The tradition was invoked in the eighteenth century to distinguish between the realm created in central Arabia and other provinces of the Ottoman Empire. Similarly, in the nineteenth century the land that fell into the hands of the invading Egyptian troops who landed on the shores of the Arabian Peninsula was regarded as an unsuitable abode for true Muslims, who were therefore required to emigrate to the land where authentic Islam still prevailed.[40] Finally, in the twentieth century, the modern Saudi state was founded as a result of invoking the tradition of *hijra*, which required true Muslims to leave not only their traditional land but also way of life in order to migrate to the land of Islam, the Saudi–Wahhabi realm.[41] Abode in this land of Islam became compulsory, while travelling to the land of non-Muslims – a wide category that included not only Christians and Jews but also other Muslims – is forbidden. The fact that other Muslims were known to be part of *ahl al-qibla* (people who face Mecca for prayer) did not suffice to make their territory permissible as an abode for true Muslims. This distinction was based not

just on a physical migration but also on a moral one, that involved abandoning the realms of blasphemy, religious innovation and, ultimately,
misguidance. The migration includes prohibitions and restrictions on
travelling to such blasphemous areas in times of peace. This application
of the concept of migration was closely associated with the *'ulama* of
Riyadh and its environs, who were most radical in their distinction
between the land of Muslims and that of non-Muslims. In pre-oil Arabia
such areas had no commercial interest. In other towns in central Arabia –
for example, Unayzah and Hayil – where there were more developed
commercial interests with the outside world, scholars were more lenient
in applying the prohibition on travel to the land of infidels. The commercial interests of these two towns required such a moderate theological
position.[42]

With the growing number of Saudi students sent on government schol-
arships to study in the land of blasphemy, the West, Ibn Baz was asked for
a religious opinion regarding the permissibility of such behaviour. The
following dialogue is recorded in his famous collection of *fatwa*s:

Q: In recent years young men travel to the land of blasphemy to study, do you
   think they need a special Committee to instruct them in good behaviour?
IBN BAZ: No doubt travelling to the land of blasphemy is a very dangerous
   matter. Its negative consequences are enormous. I have issued opinions
   warning against this danger. If there is no way of avoiding this travel, it is
   better to send old men who have in-depth knowledge of their religion. Also it
   is important to send with them pious people to watch them abroad.[43]

Ibn Baz saw great danger in sending the youth of the country to study in
the West. This also applied to those traders and entrepreneurs who
sought to establish commercial networks in distant non-Muslim lands.
He ruled that to avoid a great danger, the process must be under the
control of those who know religion.

But what is the ruling regarding inviting infidels and blasphemous
people into the abode of Muslims? What is Ibn Baz's opinion regarding
the millions of foreign workers who have been a constant feature of Saudi
Arabia since the discovery of oil in the 1930s? These questions became
urgent as Saudi Arabia hosted more than 6 million foreign workers by the
end of the twentieth century and over 8 million foreigners in 2004. Ibn
Baz gave his opinion:

Q: What is your opinion regarding institutions that import *kafir* labourers?
IBN BAZ: It is prohibited to import *kafir* labourers to the Arabian Peninsula
   because the Prophet advised to 'Remove the infidels from the Arabian
   Peninsula'. He also said that no two religions should coexist in this land . . . We
   drew the attention of *wulat al-amr* [rulers] to this important matter in various
   media programmes and newspaper articles. The infidels are not meant to

make the Arabian Peninsula their place of residence. Also it is prohibited to give them nationality. They should not be allowed to practice the rituals of their religion. It is also prohibited to import them as labourers. Muslim labourers should be used instead. *Wali al-amr* can ask infidels to work here only in those situations where a Muslim cannot be found to do the job. After they perform this function, they should be deported to their country. This follows the tradition of the Prophet who allowed Jews to stay in Kheybar because of a need but Caliph Omar deported them when there was no need for them.[44]

As demonstrated by this opinion, Ibn Baz invokes two Prophetic traditions, one related to the obligation to remove infidels from the Arabian Peninsula, and the second to the fact that no two religions should coexist in this territory. A literalist interpretation of these Hadiths predisposes Ibn Baz to rule out reliance on infidels for labour. He, however, goes further than this. A Muslim should not initiate the act of greeting infidels during social and informal encounters,[45] but according to Ibn Baz, withholding greetings is not enough; he goes as far as ordering Muslims to nourish *bagdha'* (hatred) rather than *mawada* (affection) in their hearts for infidels.

Ibn Baz allowed the ruler some freedom in applying the Prophetic tradition. If special skills are required that only infidels possess, the ruler is allowed to import them for a short time, after which he is obliged to expel them. Ibn Baz's uncompromising view on economic and personal relations with infidels is at odds with his extremely flexible position regarding calling upon infidels for military assistance against fellow Muslims. His famous *fatwa* justifying inviting American troops to Saudi Arabia to liberate Kuwait from the army of Saddam – an infidel in his opinion – is a clear case of political pragmatism. Again, Ibn Baz demonstrated with clarity the position of official Wahhabiyya, which is radical in its judgement of social matters but extremely accommodating of political decisions made on the basis of expediency and necessity.[46]

To preserve the Saudi state, Wahhabi *'ulama* stretched the limits of Salafi theology; self-preservation, rather than the literal interpretation of scripture, was the ultimate criterion. Official *'ulama* confirmed political decisions, yet in social matters they expressed an uncompromising and coercive role, perhaps a substitute for loss of authority over rulers. Violence in Saudi Arabia in the twenty-first century is the outcome of contradictions in religious discourse. While an ordinary Muslim is not meant to greet infidels in the streets, host them in his country as labourers except if they are invited by the ruler and never travel to their lands unless under supervision, he is allowed to fight behind their army generals in the battlefield. Official Wahhabi scholars retained the social aspect of *al-bara'* (dissociation from infidels), which relates to personal relations between Muslims and non-Muslims represented in nourishing hatred and rejecting friendship, but they endorsed and even legitimised political *wala'* (subservience) to so-called infidels, exemplified by their total silence over Saudi foreign policy, foreign military bases in the country and other manifestations of Saudi alliances with the West. Again, Wahhabi discourse embodied contradictions that freed the political sphere from their jurisdiction while maintaining their control of the social.

The above-mentioned Prophetic traditions have become famous slogans adopted by Saudi Jihadis in their struggle against so-called infidels. After 11 September, and the outbreak of violence inside the country, this Hadith tradition underwent a reinterpretation. As Jihadis waged war under the banner of removing infidels from the Arabian Peninsula, in 2004 Sheikh al-Obaykan offered an interpretation that accommodates infidels rather than denounces them. He offers five clarifications. First, the land specified in Hadith refers only to the two holy mosques (Mecca and Madina). Second, the verb 'remove' applies to infidels who have permanent places of worship – for example, churches. Third, the Hadith addresses rulers rather than people, Fourth, infidels should be removed but their honour and wealth should be protected while removing them. And fifth, their removal is related to *maslaha* (interest). Al-Obaykan's interpretation implies that infidels in Saudi Arabia are *mu'ahadin*, enjoying a contractual relationship guaranteed by the ruler and the subjects that makes the shedding of their blood forbidden. This is one of the reinterpretations that official Wahhabi scholars are currently engaged in formulating in response to outside pressure and local Jihadi violence.[47]

Takfir

The second mechanism deployed in consolidating and expanding the political realm was excommunication. The practice of *takfir* against those whose Islam does not correspond to that defined by the state *'ulama* not only controlled social and religious 'deviance', as defined by Wahhabi interpretation, but also expanded the political realm under the pretext of correcting the blasphemy of others.

While there is extensive debate and documentation of Muslim opinions regarding the status of non-Muslims and near consensus over the terminology used to refer to them, depending on whether they are people of the book or others,[48] the labelling of other Muslims as *kafir* has always been problematic in Islamic history. Excommunication of other Muslims is a practice that draws the boundaries in between Muslims rather than dividing Muslims from non-Muslims. In practice it amounts to symbolic violence against the 'enemy within' by drawing on religious discourse and evidence, usually by an expert – a judge or religious scholar – in order to remove an insider from the community of the faithful. Historians of the Islamic tradition emphasise that *takfir* was common in the small study circles of religious scholars, especially in the medieval period. They agree that it remained confined to a limited circle of scholars who accused each other of blasphemy and heresy.[49] This practice became problematic, threatening internal dissent and precipitating chaos and discord. The historical case of the Kharijites, who excommunicated both the Caliph Ali and governor Muawiya, thus precipitating political chaos and dissent, is viewed with fear and abhorrence by Muslims up to the present day.[50] It is also argued that when 'mobs', a reference to people with little or no knowledge grounded in serious study of the Islamic tradition and jurisprudence, participated in the definition and labelling of others as *kafir*, disaster was bound to happen. Moreover, the intervention of political authority – for example, the ruler and his manipulation of excommunication for purely dynastic purposes such as the elimination of competitors and rebels – was bound to endow this practice with new and dangerous dimensions. Many early religious scholars warned against such intervention and foresaw its potential detrimental consequences. Some scholars felt uncomfortable with both mass excommunication (*takfir al-'umum*) – for example, when whole communities of Muslims are labelled *kafir* – and specific excommunication (*takfir al-mu'ayan*) – that is, labelling one individual as *kafir*. Others considered failure to identify a *kafir* as an act of *kufr* (blasphemy), thus making it incumbent on people of knowledge to identify a *kafir*. This latter position tends to be dominant in Wahhabi teachings.

In extreme cases the act of removing the *kafir* from the realm of the community is not only symbolic but real – for example, a death sentence after being given the opportunity to repent. While excommunication remains the prerogative of a small circle of religious experts and judges, the punishment of the person accused of *kufr* is usually the responsibility of political authority. The ruler is responsible for *iqamat al-hadd* (punishment). Excommunication can eventually lead to action against a person labelled a *kafir*, whose blood can be shed, wealth confiscated and marriage annulled. In general, excommunication removes the individual from the realm of the Muslim community.

Excommunicating Muslims as groups was a mechanism for state expansion in the Wahhabi tradition. Muhammad ibn Abd al-Wahhab declared, 'I excommunicate the one who knows the religion of the Prophet, and then he insults the religion, and forbids people to follow it, and becomes an enemy of those who know religion. This is the one that I excommunicate.'[51] Ibn Abd al-Wahhab refutes the accusation that he was excessive in excommunicating whole communities. In response to a question about excommunication and violence, he explains that those who do not declare faith and perform the remaining four pillars of Islam (Prayer, fast, alms, and pilgrimage) are *kafir*s. He specifies four categories of *kafir*. First is one who knows *tawhid* but does not act according to its principle. This is a *kafir* whom we fight as a result of his blasphemy (*'nuqatiluhu bi kufrihi'*). Second is one who knows *tawhid* but insults religion and prefers polytheists to monotheists. Third is one who knows, loves, and follows *tawhid*, but hates those who accept it. Fourth is one who knows *tawhid* but whose own people (for example, family or local community) are polytheists; he supports them against monotheists because he is fond of them and cannot leave them.[52]

In the Wahhabi tradition, *nawaqidh al-Islam* (factors that remove a person from the realm of Islam) are polytheism; association with God; failing to excommunicate polytheists; preferring another authority to that of Islam; hating part of the Prophet's message; ridiculing the Prophet's message; sorcery; assisting infidels against Muslims (under the concept of *al-wala' wa 'l-bara'*); excluding some people from the rule of Islam; and disrespecting Islam's teachings. The violation of one of the above removes the person from Islam, (*'kufr mukhrij min al-milla'*).[53]

However, it is well documented that Muhammad ibn Abd al-Wahhab and his later disciples followed a well-known formula in addressing other Muslims and calling upon them to become true Muslims by abandoning their *shirk* (polytheism). In a letter to all Muslims, Muhammad ibn Abd al-Wahhab says: 'The polytheists of our time are more numerous than the infidels at the time of the Prophet. They call upon angels, saints and pious people asking for forgiveness . . . Muslims know that *tawhid* is worshipping God. This is the religion of the messengers starting with Noah and the last one is Muhammad.'[54] This is clear evidence of *takfir al-'umum*, general excommunication of other Muslims.

Twentieth-century Wahhabi letters to other Muslims often start with a known formula. An example is a letter by Sheikh Muhammad ibn Abd al-Latif in 1918. The sheikh begins: 'From Muhammad ibn Abd al-Latif to the people of Asir, Hijaz and Yemen, may God guide them to Islam', implying that they are not true Muslims. As for the people of Najd, 'they had been subjected to the work of Satan and they succumbed to his bad ways'; for example:

They visited the tomb of Zayd ibn al-Khattab to ask for favours, their women were immoral. When their husbands were absent they visited palm trees and other trees, one of which was called Tarafiyya. They hugged the trees and asked favours. In Deriyyah itself, before the *da'wa*, there was a man called Taj who claimed holiness. People came to him asking for favours . . . In Taif, the tomb of Ibn Abbas was a place where associationist practices were performed, In Madina, the same associationist practices prevailed. In Egypt, paganism and associationist traditions prevailed. Also in Yemen, Sanaa, Hadramawt, Aleppo, Damascus,

Mosul, the land of the Kurds, and Mashhad, In general in all these lands clear *kufr* was demonstrated.[55]

In 1918 Sheikh Muhammad ibn Abd al-Latif wrote a letter describing his horror over the blasphemy he witnessed in the Hijaz:

Our rightful Imam, the glorious most respected, the one who has happiness and authority Abdulaziz ibn Abdulrahman ibn Saud, may God elevate him and keep him for Muslims to teach what God instructed his slaves. We have come back from the land of Hijaz and we have seen how Satan lived in this land among its people. Your people abstained from seeing light and guidance. They have fallen into a dangerous ignorance. They are on the verge of a burning hell. They worship tombs and trees. They venerate dead saints. This is the religion of the people of the first age of ignorance to whom the Prophet was sent.[56]

It is certain that the frequency of excommunication fluctuated according to the requirements of specific historical and political contexts rather than theological concerns. The above letter demonises Hijazis and reprimands them for their polytheism, certainly a justification for attacking them in the name of Islam and correcting their so-called Satanic religious practices. Although the practice of labelling other groups of Muslims – for example, Shi'is, Sufis, Ismailis and even other Sunni Muslims – as *mushrikun* (polytheists) or *mubdi'un* (innovators) continued throughout the twentieth century, specific individuals within these communities were rarely branded as such. Throughout the second half of the twentieth century, the practice of excommunicating specific individuals was more or less under control, for obvious reasons.

There were isolated occasions whereby a religious scholar issued an opinion describing someone as *mulhid* (atheist) and, by implication, a *kafir*. Scholars who applied such labels to an individual – especially among those called *'ilmaniyyun* (secularists) – engaged in the controversial and dangerous practice of *takfir al-mu'ayan*, the excommunication of specific individuals. Saudi writers who are considered to transgress and use language deemed offensive against religion are often targets of the practice of *takfir*: for example, Abdullah al-Qasimi, Ghazi al-Qusaybi and Turki al-Hamad. Abdullah al-Qasimi (1907–96) moved from Wahhabiyya to atheism, and was excommunicated as a result. According to his biographer, al-Qasimi lived in Cairo, possibly under the patronage of a Saudi prince, until his death.[57] Princes often provided refuge for excommunicated persons. King Abdullah (2005–) took the novelist Turki al-Hamad under his patronage although he was labelled *kafir*. In 2006 al-Hamad declared that King Abdullah offered him his pen as a gift. Religious scholars who offer alternative religious interpretations or question the premises of the Wahhabi tradition can also be subject to the *takfir* ruling – for example, the Sufi sheikh Muhammad Ulwi al-Maliki

(d. 2004), regarded by the Committee of Senior Ulama as *dhal* (one who has gone astray), and described as belonging to the religion of blasphemy (*millat al-kufr*).[58] Sheikh al-Maliki was suspended from preaching and teaching in the Hijaz. Another sheikh who challenged Wahhabi interpretations, Hasan Farhan al-Maliki, discussed later in this book, was also subjected to a similar ruling. However, punishment – usually a death sentence after the offer of repentance – rarely followed such judgments. The political authorities either ignored such rulings or offered protection to those labelled blasphemous by their own religious institution, another manifestation of the contradiction between Saudi religious rhetoric and reality. The determining factor was political expediency rather than religious opinion, and the Saudi royal family and the religious establishment were accomplices in enforcing control. The damage to individuals and their reputation was, however, great. Ordinary Saudis had to navigate a difficult terrain of contradictions between religious doctrine and political expediency.

Saudi religious scholars easily practised *takfir* against other Arab leaders, such as Nasser, Qadafi and Saddam, as well as Khomeini, all of whom challenged Saudi royal politics. Sheikh Ibn Baz clearly stated that 'Saddam is *kafir*, even though he says there is no God but Allah, and even though he prays and fasts. As long as he does not abandon his Ba'thist atheism and repents, he will remain a *kafir*.'[59] Such opinions were extremely important for the political leadership as it embarked on a war to liberate Kuwait from Saddam's army.

Throughout the history of the present Saudi state no ruler has ever been labelled *kafir*. Most Wahhabi *'ulama* would accept a usurper because they believed in the legitimacy of seizing power by force: 'a tyrannical sultan was better than perpetual strife'.[60] In the twentieth century, the legitimacy of Ibn Saud was questioned by the Ikhwan in 1927. While the Ikhwan did not practise *takfir al-mu'ayan* against Ibn Saud, they clearly considered some of his actions, especially his alliance with and subservience to Britain, as acts of *kufr*.[61] The same position was adopted by Juhayman al-Otaybi during his rebellion in the Holy Mosque in 1979 as he demonstrated in his *rasa'il* the blasphemous practices of the Saudi regime.[62] More recently, a similar ruling was passed on the Saudi regime with the publication of *al-Kawashif al-jalliyya fi kufr al-dawla al-saudiyya* (Clear Evidence of the Blasphemy of the Saudi Regime). While the author, known as Abu al-Bara al-Najdi (Asim al-Barqawi al-Maqdisi), was not Saudi, the book draws heavily on *aimat al-da'wa al-najdiyya*.[63] Two other books by Saudi dissidents drew similar conclusions relating to the blasphemous nature of the regime while refraining from naming individuals within it as *kafir*.[64]

The history of excommunication entered a new phase. Young *ʿulama* and political activists whose writings indirectly implied that the Saudi regime itself is blasphemous cited the practice of association with unbelievers against believers and *al-hukum bi ghayr ma anzala allah* (rule which does not comply with God's revealed message). Western-style banking is often cited as an example of violating the revealed message. In such dissident literature not identifying a *kafir* is considered *kufr* in itself, a typical Wahhabi position.

State Wahhabiyya refrained from excessive application of *takfir* against specific individuals inside Saudi Arabia. Even when religious scholars issued opinions in which they excommunicated a specific person, the state often ignored them. However, the social impact of such opinions remained extremely important and the consequences for the accused were grave. Wahhbai discourse stretched the limits when excommunicating whole communities of other Muslims or other Muslim leaders who challenged Saudi authority in the Arab world. Excommunication remained one of the most controversial issues debated between Wahhabi scholars and their opponents. While some of their opponents accepted their pure monotheism and other matters related to religious practice and worship, they challenged the Wahhabi interpretation of excommunication. With the strong emphasis on total obedience to the ruler, excommunicating him becomes the only mechanism justifying armed rebellion.

Jihad

The third mechanism consolidating the state was *jihad*, the 'struggle in the way of God'. In Wahhabi interpretations, *jihad* was defined and executed in several ways, violence being only one of them.[65] Armed *jihad* under the banner of the ruler is considered an aspect of obeying him. While most Wahhabi scholars believed in peaceful *daʿwa*, they privileged *jihad* wars against a whole range of so-called infidels, a category that included several Muslim groups, nationalities and sects. While the position of the founder of Wahhabiyya on *jihad* is well documented,[66] it is important to focus on how the duty of *jihad* was articulated by twentieth-century official Wahhabi scholars.

In contrast with the antagonistic attitude towards other Muslims, who were regarded as worse than the infidels of Quraysh during the times of the Prophet, official Wahhabiyya not only cooperated with but also accommodated Christians, who came to Arabia with the approval of the ruler. For example, Wahhabi scholars who surrounded Ibn Saud in Riyadh early in the twentieth century had no qualms about the British officer Shakespear fighting side by side with Ibn Saud's Ikhwan troops, who played an important role in consolidating his rule under the banner of enforcing monotheism. Shakespear died in battle while he was in Ibn Saud's military camp in 1916.[67] In the 1920s *jihad* against other Muslims – for example, the people of Qasim and Hail – was fought with subsidies that clearly came from the purse of so-called infidels: the British government.[68] When it became clear to the Ikhwan that their ruler, the rightful Imam to whom they swore allegiance, was obviously operating within the British sphere of influence, they rebelled against him, an incident that threatened to undermine the newly created realm. Their rebellion was not, however, solely about relations with infidels. It was primarily a rebellion against their marginalisation after they secured the ream for Ibn Saud. The Ikhwan rebellion was motivated by worldly matters and power sharing. However, in the rhetoric of the rebels, it was above all a protest against the violation of one of the ten principles that remove a Muslim from Islam: *al-wala' wa 'l-bara'* (association with Muslims and dissociation from infidels), a principle at the heart of Jihadi struggle in the twenty-first century. While the rebellion failed to achieve its objectives, it nevertheless created a schism within the Wahhabi religious community that has not yet been repaired, namely the division between those pragmatic Wahhabis who were close to political authority in Riyadh and those who maintained their autonomy and allegiance to God rather than worldly authority. Unfortunately, there is no elaborate historiography of the religious scholars who sided with the Ikhwan rebels, a function of the triumph of the state in eliminating their rebellion.[69] Although the Ikhwan fighters were defeated by 1930, the religious heritage that justified their rebellion remained a dormant trend within Wahhabiyya. The *'ulama* who sympathised with the Ikhwan rebels in their hearts remained marginal; nevertheless, their interpretations continued to erupt in the public sphere against a background of strict government control and co-optation. Contemporary Jihadi Sheikh Nasir al-Fahad, whose work on the blasphemy of assisting Americans in their wars against Muslims will be discussed later in this book, is but one young religious scholar whose intellectual genealogy includes important figures among *aimat al-da'wa al- najdiyya*, from Muhammad ibn Abd al-Wahhab to Safar al-Hawali.

After the Second World War, Saudi Arabia moved from the British sphere of influence to that of the United States. Official Wahhabiyya remained silent on the political alliance with the USA and its various phases throughout the twentieth century. Both oil wealth and the institutionalisation of religious discourse proved to be influential weapons against dissenting voices within the Wahhabi tradition. However, neither was totally successful.

On one occasion, before he became grand mufti, Sheikh Ibn Baz criticised the influx of what he called the infidels, who in the 1940s were mainly American engineers working on agricultural projects in al-Kharj, where he was judge. Ibn Baz was summoned to the court of Ibn Saud, where he was told not to interfere in such matters.[70] However, Ibn Baz remained a strong believer in keeping the Arabian Peninsula free of infidels and other religious traditions, in respect for the Hadith cited earlier. Nevertheless, he expressed great tolerance for 'infidel' soldiers defending the realm in his *fatwa* justifying the invitation of foreign troops to liberate Kuwait in 1990–1. This controversial *fatwa* has been subject to scrutiny in several studies, but most agree that those who produced it 'were discharging an odious duty wanted by none. But discharge it they did. After all, the *ulama* were in the business of defending the realm and they were not going to repeat the mistakes of yore where ideological purity came at the expense of practical survival.'[71]

Official Wahhabi discourse denounced infidels without specifying the USA, even in the explosive context of the Palestinian–Israeli conflict. Since 11 September, mosque *imams* have been prohibited from mentioning the USA by name in their supplication during Friday sermons, which traditionally include a denunciation of the 'enemies of Islam' and a call for the victory of Muslims. In 2001 the war on Afghanistan by the USA was conducted without the official Wahhabiyya being able to denounce it as an attack on Muslims. Only dissident Wahhabi *ulama* denounced the war, and described it as a new Crusade.[72] The Saudi regime was one of the first to recognise the Taliban state, but was also one of the first to end diplomatic relations with the Taliban, just before the American invasion took place.

Since the invasion of Iraq by US troops in 2003, official religious scholars have denounced resistance in Iraq as an illegitimate war, refusing to call it *jihad*. Despite the silence of the religious establishment on the issue, Chief Justice Sheikh Salih al-Lohaydan was caught on tape preaching to a Saudi audience that the situation in Iraq requires *jihad*: 'If someone knows that he is capable of entering Iraq in order to join the fight, and if his intention is to raise up the word of God, then he is free to do so.'[73]

The release of this tape coincided with Crown Prince Abdullah's visit to Crawford, Texas in April 2005. It was obvious that this tape was meant to embarrass the Saudi leadership at a time when Saudi–US relations had suffered a setback after 11 September. Sheikh al-Lohaydan was quick to issue a letter clarifying his position regarding violence in Iraq, which he refused to describe as *jihad*.[74] He withdrew his early enthusiasm for *jihad* in Iraq, which was clearly represented in the smuggled tape. He attributed the release of the tape to what he called the 'enemies of Islam', the

Washington-based, Shiʿi-run Saudi Institute, an organisation that claims to defend democracy and human rights in Saudi Arabia.[75] While al-Lohaydan denounced the Saudi Shiʿis as being behind the tape, he condemned the killing of members of Iraqi Shiʿi National Guard at the hands of the Iraqi resistance. Al-Lohaydan's clarification reflected the political pressures that were exerted on the Wahhabi establishment, especially after clear evidence suggesting the participation of young Saudis in the fighting in Iraq, which increased in 2004–5.

It is ironic that the call for *jihad* (with the tongue, heart and sword) was historically launched against fellow Muslims whose Islam was seen as corrupt or misguided, a situation that puts such Muslims in a category worse than the polytheists of Quraysh. It is a historical fact that most Wahhabi violence has targeted other Muslims rather than non-Muslims. This is not surprising, given that Wahhabi discourse continued to denounce Muslims whose Islam deviated from the true path as *ahl al-dhalal* (those who have gone astray). Punishing errant Muslims should be harsher, according to Wahhabi interpretations. And resisting foreign occupation – for example, in Afghanistan and Iraq – is regarded by official Wahhabi scholars as illegitimate violence.

Hijra, *takfir* and *jihad* were three mechanisms used not only to enforce the boundaries of the pious state but also to ensure total obedience to rulers. While *hijra* advocated migration to the pious realm, *takfir* encouraged expulsion from it. *Jihad*, both peaceful and violent, rendered life a perpetual struggle in the way of God, but in reality it was transformed into a political strategy applied only to enhance the authority of the rulers. The three concepts were emptied of their religious meaning and turned into political weapons to consolidate the realm and its moral guardians, the *ʿulama*. Official Wahhabi *ʿulama* turned their backs on the scholar who had served as their role model, Taqi al-Din Ahmad ibn Taymiyya (1263–1328), who is described as the model of the critic-scholar. In matters political, Wahhabi *ʿulama* followed the model of realist Mamluk scholar Badr al-Din ibn Jamaʿa (1241–1333), who preached 'obedience to any lawfully constituted authority'.[76]

Political innovations

In the process of establishing a state, Wahhabiyya confirmed several political innovations that have accompanied the development of Islamic history and civilisation. Wahhabiyya is described as a religious revivalist movement, but it certainly did not offer any political vision or theory different from those already in place within the Sunni tradition. In a desperate attempt to safeguard itself against annihilation of the religious call, marginalisation of the Najdi class of *'ulama* and the disintegration of the Saudi realm, Wahhabiyya supported and defended, with text and practice, two of the most controversial but dominant political innovations in Islamic history: hereditary rule and absolute obedience to political authority. It eventually deprived the Muslim community of its right to have a say in political matters. The only legitimate criticism of political authority was initiated in secrecy, between scholars and rulers: the latter are not in theory under any obligation to act according to the advice of the former.

During an encounter between Muhammad ibn Abd al-Wahhab and Muhammad ibn Saud in 1744, the former confirmed the latter in the position of *imama* (leadership of the Muslim state), and confirmed his descendants in their role as future Imams. It is reported that in Deriyyah around 1744 Muhammad ibn Abd al-Wahhab said to Muhammad Ibn Saud: 'The people of Najd are now ignorant polytheists, divided and diverse. They fight each other. I hope you will be the Imam around whom Muslims can gather and your children after you become successive imams. The Imam [Ibn Saud] welcomed him and gave him shelter.'[77] Wahhabiyya confirmed two mechanisms for the foundation of political power: *istila'* (seizing power by force), and *ta'iyyin* (the appointment of a successor by the current ruler (hereditary rule), while paying lip service to the third principle: *shura* (consultation).[78] The oath of allegiance (*bay'a*), normally given by both a loosely defined group called *ahl al-hall wa 'l-'aqd* ('the people who tie and loose') and the *ra'iyya* (subjects) became a dramatic ritual of obedience, and even more so with the advent of new communication technology.[79] Muhammad ibn Abd al-Wahhab decreed that it is compulsory to 'listen to and obey the ruler, even if he is a despot (*ja'ir*) and debauched (*fasiq*), as long as he does not order people to disobey God. People should gather around the one who assumes the caliphate and accept him. If he got the caliphate with his sword, he should be obeyed. Rebellion against a usurper is forbidden.'[80] As a Salafi movement that draws on the tradition of the pious ancestors, Wahhabiyya did not give sufficient significance to the succession of the first caliph, which other contemporary Salafis consider as the first *shura* experience in Islam. This sets the Wahhabi movement apart from other Salafi trends, especially contemporary variants that question the principle of total obedience to rulers and hereditary rule. Wahhabiyya is also different from the nineteenth-century modernist Salafiyya, which insisted on giving the *umma* an important role in the decision-making process.[81]

While twentieth-century Wahhabi scholars were constantly preoccupied with questions of ritual performance, tomb-visiting, intercession and other so-called polytheist innovations, they failed to produce a single treatise on the nature of the Islamic state and political authority. This was partly because they seriously believed in the Islamic nature of the state they had created, and then felt that there was no need to provide religious theorising for something that already existed, and partly because of the sensitivity of political theorising in Saudi Arabia, even that originating in religious circles. Ignoring Islamic political thought has been a feature of Wahhabiyya since its inception.[82] As a revivalist movement similar to other eighteenth-century movements, it was concerned above all with religious rather than political reform. Its most famous scholars were *fuqaha'* (jurists) and *qadis* (judges) rather than political ideologues. Its low-ranking preachers were *mutawa'a*, volunteers who disciplined bodies and souls even though they had very little literacy and knowledge of their own religious sources. Historically, the majority of the *mutawa'a* were *hafadhat Quran*, people who memorised the Quran or sections of it and had no other religious training.[83] According to Muhammad ibn Abd al-Wahhab's biographer, the sheikh did not concern himself with writing treatises discussing the nature of the Islamic *imama* (leadership of the Muslim state).[84] The *hakim* (ruler) and his characteristics are mentioned in passing. The ruler is also mentioned in the context of elaborating on *taghut*, a word literally meaning 'idols' but often translated as 'despot', with an obvious association with oppression, *tughyan*. In discussing the five types of *taghut*, Ibn Abd al-Wahhab lists the following categories: first, Satan, who calls people to worship those other than God; second, the despotic ruler who changes God's law; third, the ruler who does not govern in accordance with the revealed message of God; fourth, the one who claims knowledge of the unknown; and fifth, the one who accepts worship instead of God.

Most Wahhabi scholars do not go beyond the Sunni tradition, specifying that the ruler should be a free Muslim male. He should also be just, knowledgeable of *shari'a* and capable of public administration.[85] If such characteristics are present in a person from Quraysh, the Prophet's tribe, then he has priority over others; otherwise the position is open to all Muslims. Some scholars insist that Arab descent is preferred. The ruler is appointed as a result of the consensus of *ahl al-hall wa 'l-'aqd*, a reference to people of knowledge, as well as other important members of society. The current ruler can also appoint a successor, or a future ruler can seize power by force. In all situations, he must be obeyed.

One can only speculate on why Wahhabi discourse fell short of producing a political treatise that deals with urgent matters related to the Islamic polity. Perhaps its early and later advocates were unprepared for such an intellectual luxury in a context characterised by their geographical and social marginality in the Muslim world.[86] Perhaps Wahhabi scholars regarded their movement as too all-encompassing and holistic to be concerned with a limited area such as state and polity. However, it is clear that Wahhabi religio-political discourse failed to rise above its own social and environmental context. In political matters, Wahhabi scholars confirmed social rather than religious practices. Hereditary rule was one such practice that dominated political life among the sedentary population of the region where Wahhabiyya originated.[87] In political matters, Wahhabiyya confirmed *al-mawruth al-ijtima'i* (inherited social tradition) rather than challenging it. Another reason relates to Wahhabi suspicion of the masses, the *umma*, who are believed to degenerate easily into religious laxity and blasphemy. The *umma* can in no way be given a say in important matters such as politics. Although Wahhabi scholars reiterate the traditional formula that the *umma* does not consent to wrong decisions (*'la tajtami al-umma 'ala dhalal'*), in practice they took it for granted that the *umma* is potentially wrong. In their political preaching Wahhabi scholars continued to invoke a group that remains not so well defined, 'those who tie and loose', a significant unelected body in which they must be the dominant majority to correct *al-dhalal* (debauchery).

It is clear from the copious body of Wahhabi literature devoted to matters related to creed and worship that the movement's stated objective remained the purification and renewal of faith through the reform of religious practices. This preoccupation was conducive to the political hegemony of the state. Yet Muhammad ibn Abd al-Wahhab also implemented a vigorous application of the *shari'a*, which was very much dependent on the establishment of a pious state.

Ibn Abd al-Wahhab's understanding of the Islamic state was limited to applying *shari'a* and fighting religious innovation, without paying attention to the most important pillar in state formation – the principle by which a ruler is chosen, made accountable and changed if transgression from the true path is apparent. In fact, Wahhabi discourse rules out the possibility of the *umma* actively changing the ruler. While any violent rebellion is abhorred and prohibited, unless it is initiated by advocates of the movement, there is room only for an unbinding advice, with the hope that this would change any behaviour or policy not in accordance with the revealed message. In the Wahhabi worldview, the rightful ruler is the one who calls for and leads prayer (*uqim al-salah*). Only if such a ruler prohibits the performance of prayer can Muslims contemplate a hypothetical rebellion, which, as far as Islamic history is concerned, is without precedent. Even when Muslim territories fell under foreign and non-Muslim rulers, it was rare that Muslims were not allowed to perform communal prayer. Wahhabi perception of political issues had always been determined by a reiteration of selected medieval Muslim treatises that highlighted acquiescence and submission. While most Wahhabis revere the medieval jurists Sheikh Ahmad ibn Hanbal and Ahmad ibn Taymiyya, it is ironic that they have not followed their footsteps in some political matters. In politics, Wahhabi scholars overlooked revealed religious discourse, *al-munazal* (i.e. in the Quran), in favour of a politically subservient approach that endorsed constructed and interpreted religious discourse, *al-mu'awal*, which belonged to a later generation of Sunni *'ulama*.[88]

In Wahhabi discourse, the survival of Muslim society is dependent on the strength of the state. Without the call, the state loses its *raison d'être*, and without the state the call is weakened and risks being undermined by the return of the forces of misguided Islam and the confounding of the permissible and prohibited. Consequently, the Islamised person and *umma* are constantly at risk of regressing to the *status quo ante*, the age of ignorance, in terms of personal piety, worship and societal relations. The concept of *jahiliyya* (the age of ignorance) was an integral part of Wahhabi discourse from the eighteenth century. Muhammad ibn Abd al-Wahhab wrote a book that deals with aspects of the so-called ignorant society. The age of ignorance was a label used to describe the population of Arabia at the time of the call of Ibn Abd al-Wahhab. In *Masail al-jahiliyya*, Ibn Abd al-Wahhab described a series of beliefs and practices associated with the age of ignorance, which prevailed before the call of the Prophet. The message was clear: the first age of ignorance was being repeated in Arabia in Ibn Abd al-Wahhab's time. Ibn Abd al-Wahhab described the population of his time as being 'worse than the *kafirs* of Quraysh', who were known to 'disobey *wali al amr* [the ruler]'. Among the people of ignorance, 'refusing to obey the ruler is a virtue, some made this practice a religion. The Prophet ordered them to be patient when confronted with the repression of rulers. He ordered them to listen to such a ruler, obey him, and advise him.'[89]

Wahhabi discourse preceded modern twentieth-century Islamist theorisations of the concept of the age of ignorance, the most famous of which was that of Egyptian Muhammad Qutb.[90] In Wahhabiyya, the personal, social and political were interrelated in a web that required the control of the person and society by the state and religious scholars. The question of obeying both the state and the *'ulama* is therefore crucial. Theorising obedience is perhaps the only exception to the rule in the Wahhabi tradition –its general neglect of theorising politics, as discussed earlier.

In the Wahhabi worldview, three levels of obedience have equal status: obedience to God; obedience to the Prophet; and obedience to those charged with authority, defined as the princes (*umara*) and the people of knowledge (*'ulama*). In a lecture delivered at the Great Mosque in Riyadh, Grand Mufti Sheikh Abdulaziz ibn Baz interpreted an important Quranic verse cited above: 'O ye who believe Obey Allah, and obey the Messenger, and those charged with authority among you.'[91] The title of the lecture was 'Explaining the Rights of Those Charged with Authority'.

He stated that the route to happiness and guidance is obedience to God, the Messenger and those charged with authority. Obeying those in authority follows on from fulfilling the obligation to obey God and the messenger. He defined those charged with authority as the *umara* and *'ulama*. Obedience must be to *ma'ruf* (that which is known in *shari'a*); no obedience is permitted to *ma'siyya* (sins).[92] In this interpretation, Ibn Baz follows a well-established tradition. Early Wahhabi scholars confirmed 'that a Muslim should obey the rightful imam regardless of whether he is *fajir* [despotic], or *fasiq* [debauched], offer him *zakat*, perform *jihad* under his banner, give him booty after battle, and never rebel against him using the sword. A final word, obey him until God finds you a way out. Any rebellious person is an innovator and a rejectionist who abandons the community, threatening dissent. A final advice is given to the true Muslim. Hold yourself during dissent because it is a prophetic tradition.'[93] Moreover, the prohibition of violent rebellion is extended to include public criticism of the ruler.

Although Ibn Baz's interpretation of the Quranic verse on obedience to rulers is the one adopted by the Saudi–Wahhabi religious establishment, it is not the only interpretation possible, nor is it the only one acceptable to all Sunni scholars. According to one Salafi source, Ibn Baz's interpretation of the Quranic verse overlooks the absence of the verb obey, *atiu*, when the text refers to the third element in the chain of obedience, *uli al-amr* (those charged with authority). The sura orders Muslims to obey God, and obey the Prophet, repeating the verb 'obey'. However, obeying rulers is added using the letter *waw* ('and') in Arabic. Some interpreters of the text argue that obeying the leader cannot be placed on equal footing as obeying God and his Prophet, and that this is demonstrated by the absence of the verb 'obey' before the order to include *uli al-amr* in the sura.[94] With the outbreak of violence and calls to disobey a ruler who fails to demonstrate his Islamic credentials and pursue an Islamic policy, Ibn Baz's interpretation of obedience to the ruler remains an important weapon against dissidence and rebellion. Obedience is a constant theme that dominates religious programmes. Rebellion encompasses a wide range of acts in official Wahhabi discourse. At one end stands violence (*khuruj bi 'l-sayf*), while at the other, writing an article critical of the regime, sending an informative fax or advising the ruler in public are glossed as acts of *khuruj' ala wali al-amr* (rebellion against the ruler). Recently, actions such as expressing an alternative political vision or signing a petition calling for reform have been defined as *khuruj 'ala wali al-amr*, according to Wahhabi judges.[95]

The interpretation of the Quranic verse relating to obeying those charged with authority, now considered part and parcel of obeying God and his Prophet, automatically outlaws armed rebellion against rulers, except in very limited circumstances. Most twentieth-century Wahhabi scholars insist that rebellion can be sanctioned in certain limited situations, but in practice they refrain from clarifying the conditions that allow such rebellion to take place without violating creed and faith. If the ruler displays *kufr bawwah* (obvious blasphemy), for example forbidding the performance of public prayers in mosques, the question of whether armed rebellion may or may not be justified is left unanswered, although hypothetically forbidding prayer is an act of blasphemy that justifies armed rebellion.

Responding to a question regarding whether a ruler who issues new secular laws deserves to be reprimanded or even disobeyed, Sheikh Ibn Baz replied that if new laws do not contradict *shari'a*, it is permissible for the ruler to do so, as there might be good for Muslims behind such new legislation. However, if legislation contradicts or replaces *shari'a*, this is not permissible. He gives the example of suspending punishment for acts such as fornication, alcohol consumption and theft. If the ruler suspends *shari'a* in such cases, he is regarded as *kafir* (blasphemous). How do Muslims deal with a ruler who suspends *shari'a* or enacts legislation that contradicts it? Ibn Baz confirms that good Muslims should obey such a ruler in *ma'ruf* (that which is known in *shari'a*) and not in *ma'siyya* (sin), until God changes him ('ubadilu hu allah').[96] Note that Ibn Baz does not contemplate confronting the ruler even if he suspends divine law or introduces legislation that does not conform to *shari'a*. He emphasises obedience to such a ruler until God decides to replace him or repudiate his actions, thus ruling out the possibility of the community taking any active political position. In this official Wahhabi political worldview, political activism is *khuruj 'ala al-hakim*, an abhorred rebellion that leads to chaos and discord, thus threatening religion. A good Muslim should wait for God to act in this particular situation, a position that represents the views of some but not all Sunni scholars. This interpretation is conducive to the rule of sultans and hereditary office, and historically such interpretations flourished in royal courts. Ibn Baz is a later addition to the chain of religious *noblesse d'état*.

While not distinguishing between various forms of armed rebellion and peaceful criticism, in general official Wahhabi scholars confuse political rebellion (*khuruj siyasi*) with religious rebellion that challenges creed (*khuruj 'aqa'idi*).[97] The first type is a rebellion against worldly power, and its permissibility is subject to debate among Muslim scholars, whereas the second is a rebellion against the divine message, where there is a near-consensus among scholars that it is forbidden. This confusion among official Wahhabi scholars regarding *khuruj siyasi* contributes to the mystification of politics, thus granting sanctity to those charged with worldly authority, for example the *umara*, and those in charge of interpreting the divine message, the *'ulama*. Peaceful political activism, passive resistance and armed rebellion are confused and rendered prohibited behaviour punishable by God and state. Under the patronage of the *umara*, Wahhabi *'ulama* sealed the fate of political activism, both armed and peaceful, by describing it as sinful behaviour that challenges creed (*al-'aqida*).

The overwhelming importance of submission to the ruler, once such submission was equated with submission to God and the Prophet, silenced any questioning of the role of those in power or criticism of their policies. In its extreme manifestation, this theological position encouraged total acquiescence and discouraged even the mildest public criticism of those charged with authority. Open criticism or even evaluation of the role of the ruler is confused with *al-sabb* (insult), an unforgivable great *munkar*, an evil calling for evil. Having established the obligation to obey the rulers and people of knowledge, Sheikh Ibn Baz gave a religious opinion regarding those who 'insult the *umara* and *'ulama*'.[98] The subjects (*al-ra'iyya*) are under obligation to praise the ruler rather than criticise him, and to applaud his deeds rather than expose his faults. In the same interview, Sheikh Ibn Baz was asked whether the 'word' (*al-kalima*), implying public advice using the press for example, influences the country's security, especially that which comes by fax from outside and is issued by those 'who bear grudges against the land and its people of authority'. Sheikh Ibn Baz described this kind of word as the worst evil, which must be avoided.[99] The sanctity of the *umara* that Ibn Baz promotes is shared by the *'ulama*, mainly those tied through state institutions to the ruling group. Criticising them amounts to insulting them.

A contemporary popular version of the emphasis on subservience to the ruler continues to appear in Saudi-approved internet discussion boards. Sheikhs post articles and treatises on how to deal with rulers according to the Islamic tradition, drawing on a style that invokes the words of God (Quranic verses), Hadith and the sayings of a long list of pious *'ulama*, all arguing that it is incumbent upon a Muslim to obey the ruler. In one article, Sheikh Osama al-Otaybi cites three sources to authenticate the obligation to obey by grounding it in solid Islamic Salafi sources. The message targets the 'young' who are in his opinion confused about what is expected of them. He lists several obligations that a Muslim should respect in relation with the ruler. A Muslim is under the obligation to give the ruler the oath of allegiance; listen and obey; respect him; ask God to protect him and refrain from asking God to harm him; pray behind him; give him *zakat*; perform pilgrimage and *jihad* with him; advise him in secrecy not in public; abstain from insulting him; remain within the consensus of the community; and never rebel against him, even with the word. Failure to do so consigns a person to the realm of the pro-hibited. Again and again official Wahhabis confuse religious and political rebellions. They also confuse peaceful resistance with armed rebellion. Such treatises always end with a clear message. Al-Otaybi concludes his message to the youth of the country:

It is clear that the rulers of the Saudi state must be given the oath of allegiance. This is an obligation. The people who tie and loose have given the king the *bay'a*; therefore, all Saudis are under the obligation to give it. The rulers of the Saudi state must be respected. You must supplicate asking God to protect them. You must pray behind them and pay them *zakat*. You must perform the pilgrimage and *jihad* with them. You must advise them secretly not in public. You must not gossip about them. You must not insult them and show their sins. It is forbidden to rebel against them. You must not help those who rebel against them even with the word. I ask God to protect them and guide them to all good for the country and the people.[100]

If ever the *'ulama* want to express reservations on policy and policy makers, such expression must follow an acceptable and legitimate formula. Advising the ruler (*nasiha*), writing to him (*mukataba*) and alert-ing him (*tanbih*) must be performed in secrecy, initially taking the form of 'congratulating' and 'praising' him for his good behaviour, and mildly encouraging him to reconsider matters relating to policy. All this should be done away from the gaze of the masses or the press for fear of under-mining the stature of the ruler. Sheikh Ibn Baz abhors the idea that the ruler's *'uyub* (faults or shameful behaviour) should be discussed using a public platform such as mosque minarets or transmitted by faxes to the public. Later official scholars emphasised that resorting to the media to criticise the *umara* and *'ulama* is also forbidden, a clear reference to Saudi opposition radio stations al-Islah and al-Tajdid, which broadcast from London in 2003. Alternative views on the form and substance of advice to rulers insist that secret advice is suitable only when *ma'siyya* (sin) is secre-tive. However, when sins are public, they deserve a public response from the Muslim community. Furthermore, in the absence of legitimate chan-nels and institutions for the delivery of advice, the *umma* must express criticism in the public sphere.

Such uncompromising insistence on total submission to political authority consolidated the powers of the state and those who grew in its shadow, the *'ulama*. The emphasis on total obedience neutralises any political activism that might challenge the leadership, and has serious political consequences. Saudi dissidents who objected to the ruler or aspects of his behaviour have resorted to *takfir* (excommunication) of the ruler in order to justify their disobedience. Disobedience becomes permissible only in a situation where the ruler is labelled *kafir* (blasphemous). Wahhabi dissidence in 1927, 1979 and the 1990s was justified on the basis of the ruler displaying *al-kufr al-bawwah* (clear blasphemy). Jihadi discourse in the twenty-first century is entirely grounded in a theological position that allows dissidence and even armed struggle against a 'blasphemous' ruler. In the absence of other means of expressing difference, criticism or disagreement with the ruler, excommunicating him becomes the only possible mechanism; violence becomes the only means of changing the situation.

Having nurtured political acquiescence and promised divine punishment for those who disobey the ruler, Wahhabiyya itself thrived on state-sponsored modernisation and oil wealth. It was propagated and enforced not only in mosques, scholars' study circles and pious shopkeepers' private *majlis*, but also in ultra-modern university lecture halls, international conferences, pan-Islamic organisations and, since the 1990s, internet websites and satellite television.

In summary, official Wahhabi religio-political discourse was characterised by a number of principles. These included accepting the legitimacy of the ruler regardless of how he seized power; denial of the *umma*'s political participation, as it is innately wrong; granting the ruler unlimited powers in politics; allowing various powerful rulers to contest power without interference from the community; refusal to distinguish between armed rebellion and political change by peaceful means; confirmation of the permissibility of giving secret, non-binding advice to rulers; and neglected the accountability of rulers. Official Wahhabi discourse produced consenting subjects rather than citizens.

Engaging with modernity

Before mid-twentieth century, Wahhabi *'ulama* were literate men in an illiterate society. With the establishment of the state and the advent of oil wealth and mass education, they became one group among several capable of articulating religious ideas and interpretations. Their engagement with modernity centred on formulating opinions on whether aspects of modernity were permissible or prohibited. In addition to their long-established expertise in creed and ritual purity, official *'ulama* developed religious rulings regarding technological aspects of modernity (cars, aeroplanes, radio, television, cassettes, faxes and the internet), and its economic challenges (banking, insurance and other new economic innovations). Socially, official Wahhabi scholars devoted considerable energy to issuing opinions that maintained strict control over men and women. Their *fatwas* on sex segregation, women's attire, false eyelashes, sports centres, body massage, hair removal and other innovations related to social and physical femininity are notorious.[101] A survey of volumes of Wahhabi *fatwa*s, together with thousands of sound bites on local and satellite Saudi television channels, indicates the centrality of ritual practices in Wahhabi thought and expertise, used to control the social sphere. These *fatwa*s reflect a desperate attempt by the ʿ*ulama* to remain relevant in a changing world.

These *fatwa*s also demonstrate the failure of Wahhabi ʿ*ulama* to engage with modernity beyond formulating opinions on the permissible and the prohibited in the social sphere and in ritual practice. These concerns stem from their desire to control an Islamised public sphere, taken to measure the piety of state and society.

Modernity paved the way for the emergence of the young, articulate, computer literate and cosmopolitan Wahhabi scholar. Today most official Saudi ʿ*ulama* and preachers have their own websites. The Wahhabi message is no longer preserved in handwritten chronicles and epistles, copied on small wooden boards or paper, which was in short supply only half a century ago. Today the tradition is continued in polished and elegantly bound high-quality volumes, CD ROMs, and internet web pages.

The life expectancy of the interpreters and guardians of the Wahhabiyya is stretched beyond the imagination of their predecessors, who until recently suffered blindness and chronic deadly illnesses, including cholera, chicken pox and measles.[102] Today state ʿ*ulama* travel abroad for medical treatment, live in luxurious villas, receive substantial sums of money for their noble services to political authority, Islam and Muslims, and preside over committees, charitable organisations and international religious conferences attended not only by the faithful from the main local historic centres of Wahhabi religious learning, but also from places as close as Mecca and Medina and as far away as Jakarta, New Delhi, Lagos and London. The image of the blind, miserable and poor scholar, living on a meagre income in return for religious services, has given way to wealthy guardians of the tradition, who are seen on television screens greeting princes and international delegations visiting the country. The early scholars whose names were linked to entrepreneurial commercial families are now wealthier, more influential and more connected with the world of power, money and scholarship, thanks to a solid alliance with the ruling family and generous handouts that cement loyalty and dependency. Being part of religious industry and bureaucracy has proved to be a good mechanism for social and economic mobility. While modern society needed scientists, doctors and engineers, it also needed religious scholars to ensure that no blasphemous aspects of modernity are incorporated or endorsed.

Wahhabi ʿ*ulama* today play an important ceremonial role in the patina of Islam that covers Saudi society. Scholars distinguished by their beards, special headgear that is not tied by *'uqal* (head-rope), and ankle-length *thawb* (male robes) have become an indispensable chorus in the drama of power that unfolds daily on Saudi local and satellite television and in the print media. Senior princes must be seen greeting important scholars during all national events, just as they need to be seen distributing prizes to students who have excelled in memorising the Quran and *shari'a* sciences. Religious scholars rush to greet princes at airports and in glamorous public places surrounded by media and well-wishers. They play the role of ritual elders who claim the power to interpret sacred texts, sanction power and enchant the audience.

Official Wahhabis accepted and endorsed aspects of modernity only if these fell under their control. For example, after objecting to female education in the early 1960s, they accepted it after being put in charge of the female curriculum and schools.[103] Similarly, in the early 1960s they objected to television, but later agreed to it when they were assured that they would dominate broadcasting. In the 1990s they denounced satellite television, but later endorsed it after they were guaranteed constant appearances on religious programmes. Today they have their own television channels, for example Iqra and al-Majd. They originally denounced the internet as immoral, but since 1998 they have become active participants in cyberspace through personal websites and discussion boards. After decades of considering elections *bid'a* (an un-Islamic alien innovation),[104] in 2005 they not only accepted partial municipal elections but endorsed and patronised the candidates. Important scholars visited contestants in their campaign tents and made it known that they offered informal certificates of good conduct (*tazkiyya*). It is unlikely that they would object to general elections if they are promised control over the process, a development that would also be welcomed by the political authority.

The innovations of modernity, together with communication technology, have allowed both the consolidation and contestation of official Wahhabi discourse. Official Wahhabiyya has showed great flexibility and pragmatism. However, this was entirely dependent on the gains that would accrue to its most prominent figures as a result of accepting and legitimising innovations. While modernity consolidated and spread Wahhabi discourse both in Saudi Arabia and abroad, it resulted simultaneously in its contestation. Both advocates and critics of Wahhabiyya have endorsed modern technology for the promotion of their message. While the means for the dissemination of Wahhbaiyya has become ultra-modern, the message remains far removed from the spirit of political modernity.

Official Wahhabi *'ulama* have failed to deal with the political and ethical aspects of modernity. Politics has remained a prohibited field, discussed only by *al-khassa*, a minority of chosen people, mainly the *umara* and themselves, who are endowed with the ability to interpret sacred texts and advise the ruler accordingly. However, this ability to interpret the sacred is now shared with a whole range of other non-official *ulama*, intellectuals and laymen, all a product of increased literacy and education. Official Wahhabiyya has watched the proliferation of religious discourse with great alarm.

Wahhabi scholars preferred to leave politics to the state while concentrating on matters related to *fiqh al-halal wa 'l-haram* (jurisprudence of the permissible and the forbidden) and *fiqh al-ʿibadat* (jurisprudence of worship). Traditional Wahhabiyya shied away from engaging with obvious and important polemics related to the nature of the Islamic state, the selection of the Muslim ruler, the status of kingship in Islam (*al-mulk*), the accountability of rulers and other political matters. No important theological doctrine was developed in these areas because of their political sensitivity, which such intellectual exercise would expose. Wahhabi *ulama* continued to reiterate opinions of selected scholars of the medieval period without serious engagement with contemporary political issues. Their excuse was that they are Salafis, following in the footsteps of an earlier generation of pious ancestors.

The official *ulama* failed to reflect on their own role in the modern Saudi state. They refrained from critically examining this role and tracing its evolving nature. Simply content with being guardians of the moral order while leaving political power in the hands of the ruling family and an expanding class of bureaucrats and technocrats, they lacked self-consciousness and awareness. The Saudi *ulama* accepted the *de facto* separation between religion and politics, while adopting a narrow definition of religion as all matters relating to personal conduct and *ʿibada* (worship). They excelled in controlling the social sphere while leaving the political field in the hands of the state. The Wahhabi *ulama* contributed to the consolidation of a state that is politically secular and socially religious. This enigmatic duality is an important feature of the contemporary Saudi regime, often overlooked in scholarly work on the country.

Traditional *ulama* engaged with modernity through the prism of the permissible and prohibited. This is not surprising given their training and expertise. After all, their occupation requires them to formulate such opinions. However, their only engagement with contemporary problems has been to condemn modern society for its alleged corruption, consumerism, moral laxity and degeneration. The view that society consists of potential sinners cannot be conducive to any form of democratic government or political participation. How can society give its opinion on important political matters when it is potentially *dhal* (astray or debauched)? This position stands in opposition to the Prophetic tradition, which clearly states that Muhammad's *umma* cannot agree upon error. Official Wahhabiyya coerced society morally, symbolically and physically in order to ensure its 'Islamisation', thus theoretically ensuring good Islamic government and political acquiescence. This position served the interests of the state, since the state was keen to be seen as guarding the Islamic moral order.

Official *'ulama* were far removed from urgent issues that dominated the intellectual scene in the Arab and Islamic world such as questions of social justice, political participation, the rights of women and minorities, the relationship between the modern nation-state and the wider Muslim world, relations with the international community, membership in international organisations and other urgent matters that flooded public debate in the second half of the twentieth century. Official Wahhabis remained oblivious to these matters while celebrating the Muslim state created under the banner of the Al-Saud and allegedly according to the principles of *tawhid* (the oneness of God). The failure of official Wahhabiyya to engage with the more problematic political aspects of modernity, in addition to its rejection of other Muslim traditions, led to the movement becoming a contested religious field in its own society and by people who claim to be Salafis. Today official Wahhabiyya is entangled in serious intellectual battles with diverse opponents, some of whom are its previous disciples (for example Sahwis and Jihadis) whereas others are historical enemies (for example Saudi liberals, Shi'is, Sufis and Ismailis). In Saudi Arabia today, official Wahhabiyya is one Salafiyya among others.

The relationship between religion and politics in Saudi Arabia clearly illustrates that the state is not a 'theocratic unitarian state', as described by an earlier generation of scholars and often repeated in the Western media.[105] The Saudi regime is a hybrid formation that subjects religion to political will. It is neither fully secular nor religious. It is a pragmatic entity that has survived as a result of the strength of the power of oil and mystification, both internal and external. It is best described as a post-modern pastiche. The gap between the social sphere controlled by religious scholars and the political sphere controlled by royalty is responsible for serious contradictions experienced at the level of the individual and society. It is this contradiction that is a fertile incubator for the violence that is unfolding in Saudi Arabia. While some Saudis continue to regard their Islamised social public sphere as a reflection of Islamic government, others are aware of the contradiction between rhetoric and reality. In debating this reality some have resorted to the word, whereas others have preferred the sword. In both situations, the consenting Wahhabi religio-political discourse carried the seeds of its own contestation.

2　Re-enchanting politics: Sahwis from contestation to co-optation

> We, the youth of Islam, were able to dismantle the circle of subservience to the West, reject its deceiving civilisation, know its conspiracies, but so far we do not know the reality of who we are . . . I am surprised that the vanguards of the Islamic call think that the religion of the people of Sunna and *jamma'a* is about theoretical propositions relating to the unknown world rather than about a call for reform and change.
>
> Sheikh Safar al-Hawali, *Sharh*, p. 9

Official Wahhabiyya created consenting subjects. Wealth allowed the Saudi regime to consolidate aspects of religion in the public sphere while pursuing gradual but determined political secularisation.[1] Saudi society and the public sphere were 'Islamised' while politics and the modern state remained an autonomous field beyond the reach of most senior religious scholars. Official *'ulama* developed a discourse that sanctioned this schism. The Wahhabi tradition described in the last chapter ensured that politics remained in the hands of those who claim to know people's interest. The guiding principle was – and still is – 'al-hukam a'lam bi al-maslaha' (the rulers know the public good). Official Wahhabi scholars removed not only themselves but the rest of society from political matters. They prohibited engagement in public affairs. Their religious discourse, especially that which confirmed the potential corruption and blasphemy of the *umma*, reinforced the marginalisation of the public and their exclusion from the political decision-making process. Under the banner of the state, official Wahhabiyya refined and consolidated a religious discourse that disenfranchised society and disenchanted politics.

The official Wahhabi tradition led to the consolidation of a society predominantly preoccupied with ritualistic Islam. Society evolved into a community of the faithful who vigorously engage in controlled *'ibadat* (rituals of worship), both communal and individual, that are regularly displayed in the public sphere. Such display is strictly controlled, and any deviation is condemned as innovation. Prayer, fasting and pilgrimage have been turned into spectacles regularly dramatised on local and satellite television channels. The enchantment of society, however, was restricted to the level of religious practice. In politics, only an enchanting rhetoric was retained while state practice attested to a different reality. In its propaganda, the Saudi regime reiterates that it is *dawlat al-tawhid* (the monotheist polity) that governs according to the revealed message of God. In practice, many Saudis see a different reality.

Nothing exemplifies the enchantment of Saudi society like a local television programme called Fatwa on Air, a special performance normally hosting a religious scholar who responds to questions posed by the public. The programme started in the 1960s and continues to the present day. A scholar issues religious opinions regarding the questions asked. Callers usually ask very specific questions. A woman wants to know whether menstruating for three weeks qualifies as menstruation, thus preventing her from performing prayers. A man asks whether it is permissible to borrow money to allow his mother to perform the pilgrimage. A third person asks whether high heels are permissible for women and whether diamond rings are a legitimate accessory for men. The repetitiveness and regularity of these television programmes confirm Saudi society as obsessively concerned with the ritualistic aspect of Islam. Such programmes reduce a world religion to a set of prohibited and permissible actions for the sake of demonstrating the religiosity of power. Questioning, offering advice to or criticising the political authorities is prohibited on television as much as it is elsewhere.

With the spread of new communication technology such as the internet, Saudi religious scholars who have their own websites often include a subsection, entitled 'Fatwa on line', where they respond to questions often very similar to, if not more daring than, those posed by television viewers. These sites are very popular, and continue to grow. Recently, a single young Saudi posed a question to an important and famous religious scholar regarding whether he could have sexual relations with his Filipino maid. He asked whether in this modern day a maid imported from abroad and receiving a monthly salary can be considered *jariyya*, a female slave, with whom sexual relations are licit in Islam. Women pose questions whether cosmetic surgery, false eyelashes, trousers and high heels are permissible. Religious scholars always find answers either based on a clear textual reference from the Quran or Hadith or using other methods for arriving at a ruling.

The procedure for issuing a religious ruling follows a well-known formula. It starts with 'God said', thus citing one or two Quranic verses, then 'the Prophet said', citing a Hadith, followed by quotations from the sayings of *al-salaf al-salih* (the pious ancestors). In most cases the three citations can easily be provided. However, new areas of social life for which there are no clear verses to be cited are dealt with differently using *ijtihad* (exertion in search of religious ruling) and *qiyas* (deduction by analogy) or other well-known methods. On television, it is almost impossible to come across callers who openly question religious scholars on public issues relating to government policy, religious interpretations or any contested and controversial topics. Callers avoid political issues such as democracy and Islam, human rights in Islam, and how to deal with differences in religious interpretations. No discussion of obedience to rulers, the nature of public advice to rulers or other politically sensitive matters is expected. *Fatwa*s are always concerned with the minute details of everyday life such as personal piety or relations between individuals. Relations between ruler and subjects are often discussed in public lectures where an audience listens to lectures calling upon the faithful to obey. These lectures faithfully repeat the discourse discussed in the last chapter.

The state is heavily involved in the religious sphere, not only as sponsor but also as controller. Princes are always seen distributing prizes among people who serve religion, for example clever boys who memorise the Quran at an early age, scholars who write religious treatises denouncing the enemies of the regime, preachers who dedicate their lives to spreading the official Wahhabi version of Islam, and so on. Princes often donate vast sums for visible and prestigious Islamic projects that add to their standing both locally and internationally. Saudis experience an enchanted world and a mystified public sphere with several thousand religious specialists contributing to maintaining this state of enchantment. It is estimated, however, that of the approximately one million sermons and religious lessons in mosques, only 300,000 are authorised by the Ministry of Islamic Affairs.[2]

Issuing *fatwa*s and religious instruction in general have been transformed into highly professional activities that needed an expanding specialist religious bureaucracy, educational institutions and organisations. The 'people of knowledge' are no longer a small coterie, educated in Riyadh and drawn from its environs. By the end of the twentieth century, the category included – in addition to the Najdi–Wahhabi core – thousands of *'ulama*, preachers, educators, university lecturers, ideologues and others who came from various regions.

While official religious knowledge prepared a generation of consenting subjects, in addition to *'ulama*, religious teachers and preachers, a doctorate in religious studies was a novelty that accompanied the establishment of the 'religious university'.[3] Saudi Arabia had never had the equivalent of al-Azhar, al-Qairawan or al-Najaf, where an ancient tradition of religious learning was established. In modern times, the informal study circles that flourished in the main holy cities, Mecca and Madina, lagged behind their counterparts in other parts of the Muslim world. Oil money allowed

Saudi Arabia the luxury, prestige and legitimacy associated with the most sacred of knowledge: religious education.

The first Islamic university was established in Madina in 1961. In the 1990s, with a budget over $US50 million, the various faculties had 378 members of staff specialising in linguistics, Islamic literature, jurisprudence, Islamic law, *shariʿa*, Hadith, *daʿwa* and other branches of religious studies.[4] According to Saudi sources, in 2000–1, more than two thousand students were registered at the university; 80 per cent of the total enrolment were Saudis, with the remaining students coming from more than seventy countries.[5]

In Riyadh, Imam Muhammad ibn Saud Islamic University was granted university status in 1974 to cater for a local rather than an international student population. Various religious colleges in Riyadh, such as the Scientific Institute founded in 1950, and other small colleges in Qasim were consolidated under the umbrella of this institution. With a budget of $US280 million in 1990, the university had branches in several cities, producing a total of over twenty thousand graduates every year.[6] In 2000–1 the university had more than 1,300 teachers and more than 23,000 students, of whom 643 were female.[7]

In the early 1990s the Islamic University granted 131 doctorates and the Imam University 264. While the universally accepted definition of a doctorate assumes originality and critical thinking, a doctorate from one of these universities may not meet these criteria. It is argued that 'research is commonly invoked and methodology courses are prescribed, but the success of these efforts is uncertain, especially since the parameters of research – the implicit "red lines" of permissible enquiry – are understood . . . real controversy is avoided, and any hint of criticism of government policies is non-existent'.[8] Like religious television programmes, many doctoral theses are studies of the minute details of worship.[9] Others deal with sectarian differences among Muslims, confirming that the 'other' is either outside Islam or an innovator. The red lines that are never crossed by graduate students are often related to the religio-political Wahhabi discourse, which remains unchallenged at least in a Wahhabi university. However, as the university aimed to generate consent, contestation was a by-product.

A doctorate in religious knowledge was a total innovation in the Wahhabi tradition; nevertheless, it symbolised the transformation of the consolidation and transmission of this knowledge. Historically not many Wahhabi *ulama* engaged in writing theoretical treatises. The previous generation of *ulama*, including Muhammad ibn Abd al-Wahhab himself, were 'problem-solvers' and jurists rather than religious intellectuals. With the arrival of the modern university, religious knowledge moved from the traditional study circles in the mosques and small *ma'ahid* (institutes) of Riyadh, Buraydah, Unayzah and Hail, where established religious figures taught their followers, to the modern surroundings of the urban university where a new modern-style education was adopted.[10] Religious universities, in addition to other centres of higher learning where a religious education is a compulsory component of the curriculum, produced not only the modern religious scholar but also the Islamic intellectual. The latter may or may not have specialised in religious knowledge but has enough understanding of the tradition to articulate opinions and offer interpretations.

Historically, major centres of religious learning in the Muslim world were truly transnational spaces where a tradition evolved as a result of the cross-fertilisation of ideas and scholars who had roots in different parts of the Islamic world. Mecca, Damascus, Baghdad and later Cairo where most of the Sunni Islamic tradition was produced over generations were real transnational centres. Al-Azhar in Cairo was the Mecca of Sunni scholars. Minor centres in North Africa and the Near East were not in a position to compete with al-Azhar.

Riyadh, with its religious institutes and newly established religious universities, and even Madina, where the first Islamic university was founded in the country, could not initially compete with the early centres of religious learning in the Arab world. Although Saudi Arabia received hundreds of scholars and thinkers from the Arab and Islamic world, its official *'ulama* resisted any opening up to other Muslims, who were defined as 'foreign'. They welcomed foreign *'ulama* only to convert them to their cause. They refrained from debating with other Muslim scholars as they applied the principle of *hajr al-mubta'di* (the ostracisation of innovators): those who could not be 'converted' must be ostracised. They feared that such foreign scholars might not conform to Saudi religious interpretations. Foreigners had to be 'controlled' and 'guided' to avoid corrupting the local tradition. Educational institutions and religious instruction were from the very beginning put under the control of local Najdi *'ulama*. Foreign educators were enlisted to 'deliver' the curriculum rather than interpret it. The latter was the prerogative of a closed circle which was not even open for Saudis outside the traditional religious centre, let alone (Arab and Muslim) foreigners. The state allowed its *'ulama* to administer and control the dissemination of religious knowledge by foreign instructors to ensure that the latter did not promote any religio-political interpretations that could threaten the discourse of consent or introduce religious innovations. The state rewarded the *'ulama* who were in charge of perpetuating and refining the discourse of consent by granting them a monopoly over religious interpretation. It was in the interest of both the state and the *ulama* to maintain control and surveillance. The religious establishment, staffed by loyalist Wahhabi–Salafi *'ulama*, resisted any manifestation of, for example, imported foreign (Egyptian and Syrian) Ikhwani (Muslim Brotherhood) ideas into the classroom and the mosque to safeguard against contestation. However, an undeclared 'hidden war' was raging in study circles, intellectual centres and even summer camps between local official Wahhabi Salafiyya and so-called 'foreign' interpretations. The war ceased to be hidden after 11 September when official Saudi religious discourse started openly to attack the foreign Muslim Brotherhood and other *haraki* Islamists. According to one author, to function in Saudi Arabia one must wear the Salafi cloak like an official uniform'.[11] In fact, many Egyptian and Syrian religious scholars and educators did adopt Saudi attire. They looked Saudi but spoke in their local regional accents. Many abandoned the Egyptian or Syrian headgear associated with religious scholars in favour of the Saudi 'Salafi–Wahhabi' uniform, consisting of a rather short shirt and head cover, always worn untied with a head-rope. Unlike their colleagues who remained at home, they stopped trimming their beards.

Society and local scholars remained suspicious of the Islam of 'others', namely other Saudis and the newly arriving Muslim immigrants and exiles. The latter were employed as teachers and religious instructors and were under strict orders to respect the 'Saudi religious curriculum'. Their integration remained fraught with tension and suspicion inside Saudi Arabia. Immigrants, especially those who belonged to the Egyptian and Syrian Muslim Brotherhoods, refrained from questioning Saudi–Wahhabi religio-political interpretations, if they wanted to remain in their jobs. Occasionally an immigrant *'alim* or Muslim thinker would be expelled, or 'sent abroad' on a religious mission. While Saudi Arabia adopted an 'open-door policy' towards the Muslim Brotherhood in the 1960s, to serve its own battle against Nasserites and Ba'thists, immigrants knew that they could not openly contest the religious interpretations of their host. Several scholars assimilated Saudi religio-political discourse in their own worldview. This resulted in the emergence of hybrid and cross-fertilised religious interpretations.

Modernity brought the university, which in turn produced individuals who were not only religious in the traditional ritualistic sense of the term but also conscious of their religious knowledge. The university produced graduates who could articulate this consciousness and express it in a modern language that appeals to a public wider than the traditional specialist *'ulama* study circle. It produced interpreters of religion who engage with the social and political realities of contemporary society. This engagement distinguished the new *'ulama* and intellectuals from the previous generation that dominated the religious scene in the pre-oil era. The university, together with printing and audio media, allowed the dissemination of religious knowledge to a wide audience. The religious text became available beyond the limited study circle of scholars. Moreover, the same university produced people who 'are not bound by traditional norms and rules of religious discursive activity . . . the modern intellectual will be able to read deeper into the text in a critical, imaginative manner'.[12]

With the formalisation and modernisation of the environment in which religious knowledge develops, highly articulate voices appeared, aware of the wide gap between the enchanted Islamised consenting public sphere and the secularised political domain. For this generation, the dramatised ritualistic Islam was simply not enough. From within the Wahhabi tradition and among people who were brought up on its teachings, voices emerged that expressed uneasiness about the evolution of Wahhabiyya under state control. It is important to emphasise that not all those who expressed this uneasiness are young men. Some important figures are old members of the previous *ulama* generation, thus belonging to the traditional Wahhabi *ulama* group. While most of the new generation of *ulama* and intellectuals endorsed Wahhabi social conservatism, they were uncomfortable with the religio-political aspect of that tradition. This new generation refers to itself as *shabab al-sahwa* (the youth of the awakening), or Sahwis (the awakened), a self-adopted appellation that carries multiple implications. While Wahhabiyya was in general a name imposed by outsiders on the teachings of *aimat al-da'wa al-najdiyya*, the name Sahwa is willingly adopted by those who regard themselves as part of it – the Sahwis themselves. In this chapter, I trace the changing nature of Sahwa and its evolution from contestation to co-optation.

The meaning of Sahwa: re-enchanting politics

Several studies have now traced the development of the new Sahwi trend in Saudi Arabia since the 1990s. Studies in Western languages offered detailed biographies of famous Sahwis such as Sheikhs Salman al-Awdah, Safar al-Hawali and Nasir al-Omar, documented their rhetoric and followed their engagement with politics over a critical decade in the history of the country. Most previous research focused on Sahwis as a local Saudi variant of political Islam, Islamists and recently radical Salafi groups. Saudi sources also identified Sahwa as a manifestation of what is pejoratively referred to by Saudi liberals as Islamawis, defined as an uncompromising group who 'use' and 'abuse' Islam in pursuit of ideological aspirations and political careers.[13] In most liberal and official Wahhabi discourse, Sahwa is seen as a product of alien religious interpretations and Islamist political movements, mainly the Egyptian and Syrian Muslim Brotherhood, Qutbist[14] ideologies and Jihadi trends. It is ironic that both Saudi liberals and official religious scholars detest Sahwa and Sahwis. Both realise the threatening potential of Sahwis who call not only for the Islamisation of society, as society is already Islamised, but – more importantly – for the deconstruction of the quiescent official Wahhabi discourse and its replacement with a discourse of contestation. Liberals and official Wahhabis both fear the revolutionary potential of Sahwi religio-political discourse, which threatens to dismantle the monopoly of liberals over the affairs of state and the official *'ulama* over the religious domain. Sahwis are detested because they undermine the age-old division between the religious society and secular politics. In short, they threaten the schism that grew and flourished under the state and official Wahhabi religio-political discourse. A Saudi preacher by the name of Musa al-Abdulaziz, the editor of a very marginal magazine called *Salafiyyah*, declared that liberals are closer to Islam and Salafiyya than Sahwi Qutbis. He argued that liberals have a better instinct (*fitra*).[15]

Traditional and official Wahhabi scholars are scathing in their attacks on Sahwis.[16] My intention here is to consider Sahwa as a state of mind and a plan of action. Sahwa is built on a realisation that ordinary man can be at the centre of his own destiny. Sahwa is neither creed nor worship; it is neither religion nor politics: it is both.

Sahwis are a loose and fluid sub-group within the community of the faithful who from the 1970s strove to establish a distinct identity for themselves. The mentors of the first generation of Sahwis were in fact the traditional Wahhabi *'ulama*, assisted by a group of Arab religious scholars and educators, mainly from Egypt and Syria, who migrated – voluntarily or involuntarily – to Saudi Arabia in the 1960s. Two Arab *'ulama* are often cited as influencing Sahwa: an Egyptian, Muhammad Qutb, the brother of Sayyid Qutb; and a Syrian, Sheikh Muhammad Surur Zayn al-Abdin. Both taught in Saudi educational institutions in the 1960s. While some studies have highlighted the influence of these 'foreign' scholars who settled in Saudi Arabia, it is important to examine Sahwism as an autonomous Saudi phenomenon that lies at the heart of political activism in the country. While Sahwis may have been influenced by outside intellectuals and religious scholars, they are a manifestation of a local evolution in Saudi society that began in the 1970s. While external influences on Sahwis are often exaggerated, the way Saudi Sahwis, especially the Salafis amongst them, influenced other Islamists abroad is often ignored. Some famous Saudi Sahwis are no longer local figures; their lectures are heard among Muslims worldwide. Saudi Sahwis have blurred the boundaries between the local and the global. One can read their publications anywhere in the world, and access their mosque sermons, seminars and lectures on the internet. Today one can easily switch from Sheikh Ibn Baz's lecture on obedience to *wali al-amr* to Salman al-Awdah's lecture on the fall of nations, passing by Nasir al-Omar's sermons on resistance in Iraq.

In an increasingly connected world, it is very difficult to identify the boundaries between the local and the global. There is no doubt that the Sahwa was influenced by external ideas. Nevertheless, it is grounded in local discourse, and later spread its influence beyond the geographical territory of its own homeland. More importantly, Sahwi thought is a hybrid tradition that rediscovered the revolutionary potential of Wahhabi religio-political discourse and rearticulated it in a modern language accessible to all. This rediscovery was perhaps assisted by various outside influences that arrived in Saudi Arabia in the second half of the twentieth century. It may well be that Qutbi or Muslim Brotherhood discourse and figures facilitated this rediscovery. The Muslim Brotherhood may have had an important influence, but to forge a causal relationship serves only political purposes, for example absolving Saudis from any responsibility for violence. The aim here is not to blame an external group or ideology for 'radicalising Saudi youth' or 'leading them astray', as often claimed in official Saudi statements, but rather to show the complexity of the religio-political field and how it may evade simple reductionist causal explanations.

In the Saudi context Sahwa is a movement that strives to re-enchant a politically dis-enchanted world. According to Sheikh Salman al-Awdah, Sahwa is concerned with *inkar al-munkar alanan* (disavowing the abominable in public). This is a political act that is guided by religious interpretation. In Saudi Arabia only the state and its official *'ulama* have the right and power to reject the abominable. Al-Awdah challenges this view, as he considers it the responsibility of all.

A Sahwi has an awareness of his religiosity which distinguishes him from those whose religiosity is habitual and traditional. Sahwis do not simply perform religious rituals out of habit; they often exhibit an awareness of their engagement, not only with such rituals but also in public affairs. For the majority of Sahwis, Islam is not simply a set of repetitive rituals (*'ibadat*): it is a psychological state and a blueprint for social and political engagement with the contemporary world. Islam is a project whose realisation starts with the self through *iltizam*, commitment not only to the prescribed five pillars of the tradition but also to what is considered its 'essence'. Bringing out the so-called 'essence' requires a vision of the present and future that privileges religious texts and identity. This tends to be ignored in discussion of Sahwis. It is often argued that the discourse about the return to the tradition of the great pious ancestors represents nostalgia to the glorious past – in the language of Saudi critics of Sahwa, a desire to return to an archaic and pre-modern existence. This is an inaccurate understanding of the Salafi Sahwi rhetoric that invokes the past. Salafi Sahwis use the rhetoric of the past to manipulate the present and build the future. They are grounded in current concerns. Sahwis use modern technology to disseminate a modern message, although this message is grounded in the rhetoric of the past and the ancestors. Like a tribe's obsession with genealogies, Sahwis' 'obsession' with the past is rooted in contemporary society and modern concerns. Aidh al-Qarni, a famous Sahwi sheikh, defines the Islamic awakening as 'renewal of religion while retaining its authenticity. It means that we return to religion in order to deal with contemporary and very new concerns that dominate civilisation and society . . . Sahwa means to return to the roots after a long period of *ightirab* [alienation, exile] and static existence.'[17] While Sahwa may represent itself through increased commitment to ritualistic Islam, it is above all a state of mind that allows a Muslim to have Islam and only Islam as a reference point for all aspects of life, including public political affairs. At the individual level, Sahwis have a commitment not only to the salvation of the self but also to society.

Sahwis include formally trained religious scholars who qualify as members of the *'ulama* class, in addition to ordinary men. Some Sahwis are scientists, doctors, engineers, chemists, writers and journalists, but may have studied religion as part of their education. They all therefore have some degree of religious knowledge that enables them to articulate opinions on religious texts. This puts them in the category of what is known as Islamic intellectuals, who constitute a category between the traditional *'ulama* and laymen. They do not qualify as religious scholars, who can issue *fatwas*, yet they have enough knowledge of the tradition to invoke its texts and interpretation as need arises. Unlike those who are traditionally religious, they are aware of the multiplicity of interpretations and meanings that can be attributed to the religious text. This does not mean that Sahwis can be automatically considered strong believers in the diversity of religious interpretation. It simply means that they are aware of the diversity, although they may not accept it. They can be as dogmatic as any other social category in Saudi society.

All Sahwi intellectuals are products of the modern education system in Saudi Arabia and a substantial number hold doctorates in various branches of the sciences. Many Sahwi intellectuals follow a Sahwi sheikh, a scholar upon whom they depend for *'ilm shari'* (*shari'a* knowledge), inspiration and authenticity. By claiming to be among the followers of a Sahwi sheikh, they seek recognition by proxy. Such a Sahwi intellectual would often be known as *mufakir Islami* (a Muslim thinker). They are rarely referred to as *muthaqaf* – an intellectual who is often associated with acquiring Western knowledge, especially in the arts, humanities and social sciences. Sahwi intellectuals disseminate their ideas in books, newspaper articles, sermons, lectures and sometimes their own websites. While their position between laymen and *'ulama* can be an advantage in an increasingly literate and connected society, it also carries a problematic ambiguity. Sahwi intellectuals defend their venturing into religious interpretation on the basis that in Islam there is no such category as *rijal din* (clergy), as each Muslim is required to know religion. In the opinion of many Sahwis, the word *'ulama* simply refers to those who know, regardless of the substance of their knowledge.

Saudi Sahwis are engaged in this world, especially its politics. All Sahwis subscribe to the view that the world can be changed, modified, altered and improved by communal human action that draws on religious sources, mainly the Quran and the tradition of the Prophet. Organising society in small groups, attending lectures, debating politics and religion – and even secret meetings – are all legitimate means to engage with public affairs. Above all, Sahwis strongly believe in their right to issue public advice on current affairs, and openly to criticise government policies, thus violating an important official Wahhabi dogma. They believe that the duty of publicly disavowing the abominable (*inkar al-munkar*), including telling the ruler that he has committed an abominable act or violated the rule of *shari'a*, is incumbent upon all Muslims, rather than a small coterie of *'ulama*. Sahwis criticise the religious establishment for publicly condemning the abominable only if committed by laymen, and since the early 1990s, Sahwis have distinguished themselves by carrying out this duty, and especially by condemning abominable or inappropriate actions on the part of the rulers.

Sahwis do not subscribe to a single well-defined political party or organisation. They may belong to various Islamist movements. There are, for example, groups identified with the Muslim Brotherhood in its two variants: followers of Hasan al-Banna and those of Sayyid Qutb. These tend to be concentrated in several national and pan-Islamic organisations, in addition to universities and intellectual circles. It seems, however, that in general the Saudi Muslim Brotherhood have remained conspicuous by their absence. They have stayed away from populist politics and remained an intellectual trend without a wide populist public base. However, this assessment remains impressionistic and is based on a description by Saudi Ikhwanis of their own position on the religio-political map of Saudi Arabia.[18]

There are also groups whose political orientation derives from the Syrian sheikh Muhammad Surur Zayn al-Abdin, a Salafi Ikhwani scholar, who separated from the Syrian Muslim Brotherhood and set up his own tradition. It is often claimed that his followers in Saudi Arabia are the most numerous among Sahwis. His tradition will be discussed later in this chapter, but suffice here to say that the sheikh's name is often mentioned in conjunction with discussion of the Saudi Sahwa.

Other Sahwis follow global political movements, for example Hizb al-Tahrir and al-Qa'ida. Supporters of the Movement for Islamic Renewal, al-Tajdid, based in London and led by Muhammad al-Masari, adopt the intellectual orientation of Hizb al-Tahrir. Al-Qa'ida in the Arabian Peninsula invokes a clear association with Osama bin Laden. Its followers are often called Salafi Jihadis.

Regardless of their political affiliation, most Sahwis are easily identified as *haraki* Islamists. The fact that political parties are banned in Saudi Arabia makes it difficult to identify the main political trends and their membership. Not many Sahwis will voluntarily declare their party affiliation, if they have one. However, with the arrival of the internet in 1998, Saudi Sahwis made the most of this new communication technology to create virtual communities that share similar religious and ideological orientation. The well-known among them have their own websites and discussion boards, while their followers contribute to the debate under pseudonyms as a protection against arrest and other hazards. Some Sahwi *ulama* have their own electronic newsletters.

The Saudi awakening is about the realisation that it is religiously incumbent on society to be engaged with politics. *Sahwa* is contrasted with an opposite state of mind, *gafwa* (deep sleep), comparable to inertia and indifference. Sahwis are political activists. They do not accept that calling for the oneness of God (*al-tawhid*) is the primary purpose of Islam, a position that distinguishes them from the religious establishment. In the opinion of one Saudi, the Prophet called for the declaration that 'there is no God but Allah and Muhammad is his messenger', not for the establishment of an Islamic state.[19] Therefore, purifying religious practice from *shirk* (blasphemy) becomes the primary obligation. For Sahwis, the Islamic call is a call for the establishment of the Islamic polity, and the application of *shari'a* (*tahkim al-shar'*). Their philosophy goes far beyond purifying religion from heterodoxy.

Neither the *ulama* nor the intellectuals among the Sahwis shy away from venturing into territory often regarded as taboo in Saudi Arabia. Sahwis volunteer public interpretations of foreign relations, international politics and the role of Saudi Arabia in the world, all traditionally the prerogative of a small coterie of royalty and assistants, who operate behind closed doors. Sahwi *ulama* write both theological treatises and political pamphlets concerned with world affairs.[20] Sahwis challenge the official worldview that politics is the prerogative of the ruler and his entourage. They believe that public affairs are the concern of the community of the faithful, and see themselves at the centre of *al-sha'n al'-am* (public affairs). Sahwis initially claimed that the appearance of an Islamised society does not automatically mean an Islamic polity, although it is essentially the first step towards creating one. An Islamic polity needs more than ritualistic Islam. Its realisation requires Muslims to be vigorously engaged in public affairs through communal organisation and activism, a vision that is challenging to both the state and the official religious worldview described in the last chapter. Sahwis blur the boundaries between religion and politics – boundaries that the official Wahhabi establishment managed to keep separate, with the sanction of the Saudi regime while retaining the rhetoric of the monotheist state (*dawlat al-tawhid*). Blurring the boundaries between religion and politics makes it incumbent upon Sahwis to take a position vis-à-vis political authority and the guardians of the official Wahhabi tradition. This, they claim, is guided by an interpretation of the religious texts.

Sahwis differ in their attitude to political authority. In general, they can be divided into two camps, those who accept it as legitimate government, but in need of reform, and those who reject it altogether as an illegitimate authority. Those who publicly accept the legitimacy of the Saudi regime strive peacefully to 'influence' it and make it correspond more to their vision of the rightful Islamic polity. Those who reject the existing authorities altogether work towards undermining and eventually overthrowing the regime, by either peaceful means or violence. All Sahwi sub-groups are a product of the Sahwi belief in the ability of the individual and society to change the world through various means. All Sahwis share the belief that the existing government is imperfect.

All Sahwis have reservations about the religio-political discourse of the official Wahhabi establishment that denounces their political activism, and have a contentious and strained relationship with its main figures. They have problems accepting some aspects of this tradition as it became institutionalised in Saudi Arabia in the last decades of the twentieth century. Sahwis who are Salafis accept Muhammad ibn Abd al-Wahhab's theology but may have reservations regarding the current Saudi state and its 'ulama. Such Sahwis glorify the first state of the eighteenth century, but have serious reservations about the current one. Some argue that the present regime has failed to fulfil the spirit of the early message. They point out that current Wahhabi 'ulama have abandoned the teachings of an early generation of strong and brave 'ulama who maintained their independence vis-à-vis previous Saudi imams and kings.

All Sahwis challenge the official religious interpretation that disenfran-chises society when it comes to political matters. They do not accept that only a small group of people distinguished by either their religious knowl-edge or secular expertise has the right to monopolise state policy and strategy. They aspire towards greater say in urgent social, political and economic issues. While the Sahwi *ulama* aspire to replace the traditional *ulama*, intellectuals among them aim to occupy a privileged public posi-tion in state bureaucracy and apparatus.

Nevertheless, the boundaries between the various Sahwi positions have always been fluid and unclear. In a country such as Saudi Arabia, where censorship of the religious and political domains remains very strong, it is extremely difficult for any analysis to go beyond what is publicly declared and stated by outspoken Sahwis. Throughout this research many Sahwis have pointed my attention to the fact that Sahwis who publicly accept the Saudi regime denounce it in the privacy of their closed meetings. During the 1990s several Sahwi activists were put in prison for expressing politi-cal views that undermined government decisions, an episode in Saudi history that is now well documented.[21] Several Sahwi *ulama*, for example Safar al-Hawali and Salman al-Awdah, and other Sahwi intellectuals, such as Abdulaziz al-Qasim, Muhammad al-Hodhayf, Muhsin al-Awajy, Saad al-Faqih and Muhammad al-Masari, spent some time in prison as a result of activism that was deemed challenging to the government. Government oppression of such figures was not challenged by the official Wahhabi tradition, especially Grand Mufti Abdulaziz ibn Baz. In the early 1990s, Sahwis were considered *personae non gratae* who undermined unity and cohesion among the believers. While most intellectuals spent a short time in prison, some Sahwi *ulama* were jailed for over five years. Most activists lost their previous jobs and were banned from public preaching, lecturing and study circles. Sahwis remember the 1990s as the decade of imprisonment, which, although characterised by loss of per-sonal freedom and rights, was also a time that allowed many of them to build a symbolic capital manifested in popularity, prestige and fame. Imprisonment fixed Sahwis in the historical imagination of their follow-ers as courageous activists who sacrificed personal benefit in the pursuit of public good. Their opponents, mainly Saudi liberals and official gov-ernment spokesmen, often hold them responsible for radicalising the young population and creating the grounds for the violent Jihadi trend.

One Sahwi group among others

As mentioned earlier, pluralism, more recently amounting to fragmenta-tion and even hostility between various Sahwi groups, is one important aspect of the Saudi Sahwa. One influential Sahwi sub-group is often referred to in the public sphere as Sururis, a reference to followers of Syrian sheikh Muhammad Surur Zayn al-Abdin, hereafter Muhammad Surur. This appellation is rejected by both the sheikh himself and by those who may have drawn on aspects of his thought. The sheikh states: 'I do not know of a group called Sururi. I have never been responsible for such a group. If somebody says to me "I am a Sururi," I will disown him.'[22]

The name Sururi is, however, retained by outsiders, either to emphasise the 'foreignness' of this sub-group or its *hizbiyya* (adherence to party politics). In this section I shall draw a picture of the sheikh's intellectual heritage as a prelude to discussing the evolution of Saudi Sahwis who are often identified by outsiders as being his followers. Sheikh Muhammad Surur may have inspired some Saudi sheikhs while he was a religious teacher in the religious institutes and schools of Buraydah, the home town of Salman al-Awdah.

Sheikh Muhammad Surur came to Saudi Arabia in 1965. He is known as a Syrian Muslim Brotherhood supporter who had fled his country under the pressure of the Ba'th party. He is also known to have founded his own movement, which split from the Syrian Muslim Brotherhood. However, his ideas, published in several books, journals and on his al-Sunnah website, demonstrate a strong Salafi orientation mixed with the organisational capabilities of the Muslim Brotherhood, hence the name Salafi Ikhwani. A central feature of his religious view relates to a critical stance vis-à-vis 'official *'ulama'*, in the Muslim world in general as well as in Saudi Arabia. After spending eight years in Saudi Arabia, it seems that he left, or was asked to leave, around 1973.

In most accounts of the influence of 'outside agents' on the Saudi religio-political field, Sahwis are portrayed as unquestioning followers of Islamist exiles from Syria and Egypt, including Sheikh Muhammad Surur. Gilles Kepel tends to reiterate this view.[23] He depicts an image of Saudi Sahwis as passive recipients of a foreign, politicised Islam that grew in response to Ba'thist and Nasserite oppression and was brought to Saudi Arabia by exiles. This view is also held by the Saudi regime. Perhaps Kepel's inability to realise the full potential of Wahhabi discourse and the social evolution of Saudi society in the 1970s made him reach such unjustified conclusions. In his account, he does not entertain the possibility that Sheikh Muhammad Surur himself and many other exiles may have themselves incorporated aspects of Salafi Wahhabi thought which they initially did not subscribe to. This remains a possibility that cannot be ruled out. An examination of the Syrian sheikh's writings reveals clearly that he incorporated aspects of the Salafi Wahhabi tradition, given his references to several Najdi scholars. Saudi Sahwis remain autonomous agents who can mix and match rather than blindly follow this Syrian Salafi sheikh, or any other foreign sheikh.

On a rainy London morning, Sheikh Muhammd Surur received me in the company of his young son. After a couple of hours, a friend and a colleague of the sheikh joined us. I had already asked the sheikh whether he would allow me to interview him. When I assured him that the interview would not be used for media purposes but was part of an academic study, he agreed. The sheikh was an imposing old man with a long Salafi beard. He wore what appeared to be a Saudi *thawb* (white dress) and *ghutra* (white headcover) which hung down on his shoulders without the traditional black *'uqal* (tying rope), an attire very different from that worn by traditional Levantine religious scholars. All items of clothing indicated a strong association with Salafism rather than the Muslim Brotherhood. The sheikh wore the symbols of an intellectual stand and a religious identity. A sense of wisdom and serenity emanated from him as he talked to me about his experience in Saudi Arabia, always avoiding eye-contact, in fulfilment of *ghadh al-basar* (lowering the gaze) in the presence of a woman. In the context of cosmopolitan London, he could be mistaken for an oriental mystic or sage. However, he was far removed from mysticism.

The sheikh was grounded in the real world, and fully conversant in its affairs. He combined religious knowledge with an ability to deal with current affairs. He runs a publishing house in Birmingham and a website. He left his homeland in Hawran (Syria) under political pressure, and moved to Buraydah in 1965. In 1973 he went to Kuwait, then moved to London in 1983. He later moved between London and Birmingham. In 2004–5 he left London permanently, and moved to Amman. Muhammad Surur is a transnational Salafi sheikh par excellence. He may move and build encapsulated niches around himself, but does not aim to integrate himself in the wider culture in which he finds himself.[24]

The sheikh's assessment of the relationship with Saudi *'ulama* since the 1960s highlights a process whereby 'we influenced them and they influenced us', which is probably a more accurate description than the one often acknowledged by outside observers. He holds a high opinion of Sheikh Muhammad ibn Ibrahim ibn Abd al-Latif Al-Shaykh (d. 1969), mentioned in the last chapter. He values the independence of this Saudi mufti, maintained because he was not 'an employee of the government'. He was a responsible man. Even King Faysal, who was the strongest of all Saudi kings, used to fear him. When he died Saudi Arabia did not have a mufti for almost twenty-five years. People wanted to divide and distribute Ibn Ibrahim's heritage. In the early 1990s Ibn Baz became a mufti but he was not like Ibn Ibrahim. After Ibn Ibrahim the mufti became an employee of the government.'[25]

According to Sheikh Muhammad Surur, the independence of the *ulama* should be protected and cherished. This protection can be achieved through the establishment of what he calls *jami'at al-'ulama*, an *ulama* association that is not subservient to the state. He adds: 'This association must have financial independence and must be in control of endowments. But the state does not want this. It wants to control everything. The *ulama* association should be different from *hayat kibar al-'ulama*, the Council of Senior *ulama*.' On the obligation to obey the ruler, Sheikh Muhammad Surur believes that rebelling against a ruler with the sword (*khuruj bi 'l-sayf*) is *fitna*, a cause for discord among Muslims. He argues: 'I was against Jihadi movements that fought Arab regimes because they precipitate internal struggle. But I am also against formulating an Islam that suits the ruler.'[26]

The sheikh distinguishes between two types of Salafiyya, preferring to call them *hizb al-wulat* (loyalists) and *hizb al-ghulat* (radicals). He positions himself as a Wasati, a free Centrist, an affiliation that became prominent in Saudi Arabia after 11 September, as we shall see later.

Hizb al-wulat, the loyalists, believe in unconditional obedience to [those] whom they consider to be rulers of Muslims. Their followers are chaotic; they are incapable of controlling their members except in obeying the ruler. In Saudi Arabia, the loyalists appeared after the Gulf War [1990] and their main preoccupation is to destroy the real callers for Salafi thought. They work hard to spy on free *ulama* and report them to the authorities. Their sheikh is Rabi al-Madkhali. He uses the name Qutbi and Sururi to refer to all those who disagree with him. We cannot distinguish between al-Madkhali and the policies of his government. The loyalists denounce all those denounced by the government. This party claims that the princes know better and politics is their own business only. The loyalists accuse other Salafis of ignoring the call for *tawhid* and focusing more on *hakimiyya* [rule of God], which they claim led to political dissent and confrontation with the rulers.[27]

The sheikh distances himself from *hizb al-ghulat*. Here he distinguishes between the ancient radicalism that plagued Islamic civilisation (for example the Kharijites) and the new contemporary manifestations of radicalism. What concerns us here is the new radicalism, described by the sheikh as a product of prisons, torture and oppression of Muslims. He details cases of oppression in Syrian and Egyptian prisons to conclude that these cases encouraged radicalism, and outlines the characteristics of the radicals: they shed the of blood of their opponents; they are not qualified to issue *fatwas*; and they monopolise truth and interpretation. Contemporary radicals are young and inexperienced men. They are distinguished by an ability to recite Quran and Hadith without serious reflection on their meanings. They use violence indiscriminately, blowing

up Muslim civilians and attacking the *ulama* who challenge their interpretations. The sheikh laments the polarisation of the Muslim community between the loyalists and the radicals.

In one of his publications, Sheikh Muhammad Surur defends the
concern with *hakimiyya* (sovereignty, rule of God) by referring to
the work of Muhammad ibn Abd al-Wahhab. According to Sheikh
Muhammad Surur, Muhammad ibn Abd al-Wahhab regarded those who
prefer the rule of *taghut* as *kafir*s. He asks whether 'the loyalists are aware
of Muhammad ibn Ibrahim's epistle in which he stated that the rule of
shari'a is an aspect of worshipping God alone. It is the struggle where
swords have been used.'[28]

According to the Syrian sheikh, Saudi loyalists condemned the free
Wasati Salafis. Asked about the future of *ulama* in Saudi Arabia, he
declared that 'Sheikh Safar al-Hawali and Salman al-Awdah are the
future generation, the real *ulama*'. They must resist the conspiracies of
the sultan. On the rule of the sultan, the sheikh writes:

> The sultan is mischievous. He uses his intelligence services and his resources to
> lure the *ulama*. He offers them important posts and promises to work with them
> to initiate reform. After the *ulama* fall in his hand, they become accustomed to
> seeing sins. They redefine the forbidden and the permissible. They accuse all
> those who disagree with them. They call his opponents Kharijites, innovators,
> radicals and terrorists.[29]

Sheikh Muhammad Surur says that the sultan's *ulama* should follow the
example of those who resist political authority. He cites examples of early
pious *ulama*, such as Abu Hanifa, Malik ibn Anas, Sufyan al-Thawri,
Ahmad ibn Hanbal, Imam Bukhari, Imam Nawawi, and al-Iz ibn Abd al-
Salam, and says that contemporary *ulama* should be informed by Ibn
Taymiyya's famous statement, 'I am a man of religion not a man of state,'
thus emphasising that the *ulama*'s main concern should be loyalty to
faith rather than state. The sheikh encourages participation in elections,
although he himself has no interest in directly participating in the political
process. He remains an *'alim*.

The sheikh places himself between the loyalists and the radicals, a
position which is adopted by some Saudi Sahwis. The central feature of
his approach is the combination of *'aqida* (creed) and a serious engagement with politics and public affairs. This means that if ever there is a
Sururi trend, it will be distinguished by a vigorous commitment to
Islamic creed and practices combined with political involvement. This is
contrasted with two other trends: the official Wahhabi tradition, which
concerned itself primarily with creed rather than politics; and the traditional Muslim Brotherhood, which is primarily concerned with politics
rather than the purification of faith and the enforcement of orthodoxy.

Sheikh Muhammad Surur combines creed with politics, thus revolutionising both traditional Salafiyya and the Muslim Brotherhood.[30]

11 September: an accused and divided Sahwa

As the two most famous Sahwis, Sheikhs Safar al-Hawali and Salman al-
Awdah, were released from prison in 1999, they and their followers were
caught between loyalty to call and loyalty to state. The first required disavowing the abominable in public. The second demanded an acquiescent
position, in practice amounting to either withdrawal from public life or a
positive sanctioning of government policies. As Sahwi sheikhs they continued to believe in their duty to change the world by action, including the
spoken and written word. The world they thought was in need of change
was not only social but also political. The experience of prison granted
the sheikhs a glorious status in the eyes of their followers. Those Sahwis
who fled the country in the early 1990s, for example Saad al-Faqih and
Muhammad al-Masari, reconstituted their separate movements in exile
but continued to play the role of advocates for the Sahwi sheikhs while the
latter were still in prison. After their release, the Sahwa faced a serious
challenge, represented by the attack on New York and the increase in
Jihadi violence in Saudi Arabia afterwards. After 11 September, Sahwis
were prime suspects. Three groups denounced them: certain princes
within the Saudi regime; the official religious establishment; and Saudi
liberals. When Sahwis publicly condemned Jihadi violence inside Saudi
Arabia, they incurred the wrath of followers of this trend.

Minister of Interior Prince Nayef accused the Muslim Brotherhood
variant of the Sahwis of standing behind the violence in Saudi Arabia. He
repeatedly claimed that the inspiration for violence is alien to Saudi
Arabia. According to Prince Nayef, violence is imported from Egypt by
those who were welcomed in Saudi Arabia in the 1960s. A member of the
Shura Council, Muhammad al-Zulfa, repeated the prince's accusation.
He argued that the Muslim Brotherhood introduced radical Islam into
Saudi Arabia in the 1960s, a rather surprising comment by a historian.[31]
The governor of Asir, Prince Khalid al-Faysal, directly accused the
Sahwis of being responsible for the 'new religious trend', which generated
violence in recent years. In several newspaper articles and television interviews, he made it clear that 'the extremist ideology is alien to us. It spread
in schools, mosques, and everywhere. In our schools and mosques there
are young men who deliver sermons as though they are senior clerics.'[32] In
a speech given in Abha, the prince claimed that those who are now
calling for Wasatiyya, the middle path, are 'the very ones who disseminated the thought of Sayyid Qutb and al-Mawdudi, and they are among

the students of Muhammad Qutb'.[33] Many senior princes capitalised on the events of 11 September and later local violence to condemn Sahwa and settle old scores. This was to be expected, as the regime could not tolerate any intellectual or religious trend that questions its policy or threatens its survival. However, we should not take individual princely attacks on Sahwa to be representative of the government's position.

In response to 11 September, official Wahhabis redefined the meaning of 'Sahwa' in terms of increased religiosity in the public sphere and more commitment to ritualistic Islam, thus emptying Sahwa of its most obvious meaning: political activism that reaches beyond religious rituals. Official Wahhabiyya, which had always regarded Sahwis as either competitors or adversaries, was quick to issue its own condemnation. A senior scholar, Sheikh Abdulmuhsin al-Obaykan, had his own views on the Sahwis. He reiterated that violence is a product of alien ideas that have dominated Saudi Arabia's intellectual field.[34] He disseminated these ideas on the pages of the London-based Saudi newspaper *al-Sharq al-Awsat*. In 2005 a Saudi Salafi sheikh, Musa al-Abdulaziz, argued that the Muslim Brotherhood conspired to ruin Saudi Arabia's amicable relations with the USA when they attacked New York and enlisted Saudis for the attack. He praised Saudi liberals whom he described as closer to the spirit of Islam than Sahwis, especially the Qutbis. He chose to denounce Sahwis in the context of an interview broadcast on a liberal Saudi-owned satellite channel.[35] Another well-known religious scholar, Rabi al-Madkhali, who had always been hostile to Sahwis, argued that 'Sahwis (Ikhwanis and Qutbis) are more dangerous than the *kafir* groups fought by Muhammad ibn Abd al-Wahhab in the eighteenth century. Qutbis disguise themselves under the label Salafiyya but they are worst than the obvious *kafir*s. Muslims cannot be deceived by real *kafir*s but they are deceived by those innovators who lead people astray.'[36] This is a typical position that draws on early Wahhabi religious texts, which always insisted that other so-called Muslims are worse than the *kafir*s of Quraysh. Al-Madkhali and his followers resorted to lectures and tapes to propagate their message against Sahwis. The attack on New York, which resulted in Western media becoming increasingly critical of Saudi Arabia, along with local violence, freed traditional Salafis from any constraint when attacking those who are their brothers in creed but opponents in political orientation.

Many Saudi writers joined in the denunciation of Sahwa and its advocates. After 11 September, the most critical voices were those of ex-Sahwis, who 'revised' their views and began to distance themselves from radicalism. After 11 September, the catchphrase among Saudi Islamists was *taraju'at*, reconsideration of previous opinions, thus invoking the same phenomenon that dominated the Egyptian Islamist scene almost a decade ago.[37] After several years of flirting with radicalism and excommunicating other Muslims, well-known figures who had spent time in prison, such as Mansur al-Noqaydan and Mishari al-Thaydi, moved from radicalism to calling for a reconsideration of Sahwa, and even Wahhabi doctrine, while still under the age of thirty. They published their revised positions in both traditional and new media. Western media quickly adopted their stories and hailed them as brave and courageous men who shed radicalism and terrorism.[38] Inside the country, they incurred the wrath of several groups, including, of course, their ex-comrades. Against official rhetoric blaming 'foreign Muslim Brotherhood' influence on young Saudis, al-Noqaydan wrote that radicalism is a local product and had nothing to do with alien ideas. He argued that violent Jihadis draw not on Muhmmad Qutb, Abu Ala al-Mawdudi or Hasan al-Banna but on Ibn Hanbal, Ibn Taymiyya and Najdi scholars such as Ibn Abd al-Wahhab, Ibn Sahman and Ibn Atiq. He concluded that radical thought is in fact rooted in Saudi Arabia.[39]

Locally, in an article entitled 'Sururis and Jihadis: The Raging Wolf and the Buried Snake', Khalid al-Ghannami, a young writer recently turned to liberalism, argues that the two Sahwi trends (Jihadis and Ikhwanis) are related intellectually 'but one prefers to kill openly while the other remains hidden until it is safe to emerge from its hole'.[40] This was one of the most direct accusations against Sururi Sahwis, holding them responsible for the spread of violence, radicalism and intolerance among the youth of the country. Al-Ghannami claims that Sururis are dormant *takfiri*s (practising excommunication of other Muslims), although they do not call for armed rebellion – at least openly – against the rulers or those who differ from them. He claims that they differ from violent *takfiri*s, those who resort to the sword. The latter tend to be simple and young, and have no detailed knowledge of religion except for memorising verses of the Quran and the Prophet's tradition. However, those ignorant young men are easily converted back to the right path, as they are loosely organised and tend to operate alone without an umbrella organisation. In the author's opinion, Sururis are the womb that produces violent individuals. He compares the movement to a snake hiding in a hole.

Another author, Saud al-Qahtani, argues that 'Sahwis were able to construct Islamic discourse relating to political, social, psychological, and intellectual matters'. This was beyond the ability of traditional Wahhabi *'ulama*. Sahwis were loyal to the religious dimension of Wahhabiyya but disloyal to its political views. According to this author, Sahwi preaching eroded the concept of obedience to *wali al-amr* and encouraged rebellion.[41] Al-Qahtani identified the most important aspect of Sahwa as its rejection of the absolute obedience to rulers promoted by Sheikh ibn Baz.

He argued that Sahwis remained Wahhabis in their creed but in their political views they adopted the Ikhwani intellectual activist heritage.[42] In his opinion Sahwa is an unofficial political party, independent and hegemonic. He described it as a new church, monopolising religious interpretation and demonising its opponents.

One of the most scathing attacks on Sahwa was voiced by Muhammad ibn Abd al-Latif al-Shaykh, who argued that 'official Wahhabiyya is a call that resulted in the birth of the Islamic state. Traditional Wahhabis protect the state whereas Sahwis destroy it. The first manipulates religious texts to support the state while the latter manipulates religious texts to destroy it.'[43] Official Wahhabiyya is seen here as a religious interpretation that promotes the state and builds a nation, whereas Sahwa is presented as a discourse of destruction, fragmentation and discord. Today official discourse tries to convince the world that Wahhabiyya is a tradition of tolerance and respect while the alien Sahwi ideas are a religion of violence and confrontation. Some scholars in the West adopt this official Saudi discourse.

These accusations, however, ignore the complexity of the process by which various Sahwi Islamist groups can be classified and how their discourse can easily change in response to political contexts. Sahwis draw on a complex and fluid religio-political discourse that generated several subgroups, at any one time agreeing on some issues and differing on others. Western scholarship on Saudi Islamists, however, continues to search for neat categories with the hope of identifying groups that easily fit readymade labels such as 'traditional', 'radical', 'moderate', 'reformist', 'Islamo-liberal', 'rejectionist', 'Jihadi' and others.[44] The Saudi Islamist field proved to be both diverse and difficult to classify. As long as open and organised groups are forbidden, Sahwis will remain difficult to identify as belonging to clear-cut political parties and organisations. Sahwism is a fluid philosophy that responds rapidly to changing local and international politics. As such, individuals can easily situate themselves in one category while retaining the ability to move between groups. Moreover, any attempt to situate Islamist political discourse in one tradition – Wahhabi, Ikhwani, Qutbi, Salafi Jihadi or any other – proves to be a futile attempt in the search for origins. While Saudi Arabia had its own religio-political discourse, it influenced and was influenced by several other interpretations.

Accusations and counter-accusations mirror a witch-hunt that must be understood in the context of international politics and official Saudi attempts to absolve the regime and its Wahhabi foundation from any responsibility for terrorism. The regime obviously seeks to establish not only its innocence but also that of its religious establishment. In February

2005, the regime took the lead in organising an international counter-terrorism conference, depicting itself as a victim of terrorism in a desperate attempt to dispel the accusations of sponsoring or harbouring terrorists that erupted in Western media after 11 September.[45] Any outside accusation is often portrayed by the regime as an onslaught on Islam, in an attempt to dilute the criticism and rally support from a wide constituency. By so doing, it mobilises nationalism and religious sentiments in its own support. Outspoken princes and officials deny that there is such a thing called Wahhabiyya and therefore that Wahhabi discourse can be responsible for violence.

While these accusations did not subside in the years that followed 11 September, a new, more important, development began to crystallise. In order to survive the wave of demonisation, the Sahwis had to prove their innocence. In Saudi Arabia, there was only one way to do so.

Sahwa: from contestation to co-optation

The events of 11 September coincided with a weak and discredited official Wahhabi establishment that had just lost two of its most important figures, who had dominated religious discourse for almost half a century. Sheikh Abdulaziz Ibn Baz, the grand mufti, and Muhammad al-Uthaymin, a member of the Council of Senior Ulama, died of old age in 1999 and 2001 respectively. The government appointed Sheikh Abdulaziz Al-Shaykh as grand mufti. However, it was obvious that the new mufti had neither the intellectual vigour nor the prestige enjoyed by Ibn Baz prior to his two most controversial *fatwas*, the 1990 *fatwa* legitimising the invitation to foreign troops and the 1993 one legitimising peace with Israel. At the beginning of the twenty-first century the official Wahhabi establishment seemed weak, fragmented and less credible. It had lost its monopoly over religious knowledge with the advent of the modern university and the appearance of multiple religious interpretations. It retained the support of the regime, and in return it supported the regime. Yet there emerged a religious vacuum ready to be occupied.

Although senior princes attacked Sahwis in public, the regime enlisted famous Sahwis to perform two tasks – one intellectual and one practical. The first involved preaching the religious discourse that denounced Jihadis as activists who failed to understand the meaning of *jihad*. The second task involved negotiating with Jihadis in the hopes of delivering them to the regime. Sahwi figures 'volunteered' to bring back those who had gone astray, mainly Jihadis who used violence against the state and people. Only famous Sahwi scholars such as Safar al-Hawali and Salman al-Awdah were able to play the double role of preaching against violence and neutralising violent actors. Less prominent famous Sahwis became so co-opted by the regime that they lost the credibility among their own followers, let alone their ex-comrades, to play any significant role. Others removed themselves from the public eye.

If the 1990s were years of contestation, the twenty-first century started with Sahwis moving towards mediation. Far from losing their popularity after prison, Sahwis remained active in two domains, one domestic and one international.

The domestic political front

At the domestic level, the state is aware of the continuing popularity of famous Sahwi sheikhs, whom it imprisoned almost a decade ago. Such sheikhs were younger than members of the religious establishment, more accessible and more engaged with current affairs. Most importantly, they were not so obviously connected to government bureaucracy. In order to be rehabilitated after release from prison, Sahwis, both sheikhs and intellectuals, showed good intentions by pursuing the official agenda. The agenda was to defeat Jihadis, condemn violence and praise the regime – or at least abstain from criticising it. In the official view, it was assumed that Sahwis were 'so close' to Jihadis ideologically that they could be enlisted in pacifying them and delivering them to the state. The Sahwis had no choice but to succumb to government pressure and deliver.

As popular quasi-'independent' 'ulama, al-Hawali and al-Awdah served the agenda of the government in an efficient way while aiming to be rehabilitated after the years of confrontation with the regime. Today a quasi-independent and loosely organised Sahwi establishment serves the state better as a result of its relative freedom. At the same time the government realised that it is beneficial to maintain two religious establishments, one traditional and one Sahwi, thus upholding the divide-and-rule principle. It seems that the state can accommodate two religious establishments only if they are both willing to serve its own interests. After 11 September, the state wanted to mobilise both establishments against the common enemy, the Jihadis and the Islamist opposition abroad, both sprung out of the awakening itself.

Both al-Hawali and al-Awdah are Salafi sheikhs who accept the credal aspects of Wahhabiyya and the sanctity of Muhammad ibn Abd al-Wahhab but may have reservations on whether the contemporary Saudi state is still faithful to his teachings. Both went further than the traditional Wahhabi scholars were prepared to go. Sahwi sheikhs retained the Wahhabi interpretation of creed but combined it with political activism. In this way, they can be considered closer to the ideas of Sheikh Muhammad

Surur than to official Wahhabiyya. They were distinct from their Wahhabi masters not in matters related to creed but in practice.

It is important to note that Sahwis' relationship with the government and the Wahhabi establishment went through a period of contestation (1990–4), imprisonment (1994–9) and co-optation (from 1999). The first and second phases are well documented.[46] Sahwis initially avoided confrontation with the religious establishment until around the time of the Gulf War in 1990–1. After that, they generally refused to accept the legitimacy of the *fatwa* initiated by Ibn Baz in 1990 sanctioning the invitation of foreign troops to defend the country and his 1993 *fatwa* legitimising peace with Israel. As Sahwis adopted a defiant, anti-American mood and critical position vis-à-vis the government, they were imprisoned. We should focus here on the third phase, which followed their release from prison in 1999.

After 11 September and the wave of violence that swept Saudi cities, it was clear that leading Sahwis were put on the defensive. At this critical time, the relationship between the government and Sahwis was characterised by mutual interdependence. With the accusations continuing, Sahwis distanced themselves not only from the global discourse of Osama bin Laden and local Jihadi ideologues, but also from dissident Saudi Islamists abroad. Immediately after one of the most devastating terrorist attacks, in May 2003, al-Hawali, al-Awdah and many other Sahwi sheikhs issued a statement condemning the attacks and denouncing the Jihadis as ignorant and misguided young men. It has since become routine to issue such statements after every terrorist attack in Saudi Arabia and abroad. As the government issued its terrorist wanted lists – three lists were released by June 2005 – Sahwi sheikhs called upon Jihadis to give themselves up and avoid further bloodshed and discord.

In order to absolve themselves from any responsibility for the resurgence of *jihad* and Jihadis, Sahwi sheikhs endeavoured to issue clarification statements in which they defined the Sahwi position on *jihad*. On Salman al-Awdah's Islamtoday website, an article appeared in which the author explains the position of Sahwa on this important Islamic obligation. The author argued that *jihad* is one of the most noble duties, and Jihadi education is a legitimate obligation that must be performed by Muslims. He added: 'No Sahwi abandoned this obligation. In fact they are proud of calling for it and are passionate about it. However, Sahwis distinguish between *jihad* as a value and a principle and its application on the ground in countries like Egypt, Algeria and especially Saudi Arabia.'[47]

Sahwis clearly stated that violence in Saudi Arabia under the slogan 'removing infidels from the Arabian Peninsula', which became the motto of al-Qa'ida in the Arabian Peninsula, is illegitimate. On the same website, Sheikh Abd al-Wahab al-Turayry clarifies this motto, which rests on a famous Prophetic Hadith, the subject of great discussion in the following two chapters. He asserts that this is an authentic and strong Hadith attributed to the Prophet. He argues that the Prophet did not object to the physical presence of Jews and Christians in the Arabian Peninsula, but that he ordered Muslims not to allow them to make this region their permanent home or abode. Their presence should be temporary/accidental (*tari'*). This temporary presence should be subjected to contractual arrangement, and in return infidels should be given peace. This Hadith should not be interpreted as a licence to kill infidels and shed their blood. Removing them does not mean killing them. Also the Prophetic tradition is not addressed to ordinary people but to *wulat al-amr*, leaders of the community who are required to act in this situation. Al-Turayry reminds his readers not to allow their anger and frustration over Western injustices against Muslims to let them misinterpret the sayings of the Prophet. He warns young Muslims that the presence of infidels was accepted by early knowledgeable *'ulama* (including Muhammad ibn Ibrahim, Abdulaziz ibn Baz and Muhammad ibn Uthaymin), who better understand the meaning of the Hadith. Their tradition should be followed, he concludes.[48] This interpretation, as we shall see later in this book, is contested by Jihadis. Here the Sahwi sheikh takes away the responsibility for removing infidels from the Peninsula from the hands of ordinary Muslims and makes it the sole prerogative of the ruler, thus confirming official Wahhabi views that 'al-umara alam bi al-maslaha' (princes know better).

Sahwis are aware that in the public sphere they are 'mistakenly considered to be the political wing of Jihadi movements and those calling for armed struggle'. They are bitter about the alleged cooperation of the official religious establishment with Saudi liberals in order to link Sahwis to the violent Jihadis. However, in the context of Saudi Arabia today, Sahwis have had to revise their position and avoid open confrontation not only with the religious establishment but more importantly with a state that is willing to deploy all its coercive power against those who disagree publicly with its policies or put pressure on it to take action it does not want to take.

Against the background of the most violent years in Saudi history, Safar al-Hawali launched a campaign 'to resist aggression' against Muslims. He chose the context of an interview for a programme called Bila hudud (Without Frontiers), with al-Jazeera on 5 November 2003 to announce 'al-himla al-alamiyya li muqawamat al-udwan', an international campaign to resist aggression.[49] The campaign was initially called Mecca but later changed its name. In this television programme, the sheikh declared that '*wali al-amr* is a father and we are his sons'. The campaign had several stated objectives. It was meant to educate people; resist aggression using legitimate means; clarify the true spirit of Islam by showing its humanitarian and moral message; and coordinate social and governmental efforts to fulfil these objectives. Al-Hawali promised cooperation with international institutions that reject injustice and oppression. There was also a hint that cooperation with international churches and those who respect Islam is desirable. The campaign also promised to include other non-Saudi Islamist personalities such as Fahmi Huwaidy and Muhammad Amara, both Egyptian intellectuals associated with modernist Islam rather than traditional Salafi thought.

The campaign aimed to curb the spread of violence in Saudi Arabia and demonstrate loyalty to the regime. Sheikh al-Hawali called upon Jihadis to give up their weapons and abandon armed struggle. He declared: 'We call upon the youth of the country to use the language of the tongue [words] rather than swords', and added, 'We must instruct the youth to fight the real enemy of the *umma*.' The sheikh reminded the audience that the Saudi government was to announce an initiative accepting negotiation and reconciliation with the hope of granting amnesty to the youth. He referred to Jihadis as 'our brothers who belong to the Jihadi trend'. He said that the success of the campaign was dependent on a general amnesty, trials for those who torture prisoners, the reinstatement of those who had been expelled from their jobs and respect for people's rights. Al-Hawali offered his religious skills and power of persuasion to avoid further discord. However, he presented himself as someone who could 'negotiate' on behalf of the government if it would be willing to treat him appropriately and listen to his own demands. He was not proposing to play the role of envoy or employee of the regime. His confidence was perhaps based on the backing of Shabab al-Sahwa, the Sahwi youth movement.

Using his personal popularity, al-Hawali was able to convince a few al-Qa'ida suspects such as Ali al-Faqasi to give themselves up to the authorities with the hope of amnesty, or at least a lenient sentence. Al-Hawali's call to another Jihadi ideologue, Faris al-Zahrani, was, however, unheeded. As a Ghamdi from al-Baha, al-Hawali used his tribal connections to lure famous Jihadi ideologues from the same tribe to give themselves up after the government promised fair trials to those involved in violence and amnesty to those without criminal records.

The Saudi government denied that Safar al-Hawali or any other group played a mediating or negotiating role. The fact that Sahwis were negotiating with Jihadis was, however, confirmed by the spokesman of the campaign, Muhsin al-Awajy, at American Arabic television station al-Hurra in May 2004. Al-Awajy justified the government's denial by saying that 'governments do not like to admit negotiating with terrorists. They have their own reasons.' Many Sahwis argue that had the state given Sahwis more freedom, recognition and visibility, they would have absorbed the radical Jihadis before the outbreak of violence. In discussing Jihadi violence, the Sahwi sheikhs acting as negotiators avoided outright condemnation and preferred to describe Jihadis as 'ignorant young men who rebel against elders'. This is contrasted with official rhetoric that depicts Jihadis as 'criminals' and 'thirsty bloodsuckers'. Sahwis hint at the difficulties they face in their mediation role, which they attribute to the previous failure of the justice system and its lack of transparency and independence.

Playing the role of mediators involves delivering those who threaten national security to the state with the hope of scoring political gains. However, the sheikhs have emphasised the difficulties they face as they try to convince Jihadis to return to the right path and abandon violence. In the media, al-Hawali pointed out that the Saudi judiciary is not totally independent, a factor that may influence the way Jihadis responds to mediation. He noted that some judges might be ignorant of the changes that have swept society. He also announced that some judges might issue sentences that contradict *shari'a*. Al-Hawali concluded that the Sahwis are seeking reconciliation between Jihadis and the state as a step towards reform.

While Sahwi sheikhs continued their efforts to bring Jihadis into the fold, they directed their attention to another group of dissidents who had sprung from their own ranks. The Movement for Islamic Reform in Arabia (MIRA), led by Saad al-Faqih, and the Movement for Islamic Renewal, led by Muhammad al-Masari, both based in London, emerged as two separate opposition movements out of the Committee for the Defence of Legitimate Rights in Arabia in the mid-1990s. The two movements had one common denominator: both rejected the Saudi regime and considered it impossible to reform; both called for the removal of the regime altogether. The two movements have other significant political and religious differences, however.

The Movement for Islamic Reform was a product of Sahwa. Throughout the 1990s it publicised the plight of the imprisoned Sahwi *'ulama* and their followers. With the outbreak of violence in Saudi Arabia after 11 September, Sahwis launched a demonisation campaign against MIRA and its director. A previous Sahwi comrade, Muhsin al-Awajy, took the lead in launching personal attacks on Saad al-Faqih. He never tired of calling upon al-Faqih to repent and return home. After a successful call for a demonstration in support of respect for human rights and the freeing of political prisoners in Riyadh in October 2003, Saad al-Faqih called from London for several demonstrations to take place in Saudi cities in December 2004. Sahwi *'ulama* issued a statement against those 'based abroad who want to undermine our security and prosperity'. Sahwis adopted the official Wahhabi view condemning demonstrations as illegitimate political activism. In January 2005 forty-one sheikhs signed a statement denouncing 'actions that cause *fitna*'.

Sahwis demonstrated their good intentions once again when important figures participated in the National Dialogue Forum, together with people they had previously regarded as a threat to Islam and Muslims, mainly Saudi liberals and groups whom they had previously considered to be outside true Islam, such as Shi'is. Sahwi names appeared among lists of invited participants in several meetings of the National Dialogue Forum. Several Sahwi signatories endorsed the content of an important declaration called How We Can Coexist. They reiterated the sanctity of human life, condemned imposing religion by force, and called for respect of the other. The declaration emphasised that the United States continues to dominate the Muslim world, a factor that explains the animosity. The declaration calls upon the West to 'realise that most of the Islamic movements throughout the Muslim world are essentially moderate . . . We are committed to fighting against terrorism.'[50] While this declaration was definitely targeting the outside world in an attempt to explain and clarify the position of a wide section of Saudi society, including Sahwis, other Sahwi efforts were a response to local developments.

One outcome of 11 September is the fact that Wahhabiyya became a contested religious discourse in its own home and among those who have been brought up on its teachings. While official Saudi propaganda continues to deny the very existence of a religious discourse that can be described as Wahhabi,[51] Sahwi *'ulama*, intellectuals and political activists are currently engaged in an unofficial debate about the Wahhabi movement. In the public sphere there is a serious effort to discuss religious discourse, without actually naming this discourse or even referring to the teachings of Wahhbi *'ulama* over the last 250 years. Such efforts are portrayed as attempts to renew religious discourse (*tajdid al-khitab al-dini*) or reform social heritage (*islah al-mawruth al-ijtima'i*), in the context of 'drying up the wells of terrorism'. This debate remains in great measure hesitant and superficial in the official public sphere, because it lacks an open declaration about the sources of terrorism without invoking outside influences and other foreign agents. A more open and honest debate flourishes in printed books published outside Saudi Arabia and in internet discussion boards. Only occasionally does a glimpse of this frank and sometimes daring debate erupt into the official Saudi public sphere. It is interesting that Sahwis have participated in this debate, now that the official Wahhabi establishment has lost some of its credibility. More importantly, the regime has sanctioned and even adopted 'revisionist' positions.

In one session of the National Dialogue Forum and after several critical articles that appeared in the Western press denouncing the Saudi religious curriculum for spreading hate against the West, Sheikh Abdulaziz al-Qasim, a young Sahwi who spent some time in prison in the early 1990s, presented a research paper which tested the hypothesis that the religious curriculum produced radical young people. A grandson of an important Salafi Wahhabi religious scholar associated with editing and publishing the monumental sixteen-volume Wahhabi collection of religious opinions *al-Durar al-saniyya fi al-ajwiba al-najdiyya*, al-Qasim presented his evaluation of the curriculum. He had been involved in the establishment of the Committee for the Defence of Legitimate Rights and the circulation of the Memorandum of Advice in the 1990s. In his research paper, al-Qasim asks, 'Where is the Fault?' His response confirms that Saudi religious education, which draws heavily on Wahhabi texts and interpretations, falls short of being appropriate for modern times. The judge does not name any famous religious scholar whose interpretation is considered inappropriate. Yet it is clear that al-Qasim is critical of the official Wahhabi tradition as it unfolds in the school curriculum. However, in al-Qasim's evaluation of the Saudi curriculum, Muhammad ibn Abd al-Wahhab and later scholars remain a taboo. His references draw on the various books used in schools without naming the original sources upon which the curriculum draws. The reader is left to wonder how the curriculum is formulated and who the original intellectual authorities behind the school texts are. Al-Qasim concludes that 'it is an exaggeration to claim that our religious curriculum bears the responsibility for violence against the West. In fact the faults of the current education poison relations between Muslims more than between Muslims and non-Muslims.'[52] While this is a clear condemnation of the Saudi religious curriculum, it falls short of apportioning any blame to the original masters and their disciples. Furthermore, al-Qasim could not voice a single word of criticism against the religio-political discourse or the role of the state in enforcing and financing this discourse. His assessment of religious education fell short of highlighting the contradiction between Saudi religious discourse and the reality of politics. This policy paper, together with media statements and other short publications, allowed the ex-Sahwi to redefine himself. Nowadays, after.every terrorist attack, al-Qasim and other Sahwis are given a platform to denounce violence and renew their allegiance to the regime. In one interview, he declared: 'There are problems of corruption but the royal family represents an equilibrium for stability. It is not in the interest of anybody in society to have the state destablised.'[53] Today al-Qasim is regarded as a 'modernist' sheikh or as an Islamo-liberal, although both labels are perhaps likely to be rejected by al-Qasim himself. Other Sahwis denounced al-Qasim's assessment of the education curriculum as misguided and inaccurate. In a long review of al-Qasim's policy paper, Sheikh Salman al-Kharashi launched a detailed refutation of the argument and concluded that any change to the curriculum could be interpreted as succumbing to outside pressure and a threat to Islam.

With the taming of their political discourse and the obvious willingness of Sahwis to work with the government, it seems that the only domain left in which to express 'independent' and 'defiant' views was the social and educational realms. In response to al-Qasim's assessment paper and the willingness of the government to change the education curriculum under what appeared to be American pressure, 156 *'ulama*, the majority of whom were Sahwis, issued a statement denouncing any attempt to change or modify religious education.

After 11 September, having lost all ability to resist the regime at the political level, Sahwis devoted all their attention to resisting social change. Today Sahwis 'resist' by rejecting and obstructing social change, especially that which they define as 'coming from abroad' or which corresponds to Saudi liberal agendas. Some Sahwis have focused their defiance on two areas: women and minority rights.

The social and political emancipation of Saudi women became the contested arena between the government and opposition groups. Having lost their ability to re-enchant politics, Sahwis pursued conservative interpretations of the status of women. Safar al-Hawali issued a religious opinion after being asked by someone from his home town, al-Baha, whether girls should be sent to Mecca and Jiddah for higher education, as al-Baha does not have a university. Al-Hawali answered:

I say what is the benefit of continuing education and what is its value? Girls are born to become mothers and educators of the future generation. If a woman stayed at home, did not beautify herself, and performed her religious duties, and obeyed her husband, she will be the queen in her kingdom. This is true happiness that all women, including Western *fajirat* [immoral women], aspire to. *Kafirs* in the West are beginning to wake up and provide women with subsidies if they stayed at home and raised their children. But we are going back on ourselves by asking women to go out of their houses . . . Working women get tired. They menstruate every month, they become weak. They have nervous breakdowns. To serve the nation, women must stay at home. They should not go to Jiddah in search of a university. The dormitories are full of *fasad* [corruption] and mixing.[54]

On another Sahwi website, an opinion on women's participation in elections was posted to coincide with the first Saudi municipal elections in

February 2005. In this first round, Saudi women were completely absent as candidates and as voters. A Sahwi sheikh responds to a question regarding whether the old classical *bay'a* is comparable to modern elections and whether women's participation in offering *bay'a* to the Prophet can be understood today as a way of justifying their participation in modern elections. The sheikh replies:

> *Bay'a* is not the same as elections. Early Muslim men and women did not 'elect' the Prophet; they believed in his message and his prophecy. They offered *bay'a* for that. I do not know of women who offered *bay'a* to the early caliphs as this was not their business. Elections are concerned with choosing someone to perform a task. It is a modern phenomenon guided by a special law and place.[55]

Sahwis appropriated gender relations and positioned themselves as 'guardians' of the values and rights of women, a position they share with Jihadis, as will be demonstrated in the next chapter. The state and the official religious establishment also appropriate women's issues, and both claim to guard the women of the country. Today some Sahwis resist through adopting a conservative view towards female education, participation in elections and other matters. Others, like al-Qasim, show greater flexibility in dealing with women's issues. Al-Qasim tries to draw a line between religious rulings and social tradition. He sometimes argues that religious scholars do not always make that distinction, thus prohibiting certain issues when there is no clear textual reference or injunction. This line of analysis is adopted by Sheikh Salman al-Awdah, who for one month appeared daily on MBC satellite television, to propagate new interpretations. Al-Awdah is now positioning himself as the rational and modern voice of Islam in Saudi Arabia. This confirms the view that Sahwis are political actors before being religious agents.

Sahwis seem to conduct their resistance by adopting a critical stance vis-à-vis calls for greater recognition of minority rights, which have come from abroad and from the minorities themselves. The government seemed responsive to such calls in an attempt to contain potential dissidence. In 2003 a group of Shi'i activists sent a petition to the crown prince calling for greater religious freedom, equality and partnership. Safar al-Hawali wrote a scathing refutation of their demands under an ironical title. In 'When the Minority Rules over the Majority', he states:

> In this country Shi'is are born Shi'is, practise their tradition and die as Shi'is. Nobody asks them to change their beliefs. This is freedom. There are other minorities that do not call for having a minister or a politician representing them. The Shi'is adopted a tone that seeks revenge not dialogue. They either want a Shi'i government that imposes Shi'ism on all or a secular government that allows everyone to fight for his religion under the false pretext of freedom. A civil war will then be imminent. Shi'is imply that if not given their rights they will cooperate

with foreign governments. This reminds us of al-Alqami who was an ally of foreign invaders and conspired to kill the Abbasid Caliph . . . We are concerned that Shi'is find the right path so that they can escape misery in the afterlife. We support their worldly demands and they should take these demands to the relevant government agencies. But we should discuss with them the true nature of monotheism, dissociation from blasphemy and recognition of our four Caliphs.[56]

Al-Hawali then highlights his concern over Shi'i claims that they are deprived and excluded. He argues that if Shi'is are poor,

it is because of the exploitation of their own religious scholars who extract one fifth of their income for their own purposes . . . The people who really deserve to be given their rights are the people of Tihama, between Jiddah and Yemen [al-Hawali's own region], which has a fraction of the services that the Shi'is have in their own area. Succumbing to Shi'i pressure will lead to other groups, for example Hijazi Sufis who are now allies of certain ruling families in the Arab world, to ask for the internationalisation (tadwil) of the Hijaz under the leadership of the Ashraf, whose claim for leadership together with the tribe of Quraysh, may be supported by religious texts.[57]

In denouncing Shi'i demands, al-Hawali sends a strong warning signal to the government. He projects these demands as misguided and possibly directed from abroad to undermine the unity of the Saudi state and eventually lead to its disintegration. His references to the possible return of the rule of the Sharifs and Quraysh touches a very raw nerve in the ruling family, as the Sharifs of the Hijaz were the major contestants for leadership, not only in the Arabian Peninsula but beyond that. His message is clear and direct. As a Sahwi, he defends the realm under the banner of the Al-Saud, and any concessions to so-called religious minorities will no doubt lead to undesirable consequences. His discourse focuses on other deprived regions in the north and south, which according to recent research are subject to exclusion and marginalisation.[58]

On the domestic front the previous confrontation and contestation between Sahwis and the government have subsided and given way to negotiation and mediation. It remains to be seen whether the truce will hold. Accommodation is definitely maintained while the security situation is still unstable. More Jihadi violence will no doubt bring the state and Sahwis closer. Each will try hard to postpone exerting unbearable pressure on the other.

The regional and international front

Sahwis today face the same fate as the official religious establishment. They cannot voice serious critical political opinions on domestic issues. However, they have found enough regional and international fronts to re-establish their credibility against the background of co-optation experienced in the domestic arena.

In order to compensate for their co-optation at home, Sahwis turned their attention to regional and international conflicts. At the regional level, they remained faithful to their 1990s anti-American rhetoric without invoking *jihad* in Saudi Arabia or removing infidels from the Arabian Peninsula. The increasingly unfavourable reporting on Saudi Arabia in the Western media following 11 September was countered locally by anti-Americanism that dominated most Sahwi publications, as well as others. Criticising American policies in the Middle East on the pages of the local Saudi press was mistakenly considered as genuine 'freedom of expression'. The so-called Riyadh Spring in 2002–3 was partly about the freedom to criticise the USA rather than the regime. Sahwis eagerly participated in the denunciation of the USA.

Having curbed their confrontational discourse at home, Sahwis channelled their Jihadi rhetoric to other hot-spots in the Muslim and Arab world, of which there were several. Mainstream Sahwis objected to the attack on Afghanistan and the demise of the Taliban in 2001–2. However, many did not dare openly support the Taliban or express sympathy for a state that hosted Osama bin Laden. Scholars who overtly denounced American aggression against the Taliban proved to belong to the Jihadi sub-group, mainly associated with sheikhs such as al-Khodayr, al-Oqla and al-Fahad. Suffice it to say that the majority of mainstream Sahwis remained silent while warning against providing any logistical help to the invading American army. As one of the main objectives of the US campaign at the time was to capture Osama bin Laden, many Sahwis kept a low profile, given the Saudi government's denunciation of the al-Qa'ida leader. Any objection to the campaign would have been immediately understood as sympathy for Bin Laden. Sahwis restrained themselves at a time when their reputation was being tested. Some wrote about American aggression, mainly on the internet, denouncing the killing of Muslims and glorifying resistance as if to maintain Sahwi reputation among their followers. Few Sahwi sheikhs issued statements calling upon Muslims to go for *jihad* in Afghanistan in a way similar to previous *fatwa*s regarding *jihad* against the Soviet Union in the 1980s. Famous Sahwi sheikhs had reservations even on that first experience of *jihad*.

Many Sahwis had preferred young Muslim men to stay at home and deal with the deteriorating domestic situation. It was rumoured that famous Sahwis, for example Safar al-Hawali, opposed the participation of Saudis in the Afghan *jihad* against the Soviet Union while the official Wahhabi establishment represented by Ibn Baz encouraged it as *fard kifaya* (an obligation performed on behalf of the whole community).

Al-Hawali is known to have warned against the consequences of sending young men to Afghanistan to fight the Russians, pointing out that Afghanistan was a trap for young Muslims. It is claimed that he anticipated the negative outcomes of the Afghan *jihad*.[59]

The US occupation of Iraq and the fall of Baghdad in April 2003 proved to be a different matter. Given that the Saudi government was trying hard to rebuild amicable relations with the USA and recast itself as a moderate force in the region, Sahwis, by strongly endorsing the anti-war attitude, proved that they could still embarrass their government.[60] Groups including radical Jihadis, Islamist Centrist reformers, religious scholars and exiled Islamists all advocated a total rejection of the war, which was condemned with such slogans as a 'Christian–Zionist imperialist plot' and a 'New Crusade'.[61] The fragmentation and pluralism of Sahwa melted away with the collapse of Saddam's statue in the central square of Baghdad. At the same time, Sahwi differences disappeared, as they all shared an overwhelming rejection of Saddam Hussein, seen as the 'other face of American imperialism'. A famous Sahwi scholar, Nasir al-Omar, wrote an extended essay entitled, 'Waylun lil 'arab min sharin qad iqtarab' (Arabs, Beware of an Approaching Evil). He raised seven points relating to the Iraqi crisis:

1. The war is not between Bush and Saddam or the American government and the Ba'th regime. It is yet another episode in a series of crusades announced by Bush. The first one took place when America used Saddam to hit Iran, followed by the Gulf War of 1990, followed by the American invasion of Afghanistan.
2. Our enmity against Saddam and his atheist regime is not a justification for the war.
3. The war on Iraq is an unjust crime and Sunni Iraqis will bear the heaviest loss.
4. It is an Islamic obligation to support our brothers in Iraq rather than support the regime.
5. A serious disaster stems from the relationship between the Muslim *umma* and its illegitimate governments, which have supported American interests throughout the modern period.
6. The responsibility for resisting this invasion falls on Muslims, who should abandon their preoccupation with trivial matters and concentrate on the real issue – that is, resisting the invasion.
7. American strategic plans for the Muslim world are long term. America will use all means available to dominate the Muslim world. Therefore, Muslims should resist by applying all means, including education, military confrontation, economic pressure and social and psychological force.[62]

Saudi Sahwis issued a joint declaration whose signatories included Muslim scholars and professionals from Pakistan, Sudan, Yemen, Morocco and Palestine. The declaration summarised their position:

America's objective in this war is to destroy the Muslim identity of the region and replace it with American culture. America seeks to control the economic wealth of the country to cover up its failure in Afghanistan. It also aims to occupy the region with more war and unrest to protect the security of Israel and destroy the Palestinian uprising.[63]

The overwhelming Islamist consensus concealed latent divisions within the outspoken groups. Sahwis asked whether the Saudi government and the established religious scholars would issue a *fatwa* supporting *jihad* in Iraq, thus bringing to mind their position during the liberation of Afghanistan from the Soviet Union. Hardline Islamists, often working abroad or clandestinely, exposed contradictions in the official Saudi position and among the established *'ulama*, none of whom called publicly for a *jihad* in Iraq. Throughout the Iraqi crisis the official religious establishment refused to give a religious legitimacy to resistance in Iraq. Sahwis were disappointed as several official religious scholars declared that the violence against civilians in Iraq is not *jihad*, and should be denounced as *fitna*. This did not deter Sahwis, who were enraged by the level of American aggression against the Sunni cities of Iraq, from issuing their own *fatwa*.

In November 2004 and with American troops tightening their grip over the Iraqi city of Falluja, twenty-six *'ulama*, mainly Sahwis, issued a statement denouncing American aggression and legitimising resistance by calling it *jihad*. The list of signatories included famous names such as Safar al-Hawali, Salman al-Awdah, Nasir al-Omar, Sulayman al-Rushudi, Said al-Ghamdi and Awadh al-Qarni.[64] The statement, entitled 'Saudi Ulama Letter Regarding Jihad in Falluja' and published on several Sahwi websites, classified resistance in Iraq as *jihad daf'i* (defensive *jihad*), an obligation that is incumbent on every capable Iraqi male. The signatories clarified that this *jihad* does not need to be fought under the banner of a known leader, as each individual must take the initiative and resist foreign domination. The statement also called upon Iraqis, both Sunnis and Shi'is, to unite and avoid the disintegration of the country. Jihadis are advised to protect innocent civilians and their property. The statement urged Iraqis not to cooperate with the US army and to protect Jihadis.

Sahwi sheikh Salman al-Awdah openly declared that Iraqis must resist foreign occupation, but issued clear statements against Saudi participation in the Iraqi resistance. He called it a legitimate Islamic duty that is also sanctioned by international law.[65] He added that Iraqis should physically help the resistance while the rest of the Arab and Muslim world must support this effort in other ways, for example in international forums. However, al-Awdah advised against Saudi men joining the *jihad* in Iraq. He argued that if non-Iraqis participate in this *jihad*, they may cause chaos because of lack of coordination. Foreign Jihadis might have agendas that are not compatible with local concerns and orientations. *Jihad* in Iraq must have a clear objective, i.e. throwing out foreign occupation. Those who have grand objectives such as establishing a Muslim polity or reviving the caliphate are dreaming.

Was Sahwi denunciation of the American occupation of Iraq a hesitant attempt to regain credibility after a period of acquiescence – even subservience – to the regime? Sahwi sheikh Safar al-Hawali still commands respect among his followers. In June 2005 he was admitted to hospital in Mecca after a serious stroke. He was later transferred to a hospital in Jiddah. His illness coincided with King Fahd's admission to hospital after several years of ill health. Saudi internet sites were preoccupied with the illness of the Sahwi sheikh, while the King's deteriorating health went almost unnoticed. Prince Sultan (since 2005 Crown Prince) offered to send Sheikh al-Hawali abroad for treatment. After years in prison and a long time as a 'suspect', Sheikh Safar was 'rehabilitated' by the regime. It remains to be seen whether his illness will precipitate a complete withdrawal from public life. It seems unlikely that the sheikh will be able to resume his normal activities. There is no doubt, however, that his legacy will continue to inspire many Saudis. Safar al-Hawali will go down in history as the Ghamdi sheikh who was truly caught between the state and the call. He will also be remembered as a sheikh who penetrated the circle of *aimat al-da'wa al-najdiyya* despite sharing neither the geography nor the genealogy of this group. Al-Hawali honoured the intellectual heritage of the early Wahhabis but had serious reservations about his contemporaries, especially those directly tied to government agendas. The state broke his will but failed to undermine his popularity among his followers completely.

A triumphant or bitter and twisted Sahwa?

Sahwi *'ulama* such as Safar al-Hawali and Salman al-Awdah were able to retreat into their *shari'a* knowledge and protect themselves against further loss of credibility resulting from increasing association with government agendas. After all, they can claim that they are men of religion rather than men of state. Regardless of whether it was acquired in a traditional setting or a modern university, religious knowledge still commands respect in Saudi Arabia.

By 2005 most Sahwi activists seemed to be enjoying far more freedom than they had had in the early 1990s. They have gained access to media channels, and some Sahwi groups have their own satellite television, electronic newsletters, discussion boards and other communication channels. After almost a decade of confrontation, Sahwis and the state reached a modus vivendi. Sahwis accepted the old schism between the secular state and the religious coterie. They retreated into their educational programmes, thus socialising society into Islam while leaving politics to the government. Today they concentrate on healing society and its ills. In a manner reminiscent of their mentors, the official Wahhbi establishment, they blame society's ignorance, tribalism, corruption, regionalism, opportunism and other negative traits for social problems. While a previous generation of *ulama* reprimanded society for exhibiting *shirk* (blasphemy and heterodoxy), today the same society is condemned for allegedly immersing itself in modern sins resulting from either its traditional social organisation (tribalism) or its enthusiasm for Westernisation and modern innovations. Sahwis have moved from blaming the regime for the ills of society to blaming society itself, as a way out of a dilemma. Reforming society is today an alternative to reforming the state. But can society be reformed according to Sahwi agenda without fundamental political change? After all, their early 1990 petitions demanded an overhaul of the Saudi political system rather than the transformation of society. Will a reformed society take the lead in establishing the rightful polity that Sahwis aspire to? Many Sahwis believe that reforming each part (the individual) of society will lead to a better whole. While this logic is sound, it cannot be taken for granted that such a reformed society will automatically lead to a reformed pious Islamic state.

When Sahwis venture into domestic politics, their rhetoric is general and ambiguous. Today they criticise 'all Arab regimes', when they really mean the Saudi one. Sahwis started out with an attempt to re-enchant politics, but they failed miserably. They have readjusted their rhetoric in response to a local and international context that considers revolutionary political change a kind of terrorism. While Sahwis never admit that they have changed their position on several important issues, it is obvious that they have. They have increased their visibility as a group while individual members are co-opted and rewarded. Today Sahwis call for Islamising society and applying *shari'a*, but refrain from criticising the government for introducing new legislation or removing judicial decisions in certain areas from the hands of *shari'a* courts. In Saudi Arabia, there are several legal systems, each applying to an area of public life. While personal law remains in the hands of *shari'a* courts, the economy and the media are dealt with according to new legislation, often referred to as *nidham*.

Sahwis call for reform in Saudi Arabia but condemn any attempt to exert pressure on the government through demonstrations or public criticism. They condemn America's aggression against Muslims, but never hint that the Saudi royal family is one of the Arab and Muslim regimes most loyal to the power they define as the 'aggressor'. They celebrate a transnational Islam while respecting national boundaries. They glorify the Muslim *umma*, which is bound only by religious bonds, but unwillingly accept man-made national boundaries. In their rhetoric, the establishment of a Muslim polity is an unrealistic dream, and so is armed struggle against the so-called enemies of Islam. In the present circumstances, the imbalance in power between Muslims and the 'dominating' nations requires Sahwis to resist aggression by non-violent means. In return, Sahwis have gained the trust of the regime. They are no longer the first enemy. The Jihadis, together with other peaceful Islamists abroad, occupy this position.

Sahwis are more vocal when they launch verbal attacks on the West, especially the United States. The latter gave them plenty of opportunities in Afghanistan, Iraq, Guantánamo Bay and Abu Ghraib. The American media's negative portrayal of Saudi Arabia and its religious education required a counter-campaign to resist the various manifestations of 'outside aggression'. Sahwis retained the language of the 'crusades' and the 'clash of civilisations'. They gave 'independent' opinions on *jihad* abroad and volunteered *fatwas* that made it compulsory in 'occupied territories' but forbade it in their own homeland. They distinguished between 'killing Americans' in Iraq and slaughtering them in Saudi Arabia. They sanctioned Iraqi men fighting the occupiers but had reservations regarding Saudi men travelling to the battlefield. As public figures who were given the green light to express opinions, Sahwis were interviewed by the international media, including the CNN, BBC, Reuters and AFP. They presented themselves and were presented as the Islamists of Saudi Arabia. Sahwi sheikhs formed a quasi-independent religious establishment – more accurately a church in waiting. Some have argued that the Sahwa was able to 'impose' itself on the government. This has manifested itself in government recognition of Sahwi figures, who now enjoy more freedom to express the 'diluted' statements mentioned above. Others see the Sahwa as a co-opted movement that has succumbed to government pressure without any obvious gains – for example, achieving aspects of the reform they called for in their famous 1990 Memorandum of Advice.

With the accommodation between Sahwa and state, Sahwi intellectuals are perhaps less fortunate than Sahwi *ulama*. Some of those who count themselves as Sahwi Islamic intellectuals seem to be less able to withstand the price not only of changing their views but of openly supporting government agendas. The pragmatism shown by Sahwi activists – some would say opportunism – could not be justified on the grounds of revising religious texts or offering new interpretations. After all, the 'ulama are known to be mujtahids (entitled to give individual opinions) – if they formulate a wrong opinion, they are granted one reward; if they are right, they are granted two rewards, according to the Prophetic tradition. This statement is not extended to include Sahwi activists, whose change of views and accommodation – and even support – of government can only be interpreted as political manoeuvring, pragmatism and opportunism. To avoid being labelled opportunistic or pragmatic, some Sahwi activists have retreated from the public eye, choosing a quietist position. Others have become unashamedly entangled with the regime while launching a bitter campaign against their ex-comrades.

One example was Sahwi Muhsin al-Awajy, who today not only defends Sahwa against its enemies, but also defends the state. A specialist in agriculture and holder of a doctorate in this subject from a British university, he is different from the famous Sahwi sheikhs. His regular appearances in the media, his website and his various articles have gradually eroded a symbolic capital, gained as a result of having been a political activist involved in the work that led to the release of the Memorandum of Advice and the Committee for the Defence of Human Rights in Arabia in the early 1990s. He was sentenced to fifteen years in prison but released after four years. He lost his university job and had his passport confiscated. After 11 September, he emerged as an unofficial spokesman of the Sahwa – but also of the government. Between 2004 and 2005, al-Awajy specialised in launching personal attacks on a whole range of activists, Sahwis and liberals, both men and women.[66] As he claimed to be involved in 'negotiating with Jihadis', he appeared on Arab satellite television, especially al-Jazeera, to comment on government success in pacifying terrorists, dismantling violent cells, negotiating with Jihadis, and praised official wisdom in dealing with the security problem. Al-Awajy played the role of the unofficial spokesman of the Ministry of Interior. While the government imprisoned several Saudi intellectuals, activists and religious scholars who volunteered comments on al-Jazeera without permission, he had official approval.[67] When Saudi human rights activists and lawyers criticised the government's record on freedom of expression, al-Awajy praised the regime for its understanding and tolerance. He labelled all those who call for reform from abroad as either agents of Western domination, corrupted liberals or revenge-seeking persons determined to undermine the umma's security and prosperity.[68] Regarding those who call for reform from within Saudi Arabia, al-Awajy proposes sorting out the real reformers from those who undermine religion and state. Several days after the government sent Abdullah al-Hamid, Matruk al-Falih, and Ali al-Damini, three reformers associated with calls for constitutional monarchy, to prison for writing petitions that al-Awajy himself had signed, he wrote in the local press: 'We denounce those who have contacts with foreign powers especially the crusades. We must choose the hell of our own society rather than the heaven of the colonialists.'[69] Al-Awajy repeated the government's accusations against the three imprisoned reformers.

While in his media statements and publications, al-Awajy claims to be close to Sheikh al-Hawali, the latter in an interview hinted at a personal dispute between them, which al-Hawali prefers to leave buried. Has the main pillar of the Sahwa disowned al-Awajy? Or is al-Hawali's response a way of reprimanding a follower who has gone a bit too far? It is impossible to know as long as al-Hawali remains silent. Al-Awajy's constant references to Sheikh al-Hawali and his invocation of the name of this religious scholar are desperate attempts to regain some kind of legitimacy and recognition at a time when his credibility was seriously eroded. While some Sahwi religious scholars retained some kind of dignity deriving from their religious capital, al-Awajy represents the section of Sahwa that has become 'bitter and twisted'.

In 2001 al-Awajy set up a website called al-Wasatiyya. He posts his articles on this site, which has a discussion board dealing with social, religious, political and contemporary affairs. Al-Awajy's website allows the posting of serious criticism of the Wahhabi tradition, discussion of minority-related matters, criticism of the royal family and other controversial issues. It does not, however, seem to be very popular. After reasonable success in 2001–2, it seems to have lost much of its credibility. Topics on the site do not change regularly, while the number of visitors at any particular moment remains small compared to other Saudi-run websites and discussion boards. Al-Awajy's articles dealing with domestic issues receive mixed responses, including some highly negative personal comments about him. His domestic articles receive damning comments on other Islamist and liberal discussion boards. Publications that glorify Jihadi resistance to the American occupation of Iraq are positively received. Those articles dealing with foreign matters appear as a desperate attempt to regain some of the lost credibility on the domestic front. In Saudi Arabia, like much of the Arab and Muslim world, denouncing American policies, especially neo-conservative strategies, is always hailed as an honest and brave position, a cathartic mechanism that guarantees positive responses among a population that is still deprived of freedom to evaluate the policies of its own government.

One might argue that the mixed responses to al-Awajy's views are only natural, as Saudis are just beginning to learn how to voice their opinions in the public sphere after years without any dissident voices or frank evaluation of public figures. However, in al-Awajy's case, mixed responses are symptomatic of many negative developments that the Sahwa is trying hard to contain. It seems that there are numerous specific reasons behind the mixed responses that al-Awajy has received. As a Sahwi he incurs the wrath of both Saudi liberals and the official Wahhabi establishment. The latter became more critical as he began to voice criticism of the Wahhabi tradition under the guise of 'renewing religious discourse', a cliche catchphrase that masks criticism of official Wahhabiyya without naming it. As an ex-Sahwi, al-Awajy must have had reservations about the official religious discourse that created consenting subjects. However, as he went further in his criticism to accommodate moderate or less conservative views on society, women and the Shi'i minority, he incurred the wrath of not only the Wahhabi establishment but also his own Sahwi comrades. When he condemned Jihadi violence in his articles, he incurred a severe blow from Jihadis themselves, who denounced him in a long treatise published in al-Qa'ida electronic journals and discussion boards.[70] When he publicly condemned his closest Sahwi comrades outside Saudi Arabia, he revealed an opportunism that was linked to his close relations with the regime. Today al-Awajy's controversial and ambiguous status among various groups in Saudi society is symptomatic of the problems faced by Sahwi activists as they were drawn into government agenda. Loss of credibility at a time when no obvious gains were visible was bound to accompany Sahwa's shift from confrontation with the regime to accommodation, and an ongoing co-optation. A Saudi commentator on al-Awajy's latest transformation argues: 'Al-Awajy burnt all his boats. He is standing all alone on the sandy shores of hope. He disowned Wahhabis and they disowned him. He was disowned by terrorists who rejected his mediation. One terrorist described him as the fertiliser specialist [a reference to al-Awajy's doctorate in agriculture], a crow who leads people to the corpse.'[71]

While 'burning all boats' accompanied co-optation by the government, other Sahwis have gradually drifted towards the Jihadi trend. The story of Lewis Atiyat Allah in this book is an example of a Sahwi who abandoned Sahwa in favour of the Jihadis. Other Sahwis abandoned the local variant of the awakening in favour of other Saudi Islamists abroad. A third group preferred to move out of Islamism altogether and join Saudi liberals, becoming examples of 'courageous and brave revisionists' who enjoy reading Martin Luther King and other enlightened characters. Under state oppression and co-optation, the Sahwa fragmented.

In June 2005, while Sheikh Safar al-Hawali was fighting for his life in a Jiddah hospital, the government announced its third list of wanted terrorists. Immediately, another Sahwi sheikh, Salman al-Awdah, stepped into the vacuum. He called upon the suspects to give themselves up in a manner reminiscent of Safar's approach. The Sahwa was confirmed in its new mediating role.

It remains to be seen whether Sahwi 'ulama will be crowned as the new religious establishment that will dominate the Saudi religio-political field in the twenty-first century. However, it seems that the Sahwa serves the regime better if it remains outside the circle of official religio-political discourse. Perhaps the state has realised that it is more beneficial to keep two religious establishments. An official one can curb Sahwi influence by resorting to the old conviction relating to the obligation to obey rulers and advise them privately. The official religious establishment remains in control of the courts that may in the future deal with dissident Sahwis and others. It remains important for the socialisation of the next generation of acquiescent subjects. On the other hand, an unofficial Sahwi establishment can mediate between the state and Jihadis, absorb social unrest among the youth, and channel local revolutionary sentiments abroad.

After 11 September Sahwa began to devour its own children. It might seem that the earlier contestation which gave way to co-optation led to the state being the obvious winner while the official religious establishment was the obvious loser. However, the Saudi scene is more complicated than that, and is less likely to generate clear-cut boundaries between winners and losers. Sahwi 'ulama initially sought the blessing of official 'ulama, but later they competed with them. The official 'ulama seem to have lost their monopoly not only over religious interpretation but also the hearts and minds of many young Saudis, while remaining in control of a huge religious bureaucracy including education and the judiciary. It seems that the Saudi regime is grooming Sahwi sheikh Salman al-Awdah to rise to eminence, with the help of pan-Arab media, mostly sponsored by Saudi money.[72]

3 Struggling in the way of God abroad: from localism to transnationalism

It was the right thing for Saudi Arabia to send Jihadis to Afghanistan. All Saudi Jihadis came back in 1992. They were nice people. We did not have *takfiris* in Saudi Arabia. *Takfiris* were all produced in Afghanistan. The worst among them are in London. The likes of Abu Hamza, Abu Qatada and al-Masari are the worst ones.

Jamal Khashogji, spokesman for Prince Turki al-Faysal, Saudi ambassador in Washington (Idhaat, al-Arabiyya TV Channel, 14 September 2005)

He was young, enjoying his seventeenth spring when he told his mother that he is going to Afghanistan. She begged him not to go but he always said, it is *fard 'ayn* . . . it is *fard 'ayn*. Sheikh Muhsin issued him a fatwa that he did not need his father's permission because it is *jihad daf'i* to defend Muslims against an aggressive enemy.

Year later the mother turned the radio off as Sheikh Muhsin was instructing parents to protect their children and prevent them from going to those places where they learn to excommunicate rulers.

Mr Jamil was talking on television about terrorism and Jihadis. Years ago he went to support Jihad in Afghanistan. One of the girls watching the television show spat on this *jasus* (spy). Ahmad said that Mr Jamil was clandestinely spying on the Jihadis while pretending to be a voluntary aid worker.

Muhammad al-Hodhayf, *Nuqtat taftish*

To say that Saudi Arabia was a zone free of *takfiris*, a label that is used to describe those who excommunicate others (as individuals or en masse), implying an uncompromising Islamic position, is an unconvincing statement. As mentioned earlier, the Saudi regime itself was founded on 'excommunicating other Muslims', an exercise in demonising the population of Arabia – mainly all those Muslims who resisted its hegemony. Saudi official *'ulama*, under state patronage, have practised *takfir al-mujtama'* (the excommunication of a whole society) since the eighteenth century. The early letters of *aimat al-da'wa al-najdiyya* attest to a strong tradition of denouncing other Muslims. Yet throughout their history, the *aima* refrained from excommunicating specific rulers, descendants of the Al-Saud. On one occasion, one Saudi ruler was described as *baghi* (usurper), rather than *kafir*, when he sought help from the Ottomans against his brother in the 1870s.[1] Similarly, the Ikhwan rebels of the 1920s fell short of describing Ibn Saud as *kafir*.[2] In 1979 Juhayman al-Otaybi did not excommunicate specific Saudi rulers, although he declared the regime as a whole a *kafir* regime.

As Wahhabi religious discourse travelled to Afghanistan and other destinations, it carried with it the practice of excommunication. While contemporary Islamists (for example, Egyptian Jihadis)[3] had already developed such theological positions, Saudis had their own contribution to make. In 1979, Juhayman al-Otaybi's movement was clearly a local tradition rather than an import from other Islamist movements. The Afghan experience only sharpened the Saudi *takfiri* tradition. In Afghanistan *takfir* was used against those who initially theorised it: the official Saudi *'ulama* and their sponsors, the Al-Saud. Saudis did not need to travel to Afghanistan to 'learn' the discourse of excommunication. They carried it with them. In Afghanistan, they simply applied it to their own rulers.

Before Wahhabi discourse could be refined, or even freed from the domination of the state, it travelled to distant locations very different from its original habitat. Not even the influx of Muslim scholars to Saudi Arabia in the 1960s, the majority of whom arrived as immigrants or state guests delivering sermons in prestigious government-sponsored Islamic conferences and universities, provided sufficient conditions for its universalisation. Saudi religious discourse travelled to Africa, Europe, Asia and North America. This transnationalisation took place in times of both peace and war. It is important to emphasise that this transnationalisation was initially dependent on Arabs and Muslims, who were either sent from Saudi Arabia itself or were inhabitants of these foreign destinations. In the 1980s the situation became slightly different with the maturation of a literate Saudi 'religious' generation that was sent abroad to spread the call.

At this juncture Saudi religio-political discourse was severely inhibited by its overwhelming parochialism, which meant that it lacked a universal orientation, and its premature transnationalisation under the auspices of the modern state meant that it did not find an easy reception out of Saudi Arabia. Most Saudi religious scholars never travel abroad, and not a single one rose to international eminence and gained recognition among Muslims worldwide, despite massive resources. (Egypt, for example, produced *'ulama* who gained pan-Islamic reputations; the contemporary Egyptian Sheikh Yusif al-Qardawi is perhaps a late addition to the list.) Only with oil wealth did Saudi religious scholars achieve eminence abroad. Moreover, Wahhabi discourse failed to engage with the intellectual and political problems that occupied Muslim scholars, thinkers and activists throughout the twentieth century. It was very much concerned with ritualistic aspects of worship at the expense of developing universal messages or responses to the challenges of modernity, apart from prohibiting or permitting the use of some technological innovations. Under the patronage of the state the Wahhabi tradition failed to tackle issues related to social justice, the role of women and minorities, the Islamic state, political consultation, elections and participation. These remained taboo topics. Wahhabi discourse excelled in theorising the confrontation with the 'infidel' West, rejection of other Islamic traditions (for example other Sunni interpretations and those of the Shiʿis) and glorification of the concept of *jihad*, without being able to put its theories into practice inside the country.

The transnationalisation of Saudi religious discourse created a volatile situation, with dramatic consequences not only for Saudis but also for the receiving societies. The discourse of exclusion and demonisation of other Muslims and 'infidels' developed by Saudi official *ʿulama*, while extremely important for mobilising Jihadis in a war situation, proved disastrous in times of peace elsewhere.

The premature transnationalisation of Saudi religious discourse involved the worldwide propagation of local Saudi religious interpretations. These are the intellectual product of people with genealogical links to *aimat al-daʿwa al-najdiyya*, the majority of whom were and are drawn from the oases and towns of central Arabia, especially Qasim and the area around Riyadh. Most of the so-called higher *ʿulama* had never travelled outside Saudi Arabia, and many of those who occupied the highest posts were blind, a handicap that could not be overcome in a world dominated by images and visual media.[4] Being blind is not necessarily a serious disadvantage, but it added to the parochialism and localism of this discourse. Although this discourse is founded on the assumption that it is an embodiment of the universal tradition of *ahl al-sunna wa ʾl-jamaʿa*, it failed to develop beyond its localism. It should not be forgotten that part of this localism was related to the fact that the discourse grew in the shadow of a political power desperate for legitimacy. From its early days, creating consenting subjects and legitimising the status quo left their marks on this religious tradition. When Wahhabi religio-political discourse began to be transnationalised in the last decades of the twentieth century, it travelled with its potential for both consent and contestation. Both at home and abroad, it carried the seeds of its own mutation.

A critical year: 1979

After the defeat of Egypt in 1967, Saudi Arabia enjoyed a short period of being seen as the centre of the Arab Islamic world. Its newly acquired wealth, religious rhetoric and the symbolism of its geography created the conditions for the country's pre-eminence. After a long period of claiming the special status of a pious Islamic state, Saudi Arabia was able to impose itself on the Arab–Islamic scene thanks to its wealth. President Sadat's peace treaty with Israel, a move against Arab consensus at the time, facilitated Saudi Arabia's triumphant rhetoric as the guardian not only of the two holy mosques but also Muslim interests worldwide. In the Arab world, Egypt was no longer a competitor. After Sadat's visit to Israel, the Saudi regime crowned itself as the sole defender of Arab and Muslim causes. This monopoly proved to be short-lived.

In 1979 Saudi Arabia faced the challenge of Iran, which, after the revolution, was ruled by mullahs who, like the Saudi *noblesse d'état*, claimed to apply the *shari'a* and defend Islam and Muslim causes. However, while Iranian mullahs became the state itself, their Saudi counterparts accepted a 'secretive advisory role', under the patronage of the state. Jealous of their counterparts in Iran, Saudi Sahwis asked for a greater role, which led to confrontation with the regime by the early 1990s. Iran, whose Shi'i tradition had always been denounced by Saudi *ulama*, became a competitor. Saudi Arabia and Iran struggled to win the hearts of Muslims; each paid vast sums to promote religious literature that denounced the other. Both competed to sponsor religious education, mosques, Islamic conferences and other highly visible projects outside their territories. Sectarian differences between Sunnis and Shi'is had always been divisive in Islamic history, but from now on the politicisation of sectarian identities in Saudi Arabia as well as in the Gulf, Pakistan, India and other Muslim areas became more visible and volatile, thanks to Saudi and Iranian interventions. The 1980s were known as the decade of increased sectarian tension, which the Saudi–Iranian political rivalry only aggravated. Iranian revolutionary rhetoric denounced 'imperialists and their agents' in the Muslim world. The Saudi regime felt the pressure. While Saudi religious discourse denounced Western infidels, the Saudi leadership was moving closer towards Western agenda. Its own Eastern Province Shi'i community rioted and demanded equality and recognition.[5] While these riots were severely suppressed, the danger from Iran took a new dimension with the onset of the Iran–Iraq War. The American intervention in Iraq in 2003 exacerbated the confrontation.

The year 1979 also saw Islam and Muslims 'being humiliated' by the forces of atheism in a Sunni-majority country. The Soviet Union, long branded the enemy of Muslims in Saudi official religious rhetoric, occupied Afghanistan. The occupation of a Muslim country by 'infidels' offered Saudi Arabia a golden opportunity to consolidate its reputation as defender of faith and the faithful. While the liberation of Afghanistan from Soviet occupation was a Western goal, adopted by the USA and its allies in the context of the Cold War, it inevitably became a Saudi project. The USA had always defined the danger for Saudi Arabia as coming from Communist Russia. A Saudi religio-political discourse that glorified *jihad al-daf'i* (a struggle to defend Muslims against aggressors) but had had to be content with theory rather than practice since 1932, was now given an opportunity to redirect religious zeal abroad.

A chilling message was sent to the Saudi regime with Juhayman al-Otaybi's seizure of the Mecca mosque in 1979: the regime was no longer Islamic, at least in the eyes of the small group who took sanctuary in Mecca.[6] Instead of continuing the tradition of *jihad* against infidels, Juhayman accused the regime of cooperating with infidels, introducing their ways of life into the country and promoting peaceful relations with them – all actions that were considered a violation and a nullification of faith. Juhayman's movement was at the time considered a form of revival of the discourse of *ahl al-hadith* and the Saudi Ikhwan tradition. Juhayman's discourse was grounded in the Wahhabi tradition. The Saudi government was taken by surprise by the outburst of fanaticism that erupted violently in the most sacred of territories. It hoped that redirecting this zeal abroad would be both a confirmation of Saudi religious credentials and a way to absorb local discontent and contestation. With the accession of King Fahd – hardly an example of the pious Muslim Rightful Imam – to the throne in 1982, the Afghan *jihad* seemed God sent. It became a political strategy for turbulent times.

Transnationalising Saudi religio-political discourse took place at a critical historical moment, when three factors, all with the potential of eroding Saudi religious credentials, pushed Saudi Arabia in that direction. Iran, Afghanistan and Juhayman sent a wake-up call to the Saudi regime. The government had to be seen to be supporting Muslim causes.

Struggle in the way of God abroad

Phase 1 (the 1980s): early transnational encounters

The first phase of *jihad* abroad (1979–89) was perhaps dominated by Saudis who remained loyal to their sponsors.[7] Throughout the 1980s Osama bin Laden was the sheikh of *jihad*. According to Sheikhs Ibn Baz and al-Uthaymin, he and other famous Jihadis such as the Palestinian Abdullah Azzam were true believers who fought the infidel Communists, and Bin Laden performed the obligation of *jihad al-daf'i*. When Osama bin Laden was furthering the US–Saudi project in Afghanistan, he was a 'nice' Jihadi, to use Khashogji's words. In the

1980s, Saudi Jihadis participated in the war to liberate Afghanistan from atheist Communism under the blessing of several sponsors, including the Saudi government and the official Wahhabi establishment. To contain the rising religious enthusiasm of a whole generation of young Saudis, the government decided to facilitate the export of its own young subjects to the land of war. Afghanistan became the land where one sought martyrdom. The highest religious authority, Sheikh Ibn Baz, sanctioned this *jihad* against Communism: 'We thank God who is generous. He allows us to issue a *fatwa* stating that one should perform *jihad* in Afghanistan against the enemies of religion. Muslims from all over the world came to help, asking for reward and for heaven. *Jihad* was confirmed in its global Islamic image.'[8]

In an interview published in *al-Mujahid*, Ibn Baz clearly pronounced liberating Afghanistan from Soviet domination to be a legitimate *jihad*, performed against an infidel state that invaded Muslim territory, and that all Muslims were under the obligation to support it. He declared it *fard 'ayn* (an obligation incumbent on all Muslims) in Afghanistan and *fard kifaya* (an obligation that must be performed by a sufficient number of other Muslims) elsewhere.[9]

In addition to *jihad* in Afghanistan, Ibn Baz clarified the concept of *al-wala' wa 'l-bara'*, association with Muslims and dissociation from infidels. In his view this involves loyalty and obedience to pious Muslims and dissociation from infidels, by showing enmity towards them. Hatred and enmity do not involve injustice towards infidels or attacking them if they are not fighters.

Hatred and enmity mean to hate them in your heart, never to take them as friends. Muslims should not hurt them. If they greet you, you should return the greeting. You should also preach to them and guide them to the Good. Jews and Christians are people of the book. They should be given *aman* [peace], unless they do injustice, then they should be punished. One can also give them charity.[10]

Official *'ulama* provided the theological discourse in support of the *jihad* project, disseminating the information in print and visual media and in sermons. The state promised logistical support and financial resources. For the regime *jihad* in Afghanistan was a political strategy rather than a religious obligation. State support involved various activities ranging from subsidised air tickets to multi-million-dollar projects in support of combat operations and relief efforts. It was reported that between 1980 and 1990, Saudi Arabia gave nearly US$4 billion in official aid to Jihadis in Afghanistan. This figure does not include unofficial aid from Islamic charities, donations by princes, private funds and mosque collections. The regime initially relied on already existing Muslim Jihadis and charitable networks and leadership, but later created its own network and personnel. At the beginning of the Afghan *jihad*,[11] Saudi Arabia enlisted Abdul Rasul Sayyaf, an Afghan long settled in Saudi Arabia, to set up a pro-Wahhabi Jihadi party, Ittehad-e-Islami (Islamic Unity Party) in Peshawar.[12] Saudi Arabia opened itself to Afghan and Arab Jihadi leaders to recruit, preach and raise funds in support of expelling the infidels from the land of Islam. In addition to wealth, globalisation, easy travel and communication technology created a religious effervescence that was difficult to control, even by those who had initially planned the process.

Osama bin Laden was key figure. A man of piety and wealth, standing outside the Saudi tribal system, in debt to the regime for his family's financial empire, and truly modern, he was an ideal choice.[13] Initially acting on his own initiative, he put his wealth in the service of the cause. The Saudi regime, which could not have chosen a strong tribal sheikh with thousands of followers who might invoke the rhetoric of tribal solidarity in response to calls for *jihad*, immediately noticed – and enlisted – him. The regime perhaps remembered the consequences of mobilising the tribal population for *jihad* and using tribal sheikhs to lead the struggle in the early decades of the twentieth century. Such personalities cannot be easily controlled, given the potential strength afforded them by their deep roots in society. The Ikhwan rebellion of 1927 was still alive in the historical imagination of Saudis. Although the Saudi regime had eliminated the leaders of the rebellion, it took a long time to reconcile with their tribal sections. It could therefore not tolerate a rising tribal star who could in the future challenge the rule of the Al-Saud, especially if such a personality had acquired a reputation for defending Islam and Muslims. The Saudi Afghan project was better served by someone in a state of liminality, a Saudi but not a Saudi, neither here nor there. These qualities made Osama bin Laden the ideal choice in the eyes of the Saudi leadership. It must be said, however, that the qualities that endeared Osama to the Saudi regime in the early 1980s were his greatest strength in a global Jihadi project. He captured the hearts and minds of Saudis belonging to different regions, tribes and backgrounds – in addition, of course, to other Muslims.

Osama bin Laden was able to rise above the localism of *aimat al-da'wa al-najdiyya* and their parochial discourse, and gain a pan-Islamic reputation. While not a single Wahhabi scholar gained worldwide eminence in the pre-oil era, Bin Laden succeeded. This eminence was not a result of high-level scholarship in religious knowledge or extraordinary military skills, but rather that, having no obvious roots in Saudi Arabia, Bin Laden was able to play the role of mediator between various groups. He had his Islamic credentials and wealth without being associated with one social group. These qualities made Bin Laden appealing not only to Saudis seeking martyrdom in Afghanistan but also to other Arabs and Muslims who responded to the call for *jihad*.[14] Studies of Bin Laden exaggerated his foreignness and marginality in Saudi society, and downplayed his influence and charisma.[15] Events since 2001 have proved the inaccuracy of these evaluations.

Having been guided by Sheikh Ibn Baz's religious rulings and government logistical support, young Saudis left the country, seeking an honourable death for the cause. Even women, who were excluded from any public role in Saudi Arabia at the time, enlisted themselves or were enlisted by their male relatives in the struggle against infidels. It was reported that wives joined their husbands and engaged in preaching and charitable work, helping Jihadi female relatives and orphans. *Da'iyyat* such as Fatimah Nasif and Samira Jamjum travelled to Afghanistan.[16] While there is no precise documentation and statistics regarding the exact number of Saudis who participated in the Afghan war as fighters, a figure of 30,000 is often cited. However, the number of Saudis who participated in non-combat capacity – as preachers, recruiters, fundraisers, medical assistants, charity and relief workers – must have far exceed this figure. While a substantial number of men were full-time Jihadis, the majority must have been part timers. It was reported at the time that many Saudi men visited Afghanistan and Pakistan during the long summer holiday, a visit that may not have necessarily led to a long-term or full-time commitment. The economic slump of the mid-1980s and the rising unemployment among young men acted as a push factor. However, redirecting religious zeal to Afghanistan only delayed the confrontation between the Saudi regime and its increasingly politicised religious scholars and youth.

Afghanistan offered young, old, middle-aged and wealthy men and women an opportunity to break the monotony of life at home, where independent political activism is banned and local leadership is curtailed by an authoritarian regime that forbids initiative except that which can be controlled and used in pursuit of its own agenda. Having been subjected to decades of preaching obedience to rulers who know the 'public good', for the first time in their modern history Saudis were offered the opportunity to engage in political – and even military – activism. Although the regime boasts about supporting the Palestinian cause and regularly publishes statistical evidence, the Afghan *jihad* was a totally different experience. Although it took place under government supervision and control, it gathered its own momentum in Afghanistan, and began to free itself from this control. The Saudi regime succeeded in redirecting political and military activism abroad, while reviving its own credibility and legitimacy at home. However, the evolution of the Afghan project proved more complicated. The transnationalisation of the localised Saudi religious discourse led to unintended consequences.

Saudi youth who left for Afghanistan returned with a sense of their worth and empowerment. Their post-liberation narratives glorified their heroic role in defeating the forces of atheism. The encounter was described as the triumph of Islam over Communism, while in the West it was described as the victory of Western democracies and values over totalitarian regimes, under the idiom of the 'end of history'. Young Saudi men reinvented themselves as *ahfad al-sahaba*, the descendants (grandsons) of the early pious companions of the Prophet. In the twentieth century, the descendants of the Jihadi Ikhwan who had 'unified Arabia' under the banner of Ibn Saud and become 'consenting subjects' thanks to several decades of preaching emerged from the Afghan experience with a new identity. Sons perpetuated the old glory of their fathers and grandfathers – not in Saudi Arabia this time, but abroad. Doing the same thing in Palestine remained a project that Saudis dreamt of, but did not undertake. The young men's return to Saudi Arabia was to be seen only as *istirahat al-muharib*, a temporary period of rest after an arduous and most dangerous but rewarding combat experience. While the majority were content with this experience, others were restless. They searched for future similar encounters. Religious imagery was reinvoked and fused with modern rhetoric, drawing on stories glorifying martyrdom, camaraderie, Stinger missiles, near-death situations and miraculous survival. Those who visited Jihadi relatives in Afghanistan returned to Saudi Arabia with mythical images glorifying the 'Vanguards'. In such narratives, myth and reality combined to paint a magnificent heroic narrative. Young men proved themselves in the battlefield as *murabitun 'ala al-thughur* (fighters for faith who are tied to the fortresses), and gained recognition that eventually undermined the *qa'idun*, those left behind, mainly fathers. Images of the *ghazu* (raid) were documented in poetry invoking continuity with a glorious Islamic past. In a society where parental authority – especially that of fathers – is paramount, young men returned with their own sense of worth achieved as a result of participation in a real life-threatening experience. They had their own poetry, composed and learned in distant lands. Their transformation emasculated their fathers, who had already been undermined by the religious discourse of acquiescence and the authoritarian state that nourished and perpetuated this discourse. For the first time since 1932, young Saudi men proved that they too could be heroes, scoring victories of international significance. A deep sense of patriotism and self–worth flourished, expressed in an Islamic idiom.

Official *'ulama* who theorised *jihad* and urged Muslims to take part were from now on heirs of the Prophets (*warathat al-anbiya'*), flames that kept the message alive. They were reconfirmed in their status as wise sages who deserve due respect and recognition in this world while God would reward them in afterlife. Having been patronised and controlled by the state, they proved that they were capable of mobilising people for a just cause. They temporarily regained a fraction of their lost glory as people whose first allegiance is to God rather than the state that employed them. Ibn Baz, who in 1979 had authorised the storming of the Holy Mosque in Mecca where Juhayman took refuge, briefly regained his prestige.

The regime also emerged triumphant. It glorified its contribution to Muslim causes. Most importantly, it was able to rebuff Iran's revolutionary rhetoric and accusations. The defeat of Iran and its revolutionary mullahs was a project that needed to be achieved, not only in the battlefield where the Iraqi and Iranian armies met, but also in the minds and hearts of Muslims. Official propaganda depicted Iran as the regime that fought Iraqi Muslims while the Saudi regime liberated Muslims from evil Communists. Iran's Shi'i faith assumed new political significance. The ancient Sunni Islamic discourse demonising the Shi'is as those who insult the early caliphs, the descendants of aggressive al-furs (Persians) and blasphemous and treacherous Majus, assumed new meaning in the context of confrontation between the Saudi regime and Iran.[17] While Saudis became the grandsons of the early companions of the Prophets, the Shi'is were the grandsons of al-Alqami – or, even worse, the offspring of mut'a (temporary marriage),[18] the by-product of adultery in Saudi popular imagination. Wahhabi religious discourse provided the religious language that was politicised in the context of rivalry between two states desperately fighting for supremacy in the Muslim world in general, and the Gulf region in particular. Saudi negative images of Iran and the Shi'i tradition resurfaced with the Iraqi crisis in 2003.

In Afghanistan, Wahhabi discourse encountered a plethora of religious interpretations, schools of Islamic jurisprudence and forms of worship, in addition to contemporary Islamist political interpretations. It came into contact with the dominant Deobandi tradition in both Afghanistan and Pakistan, which was perhaps closer to Wahhabiyya than any other Sunni tradition in Asia.[19] Both Wahhabi and Deobandi traditions had grown up in the context of the encounter between the Muslim world (the Arabian Peninsula and India) and Britain. This had shaped the two movements' outlook and interpretations.

In Saudi Arabia haraki Islam was still an underground movement, in the form of a revival of faith and more commitment to Islamic appearances. In the early 1980s, Saudi Islamists were preoccupied with resisting modernity and Westernisation. In Afghanistan, they encountered open Islamic political activism in the context of a war situation. For the first time Saudis had the experience of Islamist political parties and military groups working openly.

By the time they arrived in Afghanistan, Saudis had already been exposed at home to current Islamist thought, as discussed in the last chapter. In addition to the survival of the local Ikhwani tribal tradition (represented by Juhayman's followers), Muslim Brotherhood literature (for example, Bannais, Qutbists), Salafi Jihadis, Hizb al-Tahrir and Pakistani Islamism – especially that related to Abu Ala al-Mawdudi – had circulated in Saudi Arabia since the 1970s.[20] Yet Saudis had never before experienced open political activism, rivalry and competition. In the early 1980s Saudi Islamists debated how to resist corrupting Western influences and guard the authentic tradition against liberal and secularist Saudis. All Islamist trends operated as underground movements at that time. In Afghanistan the debate was about how to fight Communist infidels and their local agents. Most importantly, the debate was also about how to establish the pious Islamic state. Saudis were armed with a religious discourse that allowed them to achieve the first objective, i.e. resisting infidels through the discourse of *jihad al-dafʿi*, but the majority must have thought they already belonged to a pious state. Nevertheless, the first Afghan experience allowed Saudis to reflect on their own state, to see it from a new perspective, one that was changed by the fog of war and the euphoria of fighting and defeating the enemies of Islam. Questioning the credentials of their own pious state back home must have occurred to many Saudi Afghans as it occurred to Juhayman's followers. Did Saudis go to Afghanistan to gain military skills that would enable them to create the pious state upon their return?

Phase 2 (the 1990s): from excommunicating society to excommunicating rulers

The withdrawal of Soviet troops from Afghanistan in 1989 closed the gates of *jihad* in this country for both Saudis and other Muslims, thus marking the end of the first phase.[21] Saudi warriors and their leaders returned home. From now on they were identified as the Saudi Afghans, a subgroup of the Arab Afghans. Upon arrival at home, they were treated as heroes who had defeated the Evil Empire. The welcome was, however, only a passing moment of joy and recognition. While the Jihadi heroic narratives continued to inflame the imaginations of those who had been classified as *qaʿidun*, a bleak future awaited the returnees. Like other Arab states, Saudi Arabia had no exit strategy or reception programme to facilitate the reintegration of the Saudi Afghans in society. The rising preeminence of Osama bin Laden and his confirmation as the undisputed sheikh of *jihad* and the Jihadi fervour that crystallised around young Saudi Jihadis were carefully watched by the regime.

The second phase was perhaps the most dangerous for the Saudi regime and its religious establishment. It was during this period that a transnationalised Saudi–Wahhabi religious discourse turned its attention to its early mentors, not only to dismantle their monopoly over religious interpretation but more importantly to challenge the regime that sponsored them. This sponsorship is described as leading to a corruption of the authentic Islamic tradition. In this second phase Osama bin Laden took the lead in denouncing both the Al-Saud and official *ulama*. While Bin Laden was not a religious scholar, he spoke the language of scholars and fused this language with political rhetoric, thus inflaming the imagination of both Saudi youth and other Muslims around the world. While official *ulama* remained parochial and without a pan-Islamic reputation, Bin Laden assumed such status.

In 1990 Saddam Hussein invaded Kuwait. Osama bin Laden volunteered his services and those of his Jihadis to liberate Kuwait and fight the infidel – Saddam. Having demonstrated his military skills and acquired new expertise in the mountains and cities of Afghanistan, Bin Laden thought that he and his followers were better positioned to launch another *jihad* close to home; after all, Saddam had already been declared *kafir* by Sheikh Ibn Baz. The Saudi regime refused the offer. It was doubtful whether the Jihadi returnees were a match for Saddam's army, and the regime preferred an international coalition to liberate Kuwait and protect the kingdom. Armed with the Council of Senior Ulama's famous *fatwa* legitimising the participation of foreign troops, King Fahd told his subjects that an international coalition of armies would perform the task. Having 'defeated' the infidel Communists in Afghanistan, many Saudis found it difficult to seek assistance from Western governments to resolve a conflict between Muslims. Saudi *ulama* debated the official *fatwa* issued by the religious establishment. The previous prestige of the religious establishment, which had been gained as a result of supporting *jihad* in Afghanistan, quickly withered away. Senior *ulama* lost their credibility – for ever, this time.

After being put under what amounts to house arrest in Jiddah, Bin Laden secretly left the country with the help of family members. The Saudi Afghans dispersed inside Saudi Arabia and abroad, while waiting for other potential *jihad* destinations. Kuwait was liberated, but the foreign – mainly American – troops remained in Saudi Arabia, a fact that from now on became the axis around which the Islamist opposition to the Saudi regime revolved in all its shades and orientations. The question that was theoretical in Afghanistan – the nature of the pious Islamic state and its relations with 'infidels' – began to be posed in the context of discussing the Saudi state itself. Osama bin Laden was again a key figure, just at the time he was stripped of his Saudi nationality (in 1994). The young Saudi Afghans became fugitives, a pariah group searching for shelter or another *jihad* destination. While some followed Bin Laden to Sudan, the majority remained in Saudi Arabia or travelled to Chechnya, Bosnia and Kashmir. Their hero, Osama bin Laden, became *persona non grata* in Saudi Arabia. From now on Jihadis were defined as *al-fi'a al-dhalla* (the group that has gone astray). Violent attacks in Riyadh in 1995 killed many Americans. It was the first major anti-American action inside Saudi Arabia. In 1996 al-Khobar was bombed. While nobody claimed responsibility for either attack, it was assumed that Bin Laden and his Saudi Afghans may have been responsible. Violence confirmed the status of the Saudi Afghans as a threat to the regime. In public it tried to link the violence to Shi'i dissidents, but without success.

Osama bin Laden was expelled from Sudan, and returned to Afghanistan after the rise of the Taliban regime in 1996. Although Saudi Arabia maintained friendly relations with the Taliban and promised substantial aid, the regime initially did not put pressure on the Taliban to deport Bin Laden. According to Rashid, only when Prince Turki al-Faysal, in charge of intelligence services at the time, was personally insulted by Mullah Omar in Kandahar did the Saudis curtail diplomatic links with the Taliban. In other words, Saudi policy towards this impoverished polity was dictated by a personal insult.[22] Saudi Arabia withdrew its recognition of the Taliban only months before the USA launched its attack on the country in 2001.

Young Saudis followed Bin Laden to Afghanistan. Once again it became a haven for those who were pursued by the security forces at home. It is at this time that a religious discourse that is more focused on the Saudi regime began to emerge. It advocated excommunicating the regime as a whole, or individual figures within it, or both. Osama bin Laden's various speeches and media statements confirmed that he was working for the overthrow of the Saudi regime, which had brought 'infidels' to the Arabian Peninsula against the Prophetic tradition. As we shall see in the following chapters, this tradition became central in the struggle of Jihadis against the Saudi regime. By September 2001 Bin Laden had become the regime's chief enemy. It was facing one of the most violent episodes in modern Saudi history, with suicide bombing, confrontation and shoot-outs between members of the so-called *al-fi'a al-dhalla* (the Jihadis) and security forces.

Osama bin Laden's activism against the Saudi regime in the 1990s is now well documented.[23] I shall focus on a long speech delivered in

December 2004, in which he outlined his position vis-à-vis the regime and official ʿulama. The speech was delivered after several violent attacks shattered peace and security in Saudi cities. Al-Qaʾida in the Arabian Peninsula claimed responsibility. It was assumed that it had direct links with Bin Laden. This speech addressed 'Muslims in *bilad al-haramayn* [the land of the two holy mosques] in particular and the Muslim world in general'.[24]

The speech addresses three categories of people: *hukam al-riyadh* (pejoratively the rulers of Riyadh); *ahl al-hall wa 'l-ʿaqd* (those who tie and loose); and Muslims – Bin Laden avoids the term Saudis, as such an artificial category does not feature in his discourse. In this political speech there is fusion of Quranic verses, Prophetic sayings, citations from famous past and present ʿulama and poetry. It demonises the Saudi rulers, reprimands official scholars for their acquiescence, exposes Saudi 'conspiracies' against Muslims and defends Jihadi violence in Saudi Arabia even though it killed Muslims as well as 'infidels'.

Bin Laden explains why he and the Jihadis practised *khuruj ʿala al-hakim* (rebellion against the ruler), a direct challenge to the Wahhabi tradition which forbids such rebellion. He explains:

Al-imara [rulership] is a contract between *raʾi* [ruler] and *raʿiyya* [followers], which entails rights and obligations on both sides. It can be nullified under certain conditions. When a ruler commits treason against his religion and people, the *imara* is no longer valid. A century ago, the Al-Saud jumped on people's necks without their consent or consultation but with British support. Today these rulers practise oppression and theft of public money. People have woken up from their sleep. They are determined to take their rights. You, the Al-Saud, have only two options: first, either return people's rights to them in a peaceful way and leave the country to choose a Muslim ruler who rules according to the Book [Quran] and Sunna [tradition of the Prophet]; or second, refuse to return these rights and continue to pay your mercenaries to oppress people. Remember what happened to the shah of Iran and the Romanian president. We in al-Qaʾida do not compete with you for worldly privileges but we do not accept that you commit acts that are considered *nawaqid al-iman* [acts that nullify faith], for example ruling not according to the word of God and subservience to infidels.

According to Bin Laden, the Saudi regime moved from committing *ma ʿasi* (minor sins) and *mubiqat* (grave sins) to violating some of the ten principles of faith when it practised subservience to infidels (*tawwali al-kuffar*), and assisted them against Muslims, in Afghanistan (2001 War on Terror) and Iraq (2003 American occupation). This subservience is a major theme in local Jihadi discourse, as will be shown in the following chapter. In Bin Laden's speech there is no scope for reforming the Al-Saud. According to him the Al-Saud 'are part of an international blasphemous alliance whose main objective is to enslave Muslims'. The theme of subservience to infidels recurs when Bin Laden attacks Crown Prince

Abdullah, who in 2003 called upon Saddam to step down in order to prevent a bloodbath in Iraq. In other words, 'the Crown Prince suggested that Saddam peacefully hands over Iraq to the Americans. This is the advice of the *'arabi amir* [the Bedouin prince]'. Bin Laden plays on the imagery of the ''*arabi*', defined in the Quran as the worst *kafir* ('al-'arab ashadu kufran'). He invokes strong Prophetic language when he calls Prince Abdullah '*al-ruwaybidha*', an insignificant person who talks about public affairs. Bin Laden's rhetoric draws on both the Quran and the Hadith to project an image of the Saudi leadership as immersed in *kufr* (blasphemy).

Bin Laden asserts that he is not after worldly matters and wealth. He explains that 'we left all this behind. We left our land not because we suffered poverty. We have been away for a long time but we long for the Hijaz.' At this juncture he cites a poem demonstrating his longing for this territory:

> The love of Hijaz is in the depth of my heart
> But its rulers are wolves
> I found home and friends in Afghanistan
> God is the one who provides a livelihood

His message to 'those who tie and loose' includes advice to migrate in order to liberate the self from

illusory restraints and psychological pressure exerted by the regime. Only then you can perform your duties, lead the *umma* and organise its activities. If you delay this mission, you complicate matters further. Young Jihadis will take the initiative to interpret texts (*ijtihad*), in order to justify armed rebellion against rulers. This must be a joint effort and the *'ulama* must help convince the ruler to step down in order to avoid further bloodshed.

Bin Laden here reminds the *'ulama* of their role in the early 1960s as mediators between King Saud and his brother Faysal. According to his narrative, the *'ulama* convinced King Saud to step down and avoid further conflict. Bin Laden urges the *'ulama* to play a similar role, this time to convince the Al-Saud to leave the country to the people. One senses that in 2004 bin Laden was worried about the proliferation of *jihad* and its privatisation in the absence of grass-roots *'ulama* to guide and direct Jihadis. The violence that erupted in Saudi Arabia in 2003–4 was in need of justifications and theological sanction, both the prerogative of the specialist *'ulama*. Perhaps Bin Laden's call to the *'ulama* to take the initiative and provide guidance stemmed from concern about inexperienced Jihadis who might go too far in 'privatising' the obligation of *jihad* without central command or supervision.

Regarding Jihadi violence, Bin Laden asks a series of rhetorical questions.

Who are those who hold the thought that the regime describes as having gone astray, the so-called contemporary Kharijites? Are they Khalid al-Mihdhar, Salim al-Mihdhar or Nawaf al-Hazmi, who left Mecca to attack America? Are they King Fahd, who attacked Mecca with tanks when a small group of Muslims took refuge in the holy sanctuary? The regime could have negotiated with them [Juhayman's group] but the enemy of God, King Fahd, preferred to attack the mosque. I remember the marks left by tanks on the Haram's floor and the black smoke coming out of minarets. Are the Al-Saud the ones who command virtue and prohibit vice or are they the ones who corrupt Muslims using the media? Are they the ones who defend the honour of Muslims in Iraq, Afghanistan, Palestine, Kashmir or Chechnya? Or are they the ones allied with infidels and those who steal Muslims' wealth? Who has violated the sanctity of the Land of the Two Holy Mosques? Are they the Jihadi youth or the security forces who killed innocent people in the poor neighbourhood of Rasifah in Mecca so that the land can be confiscated by the Minister of Interior?

Bin Laden reminds his audience that those who rebelled against the Ottomans early in the twentieth century, a reference to the Saudi state, deserve to be called Kharijites. Calling the Wahhabi movement a Khariji movement echoes early Sunni positions among the *'ulama* of Damascus and Baghdad, who abhorred the movement's rebellion against the Ottoman Empire. He addresses Saudi rulers: 'Your father Ibn Saud rebelled against the Ottomans and you yourself rebelled against your brother Saud. Your *'ulama* never condemned your acts. Let's remind you of the massacre in Taif when your people practised *takfir al-'umum* [excommunicating whole communities]. Your father told his soldiers that Hijazis were *kafir*s therefore killing them was *jihad*.' Bin Laden rejects Saudi accusation that he and his followers practise wholesale excommunication. In fact he tells his audience that the Al-Saud and their early followers did exactly that in the Hijaz. This language rejects early Wahhabi discourse that justified the killing of Muslims in the Arabian Peninsula under the banner of spreading monotheism, according to the official narrative.

This leads us to question descriptions of Osama bin Laden as a puritanical Wahhabi[25] or a 'product of traditional Saudi Wahhabism'.[26] He does not embrace the official Wahhabi tradition or agree with the state narrative produced by the *'ulama* who described the population as being in a state of *kufr* before the rise of the third Saudi state. Had Bin Laden been a Wahhabi, he would not have challenged the most important pillar of the Saudi–Wahhabi foundation myth. He would not have disputed the right of the Al-Saud to rule over Arabia, a right that was granted to them by Muhammad ibn Abd al-Wahhab himself. While those who study Bin Laden's speeches and statements might describe him as a Wahhabi, we must see him through the eyes of one of his supporters.

A Saudi supporter argues that Bin Laden could not possibly be a Wahhabi. He lists four reasons in support of his opinion. First, 'Bin Laden and al-Qa'ida rebelled against the Al-Saud regime, an act that has never been performed by Wahhabis. While most Wahhabis would occasionally "criticise" the rightful Imam, hoping to reform him, they would prohibit advising him in public, let alone carrying arms against him.' Second, 'Bin Laden aims to restore the Islamic caliphate while the Al-Saud and Wahhabis were the first to have undermined the Ottoman Empire'. Third, 'al-Qa'ida and Bin Laden fight only those who undermine Islam while the Saudis and Wahhabis fought Muslims who do not accept their jurisprudence'. And fourth, 'unlike Wahhabis, Bin Laden and al-Qa'ida do not distinguish between the various schools of Islamic jurisprudence'. The author concludes that Bin Laden did not rebel against the Saudi regime in order to restore the early Wahhabiyya, which clearly claims that the Al-Saud must rule Arabia for ever in accordance with hereditary rule and that the mufti of Saudi Arabia should be a descendant of Al-Shaykh family. Al-Qa'ida is 'wider than the narrow local Wahhabi tradition, which excelled in dividing rather than uniting Muslims'. Bin Laden's supporter asks why today 'Muslims sanctify Muhammad ibn Abd al-Wahhab who brought the Al-Saud corrupt rulers to power and considered rebelling against them a form of blasphemy'.[27]

Bin Laden's attachment to the Hijaz is clear, especially when he reminds his audience of the atrocities committed there by Saudi–Wahhabi forces. It is perhaps more accurate to claim that he was a product of the context of the Hijaz rather than the narrow, localised Wahhabi religious tradition of Najd. While the Hijaz was systematically Wahhabised and Saudised in the twentieth century, the region retained some of its previous cosmopolitan and pan-Islamic outlook. Bin Laden himself and the migration of his father to this area attests to this history, with its deep-rooted transnational connections. In the past the Hijaz received migrants not only from Hadramawt, Bin Laden's ancestral land, but also from distant Muslim territories as far away as Indonesia. These migrants always brought with them their intellectual traditions, which were defined and redefined in the holy land as they intermingled with Muslim scholars who were resident in Mecca and Madina.[28] It is the cross-fertilisation of religious thought in the Hijaz that produced Bin Laden, who cannot be anchored in one locality or intellectual tradition. In his quest for the return of the pious Islamic caliphate, with the Hijaz as its central core, Bin Laden regards Ibn Saud's rebellion against the Ottomans under British orders a form of Kharijite behaviour. While many Muslim scholars doubt whether the Ottoman Empire, especially in its later years, represented the desired Islamic caliphate, Bin Laden's political speech naturally overlooks the body of literature produced by Muslim scholars who subjected the Ottoman experience to *shari'a* rulings. Many concluded that it was not only an aberration of the concept of the caliphate, but was also a system of *kufr* and innovation.[29] Bin Laden deconstructs one of the fundamental religiously sanctioned myths of the Saudi state, namely that this is the state of monotheism, which brought the people of Arabia to true Islam. He claims that the Saudis contributed to the fall of the Ottoman Empire without replacing it with a legitimate alternative. While his dream is to establish a caliphate with the Hijaz as its core, contemporary official Wahhabi discourse has limited ambitions.

Bin Laden has used arms against both the West and the Saudi regime and has proved that he is capable of inflicting great damage to both. His influence in Saudi Arabia is often downplayed, for obvious political reasons. Some argue that his lack of a solid tribal genealogy in the country prevents him from developing real influence. But perhaps a new generation of Saudis find this so-called disadvantage his main asset. They may be truly tired of the rigid tribal hierarchies and grading system that dominate Saudi society, which a priori defines people's status, privilege and even financial prospects in a regime that continues to play on tribal divisions. Bin Laden surpassed tribal solidarity groups as he brought a Harbi, Otaybi, Zahrani and Ghamdi – not to mention Egyptians, Yemenis, Palestinians and Algerians – together in a joint adventure, not only in Afghanistan but also elsewhere in the world. It was Bin Laden who challenged the apartheid system that separated 'Saudis' and 'immigrants', the million or so Muslim workers that the Saudi regime struggled to keep under control and deprive of all rights. Western expatriates enjoyed privileges and rights that Muslim immigrants could only dream of. Bin Laden himself was a descendant of an exceptional immigrant who managed to 'assimilate' while thousands of other Muslim labourers were kept outside society, confined in segregated residential compounds, if they were professionals, or shanty towns that circled Saudi cities. It is surprising that, given his appeal, some analysts have argued that for the majority of Saudis Bin Laden was the 'other'. This may have been true for those 'inside' the Saudi system, but his rhetoric certainly strikes a chord with a growing marginalised population who lack equal access to resources. Bin Laden himself was inside this system, but he rebelled against its rigid hierarchies, nepotism and corruption. He and his wealth represent the shift in Saudi Arabia from a society dominated by inherited status to one that is gradually embracing achieved status. Being the 'other' seems to have guaranteed the survival of Bin Laden's reputation, if not influence, on young Saudis – not only in Saudi Arabia, but also elsewhere. In today's world it is impossible to measure this influence accurately let alone quantify it.

Despite hundreds of books and intelligence reports, understanding the Bin Laden phenomenon is one of the most difficult tasks contemporary scholars face. It is easy to say that he is a puritanical fanatical Wahhabi. It is also easy to describe him as a non-Saudi terrorist who fell under the spell of Egyptian Jihadis, an interpretation which suits the Saudi regime as it struggles to absolve its own religious establishment from any responsibility for world terrorism. It is not surprising that the Bin Laden phenomenon is entangled with political polemics rather than sober interpretations of a complex religious and political field, made even more so as a result of new communication technology, transnationalisation and easy travel and movement. Bin Laden is an evolving phenomenon and it will continue to be so in the foreseeable future.

London: contesting Wahhabi religio-political discourse

Contesting Saudi religio-political discourse did not take place only in Afghanistan. The religio-political literature of rebellion and resistance against 'despots' who corrupt Islam was produced and published in other places as well, with Muslims of diverse nationalities contributing to its formulation. In the mid-1990s, London was a refuge for dissident Islamists facing imprisonment and torture in their own countries. While a small minority were real Jihadis, trained in the art of using weapons, the majority were theoreticians and interpreters of *jihad*, who disseminated their ideas in a tolerant, 'connected' context, with easy access to old and new media. In the name of freedom of expression, British tolerance and multiculturalism, the British authorities turned a blind eye to their activities. This was a political strategy – to watch, control and provide 'British Spooks with a great photo opportunity', in the words of a realist scholar who is not fooled by spin or rhetoric.

London thus became one of the most important centres of debate over Saudi religio-political discourse.[30] Bin Laden's envoy Khalid al-Fawaz established the Advice and Reform Committee there in 1994.[31] The influence of this committee was limited, however, as al-Fawaz was later imprisoned in Britain. More influential was the counter-theology offering revolutionary interpretations of the original Wahhabi texts that flourished in the British capital. Saudi and non-Saudi '*ulama* and political activists based in London and elsewhere contributed to the production and dissemination of this counter-religio-political discourse. London became the space where the production and distribution of dissident literature took place. What such activists did in London was not to 'invent' radical discourse or 'learn' it, as claimed by Saudi propaganda. Rather, they turned the original Wahhabi discourse against those who initially sponsored and promoted it worldwide. Their aim was to prove that had Muhammad ibn Abd al-Wahhab been alive, he would have excommunicated the current Saudi regime. This counter-discourse invoked neither the standards of democracy nor universal human rights. Instead, it reinterpreted the criteria of the Saudi religious establishment to excommunicate it. Several publications showed how the regime fell short of complying with its own Wahhabi rhetoric.

In 1994 a book entitled *al-Kawashif al-jaliyya fi kufr al-dawla al-saoudiyya* (Clear Evidence of the Blasphemy of the Saudi Regime) by Abu al-Bara al-Najdi (allegedly an alias for Jordanian Palestinian Abu Muhammad al-Barqawi al-Maqdisi (b. 1959)), was reprinted in London by an anonymous publishing house called Dar al-Qasim, thus invoking the heartland of the Wahhabi tradition. Al-Maqdisi's case is a clear illustration of how Saudi–Wahhabi religio-political discourse was adopted by a non-Saudi Islamist, thanks to transnational religious networks, easy travel, fast communication and the proliferation of Saudi-sponsored centres of religious education. Rather than bringing an alien Islamic tradition to Saudi Arabia, as claimed by Saudi officials and Western writers, al-Maqdisi fell under the influence of the religious discourse that originated in Saudi Arabia.

Al-Maqdisi lived in Kuwait where he frequented Islamist circles until his deportation to Jordan after the Gulf War of 1990–1. In the mid-1980s he travelled to Peshawar where he developed a Salafi–Jihadi discourse. According to several accounts, he visited Madina in the early 1980s, immediately after the dispersal of Juhayman's followers. During these visits, he fell under the influence of Juhayman's underground supporters. According to al-Noqaydan, al-Maqdisi also visited Buraydah in Saudi Arabia in the early 1990s.[32] Al-Maqdisi returned to Jordan in the mid-1990s, and was imprisoned in 1995. In 2005 he was still serving a prison sentence in a Jordanian prison. He was released for a short period, but was later returned to prison after an interview with al-Jazeera television. Al-Maqdisi's book could have been written by any Salafi sheikh in the British capital or elsewhere, such as Abu Qatada, another Jordanian of a Palestinian origin who in 2005 was in Belmarsh prison; or Hizb al-Tahrir's Omar Bakri, who returned to Lebanon in 2005 after the 7 July London bombings; or Abu Hamza al-Masri, a veteran of the Afghan Jihad who in 2006 was serving a prison sentence in London. It is alleged that al-Maqdisi's book circulated in Afghanistan before its republication in London.

The fact that the author chose a pseudonym ending with al-Najdi reflected a desire to authenticate this revolutionary theology by anchoring it in the heart of the Arabian Peninsula, the land of Wahhabiyya.

Al-Maqdisi endorsed Wahhabi interpretations and its symbolic attire. The book relies heavily on citations from the intellectual heritage of Muhammad ibn Abd al-Wahhab and *aimat al-da'wa al-najdiyya*. Anecdotal evidence suggests that Bin Laden ordered the writing of this book in an attempt to bring the struggle closer to Saudi Arabia. Only if the regime is declared *kafir*, a declaration that is dependent on religious evidence, can Saudis rebel with arms against the regime (*khuruj bi 'l-sayf*). The content of the book was drawn from the religious rulings of the early and latter Wahhabi *'ulama*, thus making it more accessible and acceptable to Wahhabis themselves. It spoke the words of their own *'ulama*, but the words were this time turned against the regime itself. The main point was that by its own Wahhabi theology and standards, the Saudi regime is guilty of blasphemy. The author wanted his readers to reach the conclusion that had Muhammad ibn Abd al-Wahhab been alive, he would have issued a *fatwa* convicting the Al-Saud regime of *kufr*.

Official *'ulama* ignored the book when it first appeared in 1989, and continued to do so for almost a decade after its publication. Some thought that a response would give the book more publicity than it actually deserves. However, with the outbreak of violence in Saudi Arabia in 2003–5, it was reported that many Jihadis had read the book. A pro-official *'ulama* website called al-Radd (response) published a piece denouncing the book and deconstructing its theological evidence.[33]

In the book, Abu al-Bara al-Najdi claims: 'I am a Sunni Arab Muslim not a Shi'i *rafidhi* [rejectionist] or a Communist.' This is aimed at shattering the claims of the regime that criticism comes only from Shi'i 'rejectionists' or atheists. In his words, 'the regime is blasphemous if judged by the standards of the early Wahhabi *'ulama* themselves'.[34]

Abu al-Bara argues that one must distinguish the current Saudi regime from the early people who carried the flame of monotheism under the banner of Muhammad ibn Abd al-Wahhab. One must also distinguish between the evil, subservient *'ulama* of today and Muhammad ibn Abd al-Wahhab, whose teachings they claim to follow.

The book starts with the epic of the Ikhwan fighters, the foot-soldiers of Ibn Saud. The author narrates a history that glorifies those fighters and demonises Ibn Saud, the 'symbol of conspiracy and subservience to Britain at the time'. He moves on to identify the characteristics of the blasphemous regime that evolved in the twentieth century. It does not apply Islamic law, maintains amicable and subservient relations with infidels, plunders public wealth, cooperates with Gulf and Arab *tawaghit* (despots) against their own Muslim population and joins international *kufr* organisations, for example the United Nations and other regional and international forums.

The author argues that the regime introduces new legislation (*nidham*) to replace *shariʿa*. He reminds his readers of Muhammad ibn Ibrahim's epistle (*Tahkim and qawanin*), in which he condemned the introduction of new legislation that contradicts, or has no grounding in, *shariʿa*. He claims that the suspension of *shariʿa* punishment (*iqamat al-hudud*) is characteristic of the blasphemous regime, and reminds his readers of Sheikh Muhammad ibn Ibrahim, who wrote to the king demanding the sacking of a judge in Yanbo for smoking: 'It became clear to us that the *qadi* smokes in the court. He delays people's cases. The *maslaha* [public good] requires that he is forced to resign. We hope that your majesty complies.'[35]

The grave sins of the regime must be remedied. Abu al-Bara introduces a 'way out of discord' (*makhraj min al-fitna*). He asks, 'What is to be done?' The solution proposed is that put forward by the Wahhabi establishment several decades ago, namely *hijra* (migration) and *jihad*, citing two Quranic verses, one urging Muslims to migrate, the other instructing them to perform *jihad*. The latter suggestion is justified on the basis that Muslims were urged by the Prophet to kill if they witnessed *kufran bawahan*, clear and obvious blasphemy that can be documented with evidence. Abu al-Bara warns Muslims not to be deceived by those who declare that there is no God but Allah. A Muslim must dissociate himself not only from all action that is potentially blasphemous but also from subservience to others. At this junction, he introduces citations from *aimat al-daʿwa al-najdiyya*, who urged people to excommunicate the blasphemous, fight them and rebel against them, starting with the words of Muhammad ibn Abd al-Wahhab, Muhammad ibn Abd al-Latif, and Hamad ibn Atiq.

As the book appeared after the end of the first *jihad* experience, the author reflects on the Saudi role in this *jihad*. He depicts official Saudi involvement in the Afghan *jihad* as an attempt to control the parties involved and prevent the rise of the 'real Islamic state'.

The regime spent millions for this purpose. It patronised Jihadis who were prevented from reading any literature that denounced the blasphemous Saudi regime. It even set up a residence compound for Saudi Jihadis, called *al-bayt al-saudi*, to prevent its own citizens from mixing with Muslims. They prevented the publication of manuals teaching Jihadis how to fight guerrilla warfare in cities because the regime feared that they would apply these methods in Saudi Arabia. When Saudi Jihadis returned home, their books were confiscated at the airport. They were put in prison. Saudis spend millions to appear as defenders of faith. In fact, they want to keep *jihad* away from the country. We pray to God to destroy the regime at its own hands.[36]

Abu al-Bara's book was only the beginning of a series of dissident publications that appeared in London, all challenging the Saudi religio-political discourse that was propagated by the state. In 1995 Saudi Hizb al-Tahrir dissident Muhammad al-Masari published a book entitled *al-Adilla al-qatiyya 'ala adam shar'iyyat al-dawla al-saudiyya*, in which he denounced Wahhabiyya itself. Al-Masari confirms that Abu al-Bara's book contains the full evidence in support of its main thesis, i.e. the blasphemy of the Saudi regime. However, he argues that Abu al-Bara's book is not satisfactory because it contains inappropriate language in addition to extensive discussion of minor issues such as smoking. In al-Masari's words the author 'like other Salafis fails to distinguish between absolute issues where there is consensus and where the label *kufr* can be applied and other issues where there is difference of opinion and can be subjected to *ijtihad* [interpretation]'.[37] Al-Masari proposes subjecting the whole regime, rather than individuals within it, to *shari'a* in an attempt to judge its Islamic credentials. There are criteria specified as absolute requirements for the legitimacy of Islamic political leadership: first, rule according to the revealed word of God, which excludes a ruler as a source for legislation; second, enable Islam to flourish and its rituals to be performed; third, associate with Muslims and dissociate from infidels – a position that defines international relations, to use modern terminology; and fourth, apply *shari'a* rule rather than simply admitting its relevance. According to al-Masari the Saudi regime fails to comply with these four conditions.

The Saudi regime, according to al-Masari, suspends *sha'air al-Islam* such as *jihad*. It does not forbid usury and vice. In fact, he claims that the regime actually promotes vice. Although there is a committee that is supposed to promote virtue and prohibit vice, its functions are distorted. He argues that the regime inherited this committee, which it kept not because it cares about the obligation but because it fears the consequences of abolishing the institution. The committee establishes the appearance of an Islamised space rather than its message. Therefore, the regime uses the committee to distort the image of Islam rather than to prevent vice and promote virtue. It fights the obligation incumbent upon Muslims to debate their political, military, economic and social affairs. It accepts only preachers who instruct their audience in matters related to personal worship. This observation confirms the establishment of an Islam that is obsessed with *'ibadat* (rituals, personal worship), at the expense of bringing out other aspects of the Islamic tradition, a theme that is at the heart of Sahwi activism. He criticises both Al-Saud and Wahhabi *'ulama*:

The Al-Saud spread a distorted Islam. They allow their *'ulama* to condemn the so-called innovators who perform *shirk* near tombs, worship dead saints, trees, stones and sand. They forbid the *mawlid* [celebration of the Prophet's birthday], which is an issue subject to difference in opinion rather than consensus among scholars. These issues become the main focus of preaching. Yet the blasphemy of rulers who introduce secular laws, their glorification and their subservience to infidels are hardly condemned by such *'ulama*.[38]

Like Abu al-Bara, al-Masari exposes the dark side of official Saudi engagement with the Afghan *jihad*. He argues that the regime suppressed those Arab Afghans who questioned the legitimacy of their despotic rulers. Their aim was to control the Jihadis and make them subservient to King Fahd rather than support them in their efforts to fight the Communists. He cites the example of the regime paying tribal groups in Afghanistan to block the travel of the Arab Afghans, especially Saudis, to reach training camps where debate about the Islamic credentials of King Fahd regularly took place. The Saudi regime, according to al-Masari, patronised the Afghan leaders in order to ensure that the outcome of the struggle did not challenge its own credibility. Al-Masari points out that the Saudi regime manipulated the Afghan Jihad and sent spies to report on Saudis, a theme that is so well articulated in Muhammad al-Hodhayf's novel, Nuqtat taftish, cited at the beginning of the chapter. Al-Hodfayf's character Jamil, who is now concerned with demonising Jihadis, was a spy acting on behalf of the Saudi project in Afghanistan. Al-Masari admits that Saudi Jihadis returned to Saudi Arabia with a new understanding of their own so-called pious state:

Having acquired training in weapons and combat, having read hundred of books denouncing the despots, having mixed with the real preachers, Saudi Afghans returned with a different face. They acquired and internalised the thought that excommunicates rulers, their supporters, and aides. The excommunication tradition was not new. Only its application to the Saudi regime is new. The young Saudi Afghans returned having lost trust in the regime's *'ulama*, 'regardless of the length of their beards and age'. The *'ulama* retaliated by condemning those young men and accusing them of spreading *fikr shadh* [perverse thought]. The youth left thinking that they were tied with an oath of allegiance to the Al-Saud (*fi unuqihim bay'a*), but when they returned they realised that this was an illusion.[39]

Having evaluated the current Saudi regime, al-Masari concludes by contesting the Wahhabi movement itself and its founder, Muhammad ibn Abd al-Wahhab. He not only scrutinises the Wahhabi religio-political discourse but also the relationship between the Al-Saud and the Wahhabi *'ulama*. This necessitates a return to the original pact between the reformer and Al-Saud. Al-Masari praises Ibn Abd al-Wahhab's concern over purifying faith from blasphemous practices but he criticises the reformer on four grounds:

First, the reformer overlooked the fact that the *sultan* [ruler] is not allowed to collect money from his subjects except that which is specified in the Quran and tradition. Second, hereditary rule contradicts Islam. Third, the reformer's commitment to limit his allegiance to Al-Saud anchors the call to monotheism in localism and prevents its universalisation. And fourth, granting the Al-Saud the right to political leadership and the *'ulama* the right to decide in religious matters are unacceptable measures that lead to secularisation and the creation of *kahanut* [a clergy], both are un-Islamic.

Al-Masari concludes that the Wahhabi reform movement degenerated into 'a local Najdi regional call that is also racist (*'unsoriyya*). It failed to rise above its localism and preach a universal message.'[40]

Transnationalisation in peaceful contexts

Saudi involvement in Afghanistan was only one context of the transnationalisation of its religious discourse. For the Saudi regime the transnationalisation of *da'wa* (call) became a political strategy rather than a mere religious obligation. Under the guise of religious duty towards other Muslims, the regime sought to establish its credentials among communities worldwide. It patronised Muslim regimes in various parts of the world, but its religious transnationalism was meant to reach the grass-roots level in order to control it and prevent it from contesting Saudi status and hegemony. While the Saudi government knew that it was difficult for impoverished Muslim states to contest Saudi hegemony, it feared the people in those states. Charity and education proved to be powerful mechanisms: the first bought dissenting voices, while the second aimed to control the minds and hearts of Muslims from Detroit to Jakarta.

Exporting the call involved the transnationalisation of Saudi religiopolitical discourse before it achieved a degree of sophistication suitable for an international Muslim audience, especially among Muslims in the West. The parochial local discourse was exported before it was able to produce all-encompassing and less exclusivist interpretations. The arrival of Muslim immigrants in the 1960s who worked in education and religious institutions inside Saudi Arabia had done little to broaden the scope of the Wahhabi message.

From the 1970s the official Saudi religious discourse travelled abroad to peaceful locations in Europe, America, Africa and Asia. Under the auspices of the Saudi regime, mosques, charitable organisations, religious schools, research centres and *da'wa* institutions were set up abroad. These grass-roots bodies differed from the formal and institutionalised activities that were represented by the Organisation of the Muslim Conference, the Muslim World League and other Islamic economic and financial organisations and bureaucracies that were sponsored by the Saudi government. The transnationalisation of Saudi religious discourse reached Muslims abroad as a result of educational programmes (in mosques, research centres and schools) whose main function was to disseminate religious knowledge produced by *aimat al-daʿwa al-najdiyya*. The *fatwa* volumes of Ibn Baz and al-Uthaymin, the most eminent Saudi scholars of the last two decades, could be found in small, shabby Islamic bookshops in Washington, London, Paris, Madrid, Lagos, Jakarta and other cities. While Muslims visiting Mecca could pick up a free copy of *fatwa*s relating to pilgrimage, prayer, fasting and how to visit the Prophet's mosque in Madina without committing 'blasphemous acts' such as supplication or sacrifice to other than God, they can now receive such literature in their home countries, where Saudi-sponsored Islamic education centres distribute it freely. Members of the Council of Senior Ulama, together with minor scholars and recently appointed staff in religious universities, wrote these *fatwa*s, not only for local consumption, but also for other Muslims abroad, and even potential converts.

Saudi Arabia exported vast religious literature that fell into four categories: first, the *ʿibadat* literature, whose main objective is the codification of the practice of Islamic rituals according to Wahhabi interpretations; second, literature that denounces the practices of other Muslims (including those who perform rituals differently or believe in other interpretations); third, literature dealing with Muslim women; and fourth, literature defining relations between Muslims and non-Muslims. Any Saudi-sponsored religious centre abroad had sample literature covering all these areas. What concerns us here is not the literature that deals with *ʿibadat* and how they should be 'correctly' performed (for example, prayer and fasting) but with the political implications of such literature.

First, Muslims who contemplate visiting Mecca and Madina for either the pilgrimage or *ʿumra* (minor pilgrimage) receive a leaflet instructing them on how to perform *al-ziyara* (the visit). A leaflet published by a religious centre in Madina found its way to one Saudi-sponsored religious centre in London. The leaflet explains the rules guiding the visit. It was written by a lecturer in religious studies in Saudi Arabia who worked under the editorship of Sheikh Abdullah ibn Jibrin, one of the most eminent *ʿulama*, whose name was associated with the crystallisation of the Sahwi trend. It includes a warning against some of the *mukhalafat* (errors) committed by Muslims upon their visit to the Madina mosque. There are seven permissible acts:

1-It is permissible to travel for the purpose of praying in the mosque.
2-It is permissible to travel to pray even if the visit has nothing to do with the pilgrimage.
3-When a Muslim arrives in the mosque, he must enter it with his right foot and say the name of God, in accordance with visits to mosques in general.
4-A Muslim must pray, kneeling twice for salutation.

5-After prayer a Muslim must go to the tombs of the Prophet, Abu Bakr and Omar and greet them. He must not spend a long time there. He must leave immediately.
6-It is *mustahab* (desirable) to perform ablution at home and visit the Qubba mosque and pray.
7-It is desirable to visit the Baqi cemetery and the tombs of the martyrs of Uhud.

The document warns Muslims that building on tombs or constructing mosques on them is one of the greatest prohibited acts.[41] Muslims are warned about the following:

1-Travel with the objective of 'visiting' the Prophet's tomb is prohibited. A Muslim must travel with the objective of praying in the Prophet's mosque.
2-Tomb visits are for men only. Women must not visit them.
3-Touching (*tamasuh*) minarets or stones, and kissing them or circling around them is an abominable innovation.
4-Intercession is strictly prohibited. No one must ask the Prophet for favours.
5-Raising the voice with supplication near the tomb is prohibited.[42]

The appendix of the leaflet explains the two types of *shirk* (blasphemy). The 'great association' (*shirk akbar*), which removes the individual from Islam, consists of supplication to other than God, sacrifice to other than God, circling around tombs, and rule not according to the revealed word of God. 'Minor association' (*shirk asghar*), which is great but falls short of removing one from the realm of Islam, involves swearing by a name other than that of God, and saying 'God and so and so willing', which implies equality between the will of God and that of a person.

Needless to say, the permissible and prohibited during visits to the Prophet's mosque in Madina reflect boundaries that early Wahhabis erected around themselves. These revolve around the way a true Muslim must worship, and are clear markers of identity. The regulation and control of worship rituals such as visiting the mosque distinguish between the faithful, who are part of the community, and those other Muslims who are by definition outside the realm of true Islam. Those who do not follow the rules risk committing not only minor religious innovations but also acts that remove them from Islam altogether. Such people cannot be excused on the basis of 'ignorance'. Receiving this leaflet abroad and complying with its rules removes any such excuse.

Regulating and controlling ritual practice outside Saudi Arabia is a preemptive measure that guards against potential acts of blasphemy and defilement in sacred territory, which must remain free of manifestations of *shirk*. The theme of defilement of Arabia by religious practices that do not conform to the Wahhabi rules is but one possible menace that the transnationalisation of Wahhabi discourse was meant to prevent. Defilement can also take place as a result of 'infidels', defined as *najs* (impure), being stationed on its territory, a theme that al-Qa'ida Jihadis excelled in developing and which became the slogan under which they fought and killed infidels in residential compounds. Again Jihadis took Wahhabi discourse to its logical political conclusions. They neither invented this discourse nor imported it from other Islamists movements.

Second, it is considered important, to safeguard against further defilement of the Land of the Two Holy Mosques, that creed literature is distributed abroad. Muslims intending to visit Saudi Arabia find collections of *'aqida* books in Saudi-sponsored religious centres abroad. *Fatwas in 'aqida* is a small booklet by Sheikh Ibn Baz that sums up important Wahhabi opinions on creed. It starts with a statement about the blasphemy that is exhibited by other Muslims (these days), for example 'the blasphemy that takes place near tombs'. Sheikh Ibn Baz explains:

Shirk and innovation take place in many countries near tombs. This includes asking help from the dead to heal the ill, or supplication to be victorious against enemies. All this is great *shirk* that removes Muslims from Islam . . . Prophets, angels, pious men, *jinn*, spirits and idols have no powers. To call upon them is *kufr* . . . To pray near tombs or build minarets above them is *shirk* innovation. According to the Prophet, God cursed Jews and Christians because they converted their prophets' tombs into places of worship. All Muslims and their governments must be warned against this great blasphemy.[43]

Sheikh Ibn Baz gives his opinion on hypocrisy (*nifaq*), as it has 'become so common among Muslims and is now used to fight Islam and Muslims'. The hypocrisy of a Muslim amounts to 'the enemy within', who publicly professes Islam but secretly works to erode the faith of Muslims and undermine their hegemony. The sheikh describes this malaise:

Munafiq [hypocrites] are mentioned in the Quran. They represent a great danger to the *umma*. They fall within two categories. First, those who practise 'creed' hypocrisy (*nifaq 'aqadi*). They are more *kafir*s than Jews, Christians and pagans. They are so dangerous because they are difficult to discover. Second, those who practise practical hypocrisy (*nifaq 'amali*), which involves pretending to pray and believe in God but in secrecy they lie, commit treason, and do not perform communal prayer.[44]

Again the theme of hypocrisy as explained by Ibn Baz is picked up by Jihadis, as will be demonstrated later in the book. While Ibn Baz describes ordinary Muslim hypocrites as drawing on Quranic and Hadith evidence, Jihadis apply the concept to people in positions of authority and leadership, *al-hakim al-munafiq* (the hypocrite ruler): the Saudi king.

Third, Saudis export a vast literature on women. The Saudi regime depicts itself as the guardian of women's honour, a claim now contested by those who oppose the regime. Nevertheless, exporting Wahhabi guidance to Muslim women worldwide is an extension of the domestic obligation. In both exported and domestic religious discourse, Muslim women are considered elevated creatures, who have rights and obligations. Most literature sets Muslim women in an honourable space above *jahili* and Western women. In both the age of ignorance and the contemporary West, women are described as oppressed and abused, and Muslim women are depicted as enjoying more rights and respect. Women, however, are seen as potential weak elements (*da'if*). Because of this alleged weakness, the enemies of Islam (the *kafirs*, hypocrites and Westerners) use Muslim women to corrupt the *umma*. This makes women dangerous and susceptible to corruption. In one volume sent to London and dedicated to educating Muslim women, Sheikh Salih al-Fawzan writes:

The enemies of Islam and those who have illness in their hearts want Muslim women to become a cheap commodity to be purchased by those with satanic desires. They want women to be a displayed commodity to see her beauty. They want her to leave her house and family and work as a nurse in a hospital, an air hostess on a plane, a teacher in a mixed school, an actress in a play, a singer and a television presenter. The enemies of Islam use the media to lead Muslim women astray. Women have left their real jobs in the house. Husbands are now forced to bring foreign maids to bring up children. This caused discord and evil.[45]

Issues relevant to Muslim women's education involve *ahkam* (rules) concerning the body. The focus is on biological functions (menstruation, other types of bleeding and birth), dress and the veil, worship (prayer, fasting, pilgrimage), marriage and relations with men. No educational material on women's general rights in Islam is included. Al-Fawzan's contribution to Muslim women's education is concerned with the biological female life cycle (birth, marriage and death), purity and ablution, and covering the body in order not to cause chaos or lead men astray. The obsession with the female body rather than female rights is symptomatic of the general political atmosphere, which aims to perpetuate acquiescence. Women potentially undermine state piety and virtue, therefore they need to be controlled. Controlling women is thus an extension of the religio-political orientation of the Wahhabi tradition. The discourse that is directed towards women produces not only acquiescent females but also dependent women, whose biological functions cannot be handled without consulting a male religious scholar. Women's dependence on continuous *fatwa*s dealing with the minute details of their bodily functions and worship ensures control in this life and salvation in the afterlife.[46]

This obsession with the female body and exclusion of other relevant educational material has gained official Saudi religious scholars a pejorative title. Their opponents, both Islamist and liberals, secretly refer to them as *mashaykh al-haydh* ('the sheikhs of menstruation'). Today, their female educational literature is a contested discourse both inside Saudi Arabia and abroad. As the regime and Wahhabi ʿulama claim the privilege of defending women's honour, opposition forces and dissidents' voices equally use the issue of women to contest the ʿulama's authority.

The fourth type of literature educates Muslims in how to handle relations with infidels. Among Muslim minorities in the West, the obligation to protect the faith and educate Muslims, who are believed to face daily challenges to their identity, is regarded by Saudi religious scholars as an important duty of Muslim governments. In a pamphlet entitled *Muslim Minorities: Fatwa Regarding Muslims Living as Minorities*, Shaykh Abdulaziz Ibn Baz and Shaykh Muhammad al-Uthaymin invoke a Quranic sura in which Muslims have a duty to 'invite to the way of your Lord with wisdom and exhortation and argue with them in a way that is better'.[47] With regard to Muslim minorities, the two scholars insist that Muslim governments should 'send to them whoever can assist them in achieving this and ask them to send people to Islamic countries to learn knowledge. There should be, therefore, an exchange of people between those Muslim minorities and the Muslim societies in order to activate them and help them in all their affairs'. The responsibility of such an exchange lies with political leaders and religious scholars: 'The rulers of Muslims everywhere as well as the scholars and the rich must expend whatever they can to assist the Muslim minorities. They must be good to them, help them to understand their religion and help them to acquire complete freedom to manifest the rites and practices of Islam.'[48]

In Saudi Arabia the Permanent Committee for Scholarly Research and Ifta is in control of religious interpretations. Before the millennium celebrations in December 2000, the committee offered 'an Islamic opinion regarding celebrating this occasion, exchanging cards with the "unbelievers", and having days as holiday during the period of this event'.[49] It gave nine reasons to 'make Muslims aware of the misguidance deliberately condoned by the People of the Book' and urged Muslims worldwide to shun the celebrations because

1-Jews' and Christians' theories about the millennium are against the Islamic true revelation, and are merely an illusion. 2-Celebrating the millennium makes Islam appear as similar to other false religions. 3-It is prohibited to imitate the non-believers. 4-Imitating the non-believers in the exterior behaviour leads to some kind of love and support to them in the interior. 5-Celebrating with the non-believers is a sin, a trespassing of the borders of Allah. 6-It is unlawful to advertise the event electronically and in print media. 7-There is no Islamic evidence that those dates (of the Millennium) have any precedence over other days. 8-Congratulating each other or the non-believers is unlawful. And finally 9-Muslims should commit themselves to the Muslim calendar.[50]

The banning of Muslim participation in the millennium celebrations draws heavily on the opinion of the committee and the *fatwa* of Sheikh Abdulrahman ibn Abdulaziz al-Sudays, the imam of al-Furqan mosque in Mecca, copies of which are distributed in London and elsewhere.[51] The committee that bans sending a greeting-card to an 'infidel' is the same one that in 1990s issued a *fatwa* legitimising calling upon 'infidel' states to assist in fighting another Muslim state. Members of the same committee also issued *fatwa*s banning women from wearing jeans, because this would count as pious Muslim women 'imitating infidels' (*tashabuh bi 'l-kuffar*). The contradictions of the official religious discourse contribute to its loss of credibility and contestation.

In 2004 al-Sudays delivered a sermon in London's East End mosque, where he talked about tolerance and accepting the 'other', now clichés that summarise the transformation forced on the Saudi regime and its *ʿulama* after 11 September.[52] It was doubtful whether his early 2000 *fatwa* was forgotten; Western governments eager to maintain amicable relations with a regime in control of 25 per cent of world oil reserves kept a blind eye, but the intellectual and psychological effect of contradictory religious discourse on young Muslims in Europe and elsewhere is perhaps similar to that among young Saudi men and women. Contradictions do not make for balanced lives, and Saudi society experiences far more than any other society, thanks to Wahhabi discourse and excessive and sudden wealth.

Wahhabi religious interpretations relating to worship and creed can be popular abroad. They can be seen as rational and methodological, and as founded on certainty and clear-cut categories. They reflect an obsession with sacred texts, easily accessible in both print and electronic format. These texts can be interpreted without mediators; thus in theory the discourse offers the possibility of dismantling the traditional authority exercised by fathers, religious scholars and pious men. Wahhabi interpretations call for the rationalisation of worship, minimalist rituals, equality between Muslims, and the rejection of sorcery, superstition and innovations. In theory they preach a sober rather than an animated religion. They offer certainty in a world dominated by fluid categories and multiple interpretations. Certain Muslim university students worldwide may appreciate their clarity, purity, certainty and authenticity. They may also appreciate the absence of ambiguity and hesitation. The discourse allows them to imagine a glorious Muslim past which appeals to defeated Muslims and marginalised youth as well as to wealthy and educated men and women.

Saudi Wahhabi discourse creates the illusion of empowerment, an empowerment that is achieved by complying with rigid rules and *fatwa*s that regulate almost every aspect of one's life, body and relations with others. It is the new 'science' of young Muslims.

The transnationalisation of this discourse can also create moments of confrontation among the recipients.[53] As it aims to standardise belief and worship, it risks obliterating local traditions and interpretations, undermine local power relations, threaten age-old hierarchies and create new ones. Its spread has tended to Muslims split rather than unify them. Its uncompromising and dogmatic nature leaves no room for the middle ground.

The premature transnationalisation of Saudi Wahhabi religious discourse, initially to Afghanistan and later to other destinations, led in some instances to the promotion of the authority of the Saudi regime and its Islamic credentials. Paradoxically, it also led to contestation of this authority and even undermined its security.[54] It can be said that there are unintended consequences of religious transnational connections. Wahhabi religio-political discourse is anchored in a specific context, but as it has flowed beyond this it has developed its own momentum, escaping the control of those who initially engaged in its promotion. Such forays into the wider world can turn into embarrassment, leading to international crises, which threaten to destabilise foreign policy, inter-state relations and contemporary international relations. The events of 11 September are a clear example.

The transnationalising of Saudi religious discourse proves that locally produced traditions and individuals undergo a transformation as they travel to other destinations. Sometimes it is difficult to argue that these traditions themselves are anchored in a specific locality and discourse, as many of them are products of interpretation and diverse influences.[55] The Saudi Afghan experience was perhaps one of the most important experiences for the younger generation. Although the regime tried hard to contain the Afghan *jihad* by patronising and subsidising it, together with other states and intelligence services, it failed miserably in controlling the outcome and consequences. A cross-fertilisation of religious discourse in Afghanistan, London and many other places contributed to bringing out elements of Wahhabiyya that the regime had endeavoured to suppress for several decades. Away from home and under the fog of war, Saudi Afghans took Wahhabi religio-political discourse to its logical conclusion. Similarly under the fog of London, which allowed greater freedom, the same discourse was interpreted and reinterpreted to condemn those *umara* and *'ulama* who claim to be guided by such discourse.

4 Struggling in the way of God at home: the politics and poetics of *jihad*

> Remove the polytheists from the Arabian Peninsula.
>
> Prophet Muhammad, Hadith
>
> How can *jihad* be an unlimited good in the lands of other Muslims but a corruption in the Arabian Peninsula?
>
> Sheikh Yusif al-Ayri (d. 2003), leader of al-Qa'ida in the Arabian Peninsula

In the twenty-first century, Saudi society is struggling over religious interpretation, which seems to be at the heart of political activism. As the struggle unfolds, it is accompanied by strife among various groups and confrontation between those groups and the state. Traditional *'ulama*, Sahwi sheikhs, Jihadis and laymen debate religious interpretations; not all subscribe to non-violent dialogue. Since 1990 violence has become the dark side of the Saudi religio-political debate. Various contestants challenge each other in a desperate attempt to control interpretations of religious discourse. The debate intensified after 11 September.

With American military power closing the gates of *jihad* in Afghanistan following the demise of the Taliban regime in 2001, the struggle of Saudis for the way of God came home.[1] Many Saudi Jihadis who travelled for the second time to Afghanistan, where Osama bin Laden had lived between 1996 and 2001, returned to Saudi Arabia. After the toppling of the Taliban, the dismantling of al-Qa'ida training camps and the arrest or flight of Saudi trainees, it seemed to many observers that the War on Terror, led by the USA and a number of supporting countries, was proving successful. Yet several countries in the region experienced waves of violence. Between 2001 and 2005, Saudi Arabia witnessed the worst violence in its modern history, conducted under the rhetoric of expelling infidels from the Arabian Peninsula and removing the despots, known in Jihadi discourse as *tawaghit* of the Land of the Two Holy Mosques.

On 12 May 2003 a major bombing took place in Riyadh; thirty-five people were killed and hundreds injured. On 8 November 2003 car bombs devastated al-Muhayya residential compound, killing over twenty

134

people and injuring many residents. On 21 April 2004 the building of the security forces in Riyadh was devastated by car bombs. On 2 May 2004 four attackers killed several Western workers in the industrial city of Yanbo. In the same month, another attack on offices and residences of oil company workers took place in al-Khobar in the Eastern Province. Before the end of 2004, on 6 December, the American consulate in Jiddah was attacked. A few days later, a car bomb exploded in the Ministry of Interior buildings in Riyadh.[2] In 2005 regular shoot-outs between Jihadis and security forces continued.

These bloody attacks were major events that marked a turn in the Jihadi project. They announced the arrival of the *jihad* campaign in the Land of the Two Holy Mosques, as the Jihadis called it. In addition, not a week passed during this period without the government announcing major success in capturing arms and killing suspected terrorists in the major cities, the mountains around Mecca and the farms of Qasim. Many people, referred to as armed and violent suspects, were killed in shooting incidents between Jihadis and the security forces. In 2005, Dammam saw the worst shoot-out between security forces and Jihadis, who took refuge in one building. There was no doubt that the struggle in the way of God had returned home after several years in the diaspora.

The rhetoric of Jihadis, the legitimising narrative of violence, drew on the sacred Quran and the Prophetic tradition, citing Hadiths calling upon Muslims to remove associationists or polytheists from the Arabian Peninsula – a reference to Westerners, mainly Americans. It is ironic that the struggle continued even after the USA and the Saudi government announced that most American troops stationed in Saudi Arabia had been moved to neighbouring Gulf states, mainly Bahrain and Qatar, in 2003. However, some American military bases remain in Saudi Arabia. As it unfolded, the struggle proved to be more complex and nuanced than simply a strategy to purify the land of Islam from infidels. The symbolism was, however, potent. The rhetoric of the struggle grew in a specific political context and is inspired by its own politics and poetics.

Throughout the 1990s, while the famous Sahwa *'ulama* were behind bars, a strong indigenous Jihadi trend took shape, which does not represent an external religious tradition, both politically and ideologically, as often mistakenly claimed by the government, traditional *'ulama* and Saudi media. While several successful scholarly works have attempted to trace the indigenous historical and religious roots of contemporary Jihadi discourse,[3] other works dissociate Jihadis from the indigenous Saudi–Wahhabi interpretations.[4] In official Saudi discourse, Jihadis are often referred to as Kharijites, or those who have gone astray (*al-fi'a al-dhalla*).

The quest to identify the local origins, causes and intellectual roots of Jihadism could have been a legitimate exercise at a time when Saudi Arabia was more isolated from the outside world. However, the country has now been drawn into the political, economic, intellectual and religious exchanges of other places. Easy travel, the internet (since 1999), satellite television and the media in general connect Saudis to other places and people. While Saudi Arabia received ideas and religious interpretations from abroad after opening its borders to Islamic trends since the 1960s,[5] it proved to be equally capable of initiating its own transnational religious flows to distant locations, thanks to a vigorous campaign of proselytising and royal patronage.[6] Saudi religious discourse was internalised by a whole generation of students who flocked to Saudi Islamic universities in Madina and elsewhere.[7] It is probably inaccurate to describe religious discourse inside the country since the 1970s as purely Saudi. It is equally unconvincing to describe the Islamic discourse that one encounters in London, Washington, Jakarta, Kabul and Peshawar as purely Saudi–Wahhabi. At the same time, one cannot argue that Jihadism in Saudi Arabia is an alien intellectual trend imported from other Islamist movements and locations.

Whether they draw on local religious tradition or imported politicised religion from other places, all Saudi Jihadis make use of locally produced religious knowledge and interpretations. Furthermore, regardless of whether the inspiration for, or even the orders to engage in, violence come from outside – for example, al-Qaʾida or other global Jihadi movements – it is certain that there is a strong local dimension to the Jihadi trend. Religious theoreticians of *jihad* (for example, some *ʿulama*), interpreters (Islamist intellectuals) and those who carry out violent acts such as suicide bombers and other young militants are all Saudis, with the exception of a handful of activists who belong to other Arab countries and whose names have appeared in Saudi wanted terrorist lists.[8] To attribute the outbreak of violence in Saudi Arabia in the twenty-first century to outside agents such as a global terror movement is to miss the fact that this violence has its own local religious codes, meanings, politics and poetics which resonate in some Saudi circles. The violence associated with the Jihadi trend affirms that it is part of a 'highly meaningful relationship with divinity'.[9] Violent actors are understood as culturally authentic and significant rather than examples of the absence of such significance.

The terrorist attacks of the 1990s, which increased in frequency and magnitude in 2003–4, are not senseless and aimless acts by a group of alienated youth, often described in official religious and political circles as *khawarij al-ʿasr*, contemporary Kharijites. Perpetrators of violence are guided by cultural codes that draw on sacred texts and interpretations by religious scholars who claim to return to an authentic Islamic tradition, found not only in *al-kitab wa 'l-sunna* (the book and the deeds of the Prophet) but also in medieval and more recent commentaries on the texts by famous religious authorities among *aimat al-da'wa al-najdiyya*. Jihadi violence is not at the margin of religious interpretation, but is in fact at its centre, hence the difficulties in defeating the rhetoric of *jihad* in the long term. Jihadi violence, until now dormant in many cultural and religious interpretations, has recently erupted and claimed many lives.

A more fruitful approach to interpret the Jihadi trend and the violence associated with it must start with a number of assumptions. First, Jihadism is a cultural expression grounded in strong religious interpretation that is indigenous to Saudi Arabia. Second, even if Jihadism in Saudi Arabia is a function of global terror networks and transnational religious and political flows, it grows in a specific local context with its own cultural codes and experiences. Third, Jihadism is not an affirmation of alienation, anomie, criminality, economic deprivation and social marginalisation, but an affirmation of a pledge to superiority and the belief in one's ability to change the world by action. It is often understood as a sign of the break-down of 'traditional' society, loss of identity as a result of increased urbanisation and modernisation, or self-destruction and annihilation. It may grow in a context characterised by negative conditions of poverty, marginalisation and alienation, but one should not confuse context with cause.

It seems that Jihadism, together with the violence associated with it, has been brought from the margins to occupy a central place in the religious map of Saudi Arabia. In Jihadi discourse, changing the world by action is not a reflection of defeat, but an expression of empowerment felt by young militants, ideologue *'ulama* and other Islamist intellectuals. Unless the perpetrator's view forms part of our own understanding, interpreting the Jihadi trend will escape us. It is also essential to consider the role played by the Saudi regime in creating a context that allows it to grow. In many respects, the violence of the Jihadis represents a mirror reflecting the violence of the state and its official *'ulama*.

Taking Sahwa to its logical conclusion: *qa'idun* vs. *mujahidun*

The Jihadi trend is often seen as the logical conclusion of the Sahwi movement that openly dominated the Saudi religio-political scene throughout the 1980s and 1990s.[10] While it was clear that the religio-political awakening included diverse movements and trends, it seems that there was a common source of inspiration and an agreement on basic principles. However, one of the most difficult tasks is to draw the boundaries between various Islamist groups. While there is common ground, they seem to differ in their religious, political and strategic agendas.

The Jihadi trend was operating within a context of religious diversity. Jihadi literature does not see itself as a deviation from the sources that the Sahwis drew on in the early 1990s. However, the release of famous Sahwi *'ulama* from prison and their subsequent interpretation of *jihad*, which limited it to peaceful cultural, civilisational and religious struggle under the banner of *wali al-amr* (leader of the Muslim community) marked a serious departure in the eyes of Jihadis from the main principles of *da'wa* and the early Sahwi position. Jihadis began to see themselves as the real heirs of Sahwa, carrying its banner, while those left behind or who failed to join them, both physically and intellectually, are labelled *qa'idun* (lit. 'sitting' or 'stationary': those left behind). Jihadis describe themselves as *murabitun 'ala al-thugur* (tied to the battleground).

While Jihadi and Sahwi interpretations are both grounded in Salafi religious discourse, three main differences separate Jihadis from mainstream Salafi Sahwis. An uncompromising rejectionist position towards the Saudi regime, a belief in violent resistance against Western domination, and the choice of legitimate means and targets for *jihad* (for example, the security forces and Western expatriates living in Saudi Arabia can both be legitimate targets) mark Jihadis out as a separate group on the religio-political map of Saudi Arabia.

Sahwis have reservations about the Saudi regime (*dawla*), but in public they label it Islamic. They resist Western domination by what they call peaceful civilisational means, and consider it a serious crime to kill Muslims who work for the regime – for example, members of the security forces. It has also been noted that Sahwis, after the experience of prison and the events of 11 September, have adopted a position which considers society rather than the regime to be problematic and in need of reform. Although Sahwis developed and propagated the rhetoric of Jihad and resistance to Western domination, they did not consider Western expatriates and Saudi security forces to be legitimate targets, especially after 11 September. It seems that this position is grounded in political strategy and expediency, for which they have developed elaborate judicial rulings. It is also based on their belief in the fact that an Islamised society generates Islamised government – that is, correct *da'wa* leads to authentic Islamic *dawla* – without recourse to violence. For the majority of Sahwis, *jihad* abroad (for example, in Afghanistan, Iraq, Chechnya and Palestine) is legitimate, whereas inside Saudi Arabia it is not. For example, a statement in support of *jihad* in Iraq, condemning any Muslim who cooperates with infidels' on *ithm wa udwan* (sin and aggression), was signed by twenty-six Sahwi *'ulama*.[11]

In the 1990s, and as a result of the Gulf War, the main question for the Sahwi *'ulama* was the legitimacy of calling upon the 'infidel West' to help in a war against the Iraqi Muslim army that invaded Kuwait. The famous *fatwa* of Sheikh Abdulaziz ibn Baz which legitimised the invitation of foreign troops by Saudi Arabia split the religious community and generated the dissidence described in the previous chapters.[12] However, almost ten years later, the main question became the legitimacy of Muslims assisting the infidel West in its war against other Muslims, starting with the Taliban in 2001 and moving on to Iraq in 2003, all depicted in Western discourse as part of the War on Terror. In the twenty-first century, and immediately after 11 September 2001, the West, headed by the United States, demanded that Muslim governments assist it in its War on Terror. This opened new frontiers in the quest for reforming religion and politics in Saudi Arabia. Above all, it inspired a debate regarding the legitimacy of Muslim governments assisting the enemies of Islam by killing Jihadis.

Since 11 September and the invasion of Afghanistan by US forces, a group of religious scholars came to be known in official discourse and in the Saudi press – for example, *al-Sharq al-Awsat, al-Watan* and *al-Jazirah* – as the trinity of excommunication (*thulathi al-takfir*), which consisted of sheikhs Ali al-Khodayr, Ahmad al-Khalidi and Nasir al-Fahad.[13] These sheikhs were part of a well-established intellectual genealogy that drew on the early writings of Wahhabi scholars such as Muhammad ibn Abd al-Wahhab, Sulayman ibn Abdullah Al-Shaykh, Hamad ibn Atiq, Humud al-Tuwayjiri, Muhammad al-Qahtani, Muhammad ibn Ibrahim Al-Shaykh and Humud ibn Oqla al-Shuaybi. The so-called trinity of excommunication was the young version of an old group of well-established religious scholars. It had strong genealogical links with a previous generation of Wahhabi scholars, in addition to contemporary ones. As religious scholars, they hardly referred in their writings to twentieth-century Jihadi Islamist activists and intellectuals such as Sayid Qutb or Ayman al-Dhawahiri. The latter were simply not their reference points.

In an attempt to examine the intellectual practice and the current context of excommunication and *jihad*, the writings of one of the young Jihadi scholars who emerged in the post-11 September period will be considered. Sheikh Nasir al-Fahad, who was considered part of the trinity of excommunication, wrote several pamphlets and issued a number of *fatwa*s considered a window from which to observe his thought. One of his most important treatises, *al-Tibyan fi kufr man a'ana al-amrican*, deals with religious opinion on the status of Muslims who help Americans.[14] While in the 1990s Saudi religious scholars debated the legitimacy of asking Americans for assistance in expelling Saddam from Kuwait, in

2001 the debate was about Muslims (Saudis) assisting Americans in attacking other Muslims, for example in Afghanistan. Al-Fahad does not publicly name individuals within the Saudi regime – for example, princes – as infidels, nor does he openly consider the Saudi state as a state of *kufr*. However, his writings may imply that this is the case. The obvious evidence which is often cited is Saudi relations with the USA and the regime's alleged departure from the revealed word of God. His imprisonment and later confessions on Saudi television in December 2003 reflect the regime's worries over his rhetoric and its ability to mobilise the youth of the country. While there are other religious texts dealing with 'assisting infidels' written by more established religious scholars, for example Sheikh Humud ibn Oqla al-Shuaybi's book *al-Qawl al-mukhtar fi hukm al-isti 'ana bil kuffar* (Chosen Words for the Rule Regarding Calling Upon Infidels for Assistance),[15] al-Fahad's book is easier to read and can be more accessible to non-religious specialists.

Although a graduate of one of the Islamic universities in Saudi Arabia, al-Fahad is neither an established religious scholar nor a well-known figure among the Sahwi *'ulama*, although he may have gravitated towards them in the 1990s. He was born in the early 1970s. Unusually for a religious scholar, his interest in religious matters and interpretation did not distract him from writing his own genealogy, and he published a book about his own tribal ancestors, al-Asaida, a branch of the Utayba tribe who inhabited Zilfi, a frontier town between Najd and the Gulf.[16] Al-Fahad is aware of the fact that *ansab* (genealogies) are controversial from an Islamic perspective, which tried to mould groups into a unifying religious community, suffused with the ethos of equality, and is concerned to justify documenting his lineage as being part of the Islamic tradition. He claims to have followed the middle path between an obsession with ancestors and forgetting them. Al-Fahad rejects the idea that concern with tracing genealogy should be a prelude to enforcing a hierarchical relationship between groups, an unacceptable position condemned by Islam because God insists that men are distinguished by piety. On the other hand, forgetting genealogy can lead to undesirable consequences, for example the severing of kinship ties, especially with increasing migration and dispersal. After this prelude, al-Fahad traces his own tribal ancestry, confirming his Arab Adnani origin and membership of the Rawq branch of Utayba that inhabited Najd, a tribe that more than any other contributed to the establishment of the current Saudi state. Utaybis were early converts to the Saudi cause and provided the manpower that invaded Hijaz in 1925. Their performance in early *jihad* as Ikhwan fighters, and later rebellions against the state, are well documented.

Al-Fahad is the son of a religious scholar, Sheikh Hamad bin Hamin bin Hamad bin Fahad who according to his son moved from Zilfi to Riyadh in 1374H (1944) where he assisted one of the most prominent and influential religious scholars of the current Saudi state, Sheikh Muhammad ibn Ibrahim Al-Shaykh.[17] Sheikh Muhammad ibn Ibrahim is today remembered in Salafi circles as one of the most faithful and uncompromising interpreters of the Wahhabi tradition before the official co-optation of the 'ulama by the state in the early 1970s. As mentioned earlier in this book, Sheikh Muhammad ibn Ibrahim Al-Shaykh died in 1969. Al-Fahad's father occupied various jobs in religious educational institutions, justice, and jurisdiction. He retired in 1411H (1990).

In one of the most important and comprehensive pamphlets, al-Tibyan fi kufr man a'an al-amrican (Revealing the Blasphemy of Those who Help Americans), published on his website in 1422H (2001–2),[18] al-Fahad summarised his view on the problem of association with Americans in their aggression against Muslims. The publication of the book followed the attacks of 11 September and American preparation for the invasion of Afghanistan. Muslim cooperation with Americans is regarded as kufr (blasphemy), as the title implies. The book does not mention the Saudi regime or use it as an example of regimes co-operating with Americans in their 'War on Terror'.

In the preface three Saudi religious scholars applauded al-Fahad's book and described it as a clear and accurate treatment of the subject matter. Sheikh Humud al-Oqla al-Shuaybi wrote the first endorsement of the book, confirming the intellectual genealogy of this young scholar. Al-Oqla described al-Fahad as a mujtahid belonging to the 'victorious party' and recommended his book to the public, as he found it to be 'one of the best books on the issue of the blasphemy and apostasy of those who assist Americans'. The book is endorsed by two other important Saudi sheikhs, Sulayman al-Ulwan and Ali al-Khodayr, both intellectual ancestors of the young scholar. Their praise enhances the credibility of the book at least in the eyes of other Jihadis, especially when coming from established Salafi authority figures, some of whom were members of the Council of Senior Ulama. This attests to early observations made in this book regarding the difficulty of drawing clear-cut boundaries between offfical and non-official, radical and moderate 'ulama.

Al-Fahad's book consists of three general sections: The Crusade against Islam (part I); Evidence of the Blasphemy of Those who Help Americans (part II); and A Reply to Some Misguided Opinions (part III). While al-Fahad makes a political statement about Americans and the Taliban regime in part I, he elaborates theological arguments in part II, which represents the most substantial part of the book. This section includes a sub-section in which al-Fahad lists evidence from the religious scholars of *al-da ʿwa al-najdiyya*, a reference to the Wahhabi movement and its main religious scholars since the time of Muhammad ibn Abd al-Wahhab. In part III, al-Fahad refutes some misguided opinions relating to the topic of association with and dissociation from infidels, *al-wala ʾ wa ʾl-bara ʾ*.

The book exemplifies the various aspects of al-Fahad's theological and political orientations. In addition to being a religious scholar, he poses as a political analyst who comments on current affairs which he sees through the prism of the past, tradition and the words of God. His political commentaries on current affairs expand beyond matters relating to Muslims and their history. In fact, he feels confident enough to comment on and analyse American society – despite lacking any direct contact with it – both in America or in Saudi Arabia. Al-Fahad would definitely regard visiting America as a form of an 'abode among polytheists' (*bayn dhuhrani al-mushrikin*).

In a section of the first part of the book, entitled Synopsis on America, al-Fahad paints a dark picture of American society, where moral degeneration, crime, corruption and atheism reign. America is portrayed as a land where Satan has taken refuge ('ashash fiha al-shaytan'). He cites statistics on homosexuality, illegitimate births, drug addiction, alcoholism, sexual perversion and other sins. He reminds the reader of *qawm Lut* (the people of Lut), an extinct community known in the Quran for ten deadly sins, the most famous of which is homosexuality. American society not only engages in these sins but endeavours to spread them worldwide as a result of military intervention and colonial wars, according to al-Fahad. In few pages, he depicts America as a godless country, ruled by a government of corruption and sins that does not hesitate to kill in various parts of the world, mainly in Asia, Africa and the Middle East, and listing examples of American interventions in places like Somalia, Lebanon, Vietnam and others. Al-Fahad argues that America is dangerous not only for its military adventures but also for its moral bankruptcy and corruption which it endeavours to export to other places, including the Muslim world.

In contrast, in the section in the same part (part I) entitled Synopsis on Taliban, al-Fahad paints the antithesis of America. After a brief introduction in which the religious and social diversity of Afghan society is described, al-Fahad argues that the emirate of Taliban is an Islamic government because it applied the *shari ʿa* in all aspects of life. The achievements of the Taliban are listed in terms of establishing a Committee for the Promotion of Virtue and Prohibition of Vice, promoting an Islamic media policy, prohibiting the shaving of beards, segregating men and women, eradicating opium cultivation, demolishing pagan statues in museums and elsewhere, emphasising the duty of *jihad* in the educational curriculum, and delaying the education of girls until the availability of qualified female teachers. Al-Fahad concludes that America's war on Afghanistan should be understood in terms of a crusade whose main purpose is to destroy one of the first experiments in establishing Islamic government in the Muslim world. Invoking several speeches by President Bush and other senior figures in the American administration, al-Fahad reflects an awareness of the political rhetoric of the 'enemy of Islam'. He uses this rhetoric to enhance the credibility of his own narrative and concludes that 'it is indeed a war on Islam'.

In part II, Evidence of the Blasphemy of Those who Help Americans, al-Fahad identifies two important dimensions in Islam: first, belief in one God alone (*al-tawhid*); and second, the prohibition of polytheism (*shirk*). Excommunication is a state which follows the violation of the principle of the oneness of God. Al-Fahad endeavours to prove that enmity towards infidels (*kafirun*) and dissociation from them (*bara'*) are central to belief in the oneness of God. Evidence is drawn from eight sources: the Holy Book (*al-kitab*); consensus (*al-ijma'*); tradition of the Prophet (*sunna*), sayings of the companions of the Prophet (*aqwal al-sahaba*); deduction by analogy (*qiyas*); history (*tarikh*); the words of the people of knowledge; and the words of the scholars of the Najdi *da'wa*. It is extremely interesting that al-Fahad devotes a whole section to the latter scholars and treats them as a separate category of people of knowledge. The *fatwa*s and sayings of twelve Wahhabi scholars are listed as evidence of the centrality of the duty of dissociation from infidels.

The author describes three general relations with infidels that draw on Islamic texts, history and tradition. He sketches a perception of relations between Muslims and non-Muslims that draws on ancient texts in order to guide contemporary and future relations that Muslims both individuals and states may have with infidels. First, *tawwali* is a kind of relation with infidels which removes the person from the realm of religion. It includes love of the infidel's religion, wishing them victory, and helping them against Muslims. This is a relationship of subordination and subservience to infidels. It is the most reprehensible, as it leads the Muslim himself to become an infidel.

A second relation, *muwalat*, is forbidden but does not lead to blasphemy. *Muwalat* involves, for example, respecting infidels in meetings, greeting them before Muslims, and showing them love and affection. According to al-Fahad, this relationship between Muslims and non-Muslims can be problematic, as it may develop into *tawwali*. It is perhaps accurate to describe this relationship as one of deference and accommodation shown by Muslims towards non-Muslims.

The third association, which is permissible, *mu 'amalat ja 'iza*, involves treating infidels with justice, especially non-combatants who live in Muslim lands. According to al-Fahad, the poor amongst them 'should be clothed, their hungry should be fed, and their weak should be protected. Muslims should do this not out of fear and humility but out of compassion.' Here he confirms an important Muslim tradition, namely justice towards the weak and those who represent no danger to the Muslim community.

Al-Fahad argues that Muslims confuse the three types of relations. His main concern is with the dangerous state of *tawwali*, which he explains on the basis of the writings of Muhammad ibn Abd al-Wahhab, who insisted that *tawwali* (helping infidels against Muslims) is *naqidh lil islam* (a factor that removes a Muslim from the religious community and Islam). Al-Fahad lists types of help that are forbidden, for example, help that requires the use of one's own body, weapon, tongue, heart, pen, money and opinion. This assistance is considered both blasphemy and apostasy.

After this general theological treatise, outlining permissible and prohibited relations with infidels, al-Fahad moves to contemporary politics, focusing on the American invasion of Afghanistan, described as a new crusade against Islam and Muslims. This is interpreted in light of evidence from the Quran. In a section on *shari'a* evidence, al-Fahad lists eight suras in which God informs the believers of the intentions of unbelievers who have 'plans to undermine the faith of Muslims, subjugate them and fight them until they declare their subordination and servitude'. One sura informs the believers about the intentions of Jews and Christians: 'Never will the Jews and Christians be satisfied with thee unless thou follow their form of religion' (sura al-Baqara, verse 120).

Another sura mentioned by al-Fahad prohibits intimate relations with infidels:

> Ye who believe
> Take not into your intimacy
> Those outside your ranks
> They will not fail
> To corrupt you. They
> only desire your ruin
> Rank hatred from their mouths
> What their hearts conceal
> Is far worse.   (sura al–Umran, verse 118)

With the support of evidence from sacred texts, al-Fahad describes the 'reality' of the new crusade in an attempt to emphasise the relevance and applicability of the Quranic sura to contemporary political context. In addition to invasions under the banner of colonialism (*hamlat istimariyya*), and later invasions under United Nations sanctions (*hamlat umamiyya*), he lists several examples of contemporary crusades against Muslims in Palestine, Iraq, Sudan, Libya, Lebanon, Somalia, Afghanistan, Bosnia, Kosovo, Macedonia, Chechnya and Kashmir, where Muslims have been killed. He also includes missionary activities, which are a form of 'violence as these missionaries try to "Christianise" Muslims'.

Other evidence derives from history. Al-Fahad lists *fatwa*s of famous *ulama* forbidding Muslims to help non-Muslims against Muslims. In addition to examples from medieval times, especially the era of the Mongol invasion and the responses of Ibn Taymiyya, the colonial encounter between Muslims and non-Muslims, for example in Algeria and Egypt in the twentieth century, he provides ample examples of religious scholars who spoke out against Muslims providing assistance to non-Muslims. He gives a list of theological positions from the four major Islamic schools of jurisprudence (Hanbali, Shafi'i, Maliki and Hanafi), recent *ulama* (for example Rashid Rida, Ahmad Shakir and Abdulaziz ibn Baz), and contemporary scholars (such as Safar al-Hawali). Al-Fahad implies that there is consensus among Muslim scholars throughout the ages that assistance to infidels leads to excommunication. This obviously stands in sharp contrast with Sheikh Yusif al-Qaradawi's controversial *fatwa* to American Muslims in which he declared their participation as soldiers in the American army during the invasion of Afghanistan permissible.[19]

Al-Fahad moves to the evidence of Wahhbi religious scholars, whose theological position is in his opinion the most clear and uncompromising regarding helping non-Muslims against Muslims. He describes the *ulama* of the Wahhabi call as 'the most outspoken *ulama* in this regard. They produced elaborate *fatwa* and books on the subject,' thus justifying his detailed consideration of their intellectual heritage. Al-Fahad brings the story closer to his homeland and his intellectual ancestors by citing scholars who are the guardians of the Wahhabi tradition and its most loyal interpreters. Starting with the writings of the founder, Muhammad ibn Abd al-Wahhab, he offers a survey of the opinions of those who kept his tradition alive, mainly the *aimat al-da'wa al-najdiyya*, the Najdi scholars whose work is set apart as evidence supporting the belief in the blasphemy of all those Muslims who assist non-Muslims against their fellow Muslims. The list includes the *fatwa*s of Wahhabi scholars over three centuries, starting with Muhammad ibn Abd al-Wahhab and ending with Safar al-Hawali. Al-Fahad cites a famous *fatwa* by Sheikh Ibn Baz, who warned Muslims against helping infidels, at the time 'Socialists and Communists', a reflection of the context in which the Cold War defined the enemy as the Soviet Union. In fact, as early as 1944, Ibn Baz clashed with Ibn Saud over the 'invasion' of infidels, who were at the time American contractors with the government working on agricultural and development projects.[20] Al-Fahad's celebration of the Wahhabi scholars and his line of analysis are a clear continuation of the tradition clearly represented in the work of sheikhs such as Sulayman ibn Abdullah Al-Shaykh and Hamad ibn Atiq, both of whom issued *fatwas* excommunicating those who assist infidels in wars against Muslims. In the early nineteenth century the infidels were the Ottoman sultan and his troops. In fact, both scholars insisted that punishment for Muslims who assist infidels against other Muslims should be harsher (*akhtar ghaltha*) than that meted out to infidels.[21]

This interpretation of the duty of association and dissociation as outlined by one of the most controversial Jihadi *ulama* led to his imprisonment, for two main reasons. First, the Saudi regime was not ready to tolerate such theological discourse at a time when it was under tremendous pressure from the United States to curb the spread of what was regarded as anti-American religious interpretations. Second, al-Fahad's interpretations, although coined in an abstract manner, indirectly implicate the Saudi regime, which was increasingly seen as a regime willing to offer *i'ana* (assistance) to Americans during their war on Afghanistan. American military bases in Saudi Arabia were being discussed as possible places from which to launch attacks on Afghanistan.

Al-Fahad's theoretical treatise was followed by a scathing attack on Sahwi *ulama* and intellectuals who after 11 September declared the establishment of al-Himla al-Alamiyya li Muqawamat al-Idwan (International Campaign to Resist Aggression), with the Sahwi sheikhs leading the campaign, defined as peaceful resistance against American aggression on Muslims using *da'wa* methods. Al-Fahad was specifically concerned with *Bayan al-muthaqqafin* (The Declaration of Intellectuals), which called for dialogue with American intellectuals. In a pamphlet entitled *Taliat al tankil bi ma fi bay'an al-muthaqafin min al-abatil* (Early Disparaging Attack on the Wrongs of the Intellectuals' Manifesto), al-Fahad declared that the Saudi *ulama* and intellectuals who signed the petition expressed 'defeat, humiliation, begging and demonstration of love towards the infidels'.[22] He mentions an early lecture by Salman al-Awdah entitled 'Why They Fear Islam', in which he stated the centrality of *jihad* against infidels. Al-Fahad rejects peaceful resistance and reiterates the importance of *jihad* against those who undermine Islam. His attack on Sahwa *ulama* centres on the way they abandoned their early message and instruction to Muslims, well documented in pamphlets, cassettes and public lectures. In a tone reminiscent of a student respectfully reprimanding his teachers, al-Fahad asserts that media campaigns and international treatises failed to achieve what was accomplished by the bombing of the Marines in Beirut (1983) and the Mogadishu violence; both used language that the infidels understand.

Al-Fahad asserts that there is no difference between the Soviet occupation of Afghanistan in the early 1980s and the 2001 war on the same country by the United States. He questions the argument that the first occupation required resistance through *jihad* while the latter did not. He argues that the only difference is that the 2001 situation is a battle against Americans, to which Muslim governments have become subservient. Citing Western journalists in the *Daily Telegraph* and the *Sunday Times*, al-Fahad concludes that it is a crusade against Muslims and the Wahhabiyya. Any reluctance, therefore, in helping the Taliban to resist the American invasion becomes a specific religious duty (*fard 'ayn*) on the Afghans themselves and a complementary obligation (*fard kifaya*) on other capable Muslims. This leads him to question the argument that 'we [possibly a reference to Saudis] cannot join the *jihad* in Afghanistan because we have a treaty (*mithaq*) with the United States'. Resisting the War on Terror, which started in Afghanistan, is a defensive *jihad* (*jihad al-daf'*), the best and most noble form of struggle in the way of God. In this specific context permission from the leader of the Muslim community is not even a necessary prerequisite. Afghanistan on the eve of the American invasion was a context that required the privatisation of *jihad*. The struggle in the way of God becomes the prerogative of individual Muslims as li Muqawamat take matters into their own hands.

We have seen how Jihadi interpretations of the relationship between Muslims and infidels, exemplified by al-Fahad's treatise on *isti'ana* (assistance), represents a blueprint for an understanding of international relations from a specific Islamic point of view. In this interpretation, there is no room for realpolitik, compromise or negotiation, at least in al-Fahad's approach. His theory offers three possible relationships, two of which are either blasphemous or can lead to blasphemy. Embedded in this theory is the obligation to make *jihad* rather than peace, the latter being a prerogative of Muslim compassionate behaviour towards non-enemy infidels. Using the pressing issue of the *shari'a* position on those who assist infidels, he develops the conclusion that resistance is not sufficient, but that in fact attack is compulsory in Islam. The argument draws on an intellectual genealogy, starting with the Quran, Hadith and both early and later religious scholars. Al-Fahad demonstrates that the centrality of excommunicating those who assist infidels is stressed not only by Muslim scholars worldwide but by the scholars of the Wahhabi reform movement, to which he devotes a whole chapter. The justification for violence against those who assist infidels becomes self-evident and a logical conclusion to be drawn from this treatise. Al-Fahad's book shows that in general violence is systematic and is always governed by rules and replete with meanings.[23]

Al-Fahad's views on assisting Americans and the blasphemy that constitutes such an act mirrors his opinion on a wide range of political, social, religious and sectarian issues. He dedicated several treatises to countering what he calls *shubuhat* (doubtful, misguided statements and opinions) of a whole range of scholars and communities. For example, his refutations of the claims of dead scholars (Ibrahim ibn Musa al-Shatibi al-Maliki) and contemporary ones (Sheikhs Yusif Qaradawi and Hasan al-Maliki), in addition to his Responsa to Shi'is, Sufis and Zaydis reflect his endorsement of a specific meaning of *jihad* as a total struggle against opponents, Muslims or otherwise.[24] Al-Fahad is a strong believer in the totality of Islam and its ability to provide a meaningful framework for life, and guidance on causes as noble as defending the land of Islam and faith and as small as the permissibility of using hair dye, false eyelashes, internet chat rooms and video cassettes. While it is easy to condemn al-Fahad as a radical preacher, whose words may inspire violence and terrorism and whose religious interpretations are uncompromising, it is difficult not to acknowledge that his views resonate with a substantial section of Saudi society. It is also difficult to situate his religious convictions within contemporary social scientific paradigms where the sacred is relegated to the realm of irrationality, obscurity and mystification. Al-Fahad's discourse is neither irrational nor obscure. He aims to demystify a whole range of 'misguided positions' that have replaced authentic tradition. His approach to religious interpretation reflects a desire to reform the reform movement after it has been 'corrupted'. His intellectual genealogy is neither contemporary nor foreign; yet he is totally immersed in modernity, and willing to engage in interpreting it and responding to its challenges. Although his intellectual roots have become dormant in modern times under the pressure of politics and prosperity, his discourse has erupted into both the local public sphere and the wider world, thanks to new communication technology and the internet. Saudi religious discourse was transnationalised at a time when it was not so ready for such exposure. This premature publicity is primarily responsible for accelerating the confrontation not only between Saudis but also with outsiders. Al-Fahad revisits well-known intellectual grounds, but links old arguments to contemporary concerns.

As al-Fahad's contribution to the religio-political debate through his website and electronic pamphlets came to an abrupt end with his arrest in Madina in May 2003, the struggle in the way of God at home took a nasty turn with the eruption of violence in 2003–4 and the announcement of the establishment of an al-Qa'ida branch in the Arabian Peninsula.

The struggle in the way of God in the Arabian Peninsula

While religious scholars such as al-Fahad and others wrote treatises on *jihad*, association with infidels and excommunication, the struggle in the way of God at home produced a media campaign, not only to introduce the practitioners of the duty and its ideologues, but also to win new recruits for the cause. Above all, the Jihadi media campaign was meant to defend *jihad* against a religious background which obliged Muslims to obey the ruler, even if he is unjust, in order to safeguard against chaos, death and discord among Muslims. The internet was the most popular medium, especially after Jihadi ideologues went underground, were sent to prison or died in regular confrontations between security forces and what the regime called 'suspected cells' or 'wanted al-Qa'ida activists'. Theoreticians of *jihad* expressed their views in a bimonthly magazine, *Sawt al-Jihad* (The Voice of *Jihad*), the mouthpiece of al-Qa'ida in the Arabian Peninsula. Words, images and iconography were combined to depict an organised underground movement, with a regular media outlet.[25] Furthermore, the magazine became the arena in which biographies and obituaries of the 'heroes of *jihad*' were published. The magazine, its writers and readers constituted a community joined in faith and strengthened by theological arguments.[26] On the pages of the magazine, *jihad* is celebrated in images, iconography and poetry targeting the hearts of its readers. With *Sawt al-Jihad*, the struggle became an integrated cultural whole, combining religion, politics, literature and art. While the appearance of the magazine on the internet is heavily censored and curtailed, electronic links leading to the latest issue continue to appear on discussion boards. In such an atmosphere of censorship, it becomes the duty of *al-qa'idun* (the sitting ones), i.e. those who have not joined the *jihad* for some reason, to disseminate the links to the 'voice of *jihad*'.

One of the most important functions this magazine performed was to defend the arrival of *jihad* on home soil, especially after the eruption of violence. After the Riyadh bombings of May and November 2003, a detailed document, *The Flowing Spring in Supporting Jihad in Riyadh*, edited by Saleh bin Saad al-Hasan, an alias, was published on the *Sawt al-Jihad* website.[27] It included several contributions in defence of the Riyadh bombings and in support of the theological grounds according to which such attacks were carried out. The rationale behind such publication is explained as 'dismissing the ignorant and misguided opinions of people who are now judging *jihad*. Those people do not speak with knowledge but insult our Jihadis. Despite the Saudi campaign against our Jihadis, many of whom are in hiding or in prison, God allowed justice to appear at the hands of real men who dismiss the obscurantism of the misguided people.' It is claimed that the book is the unfinished project of one important Jihadi sheikh, Yusif al-Ayri, who died in 2003. Other contributions are by Jihadis who use a mixture of aliases: tribal (Barghash ibn Tuwala); regional (Bashir al-Najdi; Abu Bashar al-Hijazi); with Islamic connotations (Abu Abdullah al-Muhajir (the Immigrant)); and invoking modern political meanings (al-Hizbi al-Mutasatir (the Hidden Party Member). These names could well be the *noms de guerre* of a single Jihadi. All contributors anchor their personae in names that resonate with a wide circle of readers by invoking tribal affiliation, Islamic heritage, regional flavour or political modernity. In addition to support from theological treatises anchored in Quran, Hadith and sayings of *'ulama*, *jihad* is an act that requires the mobilisation of passions, religious duty and tribal honour, all in the context of modernity. The propaganda of *Sawt al-Jihad* is not only meant to arouse a passionate desire to guard faith and nation, but also to celebrate and document the lives of those who die in pursuit of the ultimate death: martyrdom.

Sheikh Yusif al-Ayri (killed by Saudi security forces) is introduced as the founder of Markaz al-Dirasat wa al-Buhuth al-Islamiyya (the Centre for Islamic Study and Research) and the author of several Jihadi treatises. Sheikh al-Ayri, thought to have been the leader of al-Qa'ida in the Arabian Peninsula until his death in the summer of 2003, immediately after the first major Riyadh bombing in May, provides the basis for refuting the official anti-Jihadi opinion of Saudi *'ulama* which dominated public debate. He explains the rationale for bringing *jihad* to the Arabian Peninsula, especially after official Saudi *'ulama* justified it abroad – for example, in Palestine, Afghanistan, Chechnya and other locations – while forbidding it at home. Al-Ayri asks why *jihad* abroad is an unlimited good but is considered a cause of corruption at home. He questions why such official Saudi *'ulama* consider *jihad* a source of discord and a crime in the Arabian Peninsula, where in his opinion the conditions requiring it (both *daf'* (defensive) and *talab* (offensive) are present. Al-Ayri dismisses the opinion of the *'ulama*, both official and the so-called Sahwis, as biased, and gives several reasons for doing so. First, opinions given under threat of state violence are invalid and biased. Second, most *fatwas* against *jihad* were issued in accordance with commands from the Ministry of the Interior. Third, control of the media in Saudi Arabia prevents any unbiased consideration of *jihad*. Fourth, the Ministry of the Interior remains the only source allowed to report on the number of dead and their identity after each round of violence, in which the Ministry mistakenly claims that victims are Muslims. Fifth, the *'ulama* cannot solve the contradiction embedded in forbidding *jihad* in Saudi Arabia and commanding it elsewhere while the conditions necessitating it remain the same. Al-Ayri describes the context in which religious opinion is sought and how this context undermines the legitimacy of such opinions. He is a Salafi-turned-modernist as he 'situates' and 'contextualises' religious opinions and *fatwas*. He draws attention to the political pressure exerted on the *ʿulama* by the state in order to compromise religious judgement and produce opinions in support of state policy.

After this introduction, another author elaborates on the *shariʿa* evidence in support of the legitimacy of the violent events in Riyadh. This elaboration is presented as a response to a series of questions, drawn from current official religious and political rhetoric in condemnation of *jihad* at home. Sheikh Bashir al-Najdi refutes each question as if it was *shubuha* (a doubtful or misguided statement). The collection of erroneous statements revolves around the legitimacy of killing people with whom there is a contractual relationship requiring peace, for example civilians, women and children. He denounces other misguided statements presented to him as questions relating to the duty to announce the suspension of peaceful treaties before attacking; attacking without having been attacked first; precipitating chaos and internal discord; and undermining local peace and order. These are arguments that had dominated Saudi public debate in the media and in religious circles, all aiming to undermine the rationale of local *jihad*, and defeat Jihadis religiously, politically and morally. Sheikh al-Najdi deconstructs each *shubuha*, using proof from the Quran, sayings of the Prophet and those of religious scholars such as Ibn Taymmiyya and Ibn al-Qayyim.

On the idea that attacking American civilians in Saudi Arabia is illegitimate because they are under the protection of the Muslim ruler, Sheikh al-Najdi refuses to recognise that the Saudi king is a legitimate Muslim ruler and that Westerners in Saudi Arabia are peaceful, protected citizens. In his opinion, the regime's support for the West and its internal policies (he cites Western-style banking and moral corruption as examples) removes the ruler, often referred to as the imam, from the category of rightful Muslim rulers. 'I do not know where this imam is', says Sheikh al-Najdi. He claims that the current imam is senile (a reference to the ageing King Fahd) and unable to rule, but that the official *ʿulama* refuse to recognise his mental disability and act accordingly – that is, practise *khalʿ* (forcibly removing a ruler from office by withdrawing the oath of allegiance), an act that in the Sunni tradition is required in the case of an illegitimate or incapacitated imam. He argues that the Saudi regime cannot give *aman* (peace) to the people of the book (*ahl al-dhimma*) because it is not an Islamic government. In fact, he says that the regime pursues policies in support of the infidel's agenda rather than of its own Muslim people, citing Saudi cooperation with America in its war on Afghanistan in 2001, sanctioning Iraq throughout the 1990s and providing support for the invasion in 2003.

Furthermore, America's aggression towards Muslims in Palestine, Afghanistan and Iraq means that both the government and its citizens are legitimate targets for retaliation. In Sheikh al-Najdi's words, Americans are *harbi* (an aggressive nation). His argument reiterates that of Nasir al-Fahad who outlined the type of permissible relations with infidels. He concludes that Americans in Saudi Arabia do not qualify for *mu'amalat ja'iza*, that legal Islamic treatment preserved for non-aggressive infidels living in the land of Islam. On the question of Western women and children falling victims, he asserts that killing innocent people is illegitimate, but if they cannot be separated from the enemy, then killing them cannot be considered prohibited. It is an unintended act of murder that accompanies the deaths of those intended as the targets of the attack.

The killing of Muslims in the violence that erupted in Saudi Arabia also needed a religious opinion – not to defend it but to justify a necessary evil, in Sheikh al-Najdi's words. Against a background of revulsion and absolute prohibition on Muslims murdering Muslims, Sheikh al-Najdi faces a difficult if not impossible task – how to convince other Muslims that under certain conditions there is no escape from this tragic act of unintended murder, in modern parlance 'collateral damage'. The question whether a Muslim can kill a fellow Muslim who declares that 'there is no God but Allah and Muhammad is his Prophet' is one of the most problematic theological issues Jihadis faced after the outbreak of violence in general and the attack on the Saudi security forces in particular. This question is neither new nor resolved. Furthermore, the issue of *diya* (blood money) and *kaffara* (compensation for sinful acts) becomes problematic too. If Jihadis kill other Muslims unintentionally, are they under the obligation to pay these penalties? Sheikh al-Najdi endeavours to clarify the *shubuha* related to this complex matter. According to him, it should be dealt with under questions of *ta'wil* (interpretation of concealed meanings) and *ijtihad* (the application of reason to a religious ruling). After citing several situations involving early Muslims, *al-salaf* (the pious ancestors) whereby such unlawful killing of Muslims took place and the response of the Prophet to such acts, Sheikh al-Najdi concludes that Jihadis cannot be 'criminalised' because they did not intend to kill Muslims. Muslims killed unintentionally are considered martyrs in this specific situation. However, if they are accomplices in corruption, sin and immorality and have chosen to live with the infidels, they deserve to be fought and killed. They have become a shield for infidels and as such they themselves are wrongdoers. In a situation where good Muslims cannot be segregated from non-Muslims, Jihadis do not commit a sin by killing fellow Muslims, according to Sheikh al-Najdi: 'There is a consensus among the *ulama* that if we cannot reach non-Muslims without falling into the sin of killing Muslims, then this is permissible (*ja'iz*), as long as we fear for the lives of Muslims.'

As Jihadis brought the battle to Saudi Arabia, they unveiled a dormant schism between themselves and other contemporary *ulama* and Islamist intellectuals, whom they considered a group that would at least remain silent rather than condemn them. As the struggle in the way of God came home, Jihadis clashed with Sahwis, who not only sided with the government and official *ulama* but also endeavoured to delegitimise the project of Jihadis, by providing religious evidence proving their *dhalal* (obscurity), misguided interpretation of the duty of Jihad and other issues. While violence claimed lives in streets and residential compounds, another intellectual battle was raging on the internet between Jihadis and Sahwis.

Jihadis and Sahwis: 'the years of deceit'

While al-Fahad's treatise discussed above presented religious evidence in support of contemporary political positions, such as the question of assistance and the legitimacy of *jihad* in the Arabian Peninsula, another genre of writing has entered the public sphere, both in defence of *jihad* and in response to contemporary developments within the Islamist camp: the position of Sahwis vis-à-vis Jihadis after the events of 11 September. Jihadis debate the new 'un-Islamic' position taken by Sahwis against Jihadis and their condemnation of any violent resistance. According to Jihadis, Sahwis changed their position for political reasons. Instead of either remaining 'neutral' or celebrating and blessing the attacks, they chose to openly condemn Jihadis. Furthermore, Sahwis opted for 'peaceful' resistance to Western domination under the pretext of inequality in military power and in the absence of an Imam under whose flag *jihad* becomes legitimate. Jihadis endeavoured to overturn what they called a pragmatic and defeatist political position.

In an electronic pamphlet entitled, *Sanawat khada'a: dirasa li waqi' al-sahwa* (The Years of Deceit: A Study of the Reality of Sahwa Preachers), Yahya al-Ghamdi contributes to the debate between Jihadis and Sahwis to correct what he calls 'contradictions' in the approach and position of the latter at a time when a unified position among Muslims is more than urgent.[28] The book, written in a highly accessible non-religious tone, is a message to

the preachers whom God did not honour with breathing the air of Qandahar, Kabul, Grozny, or Jericho. To those whom God did not choose to carry the message on the heads of swords [Sahwis]. Today such preachers should at least support their Jihadi brothers with money, word, supplication, and all meagre means available to those under the rule of despots.

While the treatise addresses preachers, in fact it speaks to young Muslim men with no deep religious learning, many of whom are internet surfers looking for inspiration, assurance and allegiance. It criticises Sahwis by citing the Quran and the Prophetic tradition, together with classical Arabic poetry. It situates religious references within the context of international relations, and the words of George Bush, Safar al-Hawali, Sayyid Qutb and Osama bin Laden. The text is a pastiche, transmitted using the latest electronic communication technology. At the heart of this creation is the conflict between *murabitun* (those with experience of the battleground) and *qa'idun*. The latter are called the armchair theoreticians (*munathirun*), who have lost contact with reality and are awaiting visits by important Western journalists to assure the West that Muslims are determined to prevent future attacks on New York and elsewhere – a reference to a controversial interview with Safar al-Hawali, conducted by Thomas Friedman. Al-Ghamdi laments the Sahwis' failure to achieve excellence even in their stated field, education and the call to Islam.

Al-Ghamdi exposes the rhetoric of such Sahwis and deconstructs the rationale behind their alleged change of opinion, citing early recorded lectures by important figures in the Sahwi camp. He laments the changing perspective of Sahwis, who initially promoted a discourse in support of Jihadis, but later adopted a theoretical interpretation justifying the reluctance of *qa'idun* (those who do not participate). This change followed their experience in prison during the 1990s, which resulted – in his opinion – in complete disorientation. Al-Ghamdi attacks the inner logic of Sahwis which concentrates on the illegitimacy of *jihad* in the current context of the Islamic world. Sahwis argue that *jihad* is pointless where there is such a great military discrepancy between Muslims and 'infidels', and preaching Islam to re-Islamise society is therefore more fruitful. Furthermore, *jihad* is permissible only under the flag of a ruler. These views are strongly refuted by al-Ghamdi, who promotes an understanding of *jihad* as a compulsory duty, necessitated by the 'attack on the land of Muslims', i.e. by the United States and its allies, mainly Israel. He questions the claim that Muslims need a ruler to declare *jihad*, and laments that neither King Fahd nor President Mubarak – or any other 'Muslim' ruler – qualifies for the office of Rightful Imam, whose flag is a necessary precondition for announcing *jihad*. In terms of war strategy, al-Ghamdi argues that historically wars are not declared and fought because those who declare them are assured of victory. But he adds, 'Have the Sahwis forgotten that God is the source of victory?' The Sahwis, in his opinion, prejudge *jihad* as a failure before asking whether their so-called peaceful resistance has achieved any of its stated objectives. If ever they state that the confrontation with the West did not achieve anything apart from tarnishing the image of Islam and portraying Muslims as bloodthirsty terrorists, al-Ghamdi argues that no God-fearing religious scholar would suspend *jihad* in the present circumstances when all evidence supports the duty to resist Western domination. *Jihad* is an individual duty, prescribed to every Muslim (*fard 'ayn*), rather than a duty for a selected few (*fard kifaya*). He calls for the privatisation of *jihad* in the age of globalisation. Furthermore, *jihad* without an Imam embodies the articulation of individual duty in the face of the defeatism of the Muslim rulers. The argument is sealed with lines of poetry stating that the sword is mightier than the pen.

Al-Ghamdi refers to an important factor behind the 'defeatist' Sahwi position. He argues that God has burdened the *'ulama* with a serious defect, namely *hasad* (envy). The Sahwis could not, in his opinion, compete with Jihadis, who captured the hearts and minds of Saudi youth, especially after the successful 'raids on New York, Bali, Riyadh and other locations'. The jealousy and envy in their hearts were expressed in their condemnation of Jihadis, who proved their ability to attack and cripple the enemy, at least precipitating fear and chaos, if not victory. Al-Ghamdi points at how jealousy motivated *'ulama al-sultan* (the religious establishment) to attack the Sahwis, whose star was rising in the 1990s, but now the Sahwi *'ulama* have themselves succumbed to the 'burning feeling of jealousy and envy'. Competition over religious interpretation is a reflection of competition over status, prestige and popularity. There is no doubt that Sahwis and Jihadis fight a fierce battle over these 'worldly' matters. Religious knowledge is symbolic capital, which guarantees a material reward under the auspices of the Saudi state, especially if such knowledge confirms the legitimacy of the state. The Sahwis thought that their popularity – which had been gained at a time when Saudis, especially the young, were desperate for validating a discourse that is obviously antagonistic to both the religious establishment and political authority, in addition of course to Western hegemony in the region – was irreversible. However, after 2001, they lost some of their previous prestige, especially when they appeared to accommodate the regime. Al-Ghamdi subjects the *'ulama*, both established and Sahwis, to a sociological analysis, which takes into account political manoeuvring, group interest and relations with the centre of power. The *'ulama* as a group are no longer only a class with a special status derived from interpreting the sacred text. In fact, al-Ghamdi reduces them to a worldly group subject to human instincts and interests, which are constantly changing in response to a changing political context. The Jihadis regard the Sahwis as having joined the ranks of official *ulama* in their submission to the political authorities.

The poetics of *jihad*: body and soul

If *Sawt al-Jihad* is concerned with religious interpretations in support of *jihad* and the preparation of the minds of Jihadis, another electronic publication *Muaskar al-Battar* (al-Battar Camp), a military magazine issued by al-Qa'ida, prepares the body for such an endeavour.[29] According to the editors of this magazine, 'young Muslims do not know how to bear arms, not to mention how to use them . . . your Jihadi brothers in the Arabian Peninsula have decided to publish this booklet to serve young men in their place of isolation. They will do the exercises and act according to the military knowledge included.' It is the condition of the privatisation of *jihad*, now a duty to be performed in isolation and on the basis of private individual initiative, in the absence of a leader to carry its flag, that has given rise to the publication of *Muaskar al-Battar*. The editors insist that 'during the times of the Mongol invasion, it did not help the residents of Baghdad that most of them were *ulama* and educators'.

The Jihadis believe that the body is a vehicle, which needs to be nurtured in order to fulfil the duty. In one issue of the magazine, Sheikh Yusif al-Ayri recognises that modernity has its drawbacks, experienced at the level of the body. Obesity, the disease of the age, is a real obstacle undermining the performance of contemporary Jihadis, and as such it should be fought with a vigorous exercise routine and diet. Al-Ayri's diet is based on a balanced calorie count, resembling any diet found in books dealing with obesity and how to control it. The sheikh outlines the details of three daily meals – breakfast, lunch and dinner. The first meal of the day, *iftar* (breakfast), consists of a small amount of brown bread with butter, a glass of orange or grapefruit juice, a boiled egg and coffee or tea without sugar. The midday meal consists of soup, cheese or butter, a slice of bread, chicken or fish, salad and fruit. Finally, the evening meal is a light dinner of fish or chicken, tomato juice, half a loaf of bread, boiled potatoes, one piece of fruit and coffee or tea without sugar. Al-Ayri warns against excess consumption of red meat – beef or lamb – full-fat cheese and milk, white bread and excessive sugary fruits.

The Jihadi diet is extremely modern. It overlooks traditional cuisine and culinary tastes. In a society known for the regular consumption of rice and lamb, Sheikh al-Ayri proposes revolutionising eating habits in pursuit of *jihad*. In order to defeat obesity, the modern disease, Jihadis must subject their bodies to a strict – and modern – routine.

Diet must be accompanied by an exercise routine, bringing to mind the most advanced training often associated with gymnasiums and sports centres where the body sweats in pursuit of beauty, health and perfection. A weekly exercise routine is proposed. It involves warming-up exercises for five minutes, followed by jogging for thirty-nine minutes. The time is gradually increased to reach fifty minutes in the sixth week of the programme. While this ensures the maintenance of body weight for the average person, a different, more advanced, six-step exercise programme must be followed by those already overweight. This consists of walking for five kilometres, twenty abdomen exercises, twenty chest exercises, climbing stairs, swimming and cycling. Al-Ayri warns against excessive exercise for those who are not trained properly. Instead of doing all exercises in one day, he proposes a gradual introduction of each activity over a long period of time. His advice to Jihadis is perseverance in following the routine because 'God prefers persistent acts even if they are not numerous'. The will to fight obesity with diet and exercise is seen as sanctioned by God and required in order to prepare the body for *jihad*. A Jihadi must not only be anchored in faith and perseverance, he must also be fit for the acts required from him.

Al-Ayri says that orders and instructions can be dry and lacking in inspiration. For this reason, instructions relating to military and physical training must be interspersed with poetry, whose ultimate purpose is to 'enter the ears of Jihadis and find its way to their heart'. Only then will they respond to the call for *jihad*. In a short section entitled A Poetic Station, *Muaskar al-Battar* uses the power of rhyming words to inspire its readers. Here the magazine talks to the hearts in a way that invokes the poetics of *jihad*, as a break from long sections outlining military training, illustrated with pictures of deadly weapons.

In one poem, a Jihadi describes his journey as one with a clear destination and path.[30] This journey is illuminated by 'death, dancing at every junction'. The dancing death is sought with courage rather than cowardice, as a Jihadi never fears his destiny. Neither 'thorns' nor 'upheavals' deter him from continuing the journey as his weapon is always his determination and passion for *jihad*. The Jihadi is presented as a sword, whose shining edge exceeds the light of the sun, and those of Indian swords. He seeks heaven to satisfy his burning desire for shelter in shaded, lavish gardens. The loss of other Jihadis torments him but he expects to meet them in heaven. He has grown tired of this world with all its trappings. In response, he found the road and well of God, which guide the believer, who draws knowledge and guidance from both. He responded by 'flying to seek the way of God', despite people's call to deter him. People called upon him to stop but God called upon him to join the battle without fear or hesitation. He concludes his poem by saying that he will proceed, even alone, and despite those defeatists who ask him to remain behind. In this poem, the poetic of Jihad anchors the activity in the realm of meaningful and significant behaviour that resonate culturally, religiously and politically with a wide range of people.

Jihadi discourse encompasses a wide range of meanings. It situates *jihad* in religious interpretations, thus anchoring the duty in *shari'a* sources, as well as in analysis of world politics and international affairs, technical military training, pragmatic instructions preparing the body and poetic illuminations to create a cultural whole that is meant to appeal to both mind and soul. In such presentations, violence is no longer an isolated act with a single purpose, whether 'expelling the infidels from the Arabian Peninsula' or simply fighting the despots who do not rule according to the revealed message of God. *Jihad* is theoretically and religiously justified, militarily explained and poetically disseminated, thus creating a culture that is difficult to defeat because it evokes multiple layers of reason and faith, political awareness and international relations, and emotions and values. It plays on local and global identities, and national and religious sentiments.

Celebrations of life and death: *jihad* as performance

In a world dominated by media representations, Jihadis seem to be well prepared for disseminating powerful messages, iconography and sounds, thus satisfying a world hungry for images of death, destruction and devastation. Through several media organisations, one of which is known as Muassasat al-Sahab lil Intaj al-Ilami (Sahab Media Production), the world can see dozens of films of Jihadis in training-camps, preparing for the struggle in the way of God. While the majority of this media production is found on the internet, through links to several sites, some important films and video clips are sent to established Arab media satellite stations such as the Qatar-based al-Jazeera channel. Films are also available for purchase from commercial companies, for example Tempest Publishing, a sister organisation of IntelCentre, a Washington-based company whose stated objective is 'to assist professionals to understand and fight terrorism'. This company sells films, CD-ROMs, documents and other material related to *jihad* and terrorism to researchers, journalists, and military and security agencies.[31] Most of the items on the sale catalogue seem to be produced by al-Qa'ida, including the Arabian Peninsula branch.

One controversial film called *Badr al-Riyadh* (The Full Moon of Riyadh, a reference to the 12 May 2003 Riyadh attack), named after the battle of Badr between Muslims and Meccans, was broadcast several months after the Riyadh bombing. According to Jihadi sources, between three and four hundred thousand people downloaded the film from the internet in less than five days.[32] To understand *Badr al-Riyadh*, three important dimensions must be considered. First is the two martyrs. Second are other actors, some meant to inspire and encourage viewers – most importantly Osama bin Laden, Abu Hafs al-Masri, Humud ibn Oqla al-Shuaybi and al-Khattab, *jihad* leader in Chechnya – while others are projected as the 'malicious other', against whom the battle is waged. This category of people includes George Bush, Crown Prince Abdullah, and Minister of Interior Prince Nayef. Third, the film's message is embedded in words and acts.

This film was perhaps one of the most powerful media productions issued by Saudi Jihadis, for a number of reasons. It showed the suicide bombers of the attack of 12 May, Ali al-Harbi and Nasir al-Khaldi, in an unusual location, a private house with a sitting-room lined with comfortable cushions and colourful rugs, rather than a military camp with barbed wires and signposts. The cosy setting is a contrast to that often projected in other al-Qa'ida films with Jihadis filmed in training camps, caves and rugged mountains. Furthermore, the film portrayed the would-be martyrs in an important event that sealed their fate, *zaffat al-shahid* celebration of the martyr. The word *zaffa* is usually associated with weddings as in *zaffat al-'arus* (bride) or *'aris* (bridegroom), a common celebration which takes place within the context of Muslim and Arab weddings. The future martyrs, al-Harbi and al-Khaldi, are celebrated in a televised *zaffa* as if they are bridegrooms.[33] They are also shown in what looks like a garage where several Jihadis engage in preparing the vehicle, a jeep, for the attack. They are seen painting the jeep and changing its number plate to AZ H 314. A Jihadi explains that 314 is the number of the early Muslim fighters who participated in the battle of Badr with the Prophet.

Badr al-Riyadh documents an event best understood as a celebration of life and death interspersed with young men dancing and chanting while sporting a range of weapons around waists, shoulders and arms. The martyrs, with their bearded smiling faces completely uncovered and with their hair longer than is usual for young Saudi men, dressed in white long shirts, were filmed surrounded by a large number of hooded young men, dancing and reciting verses from the Quran and other sources. An unseen interviewer asks the would-be martyrs several questions. A sense of camaraderie and solidarity is enhanced by images of the central actors surrounded by supporters and well-wishers.

Although the film shows a celebration of the deaths of the would-be martyrs, they are seen while still alive, and partake in the jubilation. The celebration of life and death and the theme of martyrdom portrayed in the film confirm Jihadism as a theatrical performance, in which actors and audience are expected to fuse in a powerful emotional bond. While it is common for societies all over the world to separate birth and death rituals, in *Badr al-Riyadh* the boundaries overlap and are even blurred. In a single rite of passage, a Jihadi passes from life to death, then he returns to life. Death is projected as a temporary liminal phase, neither here nor there, culminating in returning to life. The theme of life and death is best expressed in a song which accompanies the celebration. The song asks participants to 'celebrate the passage of the martyr to his second home in heaven', and 'to celebrate his passage to the afterlife fully clothed, according to the tradition of the Prophet'. Al-Harbi explains that martyrdom is a transaction: God buys the soul of his slave (a human being), who sells it willingly. In a sombre voice, with his head down and his eyes fixed on the floor rather than the camera, al-Harbi recognises that the martyr may be hesitant to leave his family, friends and loved ones, but one is under an obligation to perform the noble deed, which is prescribed after the five pillars of Islam. Al-Harbi explains that death is defined as leaving life (*mufaraqat al-hayat*), but the martyr has another life in heaven. Death is a transition from life in a treacherous world to life in a generous world, where the Prophet and his companions reside. He also invokes the inevitability of death, whether 'in bed' or 'in a car accident'. Given this inevitability, he asks a rhetorical question: 'Isn't it more noble to die for the sake of God?'

The martyrs appear in the context of an interview by a fellow Jihadi, who asks them questions relating to *shari'a* evidence in support of suicide attacks, the purpose of *jihad*, the target of their actions, and their views on the USA, the Saudi state, the *'ulama* and the security forces. The interviewer brings to their attention some of the accusations of the Saudi media and officials, which portray Jihadis as killing Muslims and generating chaos in the land of the two holy mosques. The two martyrs are expected to defend the planned suicide attack on Mustawtanat al-Muhayya (the al-Muhayya settlement), a reference to a residential compound mostly occupied by expatriates. Al-Harbi invokes the terminology of 'settlement' to allude to similarities between Jewish settlements in Palestine and foreign residential compounds, inhabited by Americans and Europeans, in Saudi Arabia. The objective of the attack revolves around liberating the Arabian Peninsula from infidels, the establishment of an Islamic state, and revenge for Jihadis who are tortured in Saudi prisons or killed by Saudi security forces, such as Turki al-Dandani and Yusif al-Ayri. The martyrs lament the current transformation of the Arabian Peninsula from a land where the message of *tawhid* (monotheism) spread to other parts of the world to one from which infidel armies launch attacks, *himla salibiyya* (a crusade), on Afghanistan and Iraq.

While the general message of the *jihad* and its purpose reflect well-rehearsed arguments put forward by Bin Laden and other Jihadi ideologues, both al-Harbi and al-Khaldi fuse the grand Jihadi narrative with personal experience, life history and individual motivation. Asked why he does not go for *jihad* in areas where there is clear argument in favour of the practice, al-Harbi inserts his own personal narrative as one of the primary motivating factors behind his determination to annihilate himself. He explains that the Saudi state is a *kafir* state, practising *nifaq* (hypocrisy). While the state claims that it supports Muslim causes, it punishes those who serve their religion. He went to fight in Bosnia in the 1990s, and when he returned to Saudi Arabia he was imprisoned for one year and three months. He claims that he was tortured, left in a small cell, deprived of sleep and paraded naked in al-Ruways prison. He was shocked by both the torture of Jihadi prisoners, as a result of which some died, and the verbal abuse experienced in prison. He concludes the narrative of his personal journey to seek death by asking, 'Which Islam is this?'

The second suicide bomber narrates another personal journey. Al-Khaldi recounts several incidents whereby he and his comrades came face to face with Saudi security forces. One encounter took place in Istirahat al-Shifa where a social gathering of Jihadis was taking place. According to al-Khaldi, they were listening to lectures and engaging in recitations when armed security men attacked them. A friend died in the encounter as he was shot by security forces – for no obvious reason, according to the narrator.

In addition to the main suicide bombers, the film invokes the words of famous ideologues. Osama bin Laden's speeches, together with those of his aides, such as Abu Hafs al-Masri, and Saudi religious scholars, such as Sheikh Humud al-Oqla, provide powerful words inspiring not only the would be-martyrs but a wider circle of viewers as well. The message is to demonise and terrorise the enemy. In a clear declaration, the voice states, 'Yes I am a terrorist,' against a background of chanting:

> Crush the Pharaoh with the sorcerers
> Kill whoever is an infidel
> Make your land a graveyard
> For the defeated armies of blasphemy

If ever someone is in doubt of the meaning of terrorism, the chanting then explains:

> Prepare bows and arrows for blasphemy
> Prepare white swords

Take from our enemies red hearts and necks
Let blood flow on soil
Like a glorious river
Tell the world and repeat
This is the meaning of terrorism

The message of other characters in the film centres on the decriminalisa-
tion of the perpetrator and the humanisation of the martyr. The film blurs
the boundary between victim and victimiser, and deconstructs well-
rehearsed arguments against *jihad*. The various Jihadis in the film face the
challenge of responding to Saudi claims that they are criminals, lacking a
clear message, and in favour of killing other Muslims rather than infidels.
A Jihadi responds by asking how someone who spent twenty years
defending Muslims in Afghanistan against the Soviets can turn into a
criminal targeting Muslims. He adds that 'killing Muslims' in Saudi
Arabia would be easier than killing infidels, as the latter reside in well-
secured homes and are difficult to reach.

The film also demonises the other, the enemy, a group of world leaders
(such as George Bush), and Arab and Muslim local 'agents' of world
powers (for example, Crown Prince Abdullah and Interior Minister
Prince Nayef). Speeches by Saudi leaders are played as evidence of their
treason, and association with and subservience to infidels. In one speech,
the Crown Prince is reported as saying to George Bush that 'a small
minority (*al–fi'a al-dhalla*) poisoned our solid friendship and tarnished
the image of Islam, but we are determined to fight it with all our means.'
Al-Khalidi sends a message to Abdullah asking him to repent and stop
privileging secular intellectuals, and associating with infidels. If he does
not listen, then he faces the sword.

This film, like many other media clips that flood the internet after every
suicide bombing or attack, represents another dimension of contemporary *jihad*, which has so far escaped analysts and commentators. *Jihad* is
not only about theological treatises such as that of Sheikh Nasir al-Fahad
discussed earlier in this chapter. It is also not solely concerned with purifying the Arabian Peninsula and defeating its despots and pharaohs. *Jihad*
is a performance, celebrating heroes in a land where there are none. Saudi
youth are denied a symbol for defiance. Their local media is saturated
with old preachers calling for total obedience to the ruler, citing Quranic
verses and Hadiths discouraging individual opinion, initiative and interpretation. Such media productions require the viewer to submit, obey
and follow a single interpretation and worldview. Saudi youth surf the
internet, downloading *Badr al-Riyadh* and other al-Qa'ida productions in
search of rebellion, assertion of the self and individuality, against a well-
developed machinery whose main purpose is to censor not only the

internet but all alternative visions that may circulate in the public sphere. *Zaffat al-shahid* in *Badr al-Riyadh* is not only a celebration of life and death; it is also a ritual of rebellion and defiance, with a clear message reaching thousands of viewers. In the modern world, *jihad* is the performance par excellence. However, Jihadi films are today competing with another genre of video clips and popular culture productions that dominate Arab satellite music channels such as Prince al-Walid ibn Talal's controversial Rotana television channel. The latter proved to be extremely popular among young people not only in Saudi Arabia but in the Arab world as a whole.

Badr al-Riyadh glorifies a privatised *jihad* in a globalised world where the media create images of a monotonous world, repeat well-rehearsed arguments and promote one message, despite the fact that globalisation was expected to generate diversity and pluralism. At one level, globalisation did offer a glimpse of this hoped-for diversity, but at several others it suppressed local culture, authenticity and tradition. Jihadi discourse responds to the challenge of globalisation and its alleged discontents using the same weapon that is believed to threaten authentic tradition. The resurgence of Jihadi discourse and practice in Saudi Arabia should be understood as a local response to this globalisation. This is clearly demonstrated in Jihadi views on women, honour and shame, all believed to be under threat from the champions of the alleged globalised crusade of the unbelievers.

Gendered *jihad*: women, honour and shame

In Saudi society, women have always been viewed as symbols of the nation's piety, a barometer of its commitment to Islam and Arab tradition.[34] The state enforces this view as it polices public space under the guidance of the Committee for the Promotion of Virtue and Prohibition of Vice, in search of immoral behaviour, potentially generated by the sheer presence of women in the public sphere. Segregated, veiled women in black cloaks have become a symbol of identity in cities indistinguishable from any major cosmopolitan space in Dallas or Houston. On the one hand, the state claims to 'protect' women; it does so for its own purposes, mainly to assert its legitimacy as an Islamic state. Society also imitates the state in its obsession with restricting women, but for different reasons, mainly to guard against rapid change and alien intruders. Early in the twentieth century, the majority of Saudis perceived the presence of foreign immigrants as a necessary evil, needed to modernise the country in the absence of local skills and expertise. However, since the 1980s, this presence has become problematic – not only economically, but also culturally and politically. While economic dependence on foreign labour was grudgingly tolerated, reliance on American military assistance has generated heated debate.

Over a very short period of time, Saudi Arabia moved from a small-scale traditional society in the 1970s, in which face-to-face interaction was the norm, to a society inhabiting an urban space shared with a multinational population of Arab, Western and Asian immigrants, expatriates and workers, the majority of whom are male. Society responded to the challenge of hosting a substantial foreign population in several ways. It imposed strict segregation on its immigrant population, translated into lavish, and not-so–lavish, residential compounds and neighbourhoods where they were expected to live. It also imposed a strict code of behaviour, limiting interaction between Saudis and foreigners to the workplace, and revisited what is believed to be the last frontier in resisting penetration by the outside world: the female sphere. As a result, women paid a high price as they were seen as the last 'battlefield', to be defended, protected, sheltered, and even restricted, oppressed and excluded in pursuit of 'guarding' men's honour, and limiting the possibility of 'shame' being inflicted on men as a result of female behaviour or the violation of females by outsiders. Suddenly Saudi society became more restrictive in regulating the female sphere. While men tolerated contact with foreigners in the workplace, they did everything they could to restrict their own women's contact with outsiders, with the exception of course of Arab female teachers, instructors, doctors, nannies (in the case of wealthy women) and other indispensable outsiders, for example male drivers. Society allowed its women to be driven by foreigners, as their foreignness and low status guaranteed their inferiority to Saudi women, but restricted women from entering the public sphere, especially that which has become the sole domain of Saudi and other men. Women who previously worked in markets and fields, where they intermingled freely with men, had to be restrained as this public sphere turned into potentially hostile and alien space.

Instead of creating grounds for the amelioration of the status and rights of women, modernity led to greater restrictions on women. The state restricted female marriages to *ajnabi* (foreigners), a category that included foreign Arabs and Muslims. It also protected the strict sex segregation in the public sphere through its various law-enforcing agencies and modern technology. For example, modern communication technology has allowed strict segregation in universities, where female students see and communicate with male lecturers via videos. Children of women who married outsiders were denied nationality, thus excluding them from citizenship, the welfare state and its benefits. The state was an active agent in enforcing a restrictive code despite its apparent interest in the welfare and education of women. In 2006 new legislation required shops selling lingerie to employ women only, in a move to appease the rising Islamist discontent and ameliorate unemployment rates among women. Outspoken members of the Saudi religious establishment objected to enforcing the law. To resist female employment, they missed an opportunity to 'Islamise' the selling of female lingerie, a position that brings to mind their objections to female driving.

While the state used women as a token of its piety in a desperate attempt to enhance its own Islamic credentials, Jihadis considered women a token of their rebellion, defiance and assertion of Islamic identity, pride and autonomy. *Jihad* was not only an Islamic duty to defend the land of Islam but was also a gendered obligation to protect women from the onslaught of alien cultures, corrupting media, state oppression and Western penetration. In Jihadi discourse, *jihad* is not only a defence of Islam and Muslims but is also a resistance to local and global agents who violate men's honour and bring them shame through a systematic violation of Muslim women. Both American troops in Saudi Arabia and the Saudi state are portrayed as contributing to this violation. Examples of American 'aggression' draw on images from Afghanistan, Israel and Iraq. Israeli and American soldiers searching Muslim women at checkpoints and inside their homes give ample opportunities to illustrate the violation. Saudi state violation of women is represented through a portrayal of the state as an agent of moral corruption and secularisation via its support and sponsorship of a media empire that corrupts the youth of the nation. Jihadis claim that Saudi princes do not respect the Islamic tradition, but endeavour to normalise moral laxity, degeneration and sin. The Jiddah Economic Forums in which women participated in 2004 and 2005 brought about themes relating to the corrupting influence of the state. The picture of Madeleine Albright sitting on an armchair in the front row during the conference, unveiled and with her legs exposed, came to represent not only the 'corruption and moral degeneration' of an 'American Jewish women' but also the Saudi state. The fact that Saudi women attend these conferences and are now allowed to participate in for example the Jiddah Chamber of Commerce and Industry as voters and candidates gives more substance to Jihadi claims.

In Jihadi discourse the politics of defiance is not only anchored in Islamic duty, it is deeply rooted in the discourse about women, honour and shame. A recurrent theme centres on the association between subservience to infidels and the violation of Muslim women. The local despot is not only an oppressor who does not rule according to the revealed message of God but vigorously contributes to the emasculation of Arab men by *'ahirat al-rum* ('Roman prostitutes'), a reference to the presence of female American soldiers on Saudi soil for over a decade. The fact that Saudi Arabia was defended by American women in the Gulf War was viewed as the emasculation of its male population, especially the armed forces, a theme that is regularly reiterated in Jihadi discourse. Such images existed in Jihadi literature long before the torture of Iraqi prisoners in Abu Ghraib prison by American soldiers – both male and female – entered the public sphere in 2004. The local despot is often referred to as *dayuuth*, a strong abhorrent term describing the pimp, especially the one who trades his own *maharim* (the taboo female relatives such as mother, daughter, sister, etc.). The despot is transferred here from the realm of politics to that of morality, invoking images of sin and punishment resulting from the violation of divine law. Above all, the violation of women is attributed to the contribution of two agents: the infidels and the local despot.

Jihadi sheikh Issa al-Oshan (d. 2004), known as Muhammad Ahmad Salim, advised Saudi Jihadis against 'going to seek *jihad* in Iraq or elsewhere' and encouraged them to stay at home where they are needed.[35] He elaborates that this is not because the situation in Iraq is confused and unstable and that there is no banner to fight under, but because the priority should be the local context. Al-Oshan moves away from the duty to defend the global *umma* to the necessity of guarding against the violation of local women. He mentions a story that brought shame to a Saudi Jihadi who was fighting with the Taliban against the troops of the Northern Alliance during the American-led invasion of Afghanistan. Al-Oshan's friend told him that a Northern Alliance soldier asked him why a Saudi Arab was fighting in Afghanistan. The Saudi Jihadi answered that he wanted to defend the Muslim emirate of Taliban. The Afghan soldier replied, 'How could you come to Afghanistan while the Americans are with your sister in Saudi Arabia?' At this point in the conversation, the Jihadi felt shame. Al-Oshan argues that a Saudi cannot defend the honour of other Muslims while his own house is violated. This is a good reason to 'break the cross first in the Land of the Two Holy Mosques, to set the land on fire so that no cross could feel secure'.

As gendered discourse, *jihad* draws on cultural values, with specific reference to male–female relations, the violation of women and the obligation to defend one's honour before seeking to do the same for other Muslims. In Saudi Arabia, *jihad* is a response to the emasculation of men, who are subjected to state repression in the context of prison and torture chambers. Al-Harbi, the suicide bomber in *Badr al-Riyadh*, painfully recounts the experience of his friend in al-Ruways prison. He says that during a long and painful interrogation session, his friend and his wife (described as a respectable tribal woman, a *hurra*, a free woman (not a slave)) were subjected to the most humiliating treatment. He claims that his friend, after being paraded naked, was forced to have sexual intercourse with his wife in front of the interrogators. This not only violates the honour of the free woman as a result of an act committed by her husband, who has lost his ability to defend her honour, but also dishonours the man. Rather than being the defender of women's honour, the male prisoner, emasculated and humiliated by state agents, is turned into its violator. He collapsed, sobbing and crying, according to al-Harbi. While it is impossible to verify the authenticity of this story, it is nevertheless a powerful statement in Jihadi propaganda that plays on honour and the violation of honour. These images blur the boundaries between protector and violator of women. The helpless Muslim male is portrayed as being forced by the despot to violate his own honour.

The connection between *jihad*, on the one hand, and women, honour and shame, on the other, invokes the role of women in this duty. Are women expected to join the Jihadis? Sheikh Nasir al-Fahad provides a *fatwa* in this regard. He responds to two questions:

Q: What is the nature of female *jihad* and are women required to go out seeking *jihad*? Please answer with regard to defensive and offensive *jihad*.
SHEIKH AL-FAHAD: In general, women are not required to go for *jihad* but their exit with male Jihadis to cure the ill and the wounded and to fetch water for the thirsty is permissible. In Ibn Abbas's Hadith, the Prophet used to raid with women who look after the wounded and gain booty. Umm Atiyyah confirms that 'we used to go on raid with the Prophet to nurse the ill and there was booty for us'. Also it is permissible for women to fight directly in some situations. This is what Safiyyah bint Abd al-Mutalib did when she hit a Jew with a pole and killed him in battle. Women must get permission from their guardians before going and must be accompanied by *mahram* [a male chaperon].[36]

While there is no conclusive evidence in support of women directly participating in combat, there is ample evidence to suggest that women must be involved in other capacities, one of which is to support male relatives involved in *jihad*.[37] For this purpose, the al-Qaʾida branch in the Arabian Peninsula published *al-Khansa*, a sister electronic magazine to *Sawt al-Jihad*, named after a famous Muslim female poet who lost several sons in *jihad*. The magazine instructs women on how to reconcile *jihad* with family life. According to the editorial board, the magazine is published by an organisation called the Women's Media Bureau in the Arabian Peninsula. It owes its publication to the leader of *jihad* in the Arabian Peninsula, Abdulaziz al-Muqrin (d. 2004).[38] The magazine advises women on how to educate their children in the *jihad* culture, in addition to giving instructions in first aid and nursing the wounded, thus echoing the expectation regarding women's participation in *jihad* from an Islamic point of view. The magazine does not, however, exclude women from active combat, as the instructions in carrying and handling arms indicate.[39]

The discourse of the struggle for the way of God which encourages confrontation, resistance and domination is not only anchored in religion and politics; it is a cultural whole which defines a way of life for the Muslim male, the privatised self in a globalised world. Above all, it tackles the last line of defence, the remaining guarded fortress: women in Saudi Arabia. As gendered discourse, *jihad* not only promises liberation from the domination of 'infidels', but also a defence of the most cherished female, whose violation dishonours and shames men. Violence is generated not simply by adherence to globalised ideologies and movements but through the regional and sub-regional disputes which have their origins in the complexities of local political history and cultural practices.[40] To understand the Jihadi trend in Saudi Arabia, one must situate it in the local context. Jihadis are a response to contradictions generated by a political leadership professing adherence to Islam, while the reality attests to something different. Jihadism is today defined as illegitimate violence, but in many respects this violence is a mirror of another type of violence – that of the state. Certain types of violence can be considered legitimate, not only by the Saudi state but also by the international community. In the aftermath of 11 September and under the banner of the 'War on Terror', Saudi state violence remains more or less outside the realm of condemnation. Violations of human rights are occasionally mentioned by international organisations, but remain unproblematic for countries that claim to uphold these rights at home and encourage them abroad. While *Badr al-Riyadh* included clear references to state violence (for example, torture and humiliation in prisons), in the following section, we consider more subtle practices of indirect violence by the state.

Repentance: violence to renounce violence

State repression, manifested in long prison sentences without trial, led to *taraju'at* (going back on previous intellectual and political positions), especially by outspoken Sahwis, who after years in prison in the 1990s were transformed into a loyal opposition. When faced with the rise of local Jihadi preachers, the state used these Sahwi *'ulama* to 'orchestrate' the repentance of the Jihadis. They volunteered to play the role of mediators between the state and Jihadis. The state used the Sahwi ex-prisoners to deliver 'peace' when they offered to provide assistance in guiding the Jihadis to the right path, after straying in thought and practice.

Three Saudi Jihadi *'ulama*, Nasir al-Fahad, Ahmad al-Khalidi and Ali al-Khodayr, declared their *tawba* (repentance) in several television programmes broadcast in November and December 2003.

Nasir al-Fahad 'repented' in 2003 when Saudi television showed him being interviewed by a Sahwi preacher, Sheikh Aidh al-Qarni.[41] The programme was aimed at establishing that al-Fahad was not qualified to issue *fatwa*s, especially the one related to excommunication of 'those who assist Americans'; that Americans in Saudi Arabia are *mu'ahadin*, infidels with whom Muslims have peace as a result of an oath (*'ahd*); and that his repentance was the result of serious reflection in prison, without any pressure or coercion from the state. Al-Fahad clearly declared that his repentance was a result of lessons received in prison from people of knowledge. He admitted that he was not qualified to issue religious opinions and that it was nobler to admit error than to continue to hold mistaken views which encourage violence.

The repentance session started with al-Fahad announcing his erroneous judgment regarding the obligation to remove infidels from the Arabian Peninsula. He added that violence in Riyadh tarnished the image of Islam and Muslims, wasted resources and brought disaster. He renounced the right to give opinions on excommunication, stressing that *takfir* remains a prerogative of established *'ulama*, mainly the Council of Senior Ulama. With respect to rebelling against the ruler, al-Fahad stated that this is not justified in a country such as Saudi Arabia. He concluded that infidels in the land of Muslims should be protected and their wealth guarded because they hold visas, issued by the Saudi authorities, and the visa is a contract which brings infidels under the protection of Muslims. He rejected any call for destroying Western interests in Saudi Arabia. He added that such destruction is permissible only if *wali al-amr* declares war on infidels. Al-Fahad warned Saudi youth against the temptation to 'go out' for *jihad* in Iraq. He described the fighting as *jihad fitna*, a combat that leads to chaos and discord among Muslims. He revoked the privatisation of *jihad* and insisted that it is permissible only under the banner of a Muslim ruler, the only person who can call for *jihad*. Al-Fahad moved from being a rebel scholar to one fully endorsing the official Wahhabi religio-political discourse.

Al-Fahad renounced his earlier *fatwa* regarding the permissibility of using women and children as human shields in combat (*al-tatarus bi 'l-nisa*), a reference to the fact that women (infidel or otherwise) might be caught in violence. He argued that such a *fatwa* was current in early Islamic times but today the context is different.

In 2006, al-Fahad remains behind bars, which casts doubt over the sincerity of his apparently changed views. Perhaps the state finds it difficult to trust his televised statements. It is also possible that the Saudi government is under pressure from the United States to keep him in prison. However, the fact that al-Fahad remains imprisoned may suggest that the state does not fully trust its own propaganda. In the absence of independent reporting or access to the prisoner, we cannot rule out the possibility that al-Fahad's repentance may have been forced or staged. Therefore, no conclusive evidence can be presented here. After all, to reconsider early opinions and denounce previous convictions can be a healthy sign, but there is always room for expressing what one does not believe in. Here we enter the realm of the inner self, where assertions are difficult to make.

Several months after the televised repentance session, a letter attributed to Nasir al-Fahad and signed by him appeared on several internet sites.[42] While it is equally difficult to establish the authenticity of this letter, it carried a strong message to his audience. He clearly stated that any opinions expressed on television while he was in captivity (*'asr*) cannot be a true reflection of his beliefs. Al-Fahd refers to coercion (*qahr*), which forced his repentance, and confirms that the state holds power over him. The state, in his opinion, is the strong agent (*qawi*), while he is weak (*da'if*). He adds that the state has the upper hand, but that it cannot possibly win his heart and change his mind.

The theme of *taraju'at* and *tawba* is discussed in a pamphlet which aims to respond to the televised repentance sessions of the three Jihadi scholars. Sheikh Abdullah ibn Nasir al-Rashid argues that prisons are sites of coercion rather than compulsion.[43] It is unlikely that truth manifests itself in the despot's prison. Therefore, it is difficult to assess the status of statements made by Jihadi *'ulama* in which they renounce previous opinions. In a manner reminiscent of a tradition that does not consider confessions under duress or torture legitimate evidence, al-Rashid invokes the context of prison and torture as limiting one's free will. Any renunciation of previous opinions in such a context is defined as *taraju'at qasriyya* (forced repentance).

The repentance sessions were well publicised in official media. Intellectuals, religious scholars and laymen debated the television programmes and presented them as success stories. The main champions were the state and the Sahwi *'ulama* who helped deliver the repentance statements. So-called liberal writers presented these broadcasts as reflections of the wise spirit of dialogue adopted by the state. Others saw them as signs of the complete defeat of Jihadis. Liberal newspapers such as *al-Sharq al-Awsat* and *al-Watan* rejoiced over the end of *thulathi al-takfir* (the trinity of excommunication).[44] Some Sahwi *'ulama* warned against over using these sessions to score illegitimate gains, a reference to the way liberals commented on the television episodes. Sheikh Aidh al-Qarni applauded the Jihadi sheikhs for their courage and ability to revisit previous opinions. He argued that admitting error is better than continue to err. He used the repentance to demonstrate 'the good *fitra* [nature] of the people, who are brought up on true Islam'.[45] However, the involvement of Sahwis in the repentance dramas did not go unnoticed. Liberal writers pointed attention to the possible gains that might accrue to them as a result of their mediation with Jihadis. Several writers used the occasion to indirectly accuse Sahwis of sharing a common intellectual platform with Jihadis. One prince even went as far as accusing Sahwis of being the intellectual godfathers of the Jihadis. Sahwis were incensed by such public accusations, and one asked for a public debate with the prince to 'clarify the issues and absolve Sahwis of any responsibility for Jihadi violence'. His calls for debate were ignored.[46]

The positioning of Sahwis as 'mediators' between the state and Jihadis incurred the wrath of underground Jihadi *'ulama*, who endeavoured to defeat the Sahwis on the internet. Sahwis acquired a new label, *gafwa* ('asleep') as opposed to *sahwa* ('awakened'), thus contributing further to the rift between the various Islamist trends and enforcing a political and religious fragmentation among ex-comrades.

It is very difficult to claim with certainty that the repentance sessions, together with the royal pardons granted to Jihadis who gave themselves up to the authorities, had a positive impact on the development of events in the year that followed. In 2004 Saudi Arabia remained hostage to the Jihadis, whose attacks became more daring. The American consulate and Ministry of Interior bombings in December 2004 proved that they were still capable of hitting at the heart of the American presence in Saudi Arabia and humiliating the regime through targeting one of the most important state institutions. Repentance, especially the Saudi televised version, was confined to winning the media battle while the state tried to win the military campaign on the ground. If instruction and re-education in Saudi prisons resulted in the repentance described above, it is clear that the same prisons must have had a lot to do with producing the fiercest Jihadis. Several people who provided military and intellectual support for *jihad* had spent time in prison, for example the above-mentioned al-Harbi, Abdulaziz al-Muqrin and Yusif al-Ayri; the last two were leaders of al-Qa'ida in the Arabian Peninsula. Before his recent imprisonment, al-Fahad himself had previously been a cellmate of two other famous Jihadi sheikhs, his intellectual mentors, Sheikhs al-Khodayr and al-Oqla in al-Hayer prison in Riyadh.

Jihad: self-annihilation, purposeful behaviour or agent of modernity?

Today Jihadism is an underground movement that manifests itself in violent attacks. Its discourse is debated in rest-houses, mosques, private gatherings in the poor and crowded neighbourhoods of Riyadh and Jiddah, the elite intellectual salons, five-star international hotels, research centres and remote farms. This debate is clearly articulated in internet discussion forums and on Jihadi websites. Religious discourse comfortably intermingles with reflections on Muslim–infidel relations, contemporary politics and cultural notions about femininity, masculinity and violation of honour. The debate is supported by media productions, poetry, chanting and iconography, not to mention instruction in how to use weapons, to survive in the desert without water and food, and to seek cover within society, thus generating a cultural package that reaches much further than suicide bombers aim to. Contemporary *jihad* is a culture that flourishes in a specific historical and political context in addition to being a religious duty. It has become a privatised obligation in the age of globalisation, thanks to mass communication.

Violent acts are expressions of cultural codes imbued with great meaning for both perpetrators and victims. Rather than being at the margins of culture, violence has perhaps moved to its centre.[47] Scholars who analyse the relationship between violence and religion tend to emphasise that a cultural approach encompasses a wide range of variables that make *jihad* or any other form of religiously motivated violence authentic, inspiring and powerful.[48]

Such reflections on violence rightly situate it in the realm of culture. However, while it might have several social, economic, political and religious causes, this violence does not represent a yearning for old times, despite its rhetoric. *Jihad* is not pursued for a return to the *status quo ante*, to the glorious past and the tradition of pious ancestors. It is a culture that promises a transformation of the present to achieve a better future, and is pursued by individuals who believe in their ability to change the world. Outsiders conceive of *jihad* as self-annihilation in a world where the balance of power is clearly in favour of the West. However, from the Jihadi point of view it is purposeful behaviour. In fact, Jihadis believe that it is the only religiously sanctioned response to this imbalance.

In the context of Jihadi violence, the debates on politics and religion moved much faster than ever before. Since the early 1990s, debating religion, politics, relations with the West, the status of women, the religious establishment, the new Islamism, the ruling family, the national debt and many other urgent issues are constantly being considered by an increasingly literate population which has at its disposal multiple sources of information. The 11 September attacks increased the speed and intensity of the debate even further. Under the pressure of violence, the Saudi government was forced to respond and act rapidly. It changed the religious curriculum, sacked religious scholars, restricted charitable work, established a National Dialogue Forum and introduced limited municipal elections in February 2005. The regime presented itself as the champion of reform. While it dismisses any suggestion that its timid and hesitant reform takes place under American pressure, it will never admit that Jihadi violence may have been a wake-up call.

Jihadism is a culture of transition that may lead to a kind of modernity different from that celebrated in official discourse and often measured in ample statistics about the number of hospitals, airports, paved roads and highways. Saudi modernity brought the alien trappings of material goods, consumerism and literacy. It also consolidated a centralised authoritarian state that destroyed local political actors, with the exception of those who were willing to be co-opted. Modernity brought about increased urbanisation, dislocation and the erosion of old tribal and kinship loyalties, but failed to replace the latter with alternative modes of organisation such as independent cooperatives, associations, political parties and circles for support and representation. While Saudi modernity silenced the traditional religious diversity within Islam, it allocated massive resources for the propagation of one interpretation of religious discourse, although in the face of unprecedented proliferation of religious knowledge, it became impossible for the state to extend its control. With the centralisation of religious institutions came the decentralisation – and even fragmentation – of religious discourse. The old religious monopoly of the Salafi–Wahhabi consenting tradition began to be gradually eroded by various groups, of which Jihadis are but one.

Although modernity empowered many Saudis, it disempowered a massive population that is increasing at an unprecedented rate. Modernity generated discontent among those who could not be included in its parameters. In recent times and under the fluctuation of wealth, Saudi modernity failed to include as many people as possible. In fact, this very modernity contributed to the systematic exclusion of a wide circle of people who were able to learn its alphabet and communicate using its own language, but were for some reason excluded. It resulted in a class of dispossessed and excluded people who lacked either the right skills in a competitive market, belonged to marginalised groups and regions or failed to be part of patronage networks. However, Saudi modernity also had beneficiaries, and created an awareness and an ability to imagine an alternative existence. Modern communication technology and rapid travel speeded up this awareness and widened the gap between reality and aspirations.

The drawing of Saudi Arabia into Western modernity generated a local response with its own momentum. The country initially absorbed selected aspects of Western modernity and violently rejected others. Jihadism and Western modernity share a common belief in the ability of man to change the world. Both are sure that they hold the key to advancement and progress. However, Western modernity held reason to be the key to such advancement, whereas Jihadism invoked faith.

Jihadis may well have accelerated change but it remains to be seen whether they can survive in a time of stability.[49] The debate between those who support *jihad* and those who denounce it continues, and will probably do so for the foreseeable future. The debate is not simply about removing infidels from the land of Islam or toppling despotic regimes. It is about sincerely believing Muslim men and women and their agonising journey through a changing world. The following chapter captures a glimpse of this ongoing debate, through the life, words and thoughts of one man.

5   Debating Salafis: Lewis Atiyat Allah and the *jihad* obligation

LEWIS ATIYAT ALLAH: They will write books about me.
ABU YASIR: Why? What is your achievement?
LEWIS ATIYAT ALLAH: Nothing apart from proving that you have achieved nothing.
ABU YASIR: What have you got to say now?
LEWIS ATIYAT ALLAH: Whatever says any Lewis Atiyat Allah to another. More practical and logical proofs justifying the *jihad* option and the bankruptcy of your strategies.   Lewis Atiyat Allah, *Min buraydah ila manhatin*, p. 23

Lewis Atiyat Allah is a Saudi intellectual and Islamist activist, who has taken refuge in the bulletin and discussion forums of the internet because his message is today subject to censorship. He is also an al-Qa'ida supporter who has been forced to go underground. Lewis came to prominence under this pseudonym after 11 September, an event that precipitated a substantial schism within the Saudi Salafi scene. Since then, Lewis's articles, commentaries on current events and evaluations of the Saudi regime have appeared in several well-known Saudi internet websites and discussion boards.[1] Lewis also had his own website, which was closed down by the hosting company for security reasons.[2] It is more than likely that the virtual Lewis is currently known by his real name in the real world; he may well be a public figure. However, for fear of persecution and arrest in the country where he lives, he chose an unusual pseudonym: a Christian first name, followed by a Muslim surname.

We can only speculate on why this character chose a rather unusual nom de plume. The name Lewis brings to mind several French kings, whose names appear in Lewis's articles, together with references to Christian clergy and the church. In one article, he refers to King Fahd as 'al-malik Lewis', evoking images of dictatorship, divine kingship and alliance with a church.[3] However, the second part of his name, Atiyat Allah, anchors him in an Islamic tradition, perhaps a counter-kingship that is bestowed on the believers by Allah.

Lewis himself explains his nom de plume in a very simple manner, which reflects a rather unusual phase in his early days, when he had a sense of humour, but is now incompatible with his current Islamist preoccupation. Some time ago he travelled to the United States. He recounts the conversation he had with the immigration officer upon arrival:

IMMIGRATION OFFICER: What is your name, sir?
LEWIS: I think. Um. Well, I'm Lewis.
IMMIGRATION OFFICER: But it is not the name on your passport!
LEWIS: You can say that I'm gonna change it!
This is how I became Lewis.

Lewis's long articles are usually eagerly awaited both by many committed Islamists looking for inspiration and intelligence officers and experts on terrorism who surf the internet websites and discussion boards for *jihad* literature and al-Qa'ida supporters in an attempt to understand the phenomenon or arrest the enemy.[4]

Lewis is perhaps one of the most popular of the Jihadi Islamist internet writers.[5] One of his literary contributions on the internet received 18,576 hits. Saudi Islamists read his articles with enthusiasm. His accessible and eloquent contributions generate heated debates and counter-arguments between those who praise him and those who condemn him. Lewis also enters into dialogue with people in Saudi Arabia whose identities are known and who can afford to write under their real names as they have rejected or suspended the obligation of *jihad*. He also converses with others – usually Western specialists on terrorism, as he claims – who want to understand the duty of *jihad*, which Lewis strongly supports, enthusiastically justifies and clandestinely defends. The virtual Lewis articulates a vision in defence of *jihad* but perhaps the real Lewis suspends the duty as he cannot afford at the moment, an exposure which would no doubt lead to arrest, a fate similar to that of the Jihadi *'ulama* discussed in the last chapter.

It is difficult to know where Lewis is. Yet wherever he is, it seems that expressing open support for al-Qa'ida is taboo and has serious consequences. Under these circumstances Lewis chooses to conduct a covert *jihad*, '*bil lisan wa laysa bil sinan*' (with the tongue, not with weapons). At heart, Lewis remains a committed Jihadi, although in an open environment he would not be a foot-soldier. He is more likely to be a theoretician/strategist/interpreter of the *jihad* rather than a practitioner. He is probably a middle-aged man, in his forties. Given his writing skills, education, knowledge and style, the real Lewis is likely to be part of the political wing or the propaganda department of the Jihadi Islamist movement, providing intellectual input in support of the overall strategies.[6] However, neither Lewis nor al-Qa'ida is conventional. Lewis belongs to a trend rather than a hierarchical organisation, with an identified division of labour and clearly assigned roles. He may or may not have direct or indirect channels of communication with al-Qa'ida. However, he writes in such a way as to support and glorify *jihad*.

Both the virtual and the real Lewis can be considered *munathir wa mudafi' an al-jihad* (a theoretician and defender of *jihad*). Unlike traditional religious scholars, he writes in a modern and accessible way, reflecting knowledge of politics, international relations and an ability to analyse the world – from his point of view, of course. However, he also has a solid religious education, which enables him to intersperse his discourse with Quranic verses, Hadiths and references to early religious scholars, history and tradition.

Lewis is a committed Jihadi Salafi. He is also a hybrid in the sense that he successfully combines his religious identity and commitment to Islam with a rather deep immersion in Western discourse and languages. He is not only fluent in English, he is also an articulate reproducer of Western concepts and methodology.[7] He has mastered the art of dialogue according to Western standards, although he may not want to acknowledge his reproduction of this discourse. He also uses the method of interpretation, analysis and conventions that are common in Western discourse. In addition to his commitment to defending faith worldwide, Lewis can be regarded as a Najdi Salafi, thus locating his global religious message in the confines of central Arabia and the Wahhabi call. He may object to being labelled a Wahhabi Salafi. According to his testimony, he is the real Salafi, the one who has not been 'domesticated' by Al-Saud, pejoratively referred to in his articles as al-Sulul, a mock name which has become commonly used by the Islamist opposition in Saudi Arabia to refer to the ruling family, thanks to Lewis.[8] He may have been influenced by modern Islamist intellectuals, famous names associated with twentieth-century Islamism such as Sayid Qutb, Abu Ala al-Mawdudi and theoreticians of the Egyptian Jihadist movement, but he remains faithful to the early Wahhabi tradition, especially that associated with Muhammad ibn Abd al-Wahhab's grandson, Sheikh Muhammad ibn Ibrahim ibn Abd al-Latif (d. 1969).[9] Lewis is definitely a product of the Wahhabi reform movement and its teachings, whose Jihadi branch is now referred to in Western literature as neo-Salafis.[10] He is not, however, concerned with labels and trends. He remains in his own eyes a Muslim who follows the right path. He is local but also global, not only in his personal biography and sources of religious education but also in his cosmopolitan outlook and travel.

Lewis is a real conversationalist. He engages his opponents in intense debate, answers their queries, responds to their provocation and defends his point of view. A substantial part of his discourse is primarily directed towards his fellow Salafis, mainly those who, in his opinion, not only betrayed the Salafi movement by *ta'til faridhat al-jihad* (suspending the obligation of *jihad*), but also condemned his brand of Salafism. Since 11 September, Lewis's opponents seem to be drawn from the so-called Sururi Sahwis, discussed earlier. Others are pro-government *'ulama* and intellectuals, who openly declare their rejection of his strategy, at least in the current international context. This condemnation revolves around describing him and his likes as *khawarij al-'asr* (contemporary Kharijites), *bughat* (usurpers) and *al-fia al-dhalla* (the party that has gone astray), threatening the community by rebelling against the rightful Muslim ruler, and encouraging discord among Muslims; all carry serious religious punishments (*hudud*). It is important, however, to point out that such accusations by laymen using the internet are not necessarily grounded in serious knowledge and scholarship in Islamic studies. The majority of those who use such strong terminology in internet discussion boards are probably not aware of the historical contexts in which such labels emerged.

Lewis the person

One of the most difficult tasks in drawing the contours of Lewis's background and personality is access to the person and his narrative, which, if traced correctly, would open a window through which we can gain a glimpse of the complexity, tension and resolutions which this character has faced throughout his life. Lewis's current affiliation with the Jihadi trend is a product of an evolution and a development, all reconstructed in this chapter from information Lewis released about himself on the internet. While it is not possible to cross-check this information, I have all reason to believe that it represents an authentic and accurate description of a life that is perhaps representative of a whole generation of Saudi men born in the late 1950s and early 1960s. While Lewis is unique in his ability to articulate his thoughts and in the strength of his convictions, his biography reflects the drastic changes that have swept Saudi Arabia. In reconstructing Lewis's life history, I have no reason to consider his autobiography a fabrication. What he says about himself remains an autobiography, a selective and fully controlled narrative. My reconstruction is, however, partially mediated by my translation of the text from Arabic and my organisation of the material.

The first conversion: from Sahwi Islamism to liberalism

I was Satan's soldier then Satan became my soldier.

Lewis Atiyat Allah

Before introducing Lewis's various debates with his opponents, it is important to draw the contours of his personal journey to political activism, which is marked by his conversion from Islamism to liberalism. Like many young Saudis brought up in a world nothing like that of their parents' generation, it seems that Lewis went through a very difficult time in his youth, beautifully alluded to in the above statement. His traditional Salafi upbringing and later his commitment to the Sahwi Islamist trend gave way to liberalism.

According to Lewis, his life can be seen as a series of conversions. He had a traditional religious upbringing. His father was a Salafi and he grew up in a Salafi environment. He learnt the Quran from his father, who later sent him to Madina, where he studied in the Hadith College. He learnt three thousand Hadiths from the *Ahkam* collection. As a young man he became part of the so-called Sururi Sahwi movement in Saudi Arabia, which flourished in the 1970s and 1980s. He was a follower of Sheikh Safar al-Hawali.

Lewis says that after this brief experience of Islamism 'things happened to him', but without specifying the nature and impact of these 'things'. As a result, he admits that he lost his Islamic identity. Three years passed after he graduated from university without being able to define the meaning of 'belonging to the *umma*'. It seems that this was his first personal and intellectual crisis in life.

He abandoned his Islamic awakening and became a liberal. At this stage he began reading philosophical texts, for example the Encyclopaedia of Abdulrahman Badawi, the story of Hayy ibn Yaqthan, Descartes, Spinoza and Kant, in addition to the history and causes of the European Enlightenment and the French Revolution. He was impressed and began to condemn Islamic thought, as deep down his reference point was 'Shakespeare and Voltaire'. In his own heart Lewis considered himself as belonging to the 'victorious party', *al-umma al-muntasira* (the West). He confesses that he forgot all his Islamic education with the exception of Ibn Khaldun and his *Introduction* and Ibn Tufayl and his story 'Hayy ibn Yaqthan'. At this stage Lewis went to America.

Lewis returned to Saudi Arabia fully immersed in liberalism. He describes himself as having become 'modernist in literature and secular in thought'. He began to defend democracy, human rights and the rights of women, as defined by the West.

Lewis believes that in a previous time Satan occasionally tempted him. He immersed himself in sins to the extent that he became one of Satan's disciples, subjected to his own whims. Lewis refers here to morality and corruption as an escape from 'loss of Arab identity and faith in religion'.[11]

Following this loss, Lewis lived *ayam al-dhalal* (the days of obscurity). On one occasion, he endeavoured to use all his skills and charm to mislead a young American woman, a representative of 'the civilised world', using internet chat rooms. After several virtual encounters, the woman fell in love with him and the flowers he used to send her. She told him that she used to show the flowers to her friends and tell them that they were from her 'Arab boyfriend' who owned an oil well. She later asked him to marry her, but he declined. She then told him that she frequented an Islamic centre and had converted to Islam, hoping that he would change his mind and marry her. He declined the offer again, and began to question how he contributed in his own sinful ways to creating bad impressions about Islam and Muslims. At this juncture, Lewis wished for death.

Lewis's 'illicit' encounters with women seem to have been a foundation for his return to Islamism. In addition to being an argumentative and stubborn young man, immersed in *dhalal* (debauchery), who went as far as to preach that smoking is not *haram* (forbidden), Lewis seems to have mastered the art of flirtation to a high level. He tells us how he became an expert in using the language of eyes to lure women to smile, and perhaps more. According to him, the language of eyes is irresistible, and regardless of a woman's education and upbringing, she will eventually succumb to a glance by a charming man like himself. This did not necessarily lead to an illicit relationship, but exchanging glances would lead to mutual appreciation and smiles because 'the eye is the door to the soul', according to Lewis. He was self-confident in his abilities to 'charm and defeat an army of female resistance', wherever he found it. He practised his skills in bookshops, supermarkets and abroad.

Lewis was an experienced traveller who put his charm to the test in airports. Travelling and being with strangers were moments of excitement. He flirted with air hostesses, using a rather unusual entry into their hearts – he would discuss the ozone layer with them. When in foreign lands – Britain, for example – he sensed a 'spiritual vacuum among women', which he obligingly tried to fill on regular occasions. He would describe to an English woman how her face reflected fatigue, pain and suffering. She would respond immediately, and engage him in conversation. According to Lewis this approach is far more sophisticated and effective than starting a conversation about the weather, as English people would normally do. Lewis resists the conclusion that English women are loose or easy targets, as he stresses that many would ignore his advances.

This period in Lewis's life is described as a by-product of complete 'intellectual corruption', of which casual relations with women were one aspect. He recounts his encounters with women and his 'liberal' attitude to demonstrate the level of degeneration that he had reached before his rediscovery of the meaninglessness of life without faith. During this episode, he felt no guilt because he suspended religion as a moral force capable of halting his immersion in sin. He even went as far as denying the legitimacy of a religion, which forbids acts of immorality. At that point he introduces the term 'crisis' (*azma*) to describe his situation. He argues that it is most natural for love and closeness to develop between men and women, and admits that even talking to a woman is pleasurable. Why then does Islam restrict the interaction between men and women? He proposed a solution: moulding and modifying religion to accommodate human desires. This was his way to avoid guilt as he searched in the religious tradition for examples that would justify mixing between the sexes and more relaxed public interaction with the opposite sex. The stories of the early Muslim women (*al-sahabiyyat*) and their relations with men became his reference point in a desperate attempt to justify what he calls the contradiction between *al-shar'* (jurisprudence) and the language of the body, mainly his desires.

Lewis claims that at this stage he forgot the Quran – with the exception of some verses, which he constantly remembered in solitude. These verses summarised his newly acquired liberal convictions. Lewis felt like the *khubth* (filth) ejected by the city, described in Hadith as 'al-madina tanfi khubthuha kama tanfi al-nar khubth al hadid'. Lewis was this *khubth*. He continued to socialise with known Saudi liberals and engage with their thought. Lewis admits that he began to admire someone whom he had loathed previously when he was an Islamist Sahwi: Ghazi al-Qusaybi – Saudi liberal writer, ex-ambassador to Britain, and in 2004 Minister of Labour.

Lewis had his second crisis when he admits that he discovered 'the emptiness of their life, namely the liberals' and developed a revulsion against their gatherings. He felt that Saudi liberals are like parrots, blindly imitating the West. He believed that they were incapable of instigating any serious change. For the second time, Lewis experienced a kind of turbulence as he lost his second acquired identity as a secular liberal. He became a tormented soul, having abandoned the certainties of his first Islamic identity and his second acquired Western outlook.

The second conversion: back to Sahwa

Lewis's account of his early flirtation with liberalism and adventures with women reflects a tormented self immersed in behaviour and thoughts implicitly considered immoral. He searched for a return to salvation, a way out of his degeneration.

One day he performed his ablution and sat holding the Quran. He summarises his return to the right path:

> I did not cry as happens in the story of Prophets who repent, but I felt that I was the one addressed by the Quran. This was the turning point in my life. I continued to search in the Quran for rational proofs. I found them in sura al-anam. Finally I became like *ahl al-araf*, betwixt and between. I heard about al-Wasatiyya. I came asking about what they offer and why they are called thus. Perhaps they have ideas I can adopt. I am an ordinary person. I ask questions because I reject all artificial thoughts.

Although Lewis admits that he felt happy in his liberal days, today he feels pain and bitterness. He opted for salvation, as he felt tranquillity when he was in a public space where he lowered his gaze (*ghadh al-basar*). He also admits that suppressing his desire to look at women is not easy, but that the peace that follows is eternal, and the pleasure that succeeds hardship is everlasting. At this stage Lewis was a reformed character, a 'born-again' Muslim. He returned to Islamism but remained independent, entering into heated discussion with Sururi Sahwis, his early mentors and companions, and participating in discussion boards of the Wasatiyya internet club, coordinated by Muhsin al-Awajy. However, he was not to be satisfied by the 'methodology' of the Wasatiyya. His heart was somewhere else.

At this stage – that is, in the post-11 September period – to be a born-again Muslim was simply not enough. Lewis's personal journey to salvation became a serious mission to save his country, other Muslims and the world. From this time on, he had a mission in life. Lewis revisited the Sahwa camp, only to be disappointed by its position after 11 September.

Lewis found his salvation in a return to 'an Islam manifested in mosques, libraries, schools, universities and summer camps'.[12] The Islamic awakening (the Sahwa movement) included diverse Islamist groups and orientations, the most important of which was the so-called Sururi version, discussed earlier in this book. Lewis's involvement in the movement brought him to the conclusion that 'Saudi society and state oscillate between being totally non-Muslim in some aspects and less than Muslim in others'.[13]

Lewis admits that throughout the 1990s, he was a follower of *'ulama al-sahwa*, including, among others, Sheikhs Salman al-Awdah, Safar al-Hawali and Nasir al-Omar. His later adoption of the *jihad* obligation is not a conversion or a departure from what those scholars preached, but it takes the *sahwa* to its logical conclusion, which the above-mentioned scholars have failed to do according to Lewis, given their reaction to the events of 11 September.

The final confirmation: Lewis the Jihadi

So far we have followed Lewis through his various stages: Lewis as a Salafi; Lewis as a liberal; Lewis as an independent Islamist with connections and in communication with the Jihadis throughout the late 1990s. The final phase, discussed here, is Lewis as a confirmed Jihadi.

His position changed in the second half of the 1990s – more accurately in 1998, when he admits to having had *itisal* (communication) with Jihadis. Lewis committed himself to the Jihadi trend after 11 September 2001, when he had to make a final resolution (*yahsum al-khiyar*). The main reason for this final conversion was his disappointment with the Sahwi sheikhs, who signed a pamphlet after 11 September entitled *How we can Coexist*, which was a response to a pamphlet produced by a group of American intellectuals entitled *What we are Fighting For*.

Having been shocked by the Sahwi sheikhs' response to 11 September, Lewis wrote an article, 'Iflas al-islamiyyin' (The Bankruptcy of Islamists), which confirmed him in his position as a defender of *jihad*. This article symbolised his final break with Sahwi Islamism and conversion to the *jihad* option. Lewis argues that his abandonment of the Sahwi camp was a result of the position of their famous sheikhs outlined in the pamphlet, which, according to him, shocked all Salafis in Saudi Arabia. With 'The Bankruptcy of Islamists', Lewis came to prominence as a daring writer. He challenged the religious scholars who had dominated debate throughout the 1990s – al-Hawali, al-Awdah and al-Omar. Because of their anti-Americanism during the Gulf War of 1990, their critical stance towards the government and their imprisonment until the late 1990s, these sheikhs had become powerful symbols, capitalising on more than a decade of resistance and personal suffering. In this article, Lewis shattered the myth about these sheikhs, whose position and rhetoric changed dramatically after they came out of prison, and more so after 11 September.

According to Lewis, his eminence following the article on the bankruptcy of Islamists was accidental. He uses the image of a play in which people were bored with the monotony of the performance. In the audience there was one who was murmuring a song, possibly to overcome his boredom. When people sitting around him heard his murmurs, they asked him to go on stage and sing. He hesitated, but sang beautifully. People started to applaud, and at that moment in the show Lewis the Jihadi writer was born. The poetic of Lewis's self-assessment of his preeminence is a window from which to look at this personality. He combines two contradictory characteristics, humility and strength.

The events of 11 September 2001, which precipitated a major schism within the Salafi awakening movement, had proved to be crucial for Lewis. The Salafis were divided between those who openly supported Bin Laden (the most famous were Sheikhs al-Oqla, Nasir al-Fahad and Ali al-Khodayr) and those who distanced themselves from him without condemning him openly, for example Sheikhs Salman al-Awdah and Safar al-Hawali. There were also official religious scholars who accused Bin Laden of causing *fitna* (dissent), like the one of the early Kharijites. The Sahwa sheikhs regarded the attack on New York as a cataclysmic event unblessed by God. Despite Lewis's training and intellectual proximity to al-Hawali and al-Awdah, he decided to side with those who endorsed Bin Laden and sanctioned the *jihad* option. Lewis laments the schism within his movement, and cites the Arab poet who said:

> Ualimuhu al-rimayat kuli yawmin
> Falama ishtada sa'iduhu ramani
>
> [Every day I teach him to shoot
> When his hand became steady he shot me.]

Lewis took the preaching and teachings of *'ulama al-sahwa* to their logical conclusions when he decided to embrace the *jihad* not simply as an option but as a duty, whose fulfilment is currently the responsibility and programme of Bin Laden and al-Qa'ida. He declared the events in New York a major success and a turning-point in the struggle against American hegemony. His journey from *sahwa* Islamism to the *jihad* trend should not be interpreted as a departure from the teachings of the 1990s Sahwi sheikhs. He admits that his choice does not represent a serious departure from his intellectual Sahwi roots. The two Islamist camps – the *sahwa* and the *jihad* – differ only in practice. While they agree on the centrality of *jihad* as *faridha* (duty), they differ on the conditions of its application. They also agree that the United States is the enemy of Islam and Muslims and that it occupies the land of Muslims, especially *bilad al-haramayn* – the Land of the Two Holy Mosques, but disagree about when *jihad* should be declared, who has the right to declare it, how it should be declared and whether the conditions for declaring it are met. Moreover, there seems to be no consensus on when *jihad* ceases to be *fard kifaya* (an obligation for a sufficient number of people) and becomes *fard 'ayn* (an obligation incumbent on every individual).

Lewis's endorsement of *jihad* over whether 11 September served the Salafi cause and Muslims in general marked a departure from the philosophy of his ex-comrades. He also disagreed with their position regarding the Saudi regime. The Sahwa sheikhs and the Jihadis agree that the regime does not fully apply the *shari'a* or abide by it in all aspects of social, economic and political matters. However, the Sahwis implicitly agree not to attack the regime or harm it at present, whereas the Jihadis do not accept the strategy of a truce with the Saudi government.

Lewis does not give up hope that his early mentors, especially his intellectual masters, *'ulama al-sahwa*, will come to accept his point of view. For this reason he has entered into an electronic dialogue with Abu Yasir, one of the Sahwis, in an attempt to present his point of view and convince his ex-comrade – now intellectual opponent – that suspending *jihad* is not only un-Islamic but is also a futile policy.

Lewis Atiyat Allah and Abu Yasir: from Buraydah to Manhattan

An important and lengthy internet dialogue between Lewis and someone by the name of Abu Yasir appeared in the form of a small booklet in Arabic bookshops in London. Lewis's booklet, *From Buraydah to Manhattan*, was published in 2003 by Dar al-Riyadh, an imaginary publishing house. Previously this debate appeared on several websites.

In this booklet, an interesting debate takes place between Lewis Atiyat Allah and a fellow Salafi by the name of Abu Yasir, who belongs to the other Salafi camp, presumably another Muslim intellectual who has become 'moderate', perhaps after several years behind bars in Saudi Arabia in the 1990s. Abu Yasir challenges our characterisation of Salafis as he enters into a dialogue with Lewis. He represents the other brand of Islamism, the one associated with *'ulama al-sahwa* of the 1990s and now abandoned by Lewis. Lewis and Abu Yasir share a profound commitment to Islam, not only as a way of life but also as a solution to all problems.

Before 11 September, Lewis and Abu Yasir undoubtedly belonged to the same Islamist movement (*tayar al-haraki*), and probably knew each other very well. However, after the events, the two followed different paths. Lewis became covertly associated with the Jihadi Salafis and Abu Yasir remained part of a Salafiyya with moderate Muslim Brotherhood leanings. Abu Yasir is a *haraki*, an Islamist activist. According to Lewis, the difference between himself and his interlocutor is not in *mafahim* (understanding), but in *tatbiqat* (application). The main debate revolves around the events of 11 September and the duty of *jihad*, which led to schism within the Saudi Salafi Sahwi camp. They both see themselves as true Muslims who are opposed to the official quietist Salafi trend, represented by the Saudi religious establishment.

Abu Yasir's point of view

Abu Yasir poses a series of questions which were asked by many Saudi Salafis following the 11 September attack. These fall within two main themes. First, should *jihad qitali* (military struggle) be a priority over *jihad hadari* (civilisational struggle) to deal with the concerns of the Muslim community at this particular moment in time? Second, should the battle be taken to the USA when there is a lot of scope for educating Muslims by implementing grass-root programmes to raise social and religious awareness? The latter question deals with whether the strategy of military struggle against the 'most powerful nation on earth' is a sound tactic when contemporary Muslims have no power comparable to that of the United States. Abu Yasir's questions reflect his rejection of Bin Laden's strategy. He argues that the decision to hit America was detrimental to the Islamic *da'wa* (call). The attack was, according to Abu Yasir, carried out by 'gangsters' under the command of one person – Bin Laden – himself, without resorting to the opinion of mainstream *'ulama*. Abu Yasir questions the religious legitimacy of killing innocent people in New York who may not even support their government's policy towards the Muslim and Arab world. He believes that given the state of backwardness prevalent in Muslim countries, which have fallen under unjust rulers, attacking America did not represent a strategy but an act of anger and revenge, whose consequences were harmful. The attack led to the destruction of a young Muslim state, the Taliban government in Afghanistan, and also to aggression towards Muslims all over the world.

Abu Yasir is hesitant when it comes to endorsing the *umami* (global) approach of al-Qa'ida, which leads to overlooking *watan* (homeland) in favour of a global Muslim community. However, he does believe in the supremacy of the Muslim *umma*. He bases his understanding on practical grounds as he argues that one needs a home base in which to start an education programme, raising awareness and above all Islamising society. He does not see the benefit of wasting limited resources on battles in Kashmir, Bosnia, Chechnya and other places where al-Qa'ida is thought to operate. The Islamisation of the homeland includes preaching *da'wa*, which includes among other things the obligation of *jihad*. However, given the present circumstances of Muslims mentioned above, in practice military *jihad* has to be 'suspended' or 'frozen' in favour of cultural and educational struggle. The objective should be to create the virtuous Muslim society, which would inevitably lead to the establishment of the authentic Muslim state. Only then can Muslims think about military confrontation with a powerful enemy. In the present circumstances, none of the conditions for military struggle are met; therefore, attacking the United States was premature, foolish and detrimental.

Lewis's point of view

Lewis responds to Abu Yasir's questions and accusations in a style reflecting his familiarity with both Islamic and Western discourses. He moves easily from Ibn Taymiyya to Fukuyama, although he admits that practising Jihadis do not bother reading the latter. Lewis privileges military struggle and mocks the educational programme of Abu Yasir. For him *da'wa* is not a lesson delivered in a mosque. Even if it is the right way to raise awareness, this method has failed to end the subservience inflicted on Muslims by the superpower. According to him *da'wa* is besieged by both the United States and its local allies, the rulers of Saudi Arabia, who collaborate to suppress any activity which undermines American hegemony.

Lewis rejects the notion of *watan* (homeland) as un-Islamic. According to him, all Muslim countries and states are recent creations resulting from foreign intervention rather than an Islamic obligation or effort. This development is now taken for granted and accepted, but it should be rejected and confronted. Lewis rejects the idea of Islam based in one country. He also questions the notion of a homeland when it is occupied by American female soldiers, the ultimate humiliation.

He also rejects the importance of creating the 'institutions of civil society' through awareness, a programme adopted by Abu Yasir's movement. According to Lewis, civil society does not lead to any substantial change. He describes it as an escape from responsibility. He challenges Abu Yasir to give him examples of major historical changes that have resulted from the emergence of civil society in the Arab or Muslim world. Obviously Lewis, the supporter of *jihad*, thinks that military interventions in the form of uprisings and revolutions led to the emergence of civil society rather than the other way round.

The real educational programme, in his view, is that which emphasises the duty of *jihad*. He criticises Abu Yasir for preaching *jihad* but suspending its practice, thus arousing young people's emotions without offering an opportunity to 'practise what is preached'. The result, according to Lewis, is frustration. He mentions the position of Sheikh Safar al-Hawali and Salman al-Awdah: both allegedly advised Saudi youth against going to Afghanistan to perform *jihad* against the Soviet Union, while at the same time glorifying resistance to oppression and foreign domination.

On the decision to attack the United States, Lewis argues that Bin Laden took advice from 'majlis shura al-Qa'ida', the al-Qa'ida Shura Council. According to him, this resulted in America losing its *hayba* (authority), a success which is not well understood by the likes of Abu Yasir. According to Lewis Abu Yasir belongs to an organisation whose hierarchical infrastructure prevents him from appreciating this kind of achievement. Lewis describes the Sahwi movement as bureaucratic, rigid and hierarchical, freezing abilities as it recruits its followers on the basis of loyalty and obedience. In contrast, al-Qa'ida does not isolate itself from society – rather, it 'melts in society', using it for support and cover. Lewis concludes that the Sahwi movement can easily be eliminated by governments because it has a transparent organisational infrastructure, whereas al-Qa'ida is a real transnational movement, difficult to defeat simply because it is a loose association.

In addition, al-Qa'ida, according to Lewis, rejects hierarchical models of organisation. It acts whereas other Islamists react, resorting to the effective surprise factor. It uses the enemies' material, their weapons and ammunition, to hit a 'clear' target. Moreover, it avoids entering into polemics with other Islamist groups. Finally, it consists of a group of *fida'iyyin*, similar to those described by Ibn Taymiyya in his letter to the king of Cyprus as the ones who 'kill kings in their beds'.

On the legitimacy of targeting civilians in the USA, Lewis does not distinguish between Americans and their government. He argues that in a democracy, the government represents the will of the people. Therefore, he concludes that American civilians brought their government to power. By hitting Americans, Lewis expects America to become 'confused', lose perspective and change its policy. He demands that the USA stops supporting Israel, withdraws its troops from Saudi Arabia and abandon the Arab *taghut*s (despots) such as the Saudi leaders to the will of their own people.

Lewis comments on the limited knowledge of official Saudi *ʿulama* who mistakenly thought that they were targeted by American media when criticism of the Wahhabi movement followed the 11 September attacks. He concludes that the world does not care about such official *ʿulama*. According to Lewis, only those who defy America become famous. He gives the example of Jihadi religious scholars such as Nasir al-Fahad and Humud al-Oqla whose *fatwa*s in support of *jihad* against the USA are now famous and reported in the international media. Lewis praises those *ʿulama* for using modern communication technology (the internet) to communicate their messages, but he also sends a plea. He asks them to communicate their ideas to *al-shabab* (the young) in simple and accessible language. He laments that Saudi official religious scholars think that they live in the Meccan age, referring to the time when the Prophet Muhammad could not launch *jihad* from Mecca when he was under the rule of the blasphemous. In the Meccan age, there was no *jihad*.

From Buraydah to Manhattan is but one forum in which these two Saudi Salafis engage in a fierce debate about politics and religion. They both agree on a vision – that is, changing their country through action. Abu Yasir feels it necessary to adopt a peaceful preaching campaign to 'Islamise' society, which would eventually lead to Islamising government. According to many Islamists, an open battle with the Saudi government may have detrimental consequences. The fear of direct American intervention in Saudi Arabia to protect the oil fields necessitates a truce. Lewis, on the other hand, considers the Saudi government 'the enemy within', and totally under the thumb of the United States.

Lewis and Abu Yasir are products of the Islamist movement of the 1980s and 1990s. They draw on the same religious sources. However, the events of 11 September seem to have started a fierce battle among Saudi Salafis. This battle is fought both openly and clandestinely, in internet discussion and bulletin boards. The Sahwi camp, which has suspended the *jihad*, now has access to official media channels after almost a decade of censorship and imprisonment. Today outspoken figures in this movement are given space in official, Saudi-controlled print and satellite media. The government uses them, in addition to official *'ulama*, to discredit the Jihadis, who have gone underground.

Lewis and violence in Saudi Arabia

Saudi Salafi debate became extremely heated in 2003, which saw two major suicide bombings in Riyadh in May and November, targeting major residential compounds occupied by Westerners and other residents. These attacks, followed by one on a government security building in April 2004 and the killing of five Western workers in Yanbo and more than twenty people in Khobar in June, generated heated discussion on the internet, in which Lewis participated. The main focus of the debate was on whether such acts of violence constitute true and legitimate *jihad*.

Almost all Sahwi Islamists inside Saudi Arabia publicly condemned the violence and described it as an 'act of terror', carried out by what is often described as *al-firqa al-dhalla* (those who have gone astray) and as Kharijites; both terms invoke strong religious connotations leading to rejection and condemnation of the attackers. Among those who condemned the attacks was a small group of Sahwi activists (including Sheikhs Safar al-Hawali, Sulayman al-Duwaish and Muhsin al-Awajy), who offered to mediate between the government and activists known to have previously supported *jihad*, hoping that their young followers who had gone underground would give themselves up. They called upon the youth 'who have gone astray' to repent and come forward to face justice.

The government, however, openly rejected the proposal and continued to pursue a policy based on military confrontation with the Jihadis and their cells. It is difficult to confirm that any talks with the Jihadis did actually take place. Throughout 2003–4, the Saudi government publicly reiterated its position, and refused to negotiate with the Jihadis. However, in reality, it encouraged and welcomed the Sahwi mediation initiative. In the words of one Sahwi, the state cannot admit that it uses Sahwis to mediate with Jihadis, as this would destroy its credibility.[14]

The government used the violence of 2003–4 to project an image of the Jihadis as a group that targets society and innocent people, highlighting the fact that Muslims and Arabs were killed, especially in the November attack. When suicide bombers struck the Riyadh security building on 21 April 2004, only Saudis died. In the media battle between the government and the Jihadis, the government was able to discredit the Jihadis and expose 'their lie that they only target Westerners'. However, in April 2004, when violence struck in the Red Sea city of Yanbo and claimed the lives of five Western workers, Jihadis reasserted their early strategy of targeting Western interests and workers in Saudi Arabia. The government, under pressure because of the violence, apparently tried to appease the Jihadis by offering an amnesty period of one month (June–July 2004). A handful of suspects on the wanted list gave themselves up to Saudi embassies in Tehran and Damascus, while one or two local suspects responded to the king's offer. A key Jihadi figure, Sheikh Faris al-Shuwayl al-Zahrani, was captured on the Saudi–Yemeni border in July 2004 after refusing to give himself up to what he called the '*taghut* government'.

The obvious space for challenging both government discourse on Jihadis and that of the official and Sahwi *'ulama* was internet discussion boards. As expected, Lewis was ready to improvise, and was an active participant in this debate. In an electronic interview with *Sawt al-Jihad*, he explains and defends the Jihadi strategy in Saudi Arabia.[15] The interviewer asks Lewis whether he thinks that targeting foreigners' residential compounds might decrease the appeal of the Jihadis and turn society against them. Lewis responds that the 2003 bombings in Riyadh may dent their popularity for a short time, but that the attacks should 'be placed in the larger context of resisting Western and American domination'. He argues that Jihadis may have to resort to such strategies although it is psychologically costly and may lead to momentary decline in their popularity. According to Lewis, in the long term, Jihadis need to consider two aspects related to these attacks: first, how to prevent 'hypocrites' from achieving a media victory following violence; and second, how to stop those hiding behind a 'misguided' religious discourse from condemning Jihadis.

The interviewer asks Lewis to explain why Jihadis have not so far targeted members of the Saudi royal family – which, according to the interviewer, may avoid the problem of other innocent people being killed in future blasts. Although Lewis admits that he does not have a clear answer, he thinks that such a strategy would inevitably speed up the collapse of the Saudi regime. He argues that this is no doubt a military decision that is constantly discussed in Jihadi circles. However, he offers his explanation why such acts have not yet taken place. Jihadis, according to Lewis, may not yet be ready for the total collapse of the Saudi regime, which is a close ally of the United States. The continuity of the regime prevents the USA from attacking the country. The regime in its present configuration acts like a shield, protecting Jihadis from direct exposure to the United States which, according to Jihadis, would no doubt intervene in Saudi Arabia to protect the oil fields. Lewis thinks that limited violent attacks in Saudi Arabia would increase the pressure on the ruling family, without leading to the complete disintegration of the regime.

The violence that erupted in Saudi Arabia throughout 2003 and 2004 seems to have escalated with the occupation of Iraq and the increase in Iraqi resistance to it. While all Saudi Salafis endorsed the Iraqi resistance as legitimate defence against occupation, violence against Westerners and Western interests inside Saudi Arabia was a different and more complicated matter. As expected, official media, together with establishment *'ulama* and Sahwis, openly condemned acts of violence inside Saudi Arabia. Lewis, however, offered a different interpretation, as indicated in his commentaries on the violent events of 2003–4.

Lewis and his enemies: the *jihad* obligation explained

In addition to the internal battle that is raging electronically among Saudi Salafis, Lewis engages in a different kind of encounter, which is primarily directed towards the West. In an article entitled 'Yes Blair: It Is a Historic War', Lewis summarises his views on the war in Iraq:

Yes, you [Prime Minister Tony Blair] are right. It is a historic war and not a peripheral battle as your unwise American allies think. Look at the new weapons used by the *mujahidin* in Iraq. The weapon of kidnapping your men and women in Iraq. What happens in Falluja is a serious matter. It shows that Muslims are taking the initiative for the first time in modern history. Unlike what happened in Afghanistan in the 1980s, when *jihad* was manipulated for international political reasons, the situation in Falluja is a product of Jihadis taking the initiative and carrying out their own plan.[16]

Lewis compares two *jihad* experiences. The first took place in Afghanistan throughout the 1980s and resulted in the liberation of Afghanistan, the humiliation of the Soviet Union and eventually its collapse. Unlike other Jihadis, Lewis is aware of the international context in which this *jihad* took place; for example, he refers to the 'manipulation of the United States and other Muslim governments' of this *jihad*. His interpretation of the Afghan *jihad* invokes notions of balance of power and the Cold War conflict. He alludes to the fact that Jihadis were 'used' in this conflict to carry out the strategies of a superpower. The second case is that of Falluja. For Lewis, the Iraqi resistance in Falluja is an example of an independent 'Muslim initiative', determining without 'outside patronage' the place and time of the battle with the Unites States.

Despite destruction and death in Falluja throughout April 2004, Lewis considers the *jihad* option to be a success. He sees the Iraqi resistance as a coordinated activity which has spread *thaqafat al-jihad* (a culture of *jihad*), 'implanting the psychology and prestige of resistance and the pride of killing the blasphemous'. Lewis refers to the unexpected resistance of Iraqis in what was commonly referred to as the 'Glorious Sunni Triangle'. His interpretation of this development in Iraq centres on the fact that the resistance was a product of popular consciousness without any effort from Bin Laden's al-Qa'ida. In his opinion, by invading Iraq, the United States facilitated the spread of the *jihad* culture without any effort by al-Qa'ida.

Lewis returns to Tony Blair's description of the war in Iraq as a 'historic battle that nobody in the West can afford to go wrong or fail'. According to Blair, failure in Iraq means the return of fanatics and terrorists. Lewis agrees that failure in Iraq has a high price for the West. It involves the 'loss of all Western domination in the Muslim world achieved over the last five centuries'.

In addition to this address to Tony Blair, Lewis claims to have corresponded with Reuven Paz, senior fellow at the Centre for Global Research in International Affairs (GLORIA) in Hertzylia, Israel.[17] It seems that on one occasion, Paz accused Lewis of having fallen into *junun al-'adhama* (grandiose madness), especially after 11 September. Lewis refutes this accusation and explains that Muslims 'had an ancient grand history, which was subdued by Western domination. The 11 September attack reasserted their supremacy.' Lewis argues that the strategy of al-Qa'ida is incomprehensible to Westerners or to Paz himself, whose political thought is derived from a combination of Judaeo-Christian roots and secular capitalist principles. In contrast, al-Qa'ida's programme is above all 'mashru Islami dini' (an Islamic project devoid of secular and capitalist underpinnings), according to Lewis. This 'Islamic project' aims to undermine the existing international world order.[18]

The invasion of Iraq presents itself as the background to Lewis's commentary on the international world order. He argues that although he hated Saddam and his regime, he felt a kind of sadness over how his regime collapsed as a result of American intervention. He would have preferred al-Qaʾida men to have brought down Saddam. However, he recovered from this sadness as soon as the Iraqi resistance started inflicting heavy losses on American troops. According to Lewis, even before America expressed joy over the removal of Saddam, the resistance proved that US plans for the region would be thwarted.

Lewis introduces four prisms through which he interprets the occupation of Iraq, seen as yet another step towards thwarting American hegemony in the Arab world while increasing the credibility of the *jihad* option. First, Saddam's fall in this manner and speed facilitated the complete destruction of the secular Baʿthist ideology, thus removing one of the obstacles to the materialisation of the Islamist agenda. Second, the occupation privileged the culture of *jihad* as the option most suitable for dealing with the crisis of the Muslim world. Third, the occupation led to a trap in which the USA is the loser. The USA, according to Lewis, will lose whether it stays in Iraq or leaves. Fourth, the attack on New York was the key event that hastened the confrontation between the international world order, represented by the United States, and the Muslim world.

Lewis comes home to *bilad al-haramayn*

We have established that Lewis is an *umami* Islamist whose vision encompasses an Islamic world order which opposes and defies the current international world order, under US hegemony. His *jihad* is very much dependent on the notion of an Islamic *umma*, encompassing different races, nationalities and cultural groups. The unity of this *umma* is derived from faith rather than race. However, Lewis turns his attention to his homeland, the most sacred territory and the core of the Muslim world, the Land of the Two Holy Mosques, *bilad al-haramayn*. His homeland is central in the establishment of the Islamic world order, but unfortunately, according to Lewis, it has become, under the current Saudi leadership, a vehicle for Western hegemony. Lewis seems to blur the boundaries between the so-called national and transnational Islamists, a dichotomy that has become fashionable in several academic studies of the Islamist movement after 11 September. The first are often seen as moderate Islamists whereas the latter are considered representatives of the radical trend, held responsible for globalising *jihad* out of desperation and defeat.[19]

When Lewis 'returns' to *bilad al-haramayn*, he is transformed into a nationalist who invokes notions of sacred territory, historical responsibility and the glorious past. For Lewis *bilad al-haramayn* is not only Mecca and Madina, which are theoretically closed to non-Muslims, but the whole Arabian Peninsula. As such, the land of Islam needs to be freed from acts of defilement, manifested in the actual physical presence of non-Muslims. This foreign presence encompasses not only US soldiers and military bases, but also non-Muslim workers, especially Western expatriates. According to Lewis, foreigners, obviously regarded as profane, violate the purity of this geographical entity. Here the boundaries of *bilad al-haramayn* are seen as having become porous, allowing in the process a greater defilement and molestation to take place not only on the periphery but also in the core of this sacred territory.

For Lewis *bilad al-haramayn*'s sacredness stems from the presence of the holy shrines in Mecca and Madina as well as the fact that the last Prophet, Muhammad, appeared in this land with a sacred mission, the message of Islam. Another element in this sacredness stems from the role played by the people of this land in spreading *da'wa* (the call), starting with the early companions of the prophet, the caliphs and later generations of *bilad al-haramayn*. In addressing the people of this land, Lewis uses the term *ahfad al sahaba*, the grandsons of the early companions of the Prophet.

He calls upon the 'grandsons of the companions of the Prophet to expel the infidels from *jazirat al-'arab*', the Arabian Peninsula following the prophetic tradition. *Jazirat al-'arab* is another central term for Lewis. It invokes 'Arab' possession of a territory, which the descriptive nomenclature *al-jazira al-'arabiyya* fails to capture. Furthermore, *jazirat al-'arab* conveys a different meaning from that implied by *bilad al-haramyn*. The first invokes the centrality of the Arab dimension of the *jihad* option and the historical responsibility of the inhabitants of the Arabian Peninsula to take the lead in the struggle. When Lewis invokes *jazirat al-'arab*, there is no doubt that he is an Arab nationalist, thus exposing the tension between the universal Muslim community, the *umma*, and the particular, his own homeland. He resolves this tension by ascribing a central role to his own native land, fusing the local – his homeland – in the global project, the envisaged Islamic world order.

According to Lewis, the hegemony of the international world order is dependent on the survival of the Saudi regime in its present form, pejoratively referred to as *al-nidham al-Sululi*. This regime, he says, needs to be dismantled. Three conditions will contribute to its downfall.[20] First, the Islamic reform movement was the only voice that exposed the reality of the regime, its corruption and support of Western domination in the region. As such, this movement plays an important role in dismantling the web of lies upon which the regime bases its legitimacy. Second, internal disputes within the royal family will eventually lead to the regime's downfall. Third, regular violence like that in Riyadh in 2003 and 2004, demonstrates that

Bin Laden is preparing the ground for the collapse of the Saudi regime or a series of assassinations of key figures among the royal family.

The above factors would, according to Lewis, dismantle a regime that has 'served the West for the last seventy years', paving the way for their projects and supporting their interests. Once this essential obstacle is removed, the Islamic world order would be established. However, Lewis warns that a period of chaos may ensue in the short term. Chaos often accompanies drastic changes such as the one expected to shake the nation ('tahuz al-umma') after decades of submission, hypocrisy and evil. He also does not rule out the inevitability of *fitna* (dissent), which normally accompanies serious political and social changes. Lewis has an apocalyptic vision of the liminal period, which he describes as being chaotic and lawless. He forecasts a situation in which 'people will die of thirst, hunger and at the hands of thugs and criminals'. This is the high price that must be paid for the establishment of the Islamic world order, starting with the central core, *bilad al-haramayn/jazirat al-'arab*.

The ultimate defilement of *bilad al-haramayn*: 'when a hypocrite becomes ruler'

When the hypocrites come to thee, they say, 'We bear witness that thou art indeed the messenger of Allah.' Yea, Allah Knoweth that thou art indeed His Messenger, And Allah beareth witness that the Hypocrites are indeed liars.

They have made their oaths a screen [for their misdeeds]: thus they obstruct [men] from the Path of Allah: Truly evil are their deeds.

Quran, Sura 63, al-Munafiqun, verses 1 and 2

At the time of the Prophet, the boundaries between Muslims and non-Muslims in Madinan society were well defined. The community consisted of two categories, those who declared their Islam and were part of the Muslim *umma*, and those who remained outside it by virtue of professing other faiths. The first category consisted of those who were true believers. They declared their faith, performed Islam's rituals and demonstrated their allegiance to the Prophet and the community. But the category 'Muslims' included an ambiguous and dangerous subgroup, the hypocrites, *al-munafiqun*, who declared their faith and performed the rituals but had no allegiance to the Prophet and the community. In fact, they secretly plotted to destroy Islam and defeat Muslims. According to the Muslim tradition, *al-munafiqun* are the enemy within. They have distinct characteristics, which may or may not be easily detectable by the rest of the community of Muslims. In general the hypocrites are people who openly declare their Islam, believe in its five pillars, and are incorporated in the boundaries of the Muslim community. The earliest ones approached the Prophet, announcing their belief and acceptance of his mission. However, they used their 'insider' status, their closeness to the Prophet and their open display of piety to conceal their true selves and harm Muslims. As an enemy within, they are a 'fifth column', and serve the interests of the enemies of Islam.

The Prophet through divine revelation warned his community of the danger such groups pose for Muslims and Islam, hence Sura al-Munafiqun was revealed to draw attention to the destructive role of the hypocrites, who will always be a feature of Muslim society but who need to be exposed and expelled. During the Prophet's time, the secret of the hypocrites was exposed but God warned of their presence in the future and the responsibility of all Muslims to draw attention to their destructive influence.

One famous hypocrite in the pre-Islamic tradition was Abu Righal, who guided the army of the Abyssinian king Abraha towards the holy shrine in Mecca, the Kaaba, with the objective of destroying it. In the Islamic tradition, the Abyssinians were the rulers of Yemen and in the year of the Prophet's birth, about 570CE, we find them at the gates of Mecca threatening its precious Kaaba with destruction.[21] In the early Meccan Sura al-Fil (the elephant), the Abyssinian Christians under the viceroy Abraha Ashram led a big expedition against pagan Meccans, riding on elephants. The Meccans offered no defence, but a shower of stones, thrown by flocks of birds, destroyed Abraha's army.

In *Hina yusbih al-munafiq hakim* (When the Hypocrite becomes the Ruler), Lewis returns to the theme of hypocrites in the Islamic tradition as he recounts the famous story of another hypocrite, Abdullah ibn Sulul. Lewis argues that the most dangerous threat to early Muslims was not the known enemy – for example, Abu Jahl, whose *kufr* (blasphemy) was known and obvious. In fact, the real danger came from Abdullah ibn Sulul's 'hidden cancer that destroys the community from within'. Ibn Sulul, a Jew from Madina, declared his allegiance to the Prophet and composed poetry in his honour, but in the battle of Uhud (625), he withdrew one-third of the Muslim army, estimated at 300 men, which resulted in perplexity, confusion and the eventual defeat of the Muslims in this important military encounter with the pagan Meccans.[22] In this battle, the Meccans under the command of Abu Sufyan avenged their previous defeat in the battle of Badr. The Prophet was wounded, but Islam was not defeated, according to Lewis.[23]

Lewis asks, 'What would have happened to Muslim society had Abdullah ibn Sulul, the hypocrite, become ruler?' The Muslim tradition asserts that the presence of hypocrites within the Muslim community is not an unusual phenomenon. Nevertheless, when a *munafiq* becomes ruler of the Muslim community, the consequences are detrimental. Lewis asks his audience to imagine a hypocrite ruling over not only Muslim lands but the holiest of all – *bilad al-haramayn*. In this exercise of imagination, he outlines the intrigues of a recent 'Abdullah ibn Sulul', a reference to Ibn Saud, the founder of the kingdom, and later his sons. He lists some of the hypocritical acts of past and present. While publicly declaring faith and belonging to the Muslim community, the contemporary hypocrite uses Muslims to establish his dynastic realm. Behind their backs, he enters into alliances with the British government (a reference to early Saudi relations with colonial Britain in the Gulf). He then respects British interests and restrains Muslims from performing *jihad*. After consolidating his realm, Ibn Sulul/Ibn Saud turns his attention to his supporters, and in one battle he eliminates them after establishing his rule. Furthermore, while continuing to profess faith, Ibn Sulul/Ibn Saud introduces a Western style-banking system, charging the forbidden interest. He also conspires against all Islamist movements and causes. Lewis mentions Saudi endorsement of a number of governments – for example, Algeria, Sudan, Yemen, Egypt and Chechnya – in support of suppressing the prospect of Islamists coming to power. However, Ibn Sulul/Ibn Saud does not dare to publicly declare his *kufr*, in spite of all his wealth and capabilities. According to Lewis, the hypocrite remains weak.

In this exposure of hypocrisy, Lewis weaves together past and present. His argument is anchored in Islamic discourse and tradition. The text is full of references to the Prophet's biography and the golden age of the companions of the Prophet. Although the past is the anchor, it seems that the present is the starting-point for invoking a distant and ancient tradition. The word Salafi is well anchored in the past as it explicitly conjures up a return to the past and an orientation towards earlier tradition. However, it is clear from Lewis's exposition that the present is of great concern. The return to the past is only one way of rectifying present calamities, disorder and deviation from the right path.

The sultan's *ʿulama*: 'cursed by God and cursed by cursers'

The hypocrite does not act alone in Lewis's literary productions. He turns his attention to *ʿulama al-sultan*, the team of official religious scholars headed by the Saudi grand mufti who invokes sacred texts to sanction the words and deeds of the hypocrite ruler.[24] The *ʿulama* use their 'sacred religious knowledge' in approving the ruler's treacherous acts. For Lewis, the real *ʿulama* should play a role in exposing hypocrisy rather than lending it an air of legitimacy. In his condemnation of such *ʿulama*, there is no room for pragmatism, expediency or realism. He does not accept any argument which may justify or explain the historical support of the official *ulama* for the hypocrite ruler but rather demonstrates how they suspend certain religious interpretations and judgements. One neglected responsibility is the duty to 'expel the *mushrik*, polytheist from the Arabian Peninsula', in the Prophetic tradition. Lewis invokes a comparison with the Shi'i *ulama*, who, according to his understanding, strongly believe in the infallible imams, the descendants of the Prophet to whom they attach great deference and obedience. He argues that *ulama al-sultan* are worse than the Shi'i *ulama* because they believe in the infallible hypocrite ruler. In his reference to the Shi'i tradition, Lewis is 'ashamed of how far the Sunni *ulama* have gone in praising the rulers, invoking the concept *of tazkiyyat al-hakim* [praising the ruler]'. In his opinion, the *ulama* have distorted the reformist call of Sheikh Muhammad ibn abd al-Wahhab in the service of a ruler who happens to be a hypocrite. They have in fact 'domesticated' and 'hijacked' the reform movement to suit the political whims of the ruler, in the name of Ibn Abd al-Wahab.

Furthermore, Lewis condemns the *ulama* for their various *fatwas* justifying the prosecution of Jihadis who 'kill the infidels in the Arabian Peninsula' and questions the interpretation that such infidels represent *ahl al-dhimma*, whose blood should not be spilled by Muslims. He clarifies his point of view by adding that US military presence in Arabia is an occupation and as such *jihad* is the only means to respond to such violation of the sanctity of *bilad al-haramayn*. The central question for Lewis is how the *ulama* can issue *fatwas* justifying the killing of *ahl al-islam* and forbidding the killing of *ahl al-sulban* (people of the cross).

Lewis issues a call to the youth of the nation to abandon those *ulama* who practise *kitman* (concealing what is right as expressed in sacred texts) while revealing complete deference towards the hypocrite ruler. He urges them to point their fingers and say, 'Those are cursed by God and cursed by cursers', thus invoking a famous Quranic Sura that condemns those who practise *kitman*.

After saturating his text with religious references and Quranic verses, Lewis ventures into European history and warns against the 'historical alliance between European kings and the pope', which in his opinion had detrimental consequences for faith. He cites the French Revolution, which he interprets as a 'revolt against religion in all its manifestations, leading to rejecting religion all together and the consolidation of secular society in the West'. This interpretation of the French Revolution does overlook some substantial causal factors; however, it remains a valid reading of this historical event whose outcome is utterly condemned by Lewis. He is confident that 'the religion of God is protected, but the right path needs men to render it visible'. At the end Lewis thanks God that neither papal authority (a reference to official Saudi *'ulama*) nor despotic kings are capable of concealing the right path of Allah. Lewis's confidence is derived from his faith in God, and in the courage of Bin Laden and Jihadis.

Lewis addresses the Saudi grand mufti, Sheikh Abdulaziz al-Shaykh, a grandson of the reformer Muhammad ibn Abd al-Wahhab, and shames him by reminding him of his descent from the 'great reformer'. According to Lewis, had the latter been alive, he would have decreed a flogging for the mufti as a punishment for supporting Al-Saud's policies. Lewis declares the Mufti *fasiq* (debauched), a ruling which he thinks Ibn Abd al-Wahhab would have used to describe his grandson. He reminds the mufti of the words of Ibn abd al-Wahhab, who described the *taghut* as the ones who have gone back on religion (*murtadd*) because they permit what God forbids and forbid what God permits. Lewis reminds his audience that Islam will not flourish until Muslims announce dissociation from those people and their blasphemy.

The role of the *'ulama* in sanctioning American hegemony in Saudi Arabia is yet another proof of the co-optation of religious scholars, according to Lewis. Here he returns to the Gulf War of 1990–1 when American soldiers, including women, 'defiled the land of the Two Holy Mosques'. The *'ulama* 'sanctioned this intrusion, thus replacing a *kafir*, the blasphemous Saddam Hussein, with another *kafir*, the Americans'.

Given Saudi Arabia's sanctity and wealth, Lewis laments how Islam degenerated at the hands of the rulers. In particular he resents how *'ahl al-sunna* [Sunni Muslims] have been reduced to insignificance in the world as a result of the *'ulama*'s role'. He argues that today Saudi *'ulama* are worse than those of the Shi'is and the Kharijites because they allow the killing of Jihadis and forbid the killing of Jews and Christians. According to Lewis, the Kharijites 'left the Muslim community claiming to go back to judgement by the holy book whereas the *'ulama* today order people to obey those who do not rule according to the book'. He questions whether the 'occupying American army' in Saudi Arabia can ever be granted the status of *ahl al-dhimma* (people of the book). Finally, he encourages the Muslim youth to protect those religious scholars who refuse to be drawn into the circle of apologetic *'ulama*, giving the example of Shaykh Humud al-Oqla and his followers.

Preparing for chaos: an Imam elected by an alternative council

In interpreting Bin Laden's plan for Saudi Arabia, Lewis anticipates a period of chaos, following the gradual or sudden collapse of the house of

Saud. In order to protect the community from a state of disintegration, he urges the faithful *'ulama*, who are concerned about the future of Islam and faith, to come together and form a clandestine council consisting of the real *'ulama* and reformers (*du'at al-islah*) in a secure location. This council is expected to occupy the vacuum resulting from the expected regime collapse.[25]

Lewis, the interpreter of Bin Laden's vision, expects the United States to occupy Saudi Arabia the moment it feels that its oil interests are threatened as a result of the collapse of the house of Saud. The USA will lose its local supporters, upon whom it has been relying for the perpetuation of its hegemony. At this juncture, Lewis argues that it will have no choice but to go for a direct occupation of the Arabian Peninsula. He also introduces another possibility that would prompt the USA to deploy its troops in Saudi Arabia: a second 'spectacular attack along the lines of 11 September'. Lewis expects the USA to respond by punishing the radicals inside Saudi Arabia. The next attack, according to Lewis, will be 'creative' and unexpected in the manner in which it will be carried out. As the USA prepares for the direct occupation of Saudi Arabia, Jihadis will have had plenty of time to organise themselves, having benefited from the US occupation of Iraq, which gave them the opportunity to operate in that territory. In those circumstances, the Jihadis will be in charge of the military situation and resistance while a new council of *'ulama* elects the rightful Imam, the leader of the Muslim community.

Lewis: between admiration and detraction

There is no doubt that Lewis Atiyat Allah has established himself as one of the internet's most popular Salafi writers, whose style, arguments and interpretations are meant to address a wider audience. He presents himself as a Muslim intellectual, conversant with Islam and its tradition but also aware of politics and international relations. At one level, Lewis is a Salafi who draws on the classical sources ranging from those of Ibn Hanbal and Ibn Taymiyya to Ibn Abd al-Wahhab. At another level, he addresses history, Western intellectual heritage, international relations and the role of Islam in the modern world.

Lewis should not be understood as 'a detached observer' or a 'strategic analyst'. His discourse is a product of activism and a commitment to change the conditions of the Muslim *umma*. He remains an engaged Islamist intellectual. His Western enemies no doubt describe him as an apologist for terrorism and as someone who encourages, supports and endorses armed struggle in a global war without frontiers, specific targets or objectives and which he and his like have no chance of winning. Such opponents would also describe him as a megalomaniac, an unrealistic dreamer who would like to plunge the world into his nightmare scenarios. He would also be considered a destroyer of world peace and order, driven by subliminal hatred towards an enemy that is far superior, more rational and advanced. In Western classifications of the post-11 September world, Lewis incites violence and encourages terrorism.

Some Arab and Muslim opponents see him as a misguided person who 'poisons' the minds of young men in pursuit of an unrealistic project at a critical moment. Like his Western opponents, these people see him as an irrational misfit whose words undermine their security, prosperity and coexistence with the Western other. Some Muslims may share his emotional response to the state of degradation and humiliation, and come to lament the golden age of Muslim civilisation. In fact, this shared emotional response is the key to Lewis's fame, which means that even his enemies feel the urge to respond to his writings. For many opponents, he remains an outcast, whose enthusiasm for the cause of Muslims is not fully appreciated. In fact, his words inflame the minds and hearts of young Muslims, a situation regarded by his opponents as counterproductive, and even destructive.

Given the accessibility of Lewis's discourse, it is not surprising that his participation in internet discussion boards is eagerly awaited by a wide audience, some of whom do not hesitate to reply immediately, either in praise or condemnation. It is worth mentioning that not all those who read Lewis's articles and respond to them accept his line of thought. In addition to lengthy formal responses, represented in the dialogue with Abu Yasir mentioned earlier in this chapter, his electronic contributions generate a heated debate between those who support him and eagerly await his articles, and those who strongly condemn them. Monitoring these responses indicates that not all his respondents are particularly well informed in the two fields that Lewis masters, the Islamic and Western traditions.

Supporters praise Lewis and invoke Quranic verses glorifying and celebrating his 'sacrifices', 'commitment' and 'courage'. Others praise him for his accessible language, the clarity of his thoughts and his convincing arguments. They also call upon God to protect him from the many enemies his boldness is bound to generate. For them, Lewis is a teacher and preacher.

Those who reject Lewis describe him in very disparaging terms. Some call him ' *'ajuz* London', the old man of London, implying that he is one of the Saudi opposition figures who have taken refuge in London since the early 1990s. Others pejoratively call him 'the desktop Jihadi', a reference to his alleged lack of vitality and his incapacity to influence the course of events inside Saudi Arabia, or even beyond this one country. Some of

Lewis's attackers were his early 'comrades', other Sahwi Islamists who according to him 'failed to take their awakening to its logical conclusion as they suspended the *jihad* duty'. These people accuse Lewis of betraying the essence of the call, encouraging dissent and celebrating future lawlessness, leading the youth of the nation astray. Some trivial accusations name him as a foreign intelligence or Zionist agent, whose articles are meant to 'divide Muslims' and tarnish the image of Islam in the world.

More sophisticate deconstructions of Lewis's articles invoke the futility of the duty of *jihad* in the present circumstances, a line of argument similar to that invoked by Abu Yasir earlier in this chapter. One critic anchors his objections in strategic grounds, arguing that the loss of Afghanistan as a base was the consequence of an undisciplined struggle, targeting a powerful enemy without being able to defend one's own territory from inevitable retaliation. Such responses demonstrate that Lewis is wrong only in some strategic thinking, while his overall interpretation of the duty of *jihad* is correct.

In one electronic contribution, Lewis cites an exchange he had with Reuven Paz, senior fellow at the Centre for Global Research in International Affairs, entitled 'This is How al-Qa'ida Spoke: A Letter to Reuven Paz'. Lewis argues that Paz and the Sururi Sahwis share a common understanding of al-Qa'ida. They both condemn it as lacking a political programme. On one occasion Lewis cites Paz as having said:

I wonder whether al-Qa'ida agrees with your analysis. I had in mind the image of Osama as he sits in one of his caves reading your correspondence with this Israeli Jewish scholar [Paz] . . . My brother in humanity, Lewis, I do respect your line of analysis and your will to continue the struggle but in your writings you confuse reality with imagination. [26]

A survey of the responses to Lewis shows that both his admirers and his detractors feel compelled to address his message, which cannot be published openly in Saudi Arabia since the mid-1990s, or globally since 11 September. He has therefore taken refuge in the internet, and his ideas will most probably travel long distances in cyberspace, thanks to electronic waves.

Lewis in his own eyes

Lewis reflects on his own contribution to the cause of *jihad*. In his opinion, his main achievement is the invention of a mocking nickname for the Saudi royal family. The name al-Sulul (a reference to the hypocrite Abdullah ibn Sulul) is a powerful symbol in Muslims' religious and historical imagination. Like all such symbols, which condense meaning, the name al-Sulul powerfully evokes the 'hypocrisy' of the ruling family. Today the name is used by both Jihadis and a wide range of Islamist opponents of the Saudi regime.[27] It appears in Jihadi media clips and is repeated in international satellite television news channels when they cite Jihadi sources. According to Lewis, the name's importance will become even more revealing after the anticipated collapse of the Saudi regime, and will be associated with the royal family in a manner reminiscent of how the nicknames al-Kathab (the liar) and Abu Jahl (the father of ignorance) became an integral part of the identity of Musaylima and Amr ibn Hisham[28] respectively.

Second, Lewis admits to practising a kind of intellectual terrorism against Sahwi sheikhs by exposing their standpoint in his articles, especially in the period between 11 September and the beginning of violence in Saudi Arabia in 2003. According to Lewis, his articles influenced many young people who began to doubt the authenticity of the Sahwi sheikhs and their commitment to Muslim causes. However, he admits that after the outbreak of violence in Saudi Arabia in 2003, the Jihadis were under military and intellectual siege from the Sururi Sahwi Islamists. The government encouraged the latter to adopt an anti-Jihadi position, and even publicly defend the regime. The Sahwis had access to Saudi, Arab and international media as long as they were prepared to publicly condemn violence and attack the Jihadis.

Third, Lewis considers his articles a success in so far as they create a perception of the Jihadis that counters the negative images propagated by their enemies. According to him, he plays a role similar to that of Abdullah Azzam in the Afghan *jihad* against the Soviet Union. Lewis thinks that the modern language he uses to promote *jihad* is suitable for the current struggle against Americans.

Fourth, Lewis argues that his contributions give the *jihad* an intellectual and philosophical meaning which resonates not only in Saudi Arabia but worldwide. His rhetoric differs from that of the *'ulama* of *jihad*, whose style is judicial and may not be easily accessible to those with limited Islamic education. According to Lewis, his articles depict *jihad* as a social and civilisational duty, whereas most Jihadi literature talks of it as simply *harb 'ala al-kuffar*, a battle against the infidels with the objective of expelling them from the Arabian Peninsula. In his own self-assessment, Lewis moves Jihadi discourse to a different level of sophistication.

Evaluating Lewis: popularity against anonymity

Moving away from Lewis's subjective evaluation of his own achievement to an analytical assessment of his impact involves identifying three factors

behind his popularity: one related to Lewis as a writer; a second concerning conditions in Saudi Arabia in the post-11 September period; and a
third dealing with the relationship between the USA and the Arab world,
including Saudi Arabia. All three dimensions give a virtual and unknown
writer like Lewis unusual fame, and followers among Saudi internet users
as well as all Arabic speakers who surf the internet in search of answers to
urgent questions that dominate their imagination at a critical historical
and political moment. Lewis moved from being an unknown personality
to a major player in a virtual forum where his articles force readers to
respond, regardless of whether they agree with the message. His past and
his various personal crises – for example, his conversion to liberalism and
later return to Islamism – do not make him a straightforward popular
Islamist writer, automatically predisposed to play the role he envisaged
for himself as he entered middle age. His early personal tensions and contradictions may not have allowed him a direct entry into the world of
Jihadis. One can argue that his personal narrative may not attest to a long
association with this trend. On the other hand, it is possible to argue that
his early Islamist upbringing and his later liberalism were essential pre-
conditions for such a dramatic entry into the underground world of the
Jihadis. One can also question whether this is the final destination for
Lewis, or whether he will continue to evolve.

Lewis has become an internet Jihadi icon, despite the fact that he does
not belong to the more established community of 'ulama, Sahwis or other
formal groups. In fact, one can argue that he became so popular because
he was not a member of the 'ulama, whose stance after 11 September
changed dramatically to the surprise and shock of some of their followers.
While official Saudi media boast about ex-Jihadis – 'ulama, activists and
laymen[29] – who declare their tawba (repentance) on television screens and
move away from Jihadi and takfiri positions towards a 'moderate' Islam,
Lewis attests to an evolution in the opposite direction, towards the Jihadi
camp. Lewis's repentance – that is, the confirmation of his allegiance to
the Jihadis – does not, however, find its way to public media channels. His
story and articles remain alive in an electronic medium.

Lewis's pre-eminence relates to four personal attributes, clearly
demonstrated in his writings. He displays courage, self-confidence, hope
and an understanding of the West. He is extremely courageous in his criticism of Sahwis who in the 1990s assumed nearly sacred status among the
youth of Saudi Arabia, including Lewis himself. He dismantles the myth
surrounding these personalities, using their own weapons and drawing on
Salafi thought and proofs. His criticism remains strong and within the
limits of religious argumentation. In several articles, he defies the 'culture
of secrecy and silence' predominant in Saudi Arabia as a result of a

combination of political, religious and social factors. Political oppression – combined with powerful tribal and familial control mechanisms and religious interpretations which require total obedience to men in positions of authority and condemns 'individual' opinions believed to be threatening unity and encouraging dissent – are powerful taboos, which many prefer to remain intact. Lewis dismantles the culture of secrecy and silence cherished in Saudi Arabia, albeit under a pseudonym. Lewis's second asset is his self-confidence and belief in the strength of the Muslim community. He does not believe in self-flagellation. His articles reject defeatism and celebrate future victory. Such a style appeals to men who are tormented by what they perceive as *inhizamiyyat al-umma*, the umma's defeatist attitude. He also inspires hope and predicts future victories as inevitable for those who follow the right path. Finally, his early liberal ideas and his familiarity with Western literature put him in a privileged position regarding 'understanding the West'. He impresses his audience when he cites Lenin, Huntington and Fukuyama. Lewis appoints himself as *qadi*, judging the West and its achievement, rather than *muqalid* (follower), an imitator of Western ways.

In addition to his own attributes, Lewis's success is very much related to external factors pertaining to Saudi Arabia and Salafi schisms after 11 September. He is not a detached observer, but is immersed in his local surroundings. He has lived through several years of intense debate between various Islamists belonging to competing camps. Some, such as the Jihadis and the Sururis, are well known, but others remain clandestine and less exposed to media attention. Lewis's full understanding of these debates is reflected in his articles, most of which are responses to current affairs. His words explode at the right time and place. This connects him organically to the lives and debates of others around him. The most important debates for Saudi Islamists in the twenty-first century seem to be centred on the duty of *jihad*, the 'Islamic' credentials of the Saudi regime and how to deal with the USA. Lewis addresses these three concerns in his articles, boosting his popularity.

Lewis's popularity must also be related to the actual and perceived confrontation between the USA and the Arab and Muslim world, beginning with the question of Palestine and ending with the occupation of Iraq in 2003. In this atmosphere, internet users seem to be constantly searching for anyone who defies the USA, even if this defiance is anonymous. However, print and satellite media as well as internet discussion boards are saturated with anti-Americanism; Lewis must offer something that other writers lack. He speaks from a position of strength against a background of obvious and undisputed humiliation, weakness and defeat by American hegemony. American military strength is not only self-evident, it is on display in many settings from Afghanistan to Iraq. However, Lewis is able to expose the 'weaknesses and bankruptcy' of the superpower in ways which are not so obvious to most readers, drawing on his personal encounters with American society. The image of a naïve American woman lured by Lewis is a powerful one. He intersperses his text with humorous anecdotes and stories of situations he himself encountered while travelling abroad to deconstruct the myth about a hegemonic America whose liberalism and capitalism are nowadays projected as the last phase in the history of humanity. He empowers and emboldens others, despite his virtual and anonymous status as an internet writer.

Searching for meaning: Lewis's message

Lewis's articles contain several global and local messages. His global message has two dimensions. First, *jihad* (both defensive and offensive, military and otherwise) is a central duty which cannot be suspended depending on the historical context in which Muslims find themselves. Second, its purpose is not simply to 'liberate' Muslims from foreign domination or 'expel infidels from the Arabian Peninsula' (both themes dominate popular Jihadi discourse) but to establish Islam as a hegemonic religion, power and civilisation (*mashru haymana hadariyya*).

At the local level, Lewis has several points to make. First, he exposes the Saudi religious establishment, which claims to be faithful to the Salafi call of Muhammad ibn Abd al-Wahhab. He sends a clear message that their Salafiyya is corrupted as a result of co-optation by political authority. Second, he exposes the Sahwi Salafi discourse and shows how it has compromised itself by adopting a quietist position after 11 September. He rejects 'hierarchical Islamist organisations' which require total obedience from followers and suppress independent thinking. In such movements, obsession with loyalty, security and the safety of members tend to lead to compromise with those in positions of authority. Lewis is in favour of a *tayar* (current or trend), which is diffuse and difficult to suppress. He calls for a social movement rather than a party like the Islamist organisations. In this respect he is a populist rather than an elitist political activist. He gives the example of al-Qa'ida, which is in his opinion still strong 'horizontally' even after receiving a 'vertical' blow. It managed to inflict damage worldwide even after losing its base in Afghanistan.

Subjecting Lewis's writing to a careful reading exposes and deconstructs well-established dogma about Jihadis, often using a frame of reference which invokes notions of criminality, irrationality, ignorance, fanaticism, hatred and bigotry. Demonising the 'enemy' is a well-known strategy in the process of eliminating him. However, demonisation does not result in 'understanding', which should not be interpreted as 'justifying' or 'accepting' the internal logic that underlies the 'enemy's' behaviour. Equally Lewis and other Jihadis cannot be understood if we continue to think in terms of medieval Islamic theology – for example, referring to such groups as Kharijites or *ghulat* (religious extremists). Such theology is constantly used by the Saudi religious establishment and leadership to denounce the current threat as a religious sin similar to that of the early rejectionists who disobeyed the caliph Ali bin Abi Talib. While comparisons are misleading from both a theological and historical point of view, this discourse enhances state propaganda, which aims to discredit Jihadis by labelling them Kharijites who promote dissent by disobeying the ruler. While there are no grounds for comparing the Saudi rulers with the Muslim caliph Ali, it seems that comparing the Jihadis with the Kharijites who rebelled against him is equally implausible religiously, politically and historically.

In official Saudi discourse, activists like Lewis are often accused of wanting to repeat the Taliban experience in Saudi Arabia. However, he operates in a world far removed from that of the Taliban and the caves of the Tora Bora mountains. Lewis is just one example of a generation of urban, well-educated Muslim men, whose experience of this world is marred by a deep feeling of humiliation as a result of a perceived injustice inflicted on the Muslim world by superpowers and a well-grounded commitment to action which it is hoped will reverse this injustice and regain pride. Lewis is a modern man, and does not aspire to create an archaic, Taliban-style Muslim state in Saudi Arabia. While embracing Western science and technology, he is no doubt socially conservative, and rejects Western values and morality. Part of his project is to restore Muslim values and authenticity, while mastering the latest scientific discoveries, including the internet. Like hundreds of Islamists before him, including famous ones such as Sayiyd Qutb, Lewis has a troubled relationship with the West in which admiration, rejection and envy freely intermingle. Furthermore, by virtue of his education, possible professional training and social outlook, he does not belong to the wretched of this earth. Lewis is a real bourgeois, a pious and engaged middle-class man.

Throughout his life journey – at least the one that is available to the public through his internet confessions – it seems that Lewis acquired all sorts of meanings, but also lost others. He laments the loss of myths and roots in a world where only the 'rootless' is celebrated, the loss of local identity where only those with multiple identities are successful, and the loss of precious faith where reason is dominant. His personal biography situates him in a global world. His message and the means of its transmission are also global. But Lewis craves for his local roots. He also longs for the reinstatement of faith in this supposedly rational world. He cannot accept a world devoid of faith, God and his sovereignty. For Lewis man is a rational being and should act according to rational principles, but these actions must be guided and inspired by faith. They should emanate from the love and submission to God, and a commitment to spread his word, justice and law. He does not, however, call for an esoteric personal experience, a subjective salvation through a reinstatement of a degree of enchantment in a disenchanted world. Lewis is by no means a mystic or a Sufi in search of spells, magic and potions. Nor does he search for a psychological awakening, a retreat into or merger with the divine order. He is neither a Muslim puritan nor a mystic but is fully immersed in this world and its materialism, although he feels guided by divine power, and empowered by faith in a world where such empowerment is dismissed as emotional, irrational, misguided and even destructive.

In addition to searching for glorious roots, Lewis is committed to a constant search for a grand meta-narrative, a historical myth in which he is the central character and his faith is the motivating force. He cannot and will not accept a dismal state of exclusion from world history and humiliation by its forces. Rather than clinging to past myths about a glorious Islamic history, Lewis demands actions in this world which not only bring him back from the periphery but place him at the centre of the grand narrative about times and places. Simply put, Lewis aspires to change the world by action. His Islamism is very much a modern phenomenon, based on a strong belief in the ability to change the world. While Lewis is modern, he also reacts to the modernity that has become hegemonic not only in the Western world but also elsewhere, including his own homeland. Changing the world by action is what Lewis shares with Western Enlightenment thought.

In Western academic scholarship, real Islamist activists were studied, analysed and commented on throughout the second half of the twentieth century as part of the study of 'radical Islam', 'fundamentalism', 'Islamism' and, more recently, 'terrorism'. This became even more urgent after the collapse of Communism, when it seemed to several Western scholars that Islamism is the only remaining challenge to Western hegemony, liberal democracy and value system. Both in the West and in the Muslim world, there were those who liked to present current problems in terms of a polar opposition between the civilised West and the irrational, fanatical Muslim other.[30] This presented the West with an enemy, the 'irrational other' against whom it can define itself and draw its boundaries, while at the same time its image as a repository of reason and rationality began to be deconstructed by Western post-modern critiques. As Western rationality and modernity began to be questioned – and even condemned – by post-modern critics, the defenders of Western modernity misguidedly considered Islam to be the ultimate threat, whereas in fact the onslaught on the rationality of the Enlightenment had actually started in the twentieth century in the West itself. The West's responses to the crumbling of its own narrative about its rationality encouraged a condemnation of the other, who is now believed to be the antithesis of Western Enlightenment. The bipolar discourse of the West gave the Muslim world the opportunity to define its failure and humiliation as a product of Western aggression. Muslims themselves, through their own discourse, preferred to see themselves as that other, whom the West has condemned. Dismissing these explanations proved to be difficult, especially when the reality of the interaction between the West and the Muslim world appeared to justify an even greater belief in the credibility of the explanation – that is, the divide between 'us' and the 'other'.

Social science paradigms developed and nurtured in the age of reason searched for explanations that would situate Lewis and his like in the realm of rationality. If Lewis was a megalomaniac, a psychopath or a serial killer, then only medical science could deal with his personal problems, while criminal justice carries the burden of punishing him and locking him away behind bars or in rehabilitation centres, depending on where he is caught. However, Lewis is a social phenomenon and a political liability for the West – and, some would argue, the Muslim world and beyond. Lewis is today defined as a world menace.

Lewis is text and context. Lewis is also religion and politics. As such, understanding the phenomenon became a priority across the globe. While the humanities took care of text and language,[31] social scientists searched for the context that in all their paradigms (functionalist, Marxist, structural functionalist, modernist and post-modernist) would eventually explain the phenomenon by delineating the causes producing it.[32] In these paradigms, Lewis and his predecessors cannot remain irrational outcasts. They have to be understood as rational actors, although their actions are seen as irrational. In several scholarly works, Islamists such as Lewis are described as irrational rational actors. Part of this obsession with understanding Islamists is an obvious desire to control them and prevent others from emerging. Control can take several guises, ranging from direct military options to more subtle ways of changing the contexts that are believed to produce people like Lewis. This logic suffers from an obvious confusion between context and cause.

Identifying the context is important. Yet the methodology and assumptions used to draw the contours of the context do not seem to provide the full story behind Lewis. In fact, they tend to distort the reality of Lewis as much as the translation of *jihad* as 'holy war' distorts and obliterates the various meanings behind such a concept. Here anthropological knowledge cannot and should not confirm media and some scholarly and academic discourse which may describe Lewis as a criminal, ignorant, marginalised, alienated, peripheral Jihadi who cannot adjust to the onslaught of modernity or accept the hegemony of the West in almost all fields. Arguments about economic, social and political failures often list poverty, alienation, marginalisation, unemployment, a search for Islamic authenticity and pride; these either fail to identify the main causes or paint a distorted picture consisting of a web of causal factors. It is often believed that Jihadis emerge either from the neglected proletariat in the suburbs of big Western cities and the Muslim world or the excluded pious middle class, the dislocated and marginalised petite bourgeoisie of ancient and traditional Muslim cities, thereby holding economic deprivation and alienation responsible for producing the phenomenon. Some of the attempts at identifying the context and characteristics of Islamists are true reflections of milieu in which they grow. Yet causal relationships remain elusive.

Lewis, the Saudi Salafi, interprets the world using a dimension which includes an element often missing in social scientific Western paradigms, namely faith. With the exception of a few examples, these paradigms do not allow us to consider religion as an autonomous field and definitely have no room for religion to be considered as an end in itself. Furthermore, Western paradigms insist that religion and politics are two separate domains. In other cultural contexts, such as Saudi Arabia, the two are inseparable, at least in the minds of the majority of Saudis. If ever faith is acknowledged in Western paradigms, it is always reduced to a causal factor that may inspire a particular behaviour, orientation and dispossession while economic and material conditions are always held to be the ultimate causes. But faith is never considered an autonomous end in itself. Lewis cannot be understood without reinstating faith as an end in its own right rather than as a cause. Also, Lewis cannot be understood if we continue to consider religion and politics as two distinct fields of enquiry. At this juncture, it is important to reinstate that 'religious convictions – as are all convictions worth the name – are far too complex to be either reduced to an option in the market place of ideas or minimised as a refuge that provides emotional peace and comfort'.[33] Lewis may have sought solace in religion against a background of dislocation and confusion, but he saw in it a force that would enable him to understand the world and change it at the same time. He found in religion faith and will. As a Muslim intellectual, Lewis does not reject modernity. He reformulates it.

6   Searching for the unmediated word of God

Remove the Wahhabis from the Arabian Peninsula
al-Katib 5, anonymous Saudi internet author

Lewis Atiyat Allah is but one activist who aspires towards reformulating modernity according to his own principles. Other Saudis are equally concerned with the same questions that torment Lewis, but their preoccupation may differ in its focus and strategy. Yet they all have one common denominator: the search for the unmediated word of God. This search is at the heart of the Saudi debate in the twenty-first century.

Previous chapters demonstrated that official *ulama*, Sahwis and Jihadis are engaged in fierce intellectual battles over religious interpretation. None of these battles is likely to go as far as openly challenging the religious discourse of the ancestor, Muhammad ibn Abd al-Wahhab, or the heritage of *aimat al-da'wa al-najdiyya*. However, contesting this heritage – or at least the way it is practised, applied and interpreted by official scholars – is an ongoing intellectual preoccupation.

Traditional Saudi *ulama* regard themselves as the intellectual heirs of the reformer's heritage and as the only true Muslims. Both dissident Sahwis and Jihadis consider many contemporary official *ulama* to be latecomers who corrupted the initial original message of the reformer under the patronage of the Saudi regime. They both aspire to free religious interpretation from their monopoly. This position was particularly clear among those described previously as Salafi–Ikhwani and Jihadis. Yet not many activists openly scrutinise the interpretations of the ancestor. If they have minor reservations about the eighteenth-century message, they remain silent in the public sphere. It is assumed that the official public sphere is not yet ready for an open critical evaluation of the roots of Wahhabism. In public the majority considered the first Saudi–Wahhabi polity (1744–1818) as the exemplary monotheist state. Some extend this positive evaluation to cover the second state too (1824–91).[1] A small minority amongst them may have theological reservations on Muhammad ibn Abd al-Wahhab granting the oath of allegiance not only

211

to one Saudi ruler but also to his descendants after him, according to the alleged pact between the reformer and the ruler of Deriyyah.[2]

Against silence in the public sphere, many Saudis are concerned with Wahhabi violence, both symbolic and real, against their own Muslim society, commonly referred to as *ahl al-qibla* (the people who face Mecca for prayer), a term that includes all Muslims regardless of sect or school of jurisprudence. In alternative public spheres such as opposition publications abroad and anonymous internet discussion forums, Saudis openly denounce the demonisation of their ancestors and religious traditions. Two groups are vocal in expressing strong rejection of the Wahhabi historical and theological narrative: the Shiʿis of the Eastern Province and some of the Hijazis of the Western region.[3]

Hijazis resist Saudi–Wahhabi hegemony through revival of Hijazi identity and heritage. In this context, the restoration of a building dating back to the Ottoman period becomes an act of defiance that the regime watches very carefully. Similarly, the highlighting of the destruction of archaeological sites such as the burial places of the Prophet and his companions becomes a political act challenging contemporary religio-political domination.[4] The revival of Sufi *dhikr* (devotional recitation) circles is also an act of defiance, which the government did not spare time to suppress.[5] Since 11 September the government has turned a blind eye to such things. It can always rely on a number of official scholars who denounce Hijazis for 'worshipping graves', thus discrediting their religious tradition by associating it with *shirk* (associationist practices).

In the case of the Shiʿis, refuting Wahhabi religious discourse that denounces them as *rafidha* (rejectionists) and polytheists is the beginning of a process of regaining recognition on the religio-political map of Saudi Arabia.[6] This is disguised as a quest to be included as 'partners in the nation', the title of a Shiʿi petition submitted to the king in 2003.[7] Both Shiʿis and Hijazis search not only for recognition and partnership but for greater local autonomy as well. In a previous publication I highlighted various timid attempts by the two groups to challenge Saudi narratives.[8] It remains to be seen whether such cultural and religious activism will be translated into serious political demands calling for 'separation' from the Saudi–Wahhabi polity. So far both groups have emphasised their allegiance to the regime by playing on the theme of *wataniyya* (citizenship), a new slogan that was raised after 11 September, and the increase in Jihadi violence. The government was extremely responsive. It allocated a few places for Shiʿis and Sufi scholars in the National Dialogue Forum. When a known Sufi Hijazi scholar died in 2004, Crown Prince Abdullah visited the family and offered his condolences.

What concerns me in this chapter is how contesting the Saudi–Wahhabi heritage is today taking place from within the rank and file of people who are part of the intellectual tradition that I identified as Wahhabi–Salafi. This chapter documents how Saudi Salafis search for unmediated knowledge about religion, history and politics.

The pillars of Saudi authoritarianism

History, theology and politics are the pillars of authoritarian rule in Saudi Arabia, and enforced a tradition whereby political acquiescence is worship. While authoritarianism of course relies on the exercise of a certain degree of direct physical coercion and oil revenues, it is much more dependent on sacred narratives about the past and present. Such narratives create consent without the need to continuously exert direct repression or regularly distribute handouts. In the twenty-first century, this consent is gradually giving way to contestation.

Today Saudis have direct access to religious knowledge and alternative sources of interpretation. More people read, rather than recite, the Quran. As such they are less dependent on traditional transmission of religious knowledge, although the official religious narrative is reiterated in every public platform, including audio-visual and print media, universities and mosques. Equally, more people are aware of the multiple histories of Saudi Arabia that are available in bookshops in London, Paris, Washington, Beirut, Cairo, Istanbul and Bahrain. Many Saudis denounce the monopoly of official Wahhabi *ulama* over religious interpretation and their demonisation of other Muslims who do not share their interpretations. With increased exposure to other discourses and mass education, mainstream Saudi intellectuals and scholars are involved in a revisionist trend whose main objective is to deconstruct this monopoly and search for the unmediated word of God, the true and authentic Salafiyya that is not corrupted by *ulama* close to power. Mass education has made official *ulama* one category among several others. Searching for the unmediated word of God means dismantling religious monopolies and intellectual cartels. For many Saudi Salafis, the project represents a return to the 'true' and 'real' Salafiyya, a Salafiyya that is outside the iron fist of previous and contemporary religious scholars. It is a return to the book, the tradition of the Prophet and a narrowly defined circle of very early pious ancestors (immediate contemporaries of the Prophet, usually referred to as *al-muhajirun* (the Muslims who migrated from Mecca with the Prophet) and *al-ansar* (Madinan supporters of the early Muslim immigrants). This definition of *al-salaf* immediately excludes latter-day *ulama* and interpreters of the tradition. Many Saudis argue that this was the original project of the reform movement, the Wahhabiyya itself. Today, the quest for the unmediated word of God is also a search for unmediated historical, theological and political interpretations.

Saudis are beginning to deconstruct the three pillars of authoritarianism. A glimpse of this deconstruction is found in the writings and positions of many Saudi intellectuals, *'ulama* and others who are not yet part of an organised group or movement. Their uncoordinated efforts at articulating a critical view of history, theology and politics appeared in many unofficial forums, publications and debating circles. Those who are openly involved in presenting the clearest and most articulate revision of the pillars of authoritarianism are subjected to state repression, including suspension from their professions and imprisonment. Others prefer to remain anonymous, writing in internet discussion boards and forums.[9]

Liberating history from Wahhabi domination

In Saudi Arabia the past is a theological rather than a historical narrative. Its contours are mediated by an early generation of Wahhabi *'ulama* who were both religious scholars and chroniclers. While emerging Arab nation-states replaced their theological history with modern ideological historical narratives, Saudi Arabia continued to propagate religious narratives about the past.[10] As mentioned in the first chapter, the theological narrative about the past emphasises the blasphemy of the population of Arabia prior to the reform movement, in an attempt to justify the wars waged by the Saudi Wahhabi forces since the eighteenth century. War is justified only if Muslims fought were blasphemous. Only then does their slaughter fall within the parameter of legitimate *jihad* in Wahhabi interpretations because it is presented as a struggle against the *mushrikun* (associationists).

The Saudi–Wahhabi historical narrative is today contested. A Saudi Islamist who prefers to remain anonymous is engaged in rewriting Saudi history. During the context of several long conversations, he argued that Wahhabis were the contemporary Kharijites of the Muslim world. My informant was highly articulate and knowledgeable about both the past and the present. In addition to his professional training, he is well versed in religious matters. He endorsed calls for re-establishing a glorious Muslim caliphate. According to him, it was the Wahhabis who contributed to the downfall of this caliphate in modern times – in accordance with imperial British policy. He drew my attention to an internet pamphlet–book entitled *Who are the Kharijites?* In this book, the author, Abdullah al-Qahtani (a pseudonym), dedicates a chapter to the refutation of Wahhabi claims about the blasphemous and associationist nature of other Sunni Muslims, not only in Saudi Arabia but also in the Muslim world.[11] A compilation of theological and historical sources, the book has become a reference document for those Saudi Islamists who object to Wahhabi domination of the Salafi religious map. After all, not all Islamists in Saudi Arabia are Wahhabis.[12]

Ironically, the author relies on Wahhabi chronicles that documented the expansion of the movement since the eighteenth century.[13] However, while these chronicles glorify this expansion and consider it a *jihad* against the blasphemous and associationists of Arabia, al-Qahtani deconstructs this thesis. He hopes to demonstrate that Wahhabis were not only historical enemies of Muslims but also agents of foreign domination, mainly the British. According to al-Qahtani, Wahhabis served British interests twice. In the eighteenth century they undermined the unity of Muslims and threatened the Ottoman Empire. In the twentieth century, they ousted the Sharif of the Hijaz after the latter objected to British plans. Al-Qahtani claims that the Wahhabis were a British creation intended to undermine the Ottoman Empire, divide Muslims and weaken their unity.

Both al-Qahtani and my informant cite a book that circulated on the internet. The book is entitled *Confessions of a British Spy*, and is also known as *Memoirs of Mr Hempher, The British Spy of the Middle East*.[14] It is claimed that it was written by a man called Hempher, a British agent who allegedly met Muhammad ibn Abd al-Wahhab in Basra and convinced him to work towards dismantling the Ottoman Empire. After meeting Ibn Abd al-Wahhab, Hempher wrote, 'I was happy because I was sure that this ignorant and morally depraved man was going to establish a new sect, which in turn would demolish Islam from within, and that I was the composer of the heretical tenets of this new sect.'[15] After 2001, Hempher's book became very popular among Saudi dissidents who denounced Wahhabiyya and Saudi hegemony; references to it flooded Saudi internet discussion boards. The book is also endorsed by several dissident Sunni websites. The book, however, is a recent creation that cannot possibly reflect accurate history. It is a constructed narrative that has been revived by Wahhabiyya's opponents.

In al-Qahtani's narrative, Wahhabis are portrayed as friends of infidels and enemies of Muslims. Such depictions resonate with present concerns. Al-Qahtani invokes the past in order to explain current Saudi alliance with the West, mainly the USA. His story about Hempher substantiates his accusations.

According to al-Qahtani, Wahhabi fanaticism towards other Muslims served only the interests of the enemies of Islam. The past is invoked here to explain the present. An alleged relationship between Wahhabis and a

British spy in the eighteenth century is used as a historical precedent that set the scene for later conspiracies against Muslims in fulfilment of imperial intrigues. Several conclusions are often drawn from such references. One may argue that if Wahhabis were responsible for 11 September, then their actions contributed to demonising Muslims and Islam. The War on Terror, interpreted as a war on Muslims, would not have been launched had Wahhabis not provoked it. Other conclusions are equally possible. Wahhabis could not have been involved in the events of 11 September because throughout their history, starting with the overtures of Mr Hempher, they were friends of the infidels. Those who endorse this view argue that Osama Bin Laden could not possibly be described as a Wahhabi.

Today the past as inscribed in the Wahhabi tradition and taught in Saudi history textbooks is subjected to reinterpretation by a wide circle of Saudis. These interpreters may or may not include well-known historians, but no doubt some of them are searching for an unmediated narrative that suits their own ideological and political orientations. Revising the past means revisiting the legitimacy of the so-called 'state of monotheism'. While Hijazis, with the exception of a small minority, and the majority of Shi'is were historically opponents of Wahhabiyya and Saudi domination, today the circle is wider than that. It includes those who were brought up on its teachings but for various reasons began to challenge its historical–theological narratives. However, those who challenge these narratives face repression. It seems that Wahhabis have succeeded in enforcing the myth that without the Saudi royal family Islam is undermined, and that without the Al-Saud, Arabia would have continued to be the land of pagans and associationists. To be a good Muslim one needs to believe in Al-Saud. Revisiting the past is an attempt to prove that the Saudi–Wahhabi alliance was responsible for chaos and discord rather than unity among Muslims.

While Wahhabi expansion in Arabia is always described in Saudi narratives as conquest in pursuit of spreading monotheism among a nearly pagan society, al-Qahtani paints a horrific picture of Saudi–Wahhabi atrocities against other Muslims, both inside and outside Arabia, committed in the name of God and *jihad*. His examples start with the eighteenth century and continue to the present day. He mentions the people of Taif, a mountainous summer resort that fell into the hands of the Saudi–Wahhabi forces during the early conquest of the Hijaz in the nineteenth century and later in the twentieth century. He claims that Taif was attacked 'to liberate it from blasphemy, according to Wahhabi legends. They killed men and women, looted the city and its libraries and mosques. They killed Abdullah al-Zawawi, the Shafi mufti, Sheikh Abdullah Abu al-Khayr,

Qadi of Mecca, and Sheikh Jafar al-Shaybi.' In the twentieth century, Wahhabis fought Sharif Husayn who 'refused British orders to give Palestine to the Jews. The Wahhabis, under the leadership of Khalid ibn Loay, Faysal al-Duwaysh and Sultan ibn Bjad, attacked and sacked the Hijaz to frighten the sedentary and nomadic population.'[16]

The author reminds his readers that Wahhabis looted the holiest of all cities, Mecca. He writes, 'They never showed leniency. They left Meccans hungry. Meccans sold the jewels of their women to buy food. They starved; some ate donkeys and dead animals. The price of dog meat went up. How could they fight in Mecca when the Prophet himself prohibited violence in the sanctuary?'[17] Al-Qahtani not only highlights the plight of Hijazis, he defends the Najdi population of Arabia, which was subjected to similar atrocities and injustices. He shows that Wahhabis demonised other Sunnis and rejected their interpretations in order to justify their expansionist wars in Arabia. According to the author, Wahhabis killed Muslims in mosques after Friday prayers. He cites evidence of Ibn Abd al-Wahhab himself who described the ruler of Uyaynah, Othman ibn Muamar, as 'a blasphemous associationist. Muslims vowed to kill him after Friday prayer. He was killed in Rajab 1163AH.'[18] Al-Qahtani argues that an apostate should not be treacherously assassinated. Instead, he should be asked to repent. He concludes that Wahhabis terrorised the population in pursuit of booty rather than monotheism.

Al-Qahtani moves from history to geography when he challenges the Wahhabi 'map of blasphemy'. In Wahhabi narratives, after the conquest of Najd towards the end of the eighteenth century, the land beyond it became the land of blasphemy where religious innovations reigned. As mentioned in the first chapter, Wahhabis called upon Muslims to abandon these blasphemous regions and migrate to the land of Islam – the area under Saudi–Wahhabi domination. Invoking the Prophetic tradition which considered Najd as the land where sins will appear, al-Qahtani's historical narrative becomes theological as he quotes the Prophet to prove that the Wahhabi homeland was described as the land of earthquakes and discord, 'hunak al-zalazil wa al-fitan wa biha yatlu' qarn al-shaytan'. According to al-Qahtani, some Wahhabi scholars argued that in this Hadith the Prophet referred to Najd al-Iraq, the elevated land of Iraq, rather than Najd of Arabia. Using several quotations, al-Qahtani asserts that the Prophet meant the geographical area where false Prophets and apostates appeared immediately after the death of Prophet Muhammad: Najd of Arabia. In modern times, it was the homeland of the Wahhabis. Najd, like Wahhabi history, is today a contested region. Wahhabis consider it the homeland of the monotheists, *aimat al-daʿwa al-najdiyya*; their opponents see it as the land of past and present apostates. The latter recall the tradition of the

false prophets, for example Musaylima al-Kadhab, to establish historical continuity.[19] The theological history propagated in Wahhabi religio-
political discourse generates equally implausible counter-narratives. In the
eyes of opponents of Wahhabiyya, Najd becomes the land of blasphemy
par excellence. What evidence is better than the words of the Prophet?
The official sanctification and mystification of Wahhabiyya leads to unreasonable demonisation of its homeland and people.

Internet discussion forums are today the battleground between supporters of Wahhabi interpretations of the past and their opponents. Al-
Katib 5 contributes to the debate about history and Wahhabiyya. Like
al-Qahtani, he does not reveal his real identity. He praises the intellectual
abilities of Muhammad ibn Abd al-Wahhab, but does not shy away from
criticising some of his views. He denies that the reformer renewed faith,
because 'faith does not get old'. He contextualises the reform movement
by discussing the social and economic conditions that prevailed in Arabia
at the time. He argues that Arabia was backward, illiterate and poor.
Consequently, Ibn Abd al-Wahhab followed strict and radical interpretations of the Hanbali *fiqh* to remain on the safe side in this specific social
context. He should, however, have indicated to his followers that his
approach was suitable for that time only and should not be taken as a
standard path to be followed after him. Al-Katib 5 laments the evolution
of the relationship between the Saudi royal family, whom Ibn Abd al-
Wahhab 'installed as the political authority' and the *'ulama*, the guardians
of the *shari'a*. The latter have become a 'media front' (*jabha ilamiyya*), to
enforce the legitimacy of the regime. The *'ulama* have been reduced to the
role of poets who follow and praise the leadership. Al-Katib 5 offers his
reflections on the contemporary state:

When Abdulaziz al-Saud, the legendary leader, returned to Riyadh to establish a
'Kingdom without Borders' he was assisted by the Ikhwan, who were courageous
and loyal men, but they were also simple. They had no thinkers and *'ulama*
amongst them. We hear secular writers describing the Ikhwan as thugs and
robbers to justify their suppression after the unification of Arabia. Thugs are
usually united by a thug. Does this mean that King Ibn Saud was one of those
thugs? The Ikhwan were faithful to the principles of Ibn Abd al-Wahhab but they
confused the general principles with the minor principles.[20]

In another article, al-Katib 5 starts with a provocative title, 'Remove
Wahhabis from the Arabian Peninsula', thus invoking the Prophetic
Hadith calling upon Muslims to remove infidels from Arabia, referred to
earlier in this book. He explains:

Wahhabiyya became dormant until after the nationalist and revolutionary trends
of Nasir swept the Arab world. Wahhabiyya re-emerged with the intention of

widening its influence. It aimed to Islamise society but in fact its real objective was to increase its influence in the political field. The Saudi regime sanctioned Wahhabiyya hoping that it will serve its own interests . . . Wahhabis are used to repress those who do not agree with them. They discredit people by labelling them *kafir*s or secularists. They claim to represent Saudi society but they do not. Wahhabi *fatwa*s never condemn the state; they never object openly to usury and corruption. They never call for freedom, justice, and equality. Wahhabiyya sanctified individuals and families like Sheikhs Ibn Baz and Ibn Uthaymin. Ibn Baz allows Muslims to seek assistance from infidels to fight a Muslim state while Ibn Uthaymin forbids women to wear jeans because that is regarded as imitating the corrupt infidel West. How could Wahhabis continue to propagate contradictions? When Wahhabis clash with the regime, they quickly abandon their principles in favour of acquiescence.[21]

Al-Katib 5 exposes how the marriage between Wahhabiyya and politics was detrimental because it led to the first losing its credibility. He invokes the Afghan *jihad* as an example of how Wahhabiyya mobilised Saudi youth to serve American interests. They

advised the youth to travel to Afghanistan where they were promised to meet the sheikhs of *jihad*, Osama bin Laden and Abdullah Azzam, who were both righteous men. The Saudi government was mistaken when it antagonised Bin Laden. Wahhabis changed their mind after the eruption of violence in Saudi Arabia. Bin Laden, Azzam and Qutb are now all considered terrorists. The sheikhs of Wahhabiyya present themselves as patient preachers. In fact they preach only to increase their wealth. Wahhabis repent and ask for forgiveness when faced with the sword of Al-Saud. This is what happened to the Wahhabi Jihadi Sheikhs when they appeared on television.[22]

Al-Katib 5 refers to the crisis of Wahhabiyya during the invasion of Iraq in April 2003. He reminds his readers that the Saudi government was not in a position to support or criticise the invasion. Wahhabis preferred to preach that

the Americans were in Iraq to remove Saddam the blasphemous. Later they preached that there was no flag under which *jihad* can be launched against American occupiers. They considered the Iraqi government brought about by American occupation as *wali al-amr*, who must be obeyed. They considered resisting foreign occupation in Iraq as *khuruj 'ala wali al-amr* [rebellion against the ruler].[23]

The crisis of Wahhabiyya is but an aspect of a general crisis experienced by the contemporary state, according to al-Katib 5. His evaluation of the 1932 Saudi state highlights the 'reasons for its imminent downfall'. He lists several factors: the estrangement of the royal leadership from its social base, its subservience to the USA, its inability to improve social and economic conditions, its corruption and its injustice. He criticises the nepotism that is practised in ministries run by princes. He argues that 'princes threaten the unity of the country because they rule in the provinces as if these provinces are their personal property. Each local governor operates according to his own whims.' He cites the governor of Asir, Prince Khalid al-Faysal, who he says has turned the region into a secular emirate where dancing and singing dominate the cultural scene. 'At any turbulent moment in the future, the governor will be able to declare Asir an independent state. The Saudi royal family is digging its own grave. It shuts the door between itself and the people.'[24] Al-Katib 5's assessment of the future of the country under Saudi rule is dark, yet he claims that his allegiance, love and respect for the royal family drives him to issue this bleak evaluation of the situation.

Responses to al-Katib 5's articles vary. Some readers accuse him of causing discord and encouraging chaos. Others call him a secular agitator. More reasonable responses try to explain that he confuses Wahhabi teachings with practice, and should not blame the mistakes of contemporary Wahhabis on the original sources. His articles remain very popular, both among those who agree and those who disagree with his reasoning.

Many Saudis search for alternative reflections on the past in order to understand an uncertain present and future. This search is also a quest for unmediated knowledge. While Saudis deconstruct the Wahhabi theological narrative about history and geography, it remains to be seen whether they offer a plausible alternative narrative. Clear and convincing alternative narratives often emerge in contexts where there is genuine freedom of expression. Saudi Arabia in the twenty-first century is still far from this. Resorting to the anonymous internet discussion boards is only the beginning of the journey towards creating the right context. We will now turn our attention to those who deconstruct Wahhabi theology itself.

Liberating theology from Wahhabi domination

A second feature of the Saudi revisionist trend is a preoccupation with theological arguments. Some religious scholars aim to free the religious field from the control of one single interpretation and challenge early Wahhabi theological positions, especially those related to the alleged blasphemy of other Muslims, which Wahhabi scholars took to extremes. This stance is represented by the work of a young sheikh, Hasan al-Maliki. While al-Maliki's ideas question eighteenth-century theological positions, they are also relevant to the contemporary context. His work is not simply about how Muhammad ibn Abd al-Wahhab misjudged the Islam of his contemporaries when he branded them as polytheists and innovators; nor is it about how later disciples have corrupted his original message. Al-Maliki's work is concerned with contemporary Saudi Arabia, a place where those who claim a profound adherence to the unmediated word of God are blind followers of a previous generation of *'ulama* that has assumed sanctity. Their knowledge is mediated by the words of past and present *'ulama*. Al-Maliki endeavours to 'expose the radicals among the Hanbalis amongst us, a project which should not be portrayed as an attack on Saudi Arabia, as often mistakenly interpreted by radicals'.[25]

In a book entitled *A Preacher Not a Prophet*, published outside Saudi Arabia, Sheikh al-Maliki courageously violates a well-established and revered taboo – the sanctity of the founder of the Wahhabi movement. Al-Maliki questions this sanctity by invoking both Hanbali sources and the legacy of Muhammad ibn Abd al-Wahhab himself. Al-Maliki's book is a revisionist reading of one of the most important books written by Muhammad ibn Abd al-Wahhab, *Kashf al-shubuhat* (The Unveiling of Doubt). Al-Maliki has two objectives. First, he traces how latter-day Wahhabis departed from the main themes that were represented in Ibn Abd al-Wahhab's message. Second, and more importantly, he challenges the theological judgements and exposes the errors of Ibn Abd al-Wahhab himself.

The author reminds his readers of the reformer's strong rejection of great deference granted to interpreters of religion and his emphasis on the importance of going back to the text as the primary source. Al-Maliki considers the Wahhabi movement a revolution against the mystification of *al-awliya* (pious men). He asks, how could contemporary Saudi *'ulama* grant the reformer a status that equates him with prophets when he himself rejected such sanctity being granted to preachers and interpreters of religion? His understanding of Wahhabiyya centres on how it emerged as a movement that denounced excessive deference to interpreters of religion, yet contemporary Wahhabis showed nothing but excessive adoration of the early Wahhabi scholars. Contemporary Wahhabi *'ulama*, according to al-Maliki, practise *ghulu* (radicalism) in defending their theological ancestor. He argues that had the reformer been alive, he would have denounced this radicalism. He proposes several steps to free the religious field from a radicalism that is centred on sanctifying the founder of the movement. First, an awareness that religious interpretation is a product of human effort helps to desanctify early scholars and allows students of religion to reconsider their postulations without feeling that religion itself is threatened. Put differently, questioning early interpretations and dogma does not mean questioning religion itself. Second, an assertion that 'among human beings we only follow the Prophet Muhammad' is enough to dispel the sanctity of later interpreters.[26]

As he endeavours to challenge contemporary radicalism, al-Maliki defines the 'real' Salafiyya. In his opinion, 'we must not consider the reformer an infallible prophet. We must subject his writings to *shari'a* rule and evidence. We must not make him above *shari'a*. We must follow his words that comply with *shari'a* and reject that which does not. We must go back to *shari'a* evidence rather than men's words.'[27] Al-Maliki explains that in Saudi Arabia today there are two brands of Salafiyya, a corrupted tradition based on lies and injustices and another tradition close to the book and Sunna, propagated by people who subject the words of men to those two sources.[28] He articulates a profound quest for the unmediated word of God. He is concerned that today in Saudi Arabia, radicals preach against radicalism ('ghulat yanhawn an al-ghulu'). He asks how contemporary scholars can denounce Jihadis, who resort to the texts of early Wahhabi scholars that they themselves sanctify. He identifies the inherent problems in Wahhabi theology, which depends heavily on genealogies of knowledge. He proposes to revisit and, possibly, question the chain of transmission. This questioning, in his opinion, should not lead to questioning faith or creed. Al-Maliki proposes dissociating the sanctity of religion from the words of men. While religion is a revealed sacred tradition, knowledge about it is not. This position echoes similar arguments in the Muslim world that highlight the distinction.[29]

Al-Maliki's revisionist project is primarily concerned with the problem of *takfir* (excommunication). As Wahhabis insisted that monotheism should be exhibited in the heart, demonstrated in words and enacted in behaviour, they widened the grounds upon which a Muslim can be excommunicated. Al-Maliki questions whether Muslims can be judged blasphemous if their actions violate the principle of monotheism because they are simply ignorant. He refutes the evidence that justified claims that Muslims who may have incorporated in their rituals certain practices, such as supplication to pious men or visiting tombs, are blasphemous or polytheists, a theological position that distinguished Wahhabi interpretations from other Sunni schools. He strongly rejects Ibn Abd al-Wahhab's claim that such blasphemous Muslims are more dangerous than the *kafir*s of Quraysh in the age of ignorance. He argues that Wahhabis painted a rosy picture of Qurayshi *kafir*s, who in fact denied the afterlife, practised infanticide, allowed usury and deliberately destroyed human life, and questions whether such people can really be considered better than Muslims who utter the declaration of faith, *al-shahada*. Al-Maliki claims that the reformer was so generous towards the *kafir*s in order to justify his denunciation of Muslims who did not share his interpretations. He concludes that Wahhabis share with the early Kharijites their excommunication of Muslims who engage in *ma'asi* (minor sins), while at the same time denouncing these Kharijites. Sheikh al-Maliki proposes starting a process whereby contemporary *'ulama* do not shy away from identifying and correcting Ibn Abd al-Wahhab's errors. Self-criticism is the first step towards dealing with religious radicalism.[30]

Al-Maliki criticises the early Wahhabi position which accused whole regions of blasphemy if only a small minority exhibited it. He attributes this to the fact that from early days Wahhabiyya was a political project aimed at dominating other territories in Arabia. According to al-Maliki, the whole population of Hijaz and Asir, for example, should not be judged blasphemous when only individuals may exhibit certain blasphemous behaviour.

Al-Maliki's views were, not surprisingly, denounced by official *ulama*. He was dismissed from his job in the Ministry of Education and incurred the wrath of other Wahhabi–Salafis in Saudi Arabia. Sahwi sheikhs and Jihadi ideologues wrote epistles refuting his ideas. Some accused him of being a covert Zaydi innovator who erodes the tenets of faith from within.[31] Although he declares in his books that he is a Hanbali Salafi, he incurred harsh criticism.

Al-Maliki does not openly and directly question the religio-political heritage of the Wahhabiyya. Like Judge Abd al-Aziz al-Qasim, mentioned earlier in this book, he is concerned only with the theological aspects of Wahhabiyya. This probably explains why state reaction to his revisionist theology is relatively lenient, compared, for example, with the imprisonment of Abdullah al-Hamid, whose work directly challenges several political innovations in the official Wahhabi tradition. To find critiques of the religio-political Wahhabi tradition, one must turn to a different literature and context, a task the following section aims to accomplish.

Liberating politics from Wahhabi interpretations

Liberating politics from the control of the Wahhabi religio-political discourse is a dangerous endeavour in Saudi Arabia because the exercise challenges one of the most important and fundamental pillars of Saudi authoritarianism. Contemporary politics that demands an absolute submission to rulers became theological. Professor Abdullah al-Hamid articulated a political vision grounded in alternative religious interpretations that was deemed threatening. Al-Hamid is counted as an Islamist who among others was part of a loose group that was consulted in the process of producing the Memorandum of Advice and later establishing the Committee for the Defence of Legitimate Rights in Arabia in 1993. He was suspended from his job and was imprisoned in the 1990s. In 2003–4 he was involved in articulating drafts of various petitions calling for the gradual evolution of the Saudi regime towards a constitutional monarchy. He is best described as a member of a loosely defined Islamist intellectual trend that highlights the centrality of Islam as a reference framework for future social and political change. The trend is grounded in the emphasis on *maqasid al-shari'a* (the objectives of *shari'a*), which prioritises people's religious and worldly interest. Al-Hamid calls for a critical evaluation of Islamic *turath* (heritage) and developing the spirit of openness, pluralism and recognition of the intellectual, political and sectarian specificity of the other.[32] This approach is described as the rationalist and enlightened trend dominant among a small minority of Islamist intellectuals, mainly university professors, journalists and writers. In Western accounts, al-Hamid is described as part of an emerging trend, referred to as Islamo-liberal. Like other Saudis labelled as such, al-Hamid, however, would consider himself a Salafi.

Al-Hamid draws attention to a serious derailment of religious discourse.[33] This led to the disappearance of religious interpretations that celebrate justice and freedom. Islam, according to al-Hamid has two dimensions; one regulates *'ibadat* (worship), and the other regulates worldly matters. The first is concerned with the individual and his relation with God, whereas the second is ultimately concerned with relationships between individuals in Muslim society. The first ensures personal salvation, while the second governs the regulation of human life and association. According to al-Hamid, prayer is the most important *'ibada* that ensures personal salvation. Justice is the pillar of the second salvation, i.e. the regulation of interpersonal relations. The practice of justice is as important as performing daily prayers. At this junction, al-Hamid resorts to the Quran as he cites verses describing the obliteration of previous communities, not because they were *kafirs*, but because they paid lip service to social justice. In an attempt to retain Salafi credibility, he reminds his readers of Ibn Taymiyya's assertion that 'God makes a just *kafir* state victorious over the unjust Muslim state'. In his interpretation of religious heritage, al-Hamid argues that monotheism is linked to practising social justice. If present-day Muslims are backward, it is not because they have ceased to perform the ritualistic aspect of their religion. Backwardness is not a function of abandoning prayer. It results from neglecting the obligation to enforce social justice. This justice is linked to the practice of *shura* (real consultation by election rather than by appointment). Previous scholars whose work constitutes what is referred to as the Islamic tradition did not pay enough attention to this important reality, according to al-Hamid.

Al-Hamid attributes the neglect of consultation and social justice to several factors. First, the predominance of Umayyad–Abbasid jurisprudence that grew in the shadow of despotic rulers. Second, the role played by religious scholars who trivialised the contractual civil obligations and highlighted the centrality of ablution, supplication and Quranic recitation. Such scholars buried tolerance, freedom and equality. He concludes that slogans such as 'Islam is the solution' are doomed to fail if the Umayyad–Abbasid heritage and jurisprudence are presented as the true heritage of Islam. An Islamic renewal/reformation needs to be preceded by deconstructing Umayyad–Abbasid visions of creed, jurisprudence, civil and political obligations. 'The Islamic heritage needs to return to the holy book and the Prophetic tradition as practised by the Prophet himself and his four caliphs in order to reach an understanding of good political practice.'[34]

Al-Hamid deconstructs the meaning of *wali al-amr*, the one who determines and controls destiny. He laments how this meaning is now loaded with notions of absolute rule and despotism. Because of the heavy intervention of previous religious scholars, Muslims have succeeded in 'Islamising oppression and backwardness' under the guise of returning to the pious ancestors and guarding authenticity. Some previous *'ulama* resisted this process of Islamising repression, but later they lost their ability to resist. According to al-Hamid, Muslims inherited a tradition that considers oppression an unavoidable and necessary evil, and regards unjust leadership a natural political aspect of government. They cherished security while neglecting justice. They eventually produced the theological discourse that justified the police state, a contemporary version of old despotism. When Muslim *'ulama* issued a *fatwa* making it permissible to torture an accused person, they abandoned the civil aspect of Islam and propagated political innovation disguised under an Islamic rhetoric. Al-Hamid resorts to the words of Ibn Taymiyya's student Ibn al-Qayyim, who says: 'Satan misleads Muslims. He may show them ninety-nine doors that open paths to a secondary good but he will divert their attention from one major good. *'Ulama* were diverted from calling for just, consultative rule. Satan knows that *al-hukm al-jabri* [coercive rule] leads to oppression, poverty and sins. Satan led the *umma* astray.'[35]

Al-Hamid argues that *al-sha'b* (the people) must participate in political decisions because this is a *shari'a* principle (*asl*). He does not consider an appointed group who 'tie and loose' the real *sha'b*. The people must elect their representatives. Al-Hamid resorts to the Quran. He mentions that in the Quran God does not address the sultan even once. The Quran addresses the *umma*. Therefore, it is incumbent on the *umma* to act in pursuit of public good. Political participation must be protected by a constitution and enacted in election. The conclusion al-Hamid draws is a serious departure from the dominant official Wahhabi religio-political discourse. His understanding of the meaning of *wali al-amr* – consultation, justice, political participation and elections – threatens religiously sanctioned authoritarian rule. Al-Hamid calls for the people rather than a small circle of appointed representatives to participate in the political process. Although he does not refer directly to contemporary politics or mention the role of Wahhabi *'ulama*, his revisionist arguments cannot be read except as an attempt to liberate contemporary politics from the control of past theology as well as contemporary manifestations of previous theological positions. The challenging nature of al-Hamid's revisionist thought led to his imprisonment.

In his reconsideration of *jihad*, al-Hamid elaborates on the role of the spoken and written 'word' (*al-kalima*) in pursuing the project of political participation, consultation and election. According to him these are the objectives of *jihad madani* (a civil jihad). The just word is not simply that spoken by an *'alim* who turns up in the ruler's council to utter advice, and leaves after having cleared his conscience. The word is

that spoken from a minaret, a sermon of a preacher, a treatise of an intellectual, a play performed in theatre, and a poem that mobilises people. The word is not simply a short summary. It can be a long analytical treatise, a petition that analyses and reaches conclusions . . . Civil reform is an aspect of *jihad* in which all must participate. The *umma* must be involved in *jihad madani*. The ammunition of peaceful civil *jihad* is the pen, the tongue and social associations rather than bullets.[36]

In order to protect those who utter words of justice, they must form organisations, the seeds of an emerging civil society. Failure to do so will lead to individual activists being arrested and suppressed. Al-Hamid must have anticipated his fate, as he visited Saudi prisons several times. To guarantee their safety, reformers must reach out to a constituency. This constituency must be educated and involved in the project of *jihad madani*. This position is contrasted with the exclusionist approach of official Wahhabi *'ulama*, whose views on the masses are often tarnished by accusations of debauchery and blasphemy. Al-Hamid rejects their view, which states that the masses are 'gregarious savages who are dangerous when they are united and beneficial when they are disunited. A reformer must have a crowd (*rahat*) to protect him and support him, otherwise his words are lost and his efforts are obliterated by the forces of repression.'[37]

Al-Hamid dismantles yet another pillar of the dominant religio-political discourse, that which states that disavowing the abominable in the heart or by the tongue (secretly) is enough. He argues that this strategy does not reform a state. He uses the example of Muawiya (the first Umayyad caliph) described as *hakim ja'ir* (a despotic ruler), and Kemal Atatürk, described as *hakim kafir* (a blasphemous ruler). In both cases, change could not be achieved through the word of a small, educated minority (*nukhba*). Reforming the state is incumbent on the participation of the masses through education and guidance. He reprimands those *ulama* whose preoccupation was with jurisprudence that does not 'reform a state, does not awake the *umma*, using the pretext that Muslims must be patient when confronted with the power of the despot . . . even if he steals money and hits backs',[38] a reference to official religious discourse that draws on weak Hadiths and cites Quranic verses out of context in order to enforce and legitimise authoritarian rule, acquiescence and unconditional surrender to the will of rulers. Private advice fails to achieve its objective, according to al-Hamid. It 'is the beginning rather than the end. A despot does not usually listen. Those *ulama* who continue to defend secret advice to rulers must consider it a personal choice that is not grounded in *shari'a* evidence.'[39] If they are content with private advice, this must be their personal choice rather than a religious obligation that binds all Muslims.

Al-Hamid rules out the argument that reforming the state is dependent on the accession of a just ruler, especially when oppression becomes a regime that is entangled with a wide circle of beneficiaries. He gives the example of Umar ibn Abd al-Aziz, the Umayyad caliph celebrated in the historical imagination of Sunni Muslims as a just ruler, who could not prevent the decline of the Islamic polity although he personally had excellent qualities. To ensure reform, society must be empowered through the formation of independent civil institutions and an awareness of civil rights. He calls for the emergence of the religious thinker who renews religion to replace the traditional religious scholars. Only the first can spread awareness. As far as relations with political power, the only way is to give and take. Politics is negotiation, but society must be strong to negotiate with authoritarian rule.[40]

In this blunt critique of previous theology that justified oppression, al-Hamid does not openly mention the Wahhabi tradition, but it is impossible to read his intellectual productions without making the connection between his revisions and the dominant religio-political discourse. He is not involved in intellectual academic luxury. He aims to reform the dominant Wahhabi discourse from within. He called for reform and paid a high price for revisiting old grounds that are well established in official narratives. However, he insists on clarifying that the *ulama* are interpreters of religion rather than religion itself. Calls for reform should not be limited to those under their patronage. The *ulama* have monopoly over *fatwas*, yet it is the responsibility of society as a whole to engage in reform. Al-Hamid calls for the breaking of the monopoly of the *ulama* when he writes: 'It is not appropriate to limit calls for reform to those very religious members of society. A Muslim who exhibits *ma'asi* [sins] must not hold himself from calling for reform. Equally those *mutadayin* [religiously observant people] should not think that they are the only ones who can call for reform.'[41]

Al-Hamid blurs the boundaries between categories of people that are now well established in Saudi Arabia as he propagates the right of all in society to be engaged in the political process. Although al-Hamid is an intellectual, he is a populist one. His main concern is to dismantle the rift that has appeared in Saudi society between various categories of people, namely the so-called *mutadayin* (religious) and *'ilmani* (secular). He challenges the perception that only the former are guardians of public good and initiators of reform. Although al-Hamid is counted among the intellectuals, he does not shy away from demanding a serious engagement of the people in all their traditions, backgrounds and education to participate in reforming state and society. His efforts towards redefining heritage and freeing Islam from past and present monopolies led him to argue that contemporary associationist practices (*shirk jadid*) involve glorifying rulers and worshipping them.

Al-Hamid moved from an intellectual revisionist project to political activism in a document, 'Islam is our Constitution: A Peaceful Call for Constitutionalism and Civil Society'.[42] In this document al-Hamid identifies the origins behind the failure of reform projects. The problem lies in repression and monopolising the political decision-making process. He deconstructs the myth that glorifies the rule of *al-mustabid al-'adil* (the just oppressor), as he argues that the myth is based on a contradiction. An oppressor cannot possibly be just. The myth enforced coercive rule and blocked the emergence of consultative justice, whereby society participates fully in the decision-making process. To regard reform as an elitist project that excludes the *umma* is a position that will inevitably lead to thwarting political reform. Reforming society and state are parallel processes; one cannot be accomplished without the other.

Al-Hamid offers a reinterpretation of the role of the state, which is limited to administering people's will rather than subduing it. He challenges the view that 'wali al-amr adra bil maslaha' (the ruler knows public interest best). The state is administration while the government is the executive arm that translates people's will into action and articulates the objectives of *shari'a*. To achieve these objectives, reformers must spread the culture of civil society, through education, which in turn will lead to establishing the institutional and constitutional basis for reform. Reform is delayed in a country like Saudi Arabia because the vocabulary of constitutionalism and civil society were suppressed. Saudis should not consider the call for establishing the institutions of civil society as a call for party politics (*hizbiyya*), but for empowering society in all its sections. Al-Hamid invokes here the notion of citizenship (*wataniyya*). He argues that the national state must move society from sectarianism to an all-encompassing citizenship. The state must be capable of absorbing diversity and pluralism. According to him, this is the real meaning of the Islamic state that incorporates diversity and difference. In order to achieve serious reform, one must deconstruct the inherited Islamic political jurisprudence that grew under previous repressive and authoritarian rule. Obstacles to reform stem from the absence of jurists who are capable of articulating political reform that highlights the benefits of constitutionalism in an accessible language that draws on the holy book and the Prophet's tradition.

Al-Hamid highlights certain conditions in Saudi society that delay and may inhibit the emergence of a constitutional reformist trend. The polarisation of society between those who call for Islamising society and the advocates of modernity delays reform as neither emphasises the importance of constitutionalism. Furthermore, he laments the absence of social values that promote accepting difference, pluralism, tolerance and peaceful resolution of conflict.

Al-Hamid diagnoses the problem in Saudi society as 'the violence of the minority and the apathy of the majority'. Society has not produced the discourse of 'peaceful change'. Rather, it encouraged polarisation and radicalism. Al-Hamid recognises that by invoking the rhetoric of modernisation, the centralised state and the well-funded ʿulama were able to destroy traditional organisation and local activism within the traditional structures of the mosque, the tribe, the guild and other forms of traditional association. The state deployed substantial resources for this objective while the ʿulama provided religious legitimacy. The state failed to replace these associations with unions, political parties and modern, all-encompassing organisations. Al-Hamid acknowledges in passing that the state was powerful as it purchased the means of coercion to directly oppress and spy on its citizens.

According to al-Hamid, Saudi Arabia is at a crossroads, with two competing forces – those who practise violence and those who call for constitutional reform. He praises elements in the royal family for 'listening to reformers, for example King Abdullah and Prince Talal'. The latter failed in the 1960s when he called for constitutional monarchy because his project was elitist. Today, according to al-Hamid, the call has a wider social base. Society is ripe for this historical change. Al-Hamid overlooks the circles of power that rule Saudi Arabia, the competing and conflicting visions that dominate and sometimes paralyse the Saudi royal family.

Like many Saudi intellectuals, al-Hamid blames society, although he occasionally alludes to the role of the oppressive state in fostering the culture of polarisation, intolerance and violence. He does not give enough attention to the way the state itself, together with its available resources, were extremely efficient and active in not only eradicating calls for reform but also perpetuating the religious discourse that makes apathy, indifference and total submission to rulers a religious duty. Counting on substantial resources, the state used and deployed violence against others, especially those who did not accept its project. For the use of violence to be legitimate it needed the theorising of specialists. The *ulama* were active agents in theorising and legitimising state violence. They were the *noblesse d'état* at a time when neither intellectuals nor bureaucrats or technocrats emerged.

According to al-Hamid, there are several groups who are more likely to obstruct constitutional reform, the separation of powers and the establishment of civil society. He alludes to *al-quwa al-mutadharira* (those who are hurt by reform). He lists high-ranking officials in the judiciary. Judges are more likely than any other groups to obstruct and resist change, especially if it seems to threaten their privileges and monopolies. It is ironic that the judges he identified as obstacles to reform are the same ones who sentenced him to six years in prison in 2005. It was a Wahhabi state judge, operating under the patronage of the Ministry of Interior, who condemned al-Hamid and other reformers to several years in prison. The list of accusations was endless.

Rounds of petitions

Political activism and violence progressed hand in hand in Saudi Arabia after 11 September. Intellectuals, *ulama* and professionals engaged in dialogue aimed at strengthening calls for reform . . . A substantial number of intellectuals and political activists believed that real political reform could solve the problem of internal security, and regarded it as the only shield against terrorism and violence. They thought, correctly, that the violence had created an atmosphere in which the government was willing to listen to their demands and to the various calls for reform that had started after 11 September. Under the pressure of serious violence, the regime needed allies who would help it defeat the terrorist menace.

The regime enlisted key political activists, intellectuals and *ulama* (both official and Sahwis) in its war on terror. Even minority intellectuals such as Shi'is and Ismailis were given a platform to celebrate the common national interest that overrides sectarian and regional identities. Activists of all persuasions thought that as the government needed their aid in battling terrorism, they must extract from it not only willingness to listen to their demands but also an undertaking to implement concrete measures to ease off tension. However, they miscalculated the readiness of the government to act in accordance with their reform agenda: listening to demands was not the same as acting to promote the reformist agenda. The war on terror was in fact used as a pretext to imprison peaceful reformers, who were described as taking advantage of the violence in order to cause chaos and discord.

The intensity of political activism that gathered momentum in 2003 was dubbed the 'Riyadh Spring'; yet it precipitated a round of arrests and restrictions on political activism. Political activists of all persuasions were imprisoned for simple reasons, such as giving media interviews to Arab satellite television, signing a petition or defending political prisoners. Released prisoners signed documents forbidding them from communicating with the media. Some were banned from travelling abroad, while others had their passports confiscated. The euphoria of the 2003 Riyadh Spring gave way to disappointment and demoralisation in 2004. The common theme of all calls for reform was a serious quest for unmediated history, theology and politics. Reformers strove to free themselves from narratives of exclusion, subservience and obedience. They emphasised *wataniyya*, an all-inclusive citizenship wide enough to incorporate groups that had been marginalised or demonised. They all called for a system in which ordinary people, through elected representatives, have a major role in the political decision-making process – a revolutionary demand in the context of Saudi Arabia, where only loyal appointees enact royal will and power.

In order to articulate this reformist agenda, more than twelve petitions were submitted between 2000 and 2004 to the main senior figures in the royal family. The petitions are grouped into three categories: category I included four petitions in support of Arab causes, Palestine and Iraq being the most dominant themes; category II included six petitions calling for constitutionalism and civil society; category III included three petitions calling for respect for human rights, and recognition of Muslim minorities (Shi'i and Ismaili) and women's rights.[43] These three categories reflected concern over Saudi Arabia's position in the Arab world and a perceived lack of real solidarity with mainstream Arab causes, the deteriorating internal political scene and the status of the 'other' – religious minorities and women – in Saudi society. The petitions reflected society's frustration in the three major areas against a background of apparent government failure to respond to the three challenges. They stemmed from a general atmosphere in which revisionist trends began to be consolidated.

Saudi reformers challenged history, theology and politics as they submitted their petitions. First, they asserted their historical connection with

Arab and Islamic identity. Second, they challenged theological narratives that both excluded and demonised the Muslim other. And third, they undermined the dominant religio-political discourse that marginalised society and excluded it from the political sphere.

A series of regional and international conflicts in Afghanistan, Palestine and Iraq had led to an increase in political activism. However, one major factor facilitated this process: local Jihadi violence. As mentioned earlier in this book, the violent struggle in the way of God proved to be an agent of change. The Saudi domestic scene witnessed more political activism under the pressure of this violence than under any other factor.

In order to express solidarity with Arab causes, Saudi petitioners generated their own statements, bypassing government bureaucracy and will. For decades the Saudi government had, through its representatives and bureaucrats, articulated a vision that was described as shared by the whole society. However, twenty-first-century Saudi activists mobilised themselves to generate their own initiatives. They expressed solidarity with the Palestinian second intifada, condemned 'Sharon's violation of Jerusalem', and objected to 'Bush's War on Iraq'.[44]

The second category of petitions addressed political reform. Together with others, al-Hamid articulated the vision of constitutionalism and civil society. In his various writings he identifies five urgent principles:

1. giving priority to political reform over economic, social, educational and judicial reform;
2. grounding constitutionalism in Islamic jurisprudence;
3. promoting national unity and rejecting calls for division and partitions along regional or sectarian lines;
4. supporting the Al-Saud leadership, which guarantees *shari'a* and unity of the country;
5. addressing state and society.

In order to start the process, more than five petitions were sent to the leadership between 2003 and 2004. In January 2003, 103 intellectuals, liberals and moderate Islamists signed the National Reform Document, submitted to Crown Prince Abdullah. The list of signatories included a mixture of Islamists and liberals. Whether this was the beginning of the emergence of a united coalition of Islamists and liberals or an alliance of convenience between ideologically incompatible partners is difficult to judge.

The signatories of the reform document refrained from engaging in serious discussion of the merits of having the Al-Saud family at the top of the political system. They called, however, for radical political, economic, judicial, educational and social reforms, aimed at redrawing the social contract in such a way as to allow a wider section of society to share power and participate in the decision-making process. Their demands fall within five main areas:

1. Political reforms: the building of constitutional institutions within the parameters of what is permissible in Islam, the Quran and Sunna. This involves the formation of an elected *majlis al-shura* (consultative council) and local regional councils, an independent judiciary, citizens' rights, freedom of expression and assembly and the right to establish civil institutions, (clubs, committees and unions). The petition does not mention the formation of political parties (*ahzab siyasiyya*).

2. Economic reforms: implementing fairness and equal distribution of wealth between the different regions, controlling public spending, strengthening accountability of institutions, dealing effectively with the national debt, creating job opportunities and diversifying the economy.

3. Royalty–society relations: encouraging greater interaction between the government and society, spreading the culture of human rights, reforming public services and creating a greater role for women.

4. Reform initiatives: introducing a general amnesty for political prisoners, restoring civil rights to reformers, freedoms for intellectuals and academics.

5. Invitation to national dialogue: creating a convention or a forum for national dialogue and debate, which includes a representative sample of Saudi society.[45]

This document demonstrated that certain groups (mainly intellectuals, professionals and moderate Islamists) are willing to work with the royal family as long as it is prepared to implement reforms. Moreover, their current willingness to accommodate the Al-Saud within a constitutional monarchy is attributed to their belief that since 1932 the Al-Saud have destroyed traditional local leadership in the Hijaz, Najd, Asir and Hasa, the previously autonomous regions which are today incorporated in the Kingdom of Saudi Arabia. The reformers did not envisage any other group occupying the highest position of authority in the country. They saw two options: 'reform the Al-Saud and the dysfunctional state they have created or wait for a long period of violence followed by a radical Islamist takeover'; the consequences of either for the existence of Saudi Arabia as state and society cannot be accurately predicted. The signatories of the petition opted for the first option, namely reform the Al-Saud and work with them. It is very misleading, however, to present the reformers as a product of an autonomous and independent initiative. Their discourse is not new: it echoes earlier 1960 proposals that emerged under the patronage of Prince Talal ibn Abdulaziz. It cannot be ruled out that the constitutional reformists themselves had the patronage of key figures among a number of Saudi princes, in addition to Talal and perhaps his son al-Walid. The reformers' activism, imprisonment and release in August 2005 attests to a kind of royal connection. In fact it is almost impossible to keep the momentum of the constitutional trend without royal patronage.

The signatories of the January petition had internalised the Al-Saud's discourse on its central mediating role in Saudi society, without which they believe that the disintegration of the country is more likely to take place. While this remains the discourse that is presented in publications, some signatories argue that their decision to support a constitutional monarchy is a political strategy. Some believe that the Al-Saud are not ready to share power and will never be ready to give it up, but that if the government does not accept the demands of the January petition, particularly the establishment of an elected council, many Saudis will eventually be convinced that the moment has arrived to get rid of the Al-Saud altogether.[46]

The 2003 petitions demonstrated that a liberal group has struck an alliance with moderate Islamists inside the country. Crown Prince Abdullah invited a small group amongst them, around forty-three signatories, to attend a private session to discuss their demands. He announced the establishment of a government-sponsored dialogue forum, the King Abdulaziz Centre for National Dialogue, under royal patronage. The centre was meant to encourage various sections of Saudi society to discuss relevant contemporary issues under royal supervision.

In September 2003, another petition was released. In Defence of the Nation was submitted to the crown prince on the Saudi national day (24 September 2003).[47] The petition came after serious terrorist attacks and confrontation between Jihadis and the government. It confronts the government with the problem of violence, and links the solution to serious political reforms. It emphasises that 'military solutions' are not enough to combat terrorism, and called for a serious revision of al-khitab al-dini (religious discourse) in order to encourage pluralism and tolerance. It also called for a timetable (jadwal zamani), within which reform is to be implemented.

It was followed by a new petition at the end of 2003. This reflected the reformers' impatience with government's silence regarding previous petitions. In Call to Leadership and People,[48] reformers insisted on the urgency of constitutional reform. They also reiterated that they are partners in the nation, a plea to be included in political decisions. They criticised the suspension of real political consultation and the marginalisation of society, and emphasised that reform without institutions is unlikely to produce satisfactory results. They called upon the government to initiate change 'immediately'. This involves elections to a *majlis al-shura* (parliament) and a commitment to move towards constitutional monarchy. The signatories expressed disappointment at government responses to previous petitions. 'We reached a dead end with political leadership. Royal figures do not have the intention to implement social, economic and political reform. We say this with great sorrow. But we promise people to continue our efforts in order to prevent the ship from sinking. Then the losers are the nation and the citizens.'[49]

The Call to People involved a warning that delaying political consultation is harmful not only to society but also to religion. It seems that reformers were calling upon the *'ulama* not to obstruct change, reminding them of the duty to take part in *sha'n al-'am* (public affairs). They assured them that a constitution guarantees the application of *shari'a*, justice and equality. Institutions play a role in ensuring people's participation in promoting virtue and prohibiting vice, including favouritism, corruption and injustice.

The crown prince received the reformers and listened to their demands. Other senior princes – for example, the minister of the interior, Prince Nayef and the minister of defence, Prince Sultan – condemned the calls for reform and described them as misguided and opportunistic. They both expressed doubts regarding elections to a parliament. Prince Sultan stated that 'we can announce elections and forge them. If elections take place, they will bring illiterate and ignorant people to positions of leadership.'[50] In a speech, Prince Nayef reminded Saudis of the role of the sword in the unification of Arabia. He summoned around twenty signatories and reprimanded them. They assured the prince that the constitutional monarchy they envisage is not like the one that exists in Britain, but is similar to the political system in Bahrain, Jordan and Morocco.[51]

By March 2004 several petition signatories, political activists and lawyers had been put in prison. The government fought both Jihadis and reformers simultaneously. While repression continued through out 2004, together with another round of Jihadi violence, the government continued to invoke the rhetoric of reform. The sessions of the National Dialogue Forum, together with the promise to carry out limited municipal elections, were considered the beginning of a new era. While the dialogue sessions were meant to allow a wide section of intellectuals and activists to debate the future of the country, in reality they became yet another weapon in the war against terror. It seemed that the whole purpose of the dialogue was to gather supporters for the regime against Jihadi violence, rather than serious political reform. The regime enlisted intellectuals, activists, *'ulama* and others to have dialogues that lead to policy recommendations, but the regime is under no obligation to implement these recommendations. Up to 2005 the National Dialogue Centre organised five rounds of sessions discussing education, women, the youth and accepting the other. Against official celebration of the beginning of dialogue in Saudi Arabia that accompanied the sessions, it was reported in the official press in September 2005 that the coming 'Others and Us' session seemed to have had a less than encouraging start: 'Not even Jiddah's hot weather helped warm up the preparatory discussions . . . the participants in both the men's and women's halls of the Meridian hotel in Jiddah were almost sleepy as they read from their previously prepared papers. Some of them were seen paying more attention to the gum they were chewing or the pens they were playing with.'[52] Did the participants come to the conclusion that such sessions were futile and less likely to lead to serious change? Or was this an official reporting that disparages the participants and their apathy, perhaps to send a message of some sort?

With King Fahd on the verge of dying for more than a decade, Saudi politics and activism reached a standstill in 2005. The media campaigns surrounding local municipal elections, together with various public-relations exercises glorifying government success in killing various al-Qa'ida leaders in the Arabian Peninsula, diverted attention from the failings of the regime. Several activists were released from prison on condition they stopped all activities deemed illegal. Al-Hamid, together with Matruk al-Falih and Ali al-Damini, were sentenced to six to nine years in prison. The euphoria of the Riyadh Spring, together with the wave of petitions, stopped completely.

The regime immediately started its propaganda counter-offensive. Armed with substantial wealth, thanks to the dramatic increase in oil prices in 2004–5, it flexed its muscles after each violent encounter with Jihadi violence while its courts dealt with peaceful reformers. The rift with the USA was beginning to be mended. In 2005 Crown Prince Abdullah visited President Bush in Crawford, thus marking a return to a harmonious relationship. A televised trip to a local American supermarket capturing the crown prince munching potato chips and casually conversing with young American girls was meant to convey a new image. More serious discussions took place behind the scenes. It was announced that the US administration supports Saudi Arabia's entry into the World Trade Organisation by the end of 2005. It was assumed that Saudi Arabia was committed to trade with all partners, including Israel, a price the regime was willing to pay in order to be rehabilitated in Washington after a period of estrangement. While the American administration mildly criticised the imprisonment of Saudi reformers, the continuing bad human and women's rights record and the lack of religious freedom, it congratulated the Saudi regime for initiating a historical reform with the half-elected municipal councils. With the Iraq situation moving from bad to worse, it seemed that the tension between the USA and Saudi Arabia following the 11 September was swept under the carpet for the time being. The reform envisaged and demanded by the constitutional reform group was put on hold. The reformers' search for unmediated politics collided with the factionalism that has taken hold of Saudi royal politics in the last decade.[53]

Revisiting history, theology and politics is part of scattered intellectual attempts, crystallising among individuals and groups of people in isolation from each other. While they are all daring in their questioning of religious and political taboos, their efforts still allow room for negotiation with the regime. Al-Hamid and his colleagues hold on to the royal family and demand that it leads the reforms. They hope that Prince Abdullah, now king, and his faction within the royal family, will adopt the proposed reform. In all their petitions they consider the Al-Saud a symbolic unifying force. Reformers insist that a constitutional monarchy does not necessarily mean a British model whereby the king reigns but does not rule, although the imprisonment of some of them suggests that this is what the royal family understood from their petitions. Constitutional reformers simply consider the 'house' in need of repairs, a view that is also expressed by some members of the royal family such as Prince Talal ibn Abd al-Aziz and Saud al-Faysal. In effect, al-Hamid's proposed constitution affirms the right of Al-Saud to rule indefinitely – in fact, it provides for constitutional entrenchment of already-existing privileges and political arrangements, hardly a situation that can be anchored in an Islamic interpretation. It seems that after the present regime had exhausted its traditional theological base that had been developed by the official 'ulama over generations, al-Hamid and his colleagues are in the process of injecting the system with a new life, perhaps a prelude to the establishment of the fourth Saudi state. The constitutional reforms not only confirm but also legitimise the Al-Saud's monopoly over political decisions.

Breaking chains: the Movement for Islamic Reform in Arabia

Between 2003 and 2004, with the imprisonment of several political activists inside Saudi Arabia, some Saudi intellectuals lost hope that the anticipated political reform was possible. They remained silent, while in public they praised the limited steps taken to lessen tension, for example promises of half-elected municipal councils, and participating in national dialogues. Other Saudis listened to another, older, voice, which had been calling for serious political change since 1994. While the Movement for Islamic Reform in Arabia (MIRA) was old – it had emerged in 1996 as a splinter group from the Committee for the Defence of Legitimate Rights in Arabia – in 2003 it acquired a satellite radio station and started broadcasting not only its own programmes, but also anti-government statements. It gave Saudis inside the country an opportunity both to listen to alternative views and to contribute their own stories. MIRA called for the complete overthrow of the 'house of Saud' and its replacement with a different political system in which there is no place for hereditary rule or Al-Saud privileges. It publicised its political reform programme, which involved a serious departure from the status quo. I have discussed the movement and its political programme elsewhere. [54] In this section, only developments since 2001 will be dealt with.

The harsh measures against reformers inside Saudi Arabia seemed to increase the attentiveness of Saudis to this London-based voice. From its London headquarters, MIRA director Saad al-Faqih demands the overthrow of the Al-Saud through peaceful means such as demonstrations and civil disobedience. Al-Faqih mobilises Saudis to act in order to dismantle the political system and install an elected 'Islamic government'. He shares several characteristics with al-Hamid: both activists, together with other Islamists, were behind the Memorandum of Advice and the formation of the CDLR which led to the flight of al-Faqih to London in 1993–4. The climax of their activism in the early 1990s culminated in the famous Memorandum of Advice. Al-Faqih regards himself as part of the Sahwi Islamist trend that gathered momentum during the Gulf War of 1990–1 and led to this famous document. However, while al-Hamid remained loyal to the royal family, at least in public, al-Faqih gave up hope that it will ever respond to demands for political reform or become capable of reforming itself. While in an interview in March 1999, al-Faqih clearly stated that 'we are not ready to pull the tree with its roots yet', this did not mean that he anticipated that the ruling family was responsive to calls for reform. In October 2003, he declared that the time had come to work towards a 'surgical' operation 'through envisaging a reform programme where there is no room for Al-Saud'.[55] To put pressure on the regime and demonstrate its intolerance of peaceful political activism, al-Faqih called for demonstrations in Riyadh on 14 and 23 October 2003. The stated objectives of the demonstrations were to highlight the plight of political prisoners in Saudi Arabia to coincide with holding an international conference on human rights in Riyadh. It was estimated that around eight hundred people took part. As expected, security forces arrested some activists and demonstrators and dispersed the crowd. Another call for demonstrations in major Saudi cities was issued in December 2004. The Saudi regime surrounded the main areas where the demonstrations were planned, and prevented people from reaching them. The security forces were mobilised in large numbers to blockade areas in Jiddah and Riyadh. The demonstration failed to materialise on the designated day, although a very small number of activists managed to assemble.

Throughout 2003 and 2004 al-Faqih commented on the various petitions that were handed to the senior princes, the last of which was the aforementioned Call to Leadership and People. Al Faqih considers this petition a courageous attempt by the signatories to express their frustration with the leadership. It shows that they reached a dead end. The fact that it addressed the people as well as the leadership shows their realisation that reform cannot be achieved through addressing rulers only, and that the only hope for real reform is in raising people's awareness.[56]

When al-Faqih arrived in London in 1994 he gave the impression that he and his colleague al-Masari were acting within the Sahwi trend that was associated with the Memorandum of Advice. Immediately after settling in London, he publicised the plight of imprisoned Sahwi sheikhs such as Salman al-Awdah and Safar al-Hawali. However, after their release from prison in the late 1990s, these sheikhs moved from confrontation with the regime to co-optation, a strategy that created a rift between them and the exiled Sahwis, mainly al-Faqih and al-Masari. In a manner reminiscent of their calls to Jihadis, the released Sahwis initially called upon al-Faqih to 'repent' and return to Saudi Arabia. After 11 September and the outbreak of violence in Saudi Arabia, their conciliatory tone changed. Some famous Sahwi sheikhs – for example, Safar al-Hawali and Muhsin al-Awajy – openly denounced al-Faqih for calling for demonstrations. Sheikh Safar al-Hawali issued a public statement giving what he claimed to be religious justification for non-participation in peaceful demonstrations.

The more the rhetoric of the Sahwis inside Saudi Arabia moved towards glorifying the Saudi royal family and its centrality in the envisaged political reform process, the more that of al-Faqih moved in the opposite direction. Famous co-opted Sahwis continued to denounce him publicly. While he refrained from openly criticising and naming individual Sahwis for their accommodation and cooperation with the regime, his Sahwi ex-comrades, now adversaries, excelled in demonising him. Together with the official so-called liberal Saudi press, they launched personal attacks on al-Faqih and his followers in order to discredit them. The regime continued its efforts to silence al-Faqih's radio channel (initially known as Radio Islah, later Debate Channel and in 2006 PTV). In 2004 and for the first time, the Saudi press began to 'mention' al-Faqih by name after a long period of silence when he was only referred to as 'the so-called opposition abroad'. After calling for the October 2003 and December 2004 demonstrations on his radio channel, his photograph, together with that of ex-comrade Muhammad al-Masari, featured regularly in the local press. Official Saudi demonisation of al-Faqih took a more direct approach.[57]

Al-Faqih identifies the Saudi crisis as stemming from an absence of political participation, freedom of expression, freedom of assembly, an independent judiciary and separation of powers. In his political programme, there is no room for hereditary rule or sanctity to be granted to the Al-Saud. Al-Faqih does not believe that the royal family is an agent of unity, a symbol around which various sections of society can share meaning. He believes that the *umma* must elect its leader. As a Salafi, his quest for the unmediated word of God goes as far as to call for abolishing the office of grand mufti and calling for pluralism in issuing religious opinions – in other words, recognition of the four *madhahib*. The objective is to challenge dominant theological interpretations relating to absolute submission to political authority. He considers the official *'ulama* who perpetuate such religious interpretations as equal accomplices in enforcing authoritarian rule. His Salafiyya is one that does not recognise the authority of contemporary official *'ulama*. It only acknowledges the authority of the Quran and the Prophetic tradition.

While al-Hamid and his colleagues do not openly question the 'Islamic' credentials of the Saudi regime, al-Faqih states clearly that it is a blasphemous regime *(nidham kufr)*, that does not rule according to the revealed word of God. Al-Faqih's excommunication of the Saudi regime falls short of naming individual princes as *kafirs*, thus avoiding the problematic issue of *takfir al-mu'ayan*, the specific excommunication of individuals, which is, in his opinion, dependent on the ruling of religious experts such as judges.[58]

Since 2001 and the US War or Terror, al-Faqih and other Saudi Islamists were accused of links to Osama bin Laden by the US government. The USA claims he bought a satellite telephone for Bin Laden in 1998, prior to the US embassy bombings in Kenya. He was also accused of providing logistical support for Libyan agents on a mission to assassinate Crown Prince Abdullah in 2004. A third accusation revolved around an alleged meeting he and al-Masari had in the mid-1990s with one or two of the Jihadis who carried out the Yanbo bombing. In December 2004 the US government, together with Saudi Arabia, succeeded in putting his name on Security Council list of suspected terrorists, which led to the British government freezing his assets. The USA demanded his extradition from Britain. On various occasions, British government and Foreign Office spokesmen argued that they have no evidence against al-Faqih, and so far have resisted calls for his deportation. After the 7 July London bombings, the Saudi regime capitalised on the climate of fear in Britain and intensified its pressure on the British government to deport al-Faqih. In November 2005 the *Guardian* reported that the Saudi government was engaged in negotiating a contract to purchase Typhoon planes from Britain on condition that the latter expel al-Faqih and al-Masari. The Saudi government denied the *Guardian*'s allegations. At the time of writing al-Faqih was still broadcasting a daily evening radio programme on PTV Radio, a satellite channel, from his headquarters in north London. While his future in Britain is yet to be decided, the programme continues. His MIRA website and discussion board were suspended in July 2005, immediately after the London bombing. By September 2005 the website had returned, but without the discussion forum, which in the past had been occasionally used by anonymous participants to glorify *jihad* in various parts of the world. Al-Faqih always claimed that he had no control over material posted on MIRA's discussion board and endeavoured to remove the postings immediately after they appeared.

Is al-Faqih a covert Jihadi? Or is he a Sahwi Islamist who calls for the peaceful overthrow of a 'blasphemous' regime? Is he a believer in 'theoretical *jihad*' (*jihad nadhari*)? Or is he simply a covert propagator of *jihad 'amali* (practical *jihad*)?

According to official Saudi media, al-Faqih is an 'al-Qa'ida agent in trousers'.[59] A Saudi journalist goes as far as claiming that al-Faqih is 'a good target for Zionists and all those enemies of Saudi Arabia who recruit him and his likes to harm this land'. He asserts that according to Saudi documents, al-Faqih is linked to Zionist organisations that continue to campaign against Saudi Arabia – without, of course, presenting his readers with the evidence.[60] This opinion echoes Crown Prince Abdullah's statement after violence erupted in the industrial city of Yanbo in 2003, as a result of which several Westerners died. The crown prince described the violence as a Zionist conspiracy. It is ironic that in official Saudi discourse someone can be both an al-Qa'ida agent and part of a Zionist conspiracy against the heartland of Islam. Another Saudi author claims that al-Faqih positions himself as the al-Qa'ida spokesman in London,[61] a reference to the fact that al-Faqih is occasionally sought by Western media to give comments on current al-Qa'ida violence and Osama bin Laden.

Obviously al-Faqih does not publicly call for violent acts in pursuit of the overthrow of the Saudi regime, nor does he openly praise or glorify Jihadi violence against government buildings, Western residential compounds and innocent civilians. Callers who praise Jihadis or express support for Jihadi violence on PTV Radio station are immediately cut off. He occasionally criticises Jihadis for their 'literal' interpretation of religious texts, choice of targets and lack of a coherent political programme. On several occasions, he told his audience that Jihadis 'excel' in opposing foreign Western domination. They have a well-developed anti-Western rhetoric, but lack a complete political programme. At this juncture, he presents MIRA's programme as an alternative comprehensive blueprint for the transformation of Saudi politics and society. He positions it as the only possible alternative after the regime rejected calls for constitutional monarchy and imprisoned the main advocates. He calls for the deployment of peaceful means in the realisation of this goal.

In his commentaries on al-Qa'ida and Jihadi violence, al-Faqih positions himself as someone who adopts an analytical view. On several occasions, Western media (including the BBC, CNN, PBS and others) sought his comments on suicide bombers and violence, not only in Saudi Arabia but elsewhere. His analysis blames the Saudi regime and its policies for the eruption of violence. He also considers US Middle East policy to be part of the causes of terrorism. He unequivocally rejects the connection, made by the USA, Western scholars and Saudi liberals, between the Saudi religious curriculum, which draws on Wahhabi interpretations, and terrorism. He takes the view that the policies of the Saudi government, especially its unconditional alliance with the West, is at the heart of Jihadi violence. Furthermore, the USA, together with other Western countries, fuel this violence as a result of their foreign policy. He points to the role played by the Bush administration in giving Jihadis reasons to 'hate America', not only in Palestine but also in Afghanistan and Iraq. Following the 7 July London bombings, he wrote in the *Guardian* that restricting the freedom of Muslims in the UK and introducing new anti-terrorism legislations such as the British government package under discussion in September 2005 represent a victory for Osama bin Laden. Bin Laden longs for the creation of a rift between European governments and their resident Muslim minorities in order to give credibility to his anti-Western discourse, according to al-Faqih.[62] He argues that Bin Laden forced Western governments to abandon justice and freedom for the sake of security, elements which historically allowed the West to enjoy supremacy and domination.

What concerns us here is how al-Faqih's project reflects yet another attempt at searching for the unmediated word of God. His description of the type of 'religion' that evolved in Saudi Arabia is revealing.

He broadcast his 'caricature' evaluation of official Wahhabiyya in August 2005:

They [official religious scholars] share with Shi'is the way they revere their religious scholars. They consider them infallible. They share with Sufis their infatuation with the *tariqa* sheikh. They share with the Kharijites their willingness to describe their opponents as *kafirs*. They share with the Murjia their suspension of the duty to command virtue and prohibit vice when it comes to rulers. They refuse to criticise the rulers' bad deeds. They no longer refer to the Quran and Sunna. They always refer to what Ibn Baz and Ibn al-Uthaymin say. The words of the *'ulama* cannot be used as evidence. When confronted with a problem, we should not say 'qal ibn Baz' [ibn Baz said], we must return to the Book and the tradition of the Prophet.[63]

In his reflections on Salafiyya, al-Faqih argues that there are several meanings and usages. For the purpose of an article he wrote on Salafiyya and democracy, he argues that there are several groups claiming to be Salafis. First there are those who use it to imply that so and so is a radical or extremist. Second, there are those who use it to indicate that a group rejects *madhhabiyya fiqhiyya* (schools of jurisprudence). Third, there are those who use it to refer to political Islamist movements like the ones in Kuwait and Jordan. For al-Faqih, 'Salafiyya describes those who claim to respect *shari'a* evidence and promise to follow the methodology of the pious ancestors. Some groups and intellectuals use Salafiyya as a slogan but when it comes to practice, we discover they are not authentic Salafis. One must consider the evidence.'[64] Like other Salafis, al-Faqih is engaged in the debate about who is a Salafi.

Al-Faqih argues that under Saudi authority, the *'ulama* lost their autonomy. They became a rubber stamp to royal decisions. His daily radio show, together with the internet discussion board, are arenas for contesting the authority of the official *'ulama*, and even ridiculing their *fatwa*s. The most scathing attack is always initiated by anonymous contributors who call official *'ulama* ' '*umala*' (traitors). Al-Faqih's position vis-à-vis the *'ulama* is similar to that of a whole range of Saudi activists, intellectuals and non-official *'ulama* (both Sahwis and Jihadis). In contrast with the liberal position that aspires towards less *'ulama* intervention (official or otherwise) in the public sphere, and more liberal religious interpretations in the social sphere (for example, issues related to women), al-Faqih calls for greater role being granted to those familiar with *shari'a* evidence. For their opinion to count, they must have a degree of autonomy vis-à-vis political authority. Al-Faqih does not reject the *'ulama* altogether. He calls for a greater involvement by what he calls independent *'ulama*. According to al-Faqih, the *'ulama* should be outside the state apparatus altogether. They should derive their authority from their social base, and should organise themselves as they consider appropriate, without state interference.

While al-Faqih respects the early Wahhabi discourse of the eighteenth century and a selected chain of *ulama*, he considers later *ulama* as people who corrupted the tradition. In his opinion, the first Saudi state exemplified the power of Muhammad ibn Abd al-Wahhab in creating the Muslim polity rather than the power of the Al-Saud, an understanding that in his opinion current Saudi propaganda and educational programmes reversed.[65] He argues that the first and second Saudi states were more faithful to their religious discourse than the third state. However, the contribution of early *ulama* in the past two states is often not given enough credit in Saudi official narratives. These glorify the role of the Al-Saud in creating unity and prosperity, an approach that tends to belittle the contribution of the Wahhabi movement. If ever there is a recognition, it is usually expressed in terms of 'partnership'. Al-Faqih emphasises that 'there were several swords in Arabia in the past; none of these swords succeeded. Only the one that had the blessing of religion succeeded.'[66] His reflections on history lead him to argue that the primary force behind the establishment of the early Saudi state was the reformer: without him there would not have been an impulse for unification. Al-Faqih may have reservations on Muhammad ibn Abd al-Wahhab granting the Al-Saud an oath of allegiance that was extended to their descendants, but he does not tackle this issue publicly. It is difficult to ascertain whether this is a political strategy or a reflection of a deep conviction. He may feel that as a political movement, MIRA should not be entangled in a theological debate that would diminish its popularity among a constituency that is perhaps not yet ready for such intellectual overtures. Yet al-Faqih strongly argues against the legitimacy of hereditary leadership, which Ibn Abd al-Wahhab was known to have granted and legitimised for the Al-Saudi family. Al-Faqih avoids discussing religious matters that are divisive, or favouring one *fiqh* opinion over another. When a woman caller to Debate, later PTV, Radio criticised those *ulama* who consider *zawaj al-misyar* (secret visiting marriage)[67] permissible, he immediately pointed her attention to the fact that this matter is subject to religious debate and is not central to MIRA's programme. He adopts a similar view regarding women driving, covering their faces, and occupying position of authority. While he accepts that driving and covering the face are subject to different religious opinions, he unequivocally rejects women being put in a position of *wilaya 'ama*, (leadership), for example as president or minister. He claims that there is *ulama* consensus over excluding women from *wilya 'ama*. Other religious scholars have a different opinion on the question. In general, his position on gender issues is derived, according to him, from

the book and the Prophet's tradition. Both men and women are interpreters of this heritage, according to al-Faqih.

When it comes to the contemporary state established by Abdulaziz ibn
Saud in 1932, al-Faqih seems to be liberated from all constraints. He considers the third state to be the evil empire par excellence. However, he
acknowledges that King Abdulaziz had personal leadership qualities such
as intelligence, perseverance and charisma. For a whole week in 2004, he
bombarded Debate Radio listeners with an understanding of the past that
challenges the official narratives enforcing Saudi legitimacy. He invited
his listeners to contribute their own reflections and oral narratives that
'put the record straight'. His audience excelled in offering an alternative
historical memory that has been suppressed for so long. People from
various regions and towns, belonging to tribal and non-tribal groups,
descendants of the 1920s suppressed Ikhwan rebellion, representatives of
sedentary families in Hijaz, Najd and the Eastern Province all joined in a
chorus condemning the 'historical forgery' that the regime maintained.
Old and young men and women retold the past. They broke the silence
over 'massacres', 'torture', 'treachery' and 'hypocrisy'. While al-Faqih
offered his own version of the past, he gave others the opportunity to
imagine and articulate a different, so far untold, history. In a manner reminiscent of anonymous internet discussion boards, Saudis added their dissident voices to the written word that is yet to be claimed by identifiable
men and women. While Saudis searched for the word of God that is not
mediated by co-opted *ulama*, they longed for a past that is equally free
from the domination of the regime and its historians. If official media
channels are platforms for creating consenting subjects, Debate Radio
exemplified the 'opposite direction'. It is the voice of dissent and contestation. The majority of participants still hold on to their creative *noms de
plume*, often carefully chosen to reflect whole range of positions: the
'Jihadi Den' is a rebellious woman; the 'Bare footed' is an impoverished
man; the 'Lion' is a defiant man; the 'Stranger at home' is a man exiled in
his own country; the 'ex-Saudi' is someone who liberated himself from
'Saudi' identity. Callers are creative in choosing symbolic names to
convey a whole range of meanings including defiance, alienation, rejection, piety and determination. They continue to be followed by security
forces, however. Several raids on groups of young men who had assembled for dinner after having called Debate Radio in 2004 resulted in
arrests, the details of which were broadcast on air during the security
force raids.[68]

In addition to communicating MIRA's political programme, Debate
Radio offers a platform for attacking the royal family, the official *ulama*,
co-opted Sahwis and liberals. It allows the dissemination of MIRA's

all-encompassing reform and commentaries on current affairs. As MIRA's political programme is discussed elsewhere,[69] it is important to focus here on more recent trends that emerged with its acquisition of a media communication channel in 2003.

Al-Faqih's daily radio programme offers a wide range of topics and commentaries on past and present affairs. Sometimes he proposes alternative interpretations of economic, political and social issues. On one occasion, tribalism and tribal identity were discussed in ways that mobilised people by drawing on their tribal honour. In al-Faqih's opinion, Islam is not against tribalism as such; it is against racism. He told his audience that the Prophet called upon the tribes of Arabia to compete in defending faith rather than in fostering superiority and racism. Al-Faqih called upon the various tribes of Arabia to fulfil the Prophetic tradition and demonstrate their commitment to reform by sending in their names as individuals in support of MIRA. This was called a communal electronic demonstration, and preceded his call for real demonstrations in 2004. As al-Faqih mobilised people by appealing to their tribal identity, he emphasised equality in Islam. However, by addressing Saudis as individuals belonging to tribes rather than as Saudi citizens, he incurred the wrath of several groups. The government, together with liberals and Sahwis, accused him of playing on old tribal rivalries and ancient feuds. His ex-comrade Muhsin al-Awajy wrote a scathing attack in which he accused al-Faqih of 'sinking the ship rather than reforming it'.[70] Given the ferocity of al-Awajy's attack, it seems that al-Faqih touched a very raw nerve among government officials, who may have authorised al-Awajy's attack. Al-Faqih's response emphasised that Islam did not destroy tribal identities, but mobilised them for the public good. Invoking tribal honour on the basis of an Islamic interpretation for the purpose of political mobilisation is in sharp contrast with official Saudi narratives that demonise tribal allegiance and call upon people to offer their loyalty to the king. Tribes are only allowed to boast about their allegiance to the Al-Saud through the mobilisation of their own members. This is usually done in the context of Nabati poetry, recited in heritage festivals and addressed to the king and other princes. Al-Faqih's mobilisation is, however, very much dependent on whether tribes can be politically motivated after decades of urbanisation, migration to cities and systematic government attempts to undermine tribal economy and leadership. There is no doubt that tribalism as an identity is still prominent in Saudi Arabia, evidence of which is the enthusiasm expressed by many callers to Debate Radio, who highlighted their tribal identity and put it at the service of MIRA's programme. It is very difficult, however, to predict whether the rhetoric of tribalism and honour will eventually lead to real mobilisation. So far this does not seem to be the case. In twenty-first-century Saudi Arabia, tribes and even families are divided and polarised.

One of the novelties of MIRA's radio channel stems from its ability to question dominant understandings of gender relations. While this challenge should not be understood as leading to Western-style feminist awareness, it is definitely an attempt to offer alternative interpretations of gender, but from within the Islamic tradition. Al-Faqih does not call for 'gender equality' as understood in the West. However, he promotes what might be considered as gender complementarity, whereby men and women play complementary roles as specified and defined by *shari'a*. Al-Faqih announces that the problem in Saudi Arabia stems from confusing *shari'a* with social tradition. The official *'ulama* use restrictions on women in an attempt to increase their legitimacy, but in fact they are not capable of separating social practice from the Islamic tradition. Only a free medium for debate and discussion will overcome this problem. He gives the example of women driving, a case where the confusion between social tradition and *shari'a* evidence is clearly demonstrated. While he calls for the creation of more jobs for women and more state benefits for disadvantaged divorcées, widows and spinsters, his proposals fall short of calling for women to occupy positions of leadership, except in areas related to women. Reforming gender relations invokes a paternalistic and protective approach. Women are seen as *al-'unsor al-da'if* (the weak element), who need protection from men and the unjust state. According to al-Faqih, neither men nor women decide on women's rights. The final judgement is the Quran and the tradition of the Prophet.

In a move meant to refute the criticism of his opponents, especially those Saudi liberals who accuse him of aspiring towards a Taliban-style government, al-Faqih allowed and encouraged the participation of *islahiyyat* (female reformers) in Debate Radio. *Islahiyyat* proved to be different from the increasing number of *da'iyyat* (preachers), who by and large endorse the Sahwi discourse and its political position vis-à-vis the regime.[71] *Islahiyyat*, like other MIRA supporters, reject the regime and hold it responsible for the 'misery' of women in Saudi Arabia. Sahwi *da'iyyat* usually blame society and its misguided Islam for the current exclusion of women. Their preaching is primarily concerned with Islamic dress and worship. So far they have not demonstrated an engagement with current political affairs or articulated a vision of reform. Sahwi *da'iyyat* often assert that the problem lies in the tribal patriarchal system rather than political oppression or Islam. Suhaylah Hammad Zayn al-Abdin is such a *da'iyya*, who is very close to the government agenda. MIRA's *islahiyyat*, however, are beginning to articulate an alternative vision that establishes the connection between the status of women and political oppression. Most MIRA *islahiyyat* are not specifically concerned with issues relevant to women but offer a wide range of opinion on politics, society, the economy and foreign relations.

Women are given a platform to present their views, analyse the current situation and, more importantly, mobilise men by appealing to their Islamic, tribal and masculine honour, described as being regularly violated by the state and its agents. In October 2003 al-Faqih went as far as calling upon women to participate in the Riyadh demonstration, provided that they were veiled and protected by groups of men. He was accused by co-opted Sahwis of hiding behind a female shield (*tatarus bi 'l-nisa*), an act of cowardice. He encouraged women, together with men, to attend regular Friday prayers in specific mosques designated by the movement in an attempt to create a critical mass in such mosques without incurring state repression. This was regarded as a first step towards creating a defiant group of *islahiyyin* and *islahiyyat* without being identified by state security agents. Al-Faqih publicised the plight of Umm Saud, whose son burnt to death in al-Hayer prison, and Ghayda al-Sharif, who was allegedly subjected to humiliation by the Saudi intelligence services following the arrest of her husband. The celebration of the lives and courage of these two women and several others contributes to the creation of images of female heroines who were so 'daring in speaking truth to power'. Their experiences are regularly remembered in prose and poetry.

In general, *islahiyyat* have proved to be articulate and thoughtful. They not only discuss issues relevant to women, but also men. On various occasion, I participated in the debate and generated a wide range of responses from both men and women. The majority are young schoolteachers, students in higher education or housewives who have a good level of literacy and general awareness. They prepare presentations in advance; some speak in classical Arabic, others use colloquial language and powerful poetry. The mood is always defiant and confrontational. They draw on the Islamic tradition to challenge the domination of the royal family and its *'ulama*. More importantly, they search for religious interpretations that are not mediated by royal authority or state *'ulama*. They discuss the plight of women who are abandoned by their husbands and the state, such as widows, divorcées, spinsters and all those marginalised in Saudi society. They argue that jobs for people are not a matter of luxury; but a means of survival. They emphasise that the state must create jobs for women that respect sex segregation and Islamic tradition. One woman called for the state to employ women in the judiciary as assistants and counsellors in order to create a comfortable space for other women in an otherwise all-male forum. The *islahiyyat* want to break the chain of subservience, they want women to be treated as people with full rights and responsibilities, derived according to their vision of Islam. While they reject Western-style feminist discourse, they search for an 'authentic' Islamic alternative.

They denounce the state for forcing female teachers to travel long distances to remote schools, or even schools in other cities. They claim that this is a strategy to break up the family. The regime forces people to be so preoccupied with the details of living that they forget the real problem – oppression and corruption, according to one *islahiyya*. While *islahiyyat* call for respect and equality, they draw on *shariʿa* evidence and the tradition of the Prophet to promote a vision whereby women play an important role in society. They emphasise the connection between the marginalisation of women and political oppression. When a member of the Consultative Council, Muhammad al-Zulfa, called upon the council to debate women driving in 2005, an opinion poll on the MIRA website indicated that most participants (approximately 60 per cent) would support allowing women to drive only if the Al-Saud cease to rule the country, itself an interesting result. In this opinion poll, women's driving is conditional not on *shariʿa* evidence or social tradition, but on the overthrow of the Saudi regime. This demonstrates that gender issues in Saudi Arabia are truly a political rather than a *shariʿa* or social concern. As the Saudi regime is seen as 'morally corrupt', opposition groups emphasise piety and moral superiority. Women are central to this vision.

The participation of women in MIRA forums (internet and radio) reflects the state of frustration experienced by Saudi women in general. MIRA's *islahiyyat* denounce state-initiated reforms, for example employing women in Saudia Airlines, the Ministry of Foreign Affairs and other envisaged sectors. They reject state-sponsored reforms in the area of gender relations: often such initiatives are interpreted as a conspiracy to normalise moral corruption and degeneration. They interpret state initiatives as attempts to 'corrupt' women and destroy the piety of society. They are very critical of entertainment satellite channels owned by Saudi princes – for example, al-Walid ibn Talal's Rotana music channel. *Islahiyyat* stretch the debate on gender, yet it is important to emphasise that they do not offer a radical programme outside the Islamic tradition. As in other Muslim countries – for example, Egypt and Iran – Saudi *islahiyyat* reflect personal attempts to articulate an Islamic feminism that draws on early Muslim tradition, especially the Prophet's biography and that of early female companions of the Prophet (*sahabiyyat*), to reformulate solutions for modern and contemporary problems. They denounce traditional *ʿulama* for concentrating on interpretations that deal with women's issues such as menstruation and ablution while excluding the general plight of women in Saudi society. They call such *ʿulama mashaykh al-haydh*, 'the sheikhs of menstruation', a reference to their numerous *fatwa*s in this area. In this Islamic feminism, there is no role for state-sponsored social reforms. Most *islahiyyat* consider the state an agent of corruption rather than reform, and as a violator of women's honour rather than its protector. Examples of raids on private homes, the arrests of sons and brothers and even women themselves, provide ample evidence of this violation. According to many *islahiyyat*, the Saudi leadership exploits women after impoverishing them and depriving them of their rights. They say that it has failed to provide either economic or physical security for women, either on the streets or inside the confines of the household. They call for women's employment, as they see it as a strategy for survival for many women. Some *islahiyyat* reject the concept of *wali al-amr*, for example fathers, brothers or sons who act as guardians of women. They want to be treated as legal persons who represent themselves rather than as minors who need to be represented by others, a position that not only challenges parental authority but also political extensions of this personal and familial relationship.

It is important to compare their position with that of other categories of women in Saudi society. Some Saudi women regard the royal family as their main protector against the forces of backwardness, by which they often mean the official religious establishment that so far has denounced calls for social change. They have hopes that enlightened members of the royal family, together with moderate Muslim scholars, will crush religious opposition and initiate reforms in the area of gender. As mentioned earlier in this book, the religious establishment controls the social sphere as it is the only area left under its jurisdiction, so their hold over this last precious area of control may not evaporate very easily. Selected professional women, academics and writers were involved in presenting a petition to the royal family calling for greater freedom and recognition, in addition to signing other general reform petitions.[72] In September 2005 King Abdullah received a group of Saudi businesswomen, academics and writers to discuss matters related to the status of women in general. The discussion remained enshrined in secrecy, perhaps for fear of antagonising traditional elements in Saudi society. The controversy caused by the participation of a famous businesswoman whose veil was not tight enough – it occasionally slipped – in the Jiddah Economic Forum in 2004 was perhaps a factor in keeping the king's discussion with women behind closed doors.

MIRA's *islahiyyat* follow the news of such encounters and offer their own interpretations of the situation. In general, they regard the female signatories of petitions and those who met with the king as unrepresentative of Saudi women and as co-opted groups that the state uses to polish its image abroad. In the words of one distinguished *islahiyya*, 'the issue for me is not whether I will be allowed to drive but whether I will be able to afford a car'.[73] Women who belong to the business elite and who inherited the management of family financial companies, together with female professionals and writers, may not constitute a representative sample of Saudi women, the majority of whom remain marginalised and underprivileged.

Like other groups in Saudi society, MIRA constantly searches for uncensored spaces. If its communication arm, PTV Radio, continues without government interference, it may develop into a substantial voice. This will depend on whether al-Faqih continues to receive funds for his various activities, and on whether the British government resists Saudi or American pressure to deport him.[74] Developments inside Saudi Arabia may also influence the future of MIRA. Increased Jihadi violence, together with failure of King Abdullah to act upon at least some of the political reform agenda demanded in the various aforementioned petitions, may create a window of opportunity for MIRA.

It remains to be seen whether MIRA will be able to recruit supporters from influential groups across Saudi Arabia, such as professionals, intellectuals and foot-soldiers drawn from the various regions. Its headquarters in London is manned by a Ghamdi, a descendant of the Hijazi al-Ashraf (Abdulaziz al-Shanbari), an Otaybi, in addition to al-Faqih who claims decent from Banu Tamim. In December 2005 al-Shanbari declared that he had defected from MIRA and returned to Saudi Arabia. In March 2006 he appeared on al-Arabiyya Saudi satellite channel, denouncing MIRA and its director, while glorifying King Abdullah. One cannot rule out the possibility that the regime exerted pressure on al-Shanbari to denounce al-Faqih and accuse him of working for the intelligence services of Libya, Iran, Britain and another unnamed Gulf state, possibly Qatar. Such accusations must be understood in the context of Saudi efforts to discredit al-Faqih, one of the remaining unco-opted dissidents abroad. Al-Shanbari claimed that al-Faqih was Iraqi until the age of seventeen, a reference to the fact that al-Faqih grew up in al-Zobayr, a Sunni town in southern Iraq that has been host to several waves of Najdi migrants for the last three hundred years.

No doubt other MIRA supporters remain behind the scenes. Lists of people who have offered their allegiance indicate that a cross-section of Saudi society responded to al-Faqih's electronic support demonstration in 2004. It is difficult to asses the magnitude of MIRA in the present context of repression. Identification with MIRA, contact with or participation in its daily radio programme remain crimes punishable by arrest.

So far liberals see MIRA as a dissident political movement that draws on strict Wahhabi interpretations. They accuse it of aspiring towards establishing a Taliban-style regime in Saudi Arabia. Al-Faqih's views on gender issues and the fact that women participated not only in Debate Radio but also in the October 2003 demonstrations did little to dispel these accusations. Al-Faqih boasts that his Salafi orientation did not prevent him from using the latest communication technology to spread his message, proof of his endorsement of modernity. While using modern technology is not the same as being modern, it attests to the fact that this Salafi opposition is a product of modernity rather than a movement against it. Modernity for MIRA is defined according to its own terms, itself a proof of the possibility of multiple modernities.

When confronted with liberal accusations, al-Faqih argues that there are three categories of liberals in Saudi Arabia. First, there are those who theorise liberalism and believe in political liberties as defined in the Western tradition. He claims that he respects those people because they are consistent and tend to be critical of the royal family. These diehard liberals are almost extinct in Saudi society, according to al-Faqih. The second group is very hypocritical and subservient to the royal family despite their liberal tendencies. They only promote the social aspect of liberalism, as they call for the adoption of Western lifestyles but defend Saudi authoritarianism, justify dictatorship, absence of accountability and secrecy in politics. Those so-called liberals tend to be dominant in Saudi-owned media and government bureaucracies. He says he has no respect for such people. The third group consists of those who support MIRA but have 'overstretched' liberal social programmes. Such people are mistakenly classified as liberals because of bias in Saudi society against those who do not exhibit clear signs of religiosity. According to al-Faqih, they are in fact *islahiyyin*, who need a gentle approach in order to include them in MIRA's project.

Traditional *ʿulama* and outspoken Sahwis attacked MIRA on various occasions. Some Jihadis openly praise MIRA and its director. Others have reservations regarding MIRA's self-proclaimed peaceful strategy to over-throw the regime. Some Debate Radio callers are occasionally impatient with peaceful demonstrations or communal prayers as a political strategy. On several occasions al-Faqih cut their participation in the programme for praising violence. Most MIRA supporters seem to be frustrated with the fact that they cannot get to meet each other for fear of the intelligence services and oppression by the regime.

Will MIRA attract Jihadis who may have given up violence after the serious bloody confrontations with the regime? Such a question cannot be answered at the moment. However, it seems that by 2005, MIRA's message resonated among the unemployed and the marginalised in peripheral regions and low-income neighbourhoods. It is clear that

MIRA attracts several marginalised Hijazis, Asiris and members of the northern tribes. It may have the support of wealthy and influential members but they are not visible for obvious reasons. It remains to be seen whether MIRA through its daily broadcast can transform those atomised, disenfranchised, and marginalised young men and women into organised clandestine political activists who will in the future pose a threat to the regime. Regular demonstrations and civil disobedience may embarrass the government at a time when it may not be able, in the age of increasing exposure and globalised communication, to use force indiscriminately against peaceful, unarmed demonstrators. Any bloody confrontation with peaceful demonstrators would have serious repercussions, both internally and externally. While the government does not feel it needs to justify violence against armed Jihadis, it is unlikely that it will be able to excuse the use of violence against peaceful civilians.

Publications, political activism, internet discussion boards and live radio provide Saudis with unmediated spaces where they articulate a constant preoccupation with freeing themselves from the domination of state-approved interpretations of history, theology and politics. So far their debates have not crystallised around strong independent institutions and organisations, as these are banned, yet the anonymity and informality of the spaces various voices occupy provide alternative visions that are threatening to the regime. Such voices challenge the main pillars of authoritarianism, mainly the consenting narratives that draw on sacred religious tradition, thereby granting holiness sanctioned by texts and their interpreters to this authoritarianism. While direct repression is regularly practised, the regime censors books, jams radio stations and controls the internet.[75] The imprisonment of the constitutional reformers and regular reports on the abuse of human rights remain an embarrassment. Yet there is no doubt that the process of undermining authoritarian rule has already begun. It is difficult to bring it to a halt. The search for the unmediated word of God may eventually lead to the dismantling of authoritarian rule.

Conclusion

Literature on Saudi Arabia often starts by making the obvious observation that the regime derives its legitimacy from Wahhabiyya. Yet not many studies go further than this, for example to analyse the internal dynamics and dialectics of this legitimacy. In this book I have explored the ways in which Wahhabiyya became a hegemonic discourse under the patronage of the state. Rather than being a tradition opposed to modernity, Wahhabiyya flourished and its advocates became prosperous as a result of the immersion of Saudi Arabia in modernity. Wahhabiyya became a dominant discourse because of state patronage, oil and modernity. However, the same factors that consolidated it have led to its contestation. This has resulted in the emergence of multiple Wahhabi discourses, all constructed against the background of state control.

The creation of the modern state in 1932 consolidated a religious tradition that grew in the shadow of the sultan. After the state eliminated undesirable elements and interpretations in the 1920s, Wahhabiyya became the dominant religious discourse, whose consolidation was dependent on financial and moral support from the political elite. Wahhabi scholars developed into a class of *noblesse d'état* with its own interests and role in the political realm. This elite originated in the small oases and settlements of southern Najd and Qasim that produced religious interpreters. Until the 1970s *aimat al-daʿwa al-najdiyya* represented a close circle of people of knowledge. Against the universal claims of Wahhabiyya, mainly its assertion that it represented the authentic Sunni tradition, it remained anchored in one geographical region and propagated by people with clear regional genealogical connections.

Three important concepts, deeply grounded in the religious tradition, were deployed in supporting the project of state expansion. Relying on the tradition of the founding father, Muhammad ibn Abd al-Wahhab, the Wahhabi ʿulama promoted migration, excommunication and *jihad* to consolidate the political realm. All three concepts were conducive to political centralisation and domination. Interpretations of migration marked a physical boundary between the realm of blasphemy and the land of piety. It became compulsory for the Arabian population to abandon its own 'region of blasphemy' in favour of that of piety. The political realm was consolidated as a result of fear of death in the land of debauchery and associationist practices. To seek salvation one had to migrate to territories under the political authority of the Al-Saud and the religious authority of the Wahhabi *ulama*. Similarly, excommunication of other Muslims who lived in blasphemous places became another mechanism that consolidated the realm. Early twentieth-century Wahhabi *ulama* reinvoked the tradition of their eighteenth-century founder, who sent letters to faraway communities outlining their degeneration and religious bankruptcy. Those who did not voluntarily move to the land of piety had to be fought in their own territories to bring them back to Islam. Re-Islamising society and individual salvation were dependent on submission to the rightful Imam – the founder of Saudi Arabia, Abdulaziz ibn Saud. Those who hesitated over the exodus to piety were subjected to *jihad*, a duty anchored in sacred texts. After the activation of the three concepts, the state was proclaimed in 1932. Wahhabi discourse was successful in mystifying the world for the sake of power.

With the advent of oil in the second half of the twentieth century, the regime shared the booty with its most loyal religious scholars, now serving as judges, jurists, teachers and preachers to an increasing number of Saudis. For a brief period, the Riyadh-based religious study circles of famous Wahhabi *ulama* became the Mecca for new recruits and converts. They initially came from Qasim, Hasa and northern Najd, and later from Hijaz, Asir, the northern and eastern provinces. In a third phase, students seeking religious knowledge came from not only the Muslim world but also from among Muslim minorities in the West.[1] Most of the novices returned to their countries to preach a new faith, acquired in the heartland of Islam, under the patronage of the so-called monotheist state.

It was not long before the oil revenues were able to fund the foundation of modern religious study centres. From the 1960s schools and universities were set up across the country. Initially the staff arrived from other countries in the Arab world, especially those that produced an excess of religious educators who could not be absorbed locally or were expelled from these countries by revolutionary Arab secular regimes. Saudi Arabia adopted an open-door policy as it expanded its religious educational bureaucracy. The new recruits were seen as a shield against the revolutionary rhetoric of these Arab regimes. All were controlled and supervised by the local Wahhabi circle. Such religious educators acted on Saudi society but also reacted to the system of control already in place. They influenced and were influenced by local Saudi Wahhabi interpretations. All benefited from the oil boom of the 1970s.

Oil revenues allowed the regime to expand and purchase the latest innovations of Western modernity. Technology and easy travel facilitated the consolidation of Wahhabi discourse and widened the circle of recruits. As more Saudis entered schools and universities, many chose religious careers. The rest were inexorably exposed to religious interpretations in a systematic way. Schools, universities, radio, television, public lectures, private study circles and the media played a crucial role. After a near-monopoly over religious interpretations by the Najdi circle, recruitment and dissemination was expanded. The regime succeeded in enforcing the appearances of religiosity while politics was moving away from the control of religion and the religious.

The proliferation of Wahhabiyya produced consenting subjects, who, as I argued in the first chapter, internalised specific interpretations of sacred religious texts calling upon true believers to submit to the will of rulers, respect their wisdom and revere their policies. These interpretations rendered public calls for reform, political participation and even open discussion of public affairs akin to blasphemy. While not invented by Wahhabi *'ulama* – they had a history rooted in certain interpretations within Sunni Islam – they were reinvented, reconstructed and widely propagated.

The regime did not need to use excessive force, although it occasionally found that it had to resort to harsh measures. Under its patronage, Wahhabi *'ulama* propagated interpretations that equated obeying rulers with obeying God. If a Saudi criticised the leadership, he committed a sin, violated God's orders and challenged divine wisdom. Obedience must be extended to a group of *wulat al-amr*, an ambiguous large circle, understood to include princes and religious scholars. Official Wahhabiyya required complete submission to the wisdom of the *umara* and *'ulama*, as represented in Ibn Baz's interpretations of Quranic verses.

The discourse of consent was internalised by several generations of Saudis. With modernity, state schools, universities, mosques, the media and all communication technology propagated the discourse of acquiescence. This is not to say that Saudis consented because they were simply bribed by the 'rentier state', with its redistributive system that exchanges welfare for loyalty and submission. Although the regime did its best to buy loyalty, reward or promise to reward obedience and patronise social groups, there were more subtle forms of domination and submission. The manufacture of consenting subjects needed more than oil to lubricate an everlasting acquiescence. Wahhabi religio-political discourse preceded oil. It not only sanctified authoritarian rule, it provided shared meanings that tied people to a particular political configuration. Wahhabiyya succeeded in Islamising Saudi authoritarianism rather than society.

Saudi authoritarianism developed in the twentieth century because it was able to capitalise on a master narrative, the sum total of religio-political interpretations that assumed sanctity. When such discourse was not there or was less developed, Wahhabi *ulama* invented it for the sake of power. For more than seventy years, those who propagated this discourse were an elite class, above ordinary human evaluation and assessment. This authoritarianism was governed by highly structured sequences, narratives and rituals enacted at certain places and times. The religious discourse linked the present to the past, and present to future. As in colonial contexts, political order was to be achieved not through the intermittent use of coercion but through continuous instructions, inspection and control.[2] Saudi–Wahhabi religious discourse created consenting political subjects. It established links between divinely received wisdom and religious and political authority.

A product of state control and modernity, Saudi religio-political discourse proliferated, fragmented and challenged state authority. Unexpectedly, control under authoritarian rule produced the seeds of mutation. Wahhabiyya developed interpretations that challenged the discourse of control. As official Wahhabiyya enchanted society, rendering it more religious, and dis-enchanted politics, loud and critical voices emerged among those who had been brought up on its teachings. The Sahwis, mainly a product of Wahhabi education and modernity as experienced in universities, challenged official Wahhabi religio-political discourse as they called upon people to re-enchant politics. Sahwis contested the acquiescent discourse, a move that led inevitably to confrontation with the regime in the 1990s. While most Sahwi rhetoric was a response to what Sahwis defined as Western domination, they made linkages, subtle and not so subtle, between their local regime and Western domination. After brief periods of imprisonment, followed by a changing world situation after 11 September and a wave of violence inside the country, Sahwis were put on the defensive. They became the 'accused'. In order to defend their position, they tried two simultaneous strategies. They moderated and even stopped their criticism of the government, while a small minority endeavoured to mediate and negotiate with those defined as having 'gone astray', the Jihadis. Sahwis remain restless in Saudi Arabia despite regime's efforts to incorporate them and enlist them in its effort to combat terrorism. In the post-11 September period, Sahwis defended the regime and condemned Jihadis for their ignorance. They called upon Jihadis to give themselves up so that they could be rehabilitated and re-educated in the 'right' religious interpretations. Sahwis today refrain from challenging the government but they continue to attack the West, a safe position as long as they do not call openly for a perpetual *jihad* against infidels. They restrain their followers by arguing that only in occupied territories, for example Palestine, Iraq and Chechnya, is *jihad* permissible. Sahwi religious effervescence is now concentrated on the social sphere. Socially, Sahwis claim to defend the authentic Islamic tradition while some figures, such as Salman al-Awdah, have developed a moderate transnational religious discourse appropriate for Arab satellite television viewers. Rather like the ageing religious establishment, Sahwis see themselves as defenders of the *umma* against corrupting Western domination and cultural imperialism. Today they are a 'church in waiting'.

Wahhabi discourse was prematurely transnationalised. The process started vigorously in the 1970s and 1980s. Wahhabi interpretations travelled to Afghanistan with the Jihadis. There it went through a process of reinterpretation as it was exposed for the first time to open combat, debate and competition. With the gates of *jihad* closed in Saudi Arabia since 1932, young Saudis travelled to Afghanistan in pursuit of an honourable martyrdom.

In Afghanistan, free spaces emerged where Saudis experimented with religious interpretation. Under the fog of war, a hybrid discourse emphasising rebellion against despotic rulers matured with Osama bin Laden's patronage and the influence of other Islamist Jihadi traditions. This discourse was not invented in Afghanistan. It arrived in Afghanistan with the Saudi Afghans. Trying to identify whether Osama bin Laden is a Wahhabi seems to me a futile exercise. What is clear is that his message went further than official Wahhabi interpretations had ever been able to go. While his message is rejected by many, it is endorsed and defended by a few Saudis. His revolutionary rhetoric was developed and supported by *shari'a* evidence and the interpretations of the early Wahhabi scholars themselves. The contestation of Saudi religious discourse coexisted with official efforts to export the traditional, acquiescent interpretations. In London official Saudi religious discourse arrived to educate in matters related to worship and creed, but this education spawned interpretations that had political consequences. Both the challenging political interpretations and the consenting literature on worship proved to be popular, empowering discourses. This empowerment derives from complying with rigid rules that regulate the body and relations with the other. Saudi discourse had moved from localism to transnationalism before developing a sufficient level of sophistication suitable for an international Muslim audience. This premature transnationalisation enabled its advocates to develop its full revolutionary potential.

After 2001 debates on religious interpretations continued at home with the outbreak of violence in major Saudi cities. Jihadis developed rebellious interpretations and anchored these in the Wahhabi tradition. They confronted both official *'ulama* and Sahwis. They considered their early mentors as people who betrayed the project and failed to carry it to its logical conclusions. Jihadis did not import a new religious tradition. They simply revisited Wahhabi interpretations. They invoked symbols and meanings that resonate with society. In the style of an early generation of Wahhabi *'ulama*, young Jihadi scholars assumed the role of authentic guardians of the original message of Muhammad ibn Abd al-Wahhab. The founder's words and those of his disciples were crucial.

Jihadi activists used the internet to spread the message. This was the beginning of the privatisation of *jihad* in the age of globalisation. After each terrorist attack, Jihadis released statements and films celebrating the life and death of martyrs. In the twenty-first century, *jihad* became a performance with its own politics and poetics that draw on old meanings but is delivered and disseminated using the latest communication technology. Jihadi violence is not simply about challenging the regime and expelling infidels from the Arabian Peninsula. It is concerned with battles over religious interpretation, cultural values, national identity and the position of women. It emerges as a result of a modern orientation in which men feel they can change the world by action. Jihadis combine a longing for a return to the authentic tradition with ultra-modern concerns. Jihadi rhetoric is very traditional, yet the messages reflect issues that are a product of modernity. Jihadis are concerned with the question of loss of identity, hardly an issue in traditional societies. Their messages tended to be global, yet they are fully immersed in the politics of the locality. Such messages flourish in contexts in which aspirations are suppressed, projects are diverted and comrades betrayed. They also blossom in contexts where the gap between proclaimed official political discourse and reality is extremely wide.

Saudi Jihadi discourse emerged in an authoritarian context. Low levels of education, rising aspirations, economic deprivation, social marginalisation and suppressed dreams are the context rather than the cause. While *jihad* is commonly interpreted as a struggle for the sake of God, it is in fact a struggle over religious interpretation and identity at a time when there are several competing discourses and multiple identities. Jihadis do not seek to annihilate themselves because they are suffering alienation, sexual frustration or anomie. It seems that they do so because they strongly believe in their power and strength – both expressed in religious idiom. They are aware of the fact that after their martyrdom, some would hail them as heroes in the land of no heroes.

Through the life of one Saudi Salafi, Lewis Atiyat Allah, I traced the competing lives and identities that this personality experienced and expressed. Lewis experimented with Sahwa, abandoned it in favour of liberalism, then returned to Sahwa, only to be disappointed. He claims to have found his salvation in Jihadism. It remains to be seen whether this is Lewis's final destination. I have my doubts.

This book highlighted the consequences of state efforts to domesticate religion and its interpreters. The Al-Saud controlled religious interpretations that were carefully produced by a group of 'ulama. The latter took control of the social sphere while leaving politics to the Al-Saud and their advisers. The Al-Saud had no qualms with uncompromising religious interpretations applied in the social sphere. The more the public arena appeared to be 'properly Islamised', the more they are seen as pious Muslim rulers – or at least this is what they hoped. The 'ulama played the game according to the rules. They excelled in enforcing the outward appearances of Islam while the regime conducted its policy on the basis of pragmatism and survival, like any other government.

If ever the 'ulama interfered in the well-guarded realm of politics, it was only to repeat interpretations that consolidated power and eliminated any potential dissident voices. They interpreted peaceful dissidence as violation of Quranic verses that call upon the believers to obey God, the Prophet and wali al-amr. The state itself created the conditions that allowed mutations of the Wahhabi tradition. The more the state enforced the 'ulama's interpretations, the more this discourse proliferated. Those who excommunicate the regime itself draw on early Wahhabi sources of interpretation: when the state closed the gates of ijtihad (interpretation), society (or more accurately sections of it) opened the gates of jihad. The Saudi regime created the conditions for religiously motivated violence. Today it is struggling to convince the world that it is a victim of this violence. At the same time, it is desperately trying to convince the West that it is the only shield against this violence spreading more widely and claiming many lives, both Muslim and non-Muslim. The Saudi regime resorts to its old game. In Western contexts it demonises its own constituency for the sake of projecting itself as the sole agent of modernity, prosperity and tolerance. It relies on a circle of Western-educated princes and advisers to project an image of modernity that appeals to a West still dependent on Saudi oil. Many observers of Saudi Arabia forget the role played by these very princes and their loyal 'ulama in creating the conditions for radicalism and violence. What is meant here is not 'sponsoring terrorism' but creating the conditions that make it the only imagined solution. Had Saudis been allowed to articulate and express alternative religious interpretations, not many would have resorted to violence. Alternatively, had the Saudi leadership acted according to its professed symbols and rhetoric, not many Saudis would have described their regime as a kafir regime.

This study has captured several ongoing realities about Saudi Arabia in the twenty-first century. Despite being subject to authoritarian rule, Saudis today are engaged in a fierce debate about religion and politics, previously considered taboo topics. This debate takes place in both traditional and less traditional spaces, the latter the result of advances in communication technology. This debate is extremely modern as it reflects concerns over identity and place in the world. In a very short period, Saudis moved from a localised identity that revolved around kin, tribe, sect and region to globalisation, before consolidating a national identity. They celebrated narrow identities while at the same time they endorsed global religious belonging. They exported their narrow religious discourse before they themselves were able to cope with the pressures exerted by modernity.

The debate and those involved in it do not easily fit ready-made categories such as traditional, moderate or radical. I hope this book reflects the way those engaged in the debate can easily move from one category to another. The more authoritarian rule exerts pressure to contain debate, the more interpretations proliferate and escape the straitjacket imposed from above. As the debate disappears from the public sphere, it is bound to become more radical and dangerous. It lives in the shadow of a huge religious bureaucracy with its own privileges and power. When the official establishment became completely co-opted, Sahwis emerged to challenge its interpretations. With the co-optation of Sahwis, Jihadi interpretations emerged to challenge both. The process will continue as long as authoritarian rule continues to discipline and punish those who offer alternative interpretations. Because of the previous hegemonic status of Wahhabiyya, all will try to anchor their discourse within this so-called authentic tradition. A small minority will try to destroy Wahhabiyya altogether. This conclusion challenges the ongoing attempts by various groups to renew religious discourse under the rubric of *tajdid al-khitab al-dini* (renewing religious discourse). For this renewal to take place the right context must be dominant.

As Jihadi violence claimed many lives and triggered a wave of government repression, it must be acknowledged that it speeded up religio-political debate in Saudi Arabia more than any other event in the recent history of the country. While the official religious establishment reiterates its discourse of acquiescence, educated Saudis, intellectuals, *ulama* and laymen challenge this discourse. People who search for the original message of Salafiyya, namely the quest for the unmediated word of God, are currently engaged in redefining the religious field. It seems that not many Saudis want to reassert the consenting discourse of the official *ulama*, although they themselves continue to claim that they hold the keys to salvation. Many Saudis struggle to dismantle the three pillars of authoritarian rule, the historical, theological and political narratives propagated by the ruling elite and their *noblesse d'état*. Saudis are beginning to imagine and articulate alternative religious interpretations that promise to free them from a cumulative religio-political discourse that grew in the shadow of power. Perhaps this quest will eventually lead to dismantling authoritarian rule itself. Only then Saudis will be fully integrated in the world – not as idiosyncratic fanatical puritans, suppressed bohemian subjects or romanticised tribal desert warriors, but as free citizens able to articulate, choose and live narratives of their own making.

Notes

INTRODUCTION: DEBATING RELIGION AND POLITICS IN THE TWENTY-FIRST CENTURY

1 For recent balanced scholarly history of the Wahhabiyya, see David Commins, *The Wahhabis Mission and Saudi Arabia*, London: I. B. Tauris 2005. Other sources include Esther Peskes, *Muhammad b. Abdalwahhab (1703–92) im Widerstreit. Untersuchungen zuz Rekonstruktion der Fruhgeschichte derWahhabiya*, Beirut: Steiner, 1993; Guido Steinberg, 'Religion und Staat in Saudi-Arabien. Eine Sozialgeschichte der wahhabitischen Gelehrten 1912–1953', Ph.D. thesis, Berlin: Free University, 2000; Guido Steinberg, 'The Wahhabi Ulama and the Saudi State: 1745 to the Present', in Paul Aarts and Gerd Nonneman (eds.), *Saudi Arabia in the Balance*, London: Hurst & Co., 2005, pp. 11–34; Michael Cook, 'The Expansion of the First Saudi State: The Case of Washm', in C. Bosworth, C. Issawi, R. Savory and U. Udovitch (eds.), *The IslamicWorld: From Classical to Modern Times*, Princeton: Princeton University Press, 1988, pp. 661–99.

2 For a history of the first and second Saudi states see Madawi Al-Rasheed, *A History of Saudi Arabia*, Cambridge: Cambridge University Press 2002, pp. 14–26.

3 Bashir Nafi discusses the rise and decline of the Salafiyya that was associated with the nineteenth-century reformist modernist trend in the Arab world, mainly the project of Abduh, al-Afghani, al-Alusi and Rida. See Basheer Nafi, *The Rise and Decline of the Arab-Islamic Reform Movement*, London: Institute for Contemporary Islamic Thought, 2000, p. 45.

4 On revivalism in Islam, see Bruce Lawrence, *Shattering the Myth: Islam beyond Violence*, Princeton: Princeton University Press 1998. See also Albert Hourani, *Arabic Thought in the Liberal Age 1978–1939*, Oxford: Oxford University Press, 1962.

5 The defeat of Egypt in 1967 was a crucial moment for the shift in power to the advantage of Saudi Arabia. See Madawi Al-Rasheed, *A History of Saudi Arabia*, Cambridge: Cambridge University Press, 2002, pp. 128–34; Madawi Al-Rasheed, *Mazaq al-islah fi al-saudiyya fi al qarn al-wahid wa al-ishrin*, London: Saqi Books, 2005, pp. 9–24.

6 Muhammad ibn Abd al-Wahhab's brother Sulayman wrote one of the first critiques of Wahhabiyya in which he reprimanded his brother for excessive excommunication of other Muslims. See Sulayman ibn Abd

al-Wahhab, *al-Sawaiq al-ilahiyya fi al-radd ala al-wahhabiyya*, Beirut: Dhu al-Faqar, 1997.

7 In the eighteenth cenury the *qadi* of Mecca, Ahmad bin Zayni Dahlan, denounced his contemporary, Muhammad ibn Abd al-Wahhab, in a short responsa. See Ahmad Dahlan. *al-Durar al-saniyya fi al-radd ala al-wahhabiyya*, Beirut: al-Maktaba al-Thaqafiyya, n.d.

8 Sunni *'ulama* who were close to Ottoman officials in Damascus and Baghdad denounced Wahhabiyya in several volumes that appeared in the eighteenth century. For an understanding of Salafi–Wahhabi religious debate in Baghdad, see Hala Fattah, ' "Wahhabi" Influences, Salafi Responses: Shaikh Mahmud Shukri and the Iraqi Salafi Movement, 1745–1930', *Journal of Islamic Studies* 14/2 (2003): 127–48. For an understanding of the confrontation between Iraqi *'ulama* and Wahhabiyya, see Rasul Muhammad Rasul, *al-Wahabiyyun wa al-iraq, aqidat al-shuyukh wa suyuf al-muharibin*, Beirut: Riad El-Rayyes Books, 2005. The Azharite scholar Muhammad al-Ghazali denounced Wahhabis as ʿahl al-hadith who use less authentic hadiths to formulate religious rulings'. The Ahl al-Hadith is a group seeking literalist interpretation of the Quran and the Prophetic tradition. This school of thought was strong in a section of the Muslim community in India, where it emerged. It is often reported that Muhammad ibn Abd al-Wahhab frequented the circle of one of their scholars, someone by the name of al-Sindi, who was in Mecca at the time. Ahl al-Hadith had followers in Saudi Arabia and sometimes the boundaries between them and Wahhabis are blurred. Ahl al-Hadith rejects all schools of jurisprudence (*madhahib*) because they involve human opinion and interpretation, while Wahhabis revere Hanbali *fiqh*. Muhammad al-Ghazali promotes a different approach, associated with *ahl al-fiqh* (people of jurisprudence). See Muhammad al-Ghazali, *al-Sunna al-nabawiyya bayn ahl al fiqh wa ahl al-hadith*, 13th edn., Cairo: Dar al-Shuruq, 2005.

9 Even in present-day Turkey, considerable intellectual effort, especially in Sufi circles, is devoted to refuting Wahhabi claims and positions on important matters of religious doctrine and practice. An Arabic version of a Turkish website publicises anti-Wahhabi publications for Arabic speakers. See http://www.hizmetbooks.org/hakikat/arabic/arabic.htm.

10 Shiʿi, Zaydi and Ismaili Muslims continue to defend their tradition against Wahhabi positions that in the past denounced them as innovators. See Hasan al-Saqqaf, *al-Salafiyya al-wahhabiyya*, Beirut: Dar al-Mizan, 2005; Muhammad Mughniyyah, *Hathihi hiya al-wahhabiyya*, Beirut: Dar al-Jawad, 1982; Ayatollah Hadi Kashif al-Ghita, *al-Ajwiba al-najafiyya fi al-radd ala al-fatawi al-wahhabiyya*, Beirut: al-Ghadir, 2004.

11 St John Philby, *Arabia of the Wahhabis*, London: Constable & Co., 1928; George Rentz, *The Birth of the Islamic Reform Movement in Saudi Arabia: Muhammad ibn Abd al-Wahhab (1703/4–1792) and the Beginnings of the Unitarian Empire in Arabia*, London: Arabian Publishing, 2005. In 2005 Rentz's 1948 thesis was published by a London-based publisher acting on behalf of a Saudi research centre in an attempt to dispel Western accusations against Wahhabiyya. For a critical review of Rentz's thesis, see Madawi Al-Rasheed, review of Rentz, *The Birth of the Islamic Reform Movement*, in *Middle Eastern Studies* 12/10 (2006): 173–7.

12 Representatives of this genre of literature include Vincenzo Oliveti, *Terror's Source: The Ideology of Wahhabi-Salafism and its Consequences*, Birmingham: Amadeusbooks, 2001; Craig Ungar, *House of Bush House of Saud: The Secret Relationship between the World's Two Most Powerful Dynasties*, New York: Scribner, 2004; Bob Woodward, *Plan of Attack*, New York: Simon & Schuster, 2004; Robert Baer, *Sleeping with the Devil: How Washington Sold our Souls for Saudi Crude*, New York: Crown, 2003; and Stephen Schwartz, *The Two Faces of Islam: Saudi Fundamentalism and its Role in Terrorism*, New York: Anchor Books, 2002.

13 See Hamid Algar, *Wahhabism: A Critical Essay*, New York: Islamic Publications International, 2002; Asad Abukhalil, *The Battle For Saudi Arabia: Royalty, Fundamentalism and Global Power*, New York: Seven Stories Press, 2004; Khaled Abou El Fadl, *Speaking in God's Name: Islamic Law, Authority and Women*, Oxford: Oneworld, 2001.

14 Three Saudi sources in exile take the lead in demonstrating the excessive interpretations of the Wahhabi tradition. The electronic publications of the Washington-based Saudi Institute run by Saudi Shi'i Ali al-Ahmad, the magazine *Shuun Saudiyyah*, published by the London-based National Coalition for Democracy in Saudi Arabia, and the *al-Hijaz* magazine, published by the National Hijazi Society, all take a clearly anti-Wahhabi position.

15 Salafi Publications, a small publisher based in Canada, defend Wahhabiyya. See Haneef James Oliver, *The Wahhabi Myth: Dispelling Prevalent Fallacies and the Fictitious Link with Bin Laden*, Victoria: Trafford, 2002. See also salafipublications.com, especially electronic books that denounce the Muslim Brotherhood, which is accused of corrupting the Salafi creed and encouraging violence. For a defence of Wahhabiyya in Arabic, see the Saudi website http://saaid.net/monawein/m/24.htm (accessed 16 June 2004).

16 Iris Glosemeyer describes these efforts as a charm-offensive campaign, in which the regime mobilised its technocrats, businessmen, *'ulama* and academics to polish the image of the country after 11 September 2001. See Iris Glosemeyer, 'Saudi Arabia: Dynamism Uncovered', in Volker Perthes (ed.), *Arab Elites: Negotiating the Politics of Change*, Boulder: Lynne Rienner, 2004, pp. 141–69, at p. 157. After 11 September, the regime mobilised women to defend the realm outside Saudi Arabia as reflected in the number of Saudi princesses, academics and businesswomen who have been allowed to travel with official Saudi delegations to the USA and Europe. The daughter of King Faysal, Princess Loulouwa al-Faysal, made several appearances in Western capitals, together with Saudi academics and businesswomen. The daughter of King Abdullah, Princess Adillah, issued statements to the media, an unusual move in Saudi Arabia. Similarly, the daughter of Prince Talal ibn Abd al-Aziz was reported to have made public statements claiming that her father has the right to be considered among heirs to the throne. All female voices are meant to improve the image of the regime abroad.

17 See Natana DeLong-Bas, *Wahhabi Islam: From Revival and Reform to Global Jihad*, London: I. B. Tauris, 2004. DeLong-Bas goes as far as to argue that Wahhabiyya is a moderate religious interpretation.

18 Gilles Kepel argues that terrorism is a product of the thought of the Muslim Brotherhood exiles in Saudi Arabia. While he draws attention to the fact that

Egyptian and Syrian exiles in the 1960s were under strict orders not to 'inter-fere' in local Saudi affairs, he seems to suggest that they did. He goes further when he attributes current terrorism to their influence on the Saudi popula-tion. His evidence is drawn from the fact that Muhammad Qutb, the brother of famous Egyptian Islamist Sayid Qutb, supervised Safar al-Hawali's doc-toral thesis and the fact that the Syrian sheikh Muhammad Surur Zayn al-Abdin might have taught Sheikh Salman al-Awdah in one of the religious institutes in Buraydah in the 1960s. Both examples provide weak evidence of the radicalisation of Saudis as a result of two Muslim Brotherhood activists. The opposite argument can easily be put forward, namely that the local Wahhabi tradition, especially its emphasis on *takfir* and *jihad*, had great influ-ence on the thought of the members of the Muslim Brotherhood exiles in Saudi Arabia. See Gilles Kepel, *The War for Muslim Minds: Islam and the West*, Cambridge, MA: Belknap Press, 2004, pp. 152–96. These issues will be dis-cussed in chapter 2.

19 This confusion is common in media reporting on Saudi Arabia.

20 Steinberg addresses schisms within Wahhabiyya in the nineteenth and early twentieth centuries. He argues that there were at least two schools within Wahhabiyya, a radical one (based in Riyadh and Buraydah) and a moderate one, based in Unayzah in Qasim. Steinberg clearly illustrates that religious interpretations are grounded in socio-economic conditions. See Steinberg, 'The Wahhabi Ulama and the Saudi State'. In contemporary Saudi Arabia, it is more accurate to talk about several strands within Wahhabiyya that are not necessarily linked to a geographical region.

21 Paul Dresch makes this observation. See Paul Dresch, 'Societies, Identities and Global Issues', in Paul Dresch and James Piscatori (eds.), *Monarchies and Nations: Globalisation and Identity in the Arab States of the Gulf*, London: I. B. Tauris, 2005, pp. 1–33.

22 Bruce Lawrence rightly argues that it is unconvincing to claim that Bin Laden and his movement is an Arab version of the Red Brigades or the ultra-left groups that practised terrorism in Europe in the 1970s, or even nineteenth-century anarchists. See Bruce Lawrence, *Messages to the World: The Statements of Osama Bin Laden*, London: Verso, 2005, pp. xx. See also Faisal Devji, *Landscapes of the Jihad: Militancy, Morality, Modernity*, London: Hurst & Co., 2006. Devji rejects the comparison between Bin Laden and early revolution-ary movements. He argues that Bin Laden represents a vision that is mystical, ethical and perhaps heretical, from the point of view of mainstream Islam.

23 Dale Eickelman, 'Inside the Islamic Reformation', *Wilson Quarterly* 22 (1998): 80–98, at p. 82. See also Dale Eickelman and James Piscatori, *Muslim Politics*, Princeton: Princeton University Press, 1996; and Dale Eickelman and Jon Anderson, *New Media in the Muslim World: The Emerging Public Sphere*, Bloomington: Indiana University Press, 1999.

24 The *taraju'at* (lit. going back, repentance) of Mansur al-Noqaydan and Mishari al-Thaydi are now well known in the West. Both renounced radical-ism and made a career out of publicising their 'reformation'.

25 For internet censorship in Saudi Arabia see Human Rights Watch, *The Internet in the Mideast and North Africa*, New York: Human Rights Watch, 1999.

26 A representative report is that of Cheryl Benard. See Cheryl Benard, *Civil Democratic Islam: Partners, Resources, and Strategies*, Santa Monica: Rand, 2003. See also Angel Rabasa et al., *The Muslim World after 9/11*, Santa Monica: Rand, 2004.

27 A study of the elite in Saudi Arabia demonstrates that this kind of research is extremely difficult as a result of the Wahhabis' anti-research culture, especially if the subject of research is the religious elite itself. Muhammad al-Sonaytan attributes his less than sufficient data on religious scholars to Wahhabi reservations on research. See Muhammad al-Sunaytan, *al-Nukhab al-saudiyya dirasa fi al-tahawulat wa al-ikhfaqat*, Beirut: Markaz Dirasat al-Wihda al-Arabiyya, 2004. While it is incredibly easy to publish biographies that praise the *'ulama*, it is impossible to see them other than as pious guardians of the Islamic tradition. To say that they are a class set apart and with its own privileges and power amounts to insulting them. Similarly, as expected, biographies of kings and princes tend to promote mythical narratives.

1 CONSENTING SUBJECTS: OFFICIAL WAHHABI RELIGIO-POLITICAL DISCOURSE

1 In the twenty-first century Salafis are diverse in their political views on the legitimacy of existing governments, democracy, elections, human rights and those of women and minorities as well as many other important issues. Most importantly, they differ on the strategy that must be adopted vis-à-vis political authority. At one extreme there is a trend that accepts total obedience to rulers and prefers not to initiate any political views. In Saudi Arabia, followers of this trend are pejoratively referred to as Jamis, after a Madina-based sheikh, Aman al-Jami. At the other extreme, Salafi Jihadis call for armed resistance against unjust and *kafir* rulers. Among those who adopt violence as a strategy, there are also subgroups. One such group is known as Ikhwan Burayda. This book will cover some but not all of the dominant and well-known Salafi trends within Saudi Arabia.

2 Saudi–Wahhabi Salafis denounced the Ottoman Empire as a *kafir* regime in the time of Muhammad ibn Abd al-Wahhab. Their objections were centred on the proliferation of Sufi *turuq* (sing. *tariqa*) under the auspices of the Ottoman sultan, a blasphemy that must be rejected by good Muslims. However, it is simplistic to reduce the Ottoman–Wahhabi conflict to its religious dimension. Fattah argues that understanding the Wahhabi revivalist movement especially in the later period of the nineteenth century was closely related to the incorporation of the Gulf region in European imperial design and the shift in trade routes between Europe and Asia. See Hala Fattah, *The Politics of Regional Trade in Iraq, Arabia and the Gulf 1745–1900*, Albany: State University of New York Press, 1997.

3 Several Saudi scholars take it for granted that the Arabian population was blasphemous and chaotic prior to Wahhabi revivalism. See Abdullah al-Uthaymin, *al-Sheikh Muhammad ibn Abd al-Wahhab*, Riyadh: Dar al-Ulum, 1992; Uwaidah al-Juhany, *Najd before the Salafi Reform Movement: Social, Political, and Religious Conditions during the Three Centuries Preceding the Rise of the Saudi State*, Reading: Ithaca, 2002; Abdulaziz al-Fahad, 'The Imama vs.

the Iqal: Hadari–Bedouin Conflict and the Formation of the Saudi State', in Madawi Al-Rasheed and Robert Vitalis (eds.), *Counter-Narratives: History, Contemporary Society, and Politics in Saudi Arabia and Yemen*, New York: Palgrave, 2004, pp. 11–24.

4 Wahhabis identify Hijazis who visit tombs or build domes on graves as *quburis*, meaning grave-worshippers. This is also a pejorative way to refer to the people of Hijaz in general.

5 An example of Wahhabi historiography that was intimately tied with the movement is the work of Hussein ibn Ghannam, referred to as the Sheikh and Imam, in which one finds a classic example of Wahhabi demonisation of Arabian society together with a detailed description of the atrocities that were inflicted on this society by Wahhabi raids. Ibn Ghannam's book is one of the main historical sources on Wahhabiyya. See Hussein ibn Ghannam, *Tarikh najd*, Cairo: Dar al-Shuruq, 1994.

6 On contemporary historiography, see Al-Rasheed, *A History of Saudi Arabia*, pp. 188–217.

7 On folk Islam that prevailed among the population of Arabia, especially women, see Eleanor Doumato, *Getting God's Ear:Women, Islam, and Healing in Saudi Arabia and the Gulf*, New York: Columbia University Press, 2000.

8 For a historical and theological interpretation of this Islamic obligation, see Michael Cook, *Commanding Right and Forbidding Wrong in Islamic Thought*, Cambridge: Cambridge University Press, 2000.

9 A vivid description of both the atrocities and gains of the Wahhabis can be found in the chronicles of the movement's historians. See Ibn Ghannam, *Tarikh najd*.

10 Muhammad ibn Abd al-Wahhab, *Masail al-jahiliyya*, Riyadh: Dar al-Watan, 1408H, p. 43.

11 For a rationalist critique of 'blocking the means', see Abou El Fadl, *Speaking in God's Name*.

12 The composition of *majlis al-shura* reflects a mixture of religious scholars and technocrats. For an analysis of the first *majlis*, see Hrair Dekmejian, 'The Rise of Political Islam in Saudi Arabia', *Middle East Journal* 48/4 (1994): 627–43. For the Saudi elite in general, see al-Sunaytan, *al-Nukhab al-saudiyya*.

13 For twentieth century episodes of this dissidence see Madawi Al-Rasheed *A History of Saudi Arabia* 2002.

14 Several Wahhabi publications are used in this chapter. One important source is sheikh Abdulrahman al-Qasim (ed.), *al-Durar al-saniyya fi al-ajwiba al-najdiyya*, 16 vols., Riyadh: n.p., 2004, hereafter *al-Durar al-saniyya*, and Muhammad al-Shuwayir *Abdulaziz ibn Baz majmu fatawi wa maqalat mutanawiah*, vols. V and VI, Jeddah: al-Sabahah, n.d. [1413H], hereafter *Majmu fatawi*, in addition to several publications by Muhammad ibn Abd al-Wahhab.

15 Guido Steinberg describes the ecology of this region where the staunchest supporters of the movement originated. See Guido Steinberg, 'Ecology, Knowledge, and Trade in Central Arabia (Najd) during the Nineteenth and Early Twentieth Centuries', in Al-Rasheed and Vitalis (eds.), *Counter-Narratives*, pp. 77–102, at pp. 78–88.

16 The Banu Tamim is an ancient sedentary Arabian tribe. Its members lived in the various oases and towns from Hail in the north to Hawtat Bani Tamim in the south. Many years of sedentarisation deprived it of its tribal organisation and structure. Moreover, members of Banu Tamim are found in Gulf states, Iraq, Egypt and the Levant as a result of a long history of trade and migration. Several generations of this tribe settled in Zubayr in southern Iraq, where they formed a Sunni colony.

17 Al-Rasheed, *A History of Saudi Arabia*, pp. 49–58.

18 One of the main chronicles of Najdi scholars is Abdullah al-Bassam, *Ulama najd khilal thamaniyat qurun*, vols. I–VIII, Riyadh: Dar al-Asimah, 1419AH. See also Abdullah al-Bassam *Ulama najd khilal sitat qurun* Mecca: Dar al-Nahda, 1398AH.

19 al-Bassam, *Ulama najd khilal thamaniyat qurun*.

20 Pierre Bourdieu argues that schools produce the modern technocrat. They are the most efficient weapon of the state, creating the machinery that operates within ourselves. In contemporary Western society, of which France is an example, the school produces 'state nobility'. See Pierre Bourdieu, *The State Nobility*, Cambridge: Polity Press, 1996. In places like Saudi Arabia, we can argue that the Wahhabi *'ulama* and their educational and preaching efforts over the last century are truly a form of *noblesse d'état*, a religious 'nobility' in control of peoples' minds through their monopoly over educational institutions.

21 Alexander Bligh, 'The Saudi Religious Elite (Ulama) as Participants in the Political System of the Kingdom', *International Journal of Middle East Studies* 17/1 (1985): 37–50.

22 Abdulaziz al-Tuwayjiri, *Li surata al-layl hatf al-sabah*, Beirut: Dar Riyadh al-Rayyis, 1998, p. 474.

23 I borrow this terminology from the anthropologist Abdullah Hammoudi, who applied it in the context of Morocco. See Abdullah Hammoudi, *Master and Disciple: The Cultural Foundations of Moroccan Authoritarianism*, Chicago: Chicago University Press, 1997.

24 Sheikh Ibn Ibrahim's biography is constructed from *al-Durar al-saniyya*.

25 *al-Durar al–saniyya*, vol. XVI, p. 474.

26 al-Bassam, *Ulama najd khilal thamaniyat qurun*, vol. I, p. 244.

27 Ibid., pp. 245–6.

28 Ibid.

29 Ibid., p. 249.

30 Ibid.

31 *al-Durar al-saniyya*, vol. XVI, pp. 206–313. Sahwi sheikh Safar al-Hawali wrote an interpretation of Ibn Ibrahim's epistle, in which he highlighted the main themes that dominated the sheikh's thinking. See Safar al-Hawali, *Sharh risalat tahkim al-qawanin*, n.p.: Dar al-Kaima, 1999.

32 *al-Durar al-saniyyah*, vol. XVI, p. 206.

33 Nasir al-Fahad, www.alsalafyoon.com, accessed 26 November 2003.

34 Bligh, 'Saudi Religious Elite', p. 39.

35 See http://www.binbaz.org.sa/Doisplay.asp?f=eng0007.

36 Al-Rasheed, *A History of Saudi Arabia*, pp. 163–87.

37 Wahhabi state *'ulama* are not unique in playing this role. For a comparative study, see Muhammad Qasim Zaman, *The Ulama in Contemporary Islam: Custodians of Change*, Princeton: Princeton University Press, 2002.
38 See http://said.net/Warathah/1/hatif.htm and http;//said.net/Warathah/index/htm, accessed 10 March 2005.
39 Migration as an act of piety and survival is an integral tradition in Islam. For the early tradition of the Prophet and migration from Mecca to Madina, see Jonathan Berkey, *The Formation of Islam: Religion and Society in the Near East, 600–1800*, Cambridge: Cambridge University Press, 2003.
40 This obligation is clearly demonstrated in the early history of Wahhabiyya. See Ibn Ghannam, *Tarikh najd*.
41 Al-Rasheed, *A History of Saudi Arabia*, 2002.
42 Steinberg, 'The Wahhabi Ulama'.
43 *Majmu fatawi*, vol. V, p. 390.
44 Ibid., p. 79.
45 Ibid., p. 342.
46 On the Gulf War of 1990–1, see Al-Rasheed, *A History of Saudi Arabia*, pp. 163–87.
47 Sheikh Muhsin al-Obaykan, 'Ma'na ukhruj al-mushrikin min jazirat al-arab', *al-Sharq al-Awsat*, 25 October 2004.
48 On Muslim–infidel relations, see Yohannan Friedman, *Tolerance and Coercion in Islam: Interfaith Relations in the Muslim Tradition*, Cambridge: Cambridge University Press, 2003.
49 Patricia Crone, *Medieval Islamic Political Thought*, Edinburgh: Edinburgh University Press, 2004.
50 On the Kharijites see ibid., pp. 54–64. Current official Saudi discourse refers to al-Qa'ida agents as the contemporary Kharijites. See Omar Kamil, *al-Mutatarifun khawarij al-asr*, Beirut: Bisan, 2002.
51 *al-Durar al-saniyyah*, vol. I, p. 73.
52 Ibid., pp. 100–4.
53 Ibid., vol. VIII, pp. 89–90.
54 Ibid., vol. I, pp. 66–7.
55 Ibid., pp. 372–439.
56 Ibid., p. 565.
57 For a biography of Abdullah al-Qasimi, see Yurgen Wasella, *al-Qasimi bayn al-usuliyya wa al-inshiqaq*, trans. Muhammad Kibaybo, Beirut: Dar al-Kunuz al-Adabiyya, 2001.
58 See http://www.metransparent.com/texts/bayan hayat.htm, accessed 3 May 2005.
59 *Majmu fatawi*, vol. VI, pp. 121–2.
60 Michael Crawford, 'Civil War, Foreign Intervention, and the Quest for Political Legitimacy: A Nineteenth Century Saudi Qadi Dilemma', *International Journal of Middle East Studies* 14 (1982): 227–48, at p. 235.
61 On the Ikhwan, see John Habib, *Ibn Saud's Warriors of Islam: The Ikhwan of Najd and their Role in the Creation of the Saudi kingdom, 1910–1930*, Leiden: Brill, 1978 and Joseph Kostiner, 'On Instruments and their Designers: The Ikhwan of Najd and the Emergence of the Saudi State', *Middle Eastern Studies* 21 (1985): 298–323.

62 Rifat Ahmad, *Rasail Juhayman al-Otaybi*, Cairo: Madbouli, 2004.
63 Abu al-Bara al-Najdi, *al-Kawashif al-jaliyya fi kufr al-dawla al-saudiyya*, London: Dar al-Qasim, 1994.
64 Saad al-Faqih, *al-Nitham al-saudi fi mizan al-islam*, London: al-Haraka al-Islamiyya lil islah, 1996; Muhammad al-Masari, *al-Adilla al-qatiyya ala adam shariyat al-dawla al-saudiyya*, London: Dar al-Shariyya, 1995.
65 DeLong-Bas, *Wahhabi Islam*.
66 For a good interpretation of the tradition of *jihad* in Islam in general, see Rudolph Peters, *Islam and Colonialism: The Doctrine of Jihad in Modern History*, The Hague: Mouton, 1979; Rudolph Peters, *Jihad in Classical and Modern Islam*, Princeton: Markus Wiener, 1996. On modern Egyptian interpretations of *jihad*, see Johannes Jansen, *The Neglected Duty*, New York: Macmillan, 1986.
67 Al-Rasheed, *A History of Saudi Arabia*, p. 42.
68 Peter Sluglett and Marion Sluglett, 'The Precarious Monarchy: Britain, Abd al-Aziz ibn Saud and the Establishment of the Kingdom of Hijaz, Najd and its Dependencies, 1925–1932', in Tim Niblock (ed.), *State, Society and Economy in Saudi Arabia*, London: Croom Helm, 1982, pp. 36–56.
69 Guido Steinberg draws attention to the fact that there is almost a historical amnesia regarding the Wahhabi *'ulama* who sided with the Ikhwan rebels. See Steinberg, 'The Wahhabi Ulama'.
70 Ibid.
71 al-Fahad, 'The Imama vs. the Iqal'.
72 See chapter 4 in this volume.
73 Lisa Meyer, 'More Evidence of Saudi Doubletalk: Judge Caught on Tape Encouraging Saudis to Fight in Iraq', 26 April 2005, NBC investigation unit. See http://www.msnbc.msn.com/id/7645118/print/1/displaymode/1098/, accessed 28 April 2005. For al-Lohaydan's view on *jihad*, see Saleh al-Lohaydan, *al-Jihad fi al-islam*, Riyadh: Dar al-Liwa, 1980.
74 See http://alsaha.fares.net/sahat?128@158.LNZuqLRwb5j.3@.1dd77103.
75 See www.saudiinstitute.org.
76 John Esposito and John Voll (eds.), *Makers of Contemporary Islam*, Oxford: Oxford University Press, 2001, p. 10.
77 *al-Durar al-saniyyah*, vol. XVI, p. 348.
78 This position reiterates Islamic political theory that was promoted by medieval scholars such as Ahmad ibn Taymiyya (1263–1328) in *al-Siyasa al-shariyya fi islah al-rai wa al-raiyya*, Beirut: Dar al-Jil, 1988; Ali al-Mawardi (991–1031) in *al-Ahkam al-sultaniyya wa al-wilayat al-diniyya*, Beirut: al-Arqam, n.d. For a review of Islamic political thought of the medieval period, see Hourani, *Arabic Thought in the Liberal Age*; Crone, *Medieval Islamic Political Thought*; and Antony Black, *The History of Islamic Political Thought: From the Prophet to the Present*, Edinburgh: Edinburgh University Press, 2001.
79 Crown Prince Abdullah became king in August 2005. This was the first time that worldwide coverage of the *bay'a* was possible, thanks to Saudi-owned satellite media and international coverage. Previous *bay'a*s – for example, that of King Fahad in 1982 – were hardly televised outside Saudi Arabia.
80 *al-Durar al-saniyyah*, vol. I, p. 33 and vol. XVI, p. 153.
81 On modernist revivalism, see Hourani, *Arabic Thought in the Liberal Age*.

82 Joseph Kechichian, 'The Role of the Ulama in the Politics of an Islamic State: The Case of Saudi Arabia', *International Journal of Middle East Studies* 18 (1986): 53–71.

83 Guido Steinberg describes the low level of religious education among religious scholars in the nineteenth century. See Steinberg, 'Ecology, Knowledge, and Trade', pp. 85–94 and Al-Rasheed, *A History of Saudi Arabia*, pp. 49–58. However, the situation prevailed until the mid-twentieth century, and even today not many Saudi religious scholars have worldwide recognition for their religious knowledge. Despite the decline of al-Azhar in recent decades, it has continued to produce scholars whose reputation travelled across the Muslim world.

84 Abdullah al-Uthaymin, *al-Sheikh Muhammad ibn Abd al-Wahhab*, p. 152. For another biography of Ibn Abd al-Wahhab see *al-Durar al-saniyyah*, vols. I and XVI and Ibn Ghannam, *Tarikh najd*. In English, George Rentz relies on the latter source. See Rentz, *Islamic Reform Movement*.

85 Contrast this lack of theorising Muslim leadership with Sunni reformism in Yemen. See Bernard Haykal, *Revival and Reform in Islam: The Legacy of Muhammad al-Shawkani*, Cambridge: Cambridge University Press, 2003. On Shiʿi preoccupation with the issue of *imama*, see Fuad Ibrahim, *al-Faqih wa al-dawla*, Beirut: Dar al-Kunuz al-Adabiyya, 1998.

86 Uwaidah al-Juhany draws attention to the concerns of the Najdi population at the time of the movement. These concerns did not go beyond regulating social relations and terminating the endemic feuds between various factions in the oases of central Arabia. See al-Juhany, *Najd before the Salafi Reform Movement*.

87 Ahmad al-Katib, *al-Fikr al-siyasi al-wahhabi qira'a tahliliyya* London: Dar al-Shura lil dirasat wa al-ilam, 2003.

88 Kuwaiti Islamist Hakim al-Mutayri criticises Wahhabi positions on politics. See Hakim al-Mutayri, *al-Huriyya wa al-tawafan*, Beirut: al-Muasasa al-Arabiyya lil Dirasat wa al-Nashr, 2004.

89 Ibn Abd al-Wahhab, *Masail al jahiliyyah*, pp. 12–13.

90 Muhammad Qutb, *Jahiliyat al-qarn al-ishrin*, 14th ed., Beirut: Dar al-Shuruq, 1995.

91 Quran, Sura al-nisa, verse 59.

92 Abdulaziz ibn Baz, lecture, 1/4/1417H, see http://www.ibnbaz.com.

93 *al-Durar al-saniyyah*, vol. I, p. 348.

94 al-Mutayri, *al-Huriyya wa al-tawafan*.

95 *al-Quds al-Arabi*, 16 May 2005: a Saudi judge sentenced three constitutional reformers to a period ranging from six to nine years in prison. For further details see chapter 6.

96 Abdulaziz ibn Baz, http://binbaz.org.sa/Display.Asp?f=bz01274.htm.

97 al-Mutayri, *al-Huriyya wa al-tawafan*.

98 Abdulaziz Ibn Baz, interview in *al-Dawah* magazine, http://www.ibnbaz.com, 19/12/1415H.

99 This is a reference to the faxes of Saudi Islamist opposition in the mid-1990s.

100 See http://otiby.net/makalat/articles.php?id=104, accessed 12 May 2005.

101 Abou El Fadl, *Speaking in God's Name*.

102 See Steinberg, 'Ecology, Knowledge, and Trade' on the miserable state of health and scholarship in central Arabia in the nineteenth century.

103 Wahhabi scholars today deny that their intellectual ancestors objected to female education. They insist that they objected to the delivery of education rather than its principle.

104 According to a survey of past and present scholars' views on elections, famous Saudi sheikhs are listed as having reservations, for example Muhammad ibn Ibrahim Al-Shaykh, Humud ibn Oqla al-Shuaybi, Ali al-Khodayr and Abdulaziz al-Omar. See http;//www.almaqreze.com/ Munawaat/Namesofscholars.htm

105 Bligh, 'Saudi Religious Elite', p. 40.

2 RE-ENCHANTING POLITICS: SAHWIS FROM CONTESTATION TO CO-OPTATION

1 For detailed discussion of the sociological and political impact of the first oil boom, see Al-Rasheed, *A History of Saudi Arabia*, chapter 5.

2 *al-Sharq al-Awsat*, 18 July 2005.

3 For an account of the rise of religious and other universities in Saudi Arabia, see Andre Elias Mazawi, 'The Academic Profession in a Rentier State: the Professoriate in Saudi Arabia', *Minerva* 4 (2005):221–244.

4 Hamad al-Salloum, *Education in Saudi Arabia*, Washington: Saudi Arabian Cultural Mission, 1995, p. 70.

5 The Saudi Arabian Information Resource, http://www.saudinf.com/main/ j42.htm.

6 Al-Salloum, *Education in Saudi Arabia*, p. 71.

7 The Saudi Arabian Information Resource, http://www.saudinf.com/main/ j44.htm.

8 James Piscatori, 'The Evolution of a Wahhabi University', unpublished conference paper, Oxford, September 2003.

9 Sheikh Salman al-Awdah's doctoral dissertation dealt with ablution.

10 Piscatori, 'Evolution'.

11 Omar al-Azi, 'al-Ikhwan al-saudiyun: al-tayar allathi lam yaqul kalimatuhu bad', http://www.ala7rar.net/navigator.php?printTopic&tid=1277, accessed 8 June 2005.

12 Farish Noor, *New Voices of Islam*, Leiden: ISIM, 2002, p. 20.

13 Turki al-Hamad, *Rih al-janna*, London: Saqi Books, 2005

14 Qutbists (followers of Sayyid Qutb) refers to a variant of Egyptian Hasan al-Banna's Muslim Brotherhood movement, often described as more radical. Qutb's brother, Muhammad was a university lecturer in Saudi Arabia.

15 Musa al-Abdulaziz, interview on Idhaat, al-Arabiyya television channel, 29 June 2005.

16 Rabi al-Madkhali, cited in Muhammad Surur Zayn al-Abdin, 'al-Salafiyya bayn al-wulat wa al-ghulat', unpublished manuscript, n.d.

17 Awadh al-Qarni, interview, *Elaph*, 14 May 1426AH. See http:// www.elaph. com.

18 See several articles assessing the Saudi Muslim Brotherhood on Ikhwani website http://www.ala7rar.net.

19 Musa al-Abdulaziz, interview on Idhaat, al-Arabiyya television channel, 29 June 2005.

20 A typical text is Safar al-Hawali's letter to Sheikh Abdulaziz ibn Baz, in *Kashf al-ghamma an ulama al-umma*, London: Dar al-Hikma, 1991.
21 For a history of the Sahwis in the 1990s, see Madawi Al-Rasheed, 'Saudi Arabia's Islamist Opposition', *Current History* 95/597 (1996): 16–22; Al-Rasheed, *A History of Saudi Arabia*. See also Mamoun Fandy, *Saudi Arabia and the Politics of Dissent*, New York: St Martin's Press, 1999; Dekmejian, 'The Rise of Political Islam'; Joshua Teitelbaum, *Holier than Thou: Saudi Arabia's Islamic Opposition*, Washington: Washington Institute for Near East Policy, 2000.
22 Muhammad Surur Zayn al-Abdin, in *al-Sunna* 40 (1417H), p. 92.
23 Kepel, *The War for Muslim Minds*, pp. 170–96.
24 This theme is developed by Penina Werbner, who distinguishes between transnationals and true cosmopolitans. Transnationals are identified by their ability to move, whereas cosmopolitans master the cultures in which they find themselves. See Penina Werbner, 'Global Pathways: Working Class Cosmopolitans and the Creation of Transnational Ethnic Worlds', *Social Anthropology* 7/1 (1999): 17–35.
25 Interview, London November 2004.
26 Ibid.
27 Zayn al-Abdin, *al-Sunna* 40 (1417H), p. 82.
28 Ibid.
29 Muhammad Surur Zayn al-Abdin, in *al-Sunna* 47 (1418H), p. 93.
30 Jihadi Salafis denounce Sheikh Muhammad Surur and his '*haraki*' Islam because he refuses to accept the inevitability of *jihad* against governments. See 'Minbar al-tawhid wa al-jihad', http://www.tawhed.ws/c?i=57, accessed 5 November 2005.
31 Interview, al-Mustaqilla television channel, 30 January 2005.
32 Prince Khalid al-Faysal on Idhaat, al-Arabiyya television channel, 15 July 2004.
33 Prince Khalid al-Faysal, *al-Watan*, 7 July 2004.
34 *Al-Riyadh*, 31 January 2005.
35 Sheikh Musa al-Abdulaziz, on Idhaat, al-Arabiyya television channel, 29 June 2005.
36 Rabi al-Madkhali, in Zayn al-Abdin, *al-Sunna* (1416H), p. 95.
37 On the Egyptian *tarajuat*, see Muntasir al-Zayat, *al-Jamaat al-islamiyya ruyah min al-dakhil*, Cairo: Dar al-Mahrusa, 2005.
38 Several articles appeared in the Western press after 11 September. Some journalists glorified the 'courageous men who moved from Jihadi violence to liberalism', loyal to their government and less threatening to the West.
39 Mansur al-Noqaydan, 'al-Fikr al-jihadi al-takfiri', *al-Riyadh*, 11 May 2003. Al-Noqaydan is right in claiming that Jihadis draw on local religious texts rather than alien ideas. His story is published in the *New York Times*. See Mansur al-Noqaydan, 'Telling the Truth, Facing the Whip', *New York Times*, 28 November 2003. His story is also publicised by American journalists and on satellite television: for example, Idhaat, al-Arabiyya, 15 September 2004 and 17 September 2005.
40 Khalid al-Ghannami, 'Sururis and Jihadis: The Raging Wolf and the Buried Snake', *al-Watan*, 30 January 2005. See also http://www.daralnadwa.com/vb/showthread.php?t=144602, accessed 31 January 2005.
41 Ali al-Amim, http://www.daralnadwa.com.

42 Saud al-Qahtani, http;//www.daralnadwa.com.

43 Muhammad ibn Abd al-Latif Al-Shaykh, 'Bin Laden wa da'wat Muhammad ibn Abd al-Wahhab', *al-Hayat*, 21 March 2002.

44 The obsession with classifying Islamists has ceased to be a purely academic exercise. It is entangled with strategies and policies of governments in the West. Nothing exemplifies this like Cheryl Benard's Rand Report in which she classifies Islamists according to well-known criteria, for example their views on relations with the West, women, minority groups, elections, democracy and other social and political issues. While such classifications may be useful for the American administration, they fail to account for the fluidity and hybridity of Islamist movements in an age of increased communication and shifting boundaries. See Benard, *Civil Democratic Islam*.

45 The Riyadh Counter-Terrorism Conference (5 February 2005) concentrated on the intellectual and religious roots of terrorism, finance networks and money laundering, as well as the security dimension. One important aspect of terrorism was deliberately excluded: the role of local authoritarian regimes and their coercive force in creating favourable ground in which terrorism and Jihadi discourse become meaningful, and capable of resonating with many groups. Furthermore, the conference failed to address contradictions between state political discourse and reality, for example the contradiction between Saudi religious legitimising narrative as defender of Islam against infidels and its close alliance with the West, which is increasingly seen by Saudi Islamists as a threat to Islam. A similar conference was sponsored in London in January 2006 and hosted by the Royal United Services.

46 On the Sahwa in the 1990s, see Al-Rasheed, 'Saudi Arabia's Islamist Opposition'.

47 See http://www.islamtoday.net/print.cfm?artid=5817.

48 See Abd al-Wahhab al-Turayry, 'Dawa', http://www.islamtoday.net/articles/show-articles-contenjt.cfm?catid.

49 Safar al-Hawali, interview, Bila hudud, al-Jazeera, 5 November 2003.

50 See http://islamtoday.net/english/printme.cfm?cat-id=29&sub-cat-id=471.

51 In a BBC radio programme, the Saudi ambassador to London, Prince Turki al-Faysal denied that there is such a thing as Wahhabiyya: BBC World Service, Analysis, 13 April 2005.

52 For Abdulaziz al-Qasim's research paper presented to Saudi National Dialogue Forum, see http://metransparent .com/texts/qassem manahej.htm). For a brief mention of al-Qasim, see Stephane Lacroix, 'Between Islamists and Liberals: Saudi Arabia's New Islamo-liberal Reformist Trend', *Middle East Journal* 58/3 (2004): 345–65.

53 Reuters, 'Al-Qaida's Aim in the Kingdom Unlikely to be Achieved', Reuters, 6 June 2004.

54 See www.alhawali.com, accessed 5 May 2004.

55 See http;//www.islamtoday.net/qprint.cfm?artid=48582.

56 See www.almoslim.net, accessed 10 March 2005.

57 Ibid.

58 On the exclusion and deprivation of the northern provinces, see Matruk al-Falih, *Sikaka al-jawf fi nihayat al-qarn al-ishrin*, Beirut: Bisan, 2000. Al-Falih warns that if regional disparity in development and modernisation are not

addressed, the situation in Saudi Arabia will become volatile in the future. See Matruk al-Falih, *Mustaqbal al-saudiyya al-islah aw al-taqsim*, London: Qadaya al-Khalij, 2002.

59 Muhammad al-Awadhi, 'Safar al-Hawali: An Example of Early Understanding', http://www.ala&rar.net/navigator.php?printTopic&tid-244, accessed 5 July 2005.

60 For an assessment of the Saudi position regarding the US invasion of Iraq, see Al-Rasheed, 'Saudi Arabia's Islamist Opposition'.

61 For a Sahwi view on the war, see 'Bayan hawla al-tahdidat al-amrikiyyah lil mintaqah', at http//www.islamtoday.net/Iraq2/byan.htm.

62 Nasir al-Omar, 'Waylun lil arab min sharin qad iqtarab', at http://www.islamtoday.net/articles/show_articles_content.cfm?i.

63 See 'Bayan hawla al-tahdidat al-amrikiyyah lil mintaqah', at http//www.islamtoday.net/Iraq2/byan.htm.

64 See http://www.almoslim.net/bayanat/falogah-jehad/sings-list-main1, accessed 18 November 2004.

65 Salman al-Awdah, interview, Idhaat, al-Arabiyya television channel, 13 July 2005.

66 Al-Awajy wrote articles posted on his website attacking Saad al-Faqih, Muhammad al-Masari, Mansur al-Noqaydan, Mishari al-Thaydi, Juhayr al-Musaid, Abdulaziz al-Khamis, Ghazi al-Qusaybi and many others, including this author. In one article he called upon Prince Khalid al-Faysal, governor of Asir, to engage in a dialogue with him. When I referred to al-Awajy as an Islamo-liberal, thus citing a label propagated by a French doctoral student, he was furious. He regarded the label as an insult. He immediately posted an article in which he called me *umm al-mu'minin*, 'the Mother of the Faithful', an amusing and ironical title. In March 2005 he launched an attack on Minister Ghazi al-Qusaybi in which he accused him of destroying the Islamic credentials of the Saudi state and of manipulating King Abdullah. Al-Awajy was imprisoned for ten days. His website, al-wasatiyya, was suspended. All his articles were found on http://www.wasatyah.com. For the label 'Islamo-liberal', see Stephane Lacroix, 'Between Islamists and Liberals: Saudi Arabia's New Islamo-liberal Reformists', *Middle East Journal* 58/3 (2004): 345–64 and Stephane Lacroix, 'Islamo Liberal Politics in Saudi Arabia', in Paul Aarts and Gerd Nonneman (eds.), *Saudi Arabia in the Balance: Political Economy, Society, Foreign Affairs*, London: Hurst & Co., 2005, pp. 35–56.

67 In 2004 Sheikh ibn Zu'yar and his son were imprisoned after statements given to al-Jazeera television channel. The first commented on one of Osama bin Laden's statements while the second criticised the government's decision to imprison his father who had already served eight years in prison in the 1990s. A Saudi lawyer, Abdulrahman al-Lahim, was also put in jail after comments on al-Jazeera. He criticised the government's decision to imprison Matruk al-Falih, Abdullah al-Hamid and Ali al-Damini. The three prisoners became known as constitutional monarchy reformers. See chapter 6 for further details.

68 Muhsin al-Awajy, 'Saad al-Faqih wa muhawalat kharq al-safinah', at http://www.yaislah.org/vboard/showthread.php?t=117529, accessed 17 November 2004.

69 Muhsin al-Awajy, 'Thawabit al-islah', *al-Madina*, 26 March 2004.

70 The most damming criticism of al-Awajy was written by Jihadi sheikh Yusif al-Ayri.

71 Saud al-Qahtani, 'Hadith ma' al-Awajy', discussion with al-Awajy, 25 March 2004, at http://writers.alriyadh.com.sa/kpage.php?ka-262.

72 During the fasting month in 2005, Sheikh Salman al-Awdah appeared daily on MBC television station in a programme called Hajar al-Zawiya, Cornerstone, to discuss religious issues and current affairs. The programme may contribute towards creating a pan-Arab reputation for the sheikh. It is also a desperate Saudi attempt to portray a different face of Islam to a wide Arab audience.

3 STRUGGLING IN THE WAY OF GOD ABROAD: FROM LOCALISM TO TRANSNATIONALISM

1 On a previous conflict between one Al-Saud ruler who in 1870 sought assistance from the Ottomans, defined as apostates by Wahhabi 'ulama, see Abulaziz al-Fahad, 'From Exclusivism to Accommodation: Doctrinal and Legal Evolution of Wahhabism', New York Law Review 79 (2004): 485–519.

2 On the twentieth-century Ikhwan conflict with the Al-Saud see Habib, Ibn Saud's Warriors and Kostiner, 'The Ikhwan of Najd'.

3 The main text that is often cited as representative of Egyptian Islamist theorisation of jihad is that of Muhammad Abd al-Salam Faraj, al-Faridha al-gaiba (The Absent Duty). See Peters, Jihad in Classical and Modern Islam, 149–69 and Jansen, The Neglected Duty.

4 Anwar Abdullah, Khasais wa sifat al-mujtama al-wahhabi, Paris: La Librairie de l'Orient, 2005.

5 On the Shi'is during this period see Fuad Ibrahim, 'The Shiite Opposition in the Eastern Province from Revolution to Accommodation (Case Study: The Reform Movement in Saudi Arabia)', Ph.D. thesis, University of London, 2004.

6 The latest version of the epistles of Juhayman appeared in Cairo. See Ahmad, Rasail Juhayman. On the siege of the Mecca mosque and its consequences, see Fahd al-Qahtani, Zilzal Juhayman fi Mecca, London: Munathamat al-Thawra al-Islamiyya fi al-Jazira al-Arabiyya, 1987. See also Joseph Kechichian 'Islamic Revivalism and Change in Saudi Arabia: Juhayman al-Utaybi's letters to the Saudi people', The Muslim World 70 (1990): 1–16.

7 On the Afghan jihad and the internationalisation of the conflict see John Cooley, Unholy Wars: Afghanistan, America and International Terrorism, London: Pluto Press, 2000 and Tom Carew, Jihad: the Secret War in Afghanistan, Edinburgh: Mainstream Publishing, 2000. On Osama bin Laden and the Muslim Diaspora, see Enseng Ho, 'Empire through Diasporic Eyes: A View from the Other Boat', Society for Comparative Study of Society and History (2004): 210–46.

8 Majmu fatawi, vol. V, p. 149.

9 Ibid., p. 151.

10 Ibid., pp. 246–7.

11 For a vivid journalistic account of Saudi involvement in the Afghan project, see Ahmed Rashid, Taliban: The Story of the Afghan Warlords, London: Pan Books, 2000, pp. 196–206.

12 Ibid., p. 85.
13 It is very difficult to identify an authentic biography of Bin Laden. An incredible number of books on him and on al-Qa'ida have appeared worldwide and in several languages, most containing elements of both myth and reality. In September 2005, on-line book shop Amazon listed 320 such books. Abd al-Bari Atwan offers a reasonable account of the man and his project, based on interviews with Bin Laden in 1996. See Abd al-Bari Atwan, *The Secret History of al-Qaida*, London: Saqi, 2005.
14 Immediately after 11 September polling organisations reported that more than 90 per cent of Saudis viewed Osama bin Laden favourably. In 2005 he was viewed favourably by a large number of Muslims in Pakistan (65 per cent), Jordan (55 per cent) and Morocco (45 per cent). Anthony Cordesman cited these figures in his testimony before the US Senate Judiciary Committee 'Saudi Arabia: Friend or Foe?' on 8 November 2005.
15 The transnational dimension of Bin Laden's project is discussed in Fawaz Gerges *The Far Enemy: Why Jihad Went Global*, Cambridge: Cambridge University Press, 2005. Gerges argues that Bin Laden's followers suffered from internal struggle that developed around national and ethnic belonging. However, while these internal struggles are well documented in his book, it is also noticeable that an Islamic global identity was forged among his followers who came from all parts of the Muslim world.
16 *al-Majallah*, 9–15 October 2005.
17 On anti- Shi'i *fatwa*s see Ibrahim, 'The Shiite Opposition'.
18 *Mut'a* marriage, a temporary marriage between a man and a woman, is considered lawful in Shi'i Islam but not so in the Sunni tradition.
19 On Deobandis see Barbara Metcalf, *Islamic Revival in British India: Deoband 1860–1900*, Princeton: Princeton University Press, 1982. Ahmed Rashid discusses the role of Deobandi *madrasa*s in the formation of the Taliban. He argues that Wahhabiyya first came to central Asia in 1912 when a native of Madina introduced it in Tashkent and the Ferghana Vallley. It went on to reach Afghanistan from there and from India. See Rashid, *Taliban*, p. 85. On Saudi patronage of Asian religious circles, mainly *ahl al-hadith* and Deobandi schools since the 1950s, see Zaman, *The Ulama in Contemporary Islam*, pp. 173–7.
20 In the 1970s the writings of twentieth-century Islamist thinkers such as Sayid Qutb and his brother Muhammad, and the Pakistani Abu al-Ala al-Mawdudi, were reprinted in Saudi publishing houses.
21 On the participation of Arabs in general in the Afghan *jihad*, see Abdullah Anas, *Wiladat al-afghan al-arab*, London: Saqi Books, 2002; Muhammad Salah, *Waqai sanawat al-jihad*, Beirut: Khulud, 2002; Ayman Faraj, *Thikrayat arabi afghani abu jafar al- masri al-qandahari*, Cairo: Dar al-Shoruq, 2002; and Ahmad Zeidan *Bin Laden bila qina'* Beirut: World Book Publishing, 2003. Most of this literature draws on personal involvement or journalistic encounters with Jihadis in Afghanistan. To my knowledge, no academic assessment of the Arab and Saudi involvement in this war has appeared.
22 Rashid, *Taliban*, p. 202.
23 Osama bin Laden's activism against the Saudi regime is discussed in several recent publications. The growing literature on al-Qa'ida usually touches upon Bin Laden's opposition to the regime.

24 Osama bin Laden's speech of 15 December 2004, broadcast on al-Jazeera and other Arab and international satellite stations. The speech can be listened to on several Jihadi websites, from which the text can also be downloaded. I use the Arabic text in this book. Bruce Lawrence translated Bin Laden's statement. See Osama bin Laden, 'Depose the Tyrants', in Lawrence *Message to the World*, pp. 245–75.

25 Fandy, *Saudi Arabia and the Politics of Dissent*, p. 192.

26 David Zeidan, 'The Islamic Fundamentalist View of Life as a Perennial Battle', *Middle East Review of International Affairs* 5/4 (2001): 26–53, at pp. 26–47

27 A Saudi supporter of al-Qa'ida and Bin Laden. See internet writer Abdullah 2005, 'Hal al-sheikh Osama wa sahbuh min atba' al-sheikh Muhammad ibn Abd al-Wahhab?', http://islah200.org/vboard/ showthread. php?s=36f3c5fe3f52c7d5eb50806410640d23&t=12, accessed 15 April 2005.

28 On the presence of Indonesian scholars in the Hijaz, see Mathias Diederich, 'Indonesians in Saudi Arabia: Religious and Economic Connections', in Madawi Al-Rasheed (ed.), *Transnational Connections and the Arab Gulf*, London: Routledge, 2005, pp. 128–46.

29 For example, Saudi Jihadi sheikh Nasir al-Fahad, like most die-hard Wahhabis, considers the Ottoman caliphate a *kafir* state because it encouraged Sufism, innovations and *shirk*. Al-Fahad, who will be discussed in chapter 4,wrote a pamphlet demonstrating the blasphemy of the Ottomans. This pamphlet draws on early Wahhabi *'ulama* positions. See Nasir al-Fahad, *al-Dawla al-'othmaniyya wa mawqif da'wat al-shaykh Muhammad ibn Abd al-Wahhab minha*, at http://www.alsalafiyoon.com

30 On Saudi religious transnational connections in London, see Madawi al-Rasheed, 'Saudi Religious Transnationalism in London', in Madawi Al-Rasheed (ed), *Transnational Connections and the Arab Gulf*, London: Routledge, 2005, pp. 149–67. On the debate between national and transnational Jihadis, see Gerges, *The Far Enemy*.

31 Fandy, *Saudi Arabia and the Politics of Dissent*.

32 Mansour al-Noqaydan, 'Kharitat al-islamiyyin fi al-saudiyya wa qisat al-takfir', at http://www.saudinote.com/mansour/6html.

33 See al-radd at http://www.alradnet.com/epaper/article.php?id_net=74, accessed 18 October 2005

34 Abu al-Bara al-Najdi, *al-Kawashif*, p. 13.

35 Ibid., p. 59.

36 Ibid., p. 274.

37 al-Masari, *al-Adilla*, p. 7.

38 Ibid., p. 62.

39 Ibid., p. 154.

40 Ibid., p. 233–4.

41 Yusif al-Ahmad *Ziyarat al-masjid al-nabawi*, Madina: General Presidency of the Promotion of Virtue and Prevention of Vice, n.d.

42 Ibid.

43 Abdulaziz ibn Baz, *Fatawi fi al-'aqida*, Riyadh: Dar al-Watan, n.d., p. 5.

44 Ibid.

45 Salih Al-Fawzan, *Tanbihat ʿala ahkam takhus al-muminat* Riyadh: Wizarat al-Shuun al-Islamiyya wa al-Awqaf wa al-Daʿwa wa al-Irshad, 1412H, pp. 10–11.

46 According to a witty Saudi, Wahhabi *ulama* issued more than 30,000 *fatwas* dealing with women, more than had been produced within the Muslim tradition for centuries.

47 Abdulaziz ibn Baz and Muhammad al-Uthaymin, *Muslim Minorities: Fatwa Regarding Muslims Living as Minorities*, Hounslow: Message of Islam, 1998, p. 16.

48 Ibid., p. 19.

49 *Al-Jumaah*, 11/10, 1420H, p. 53.

50 Ibid.

51 Abdulrahman al-Sudays, *Idhaat bi munasabat am 2000* Riyadh: Dar al-Watan, 2000.

52 For an exposure of al-Sudays's contradictions, see Madawi Al-Rasheed, 'al-Saudiyya wa muslimu britaniya: idhaat al-sheikh al-Sudays bayn al-ams wa al-yawm', *al-Quds al-Arabi*, 24 June 2004.

53 For the divisive role of Wahhabi discourse among British Muslims see Jonathan Birt, 'Wahhabism in the United Kingdom: Manifestations and Reactions', in Madawi Al-Rasheed (ed.), *Transnational Connections and the Arab Gulf*, London: Routledge, pp. 168–84.

54 Despite billions spent on the Afghan *jihad*, the majority of Afghan political parties backed Saddam Hussein when he invaded Kuwait in 1990. Similarly, in Britain, where Saudi-sponsored religious institutions and charities flourished, several British Muslims supported Saddam and condemned the Saudi regime for its alliance with the West. According to Ahmed Rashid, Saudi Arabia failed to develop a national-interest-based foreign policy. See Rashid, *Taliban*, p. 199.

55 Madawi Al-Rasheed, 'Localizing the Transnational and Transnationalizing the Local', in Madawi Al-Rasheed (ed.), *Transnational Connections and the Arab Gulf*, London: Routledge, 2005, pp. 1–18, p. 9.

4 STRUGGLING IN THE WAY OF GOD AT HOME: THE POLITICS AND POETICS OF *JIHAD*

1 After Palestine, the Afghan *jihad* remains the second and most important experience that captures the imagination of Jihadis in their literature. Recently, other locations have become equally important for the second generation of Jihadis – for example, Bosnia, Kashmir, Chechnya and, more recently, Iraq.

2 For a chronology of violence in 2003 and 2004, see *Arab News*, 26 April 2004. For an analysis of violence from a security perspective, see Anthony Cordesman and Nawaf Obaid, *National Security in Saudi Arabia: Threats, Responses, and Challenges*, Westport: Praeger Security International, 2005, pp. 109–36, A more nuanced interpretation is Roel Meijer, 'The "Cycle of Contention" and the Limits of Terrorism in Saudi Arabia', in Aarts and Nonneman (eds.), *Saudi Arabia in the Balance*, pp. 271–311.

3 The assessment of the intellectual origins of Jihadis polarised the scholarly community, journalists and intelligence services. Among academics, there are

those who argue that Jihadism originates from Wahhabi sources (Abukhalil, *The Battle For Saudi Arabia*; Algar, *Wahhabism*). There are also those who argue that the ideology and practice of Jihadism is alien to Saudi Arabia; for example, Natana DeLong-Bas absolves Wahhabism from any responsibility for the intellectual roots of Jihadi thought (DeLong-Bas, *Wahhabi Islam*). Maha Azzam also argues that the Jihadi thought of al-Qa'ida is rooted in the Egyptian radical Islamist trend rather than in Wahhabi sources (Maha Azzam, 'Al-Qaeda: The Misunderstood Wahhabi Connection and the Ideology of Violence' London: Chatham House, 2003, briefing paper 1). Other analysts differ in their assessment of the origins of Jihadism. A Saudi convert from Jihadism to 'rational' Islam argues that Jihadi thought has its roots in the local Wahhabi tradition (Mansur al-Noqaydan, *al-Riyadh*, 11 May 2003). I am more inclined to agree with this assessment, although it must be admitted that transnational influences, described in chapter 3, are extremely important.

4 Traditional Salafi publications dissociate Jihadism from Wahhabi Salafi thought and insist that Jihadism derives from the Muslim Brotherhood and Qutbist agendas. See Oliver, *The Wahhabi Myth*.

5 Gilles Kepel sketches the process by which Saudi Arabia became a host to the exiled Egyptian and Syrian members of the Muslim Brotherhood in the 1960s: see Kepel, *The War for Muslim Minds*, pp. 152–96. However, hosting members of a political party with its own intellectual Islamist heritage and activism may not always translate into actual endorsement of all this group's ideas. The cross-fertilisation of religious ideas between Saudi Wahhabi thought and that of the Muslim Brotherhood, which arrived in Saudi Arabia with the flight of the persecuted Muslim brotherhood members is more complex than is often acknowledged. It is certain that Saudis benefited from the modern organisational skills of twentieth-century Islamist movements, but they brought their own tradition into the complex Islamist scene of the last half century.

6 See Al-Rasheed, 'Saudi Religious Transnationalism' and Birt, 'Wahhabism in the United Kingdom'.

7 For details on British Muslims studying at Saudi religious universities, see Birt, 'Wahhabism in the United Kingdom'. For a general overview of Saudi transnational religious networks in London see Al-Rasheed, 'Saudi Religious Transnationalism'.

8 After 11 September Saudi Arabia started issuing its own lists of wanted terrorists. The first one appeared on 7 May 2003. It had nineteen names. On 6 December 2003, it issued a list with twenty-six names of wanted terrorists. Saudi security forces killed more than half of the men mentioned in both lists. See *al-Riyadh*, 7 December 2003. For an English version of these lists, together with the names of suicide bombers who perished after each attack, see Meijer, 'The "Cycle of Contention"', pp. 301–11.

9 Anthropologist Neil Whitehead offers a nuanced interpretation of violence as a cultural phenomenon; see his remarks in Andrew Strathern, Pamela Stewart and Neil Whitehead (eds.), *Terror and Violence: Imagination and the Unimaginable*, London: Pluto Press, 2005, p. 10.

10 In several studies, Saudi writer Saud al-Qahtani expressed the view that so-called Sahwi *'ulama* are responsible for the consolidation of a violent Jihadi

trend. According to al-Qahtani, the Sahwi movement gave birth to the 'excommunication giant' (*al-marid al-takfiri*). However, in recent times it has become clear that Sahwis have been criticised by Jihadis, who attacked their main figures in several publications. See al-Qahtani, 'al-Sahwa al-islamiyya al-saudiyya' (The Saudi Islamist Awakening), at http://www.daralnadwa. com. The same interpretation of the origins of Jihadism is reiterated in the works of Ali al-Amim such as *Mashayikhna wa mashaykh al-sahwa* (Our Sheikhs and the Sahwi Sheikhs). Al-Amim shows the connection between traditional and new religious scholars and the tension in their relationship. See http://www.daralalnadwa.com. (Both sites accessed 12 December 2004.)

11 Twenty-six Saudi *'ulama* expressed an opinion on the legitimacy of *jihad* in Iraq. Sahwi sheikhs were among the signatories of a document that pronounced military resistance to the American occupation of Iraq a legitimate Jihad. See *al-Quds al-Arabi*, 8 November 2004.

12 Statement by the Council of Senior Ulama Supporting Actions Taken by the Leader Inviting Qualified Forces to Respond to the Aggression against this Country. This *fatwa* was issued on 14 August 1990 and published in the official Saudi gazette, *Umm al-Qura* (18 August 1990). For a historical interpretation of the question of using infidels to defend the land of Islam, see al-Fahad, 'From Exclusivism to Accommodation'.

13 On the trinity of excommunication, see *al-Sharq al-Awsat*, 14 December 2003 and 30 June 2004.

14 Nasir al-Fahad, *al-Tibyan fi-kufr man a'ana al-amrican*. This electronic book appeared in 2001–2: see http://66.34.76.88/NaserAlfahed/Tibyan2.htm. Most work cited here is posted on www.alsalafyoon.com and www.tawhed.ws/ a?i=12. Al-Fahad's books and biography appeared on al-ansar at http://www. alansar.co.nr/fahd, accessed 7 April 2006. This site includes all books, *fatwas* and articles by Nasir al-Fahad. All references to his work in this chapter draw on the content of several websites. The sites host several lengthy pamphlets written by him. (The sites were accessed on 26 November 2003, 5 November 2005 and 6 April 2006.)

15 Humud al-Oqla al-Shuaybi, 'al-Qawl al-mukhtar', http://www.yaislah.org/ vboard/showthread.php?t=120460 (2000), accessed 28 January 2005.

16 Nasir al-Fahad, *Mu'jam ansab al-usar al-mutahadhira min ashirat al-asaida*, Riyadh: Dar al-Bara, 1420H [2001].

17 Biographical notes on Nasir al-Fahad are constructed out of very scarce information included in his writings (al-Fahad, *Mujam ansab*) and electronic publications on his website. See http://www.alsalafyoon.com and http://www. alalnsar.co.nr/fahd.

18 The text appeared on http://www.alsalafyoon.com, accessed 26 November 2003.

19 Basheer Nafi, 'Fatwa and War: On the Allegiance of the American Muslim Soldiers in the Aftermath of September 11', *Islamic Law and Society* 11/1 (2004): 78–116. See also Basheer Nafi and Suha Taji-Farouki (eds.), *Islamic Thought in the Twentieth Century*, London: I. B. Tauris, 2004. See also.

20 Steinberg, 'Ecology, Knowledge, and Trade'.

21 Al-Katib, *al-Fikr al-siyasi*.

22 Nasir al-Fahad, 'Taliat al-tankil', http;//www.al-fhd.com/kutob.htm, accessed May 2003.

23 Whitehead in Strathern et al. (eds.), *Terror and Violence*, p. 9.

24 See the *fatwa* section and several other books on http:// www.alsalafyoon.com. See also 'Replies to the Misguided Opinions of Hasan al-Maliki' and 'Replies to the Rafidah in their Accusations of the Prophet's Companions', both by Nasir al-Fahad. Hasan al-Maliki is a controversial writer who challenges the Wahhabi tradition in an attempt to deconstruct the hegemony of Muhammad ibn Abd al-Wahhab. His book *Da'iyya wa laysa nabiyyan* (Preacher not a Prophet), reconsiders the thought and position of Ibn Abd al-Wahhab. Full details are in chapter 6. See Hasan al-Maliki, *Da'iyya wa laysa nabiyyan*, Amman: Markas al-Dirasat al-Tarikhiyya, 2004.

25 In 2004 *Sawt al-Jihad* was posted on several websites. It can be downloaded in Word and PDF format. The author was able to consult several volumes, the last of which was volume 27. Links to the magazine were posted on al-neda, al-qalah, al-tajdeed, islah, al-saha, al-qaidun and minbar al-tawhid wa al-jihad. It is difficult to give links to such sites as some are no longer accessible while others continue to change their links to avoid censorship. Jihadi literature that is cited in this chapter draws on lists of publications on the *Sawt al-Jihad* website. In addition to the magazine, the website included twenty-two electronic books, research pamphlets and letters. It also included thirteen transcripts of oral sermons. The list was posted on http://www.yaislah.org/vboard/showthread.php+t-117079.

26 According to Saudi-sponsored al-Arabiyya satellite television, the editor of *Sawt al-Jihad* was identified as the information minister of al-Qa'ida in the Arabian Peninsula, Abdulaziz ibn Rashid al-Onayzi. According to the source, he was captured by Saudi security forces in Riyadh. Al-Onayzi wrote under several names. This information is unverifiable. See al-Arabiyya's al-Ayn al-Thalitha programme, 17 October 2005.

27 Saleh ibn Saad al-Hasan edited an electronic book, *al-Nabi al-fayad fi taiyid al-jihad fi al-riyadh*, which was published on the *Sawt al-Jihad* website.

28 Yahya al-Ghamdi *Sanawat khadaa*, selected sections from *Sawt al-Jihad*, issues 5–10.

29 *Muaskar al-Battar*, vol. 3, pp. 12–14: see www.hostinganime.com/battar/b1word.zip, accessed 10 June 2004.

30 Ibid., p. 15.

31 IntelCenter Tempest Publishing: see http://www.intelcenter.com.

32 *Sawt al-Jihad*, vol. 11.

33 One Saudi commentator argues that Jihadis lure young Saudi men by invoking *zaffa*, a happy celebration for a bridegroom to be, thus playing on youthful sexual frustration and sensational themes. See Minister of Interior's spokesman, Saud al-Musaybih, *al-Yawm*, 17 January 2005. See also 'Amer al-amir al-kabt al-jinsi bayn al-jana wa al-nar', http://daralnadwa.com/vb/showthread.php?t=153503, accessed 21 April 2005. Some Saudis argue that Bin Laden and other Jihadi *'ulama* use the glorious and sensual description of heaven in the Quran to lure sexually frustrated youth into holy war. They suggest that lifting sex segregation in society would be beneficial in fighting terrorism. Novelist Turki al-Hamad plays on the same theme in his 2005

novel *Rih al-janna* (The Wind of Heaven). Saudi anthropologist Saad al-Suwayan also expressed a similar opinion. Biographies of dead Jihadis reveal that most of them are married, thus making the sexual frustration theory implausible.

34 Eleanor Doumato interprets gender in the context of national identity and monarchical rule in Saudi Arabia. See Eleanor Doumato, 'Gender, Monarchy and National Identity in Saudi Arabia', *British Journal of Middle Eastern Studies* 19/1 (1992): 31–47.

35 Muhammad Ahmad Salim (Issa al-Oshan), 'La tathhabu lil iraq' (Don't Go To Iraq), *Sawt al-Jihad*, vol. 7. This view echoes the document of the twenty-six Saudi Sahwi *'ulama* who declared resistance in Iraq a legitimate *jihad* but were hesitant regarding the involvement of Saudi youth. See http://www.yaislah.org/vboard/showthread.php?t=116031.

36 For Nasir al-Fahd's views on the participation of women in *jihad*, see 'Minbar al-tawhid wa al-jihad', http://www.alsunnah.info/r?i=996, accessed 26 February 2004. The role of women in *jihad* is also discussed by Sheikh Yusif al-Ayri in a pamphlet called *Dawr al-nisa fi jihad al-ada* (The Role of Women in Jihad against Enemies): see http://www.lajnah22me.co.uk/forums/ showthread.php?s=af496a7229141d3a08c9818715b, accessed 16 February 2005.

37 Sheikh al-Ayri explains women's involvement in *jihad* by drawing on *shari'a* evidence. See Yusif al-Ayri, 'Dawr al-nisa fi jihad al-ada', http://www.hakayk.org/vb/showthread.php?t=1665, accessed 5 November 2005.

38 *al-Khansa, Jihad Magazine for Women*, 24 August 2004 see BBC News, http://news.bbc.co.uk/go/pr/fr/-/2/hi/middle-east/3594982.stm.

39 The Saudi-sponsored al-Arabiyya satellite channel reported a story about a female Saudi Jihadi. Um Usama admitted that she was active in supporting *jihad* through participation in internet discussion forums, promoting Jihadi thought and encouraging other women to recruit for al-Qa'ida. The story cannot be cross-checked. See http://www.alarabiya.net/articlep.aspx?p=10527, accessed 27 February 2005.

40 Neil Whitehead (ed.), *Violence* Oxford: James Curry, 2004.

41 Saudi Television, Channel 22, November 2003 (Repentance of Nasir al-Fahad).

42 Nasir al-Fahd's letter from prison, 'al-Taraju' an al-taraju' al-mazum', at http://islah200.org/vboard/showthreads.php?t=122619, accessed 22 April 2005.

43 Abdullah al-Rashid, 'Hashim al-taraju'at: waqafat ma murajaat al-Fahad, wa al-Khodayr wa al-Khalidi': see http://www.islah.tv/v/board/showthread.php?s=70119943da5813b410, accessed 24 March 2004.

44 *Al-Sharq al-Awsat*, 14 December 2003 and 30 June 2004.

45 Aidh al-Qarni, statement to *al-Jazirah* daily newspaper: see http://www.al-jazirah.com/178841/fe3dt.htm, accessed 15 December 2003.

46 Muhsin al-Awajy, 'Risalah maftuhah', http://www.wasatyah.com/vb/ shothread.php?s=e2e606281f92aba2, accessed 12 June 2004.

47 See Neil Whitehead in Whitehead (ed.), *Violence*, p. 6.

48 Mark Juergensmeyer, *Terror in the Mind of God: The Global Rise of Religious Violence*, Berkeley: University of California Press, 2000, p. 159.

49 Drawing on Michael Waltzer's study of radical puritans in England, Nadir Hashemi argues that Jihadi activism, especially that associated with al-Qa'ida,

can be seen as an agency of modernisation, an ideology of a transition period. See Nadir Hashemi, 'Islamic Fundamentalism and the Trauma of Modernization: Reflections on Religion and Radical Politics', in Michael Browers and Charles Kurzman (eds.), *An Islamic Reformation?* Lanham: Lexington, 2004, pp. 159–77, at p. 170.

5 DEBATING SALAFIS: LEWIS ATIYAT ALLAH AND THE *JIHAD* OBLIGATION

1 Lewis's articles appeared on several websites. These include al-saha, al-neda, al-islah, al-qalah, al-wasatiyyah and ansar al-Islam. The most comprehensive list appeared in minbar al-tawhid wa al-jihad, which included fifteen articles. The whole collection of his articles also appeared as an electronic book, advertised by Markaz al-ilam al-islami al-alami, the Islamic International Media Centre. The links to these websites change regularly to avoid censorship, so the full details of the links are not listed here, but one can still access http://alsaha.fares.net/sahat?128@26.oxTgmRBMVIp.0@1dd61560, accessed 11 August 2004 and minbar al-tawhid wa al-jihad, http://www.tawhed.ws/a?i=130, accessed 16 June 2005.

This chapter is based on an analysis of several articles that appeared between 2001 and 2004 and is inspired by reading electronic responses to his articles. Furthermore, discussion with several Saudis who are regular readers of Lewis's work aided my interpretation of the work of this anonymous internet writer.

2 Lewis's website was http://yalewis.com. This website is no longer accessible.
3 Lewis, 'Ulaika yalanhum allah wa yalanhum al-lainun' (Cursed by God and Cursed by Cursers), http://yaislah.org/vboard/showthread.phb?.s=8fba70c25266fdec, accessed 20 May 2004.
4 In December 2004 Lewis's name appeared in the Security Council's reasons for including the name of Saudi dissident Saad al-Faqih on the list of people supporting terrorism. It was alleged that al-Faqih had 'correspondence with Lewis the Jihadi'. While the British government responded by freezing al-Faqih's assets, he was not convicted, thus demonstrating the lack of evidence available to pursue legal action against him. This shows that Lewis is known to US and international anti-terrorism intelligence agents.
5 Reuven Paz, who monitors Jihadi websites for intelligence and security purposes, admits that Lewis is the most popular interpreter of al-Qa'ida among supporters of the movement. See Reuven Paz, 'Global Jihad and the United States: Interpretation of the New World Order of Osama bin Laden', PRISM Series of Global Jihad, no. 1, http://gloria.idc.ac.il/islam/global_jihad.htm/, accessed 28 May 2004.
6 It is possible that Lewis took part in the *jihad* in Afghanistan, but I have seen no confirmation of this in his writings. He may have participated in a non-military capacity. If he did participate in the Afghan war, he would be a first-generation Jihadi.
7 Several articles by Lewis include English words current in the media and in contemporary political speech, for example 'world order', 'clash of civilisations' and other clichés.

8 This is a reference to a famous personality during the time of the Prophet, Abdullah ibn Sulul, a Madinan Jew who converted to Islam.

9 Muhammad ibn Ibrahim ibn Abd al-Latif was discussed in the first chapter.

10 On the historical schism within the Wahhabi movement, see Steinberg, 'The Wahhabi Ulama'.

11 All biographical information is based on an article by Lewis, 'Muthakarat Lewis' (Lewis's Memoirs): see http://yaislah.org/vboard/showthreadphb?s= 040943e2970, accessed 2 May 2004 and http://www.wasatiyah.com/ vb/showthread.php?s=928743f196118605121dc9a9f495a2&threadid=1689, accessed 9 August 2004. Other details are provided by Lewis in other articles.

12 Lewis Atiyat Allah, *Min buraydah ila manhattan hiwar Saudi–salafi hawl al-qa'ida wa tafjirat new york* (From Buraydah to Manhattan: Saudi–Salafi Dialogue about al-Qa'ida and the Bombing of New York), London: Dar al-Riyadh, 2003, p. 13. Two other articles by Lewis explain his position regarding the changes that swept Sahwis after 11 September. These are 'Hazimat al-Islamiyyin' (The Defeat of Islamists) and 'al-Khayar al-istratiji wa al-tarikhi li shuyukh al-sahwa' (Strategic and Historical Choice of Sahwi Sheikhs). Both articles appeared on minbar al-tawhid wa al-jihad.

13 Atiyat Allah, *Min buraydah*, p. 14.

14 Muhsin al-Awajy, on Qadaya khalijiyya programme, al-Hurra, 4 May 2004.

15 *Sawt al-Jihad*, vol. 6, Shawal 1424H (The Voice of *Jihad*, electronic bimonthly magazine).

16 Lewis Atiyat Allah, 'Na'am ya blair inaha harb tarikhiyya' (Yes, Blair, it is a Historic War), http://www.yaislah.org/ vboard/showthread.php?s= 41e916364666da7, accessed 15 April 2004.

17 Reuven Paz monitors Jihadi literature on the internet. See http://www.ocnus. net/cgi-bin/exec/view.cgi?archive=33dnum796, accessed 8 December 2004.

18 Lewis Atiyat Allah, 'Nass reuven paz ila lewis atiyat allah' (Reuven Paz's Text to Lewis Atiyat Allah), http://yaislah.org/vboard/showthread.php?s= b260db23167abc9, accessed 1 April 2004.

19 A representative study that discusses this dichotomy is Gerges, *The Far Enemy*.

20 Lewis Atiyat Allah, 'al-Hala al-siyasiyya wa i'adat tashkil al-nitham al-duwali' (The Political Situation and the Reorganisation of the International World Order), http://alsaha2.fares.net/sahat?128@148.LQ6fho1QonYO@.Idd, accessed 18 November 2003.

21 Philip Hitti, *History of the Arabs*, 10th edn., London: Macmillan, 1970

22 Ibid., p. 64.

23 Lewis Atiyat Allah, 'Hina yusbih al-munafiq hakim' (When the Hypocrite Becomes the Ruler), http://www.tawhed.ws/a?i=130.

24 Lewis Atiyat Allah, 'Ha'ula' yalanahum allah wa yalanahum al-la'inun' http://www.yaislah.org/vboard/showthread.php?s=8fba70c25266fdec, accessed 20 May 2004.

25 Lewis Atiyat Allah, 'Qiraa fi khitab al-shaykh osama al-akhir' (A Reading of the Last Speech by Sheikh Usama Bin Laden), http://www.tawhed.ws/a? i=130.

26 From Reuven Paz to Lewis Atiyat Allah, http://www.yaislah.org/vboard/ showthread.php?s=b260db231b7abc9, accessed 1 April 2004.

27 Participants in Radio Islah (Debate Channel in 2005 and PTV in 2006), the media channel of the Movement for Islamic Reform in Arabia and Tajdeed Radio, media channel of Movement of Islamic Renewal, use the name ibn Salul to refer to the Saudi royal family.

28 Abu Jahl is associated in Islamic memory with the story of the death of Abu Talib, the Prophet's uncle. It is recounted that the Prophet tried to persuade Abu Talib to declare his Islam on his deathbed, but Amr ibn Hisham (Abu Jahl) dissuaded him.

29 For example, the televised repentance session of Nasir al-Fahd and other ʿulama are well known among those who are interested in the story of the Jihadis.

30 For example, Francis Fukuyama, *The End of History and the Last Man* London: Penguin, 1992 and Samuel Huntington, *The Clash of Civilizations and the Remaking of World Order*, London: Simon & Schuster, 1996.

31 See Ahmad Moussali, *Radical Islamic Fundamentalism: the Ideological and Political Discourse of Sayyid Qutb*, Beirut: American University of Beirut, 1992; Roxanne Euben, *Enemy in the Mirror: Islamic Fundamentalism and the Limits of Modern Rationalism* Princeton: Princeton University Press, 1999; Ibrahim Abu Rabi *Contemporary Arab Thought Studies in Post-1967 Arab Intellectual History* London: Pluto, 2004; and John Gray, *al-Qaeda and What it Means to Be Modern*, London: Faber & Faber 2003. On Jihadi use of electronic media, see Gary Bunt, *Virtually Islamic: Computer-mediated Communication and Cyber Islamic Environments*, Cardiff: University of Wales Press, 2000 and Gary Bunt, *Islam in the Digital Age: E-Jihad, Online Fatwas and Cyber Islamic Environments*, London: Pluto Press, 2003. From a religious studies perspective, see Lawrence, *Shattering the Myth*

32 Gilles Kepel, *Jihad: The Trail of Political Islam*, London: I. B. Tauris, 2003; Kepel, *The War for Muslim Minds*; François Burgat, *Face to Face with Political Islam*, London: I. B. Tauris, 2003; François Burgat, *L'Islamisme a l'heure de al-Qaida*, Paris: La Decouverte, 2005; Farhad Khosrokhavar *Les Nouveaux martyrs d'Allah*, Paris: Flammarion, 2003; Farhad Khosrokhavar *Quand al-Qaida parle temoignages derriere les barreaux*, Paris: Bernard Grasset, 2006; Olivier Roy, *The Failure of Political Islam*, London: I. B. Tauris, 1994.

33 Euben, *Enemy in the Mirror*, p. 48.

6 SEARCHING FOR THE UNMEDIATED WORD OF GOD

1 For a concise historical account of the two Saudi states, see Al-Rasheed, *A History of Saudi Arabia*, pp. 14–38.

2 On the details of the pact between Muhammad ibn Abd al-Wahhab and Muhammad ibn Saud see Ibn Ghannam, *Tarikh najd*.

3 It is noteworthy that there is a Salafi tradition in the Hijaz that glorifies the Saudi expansion in this part of the Arabian Peninsula. One contemporary writer defends this tradition against the heretical Sufi circles. See Sharif Hatim ibn Arif al-Awni in http://www. Alsaha2.fares.net/sahat?128@ 80Kum1nA5kSju.0@.1dd67394, accessed 21 October 2004.

4 Hijazi architect Sami al-Angawi highlights 'Saudi–Wahhabi' violence against archaeological sites in Mecca and Madina which in his opinion aim to

obliterate not only the Prophetic tradition but also other historical episodes, such as the Ottoman era. Ex-Hijazi oil Minister Ahmad Zaki Yamani's al-Furqan Foundation promotes Islamic heritage through the preservation and publication of books that celebrate the contribution of Hijazi *ulama* and intellectuals. A monthly magazine, *al-Hijaz*, published in London by al-Jamiyya al-Wataniyya al-Hijaziyya (the National Hijazi Association), does not shy away from reviving the idea of an independent 'kingdom of Hijaz'. It publishes scathing attacks on the Wahhabi tradition and promotes an image of the Hijaz as the land of tolerance, pluralism and religious diversity. It regards the partition of Saudi Arabia a matter of time. See *al-Hijaz*, 15 August 2003 and 15 May 2005. Hijazi authors, for example the anthropologist Mai Yamani, celebrate a Hijazi identity, defined in relation to a Najdi identity. See Mai Yamani, *Cradle of Islam: The Hijaz and the Quest for an Arabian Identity* London: I. B.Tauris 2004. Western journalists celebrate the revival of these regional and sectarian identities and their emergence in Saudi Arabia. See John Bradley, *Saudi Arabia Exposed: Inside a Kingdom in Crisis*, New York: Palgrave, 2005. To say that there are regional identities that are suppressed in Saudi Arabia is one thing; to call for a separate political entity to contain these local identities is something else.

5 Hijazi Sheikh Hasan Farhan al-Maliki paid a price for reviving Sufism in the Hijaz. He was prevented from preaching and subjected to harassment. When al-Maliki died in 2004, Crown Prince Abdullah made a reconciliatory gesture to his followers as he visited al-Maliki's family in person to offer his condolences.

6 For a detailed account of Saudi Shi'i political activism, see Ibrahim, 'The Shiite Opposition'. For Shi'i promotion of diversity and coexistence between various Muslim sects, see Hasan al-Safar, *al-Tanawu wa al-taayush* London: Dar al-Saqi, 1999.

7 The full text of the 2003 Shi'i petition is found in *Rabi al-saudiyya wa makhrajat al-qam'* Beirut: Dar al-Kunuz al-Adabiyya, 2004, p. 203.

8 Al-Rasheed, *A History of Saudi Arabia*, pp. 199–215.

9 In the course of writing this book, many men and women initiated contact with me, hoping to voice opinions that are often suppressed. Their revisionist position is deemed threatening by the regime because it promises to dismantle the triangle of Saudi authoritarianism. They remain anonymous.

10 Both Syria and Iraq created modern ideological narratives about the past that draw on Arab nationalism in its Ba'thist version.

11 Abdullah al-Qahtani in http://www/alwahabiyya.20m.com/index.html.

12 As mentioned earlier in this book, some Saudi Sahwis dismiss aspects of Wahhabiyya altogether – for example, followers of Hizb al-Tahrir. Muhammad al-Masari is an example.

13 The author relies on Wahhabi scholar Hussein ibn Ghannam, *Tarikh najd*.

14 For an Arabic version of Hempher's text see htty://www.sunna.info/ antiwahhabies. See also Muthakarat Mister Humpher, *Saytartat al-inglis wa damuhum li Muhammad ibn Abd al-Wahhab*, Beirut: Dar al-Funun, 2005. For an English version, see http://www.sunna.info/antiwahabies/wahabies/htm/ spy1.htm, accessed 23 September 2005. Hempher's story is taken for granted as an authentic narrative about Wahhabi treason against Muslims.

15 Hempher, in http://www.sunna.info/antiwahhabies For an English version, see http://www.sunna.info/antiwahabies/wahabies/htm/spy1.htm
16 Abdullah al-Qahtani, in http://www/alwahabiyya.20m.com/index.html.
17 Ibid.
18 Ibid.
19 For an anthropological discussion of Musaylima al-Kadhab in Muslim history, see Dale Eickelman, 'Musaylima: An Approach to the Social Anthropology of Seventh Century Arabia' *JESHO* 10 (1967): 2–52.
20 Al-Katib 5 in http://alsaha.fares.net/sahat?128@209.45GKmXTC2ap.0@ 1dd6221b, accessed 20 August 2004.
21 Al-Katib 5 in http://alsaha.fares.net/sahat?14@71.g08Vn1PgeQ.0@.1dd639 c9, accessed 9 July 2004.
22 Ibid.
23 Ibid.
24 Al-Katib 5 in http://alsaha.fares.net/sahat?128@186.Ns4foWu9Oj.T0@. 1dd6a654, accessed 23 April 2004.
25 Hasan al-Maliki, *Qira'a fi kutub al-'aqa'id* Amman: Markaz al-Dirasat al-Tarikhiyya, 2000, p. 197.
26 al-Maliki, *Da'iyya wa laysa nabiyyan*, p. 17.
27 Ibid.
28 Al-Maliki, *Qira'a fi kutub al-'aqa'id*, p. 193.
29 For example, Iranian scholar Abdulkarim Soroush and Egyptian scholar Khaled Abou El Fadl call for this separation.
30 Al-Maliki, *Qira'a fi kutub al-'aqa'id*, p. 149.
31 Sahwi sheikhs, for example Safar al-Hawali and Jihadi Nasir al-Fahad, condemned Hasan al-Maliki. Both accused him of being a covert Zaydi. Official *ulama* share their assessment of al-Maliki.
32 See http://www.ala7rar.net/navigator.php?pname-printTopic&tid=703.
33 Discussion in this section draws on Abdullah al-Hamid, 'al-Islam halaq bi janahayn al-adala wa al-huriyyah', (Islam Flew with Two Wings: Justice and Freedom), *al-Hayat*, 30 November 2002, and Abdullah al-Hamid, 'al-Dawa wa al-mujtama al-madani: dawa ila al-ilmaniyya aw al-islam' (Call to Civil Society: A Call to Secularism or Islam?), *al-Hayat*, 29 November 2005.
34 Al-Hamid, 'al-Islam halaq bi janahayn'.
35 Abdullah al-Hamid in http://alsaha.fares.net/sahat?128@178. QYipdQLOWM. 0@.Idd7131d.
36 Abdullah al-Hamid, 'al-Jihad al-madani fi al-Islam', in http;//www.wasatyah. com/vb/showthread.php?t=19863).
37 Ibid.
38 Ibid.
39 Ibid.
40 Ibid.
41 Ibid.
42 Abdullah al-Hamid in http://islah200.org/vboard/showthread.php?s= 74aa699f20fe0086d14f70f6a046cb2&t=121.
43 Full details of the Arabic text are in *Rabi al-saudiyya wa makhrajat al-qam'*, p. 28.
44 Ibid., pp. 28–9.

45 Ibid., pp. 156–62.
46 Interview with a Saudi reformer who endorses the constitutional monarchy agenda, London, November 2004.
47 *Rabi al-saudiyya wa mukhrajat al-qam*'.
48 Ibid.
49 Ibid.
50 Al-Rasheed, 'Localizing the Transnational'.
51 Ali al-Damini, *Zaman al-sijn azmina lil huriyya*, Beirut: Dar al-Kunuz al-Adabiyya, 2005, p. 164.
52 *Saudi Gazette*, 21 September 2005.
53 Al-Rasheed, 'Saudi Religious Transnationalism'.
54 The story of MIRA is discussed in several publications. See Al-Rasheed, *A History of Saudi Arabia* and Fandy, *Saudi Arabia and the Politics of Dissent*. These publications deal with MIRA in the 1990s. In this book the evolution of MIRA as it developed after 11 September is discussed. Information here is based on monitoring MIRA weekly newsletter (*al-Islah*) in the late 1990s, media statements, radio broadcasting and website. Interviews with the director of MIRA and other male and female activists belonging to the movement provide information on this political movement and its programme. For their own security, they remain anonymous.
55 Interviews with Saad al-Faqih, London, 2 March 1999 and 6 October, 12 and 28 December 2003.
56 Saad al-Faqih in http://www.yaislah.org/more.php?id=338_0_1_0M3, accessed 1 December 2004.
57 Yahya al-Amir, 'al-Muaradha al-bahlawaniyya', *al-Riyadh*, 12 May 2004.
58 Al-Faqih, *al-Nitham al-saudi*.
59 Yahya al-Amir, 'al-Muaradha al-bahlawaniyya', *al-Riyadh*, 12 May 2004.
60 Ibid.
61 Saud al-Qahtani, 'Mujrimun bi ism al-islah', http://wasatyah.com/vb/showthread.php?s=044629ec0ee25a89a, accessed 6 January 2004.
62 Saad al-Faqih 'Give up your Freedom or Change Tactics', *Guardian*, 11 August 2005.
63 Saad al-Faqih, Debate Radio (previously Islah Radio) August 2005.
64 Saad al-Faqih, 'Itiradhat al-salafiyyin ala al dimoqratiyya', 11th meeting of Mashru Dirasat al Dimoqratiyya fi al Buldan al arabiyya, Oxford, 2001. The same article is published in Ali al-Kuwari (ed.), *Azmat al dimoqratiyya fi al buldan al-arabiyya*, London: al-Saqi, 2004, pp. 67–93.
65 Saad al-Faqih, 'al-Birnamaj al-siyasi, al-haraka al-islamiyya lil islah', unpublished manuscript, n.d.
66 Saad al-Faqih, interview, London, 3 November 2003.
67 Under the pressure of soaring bridewealth and the increase in the number of Saudi spinsters, several *'ulama* issued *fatwa*s legitimising this type of marriage, which is often conducted in secrecy. Such *fatwa*s remain controversial.
68 For full details of the raid, see Madawi Al-Rasheed, 'al-Saudiyya lahathat qabl al-itiqal ala al-hawa', *al-Quds al-Arabi*, 1 November 2004.
69 Al-Rasheed, *A History of Saudi Arabia*.
70 Muhsin al-Awajy's articles can be found on his website: see www.wasatiyyah.com.

71 A scathing report on Saudi Sahwi *da ʿiyyat* appeared in the Saudi-owned magazine *al-Majalla* (9–15 October 2005). The report accused *da ʿiyyat* of spreading a culture of death and fear. The report also argued that most of them are responsible for the psychological problems experienced by women, who are told not to enjoy life but to prepare for death and the afterlife. The report accused *da ʿiyyat* of having no intellectual sophistication as they launch into attacking the West without demonstrating how the situation of women can be improved in their own society. Needless to say the report concluded that there is an obvious connection between the preaching of *da ʿiyyat* and terrorism, a conclusion that is supported by many Saudi liberal journalists who follow government agendas. In such reports, the purpose is to condemn rather than explain and understand this new phenomenon in Saudi society, namely the engagement of women in the Sahwi project and how this is a function of a long history of exclusion and gender inequality. Whether rich or poor, *da ʿiyyat* are seriously navigating a male-dominated landscape by choosing the most secure and least controversial means, namely Islam.

72 For women's petitions to the royal family in 2003, see *Rabi ʿa-lsaudiyya wa makhrajat al-qam ʿ*.

73 Personal communication with an *islahiyya*, March 2005.

74 On 27 September 2005, the *Guardian* reported that according to a Saudi source, the Saudi regime demanded that Britain deport al-Faqih and al-Masari in return for a contract worth £40,000,000 to purchase Typhoon planes from BAE. The following day it was reported that 'Downing Street made no attempt to dispute the *Guardian*'s disclosure'. See the *Guardian*, 27 and 28 September 2005. A couple of days later an offcial Saudi spokesman denied that there was a deal being negotiated with Britain to hand over the Saudi dissidents.

75 On censoring the internet in Saudi Arabia, see Human Rights Watch, *The Internet*.

CONCLUSION

1 Muhammad Zaman discusses Saudi–Wahhabi patronage of South Asian Islam in the 1950s: see Zaman, *The Ulama in Contemporary Islam*. Jonathan Birt sketches aspects of the association of British Muslims with Saudi Arabia in pursuit of religious knowledge: see Birt, 'Wahhabism in the United Kingdom'.

2 Timothy Mitchell, *Colonising Egypt*, Berkeley: University of California Press, 1988.

Bibliography

Aarts, Paul and Gerd Nonneman (eds.) *Saudi Arabia in the Balance: Political Economy, Society, Foreign Affairs* London: Hurst & Co., 2005

Abou El Fadl, Khaled *Speaking in God's Name: Islamic Law, Authority and Women* Oxford: Oneworld, 2001

Abou Zahab, Mariam and Olivier Roy *Islamist Networks: The Afghan–Pakistan Connection* London: Hurst & Co., 2002

Abukhalil, Asad *The Battle For Saudi Arabia: Royalty, Fundamentalism and Global Power* New York: Seven Stories Press, 2004

Abu Rabi, Ibrahim *Contemporary Arab Thought: Studies in Post-1976 Arab Intellectual History* London: Pluto, 2004

Algar, Hamid *Wahhabism: A Critical Essay* New York: Islamic Publications International, 2002

Atwan, Abd al-Bari *The Secret History of al-Qaida* London: Saqi, 2005

Azzam, Maha 'al-Qaeda: The Misunderstood Wahhabi Connection and the Ideology of Violence' London: Chatham House, 2003, briefing paper 1

Baer, Robert *Sleeping with the Devil: How Washington Sold our Souls for Saudi Crude* New York: Crown, 2003

Benard, Cheryl *Civil Democratic Islam: Partners, Resources, and Strategies* Santa Monica: Rand, 2003

Berkey, Jonathan *The Formation of Islam: Religion and Society in the Near East, 600–1800* Cambridge: Cambridge University Press, 2003

Birt, Jonathan 'Wahhabism in the United Kingdom: Manifestations and Reactions', in Madawi Al-Rasheed (ed.), *Transnational Connections and the Arab Gulf*, London: Routledge, 2005, pp. 168–84

Black, Antony *The History of Islamic Political Thought: From the Prophet to the Present* Edinburgh: Edinburgh University Press, 2001

Bligh, Alexander 'The Saudi Religious Elite (Ulama) as Participants in the Political System of the Kingdom', *International Journal of Middle East Studies* 17/1 (1985): 37–50

Bourdieu, Pierre *The State Nobility* Cambridge: Polity Press, 1996

Bradley, John *Saudi Arabia Exposed: Inside a Kingdom in Crisis* New York: Palgrave, 2005

Bunt, Gary *Islam in the Digital Age: E-Jihad, Online Fatwas and Cyber Islamic Environments* London: Pluto Press, 2003

Virtually Islamic: Computer-mediated Communication and Cyber Islamic Environments Cardiff: University of Wales Press, 2000

Burgat, François *Face to Face with Political Islam* London: I. B. Tauris, 2003

L'Islamisme a l'heure de al-Qaida Paris: La Decouverte, 2005

Carew, Tom *Jihad: the Secret War in Afghanistan* Edinburgh: Mainstream Publishing, 2000

Commins, David *TheWahhabi Mission and Saudi Arabia* London: I. B. Tauris, 2005

Cook, Michael 'The Expansion of the First Saudi State: The Case of Washm', in C. Bosworth, C. Issawi, R. Savory and U. Udovitch (eds.), *The Islamic World: From Classical to Modern Times*, Princeton: Princeton University Press, 1988, pp. 661–99

Commanding Right and Forbidding Wrong in Islamic Thought Cambridge: Cambridge University Press, 2000

Cooley, John *Unholy Wars: Afghanistan, America and International Terrorism* London: Pluto Press, 2000

Cordesman, Anthony and Nawaf Obaid, *National Security in Saudi Arabia: Threats, Responses, and Challenges* Westport: Praeger Security International, 2005

Crawford, Michael 'Civil War, Foreign Intervention, and the Quest for Political Legitimacy: A Nineteenth Century Saudi Qadi Dilemma', *International Journal of Middle East Studies* 14 (1982): 227–48

Crone, Patricia *Medieval Islamic Political Thought* Edinburgh: Edinburgh University Press, 2004

Dekmejian, Hrair 'The Rise of Political Islam in Saudi Arabia', *Middle East Journal* 48/4 (1994): 627–43

DeLong-Bas, Natana *Wahhabi Islam: From Revival and Reform to Global Jihad* London: I. B.Tauris, 2004

Devji, Faisal *Landscapes of the Jihad: Militancy, Morality, Modernity*, London: Hurst & Co., 2006

Diederich, Mathias 'Indonesians in Saudi Arabia: Religious and Economic Connections', in Madawi Al-Rasheed (ed.), *Transnational Connections and the Arab Gulf*, London: Routledge, 2005, pp. 128–46

Doumato, Eleanor 'Gender, Monarchy and National Identity in Saudi Arabia', *British Journal of Middle Eastern Studies* 19/1 (1992): 31–47

Getting God's Ear:Women, Islam, and Healing in Saudi Arabia and the Gulf New York: Columbia University Press, 2000

Dresch, Paul 'Societies, Identities and Global Issues', in Paul Dresch and James Piscatori (eds.), *Monarchies and Nations: Globalisation and Identity in the Arab States of the Gulf*, London: I. B. Tauris, 2005, pp. 1–33

Eickelman, Dale 'Inside the Islamic Reformation', *Wilson Quarterly* 22 (1998): 80–98

'Musaylima: An Approach to the Social Anthropology of Seventh Century Arabia', *Journal of the Economic and Social History of the Orient* 10 (1967): 2–52

Eickelman, Dale and Jon Anderson *New Media in the Muslim World:The Emerging Public Sphere* Bloomington: Indiana University Press, 1999

Eickelman, Dale and James Piscatori *Muslim Politics* Princeton: Princeton University Press, 1996

Esposito, John and John Voll *Makers of Contemporary Islam* Oxford: Oxford University Press, 2001

Esposito, John 'Muslim Activist Intellectuals and their Place in History', in Esposito and Voll (eds.), *Makers of Contemporary Islam*, pp. 3–22

Euben, Roxanne *Enemy in the Mirror: Islamic Fundamentalism and the Limits of Modern Rationalism* Princeton: Princeton University Press, 1999

al-Fahad, Abdulaziz 'The Imama vs. the Iqal: Hadari–Bedouin Conflict and the Formation of the Saudi State', in Al-Rasheed and Vitalis (eds.), *Counter-Narratives*, pp. 11–24

'From Exclusivism to Accommodation: Doctrinal and Legal Evolution of Wahhabism', *New York Law Review* 79 (2004): 485–519

Fandy, Mamoun *Saudi Arabia and the Politics of Dissent* New York: St Martin's Press, 1999

Fattah, Hala *The Politics of Regional Trade in Iraq, Arabia and the Gulf 1745–1900* Albany: State University of New York Press, 1997

' "Wahhabi" Influences, Salafi Responses: Shaikh Mahmud Shukri and the Iraqi Salafi Movement, 1745–1930', *Journal of Islamic Studies* 14/2 (2003): 127–48

Friedmann, Yohanan *Tolerance and Coercion in Islam: Interfaith Relations in the Muslim Tradition* Cambridge: Cambridge University Press, 2003

Fukuyama, Francis *The End of History and the Last Man* London: Penguin, 1992

Gerges, Fawaz *The Far Enemy: Why Jihad Went Global* Cambridge: Cambridge University Press, 2005

Glosemeyer, Iris 'Saudi Arabia: Dynamism Uncovered', in Volker Perthes (ed.), *Arab Elites: Negotiating the Politics of Change*, Boulder: Lynne Rienner, 2004, pp. 141–69

Gray, John *al-Qaeda and What it Means to Be Modern* London: Faber & Faber, 2003

Habib, John *Ibn Saud's Warriors of Islam: The Ikhwan of Najd and their Role in the Creation of the Saudi Kingdom, 1910–1930* Leiden: Brill, 1978

Hammoudi, Abdullah *Master and Disciple: The Cultural Foundations of Moroccan Authoritarianism* Chicago: Chicago University Press, 1997

Hashemi, Nadir 'Islamic Fundamentalism and the Trauma of Modernization: Reflections on Religion and Radical Politics', in Michael Browers and Charles Kurzman (eds.), *An Islamic Reformation?* Lanham: Lexington, 2004, pp. 159–77

Haykal, Bernard *Revival and Reform in Islam: The Legacy of Muhammad al-Shawkani* Cambridge: Cambridge University Press, 2003

Hitti, Philip *History of the Arabs*, 10th edn., London: Macmillan, 1970

Ho, Enseng 'Empire through Diasporic Eyes: A View from the Other Boat', *Society for Comparative Study of Society and History* (2004): 210–46

Hourani, Albert *Arabic Thought in the Liberal Age 1978–1939* Oxford: Oxford University Press, 1962

Human Rights Watch *The Internet in the Mideast and North Africa* New York: Human Rights Watch, 1999

Huntington, Samuel *The Clash of Civilizations and the Remaking of World Order* London: Simon & Schuster, 1996

Ibn Baz, Abdulaziz and Muhammad al-Uthaymin *Muslim Minorities: Fatwa Regarding Muslims Living as Minorities* Hounslow: Message of Islam, 1998

Ibrahim, Fuad, 'The Shiite Opposition in the Eastern Province from Revolution

to Accommodation (Case Study: The Reform Movement in Saudi Arabia)'
Ph.D. thesis, University of London, 2004

Jansen, Johannes *The Neglected Duty* New York: Macmillan, 1986

Juergensmeyer, Mark *Terror in the Mind of God: The Global Rise of Religious Violence* Berkeley: University of California Press, 2000

al-Juhany, Uwaidah *Najd before the Salafi Reform Movement: Social, Political, and Religious Conditions during the Three Centuries Preceding the Rise of the Saudi State* Reading: Ithaca, 2002

Kechichian, Joseph 'Islamic Revivalism and Change in Saudi Arabia: Juhayman al-Utaybi's Letters to the Saudi People', *The Muslim World* 70 (1990): 1–16

'The Role of the Ulama in the Politics of an Islamic State: The Case of Saudi Arabia', *International Journal of Middle East Studies* 18 (1986): 53–71

Kepel, Gilles *Jihad: The Trail of Political Islam* London: I. B. Tauris, 2003

(ed.) *al-Qaida dans le text* Paris: Presse Universitaire de France, 2005

The War for Muslim Minds: Islam and the West Cambridge, MA: Belknap Press, 2004

Khosrokhavar, Farhad *Les Nouveaux martyrs d'Allah* Paris: Flammarion, 2003

Quand al-Qaida parle temoignages derriere les barreaux Paris: Bernard Grasset, 2006

Kostiner, Joseph 'On Instruments and their Designers: The Ikhwan of Najd and the Emergence of the Saudi State', *Middle Eastern Studies* 21 (1985): 298–323

Lacroix, Stephane 'Between Islamists and Liberals: Saudi Arabia's New Islamo-liberal Reformist Trend', *Middle East Journal* 58/3 (2004): 345–64

'Islamo Liberal Politics in Saudi Arabia', in Aarts and Nonneman (eds.), *Saudi Arabia in the Balance*, pp. 35–56

Lawrence, Bruce *Messages to the World: The Statements of Osama Bin Laden* London: Verso 2005

Shattering the Myth: Islam beyond Violence Princeton: Princeton University Press, 1998

Mazawi, Andre 'The Academic Profession in a Rentier State: the Professoriate in Saudi Arabia', *Minerva* 43 (2005): 221–244

Meijer, Roel 'The "Cycle of Contention" and the Limits of Terrorism in Saudi Arabia', in Aarts and Nonneman (eds.), *Saudi Arabia in the Balance*, pp. 271–311

Metcalf, Barbara *Islamic Revival in British India: Deoband 1860–1900* Princeton: Princeton University Press, 1982

Mitchell, Timothy *Colonising Egypt* Berkeley: University of California Press, 1988

Moussali, Ahmad *Radical Islamic Fundamentalism: The Ideological and Political Discourse of Sayyid Qutb* Beirut: American University of Beirut, 1992

Nafi, Basheer 'Abu al-Thana al-Alusi: An Alim, Ottoman Mufti, and Exegete of the Quran', *International Journal of Middle East Studies* 34 (2002): 465–94

'Fatwa and War: On the Allegiance of the American Muslim Soldiers in the Aftermath of September 11', *Islamic Law and Society* 11/1 (2004): 78–116

The Rise and Decline of the Arab-Islamic Reform Movement London: Institute for Contemporary Islamic Thought, 2000

Nafi, Basheer and Suha Taji-Farouki (eds.), *Islamic Thought in the Twentieth Century* London: I. B. Tauris, 2004

Noor, Farish *New Voices of Islam* Leiden: ISIM, 2002

Oliver, Haneef *The Wahhabi Myth: Dispelling Prevalent Fallacies and the Fictitious Link with Bin Laden* Victoria: Trafford, 2002

Oliveti, Vincenzo *Terror's Source: The Ideology of Wahhabi-Salafism and its Consequences* Birmingham: Amadeusbooks, 2001

Paz, Reuven 'Global Jihad and the United States: Interpretation of the New World Order of Osama bin Laden', PRISM Series of Global Jihad, no. 1, 2004, http://gloria.idc.ac.il/islam/global_jihad.htm/

Peskes, Esther *Muhammad b. Abdalwahhab (1703–92) im Widerstreit. Untersuchungen zuz Rekonstruktion der Fruhgeschichte der Wahhabiya* Beirut: Steiner, 1993

Peters, Rudolph *Islam and Colonialism:The Doctrine of Jihad in Modern History* The Hague: Mouton, 1979

Jihad in Classical and Modern Islam Princeton: Markus Wiener, 1996

Philby, Harry St John *Arabia of the Wahhabis*, London: Constable & Co., 1928

Piscatori, James 'The Evolution of a Wahhabi University', unpublished conference paper, Oxford, September 2003

Rabasa, Angel et al. *The Muslim World after 9/11* Santa Monica: Rand, 2004

Al-Rasheed, Madawi 'Circles of Power: Royalty and Society in Saudi Arabia', in Aarts and Nonneman (eds.), *Saudi Arabia in the Balance*, pp. 185–213

A History of Saudi Arabia Cambridge: Cambridge University Press, 2002

'Localizing the Transnational and Transnationalizing the Local', in Madawi Al-Rasheed (ed.), *Transnational Connections and the Arab Gulf*, London: Routledge, 2005, pp. 1–18

'Saudi Arabia and the Challenge of the American Invasion of Iraq', in R. Fawn and R. Hinnebusch (eds.), *The Iraq War: Causes and Consequences*, London: Lynne Rienner Press, forthcoming

'Saudi Arabia's Islamist Opposition', *Current History* 95/597 (1996): 16–22

'Saudi Religious Transnationalism in London', in Madawi Al-Rasheed (ed), *Transnational Connections and the Arab Gulf*, London: Routledge, 2005, pp. 149–67

'The Shia of Saudi Arabia: A Minority in Search of Cultural Authenticity', *British Journal of Middle Eastern Studies* 25/1 (1998): 121–38

Review of Rentz, *The Birth of the Islamic Reform Movement*, in *Middle Eastern Studies* 12/10 (2006): 173–7

Al-Rasheed, Madawi and Robert Vitalis (eds.) *Counter-Narratives: History, Contemporary Society, and Politics in Saudi Arabia and Yemen* New York: Palgrave, 2004

Rashid, Ahmed *Taliban:The Story of the Afghan Warlords* London: Pan Books, 2000

Rentz, George *The Birth of the Islamic Reform Movement in Saudi Arabia: Muhammad ibn Abd al-Wahhab (1703/4–1792) and the Beginnings of the Unitarian Empire in Arabia* London: Arabian Publishing, 2005

Roy, Olivier *The Failure of Political Islam* London: I. B. Tauris, 1994

Saghi, Omar 'Oussama ben Laden, une icone tribunitienne', in Kepel (ed.), *al-Qaida dans le text*, pp. 12–111

al-Salloum, Hamad *Education in Saudi Arabia* Washington: Saudi Arabian Cultural Mission, 1995

Schwartz, Stephen *The Two Faces of Islam: Saudi Fundamentalism and its Role in Terrorism* New York: Anchor Books, 2002

Sluglett, Peter and Marion Sluglett 'The Precarious Monarchy: Britain, Abd al-Aziz ibn Saud and the Establishment of the Kingdom of Hijaz, Najd and its Dependencies, 1925–1932', in Tim Niblock (ed.), *State, Society and Economy in Saudi Arabia*, London: Croom Helm, 1982, pp. 36–56

Steinberg, Guido 'Ecology, Knowledge, and Trade in Central Arabia (Najd) during the Nineteenth and Early Twentieth Centuries', in Al-Rasheed and Vitalis (eds.), *Counter-Narratives*, pp. 77–102

'Religion und Staat in Saudi-Arabien. Eine Sozialgeschichte der wahhabitischen Gelehrten 1912–1953', Ph.D. thesis, Berlin: Free University, 2000

'The Wahhabi Ulama and the Saudi State: 1745 to the Present', in Aarts and Nonneman (eds.), *Saudi Arabia in the Balance*, pp. 11–34

Strathern, Andrew, Pamela Stewart and Neil Whitehead (eds.), *Terror and Violence: Imagination and the Unimaginable*, London: Pluto Press, 2005

Teitelbaum, Joshua *Holier than Thou: Saudi Arabia's Islamic Opposition* Washington: Washington Institute for Near East Policy, 2000

Ungar, Craig *House of Bush House of Saud: The Secret Relationship between the World's Two Most Powerful Dynasties* New York: Scribner, 2004

Werbner, Penina 'Global Pathways: Working Class Cosmopolitans and the Creation of Transnational Ethnic Worlds', *Social Anthropology* 7/1 (1999): 17–35

Whitehead, Neil (ed.) *Violence* Oxford: James Curry, 2004

Woodward, Bob *Plan of Attack* New York: Simon & Schuster, 2004

Yamani, Mai *Cradle of Islam: The Hijaz and the Quest for an Arabian Identity* London: I. B. Tauris, 2004

Zaman, Muhammad Qasim *The Ulama in Contemporary Islam: Custodians of Change* Princeton: Princeton University Press, 2002

Zeidan, David 'The Islamic Fundamentalist View of Life as a Perennial Battle', *Middle East Review of International Affairs* 5/4 (2001): 26–53

SOURCES IN ARABIC

Abdullah, Anwar *Khasais wa sifat al-mujtama al-wahhabi* Paris: La Librairie de l'Orient, 2005

Abu al-Bara al-Najdi *al-Kawashif al-jaliyya fi kufr al-dawla al-saudiyya* London: Dar al-Qasim, 1994

Adonis and Said, Khalidah *Muhammad ibn Abd al-Wahhab* Beirut: Dar al-Ilm lil Malayin, 1983

al-Ahmad, Abdullah *Ziyarat al-masjid al-nabawi* Madina: General Presidency of the Promotion of Virtue and Prevention of Vice, n.d.

Ahmad, Rifat *Rasa'il Juhayman al-Otaybi* Cairo: Madbouli, 2004

al-Alusi, Mahmud *Tarikh najd* Cairo: Madbouli, 1343H

Anas, Abdullah *Wiladat al-afghan al-'arab* London: Saqi Books, 2002

Atiyat Allah, Lewis *Min buraydah ila manhatin hiwar Saudi–salafi hawl al-qa'ida wa tafjirat new york* London: Dar al-Riyadh, 2003

al-Bassam, Abdullah *'Ulama najd khilal sitat qurun* Mecca: Dar al-Nahda, 1398AH

'Ulama najd khilal thamaniyat qurun, vols. I–VIII, Riyadh: Dar al-Asimah, 1419AH

Dahlan, Ahmad *al-Durar al-saniyya fi al-radd 'ala al-wahhabiyya*, Beirut: al-Maktaba al-Thaqafiyya, n.d.

al-Damini, Ali *Zaman al-sijn azmina lil huriyya* Beirut: Dar al-Kunuz al-Adabiyya, 2005

al-Fahad, Nasir *Mujam ansab al-usar al-mutahadhira min ashirat al-asa'ida* Riyadh: Dar al-Bara, 1420H [2001]

al-Falih, Matruk *al-Mujtama wa al-dimoqradiyya wa al-dawla fi al-buldan al-'arabiyya* Beirut: Markaz Dirasat al-Wihda al-Arabiyya, 2002

Mustaqbal al-saudiyya al-islah aw al-taqsim London: Qadaya al-Khalij, 2002

Sikaka al-jawf fi nihayat al-qarn al-ishrin Beirut: Bisan, 2000

al-Faqih, Saad 'Itiradhat al-salafiyyin 'ala al dimoqratiyya', in Ali al-Kuwari (ed.), *Azmat al dimoqratiyya fi al buldan al-'arabiyya*, London: al-Saqi, 2004, pp. 67–93

al-Nitham al-saudi fi mizan al-islam London: al-Haraka al-Islamiyya lil Islah, 1996

Faraj, Ayman *Thikrayat 'arabi afghani Abu Ja'far al-Masri al-Qandahari* Cairo: Dar al-Shoruq, 2002

al-Fawzan, Salih *Tanbihat 'ala ahkam takhus al-muminat* Riyadh: Wizarat al-Shuun al-Islamiyya wa al-Awqaf wa al-Dawa wa al-Irshad, 1412H

al-Ghazali, Muhammad *al-Sunna al-nabawiyya bayn ahl al-fiqh wa ahl al-hadith*, 13th edn., Cairo: Dar al-Shuruq, 2005

al-Hamad, Turki *Rih al-janna* London: Saqi Books, 2005

al-Hamid, Abdullah 'al-Da'wa wa al-mujtama al-madani: da'wa ila al-'ilmaniyya aw al-islam', *al-Hayat*, 29 November 2005

'al-Islam hallaq bi janahayn al-adala wa al-huriyya', *al-Hayat*, 30 November 2002

Istiqlal al-qada al-saudi 'awaiquhu wa kayfiyat tazizuhu Paris: Eurabe, 2005

al-Hawali, Safar *Dhahirat al-irja fi al-fikr al-islami* Rosmalen: Dar al-Kalima, 1999

al-'Ilmaniyya Cairo: al-Tayyib, 1998

Kashf al-ghamma an 'ulama al-umma London: Dar al-Hikma, 1991

Sharh risalat tahkim al-qawanin n.p. Dar al-Kaima, 1999

al-Hodhayf, Muhammad *Nuqtat taftish* Riyadh: n.p., 2006

Ibn Abd al-Wahhab, Muhammad *Masa'il al-jahiliyya* Riyadh: Dar al-Watan, 1408H

Mualafat al-sheikh Muhammad ibn Abd al-Wahhab, vol. I: *Kitab al-tawhid*, Riyadh: Jamiat al-Imam Muhammmad ibn Saud al-Islamiyya, 1398H

Mualafat al-sheikh Muhammad ibn Abd al-Wahhab, vol. II: *Kitab al-jihad*, Riyadh: Jamiat al-Imam Muhammad ibn Saud al-Islamiyya, 1398H

Mualafat al-sheikh al-imam Muhammad ibn Abd al-Wahhab, vol. III: *Fatawa wa masa'il al-imama al-sheikh Muhammd ibn Abd al-Wahhab*, Riyadh: Jamiat al-Imam Muhammad ibn Saud al-Islamiyya, 1398H

al-Usul al-thalatha wa adilataha Riyadh: Wizarat al-Shuun al-Islamiyya wa al-Awqaf wa al-Dawa wa al-Irshad, 1421H

Ibn Abd al-Wahhab, Sulayman *al-Sawa'iq al-ilahiyya fi al-radd 'ala al-wahhabiyya* Beirut: Dhu al-Faqar, 1997

Ibn Baz, Abdulaziz *Fatawi fi al-'aqida* Riyadh: Dar al-Watan, n.d.

Hukum al-sihr wa al-kahana Riyadh: Wizarat al-Shuun al-Islamiyya wa al-Awqaf wa al-Dawa wa al-Irshad, 1421H

Ibn Ghannam, Hussein *Tarikh najd* Cairo: Dar al-Shuruq, 1994

Ibn Jibrin, Abdulrahman *Risalat al-islah* Beirut: n.p., 1424H
Ibn Taymiyya, Ahmad *al-Siyasa al-shariyya fi islah al-ra'i wa al-ra'iyya*, Beirut: Dar al-Jil, 1988
Ibrahim, Fuad *al-Faqih wa al-dawla*, Beirut: Dar al-Kunuz al-Adabiyya, 1998
Kamil, Omar *al-Mutatarifun khawarij al-'asr* Beirut: Bisan, 2002
   al-Saudiyya tahadiyat wa afaq Beirut: Bisan, 2003
Kashif al-Ghita, Muhammad *al-Ajwiba al-najafiyya fi al-radd 'ala al-fatawi al-wahhabiyya* Beirut: al-Ghadir, 2004
   Naqd fatawi al-wahhabiyya sahara n.p.: n.p., 1990
al-Katib, Ahmad *al-Fikr al-siyasi al-wahabi qira'a tahliliyya* London: Dar al-Shura lil dirasat wa al-ilam, 2003
al-Lohaydan, Salih *al-Jihad fi al-islam*, Riyadh: Dar al-Liwa, 1980
al-Maliki, Hasan *Da'iyya wa laysa nabiyyan* Amman: Markas al-Dirasat al-Tarikhiyya, 2004
   Qira'a fi kutub al-aqa'id Amman: Markaz al-Dirasat al-Tarikhiyya, 2000
al-Masari, Muhammad *al-Adilla al-qatiyya 'ala adam shariyat al-dawla al-saudiyya* London: Dar al-Shariyya, 1995
al-Mawardi, Ali *al-Ahkam al-sultaniyya wa al-wilayat al-diniyya* Beirut: al-Arqam, n.d.
Mughniyyah, Muhammad *Hathihi hiya al-wahhabiyya*, Beirut: Dar al-Jawad, 1982
al-Mutayri, Hakim *al-Huriyya wa al-tawafan* Beirut: al-Muasasa al-Arabiyya lil Dirasat wa al-Nashr, 2004
Muthakarat Mr Humpher Saytartat al-inglis wa da'muhum li Muhammad ibn Abd al-Wahhab Beirut: Dar al-Funun, 2005
al-Qahtani, Fahad *Zilzal Juhayman fi Mecca* London: Munathamat al-Thawra al-Islamiyya fi al-Jazira al-Arabiyya, 1987
al-Qahtani, Muhammad *al-Wala' wa al-bara'* Riyadh: Dar Tibah, 1422H
al-Qasim, Abdulrahman *al-Durar al-saniyya fi al-ajwiba al-najdiyya*, vols. I–XVI, Riyadh: n.p., 2004
al-Qasim, Abdulaziz *Mukashafat*, vol. I, Jiddah: n.p., 2002
Qutb, Muhammad *Jahiliyat al-qarn al-ishrin*, 14th edn., Beirut: Dar al-Shuruq, 1995
Rabi al-saudiyya wa makhrajat al-qam' Beirut: Dar al-Kunuz al-Adabiyya, 2004
Al-Rasheed, Madawi *Mazaq al-islah fi al-saudiyya fi al qarn al-wahid wa al-ishrin*, London: Saqi Books, 2005
   'al-Saudiyya lahathat qabl al-itiqal 'ala al-hawa', *al-Quds al-Arabi*, 1 November 2004
   'al-Saudiyya wa muslimu britaniya: idhaat al-sheikh al-Sudays bayn al-ams wa al-yawm', *al-Quds al-Arabi*, 24 June 2004
Rasul, Rasul Muhammad *al-Wahabiyyun wa al-iraq, 'aqidat al-shuyukh wa suyuf al-muharibin* Beirut: Riad El-Rayyes Books, 2005
al-Safar, Hasan *al-Tanawu wa al-taayush* London: Dar al-Saqi, 1999
Salah, Muhammad *Waqai sanawat al-jihad* Beirut: Khulud, 2002
al-Saqqaf, Hasan *al-Salafiyya al-wahhabiyya* Beirut: Dar al-Mizan, 2005
al-Shaykh, Muhammad ibn Abd al-Latif 'Bin Laden wa da'wat Muhammad ibn Abd al-Wahhab', *al-Hayat*, 21 March 2002
al-Shuwayir, Muhammad *Abdulaziz ibn Baz majmu fatawi wa maqalat mutana-wiyya*, vols. V and VI, Jiddah: al-Sahabah, [1413H]
al-Sudays, Abdulrahman *Idhaat bi munasabat am 2000* Riyadh: Dar al-Watan, 2000

al-Sunaytan, Muhammad *al-Nukhab al-saudiyya dirasa fi al-tahawulat wa al-ikhfaqat* Beirut: Markaz Dirasat al-Wihda al-Arabiyya, 2004
al-Tuwayjiri, Abdulaziz *Li surata al-layl hatf al-sabah* Beirut: Dar Riyadh al-Rayyis, 1998
al-Uthaymin, Abdullah *al-Sheikh Muhammad ibn Abd al-Wahhab* Riyadh: Dar al-Ulum, 1992
al-Uthaymin, Muhammad *Risala fi al-dima' al-tabiyya lil nisa* Riyadh: Wizarat al-Shuun al-Islamiyya wa al-Awqaf wa al-Dawa wa al-Irshad, 1421H
Wasella, Yurgen *al-Qasimi bayn al-usuliyya wa al-inshiqaq*, trans. Muhammad Kibaybo, Beirut: Dar al-Kunuz al-Adabiyya, 2001
al-Zayat, Muntasir *Ayman al-Dhawahiri kama araftuh* Cairo: Dar al-Mahrusa, 2002
    al-Jama'at al-islamiyya ruyah min al-dakhil Cairo: Dar al-Mahrusa, 2005
Zayn al-Abdin, Muhammad Surur *Azmat akhlaq* Birmingham: Dar al-Arqam, 1999
    'al-Salafiyya bayn al-wulat wa al-ghulat', unpublished manuscript, n.d.
    'al-Saudiyya 'ala muftaraq turuq', unpublished manuscript, n.d.
    al-'Ulama wa amanat al-kalima Birmingham: Dar al-Arqam, 1998
Zeidan, Ahmad *Bin Laden bila qina'* Beirut: World Book Publishing, 2003

INTERNET WRITERS

This list includes names of writers whose work is accessed on the internet. Some are well-known Saudi and Arab figures who write in the local media. A few are religious scholars. Others are *noms de plume*.

al-Amim, Ali
al-Amir, Omar
al-Amir, Yahya
al-Awadhi, Muhammad
al-Awajy, Muhsin
al-Ayri, Yusif
al-Azi, Omar
Abdullah
al-Fahad, Nasir
al-Ghamdi, Yahya
al-Ghannami, Khalid
al-Hamid, Abdullah
al-Hasan, Salih
Hempher
al-Katib 5
Lewis Atiyat Allah
al-Noqaydan, Mansur
al-Omar, Nasir
al-Qahtani, Abdullah
al-Qahtani, Saud
al-Qarni, Aidh
al-Qarni, Awadh
al-Qasim, Abdulaziz
al-Rashid, Abdullah

Salim, Muhammad (Issa al-Oshan)
Sharif Hatim ibn Arif al-Awni
al-Thaydi, Mishari
al-Turayri, Abd al-Wahhab

INTERNET WEBSITES

Only the names of websites are listed. Some sites are no longer accessible. For full links at the time these sites were accessed see footnotes.

Ahl al-sunnah wa al-jamaah
al-Ahrar
Ansar al-Islam
al-Awdah (Islamtoday)
Dar al-Nadwah
Elaph
al-Furqan
Haqaiq hiwariyyah
al-Haramain
Hawali, Safar
Hiwar al-Khaymah
Hizmet Books
al-Hodhayf, Muhammad
Ibn Baz
al-Islah
Islamiyyah la wahhabiyyah
Kashif
al-Khansa
La hudud
Manabir al-Jazirah al-Islamiyyah
al-Maqreze
Middle East Transparent
Minbar al-tawhid wa al-jihad
al-Mohawer
al-Moslim
Murajaat fikriyyah
al-Multaqa
al-Nida
al-Otaybi
al-Qaidoun
al-Qalah
al-Radd
al-Rasid
al-Saha
Salafi Publications
al-Salafiyoon
al-Salafiyyun
Saudi Arabian Information Resource

Sayd al-fawaid
Saudi Institute
Sawt al-ikhdud
Sawt al-Jihad
al-Tajdid
Tuwa
al-Wasatiyyah
al-Wifaq
Yalewis

NEWSPAPERS AND MAGAZINES

Arab News
Guardian
al-Hayat
al-Hijaz
al-Jumaah
al-Madinah
al-Majallah
New York Times
al-Quds al-Arabi
al-Riyadh
Saudi Gazette
al-Sharq al-Awsat
Shuun Saudiyyah
al-Watan

SATELLITE CHANNELS

al-Jazeera
al-Hurra
al-Arabiyya
al-Mustaqillah
al-Majd

Index of personal names

Index of place names

General index

Cambridge Middle East Studies 25

STORMWATER

Best Management Practices and Detention
for Water Quality, Drainage, and CSO Management

BEN URBONAS
Urban Flood Control District ● Denver ● Colorado

PETER STAHRE
Malmö Water and Sewer Works ● Malmö ● Sweden

PTR Prentice Hall, Englewood Cliffs, New Jersey 07632

Library of Congress Cataloging-in-Publication Data

Urbonas, Ben.
   Stormwater : best management practices and detention for water
quality, drainage, and CSO management / Ben Urbonas, Peter Stahre.
      p.   cm.
   Rev. ed. of: Stormwater detention. 1989, c1990.
   Includes bibliographical references and index.
   ISBN 0-13-847492-3 :
   1. Storm water retention basins. 2. Urban runoff. I. Stahre, Peter.
II. Urbonas, Ben. Stormwater detention. III. Title.
TD665.S72 1993
628'.21—dc20   92-17276
                                                CIP

Editorial/production supervision/interior design: *John Morgan*
Cover design: *Ben Santora*
Acquisitions editor: *Michael Hays*
Editorial assistant: *Dana Mercure*
Prepress buyer: *Mary E. McCartney*
Manufacturing buyer: *Susan Brunke*
Proofreader: *Mary Kathryn Bsales*

 © 1993 by PTR Prentice-Hall, Inc.
A Simon & Schuster Company
Englewood Cliffs, New Jersey 07632

The publisher offers discounts on this book when ordered in
bulk quantities. For more information, write: Special
Sales/Professional Marketing. Prentice Hall, Professional &
Technical Reference Division, Englewood Cliffs, NJ 07632.

Printed in the United States of America
10 9 8 7 6 5 4 3 2

ISBN   0-13-847492-3

Prentice-Hall International (UK) Limited, *London*
Prentice-Hall of Australia Pty. Limited, *Sydney*
Prentice-Hall Canada Inc., *Toronto*
Prentice-Hall Hispanoamericana, S.A., *Mexico*
Prentice-Hall of India Private Limited, *New Delhi*
Prentice-Hall of Japan, Inc., *Tokyo*
Simon & Schuster Asia Pte. Ltd., *Singapore*
Editora Prentice-Hall do Brasil, Ltda., *Rio de Janeiro*

To our wives and daughters

	Irena
Malina	*Tesa*
Misia	*Vida*
—P.S.	*—B.U.*

Contents

Part One Types of Storage Facilities 1

Part Four   Stormwater Quality Enhancement   309

24   Design of Wetland Detention Basins and Channels   382

25   Best Management Practices for Stormwater Quality   403

Preface

Urban stormwater engineering and management has advanced more in the last 20 years than at any time in history. Granted, the advances were possible only because the basic mathematic, hydraulic, and hydrologic principles were there to act as a foundation on which many individuals and institutions built this technology. As a part of these advances, stormwater detention emerged as one of the basic components used today in stormwater management. When properly applied, it can reduce the adverse impacts of accelerated stormwater runoff from urbanized lands by slowing or disposing of the runoff and by removing from urban runoff some of the pollutants that it is known to carry.

Although in the 1980s stormwater detention became one of the most popular and widely used best management practices (BMPs) for the enhancement of stormwater quality, a number of other BMPs are gaining popularity throughout the world. Despite appearances, many of these BMPs are another form of stormwater detention or retention. The proliferation of a number of these BMPs in recent years has sometimes occurred with little technical basis for predicting the design's performance or without a critical look at what is being recommended and how it will fit in with a municipality's ability to keep these facilities functioning over many years. As a result of the ever-growing emphasis on controlling stormwater quality, the authors have added material on stormwater quality enhancement best management practices in the second edition of this book.

This book was written with the practicing engineer and stormwater manager in mind. Practitioners should find it a useful reference. At the same time, it contains sufficient materials to serve as a textbook for a college or training course in urban stormwater engineering.

Many have contributed to the technology described in this book. The authors sincerely hope that adequate acknowledgment has been given to all contributors and sources of information. The authors particularly wish to acknowledge the Swedish Council for Building Research for its financial support of basic research that led to the compilation of much of the material contained in this book.

—Ben Urbonas
—Peter Stahre

Foreword

Stormwater: Best Management Practices and Detention, by Ben Urbonas and Peter Stahre, was originally published by Prentice Hall in 1990 as *Stormwater Detention.* The book has stood the test of fire and has quickly proven to be a practical, technically based, comprehensive treatise on this topic. Thus, a second edition is justified to include best management practices (BMPs) for reducing the discharge of pollutants found in stormwater and the design and use of constructed wetlands in urban stormwater management.

In the United States the quality of stormwater discharges and combined sewer overflows (CSO) is receiving considerable attention. This is due primarily to congressional mandates forcing local governments to look for ways to reduce the impact of CSO and separate storm sewer system discharges on rivers, lakes, streams, estuaries, and oceans. Many of the older cities in the United States have combined sewer systems, while most of the more recently developed ones have separate systems. On the other hand, Europe has mostly combined sewer systems, with some separate storm sewer systems in newer suburban communities—the CSO problem being the primary focus in Europe.

Even though stormwater quality is now receiving alot of attention, the quantity issue cannot be ignored or forgotten. The public clearly understands when their property is damaged because of urban flooding, when traffic is delayed because of flooded streets, or when lives are lost. The need to improve drainage and to control flooding has driven local governments to fund storm sewer and drainageway improvements in the past. It must also be recognized, however, that quantity and quality cannot be separated. Urbonas and Stahre clearly understand this, and *Stormwater: Best Management Practices and Detention* skillfully integrates these two concerns.

Stormwater detention is important in addressing both quantity and quality. Stormwater quantity demands allocation of space on the urban landscape. The issue, simply put, is where does the water go when it rains? Temporarily storing it, or detaining it, is a way of more effectively utilizing the available conveyance space downstream. With regard to stormwater quality enhancement, one basic approach is to detain stormwater long enough to improve its quality, regardless of whether this detention is in the form of ponds, dry basins, wetlands, or on-site swales. Detention is a common element to both areas of concern and has become an important element of urban stormwater quantity and quality management.

As attention turns to the quality of separate storm sewer discharges and CSO, the need has intensified for practical and economically reasonable ways to reduce pollutants in these discharges. Urbonas and Stahre recognized this need and have added to *Stormwater: Best Management Practices and Detention* discussions of BMPs and constructed wetlands. The addition of these subjects will be useful to a professional identifying, evaluating, designing, and implementing plans intended to reduce pollutants in and from stormwater and CSO discharges. There are a host of BMP options, but all BMPs do not apply to all situations. It is important to understand the applicability of the many BMPs to various situations and to be able to evaluate the technical feasibility, capital or initial costs, and long-term maintenance requirements and costs of each practice.

A wetland, on the other hand, can be considered a BMP when addressing water quality problems or an environmental resource in its own right. The intrinsic value of wetlands has been recognized, and in many cases it is necessary and/or desirable to create wetlands as part of an urban stormwater project.

Neil S. Grigg, in his book *Urban Water Infrastructure* published in 1986, characterized stormwater as the linking part of the urban water system in that it is at the same time a source of supply and wastewater. Stormwater is difficult to control when it arrives in amounts too large for systems to handle, but when properly managed it can replenish water supply reservoirs and groundwater aquifers and clean streets and other urban surfaces. Detention, wetlands, and other BMPs are important linking functions of the urban stormwater system. As the demands of the public change with time, engineers should not continue to practice urban drainage design as they have in the past. Therefore, engineers will need to routinely consider how to incorporate detention, wetlands, and other BMPs as integral parts of urban stormwater systems in the future.

L. Scott Tucker, P.E.
Executive Director, Urban Drainage
and Flood Control District
Denver, Colorado

Overview

1.1 DEFINITION OF STORAGE FACILITIES

The term *storage facilities* is used in this text to describe any combination or arrangement of detention and retention facilities in a combined sanitary–storm sewer system or a separate stormwater conveyance system. Unfortunately, there is no standard nomenclature to describe various types of storage facilities in this field of engineering. Therefore, it is up to each author to describe his or her terminology.

A classification for storage facilities is defined here which will be used throughout this text. It is based on the location of the facility in the sewer or flow conveyance system. This nomenclature is intended to help the reader to understand the different storage systems discussed in this book.

1.2 SOURCE CONTROL VS. DOWNSTREAM CONTROL

Since the basis for classifying storage facilities is the location in the collection and conveyance system, storage facilities can be classified as *source control* or *downstream control*. In the first case, the storage takes place far up in the wastewater or storm runoff collection system. Each storage facility is small and is located near the source, thereby permitting more efficient utilization of the downstream conveyance system. Some generalized observations can be made for source control:

- It affords great flexibility in choosing sites for facilities.
- Storage unit design can be standardized.

- Flow efficiency of the existing downstream conveyance system can be increased.
- Real time flow control can increase system capacity.
- It is difficult to monitor large numbers of storage units for proper design, installation, and upkeep.
- Maintenance and operation costs can be high due to large numbers of storage units.

With downstream control, on the other hand, the storage volume is consolidated at fewer locations. The storage facilities can be, for example, located at the downstream end of a large watershed, a subbasin of the watershed, or at a wastewater treatment plant. The following generalized observations can be made regarding downstream control:

- It has reduced construction cost as compared with a large number of source control facilities (Hartigan, 1982, 1986; Wiegand et al., 1986).
- It has reduced maintenance and operation costs.
- It is easier to administer construction and upkeep.
- Finding acceptable sites can be difficult.
- Land acquisition costs can be high.
- In combined sewer systems, fitting downstream storage into the sewer system can be difficult.
- Large dams and/or storage facilities can encounter public opposition.

There is no clear boundary of what constitutes source control and downstream control. There are storage facilities that, strictly speaking, can be classified as either of the two types. To further clarify the terminology, the classifications described earlier can be further refined. The more detailed description contains six categories of storage facilities shown as a block diagram in Figure 1.1.

1.3 LOCAL DISPOSAL

Local disposal of stormwater has gained considerable recognition and acceptance in recent years. Some communities in the United States, such as the states of Maryland and Florida, have mandated its use in new land development. The term *local disposal* is used to describe storage facilities that use infiltration or percolation to dispose of stormwater. This practice attempts to utilize nature's own way of disposing of stormwater for the smaller storm events.

Where soil is suitable, stormwater from impervious areas is conveyed to an acceptable site covered with vegetation and infiltrates into the ground.

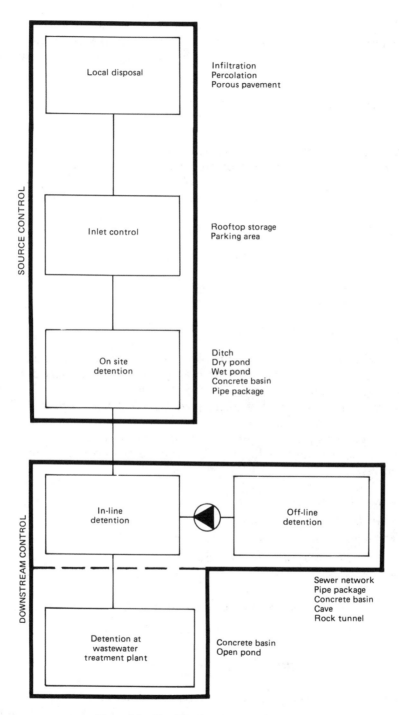

Figure 1.1 Classification of storage facilities.

If adequate infiltration sites are not available, stormwater can be routed to underground storage vaults from which water is allowed to percolate into the ground. Chapter 2 describes the principles and technology of local disposal.

1.4 INLET CONTROL AT SOURCE

Stormwater can be controlled at the source by detaining it where precipitation falls. This is done by choking off the inlets to the conveyance system. The detention volume is then obtained on properly prepared

- rooftops,
- parking lots,
- industrial yards, or
- other properly designed surfaces.

Chapter 3 describes in greater detail inlet control facilities.

1.5 ON-SITE DETENTION

On-site detention identifies an entire plethora of storage facilities which occur in the upper reaches of the flow conveyance system. The primary difference between on-site detention and local disposal and inlet control facilities is in the amount of tributary area being intercepted. On-site detention generally intercepts runoff from several pieces of real estate or from an entire subdivision. This means the water has been conveyed at least a short distance before it arrives at the detention facility. On-site detention may take any of the following forms:

- swales or ditches,
- dry basins (i.e., dry ponds),
- wet ponds (i.e., ponds with permanent water pool),
- concrete basins, usually underground, and
- underground pipe packages or clusters.

On-site detention ditches and ponds are described in Chapter 4, and concrete basins in Chapter 5.

1.6 IN-LINE DETENTION

The term *in-line* refers to detention storage in sewer lines, storage vaults, or other storage facilities that are connected in-line to the conveyance network.

In-line detention can utilize excess capacity that may be found in an existing sewer network, or it may be necessary to construct separate storage facilities to provide the needed volume. In-line detention storage may take on any of the following forms:

- concrete basins,
- excess volume in the sewer system,
- pipe packages,
- tunnels,
- underground caverns, or
- surface ponds.

Chapter 6 describes the use of existing sewer systems, while Chapters 4, 5, 7, and 8 describe open ponds, concrete basins, pipe packages, and tunnel storage, respectively.

1.7 OFF-LINE STORAGE

Off-line refers to storage that is not in-line to the sewer network or other conveyance systems. Off-line storage is achieved by diverting the flow from the conveyance system to storage when a predetermined flow rate is exceeded. The diverted water is stored until sufficient conveyance or treatment capacity becomes available downstream.

With off-line storage, one must decide how the stored volume will be emptied. In designing off-line facilities, the following must be considered:

- the holding time needed to avoid odor or public health problems;
- hydraulic capacity or the treatment capacity of the downstream system;
- the hydraulic load on the downstream system at any given time; and
- the possibility for additional inflow before the storage is emptied.

1.8 STORAGE AT TREATMENT FACILITIES

Storage at treatment facilities is a special case of in-line or off-line storage. It is designed to provide flow or waste load equalization at the treatment plant. For an in-line storage, all flow passes through it, while in an off-line storage facility the flows that exceed a preset flow rate are stored. Both types of storage are usually emptied using pumps. Sometimes detention at the treatment plant can occur in the oversized sedimentation or aeration tanks of the treatment plant. Flow equalization at a wastewater treatment plant is discussed in more detail in Chapter 9.

REFERENCES

HARTIGAN, J. P., "Regional BMP Master Plans," *Urban Runoff Quality—Impact and Quality Enhancement Technology,* American Society of Civil Engineers, New York, 1986.

HARTIGAN, J. P., AND QUASEBARTH, T. F., "Urban Nonpoint Pollution Management for Water Supply Protection: Regional vs. Onsite BMP Plans," *Proceedings of Twelfth International Symposium on Urban Hydrology, Hydraulics, and Sediment Control,* University of Kentucky, Lexington, Ky., 1985.

WIEGAND, C., SCHUELER, T., CHITTENDEN, W., AND JELLICK, D., "Cost of Urban Quality Controls," *Urban Runoff Quality—Impact and Quality Enhancement Technology,* American Society of Civil Engineers, New York, 1986.

2

Local Disposal by Infiltration and Percolation

2.1 GENERAL

The traditional method of disposing of stormwater in an urban area is to drain it away as rapidly as possible. This is done by swale, gutter, and storm sewer conveying runoff to the nearest stream or river. In recent years, however, environmental concerns have arisen, and we are beginning to question the impacts on the receiving waters of continuing to use the practice of rapid conveyance downstream.

Williams (1982) and others have reported that the traditional approach to drainage increased flooding and stream erosion. In addition, questions are being asked regarding how the traditional approach affects the natural water balance, causes adverse shock loads of pollutants in the receiving waters, or, in the case of combined sewers, contributes to treatment plant malfunction.

In response to various concerns, some communities have elected to encourage or mandate local disposal of stormwater at its source of runoff. This is done by having a portion of the stormwater infiltrate or percolate into the soil. Although this approach has received greater attention in recent years, it has, in fact, been in use for a long time. Typically, it has been used to control stormwater from individual residential lots. The advantages often cited for the use of local disposal include:

1. recharge of groundwater;
2. reduction in the settlement of the surface in areas of groundwater depletion;

3. preservation and/or enhancement of natural vegetation;

4. reduction of pollution transported to the receiving waters;

5. reduction of downstream flow peaks;

6. reduction of basement flooding in combined sewer systems; and

7. smaller storm sewers at a lesser cost.

Equally good arguments are made against the use of local disposal systems. As a result, the use of local disposal systems should be addressed on a site-specific basis at each urban community. Arguments against the use of these facilities include:

1. The majority of runoff occurs from streets and large commercial areas, and local disposal of residential lots may have little impact on runoff.

2. Soils may seal with time, leaving property owners with a failed disposal system.

3. Very large numbers of infiltration and percolation facilities may not receive proper maintenance.

4. Reliance on their operation may leave communities facing enormous capital costs in the future, if or when these systems begin to fail.

5. Groundwater level may rise and cause basement flooding or damage to building foundations.

2.2 PRECONDITIONS FOR LOCAL DISPOSAL

The ability of soil to absorb stormwater depends on the following factors, among others:

- vegetative cover,
- soil type and conditions,
- groundwater conditions, and
- quality of stormwater.

Whenever precipitation falls to the ground, some of the water will infiltrate into the soil. The process of downward movement of the infiltrated water through the unsaturated zone above the groundwater table is called *percolation*. Further movement through the ground is called *groundwater flow*.

The upper layers of soil are strongly influenced by frost, plant roots, and other external factors. Therefore, the upper soil layers can be loosened by the external factors and be relatively porous. In clay soils, the upper layers may have some porosity in the form of cracks and cavities, but the lower layers are impermeable. As a result, areas containing substantial percentages of clays

are poor candidates for local disposal through the use of infiltration or percolation. Unfortunately, the technology of water transport in soils is beyond the
scope of this book, and the reader is referred to literature on geohydrology.

2.2.1 Vegetation

Figure 2.1 schematically depicts the exchange of water in the vegetation
cover–soil complex. Much of the water that infiltrates into the soil is absorbed

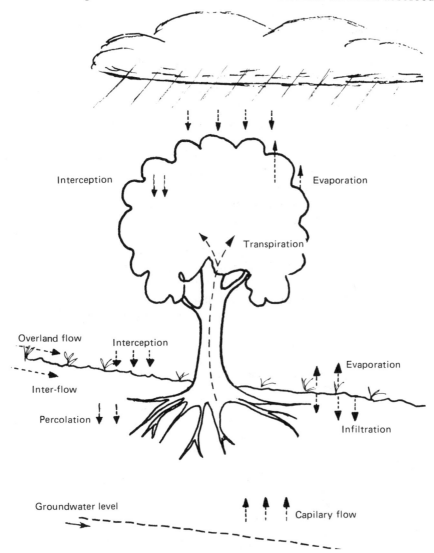

Figure 2.1   Water exchange in vegetation-covered soil.

by plant roots and is returned to the atmosphere through plant respiration. The process of returning water to the atmosphere through plant respiration and through direct evaporation is called *evapotranspiration.*

The soil–vegetation complex functions, to a certain degree, as a filter which reduces clogging of the surface pores of the soil. That roots help keep the soil pores open and facilitate the buildup of the organic soil humus layer may explain why infiltration capacities are found to be higher in older grass-covered areas and in areas of least disturbance by human activities.

2.2.2 Soil Conditions

The quantity of water that can infiltrate into soil is, to a large extent, dependent on the effective porosity of the soil. *Effective porosity* is defined as the quantity of water that can be drained out from saturated soil. The capillary-bound water is therefore not included in the effective porosity definition. Table 2.1 summarizes the approximate values of porosity for different types of soils.

Permeability is a measure of how fast water can move through a soil. Table 2.2 gives the ranges of permeability typically found in various soil groups. By knowing the permeability and the slope of the groundwater's surface, the velocity of groundwater flow can be calculated.

Soils are never truly homogeneous, and field data is needed to effectively estimate the infiltration capacities at any site. To obtain reliable estimates of infiltration, the engineer needs to know the type of soils, the vertical thickness and horizontal distribution of each type, the presence of clay or other impervious lenses, and information about groundwater. This type of information can only be obtained by a drilling and sampling program that also includes field infiltration and percolation tests and observations of groundwater levels.

TABLE 2.1 Approximate Values of Soil Porosity

Type of Soil	Percent Effective Porosity
Crushed rock	30
Gravel and macadam	40
Gravel (2 to 20 mm)	30
Sand	25
Pit run natural gravel	15–25
Till (boulder clay)	5–10
Dry crust clay	2–5
Clay and silt (below surface)	0

TABLE 2.2   Permeability of Various Soils

	Range in Permeability	
Type of Soil	Meters per year	Feet per year
Gravel	30,000 to 3,000,000	100,000 to10,000,000
Sand	30 to 300,000	100 to 1,000,000
Silt	0.03 to 300	0.1 to 1,000
Boulder clay	0.003 to 30	0.01 to 100
Clay	Less than 0.03	Less than 0.1

2.2.3 Groundwater Conditions

In addition to soils information, the engineer must also understand the groundwater conditions at a potential disposal site to determine the site's suitability. Among others, the following data are needed to understand the local groundwater conditions:

• distance between the surface of the ground and the groundwater;
• the slope of the groundwater surface;
• depth and direction of groundwater flow including zones of surface inflow and outflow; and
• variation in groundwater levels with the season.

In relatively homogeneous soils, the groundwater level essentially follows the slope of the land. Runoff patterns develop, however, as the terrain varies in slope, and regions of inflow and outflow become apparent, as illustrated in Figure 2.2. For obvious reasons, infiltration facilities and percolation facilities have to be located in the inflow regions. Attempts to infiltrate in the outflow regions will generally fail.

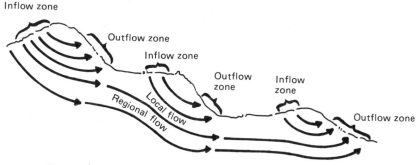

Figure 2.2   Inflow and outflow of groundwater.

2.3 ARRANGEMENTS FOR LOCAL DISPOSAL

Local, site-specific conditions often dictate the selection of what type of local disposal facilities are used. The following sections describe how various infiltration and percolation principles need to be considered in the selection of such facilities. Examples are used to describe some of the more commonly observed facilities.

Before various types of installations are described, we discuss in general the selection of the type of local disposal. Each type will depend on the goals for local disposal and will dictate how the disposal facility is designed. The variety of disposal modes can be illustrated through the use of a conceptual, so-called geometric model, shown in Figure 2.3. Because of its conceptual construction, it also describes possibilities that lack practical significance.

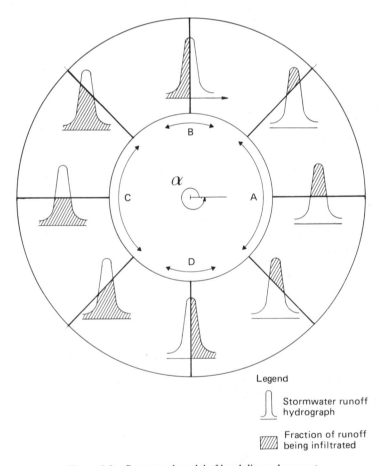

Legend

Stormwater runoff
hydrograph

Fraction of runoff
being infiltrated

Figure 2.3 Conceptual model of local disposal concepts.

The conceptual model consists of a number of schematic stormwater hydrographs located between two concentric circles. The various local disposal concepts are characterized by the radii of the circles intersecting the hydrographs. Any disposal concept can then be described with the aid of the central angle, α. Four local disposal concepts (i.e., A, B, C, and D) are described in more detail to illustrate this conceptual model.

Concept A.   Only the flow peaks of stormwater runoff are intercepted and disposed locally, while the lesser flows are carried away by the storm conveyance system. To achieve this, the storm conveyance system is designed to carry away flows up to a certain design capacity, and the excess is diverted to the local, off-line disposal facility.

The advantage of this approach is that the size of the downstream storm conveyance system can be reduced (i.e., smaller storm sewers, culverts, etc.). On the other hand, the sometimes most strongly polluted fraction of runoff is carried away instead of being disposed through infiltration or percolation.

Concept B.   The intent of this concept is to intercept and to dispose locally the front end of the stormwater runoff hydrograph. This can be accomplished by routing all runoff into an interception facility until a predetermined volume is reached, at which time the remainder of the runoff continues downstream.

The advantage of this concept is that the sometimes most polluted initial storm runoff is intercepted and disposed through infiltration or percolation. The interception volume can be made large enough to intercept many, but not necessarily all, the storm runoff events. The percentage of the runoff events that are intercepted completely depends on the volume of storage and how that volume compares to the statistical distribution of the runoff events at the site.

Concept C.   In this concept, the runoff is diverted to the disposal facility up to a preset flow rate which cannot be exceeded. This can be accomplished by routing runoff through a small diameter pipe to the disposal facility. When the pipes flow capacity or the interception volume is reached, the larger flows overflow to the downstream conveyance system.

The advantages of this concept are almost identical to the aforementioned Concept B advantages. This design approach will also intercept the entire runoff from smaller storm events. The percentage of runoff intercepted depends not only on the volume of runoff, as in Concept B, but is also controlled by the preset maximum inflow rate. As a result, the runoff from some of the smaller storms may not be intercepted completely if the runoff hydrograph has a high peak, which is possible with intense, short-duration rainstorms.

Concept D.   This concept probably has the least practicality for local disposal. It is based on the interception of stormwater runoff after a preset runoff volume has occurred or a preset amount of time has elapsed. On the other hand, this concept may have utility in a real time control of a storm sewer system where the storm sewer capacity of the downstream watershed is optimized by rapidly conveying away the initial runoff before the flow from upstream tributary areas arrives.

An analysis of local goals, objectives, and system constraints will dictate which of the aforementioned concepts best fits the needs of the site. The selection of any one of the local disposal concepts cannot be made without first understanding local needs, rules, and regulations and how the concept will fit into the total stormwater management system of the community.

2.3.1 Types of Installations

The most commonly used local disposal installations include:

- infiltration beds,
- open ditches,
- infiltration ponds,
- percolation basins,
- pipe trenches, and
- rock-filled trenches or pits,
- pervious pavement.

2.3.2 Infiltration Beds

The simplest form of local disposal is simply to let stormwater run onto a vegetation-covered surface, as illustrated in Figure 2.4. In areas with high groundwater table or fine-grained soils, infiltration can be very slow and will result in standing water. Under these conditions, it may be necessary to install subdrains, which are connected to the downstream conveyance system. This will return runoff to the conveyance system; however, its rate of flow will be significantly reduced and many of the impurities will be filtered out by the passage of the water through the soil.

2.3.3 Open Ditches

The use of *open ditches* and swales adjacent to streets, roads, highways, and small parking lots, as illustrated in Figure 2.5a, is a special case of surface infiltration. The rate of infiltration and the infiltration capacity depend on the level of groundwater below the ditch, the porosity of the soil, the suspended solids load in the stormwater, and the density of the vegetation on the surface. The sizing of surface infiltration swales is described in Section 17.5.

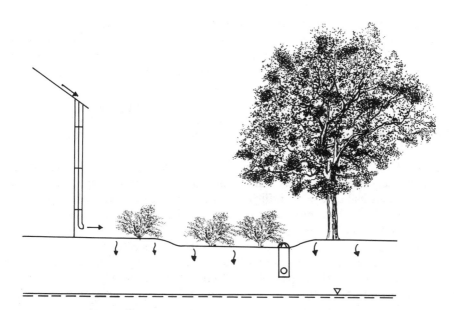

Figure 2.4   Representation of an infiltration bed.

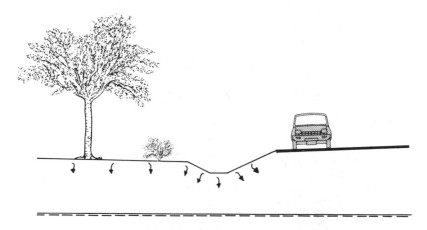

Figure 2.5   (a) Representation of an infiltration ditch.

It is often not possible, however, to infiltrate all the runoff into the ground using only swales and ditches, even when the soils and other geologic and groundwater conditions are favorable. This is because the tributary area is too large when compared to the available infiltrating surface area; i.e., the area of the infiltration surfaces is less than one-half that of the tributary impervious surfaces. Nevertheless, even when only a small part of the design storm can be infiltrated into the ground, open ditches and swales add to the array of best management practices (BPMs) that help reduce the volume of runoff and, as a result, reduce the mass of pollutants reaching the receiving waters. Open ditches and swales can be designed to flow slowly—at 1.0 foot per second (0.3 m/s) or slower—thereby also encouraging the settling out of pollutants near their source of runoff.

Good vegetation growth in open ditches is important. Vegetation reopens and reaerates soil surfaces that can become clogged with the fine sediments found in urban runoff. As a ditch or swale accumulates too much sediment, the surface infiltration rate and the ditch's flow capacity are reduced. Eventually, it becomes necessary to excavate and dispose of the accumulated sediment to restore its infiltrating and flow carrying capacities.

In a special case of an infiltration ditch or swale, a series of percolation trenches are installed intermittently, along its length, as illustrated in Figure 2.5b. The trenches are sized to intercept and dispose of runoff from a specific design storm, usually a 2-year storm. The water enters the trench from the top through a surface filter consisting of sandy soils. To reduce the chances of the sandy soil filters and the percolation trenches becoming plugged with sediments, stormwater is first directed to flow as a sheet over a buffer strip of grass. This grass strip removes some of the coarse and medium-sized sediment before stormwater reaches the percolation trench.

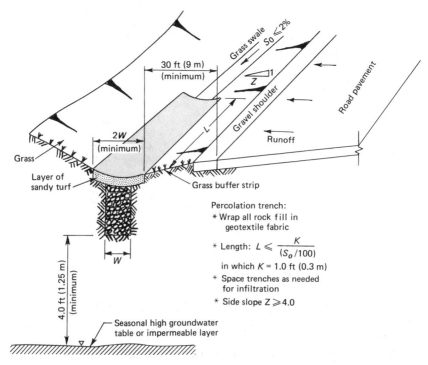

Figure 2.5   (b) Infiltration swale with a supplemental percolation trench.

Section 2.3.5 describes the use of and some of the details of percolation basins. It stresses the need to keep suspended solids from entering the percolation trench and shows how a surface inlet can be designed to remove sediment before water enters the trench. Detailed procedures for the sizing of percolation trenches are presented in Section 17.4.

2.3.4 Infiltration Ponds

Stormwater detention or retention ponds located in permeable soils may also be used as *infiltration ponds*. This concept is shown in Figure 2.6. By their nature, ponds generally have a smaller surface area, in proportion to the tributary area, than other infiltration concepts described earlier. The larger surface loading rates can cause standing water to be present for extended periods of time. Healthy vegetative growth is therefore rarely possible in infiltration ponds. As a result, the infiltrating surfaces have a tendency to plug quickly. Once plugged, runoff will spill downstream and may overload the downstream conveyance system.

Another common, yet often overlooked, cause of infiltration pond failure is the rise of the groundwater table immediately under the pond. This happens whenever a pond is loaded at rates that exceed the underlying soil's capacity to drain horizontally. Permeable soils have pore volume ratios that typically range from 0.2 to about 0.35. Thus, 1 foot (0.3 m) of water on the infiltrating surface occupies 3 to 5 feet (1.0 to 1.5 m) of depth in the soil. As stormwater infiltrates through the surface of the infiltration basin, the groundwater rises. If too much water infiltrates into the ground, it will surface above the basin's bottom. In many cases the infiltrating basin becomes a pond with a

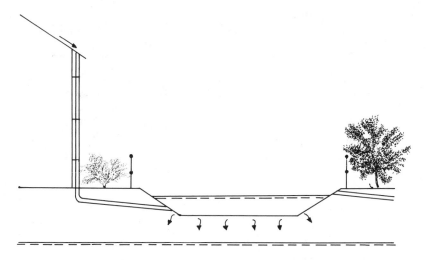

Figure 2.6   Representation of an infiltration pond.

permanent pool of water, and no amount of surface restoration activity can make it drain. To avoid such failures, the designer must estimate the level to which groundwater is expected to rise under the stormwater infiltration basin whenever the infiltrating surface area is less than 50% of the tributary impervious area. Such estimates should be based on the stormwater infiltration loadings expected to occur over a period of 2 to 5 years.

Ponds, as local disposal facilities, are less attractive than the other concepts described so far. Because of their tendency to rapidly lose infiltration capacity with time, they often become a nuisance. There are reported cases of property owners regrading their land to fill such ponds in the hope of eliminating drainage problems on their land. This often is done without realizing that their actions may be adding to drainage problems downstream.

Preventive maintenance to remove silt buildup at infiltration ponds can reduce these problems. On the other hand, this maintenance may have to be forced onto the property owners by a local government, which is politically unpopular. Thus, on-site infiltration ponds are generally destined to fail within a relatively short period of time after installation.

2.3.5 Percolation Basins

The use of percolation basins for stormwater disposal was promoted in the early 1970s. A percolation basin is constructed by excavating a pit, filling it with gravel or crushed stone, and then backfilling over the top of the rock. The rock media provide the porosity for temporary storage of water so that it can then slowly percolate into the ground. One example of this for an installation at a single residence is illustrated in Figure 2.7.

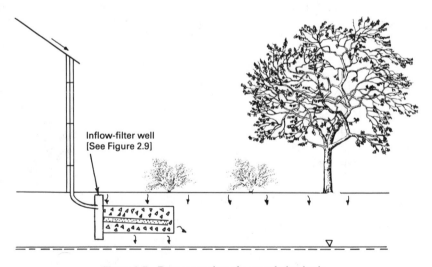

Inflow-filter well
[See Figure 2.9]

Figure 2.7 Representation of a percolation basin.

Obviously, percolation basins are only feasible if they are located in suitable soils and groundwater conditions. If the basin is located in the unsaturated soil zone, namely, above the groundwater, stormwater will percolate out of the basin and raise the level of the groundwater. Basins should not be designed to be completely or partially submerged by groundwater, as they will not function properly. If the permeability of the surrounding soil is low, it will be necessary to install a bottom drain pipe similar to the one illustrated in Figure 2.8, which is connected to the downstream conveyance system via a choked outlet.

A serious problem with percolation basins is their tendency to clog with suspended particles carried by stormwater. Once clogged, all the rock needs to be removed and replaced with clean rock, and the pit itself needs to be enlarged to remove clogged soils adjacent to the rock. This problem can be significantly reduced if the stormwater is filtered before it enters the rock-filled basin.

Filtering can be accomplished by passing the stormwater through a granular filter bed or a fine mesh geotextile material. In either case, the filter media will need to be removed and replaced from time to time, but at considerably less cost than the replacement of the rock bed. Figures 2.9(a) and 2.9(b) illustrate a filter installation upstream of a percolation basin.

Another problem that needs to be addressed in constructing percolation basins is the natural phenomenon of finer soil particles migrating into the pores of the coarse rock media. This can be prevented through the use of properly selected geotextile fabrics or the installation of granular filtering layers between the rock media and the adjacent in situ soil.

2.3.6 Pipe Trench

Pipe trench is nothing more than a special case of percolation basin. A sample installation is shown in Figure 2.10, which illustrates how stormwater is stored not only in the rock media, but in the pipe itself. All the problems associated with clogging of rock media in the percolation basin can be found

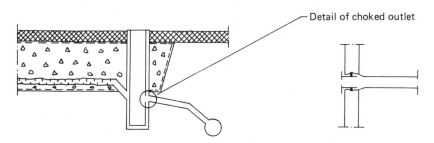

Figure 2.8   Choked bottom outlet of a percolation basin. (After Swedish Association of Water and Sewer Works, 1983.)

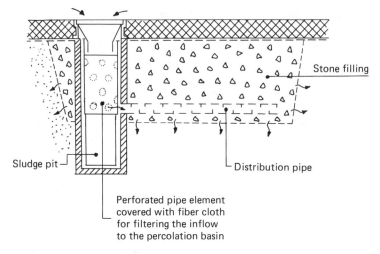

Stone filling

Sludge pit

Distribution pipe

Perforated pipe element
covered with fiber cloth
for filtering the inflow
to the percolation basin

Figure 2.9   (a) Example of an inflow well with a filter.

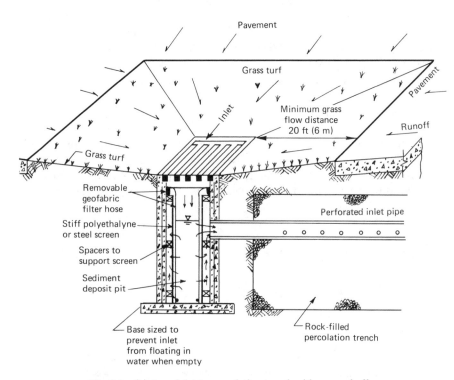

Pavement

Grass turf

Pavement

Inlet

Minimum grass
flow distance
20 ft (6 m)

Runoff

Grass turf

Removable
geofabric
filter hose

Perforated inlet pipe

Stiff polyethalyne
or steel screen

Spacers to
support screen

Sediment
deposit pit

Base sized to
prevent inlet
from floating in
water when empty

Rock-filled
percolation trench

Fig. 2.9   (b) Area inlet to percolation trench with a grass buffer.

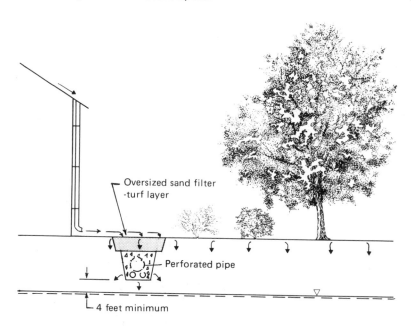

Figure 2.10   Representation of a pipe trench as a percolation basin.

in the pipe trench. Therefore, the filtering of stormwater and the prevention of soil migration into the rock media must be part of each installation in order to have a successful pipe trench facility.

2.3.7 Permeable Pavement

The term *permeable pavement* describes basically three types of paved surfaces designed to minimize surface runoff. Porous asphalt pavement and porous concrete pavement are constructed similarly to conventional pavement, the basic difference being that the sand and finer fraction of the aggregate are left out of the pavement mix. In addition, the pavement is generally placed on top of a substantial layer of granular base.

Another type of permeable pavement is constructed of modular interlocking concrete blocks with open cells. The blocks are placed over a deep layer of coarse gravel. Porous geotextile filter fabric is placed under the coarse granular base to prevent the underlying soils from migrating into the granular base. If the pavement is expected to provide local disposal, the seasonal high groundwater and bedrock under the permeable pavement must be at least 4 feet (1.2 m) below the pavement's surface. Typical cross-sections of porous pavement are shown in Figure 2.11.

The use of permeable pavement does not have to be limited to areas with permeable underlying soils unless stormwater must be infiltrated into the ground, i.e., disposed of locally. Whenever the underlying soils, groundwater

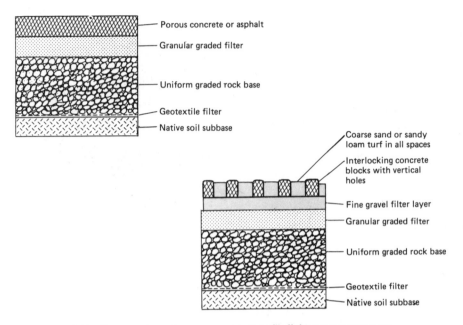

Figure 2.11   Cross-sections of porous pavement and cellular porous pavement.

depth, or bedrock does not permit local disposal by infiltration, permeable pavement can be designed to act as an underground detention facility by installing an impermeable membrane between the coarse rock media and the native soil subgrade. The granular base is drained with the aid of perforated pipe installed at 10- to 25-foot (3- to 8-m) intervals. These underdrains are connected to a nonperforated manifold that discharges into the surface drainage system through a flow regulator. The outflow regulator is designed to empty the entire pore storage volume available in the rock media within a 6- to 12-hour period.

Permeable pavement offers another alternative for local disposal or for on-site detention of stormwater. It, in effect, reduces or modifies the directly connected surface imperviousness of an urban watershed.

The long-term viability and durability of porous asphalt and concrete pavement are always of concern, especially when they are used in cold climates with severe freeze–thaw cycles. This may not be a valid concern in warm climates, such as may be found in Florida, Louisiana, Southern California, and similar locations. Discussions with several city and county engineers who have used porous concrete or asphalt pavement reveal that such surfaces have a tendency to clog and seal within 1 to 3 years. As a result, they need vigorous maintenance in the form of high-power vacuuming to retain a permeable surface, and even then they eventually seal. Once sealed, the only way to restore porous concrete or asphalt pavement is to replace it—a very expensive maintenance practice.

Interlocking cellular concrete block pavement, when properly installed, seals at a much slower rate than do the surfaces of continuous porous pavement. Cellular concrete block pavement also seems to have a good service record under all climatic conditions. However, individual blocks sometimes settle and misalign when subjected to too much automobile traffic. As a result, this type of pavement is best used in automobile parking pads adjacent to conventionally paved driving surfaces.

Another excellent use for cellular concrete block pavement is in remote or overflow parking zones adjoining shopping centers, churches, schools, and office complexes, and in other locations where large parking areas are needed. When properly integrated into the site, these permeable parking areas can also act as local infiltration areas for many of the impervious surfaces on the remainder of the development site. An example of an application of perforated block pavement can be seen in Figure 2.12, which shows a beachfront parking area on the coast of Taiwan.

Because the rock media under cellular concrete blocks is free-draining, it offers little resistance to horizontal flow. Typically, paved areas have a positive slope, and the water entering the rock media flows along the slope and can surface somewhere near the downstream toe of the paved surface. When this happens, the amount of water that infiltrates into the underlying soils is reduced and the effectiveness of this practice is diminished. To eliminate horizontal migration of water within the porous media, the cellular blocks are installed in continuous concrete cells, as shown in Figures 2.12 and 2.13. These walls arrest the horizontal movement of water within the rock media and force precipitation to infiltrate near the point where it falls.

Figure 2.12   A cellular porous paving block installation in Taiwan, ROC.

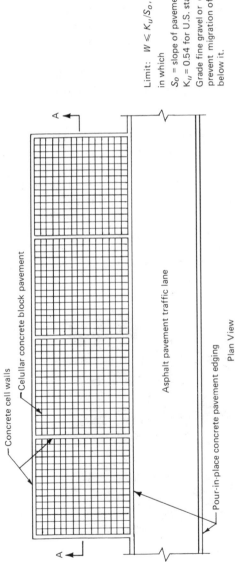

Limit: $W \leqslant K_u/S_o$,

in which

S_o = slope of pavement surface in ft/ft (m/m),

K_u = 0.54 for U.S. standard units (0.165 for SI units).

Grade fine gravel or coarse sand base material to prevent migration of this material into the gravel base below it.

Concrete cell walls

Cellular concrete block pavement

Asphalt pavement traffic lane

Pour-in-place concrete pavement edging

Plan View

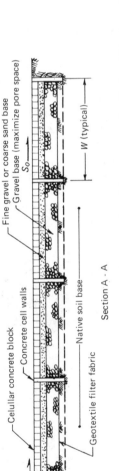

Fine gravel or coarse sand base

Gravel base (maximize pore space)

S_o

W (typical)

Cellular concrete block

Concrete cell walls

Native soil base

Geotextile filter fabric

S_o

Section A - A

Figure 2.13 Installation of modular porous paving blocks within concrete-walled cells.

2.3.8 Minimizing Directly Connected Imperviousness

Minimizing directly connected imperviousness is another process of reducing and slowing down surface runoff. It involves breaking up the surface runoff hydraulic connection of adjacent impervious surfaces to the maximum extent practicable. As a result, runoff from these surfaces has to travel over stable permeable surfaces such as lawns, slow-moving or infiltrating grassed swales, porous pavement, etc., before reaching a gutter, storm sewer, drainage channel, or receiving waterway. Rainfall infiltration into the ground is increased, and the load of suspended solids and other pollutants is reduced somewhat by their contact with grass surfaces.

This practice is most effective in reducing and slowing down surface runoff during small storms. Large storms tend to overwhelm the retention loss system and produce surface runoff, probably at a somewhat slower rate than would otherwise occur in a conventional drainage system. Since the majority of rainstorms are small, minimizing directly connected imperviousness can eliminate and reduce a significant portion of the total annual surface runoff reaching the receiving water system. Some of the water will eventually find its way into the receiving system through the groundwater system, but at a much slower rate. This practice enhances groundwater recharge and retains as much of the precipitation where it falls, just as land surfaces tend to do before they are covered by impervious surfaces.

Reduction of directly connected imperviousness does not have to be limited to newly developing areas. Some retrofitting of this practice is possible in low- to medium-density residential neighborhoods and in low-denisty office complexes. In older neighborhoods, roof gutter downspouts often discharge directly into the formal drainage system. Disconnecting these downspouts from separate storm sewers and combined sewers and letting them first drain across grassed areas reduces the directly connected impervious area in an existing urban watershed. In areas where downspouts are not connected to sewers and instead drain directly onto driveways or streets, routing these drains to discharge first onto grass surfaces also helps to reduce directly connected impervious surfaces. This form of local disposal is described in more detail in Section 25.3.1.

2.4 SPECIAL CONSIDERATIONS AND MAINTENANCE

2.4.1 General

Systematic use of local disposal of stormwater is a relatively recent phenomenon. As a result, most installations in existence today have been in operation only a few years. The Environmental Protection Agency of the United States of America (EPA, 1983) reported considerable success in control of storm runoff and pollutants through the use of local disposal devices. Removal of pollutants over the long term was estimated to range between 45% and 65% without adverse contamination of groundwater.

Because of the relatively short experience, it is still too early to draw far-reaching conclusions regarding the installations' long-term reliability or life expectancy. The following sections discuss some of the construction, operation, and maintenance lessons gained from the experience so far.

2.4.2 Quality Control in Construction

Obviously, satisfactory performance of local disposal is very much dependent on the installation being built in accordance with the designer's plans, specifications, and/or instructions. Although this is obvious, it is very common to see improper installation of local disposal facilities.

Unlike the construction of large public works projects that have full-time professional inspection, local disposal facilities, because of their small size, will often not have full-time inspection. Even if they do, according to Shaver (1986), the inspectors are often not familiar with the technology and functional relationships of such facilities. We need to recognize that a typical construction worker cannot be expected to know the special needs of these type of installations.

When selecting local disposal as a functioning part of a community's stormwater management system, proper installation inspection and quality control procedures will also have to be provided by the community. Inspectors will have to be hired and trained. They will also need to be trained to call for expert help when unforeseen field conditions are encountered that may require design changes. The importance of attempting to properly deal, on a case-by-case basis, with the installation problems cannot be overemphasized. The successful performance of the entire stormwater system depends on a quality assurance program.

2.4.3 Safeguarding Local Disposal Facilities

Infiltration and percolation facilities are usually constructed at the same time other facilities and structures are constructed. The risk of damage to these facilities is the greatest at this time. To minimize these risks, the following are recommended:

1. Locate percolation basins away from roads or construction haul routes. Heavy vehicles traveling over these basins can cause the surrounding soil to flow into the pores of the rock media.
2. Minimize the sealing of infiltration and percolation surfaces by keeping traffic off those areas where they are to be built. Also, locate other activities that could seal soil surfaces (e.g., cement mixing, vehicle maintenance, etc.) away from these sites.

3. Since runoff from construction sites is heavily laden with fine, suspended solids which clog infiltration and percolation facilities, keep runoff out of these facilities until construction is complete.

2.4.4 Maturing of Infiltration Surfaces

Newly constructed infiltration surfaces may not have as rapid an infiltration rate as more mature surfaces. This is attributed to freshly compacted surfaces and immature vegetative cover. Figure 2.14 shows an example of water standing due to reduced infiltration capacity.

After infiltration surfaces undergo freeze and thaw and the vegetation's root system loosens the soils, infiltration rates tend to increase. Use of nursery grown turf in newly installed infiltration basins can achieve the highest possible infiltration rates in the shortest amount of time after construction.

Since infiltration rates in a new facility are likely to be less than anticipated in design, the downstream stormwater conveyance system may appear to be somewhat undersized. It is wise to account for this interim period and to either slightly oversize the local disposal facility or the downstream conveyance system.

As the local disposal facilities begin to age, some of them will fail and will have to be repaired or replaced. When failures begin to occur, the downstream conveyance system will need to handle more runoff. If the conveyance system was not designed with this in mind, it will become inadequate to handle the increase in runoff.

Figure 2.14   Standing stormwater due to reduced infiltration capacity.

2.4.5 Clogging

After land development is completed, random erosion occurs at points of concentrated flow (e.g., at edge of pavement, at roof downspouts, etc.). The eroded soils are carried to the infiltration or percolation facilities and the infiltration and percolation rates are significantly reduced. Control of erosion is very important and can be accomplished through the installation of splash pads at downspouts, the use of rock or paved rundowns, and other measures. Erosion control can go a long way toward reducing the rate of deterioration of local disposal facilities.

It is not possible entirely to prevent fine sediments from entering the infiltration facilities and eventually clogging the soil pores. How long it takes will depend on the porosity of the soil, the quality of the stormwater, and how often runoff occurs. It is possible to reduce the amount of sediment through mechanical separation, such as presettlement in a holding basin. The use of filtration in advance of percolation beds, mentioned earlier, is very effective in reducing clogging.

If clogging occurs shortly after installation of infiltration facilities, it can indicate excessive sediment loads. One should check for erosion in the tributary area and for any other sources of excessive sediment. Frequent clogging may also indicate the blockage of filters at the inlets to the infiltration or percolation beds. If this is the case, the problem can be corrected by simply cleaning out the filter media.

Of a more serious nature is the clogging that will occur over a long period of time. This is due to the accumulation of pollutants in the pores of the soil and in the percolation media. This could take several years, unless there are unusually heavy loads of sediment from the tributary basin. Heise (1977) reported on an infiltration system in Denmark installed in 1950. It was designed to intercept runoff from street surfaces. Although it functioned well at first, it lost all of its infiltration capacity in 20 years. Excavation revealed that the soils were impregnated with oily sediments. Instead of replacement, a storm sewer was installed.

2.4.6 Frost Problems

Frost in the soils can adversely influence the performance of a local disposal facility. It is possible, however, to design mitigating features into an installation, but their reliability has yet to be field verified. For example, it is possible to install insulation above the stone in a percolation pit, but the filter areas at the inlets can freeze and prevent water from entering the rock media itself.

Freezing can be an extreme problem in cold climates, especially for infiltration basins. When that is the case, sufficient storage volume on the surface of the basin needs to be provided to store winter snowmelt until spring thaws reopen the infiltration surfaces.

2.4.7 Slope Stability

Because local disposal artificially forces stormwater into the ground, the possibility of creating slope stability problems should always be considered. As the water infiltrates or percolates into soils, the intergranular friction in the soil can be reduced and previously stable slopes can become unstable. Slope failures in urban areas can be disastrous. A geotechnical expert should be consulted whenever local disposal is being considered, regardless of the slope of the terrain. Such expertise is especially important if slope stability may be affected.

2.4.8 Effects on Groundwater

The forced inflow of stormwater into the ground will affect the groundwater levels and water quality in the regions where it occurs. The impact on groundwater needs to be considered and accounted for in the design of buildings. As an example, buildings with basements may not be feasible if the groundwater levels are raised above basement floor elevations. This problem may be solved by the installation of underdrains. At any rate, local disposal will have an impact on groundwater.

Local disposal may also have an impact on the quality of groundwater and may be of particular concern where groundwater is used as water supply. Studies reported to date by the EPA (1983) and others suggest that groundwater recharged by nonindustrial stormwater may not have serious water quality problems. Water quality samples taken at several sites revealed that the groundwater underneath infiltration and percolation facilities meets all of the EPA's primary drinking water standards. These findings are still considered site-specific and, as a result, are inconclusive for all conditions.

Recent findings of groundwater contamination by organic toxicants, however, leave room for concern. As our society continues to use various solvents, herbicides, pesticides, and other potentially toxic, carcinogenic, or mutagenic chemicals, many of these chemicals will enter groundwater with infiltrated stormwater. Unfortunately, the potential of these chemicals being present in stormwater runoff is ever present. And although there is no evidence of widespread contamination, as long as these chemicals are in general use we need to consider their potential presence in the stormwater runoff.

2.4.9 Care and Maintenance

As with any facility installed by humans, regular care and maintenance is needed to insure proper operation. Unfortunately, maintenance is often neglected. Often, local disposal facilities are constructed as a part of a new development and become the responsibility of the individual property owner. Maintenance or operational instructions are often not provided to the new owners.

As these facilities begin to fail, the property owners may conclude that the site was improperly graded in the first place. This "problem" may be resolved by improving surface drainage through regrading the site, or by installing drainage pipes or swales. Obviously, this defeats the local disposal concept and results in increased loading on the downstream system. It may be possible to avoid such a scenario if local authorities mandate, by ordinance, that the new owners be notified at time of sale that they are now owners of a local stormwater disposal facility. Such formal notices should also contain the operation and maintenance instructions.

Infiltration facilities, to a large extent, depend on a healthy growth of vegetation to keep the infiltration surfaces porous. Maintenance of the infiltration areas needs to include the maintenance of the vegetation growing on the infiltration zone. As the facility ages and the surface soils become clogged, the top soil layers may have to be removed, replaced, and revegetated to restore their infiltration capacity.

Maintenance of percolation facilities needs to concentrate on keeping the inlet filters from being plugged. The filter fabric and/or sand layers need to be checked frequently and cleaned when found to be excessively clogged. After a number of years it may be necessary to replace the rock media and the adjacent soils because the very fine, unfilterable particles fill the pores. Regular maintenance of the inlet filters can significantly increase the time before the percolation bed has to be replaced.

REFERENCES

American Society of Civil Engineers and Water Pollution Control Federation, *Stormwater Management Manual of Practice,* American Society of Civil Engineers, New York, 1992 (in press).

DAY, G. E., SMITH, D. R., and BOWERS, J., *Runoff and Pollution Abatement Characteristics of Concrete Grid Pavement,* Bulletin 135, Virginia Water Resources Research Center, Blacksburg, Va., 1981.

EPA, *Results of the Nationwide Urban Runoff Program—Final Report,* U.S. Environmental Protection Agency, NTIS Access No. PB84-185552, Washington, D.C., 1983.

Florida Concrete Products Association, *Pervious Pavement Manual,* Orlando, Fl., 1988.

GOFORTH, G. F., DINZ, E. V., and RAUHUT, J. B., *Stormwater Hydrological Characteristics of Porous and Conventional Paving Systems,* Report No. PB84-123-729, Municipal Environment Research Laboratory, U.S. Environmental Protection Agency, Cincinnati, Ohio, 1984.

HEISE, P., "Infiltration Systems," *Seminar in Surface Water Technology,* Fagernes, 21–23, March 1977. (In Danish).

LIVINGSTON, E. H., et al., *The Florida Development Manual: A Guide to Sound Land and Water Management,* Department of Environmental Regulation, Tallahassee, Fla., 1988.

PRATT, C. J., "Permeable Pavement for Stormwater Quality Enhancement," in H. C. Torno, Ed., *Urban Stormwater Quality Enhancement—Source Control, Retrofitting, and Combined Sewer Technology,* American Society of Civil Engineers, New York, 1990.

SCHUELER, T. R., *Controlling Urban Runoff: A Practical Manual for Planning and Designing Urban Best Management Practices,* Metropolitan Washington Water Resources Planning Board, Washington, D.C., 1987.

SHAVER, H. E., "Infiltration as a Stormwater Management Component," *Urban Runoff Quality—Impact and Quality Enhancement Technology,* American Society of Civil Engineers, New York, 1986.

SMITH, D. R., "Evaluation of Concrete Grid Pavements in the United States," *Proceedings of the Second Conference on Concrete Block Paving,* Delft, Australia, 1984.

SWEDISH ASSOCIATION OF WATER AND SEWAGE WORKS, *Local Disposal of Storm Water—Design Manual,* Publication VAV P46, 1983. (In Swedish).

TORNO, H. C., Ed., *Urban Stormwater Quality Enhancement—Source Control, Retrofitting, and Combined Sewer Technology,* Proceedings of an Engineering Foundation Conference in Davos, Switzerland, October, 1989, American Society of Civil Engineers, New York, 1990.

WILLIAMS, L. H., "Effectiveness of Stormwater Detention," *Proceedings of the Conference on Stormwater Detention Facilities,* American Society of Civil Engineers, New York, 1982.

YOUSEF, Y. A., WANIELISTA, M. P., Hvitved-Jacobsen, T., and Harper, H. H., "Fate of Heavy Metals in Stormwater Runoff from Highway Bridges," in *The Science of the Total Environment,* International Symposium on Highway Pollution, London, 1984.

3

Inlet Control Facilities

3.1 INTRODUCTION

Until the 1960s, a typical approach to stormwater drainage design was to convey the water away from where it fell as rapidly as possible. As a result, stormwater runoff was accelerated, and the flow peaks increased substantially as land urbanized. The concept of controlling runoff at its source became popular in the 1960s. The idea was to temporarily detain stormwater runoff at its source and to release it at reduced rates into the downstream conveyance system. The peak runoff rates from individual sites can be reduced by:

- increasing the travel time of runoff to the inlet, and
- detaining runoff at its source.

3.2 INCREASING THE TRAVEL TIME OF RUNOFF

The travel time of stormwater runoff can be increased by reducing the surface flow velocity and by lengthening the distance runoff has to travel. The velocity of flow on any surface can be approximated using Manning's Equation:

$$V = \frac{K_u}{n} R^{2/3} S^{1/2} \tag{3.1}$$

in which V = velocity of flow in feet per second (m/s),
K_u = 1.49 for U.S. standard units (1.0 for SI units),
n = Manning's roughness coefficient,

R = depth of flow in feet (m), and

S = slope of the ground in feet per foot (m/m).

The practical approach tells us that only two variables in this equation can be varied during design, namely, Manning's roughness coefficient n and the slope of the ground S. As an example, the slope can be reduced during site grading of new development. Reduction of slope will also increase depression storage of the surfaces. Surface depression storage retains some of the rainfall and keeps it from running off. The retained water forms puddles which eventually evaporate or infiltrate into the ground.

On the other hand, flat slopes can result in poor surface drainage, which can become a nuisance. Also, poor drainage of paved areas can reduce pavement life and increase its maintenance frequency. Such potential problems need to be evaluated before selecting what cross-slopes to use for paved areas.

It is much easier to increase the roughness coefficient of grassy areas than it is for paved surfaces. The slope of grassy surfaces can be made to undulate and thus slow down runoff velocities. On the other hand, paved areas, such as parking lots, can be interspersed with grassy areas to reduce the average flow velocities along the surface of the site.

These are simple concepts that are often not used because local drainage or paving criteria require curb and gutter at all pavement edges. Where permissible, these concepts offer possibilities for reducing surface runoff from developed sites; however, it is very difficult to actually quantify by how much. Instead of using curb and gutter, the edges of the paved areas can be delimited with precast wheel stops that permit drainage to flow onto the grassy surfaces as sheet flow.

Often, there are opportunities in site design to increase flow paths to storm sewer inlets. For example, sites can be graded to have slow surface swales that, more or less, parallel the contours and intercept runoff. Whenever this is possible, the runoff travel time is increased, runoff peaks are reduced, some of the runoff is infiltrated into the ground, and slope erosion problems are reduced. Creativity, within sound technological constraints, can help achieve good drainage, aesthetic enhancement, erosion control, and savings in the cost of construction, operation, and maintenance.

3.3 SURFACE STORAGE

More direct inlet control temporarily detains runoff at, or near, the source of runoff. Such detention can occur on flat roofs, parking lots, storage yards, and other surfaces specifically prepared for this purpose. Many of these techniques were originally introduced in the *Urban Storm Drainage Criteria Manual* originally published by the Denver Regional Council of Governments (1969). Since then, these concepts have proliferated worldwide, and examples of their use can be found in many of the industrialized countries in the world.

Source control has the potential, if properly implemented and maintained, of being an effective stormwater management technique (Urbonas & Glidden, 1983). However, one must be aware of its limitations and pitfalls, which are discussed in the following sections.

3.4 ROOFTOP STORAGE

Stormwater can be detained on a flat roof by installing flow restrictors on roof drains. Flat roofs are designed to hold a substantial live load and are sealed against leakage. Nevertheless, when a roof is used for detention, the structural design needs to account for the increased loading in accordance with the recommendations of the Uniform Building Code.

The Uniform Building Code also recommends minimum standards for the design of flat roofs, which include minimum roof slopes and maximum ponding depths. The designer should check the latest codes and standards before finalizing his or her plans. If all the UBC requirements are fully adhered to as they exist at the time this book was written, very little effective storage volume is available on rooftops. However, it is a concept that is often practiced and may be worth consideration.

A typical design for a flow restrictor that is used at a roof drain is illustrated in Figure 3.1. As can be seen, the outlet has a strainer that is surrounded by a flow restricting ring. The degree of flow control is determined by the size and number of holes in the ring. When the water depth reaches the top of the ring, it then spills freely into the roof drain with virtually no further restriction. Water ponding depth is thereby controlled to a permissible depth while providing a controlled release rate for a measured storage volume.

Rooftop detention is not without its problems. The most common is lack of proper inspection and maintenance. The flow control ring can clog with debris, such as leaves, and cause the water to pond for prolonged periods. Building owners have been known to remove these flow restrictors to eliminate the nuisance of ponding water on the roof, often not realizing that the control ring is an integral part of the community's drainage system. This happens frequently after a roof develops a leak.

A follow-up inspection and enforcement program, to insure that all roof restrictors are working, is generally not practical for a municipality. Thus, roof detention controls have a tendency to disappear with time, and their value as a stormwater management tool needs to be questioned. A routine municipal inspection and enforcement program is one way to minimize the loss of roof detention. However, commitment for such an inspection program is often not possible from the elected officials. As a result, rooftop detention cannot be expected to be effective with time in reducing flows in the downstream conveyance system.

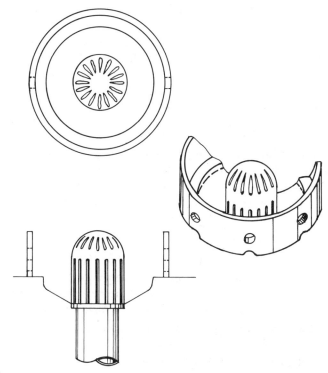

Figure 3.1   Roof detention drain control ring. (After Poertner, 1974.)

3.5 DETENTION ON PAVED SURFACES

Parking lots, paved storage yards, and other paved surfaces can be, and are, often used for stormwater detention. The advantage parking lots and other paved surfaces have over rooftops is that parking lots provide a much larger storage surface which can also pond to a greater depth. The use of parking lots as detention facilities has become very popular in some parts of the United States. The reason for this is that very little additional land needs to be dedicated exclusively for detention in a commercial development. As a result, this provides an economic incentive for the land developer to lobby for the acceptance and the continued use of parking lots as detention basins.

Unfortunately, as often happens with new concepts that catch on quickly, economic or political expediency can get in the way of sound engineering practice. Often, the decision makers embrace the idea of parking lot detention as a panacea for all drainage problems (Urbonas, 1985). As with rooftop detention, the use of parking lots for detention needs to be backed up with the staff resources to insure their continued existence and proper maintenance. Merely requiring their installation at the time of development is not enough.

Parking lot detention shares the same surface area with parked vehicles. If the detention is designed without regard for the primary use of the parking lot in mind, considerable inconvenience and damage to parked vehicles can occur when it rains. First and foremost, for the parking lot detention to be acceptable to its owners, it is necessary to insure that the lot does not pond water frequently. Also, when the lot detains stormwater, it should be inundated for only a short period of time. Thus, it is important for the designer to recognize the limitations in ponding depths and the frequency of ponding. Failure to do so can lead to owners taking action to eliminate this nuisance after experiencing flooding on their property.

Here are several rules for designing relatively successful parking lot detention. The same rules are also appropriate for detention on other types of paved surfaces.

1. Keep the frequency of ponding on the lot to a minimum. Ponding at full depth no more frequently than once every 5 to 10 years will keep the nuisance factor very low. This may require that detention of the more frequent smaller storms occur off the parking lot surface.

2. Keep the *maximum* depth of ponding during a major storm (i.e., 100-year storm) to less than 8 inches (0.2 m).

3. Locate the deepest ponding zones at remote and least used portions of the parking lot. Obviously, site layout may dictate otherwise; if so, ask the owner to determine if alternate site layout is possible.

4. Drain the parking lot ponding quickly, preferably in less than 30 minutes.

5. Keep the flow restrictors out of easy reach to reduce vandalism and to discourage owners from removing them. Use a buried pipe as the primary flow control device instead of an orifice plate, which can be easily removed.

It is clear from the preceding rules that there may exist a conflict between the stormwater management needs and these rules. For example, if the local requirements are to control frequently occurring storms (i.e., 2- or 5-year events), parking lot detention will result in frequent ponding. On the other hand, if the requirements call for the control of very large storms (i.e., 10- or 100-year recurrence frequency), then the frequency of ponding will be low.

Use of parking lots in conjunction with ponds adjacent to the parking lot or with underground storage should not be overlooked. The adjacent or underground detention facility can store the more frequent events permitting the runoff from the larger storms to back up onto the parking lot surface. As an example, this concept was incorporated into the Arapahoe County Storm

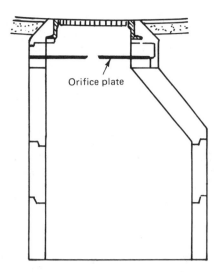

Figure 3.2   Use of control orifice plate
inside an inlet. (After Poertner, 1974.)

Drainage and Technical Criteria (1985) in Colorado. These same criteria also incorporate all of the aforementioned rules for parking lot detention and provide for multifrequency and multistage control.

There are many ways one can design a flow restrictor to control the rate of drainage from a parking lot detention. One concept mentioned in the *American Public Works Association Special Report 43* by Poertner (1974) is illustrated in Figure 3.2. This simple concept uses an orifice installed below the grate of an area inlet. There are also specialty devices, such as the hydrobrake and the flow control valve, that also can be used. These specialty devices will be described in more detail in Chapter 12.

Whenever designing detention on paved surfaces that are used for other, probably more noticeable purposes (e.g., parking of cars, storage of building materials, storage of trucks or buses, etc.), the designer needs to provide surface overflows for larger storms. These have to be built into the system to act as a precaution against the possibility that the primary outlet may become clogged, or a larger-than-the-design storm may occur. Failure to incorporate an emergency overflow can cause damage and result in liability that can otherwise be avoided. Even these precautions may not prevent damage during unusually large rainstorms, but during such events, damage is likely even if detention is not a part of the system.

REFERENCES

APWA, *Urban Stormwater Management,* Special Report No. 49, American Public Works Association, Chicago, Ill., 1981.

ARAPAHOE COUNTY, *Storm Drainage Technical Criteria,* Arapahoe County, Colo., 1985.

DRCOG, *Urban Storm Drainage Criteria Manual,* Vols. 1 & 2, Denver Regional Council of Governments (currently being published by Urban Drainage and Flood Control District), Denver, Colo., 1961.

POERTNER, H. G., *Practices in Detention of Urban Storm Water Runoff,* American Public Works Association, Special Report No. 43, 1974.

URBONAS, B. R., "Stormwater Detention, Idealism of 1960's Matures," *Proceedings of the Seminar on Flood Plain Hydrology,* Dept. of Civil Engineering, New Jersey Institute of Technology, Piscataway, N.J., 1985.

URBONAS, B. R., AND GLIDDEN, M. W., "Potential Effects of Detention Policies," *Proceedings of the Second Southwest Region Symposium on Urban Stormwater Management,* Texas A&M University, November 1983.

4

Open Ponds

4.1 INTRODUCTION

It is generally acknowledged by the stormwater management profession that urbanization increases runoff from rainstorms and snow melt. For example, studies in Denver by Urbonas show that during a routine summer afternoon rainshower, an acre of pavement will produce the same amount of runoff as would occur from several square miles of native rangeland. During an 1-inch thunderstorm, one paved acre may yield the same amount of runoff as 40 to 100 acres (15 to 40 ha) of rangeland. Clearly, urbanization radically increases storm runoff for the majority of storm events. This has a very significant effect on downstream residents and drainage systems. Detention can help mitigate, but not totally eliminate, these effects.

Open ponds are probably the most common type of detention used in stormwater management. They have the advantage of being dedicated totally to the task of stormwater management, which is not the case for rooftops or parking lots. They are also visible. This attracts attention for maintenance. Although there are examples of using open detention for control of combined sewer overflows, public health and aesthetic considerations generally limit the use of open detention ponds to the control of separate stormwater runoff.

4.2 PLANNING FOR DETENTION PONDS

When planning for a detention pond, it is not sufficient to address only hydrology and hydraulics. According to American Society of Civil Engineers (ASCE) (1985), successful detention facilities also have strong recreational or other community uses. The detention aspect is often considered secondary by the residents in the area. For these reasons, planning for detention needs also to consider the social, environmental, and recreational needs of each community.

When open ponds are planned, an attempt should be made to combine the detention use with other community uses. The following sections discuss such co-uses, along with the design considerations for each.

4.2.1 Effects on the Landscape: Aesthetics

As an integral part of the community it serves, a detention pond needs to blend into the landscape and into the community. Too often, detention ponds are installed merely as a hole in the ground (sometimes referred to as an HIG) without any redeeming landscape features.

Simple yet inexpensive measures, such as gentle side slopes, planting of trees and shrubs, and other landscaping features can transform an HIG into an attractive amenity for the neighborhood. The services of a competent land use planner and a landscape architect early in a development's planning process can help achieve more useful and attractive results.

4.2.2 Pond Environment

Ponds that have a permanent pool of water offer many attractive environmental possibilities. As urbanization occurs, there is a loss of wildlife and bird life habitat. Such habitat is replaced by manicured lawns, shrubs, and trees that offer habitat for select small birds and animals such as squirrels. It is possible to create a natural micro-environment around ponds that attract a greater variety of animal and bird life. These "natural" environmental pockets are considered by many city dwellers to be a treasure in an otherwise densely urbanized community.

Proper planning for riperian vegetation that fits the urban setting needs to be considered when designing the pond's landscape. As an example, water lilies and cattails can contribute to pond's aesthetic appeal. On the other hand, the uncontrolled spread of wild vegetation can be a nuisance to the surrounding neighborhood and become an operational and maintenance problem. Some of these problems are discussed later.

4.2.3 Recreational Opportunities

Detention basins and ponds, with or without permanent pools of water, offer many recreational opportunities in an urban setting. In Figure 4.1 we see two examples of detention ponds in Sweden. Both were planned and designed in cooperation with park officials of each community. These two examples illustrate how stormwater detention can be incorporated nicely into the land-

Figure 4.1   Examples of ponds in Sweden at two parks.

Figure 4.2   Skyline Park in downtown Denver.

scape and provide recreational opportunities for local residents between storms. Since the periods between storms generally far exceed the periods of rainfall, these facilities are available for recreational uses most of the time.

Two other examples of active and passive recreational opportunities are illustrated in Figures 4.2 and 4.3. The first shows a detention basin in the central business district of Denver. It is used by people during the day for strolling, eating lunch, or just relaxing in the sun. The attractive landscaping

Figure 4.3   Englewood High School athletic field. *(Photo courtesy of McLaughlin Water Engineers, Ltd.)*

fits the surrounding architecture and the inner city setting. Most people that use it do not realize that this three-block long basin is designed to actually reduce the storm flow rates to the available capacity of the downstream storm sewers. The second example is also in the Denver area and shows where a detention basin is used as a high school tournament athletic field. It is an off-line pond that controls floods downstream and stores water when the adjacent channel carries floods that exceed the 10-year storm.

Other examples, not illustrated here, include ponds with large permanent water surfaces that are used for skating in winter and for boating in summer. The possibilities for multiple use are limited only by the imagination and the community's desires to combine stormwater detention ponds with uses other than just storing water temporarily when it rains.

4.2.4 Removal of Pollutants

Detention basins and ponds, because they back up water, will cause suspended solids to settle. Since many of the pollutants are attached to suspended solids, ponds will remove some of them. How much is removed will depend on pond volume, inlet and outlet configuration, pond depth and shape, the time the stormwater resides in the pond, and whether or not the detention facility has a permanent pool of water.

Considerable information has been developed in recent years on the design of detention facilities for water quality enhancement. Although we still have a lot to learn before we can design them with complete confidence, there are sufficient field data to predict the ranges in the removal of settleable pollutants that can be expected from detention facilities. Since this is a topic of interest to many stormwater managers, Part 4 of this book is dedicated to the design of detention for water quality enhancement.

4.2.5 Detention in Natural Lakes

When the downstream recipient of urban storm runoff is a natural lake, a water supply reservoir, or a recreational reservoir, each of them can provide peak flow attenuation. The flow routing advantages of these water bodies, however, can extract a price in the form of water quality deterioration and adverse impacts on their natural or designated uses. Potential causes of water quality degradation and resultant concerns may include the following:

- Nutrient enrichment resulting in accelerated eutrophication. Excessive algae levels can deplete oxygen and cause fish kills. According to Wallen, Jr. (1984), these factors also have been linked to impairment of recreational uses.

- Deposits of sediments containing heavy metals and attached petroleum product will occur in the bottom.

- If salt is used to control street icing, increases in lake salinity can occur. So far, there is little documentation of this actually becoming a serious problem.

- If acid rain is of concern, the increased surface runoff from urbanization may increase the acidity of the receiving water body.

4.2.6 Safety

When we discuss safety of detention ponds or basins we are, in fact, discussing a wide range of possibilities. This topic encompasses the structural integrity of the confining embankment and of the outlet works and the safety of the people using the facility for recreation. The latter includes the need to protect people when the pond is storing runoff (i.e., operating) and during the periods between storms.

The protection of embankments against catastrophic failure due to water overtopping them are discussed in more detail later in this section. At this time, we focus on the day-to-day safety considerations for the public in the vicinity of a pond.

The designers, owners, and approving agencies need to recognize that detention ponds are a part of the total urban community's infrastructure. As a result, they need to be designed with public safety in mind. It is inevitable that people will have access to these facilities, especially if the detention facility is in a park.

We have seen public works officials overreact and completely fence detention facilities. Fortunately, there are many more examples, such as reported by Edwards (1982), Stubchear (1982), and others where detention ponds are multiple-use facilities. Although safety should remain a concern, a properly designed detention pond should be no more hazardous than an urban lake, a playground, a hiking trail, or any other recreational or park facility in a city. It definitely is a safer facility than a city street, yet no one fences off streets.

Probably the most reliable safety feature to protect the public against accidentally falling into a pond is to install gentle side slopes for all the banks and the embankment. Banks should be sloped no steeper than 4 units of measure horizontally for each unit vertically (i.e., 4:1) Slopes steeper than 3:1 should be avoided entirely unless the facility is fenced. Gentle side slopes for the first 10 to 20 feet (3 to 6 m) under water facilitate easy escape if a person accidentally enters the pond.

ASCE (1985) recommends that the designer pay particular attention to safety features around the outlet works. It recommends that outlet risers be located away from shore to discourage the public from access. Also, installation of trash racks with low entry velocities will contribute to safety during operation. Fencing, on the other hand, is less effective than it first appears, since the public, especially children, have been seen to bypass fences to access outlet areas.

Wherever possible, one should minimize the visibility of the outlet, thereby reducing its attraction potential. In some cases, installing signs warning of the hazard may be appropriate; however, signs also appear to have a limited record of success in keeping people away from the more hazardous areas. Clearly, the exact methodology will vary with its urban setting.

4.2.7 Layout of Detention Ponds

When planning a detention basin, try to lay it out so that it fits the surrounding landscape and the community. Unfortunately, there are too many examples of treating detention facilities as though they were a nuisance. As a result, they are sometimes located and designed without any regard for the community's needs or how the pond or basin may enhance the aesthetics of the surroundings. A detention facility can be designed to be an attractive and aesthetic amenity in an urban neighborhood. A side benefit of incorporating an attractive detention facility into the community's landscape is that it is more likely to receive proper maintenance.

Detention ponds should be laid out to insure that the flow entering the pond is evenly distributed across the pond so that stagnant zones do not develop in the pond. Zones of stagnation tend to become overgrown with vegetation and can increase mosquito breeding. Oblong shapes, with inlet and outlet at opposite ends, appear to be best suited for this purpose. If this shape is not possible, an elongated triangular shape with the inflow at its apex provides a reasonable alternative.

4.3 TECHNICAL CONFIGURATION

Technically, there are two types of detention facilities: those that store water only when stormwater is being detained and those that have a permanent pool of water. The latter store stormwater above the water surface of the permanent pond. We discuss technical considerations for both types of detention facilities.

4.3.1 Inflow Structure

Erosion and sediment deposition problems can develop at the inflow to the detention basin. Although it is possible to design inflow structures to minimize erosion, deposition cannot be prevented. To minimize maintenance costs, however, it is a good idea to localize much of the deposition where it can be easily removed.

To address the concerns we have just discussed, inflow structure needs to accomplish the following and have the following features:

- Dissipate flow energy at the inflow.
- Drop the inflow elevation when it enters the pond above the pond's water surface.
- Accelerate the diffusion of the inflow plume.
- Provide protection against erosion.
- Provide maintenance access for the repairs to the inlet and for the removal of sediments.
- Incorporate safety features to protect the public (i.e., gentle slopes, fencing or railing at vertical faces of the structure).
- Be unobtrusive to the public eye by blending the inlet into the surrounding terrain.

Inflow energy can be dissipated with the installation of standard energy dissipating structures. Although meant for much larger installations, some of the spillway structures developed by the U.S. Bureau of Reclamation (1964, 1974) provide good examples of design. Of course, the designer may have to scale down some of these designs. These types of structures can be modified in appearance to fit the urban setting. Two good examples of attractive baffle chutes, both located in parks, are shown in Figures 4.4(a) and 4.4(b).

Typically, baffle chutes, vertical spillways, and sloping chutes with energy dissipating basins work well as inlet structures when the inflow has to be dropped in elevation. The reader is encouraged to study the cited references and modify as needed the standard designs to fit each site. One word of caution, however: It takes considerable mass to dissipate flow energy normally found at even small installations. Do not skimp on these structures. Unless properly designed and constructed, they can fall apart very quickly.

A settling basin or a settling zone should be provided near the inlet. The heaviest sediments will settle out at this location, and their removal thereby will be facilitated. A simple design for a settling basin is to depress the bottom near the inflow structure. Stabilize the bottom of this depressed area with soil cement, prefabricated slabs, or concrete paving; however, this is not abso-

(a)

(b)

Figure 4.4   (a) Baffle chute energy dissipator in Denver. (b) An inflow structure with architectural flair in a Denver park. (*Courtesy of Urban Drainage and Flood Control District, Denver, Colo.*)

lutely necessary. A stabilized bottom provides the maintenance crews with fixed boundaries within which sediment removal is to take place.

4.3.2 Configuration of Pond Bottom

The configuration of the pond bottom will depend, to a large degree, on whether the pond will have a permanent pool of water. Bottoms with permanent pools are, in some respects, easier to design. This is especially true if the low flows are conveyed in a pipe to the permanent pool. The areas above the

Figure 4.5 Two examples of trickle flow channels.

permanent pool can then be graded relatively flat, kept clean with less effort, and can be made available for other uses (e.g., play fields, picnic tables, passive recreation, etc.) for longer periods of time.

The permanent pool can also act as the settling basin. The EPA (1983) reported that a permanent pool will cleanse stormwater of pollutants much more effectively than a detention basin without a permanent pool of water. Thus, if water quality enhancement is a goal, this configuration offers proven advantages.

Vehicular access needs to be provided to the entire perimeter of the pool to facilitate maintenance. If possible, provide gates or valves to totally drain the permanent pool. When drained, the bottom is much easier to clean and to excavate than when it is under water. This translates into maintenance cost savings.

A detention basin that stores water only during storms should have a trickle flow ditch between the inlet and the outlet. Two examples are illustrated in Figure 4.5 in which the low flow ditches are sized to carry the frequently occurring runoff and trickle flows. When large rainstorms occur, the capacity of these ditches is exceeded and the water floods the adjacent pond bottom.

The most successful installations of low flow and trickle flow channels have a concrete bottom. Concrete lining facilitates self-cleansing of the ditch and its maintenance. Drainage of the pond bottom between storms has to occur efficiently if it is going to be used for recreation. To achieve this, the bottom has to be cross-sloped at no less than 2% toward the trickle channel(s). Where high groundwater is present, the bottom may not be suitable for passive or active recreation unless subdrains are installed.

Opportunities for multiple use may be plentiful, but it is up to the designer to insure that multiple uses will indeed be possible. Poorly configured and poorly drained detention pond bottoms can foreclose recreational uses, even when such uses are desired or intended at the detention pond.

4.3.3 Slope Protection

Side slopes of the pond will tend to erode whenever the detained water surface fluctuates frequently or when there is wave action. Good vegetation will help to protect the side slopes against erosion; however, in areas of high velocities and wave attack, structural measures are needed to supplement vegetation. Figure 4.6 shows an example of rock slope erosion protection in an overflow zone. Other techniques include concrete lining, burried riprap, and soil cement.

An example of bank protection at the water level is illustrated in Figure 4.7. This type of erosion protection has to be provided when the ground slope under the water is steeper than the normal beaching slope. The use of rock or gabion has been generally successful for this purpose, while the use of hard linings, such as concrete, has had only a marginal success record.

Structural concrete, with adequate bedding and subdrainage, should also perform well as slope protection. In designing concrete slope protection, the forces of wave action and those of freeze and thaw can displace concrete slabs. The U.S. Bureau of Reclamation (1978) provides detailed design suggestions for the design of slope protection that should work well for larger urban detention reservoirs. This and other publications by the Bureau provide excellent guidance for a designer of detention ponds and basins.

4.3.4 Outlet Structure

The configuration of a pond outlet determines the type of pond (i.e., wet or dry), the storage volume, and the control the pond provides the storm run-

Figure 4.6   Slope protection near an outlet.

Figure 4.7   Slope protection at the normal water level.

off. For some time now, many detention ponds were being designed to control runoff from a single recurrence frequency of rainstorm. As a result, some ponds were sized to control, for instance, only the 100-year storm, the 10-year storm, or some other design storm. Studies by Kamadulski and McCuen (1979) and Urbonas and Glidden (1983) concluded that the control of a single frequency of runoff will not effectively control storm runoff of a different runoff probability.

The recommended method is to provide outlets to control the flows of at least two recurrence frequencies of runoff. Brulo et. al. (1984), Kamelduski and McCuen (1979), and Urbonas and Glidden (1983) have described the advantages of two-staged outlets in controlling multiple flood frequencies. Control of two widely different recurrence frequencies of storms can control runoff of other recurrence frequencies as well. It is possible to design outlets that can provide more levels of control, but each level of control adds complexity and cost. From a practical perspective, design for two levels of control, such as the 2-year and the 10-year floods, should be sufficient in most settings. If major floods are of great concern, the outlet can be designed to control the 100-year flood in addition to the other two events.

Although the goals may vary, the most common practice is to control the release rates so that the flows after land development are no larger than before land development. This is frequently specified by local ordinance or criteria which also specify the design storm or storms that need to be so controlled. The discharge rate specified by such criteria is the discharge that should occur when the storage volume occupies the volume allocated for the storm of specified recurrence frequency. If more than one level of control is desired, there is a unique design discharge that may be released for each level of storage from multiple outlets.

In designing outlets, consider the following:

- Design the outlet control orifice in a way that makes unauthorized enlargements impractical. Use of a pipe section that limits the flow rate instead of an orifice plate is one method for achieving this.
- Design the outlet for maximum safety to the public.
- Wherever possible, design for the control of two or three levels of flow (e.g., 2- and 10-year; 2- and 100-year; 10- and 100-year; 2-, 10- and 100-year; etc.).
- Provide maintenance access to the outlet.
- If possible, use no moving parts or pumps in an outlet.
- Use massive components to reduce damage from vandalism.
- Provide erosion protection at the inlet and outlet ends of the outlet pipe.
- Provide coarse gravel packing to screen out debris whenever a perforated outlet riser is used in a dry detention basin.
- Provide a skimmer type shield around a perforated riser in a wet pond to skim off floating debris.
- Always design with maintenance and aesthetics in mind.

Figures 4.8 and 4.9 contain two examples of outlets for dry detention basins. These outlets will permit the entire pond volume to drain between storms. Both provide a small drop between the pond bottom and the lowest flow control orifice to improve the drainage of the bottom.

An example of an outlet for a pond with a permanent water pond also used to control the release of the water quality capture volume is seen in Figure 4.10. After the storm is over, the water surface eventually drops to the permanent pool level. This level is controlled by positioning the openings at the desired permanent water level. Regardless of the configuration, install a gate or a valve near the bottom of the permanent pool. This will greatly facilitate sediment and debris removal from the bottom and its regular maintenance.

4.3.5 Trash Racks

As a practical matter, outlets should be provided with a trash rack to prevent plugging with debris and to provide for safety to the public. An example of a trash rack for a dry pond is illustrated in Figure 4.11. This example shows a rack that is sloped to facilitate cleaning and to reduce entrance flow velocities. Experience suggests that sloping of the rack at 30% to 50% above the horizontal plane seems to work quite well and permits "raking off" of floatables during operation.

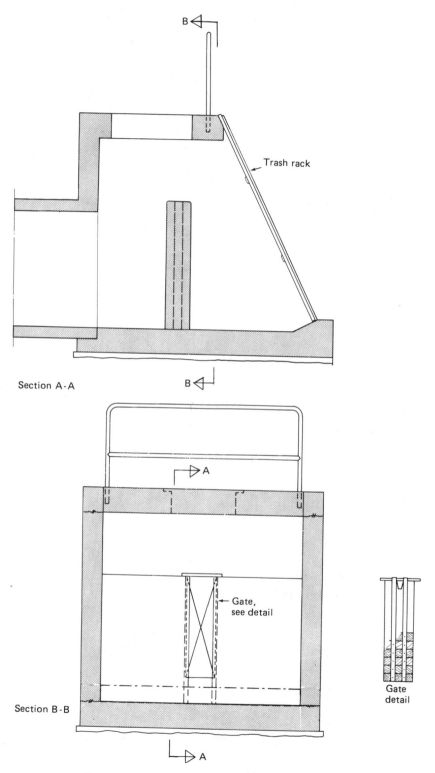

Section A-A

Section B-B

Trash rack

Gate,
see detail

Gate
detail

Figure 4.8 Outlet structure with a fixed gate control.

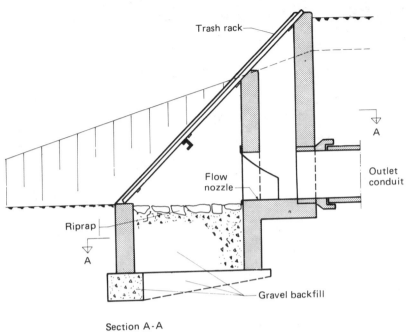

Section A-A

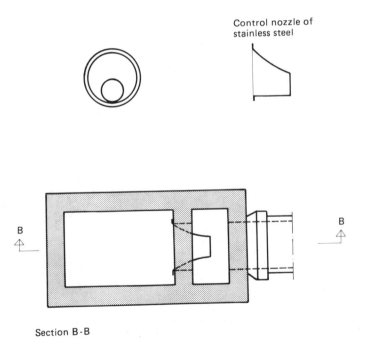

Section B-B

Figure 4.9 Outlet structure with a fixed orifice control.

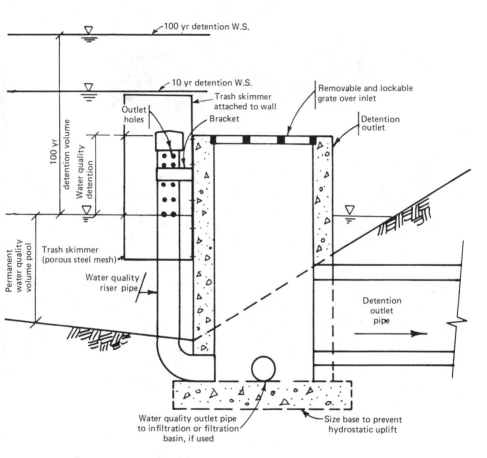

Figure 4.10 Outlet riser for a pond with a permanent pool. (After UDFCD, 1992.)

Figure 4.11   Example of a trash rack for a pond outlet.

For very small control outlets (i.e., less than 6 inches (150 mm) in diameter) the trash rack needs to have a relatively large opening. Kropp (1982) suggested that small orifice outlets be protected with a rack having a net opening of no less than 20 times the opening of the orifice. He did caution, however, to keep the spacings between openings narrower than the orifice itself. If the openings are spaced too far apart, the trash carried by stormwater can pass through the rack and plug the orifice.

For larger outlets, 24 inches (610 mm) in diameter or larger, good operational results can be obtained when the rack's net opening is no less than four times the opening of the outlet. For example, a 24-inch (610-mm) diameter outlet can be reasonably protected by a sloping trash rack having a net opening of 12.5 square feet (1.2 m²). Although this may sound large, a rack approximately 4 feet (1.25 m) on each side will provide more than adequate protection to the public and keep the outlet from plugging.

Consider the following when designing trash racks for dry ponds:

- For outlets with diameter openings of 24 inches (610 mm) or less, provide a net trash rack area that is no less than the factor recommended in Figure 4.12 times the outlet area.
- The spacing between the openings of the trash rack should be smaller than the smallest dimension of the outlet.
- For outlets 24 inches (610 mm) or more, provide a net rack area no less than four times the outlet area.
- For larger outlets, the spacing between the openings of the rack should be 6 inches (150 mm) or less to prevent a child from passing through the rack.
- Slope all racks at 30% to 50% above the horizontal to facilitate cleaning. A flat angle also permits the floating debris to "ride up" the rack as the pond level rises, thereby freeing up openings underneath.

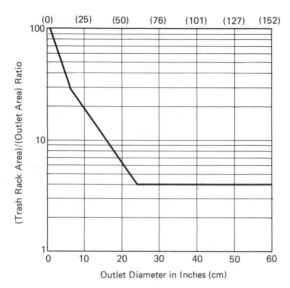

Figure 4.12 Minimum trash rack area size vs. outlet diameter. (*After UDFCD*, 1992.)

- For larger outlets, a 4- to 6-inch (100- to 150-mm) horizontal opening at the bottom of the rack will permit the smaller debris to flush through the outlet.

4.3.6 Spillway vs. Embankment Overtopping

In the 1985 report to the American Society of Civil Engineers by a task committee set up to investigate the state of the art of detention pond outlets, safety of detention outlets was particularly stressed. In addition to public safety, the committee expressed a strong concern for the protection of the detention pond dam against failure due to overtopping and due to failure at the outlet.

A detention pond behind an embankment is nothing more than a reservoir of water behind a dam. The scale may be much smaller, but the analogy holds. As a result, a breached embankment may be the cause of much more damage than would occur from flooding without the detention pond. Fortunately, many detention ponds are so small that embankment safety does not have to be an issue of great concern.

Always consider the probability of embankment failure and the circumstances under which such failure is possible when designing a detention facility. Once the overtopping flood has been identified, such as the 500-year flood, estimate the consequences of failure in light of the flooding that would occur from such a storm if there was no dam. Will the failure be rapid or will the embankment breach slowly? Will the predicted mode of failure increase the flooding damages, and to what degree? Your analysis may reveal that despite failure, flood damages would be essentially the same as those that would occur if the detention pond was not present. With this type of analysis, the designer is in a strong position to make rational and cost-effective recommendations.

An emergency spillway is always a good idea. It can be designed to protect the embankment from overtopping whenever storms larger than design storms occur or when outlets plug with debris. Clearly, a spillway designed to pass the probable maximum flood is desirable but may not be practical or possible to provide for a small urban pond. As a result, spillways for smaller ponds are often sized for less than the probable maximum flood. In those cases, the embankment can be constructed to resist sudden failure during rare and extremely large floods. One example of an attractive emergency spillway for a small detention dam is shown in Figure 4.13. Wooten et al. (1992) describe the use of *cellular concrete mats* placed on a dam face as an alternative to an emergency spillway for small dams. These cellular mats permit use of the entire dam's crest as a spillway.

An embankment overtopping analysis (described in the next section) along with incremental flooding damage analysis for floods up to the maximum probable flood can serve as a basis in setting the level of protection at each site. Under no circumstances, however, should the emergency overflow from a pond be designed to have a direct path to any buildings or other structures used for human occupancy, commerce, or industry.

Figure 4.13   An example of an emergency spillway.

4.3.7 Embankment Loss Analysis

Urban watersheds are typically small, and the amount of total time an embankment is actually overtopped is much shorter than for a large watershed. A detailed embankment loss analysis can quantify the breaching potential of an embankment for a variety of large storm events. A procedure based on the results of highway embankment overtopping studies by Chen and Anderson (1986) for the Federal Highway Administration could be used for this purpose.

Figure 4.14 shows four nomographs that can be used to estimate the soil loss rate of an overtopped bare soil embankment. Two of these provide the erosion rates for a 5-foot (1.5 m) high embankment, while the other two give correction factors for embankments under other design conditions. The procedure for estimating the erosive loss of soil is as follows:

1. Determine the height of the embankment and its soil type (i.e., cohesive or noncohesive).
2. Determine the headwater depth, h, and tailwater, t, above the embankment crest.
3. Compute t/h.
4. Using h and t/h, determine the erosion rate, E_a, from Figure 4.14 for the embankment soil type.
5. Again using Figure 4.14, determine the adjustment factors for embankment height and duration of flow.
6. Compute the erosion rate: $E = K_1 K_2 E_a$.
7. Compute the soil loss for the period the embankment is estimated to be overtopped.

The foregoing procedure may or may not provide an accurate estimate for a particular site. There are many uncertainties in its application, and it is wise to provide safety factors in design. For example, when estimating the embankment loss, you may want to assume that overtopping occurs over only a portion of the crest length.

Here are some suggestions for how to mitigate possible adverse impacts of detention pond dam overtopping whenever the emergency spillway is of less capacity than the probable maximum flood:

- Construct the embankment using erosion resistant material. For example, concrete rubble or large rock embedded in compacted clay soils on the downstream side of the dam may be able to withstand considerable overtopping for brief periods of time without sudden and catastrophic failure.

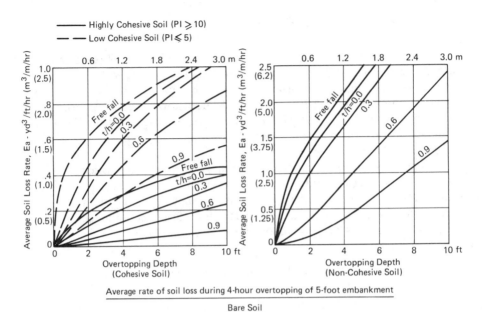

Average rate of soil loss during 4-hour overtopping of 5-foot embankment

Bare Soil

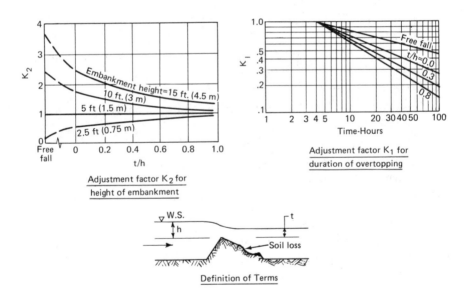

Figure 4.14 Soil erosion loss nomographs for overtopped bare soil highway embankments. *(After Chen and Anderson, 1986.)*

- Use noneroding materials on the downstream portion of the embankment such as soil cement, rollcrete, interlocking concrete elements or concrete paving.
- Design the embankment with an extra wide crest or construct a paved road on top.
- Flatten the downstream face of the dam and revegetate with native turf-forming grasses.
- Enlarge the conveyance capacity downstream of the dam.
- Excavate the pond to eliminate or reduce the height of the embankment.

4.4 OPERATION AND MAINTENANCE

If you do not plan to maintain it, do not build it. That should be the golden rule in public works. As a result, all detention ponds should have maintainability built into them. This includes good maintenance access to all parts of the ponding area for mechanized maintenance equipment. Although this suggestion may seem trivial, one of the most frequently observed deficiencies is inadequate maintenance access. Can it be built, and can it be maintained? These two questions should always be asked as the detention facilities are being designed. If the answer is no to either question, modify the design.

In this section we discuss some of the operation and maintenance considerations for detention ponds. The following topics are discussed:

- general inspection and maintenance,
- algae and aquatic plants,
- sediments,
- floating debris and pollutants,
- general housekeeping, and
- erosion.

4.4.1 General Inspection and Maintenance

The responsibility for maintenance rests with the owner of the detention pond. As part of the design, provide an operation and maintenance manual to the owner. It is a good idea for the owner to have one prepared for already existing facilities. Such a manual does not need to be complicated. It merely needs to serve as a checklist of things to look for, and to do, on a regular basis. A more detailed, but more valuable, manual could contain copies of as-built drawings for key elements of the pond, a list of replacement parts, emergency procedures in case of very large floods, names and telephone numbers of key individuals, etc. Obviously, the level of detail will vary with the size and the complexity of the installation.

At the beginning of each flood season, and after each significant storm, inspect the detention pond for damage. Pay particular attention to the embankment (i.e., dam), the outlet works, the emergency spillway, and the inlet works. Look for signs of erosion, excessive deposition of sediments, buildup of trash or debris, or any other signs of damage. Address problems immediately. What may appear to be minor damage at the time can become the weak link if another flood occurs before repairs are made.

4.4.2 Algae and Aquatic Plants

Algae and other aquatic plants will only occur in "wet" ponds, namely in ponds with a permanent water pool. Since detention ponds often receive nutrient enriched water, the possibility of them having algae and/or other aquatic plants is indeed high.

Bottom vegetation, on the other hand, occurs mostly in the shallow areas of the pond. It is thus possible to control the extent of bottom vegetation through the shaping of the pond. If it is desirable to have vegetation near the shore for aesthetics, water quality, or aquatic habitat, the pond can be made shallow near the edges. At the same time, water depths exceeding 6 feet (1.8 m) can be provided further from shore portions of the pond, thereby reducing the vegetation growth potential further from pond edges.

Although it is virtually impossible to prevent algae from growing in an urban detention pond, excessive bottom vegetation growth can be controlled through the design of the facility and by occasional harvesting. Although there are chemicals that can kill or control algae and other vegetation, their use can contaminate the receiving waters. For this reason, algae and vegetation control chemicals should be used with extreme caution.

Wherever the state wildlife or federal regulations permit consider the use of fish that eat algae and other aquatic vegetation. Their use has been occasionally successful in controlling excessive aquatic plant growth. Check with your state's game and fish personnel before deciding on their use. It may be wise to experiment first on a smaller installation to see if the fish improve the conditions in your part of the country.

Excessive algae can cause odor and aesthetic problems. Although total elimination of algae is virtually impossible, it is possible to mitigate their adverse impacts. Making the pond deeper can help in some cases, especially if the water in the pond is flushed through on a rather frequent basis. Also, the use of mechanical aerators can help mitigate the odors and reduce algae growth. If odors and excessive algae become a problem, draining the pond and cleaning out its bottom will remove some of the nutrient source entering the water column. Although not totally foolproof, this can reduce the problem until the bottom nutrients have again accumulated.

Dry detention basins should not have problems with algae growth. If, however, the basin does not drain fully, or the bottom is so flat that the bottom drains very slowly, marshy or wetland type vegetation can develop. It is not practical to mechanically mow the pond bottom when that happens, and very little routine daily maintenance can be done on the bottom of the basin. Occasionally, the entire bottom can be "mucked out" to remove excess sediment buildup, thereby cleaning the bottom every few years. If the stated goal is to reduce or to eliminate the marsh bottom conditions, then steepen the bottom slope when grading it or install subdrains to drain the bottom.

4.4.3 Sediments

Storage of runoff in basins will cause sediments to settle within them. The amount and rate of sediment deposition is a function of the source and quantity of sediments in the incoming water and their settling velocities. The rate of sediment buildup inside a basin or a pond will depend to some degree on how much the stormwater is slowed in the basin and how long the water stays in the basin.

Sediment deposition is particularly severe when land development activities are occurring in the tributary watershed. Soil erosion during the land development period, if not controlled, can quickly fill a detention pond. For this reason, it is strongly recommended that erosion control within the tributary watershed be practiced and that the detention ponds and basins be reexcavated on completion of the land development work. This practice will restore the pond's original design volume and insure that it will perform as originally designed.

The deposition of sediments in a detention basin does not occur uniformly over the bottom. The larger and heavier sediments drop out near the inlet to the pond. As the distance from the inlet increases, the bottom deposits consist of the smaller particle fraction of the sediment load. To facilitate maintenance and the removal of the deposited sediments, it is a good idea to incorporate a sediment trap near the inlet.

Removal of sediments is easiest when the pond bottom is dry. This can be scheduled during the dry season, when the pond can be drained completely. Allow sufficient time to dry the bottom soils so that mechanical excavating equipment can be used. Facilitate access for the mechanical maintenance equipment by installing access ramps that lead to the bottom of the pond. An example of such an installation is illustrated in Figure 4.15.

If it is not possible to drain or to pump the pond dry, underwater excavating techniques have to be employed. Examples of underwater excavation include hydraulic dredging or the use of a drag line or a "clam shell." Underwater excavation is much more expensive than dry excavation, a fact that needs to be recognized at the time of design. Consult with a geotechnical engineer to ascertain if the soils in the pond bottom will stabilize sufficiently,

Figure 4.15   Access ramp for maintenance equipment.

within a reasonable time after the pond is drained, to support excavation equipment. If the soils will not stabilize sufficiently, underwater excavation may be the only option.

4.4.4 Floatables

Detention pond and basin maintenance also includes the removal and disposal of floatables such as tree branches, lumber, leaves, styrofoam, litter, etc. carried to the pond by stormwater. In ponds that are designed to reduce peaks of larger storm hydrographs, the water moves rapidly through the pond and much of the floatable mass can be flushed through. In such cases, all that may be needed is an occasional debris collection and cleaning of outlet trash racks between storms.

On the other hand, floatables can be a problem for ponds (i.e., basins with a permanent pool) and for ponds and basins intended for water quality enhancement. Frequent trash pickup along the shore is needed to maintain a clean appearance. It is possible to install floating skimmers at a forebay into which the inlets empty stormwater runoff. This keeps the floatables from entering the main body of the pond, and the floatable trash is concentrated for easier removal and disposal.

4.4.5 General Housekeeping

To the public, the most important feature of any urban facility is a clean, well-maintained appearance. Because of this, it is wise to schedule frequent debris and trash removal and regular mowing of the grass around the pond and within the detention basin. The frequency of such maintenance will be governed by the specific uses of detention facilities and whether they are located close to residential or commercial areas. One cannot offer standardized guidelines for scheduling such activities, since they vary between installations and between various communities. What is important, however, is to anticipate and to budget for routine maintenance and housekeeping when new detention facilities are being installed.

REFERENCES

ASCE, *Stormwater Detention Outlet Control Structures,* Final Report of the Task Committee on the Design of Outlet Structures, American Society of Civil Engineers, New York, 1985.

BRULO, A. T., KIBLER, D. F., AND MILLER, A. C., "Evaluation of Two Stage Outlet Hydraulics," *Proceedings of the ASCE Hydraulics Division Conference on Water for Resources Development,* New York, 1984.

CHEN, Y.-H., AND ANDERSON, B. A., *Analysis of Data in Literature for Estimating Embankment Damage Due to Flood Overtopping,* Simons, Li & Associates, Inc. Report to U.S. Department of Transportation, Federal Highway Administration, DC-FHA-01, Washington, D.C., 1986.

EDWARDS, K. L., "Acceptance and/or Resistance to Detention Ponds," *Proceedings of the Conference on Stormwater Detention Facilities,* American Society of Civil Engineers, New York, 1982.

EPA, *Results of the Nationwide Urban Runoff Program,* NTIS Access Number: PB84-185552, Environmental Protection Agency, Washington, D.C., 1983.

KAMELDUSKI, D. E., AND MCCUEN, R. H., "Evaluation of Alternative Stormwater Detention Policies," *Journal of Water Resources Planning and Management Division,* Vol. 105, pp 171–86, American Society of Civil Engineers, New York, Sept. 1979.

KROPP, R. H., "Water Quality Enhancement Design Techniques," *Proceedings of the Conference on Stormwater Detention Facilities,* American Society of Civil Engineers, New York, 1982.

POERTNER, H. G, *Practices in Detention of Urban Stormwater Runoff,* American Public Works Association, Special Report Number 43, 1974.

SCHROEDER, G., *Agricultural Water Engineering,* 3rd ed., Springer-Verlag, Berlin, 1958. (In German).

STUBCHEAR, JAMES M., "Stormwater Basins in Santa Barbara County," *Proceedings of the Conference on Stormwater Detention Facilities,* American Society of Civil Engineers, New York, 1982.

UDFCD, *Urban Storm Drainage Criteria Manual,* Vol. 3 (draft), Urban Drainage and Flood Control District, Denver, 1992.

URBONAS, B. R., AND GLIDDEN, M. W., "Potential Effectiveness of Detention Policies," *Proceedings of the Second Southwest Regional Symposium on Urban Stormwater Management*, Texas A&M University, November, 1984.

U.S. BUREAU OF RECLAMATION, *Hydraulic Design of Stilling Basins and Energy Dissipators*, United States Department of Interior, Bureau of Reclamation, GPO, Washington, D.C., 1964.

U.S. BUREAU OF RECLAMATION, *Design of Small Dams*, United States Department of Interior, Bureau of Reclamation, GPO, Denver, Colo., 1973.

U.S. BUREAU OF RECLAMATION, *Design of Small Canal Structures*, United States Department of Interior, Bureau of Reclamation, GPO, Denver, Colo., 1974.

WOOTEN, R. L., POWLEDGE, G. R., and WHITESIDE, S. L., "Dams Going Safely Over the Top," *Civil Engineering*, American Society of Civil Engineers, New York, January, 1992.

5

Concrete Basins

5.1 GENERAL

Among the different types of stormwater storage facilities, concrete basins offer the greatest flexibility and are used extensively for the control of combined sewer overflow. Due to their structural nature, concrete basins can be configured into almost any geometric shape. Their main advantage is that their sides can be made near-vertical or vertical, which means that right-of-way can be minimized. Their disadvantages include poor aesthetics, high construction cost, and safety. Aesthetics and safety needs can be addressed adequately in a manner similar to what was done in the facility illustrated in Figure 4.2. Often, a concrete basin can be located in out-of-sight locations such as an industrial plant, storage yard, etc. where aesthetic concerns and safety to the general public is mitigated by the limited access to such facilities. As an alternative, concrete storage basins can be turned into underground storage vaults when site conditions so dictate.

Like most other types of storage facilities, concrete basins can be connected both in in-line and off-line to the drainage conveyance system. How they are used depends on the design objectives. Although concrete basins can be open on the top, they are most often used as buried vaults. The remainder of this section describes various flow regulating configurations that may be used in the capture, storage, and treatment of combined wastewater/stormwater flows and, for some of them, separate stormwater runoff systems.

5.2 SYSTEMATIZATION OF STORAGE BASINS FOR COMBINED SEWER SYSTEMS

Concrete storage basins for the control of combined sewer overflows can be classified into two main groups by how they are connected to the storm sewer:

- In-line storage;
- Off-line storage.

5.2.1 In-line Storage

An in-line storage basin is connected in series to the sewer. The basin is equipped with an outlet that has less hydraulic capacity than the inlet. Flows pass through the basin undetained until the inflow rate exceeds the outlet's capacity. The excess inflow is then stored within the basin until the basin is full or the inflow rate decreases.

Figure 5.1 shows a schematic representation of an in-line storage facility equipped with a spillway, which operates only when the storage volume of the basin is exceeded. The amount of treatment the inflow receives is determined, among other things, by the holding time of the water in the basin.

The advantages of in-line storage with a spillway include the following:

- one spillway;
- simple piping arrangement;
- floatables can be skimmed off at spillway;
- storage can be drained by gravity; and
- flexibility in design.

The disadvantages include:

- wide variations in outflow by gravity, and
- difficult to design to be self-cleansing.

Figure 5.2 illustrates an in-line storage where the excess inflow bypasses the basin. When the basin is full, the water in the basin backs up into an up-

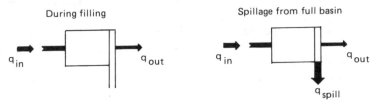

During filling   Spillage from full basin

q_{in} q_{out} q_{in} q_{out}

q_{spill}

Figure 5.1   In-line storage with a spillway. *(After ATV, 1977.)*

During filling   Spillage from full basin

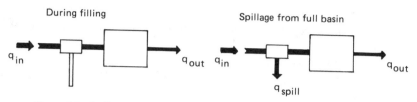

Figure 5.2   In-line storage with an upstream bypass. *(After ATV, 1977.)*

stream splitter and no additional flow can enter the storage basin. In this way, all of the smaller storms and the front end of the larger storms are intercepted. As a result, the smaller and more frequent storm runoff receives treatment. For the larger storms, the more polluted "first flush" will receive treatment, while the remainder of the runoff receives no treatment.

The advantages of in-line storage with upstream bypass include the following:

- only one, simple, splitter;
- simple piping arrangement;
- emptying of storage by gravity is likely; and
- greater flexibility in final design.

The disadvantages include:

- if storage is emptied by gravity, there is a large variation in flow;
- floatables will enter the storage basin; and
- difficult to design storage for self-cleansing.

5.2.2 Off-line Storage

An off-line storage basin is connected in parallel to the sewer pipe, whereby the dry weather flow bypasses the storage basin. During a storm, the flow depth in the sewer increases until it overflows a side channel spillway at $S1$ and it spills into the storage basin. Such an arrangement is illustrated in Figure 5.3, which also includes an overflow spillway at $S2$. Flows exceeding the storage basin's capacity spill out of the basin via this spillway.

During filling   Spillage from full basin

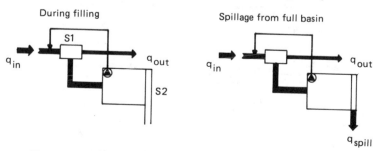

Figure 5.3   Off-line storage with a spillway. *(After ATV, 1977.)*

> The advantages of off-line storage with a spillway include the following:
> - small head loss in the parallel pipe;
> - flow in downstream storm sewer varies less than in a series arrangement;
> - floatables can be skimmed off at the spillway; and
> - the basin is dry during dry weather periods.
>
> The disadvantages include:
> - pipe layout is more complex than in series connection; and
> - pumping of the basin is often required to empty.

Figure 5.4 illustrates an off-line storage basin without a spillway. During storm runoff, when the flow exceeds a preselected level, it spills over a side channel spillway $S1$ into the storage basin. The inflow into the storage facility continues until the storage basin is full, or the flow level at $S1$ drops below the side channel spillway's crest. When the basin is full, the water level in the basin is at the same elevation as in the bypass pipe. As a result, the inflow can no longer enter the basin and bypasses it through $S2$, usually receiving no treatment.

> The advantages of off-line storage without a spillway include the following:
> - minimum head loss in the bypass sewer;
> - less flow variation in the bypass sewer;
> - no water in the basin during dry weather flow periods.
>
> The disadvantages include:
> - more complex piping arrangement is required;
> - will probably require pumping to empty;
> - floatables likely to spill out of the system; and
> - hydraulics of side channel spillways is complicated.

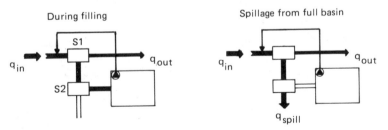

Figure 5.4   Off-line storage basin without a spillway. *(After ATV, 1977.)*

5.2.3 In-line and Off-line Combinations

The in-line and the off-line storage arrangements can be combined to work together and function as a single unit. Here, one basin functions as an in-line basin and the other as an off-line basin. By combining these into a composite unit, the advantages of both can be utilized.

Figure 5.5 shows a composite unit connected in series with the sewer system. Under dry weather conditions and during small storms, only the in-line unit is utilized. During larger storms, the in-line basin fills to capacity and the excess flow is diverted through $S1$ into the off-line basin. When both basins are full, any additional runoff then spills through $S2$ out of the second basin.

The idea behind this somewhat complex arrangement is to trap the strongest polluted stormwater in the first basin and to provide some treatment for the remainder of storm runoff. Even in the case where the capacity of the second basin is exceeded, some purification of the stormwater is expected to occur by virtue of it being detained in storage.

An arrangement utilizing a composite unit connected in parallel is illustrated in Figure 5.6. In this arrangement, the dry weather flow bypasses both storage basins. When the flow reaches a preset rate, the excess is diverted into the first basin through a side channel spillway, $S1$. The first basin does not have a spillway, and when it is full, water backs up and is diverted to the second basin through $S2$. When the second basin fills up, the excess flow then spills out of the system through $S3$.

The advantages of the parallel connection are very similar to the ones for the series arrangement, except the water stored in the first basin is assured treatment in a downstream treatment plant. One added benefit is that a more uniform flow rate to the plant is achieved. In areas where the first flush is demonstrated to contain the strongest concentrations of pollutants, the composite arrangement, whether connected in series or parallel, can achieve greater treatment efficiencies than a single storage system. However, this improved treatment is achieved by having a more complex and possibly more expensive installation.

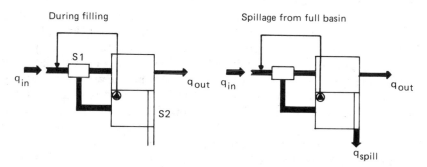

Figure 5.5 Combination storage connected in series.

During filling   Spillage from full basin

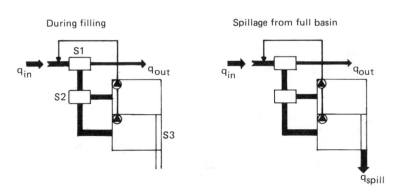

Figure 5.6 Combination storage connected in parallel.

5.2.4 In-line or Off-line Storage?

The arrangements described in this section are primarily intended for use in a combined sewer system with a wastewater treatment plant located downstream in the system. Also, most of the storage arrangements described so far can also be used for flow equalization. As such, they can reduce flow peaks to match the conveyance or treatment capacity of the downstream system.

Some treatment of separate stormwater runoff can be achieved, however, without additional downstream treatment facilities if an in-line system is employed. When storage is the only source of treatment, the operation and maintenance activities will increase, consistent with the treatment levels.

In a combined sewer system, whether an in-line or an off-line facility should be used will depend on whether the system will experience a strong first flush. In combined sewers and urban areas with flat terrain, the accumulation of pollutants in storm sewers may be the prime reason for the observed first flush. Munz (1977) observed that the first flush is strongest if the runoff flow time is less than 10 minutes. Also, according to Munz (1977), the most pronounced flushing effect in a storm sewer occurs when pipes have dry weather flow velocities between 1.5 and 2.5 feet per second (0.5 and 0.8 m/s). When the velocities are higher, very little accumulation of pollutants occurs in the storm sewer. With lower velocities, the flushing process appears to be inefficient, and flushing is not limited to the beginning of the runoff.

Also, more significantly polluted first flush is generally associated with smaller watersheds, where the mixing of flows from large areas is not present.

First flush in separate storm sewers is not always observable. As more and more data, such as that collected during the Nationwide Urban Runoff Program (EPA, 1983) become available, it seems that a strongly polluted first flush may be found in some urban centers and not in others.

Beside trapping the first flush of storm runoff, the selection of the storage system needs to consider the capacity of the downstream conveyance system, the presence and capacity of a treatment plant, and the size and nature of the watershed downstream of the storage. For instance, if the watershed between the storage facility and the treatment plant contributes much stormwater, the pollutants are best trapped and held in a storage facility which is connected in parallel. If this is not done, the effects of detention will be lost through dilution and possible spilling into the downstream system. Table 5.1 compares the conditions for the selection of a storage system arrangement for the purpose of trapping the first flush.

5.3 TECHNICAL CONFIGURATION

The physical configuration of a concrete storage basin is largely determined by site conditions. For instance, the vertical fall in the sewer system will determine if the basins will be drained by gravity or if pumping will have to be used. Also, site geometry will dictate how the installation is configured in the horizontal plan. This can be especially critical in dense urban areas where right-of-way is very limited. Fortunately, concrete storage tanks can be easily configured into any desired horizontal plan.

Concrete storage basins can be built with an open or a closed top; however, the closed basin is used almost exclusively in densely urbanized areas. A closed basin has advantages for safety and odor control, especially in combined sewer systems. Only at the treatment plant, or in isolated and fully fenced areas, is an open basin a viable option in a combined sewer system.

TABLE 5.1   Conditions for Trapping of the First Flush

Flow Time in the Watershed	
<10 min	good
10–20 min	average
>20 min	poor

Dry Weather Flow Velocity in Sewer	
<1.5 ft/sec (<0.5 m/s)	average
1.5–2.5 ft/sec (0.5–0.8 m/s)	good
>2.5 ft/sec (>0.8 m/s)	average

Watershed Condition Downstream of Storage	
No addition of runoff downstream	good
Addition of stormwater downstream:	
Parallel connection	average
Series connection	poor

After Munz, 1977.

5.3.1 Vertical Considerations

Refer to Figure 5.7 and examine some of the more important aspects of a storage basin's vertical configuration.

According to Koral and Saatci (1976), there are certain height restrictions for a cost-effective installation of concrete detention vaults. For example, the elevation difference between the outlet and the maximum storage level should be at least 7.5 to 11 feet (2.3 to 3.4 m), where the lesser depth is intended for smaller storage basins. If the suggested depths are not achieved, the basins will require excessive horizontal surface area, be more expensive to build, have less efficient flow conditions, have limited accessibility for cleaning, etc. Figure 5.8 shows the optimum vertical dimensions that were recommended by Koral and Saatci (1976).

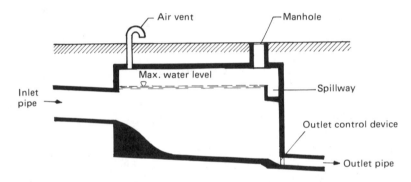

Figure 5.7   Vertical configuration of a concrete basin. *(After ATV, 1977.)*

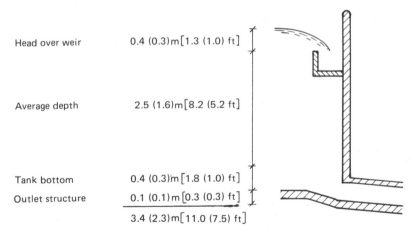

Head over weir	0.4 (0.3)m [1.3 (1.0) ft]
Average depth	2.5 (1.6)m [8.2 (5.2 ft]
Tank bottom	0.4 (0.3)m [1.8 (1.0) ft]
Outlet structure	0.1 (0.1)m [0.3 (0.3) ft]
	3.4 (2.3)m [11.0 (7.5) ft]

Figure 5.8 Minimum vertical dimensions for concrete detention tanks. *(After Koral and Saatci, 1976.)*

5.3.2 Horizontal Plan

Obviously, the area that the storage facility will occupy will depend, among other things, on the height limitations and right-of-way availability. A rectangular shape offers certain cost and maintenance advantages. Also, experience suggests that flat-bottomed basins should have their width equal to one-half to two-thirds of the length of the basin. For basins with sloping parallel grooves in the bottom, the length is determined by the distance over which the grooves can be effectively flushed clean. This is further discussed in Section 5.3.5.

Site availability, however, will sometimes dictate a variation from a standard rectangular plan. It may be necessary to design irregularly shaped basins, especially in densely populated areas. In such cases, you can expect construction and basin cleaning costs to be higher.

Round and octagonal basins can be more expensive to build; however, they offer self-cleansing possibilities often lacking in other configurations. As illustrated in Figure 5.9, by arranging the inflow tangentially and the outlet at the center, the tank can be made virtually self-cleansing.

5.3.3 Inlet Pipe

The manner by which wastewater is fed into a storage basin depends on whether the basin is in series or in parallel with the sewer. When in series, all

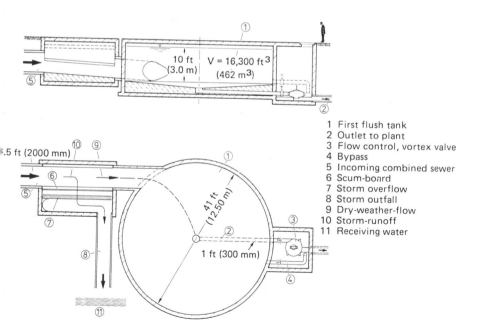

1 First flush tank
2 Outlet to plant
3 Flow control, vortex valve
4 Bypass
5 Incoming combined sewer
6 Scum-board
7 Storm overflow
8 Storm outfall
9 Dry-weather-flow
10 Storm-runoff
11 Receiving water

Figure 5.9 Round concrete basin. *(By Umwelt and Fluidtechnik GmbH, West Germany.)*

of the stormwater enters the storage basin. As a result, no separate inlet structures are needed. To gain additional storage capacity, it is advantageous to let
the water rise in the basin until it backs up into the inlet. If this is the intended
design, however, be sure that the water does not back up into nearby basements. When there is a risk of water backing up into basements, investigate
the possibility of collecting the wastewater from affected basements in a separate sanitary sewer that bypasses the storage basin.

When the basin is filled by two or more sewers coming from different
directions, combine the sewers into a single inlet pipe. If, however, multiple
inlets are necessary, then pay particular attention to the flow patterns in the
basin to insure that no unusual "dead zones" or adverse flow conditions are
created.

When the storage basin is connected in parallel, the inflow takes place
through a separate inlet structure. This structure consists of a side channel
overflow or spillway designed to function only after a predetermined flow in
the sewer is exceeded. Figure 5.10 shows one schematic example of a side
channel overflow. For a more detailed description of the analysis and design of
side channel spill structures, refer to advanced open channel design textbooks
or special literature.

5.3.4 Inflow Arrangements

Before designing an inflow structure for a storage basin, determine if

1. the basin is to provide removal of solids before the excess flow is permitted to spill to the receiving waters, or
2. the basin is going to be without a spillway.

In the first case, the inflow must be designed to enter the basin without
resuspending the settled solids. This will require energy dissipation and rapid

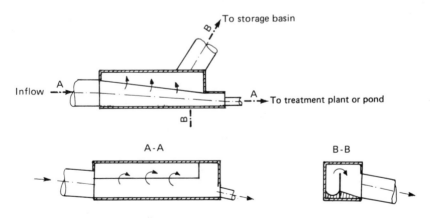

Figure 5.10   An example of a side channel overflow.

Plan   Vertical section

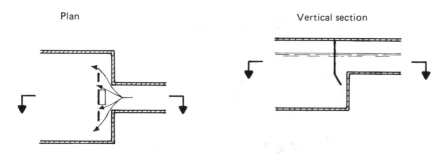

Figure 5.11   Baffle arrangement at the inlet. *(After Koral and Saatci, 1976.)*

diffusion of the inflow plume. Figure 5.11 contains an example of how the inflow plume can be diffused quickly through the use of baffles. When designing
such baffles, be careful not to create a rotating flow motion within the basin
itself.

For basins without spillways, settling of solids on the basin floor should
be avoided. In fact, the resuspension of solids into the water column facilitates
the cleaning of the storage basin. To achieve this, the inlet is designed to make
the installation as self-cleansing as possible.

To keep the sediments suspended, the energy of the inflow water can be
used to clean the basin's floor. This can be done by arranging the inlet(s) to
create as much circular flow and turbulence in the basin as possible. First, try
to maintain the inlet pipe elevation as high as possible so the water can accelerate into the basin. Next, locate the inlet(s) and the outlet tangentially to
maintain rotational flow in the basin, as in Figure 5.12.

To preserve kinetic energy of the inflow so that it can be transferred to
rotational flow, the inlet can be equipped with a parabolic profile. The water is
fed into the basin by a groove in the upstream end of the basin (see Figure
5.13) or by a sloping inlet pipe, as in Figure 5.14.

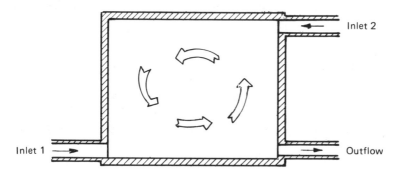

Figure 5.12   Placement of inlets and outlet to promote rotational flow in basin.
(After Malpricht, 1973.)

Figure 5.13   Example of inlet groove in a storage basin.

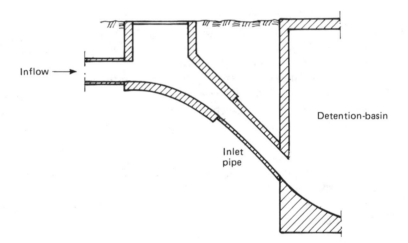

Figure 5.14   Inlet pipe profile for resuspension of solids. *(After Malpricht, 1973.)*

5.3.5 Basin Bottom Configuration

One has to expect that some sand, silts, and sludge will settle out in the basin. To expedite cleaning, the bottom must be carefully designed and constructed. Typically, we find three basic configurations that help to achieve this:

- flat bottoms,
- bottoms with multiple parallel grooves, and
- bottoms with a single continuous groove.

Flat Bottoms.   Of all the basin bottom configurations, the flat bottom is, by far, the simplest and least costly to build. Flat bottoms also are easiest to clean and best for access to all parts of the basin. On the other hand, flat bottoms do not lend themselves as readily as the other two types to automated cleaning. Figure 5.15 shows a concrete storage basin with a flat bottom.

To permit easy access to all parts of the basin for maintenance, the bottom should be sloped no more than 10%. The lower limit for this slope is 3% which is needed for good drainage of the basin floor.

Basins connected in series with the sewer are usually equipped with a bottom groove (i.e., trickle flow channel) to convey the dry weather flows. The hydraulic capacity of this groove has to be in balance with the outlet capacity. Only when the outlet capacity is exceeded, the water should spill out of the groove onto the basin floor. A low flow groove can also be used in basins connected in parallel to the storm sewer. Even in a parallel arrangement, it helps to guide the low flow and the sediments it carries directly to the outlet.

A simple way to build a low flow groove is to use sanitary sewer pipe halves, as shown in Figures 5.16 and 5.17. These pipe halves are grouted into a precast slot on the basin floor, taking care not to create sharp edges or corners. The groove itself may be located in the center or at one of the edges of the basin, as shown in Figure 5.18.

Round and octagonal basins are, almost without exception, constructed with a flat, cone-shaped bottom. Here, the bottom slopes toward the center, where an outlet is located. The dry weather flow follows a parabolic path, as illustrated in Figure 5.9 to the central outlet. This arrangement provides little interference with the circular flow within the basin.

Bottoms With Parallel Grooves.   To facilitate automatic cleaning, the basin's bottom is sometimes equipped with a number of parallel longitudinal grooves. Each of the grooves is cleaned separately by the use of flushing water. Clearly, this bottom design is more expensive to build than a flat

Figure 5.15   Concrete basin with a flat bottom.

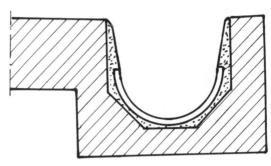

Figure 5.16   Low flow groove configuration. *(After Malpricht, 1973.)*

Figure 5.17   Bottom groove constructed of pipe halves.

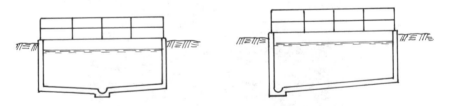

Figure 5.18   Possible low flow groove locations.

bottom. In addition, it is more difficult for maintenance personnel to move around a grooved bottom. An example of a basin with parallel longitudinal grooves is shown in Figure 5.19. Three different configurations of groove design are illustrated in Figure 5.20.

Originally, the purpose for the installation of parallel grooves in a

Figure 5.19   Bottom with parallel longitudinal grooves.

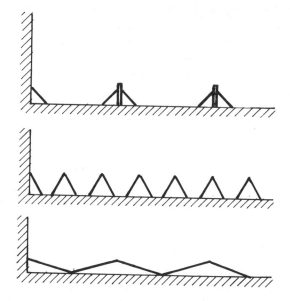

Figure 5.20   Three configurations of basin bottom grooves. *(After Koral and Saatci, 1976.)*

storage basin floor was to make the bottom self-cleansing as it empties. Experience has shown, however, that the stored water does not accelerate sufficiently to achieve adequate velocities to flush away the deposits. As a result, the bottom has to be cleaned occasionally during the dry weather periods. Cleaning is accomplished by flushing through the outlet using sediment-free water, usually one groove at a time. For this reason, the grooves need to slope at least 3% to 5% toward the outlet; the steeper the slope, the more effective the flushing.

Bottoms With a Single Continuous Groove. If properly designed, a basin with a single continuous groove can be totally self-flushing during the dry weather flow periods. In this design, the bottom has one continuously sloping groove between the inlet and the outlet. Figure 5.21 illustrates this concept, while Figure 5.22 is a photograph of an actual installation. This concept was introduced in Switzerland by Koral and Saatci (1976).

To achieve reasonable flushing velocities, the longitudinal slope has to be no less than 2%. The slope has to be increased in each U-turn to compensate for the energy loss at each bend. This means that the total vertical fall between the inlet and the outlet can become quite large. As a result, this type of a bottom is practical only for relatively small basins with volumes not exceeding 20,000 cubic feet (600 m³).

Figure 5.23 illustrates examples of some common groove configurations. Basins with this type of bottom are more costly to build than basins with flat bottoms. To reduce costs, prefabricated groove elements have been introduced in Switzerland. These elements can be incorporated into designs as an alternate, and the bidding process can demonstrate which construction technique is most economical at any given site.

Based on the experience gained in Switzerland, Koral and Saatci (1976) compiled the following set of practical recommendations for the design of basins equipped with a continuous low flow groove:

- Dry weather flow velocity in the groove should be no less than 2.3 feet per second (0.7 m/s).
- The depth of dry weather flow should be no less than 1.2 inches (3 cm).
- Maintain side slopes of the groove between 1:1 and 1.4:1.
- The head loss at each 180-degree turn is estimated at 0.4 to 0.8 inch (1 to 2 cm).

5.3.6 Outlet Structure

The outlet structure, in combination with the storage capacity, affects the size and nature of downstream facilities. Namely, the size of sewers, pumps, treatment tanks, etc. depend, to a large degree, on how the outlet and storage are configured.

Often, it is desirable to maintain the outflow constant. This is not easy to accomplish, since most outlet controls exhibit a linear logarithmic relationship between the headwater depth and the discharge. Even when the basin is emptied by a pump, the pumping efficiency can vary with the submergence of the pump.

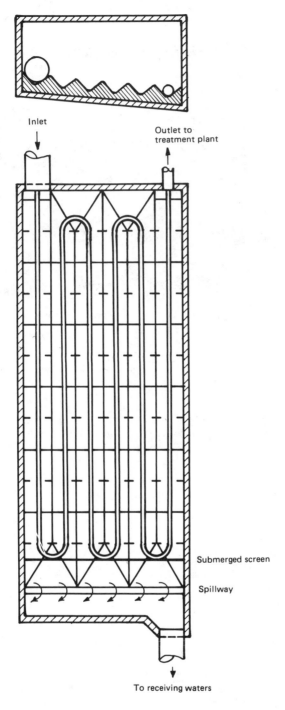

Inlet

Outlet to
treatment plant

Submerged screen

Spillway

To receiving waters

Figure 5.21 Bottom design with a single continuous groove. *(After Koral and Saatci, 1976.)*

Figure 5.22   Storage basin with a single continuous groove.

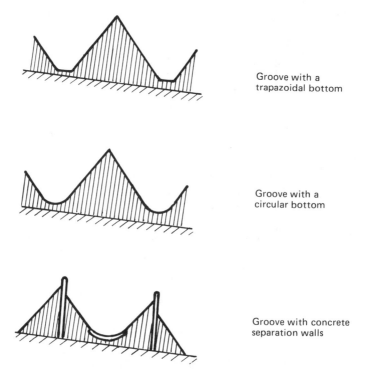

Groove with a
trapazoidal bottom

Groove with a
circular bottom

Groove with concrete
separation walls

Figure 5.23   Examples of basin bottom groove. *(After Koral and Saacti, 1976.)*

To reduce sediment buildup on the basin floor, it is advisable to reduce the period of time the water is out of the bottom groove and on the basin floor. Unnecessary shallow ponding behind the outlet also increases sediment deposition and the maintenance frequency of the facility. Depressing the outlet into the basin floor approximately 4 to 8 inches (0.1 to 0.2 m) (see Figure 5.8) can significantly reduce these types of problems.

The outflow from a storage basin can be controlled in several ways, including the use of:

- a fixed outlet orifice or nozzle,
- a choked outlet pipe,
- adjustable gates,
- pumps, and
- special flow regulators.

Because the outlet plays such a significant role in the detention process, it deserves special attention. As a result, Part 2 of this book is dedicated to this topic.

5.3.7 Spillways and Emergency Outlets

In addition to the operational outlet, concrete storage basins are typically equipped with an emergency outlet, which begins to operate when the basin is full. An emergency outlet can be a large pipe or a spillway. If the downstream sewer has excess capacity, the spilled water can be routed to it; otherwise the spilled water is conveyed, untreated, to the receiving waters.

To prevent floatables from discharging over the spillway, the spillway can be equipped with a skimmer. The skimmer is a separate structure located just upstream of the spillway, as shown in Figure 5.24.

The spillway in the storage basin should be located at the side opposite from the outlet, because the floatables often collect near the outlet. By keeping the spillway away from the outlet, the chances for floatables rising between the skimmer and the weir as the basin fills are reduced.

The emergency outlet has to be able to handle all of the incoming flow. Thus, the spillway is sized to pass the maximum inflow, without taking into account the capacity of the main outlet. The spillway's design capacity has to anticipate the possibility that the main outlet may become clogged or may have to be taken out of operation for system maintenance.

5.4 SUPPLEMENTAL PROVISIONS

When installing underground detention storage, provisions need to be made for the installation of electricity, ventilation, and cleaning water. These are needed for the operation, cleaning, and maintenance of the storage basin and its appurtenances.

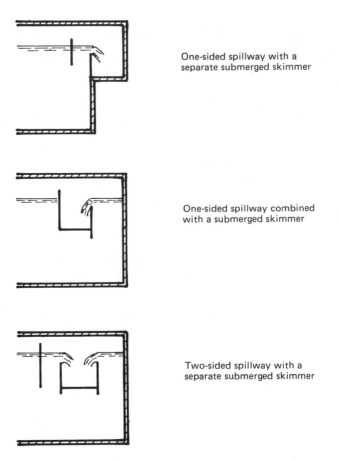

One-sided spillway with a
separate submerged skimmer

One-sided spillway combined
with a submerged skimmer

Two-sided spillway with a
separate submerged skimmer

Figure 5.24 Three examples of skimmer arrangement at a spillway. *(After Koral and Saacti, 1976.)*

5.4.1 Electrical Equipment

Electric power is needed for lighting and for the operation of pumps, gates, and other mechanical equipment. All electrical equipment has to be corrosion resistant, flood-proof, and explosion-proof. The latter is because methane gases have been shown to accumulate inside an underground storage basin in combined storm sewer systems.

Light fixtures inside the basin should be located to permit easy access for replacement. Light fixtures on walls are easier to access than on the ceiling. The circuit breakers and switches should, however, be located outside of the detention basin vault. When possible, all electrical equipment, except the lights, should be located in a special ventilated and heated room. In small installations, this can be a freestanding switch box as shown in Figure 5.25.

Figure 5.25   Freestanding electrical switch box.

5.4.2 Ventilation

It is very important to provide effective ventilation for underground detention. Experience suggests that good ventilation is accomplished when four- to six-fold exchanges of air per hour are achieved. Although the inflow and outflow pipes can provide some ventilation of the basin, their contribution is unreliable and should not be considered in the design. Also, the ventilation openings should be designed to prevent air from being trapped between the basin ceiling and the water surface.

The size of the vent openings will depend on the basin location, wind conditions, and ventilating arrangement. To achieve the desired air exchange rate, the openings should be sized for the following maximum air flow velocities:

0.8 feet per second (0.25 m/s) in wind-sheltered locations,

1.6 feet per second (0.50 m/s) in reasonably windy locations, and

2.5 feet per second (0.75 m/s) when a chimney effect is provided.

5.4.3 Cleaning Water

It is advisable to make provisions for fresh water to wash down the storage basin walls, skimmers, weirs, etc. and to flush out the deposits that accumulate on the bottom. The most common sources for this water are

- municipal water systems,
- temporary connection to fire hydrants,

- pumping from a nearby stream, pond, or lake,
- water wells, and
- water trucks.

The selection of the water supply will depend on what is most readily available or practical. For large installations, permanent water supply installations are preferable. An internal water distribution system is handy and provides easy access to all parts of the basin, as seen in Figure 5.26. When connecting to a water system, be sure to install backflow prevention valves with antisiphon devices. Backflow into a public or domestic water supply system is not acceptable and should never be permitted to occur. Be sure to also provide antisiphon devices when using nearby fire hydrants, water wells, streams, lakes, etc. as a source of cleaning water.

5.5 OPERATION AND MAINTENANCE

The concrete storage basin, especially if it is underground, will be subjected to extremely harsh operating conditions. It will be subjected to

- high humidity,
- organic sludge deposits,
- corrosive gases,

Figure 5.26 Cleaning water system in a basin.

- intermittent operation, and
- microbe and fungal attack.

Some of the operational problems can be mitigated by appropriate design. However, regular inspection and maintenance have to be provided if satisfactory function is to be maintained. The designer can facilitate maintenance, however, by incorporating labor-saving devices into the installation.

5.5.1 Manholes and Access Openings

All covered storage basins need access openings for maintenance personnel and equipment. For larger basins, a permanent stairway, as seen in Figure 5.27, can be provided. For smaller installations, a permanently installed ladder can be used, but that option is not as convenient, or as safe, as a stairway. If possible, personnel access should be from an above-ground building, as in Figure 5.28, which can also house all of the electrical controls and the valves for the cleaning water system.

Access openings should also be provided for the purpose of moving cleaning and maintenance equipment and materials in and out of the basin. One of the openings should be located directly above the outlet for cleaning when the basin is full and the outlet is clogged.

In addition to providing maintenance access, the same openings can also be used for ventilation and to admit daylight into the basin. When the openings permit sufficient daylight into the basin, electric lighting may not be necessary.

Figure 5.27   Access stairway for maintenance personnel.

Figure 5.28   Access building containing electric controls.

5.5.2 Inspection Access

It is advisable to provide separate inspection walkways inside large storage basins. These make the inspection of a basin more comfortable and facilitate more frequent visits. Two examples of how such walkways can be arranged inside of a basin are shown in Figure 5.29. To reduce costs, the use of the emergency spillway for an inspection walkway is possible. However, access will not be feasible when the spillway operates. An example of this type of an arrangement is shown in Figure 5.30.

5.5.3 Regular Inspection

A routine inspection schedule is a precondition for satisfactory operation of the storage basin. The frequency of inspection will vary with the complexity of the installation and whether or not it contains mechanical equip-

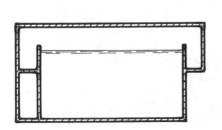
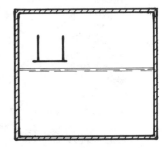

Figure 5.29   Two examples of inspection walkways. *(After Koral and Saatci, 1976.)*

Figure 5.30   Emergency spillway as an inspection walkway.

ment. In addition, inspection of the basin after each storm will reveal if the cleaning of clogged outlets or the removal of unusual accumulations of deposits is needed. Keeping a log of all inspections including dates, times, names of inspectors, and findings can help identify long-term trends and prevent major problems.

The inspector should attend to the following during each visit:

- Check electrical parts.
- Test operation of pumps.
- Check outlets for clogging.
- Check for sludge deposits.
- Inspect the water distribution system.
- Examine measuring devices.
- Look for excessive condensation.
- Look for corrosion damage.
- Look for signs of early damage or deterioration.

5.5.4 Cleaning of Basins

Because there will be sedimentation inside a concrete storage basin, it will need occasional cleaning. Proper design can facilitate this task and, in some cases, automate it. Nevertheless, supplemental manual cleaning will always be needed regardless of the design used.

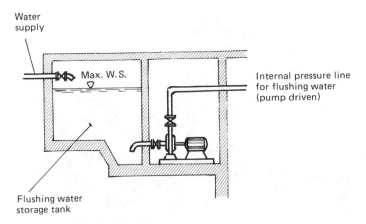

Water
supply

Max. W.S.

Internal pressure line
for flushing water
(pump driven)

Flushing water
storage tank

Figure 5.31   Flushing water storage tank. *(After Malpricht, 1973.)*

Flushing of Flat Bottoms.   Whenever the storage basins with flat bottoms have to be flushed with water, proper design of the installation will significantly ease this task. Provide a water supply with sufficient pressure to do
the job. Also, the bottom has to be properly sloped, as described earlier.

Flushing efficiency is directly related to the energy of the available
water. The pressure in a municipal water system can reach 80 pounds per
square inch. However, it often is significantly lower, and in those cases it will
be necessary to install a booster pump. The pump is usually connected to a
flushing water tank, as illustrated in Figure 5.31. Such a tank insures that the
municipal water system will not be overloaded when the pump operates. Also,
the air gap between the water inlet and the stored water insures that the stored
water will not siphon back into the municipal system.

Flushing Bottoms with Parallel Grooves.   Flushing of grooves is achieved
by running a large quantity of water in a short period of time. This rapid
application of water carries away the accumulated deposits. Obviously, the
longer the groove, the more water will be needed, so be sure to account for
this during design. Both clean water or stormwater can be used for flushing of
the grooves.

To provide this shock load of flushing water, the storage basin needs to
be equipped with special flushing tanks, which are designed to feed the water
to each groove separately. The outflow rate is regulated with gates or by the
tilting of the tank. These storage tanks can be either fixed or movable; the
latter is illustrated in Figure 5.32.

It is also possible in some cases to use the inlet pipe to store flushing
water. This is done by temporarily damming up the pipe and then rapidly

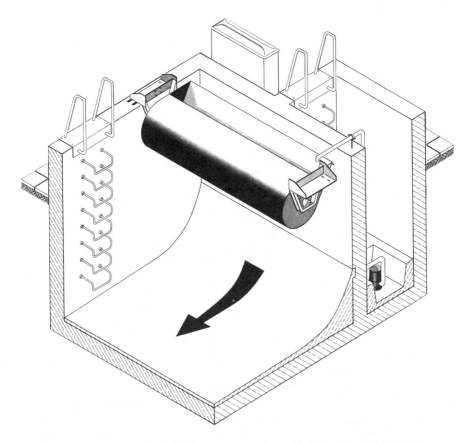

Figure 5.32   A movable flushing water container. *(By Umvelt und Fluidtechnik GmbH, West Germany.)*

releasing the water. However, when using this technique, be sure that the backed-up water does not enter upstream basements.

Cleaning with Scrapers.   When flushing with water will not remove the deposits, the use of mechanical scrapers can get the job done. This solution is expensive and is only viable when the bottom configuration can accept such equipment. The use of bottom scrapers is most common at pumping stations and at sewage treatment plants. (See Figure 5.33.)

Cleaning with Mobile Cleaning Equipment.   In certain cases, attempts have been made to clean large storage basins having flat bottoms with small mobile cleaning units. However, this technique has not yet gained wide acceptance for the cleaning of underground basins. It is, however, in wide use for the cleaning of large, above-ground installations.

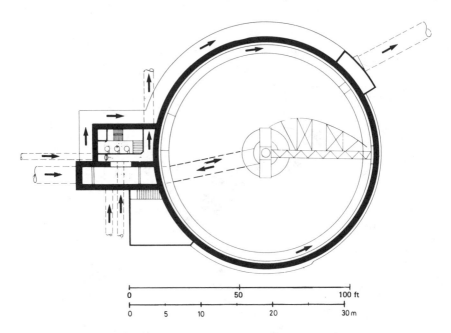

Figure 5.33   Storage basin with a mechanical bottom scraper. *(After Larsen, 1978.)*

5.5.5 Water Level Record

It is essential to record water levels in the basin to provide an operational record and future design and maintenance information. This can be done by installing a water level recorder. To calibrate and to verify the operation of the recording devices, a graduated measuring rod should be installed in a location that is clearly visible and accessible when the basin is full.

REFERENCES

ATV, *Guidelines For Dimensions, Configuration and Operation of Rain Detention Basins,* Arbeitsblatt A 117, 1977. (In German)

ATV, *Guidelines For Dimensions and Configuration of Rain Relief Installations in Mixed Water Canals,* Arbeitsblatt A 128, Second Edition, 1978. (In German)

BAYERISCHES LANDESAMT FUR WASSERWIRTSCHAFT, *Planning Aids for the Configuration of Rain Overflow Basins,* Munich, 1978. (In German)

BROMBACH, H., "Model Studies of the Self-Cleaning Behavior of Rain Overflow Basins," Wasser und Boden No. 2, 1979. (In German)

DODSON, K., AND LINDBLOM, *Evaluation of Storm Standby Tanks,* Columbus, Ohio, EPA 11020 FAL 03/71, 1971.

EIDGENOSSISCHES AMT FUR UMWELTSCHUTZ, *High Water Relief and Rain Overflow Basins,* 1977. (In German)

EPA, *Results of the Nationwide Urban Runoff Program,* Final Report, U.S. Environmental Protection Agency, 1983.

HEDLEY, D., AND LOCKLEY, J. C., "Use of Retention Tanks on Sewerage Systems: A Five Year Assessment," Water Pollution Control, 1978.

INTERNATIONALE GEWASSERSCHUTZKOMMISION FUR DEN BODENSEE, *Rain Relief Installations, Dimensions and Configuration,* Report No. 14, 1973. (In German)

KALINKA, G., "Use and Experience With Cleaning Equipment for Rain Basins," Wasser und Boden No. 11, 1979. (In German)

KORAL, J., AND SAATCI, C., "Self-Cleaning Rain Overflow Basins With Snake Grooves," Wasserwirthschaft No. 10, 1974. (In German)

KORAL, J., AND SAATCI, C., *Rain Overflow and Rain Detention Basins,* Second Edition, Zurich, 1976. (In German)

KRAUTH, K., "Recipient Relief by Treating Rain Water in Rain Water Overflow Basins," Wasserwirtschaft No. 2, 1973. (In German)

KROPF, A. "Detention Basins And Water Clarification Plants," Scheizerische Bauzeitung No. 18. 1957. (In German)

LARSEN, E., "Open and Closed Basins in Combined Systems," Seminar om Utjevningsbassenger, Marsta, 1978. (In Danish)

MALPRICHT, E. Construction and Operation of Dentention Basins," Korrespondenz Abwasser No. 5, 1973. (In German)

MASSACHUSETTS, COMMONWEALTH OF, METROPOLITAN DISTRICT COMMISSION, *Cottage Farm Combined Sewer Detention and Chlorination Station,* Cambridge, Mass., EPA-600/2-77-46, 1976.

MILWAUKEE, CITY OF, AND CONSOER TOWNSEND AND ASSOCIATES, *Detention Tank For Combined Sewer Overflow, Demonstration Project,* Milwaukee, Wis., EPA-600/2-75-071, 1975.

MUNZ. W., "Dimensions of Storm Water Basins," Gas-Wasser-Abwasser No. 3, 1975. (In German)

MUNZ, W., "Storm Basins and Stormwater Detention," Wasser/Abwasser No. 1, 1974. (In German)

MUNZ, W., "Storm Basins and Storm Water Detention," Wasser/Abwasser No. 9 and 11, 1973. (In German)

MUNZ, W., "Storm Water Overflows With and Without Detention Basins," Eidg. Anstalt fur Wasserversorgung, Abwasserreinigung & Gewasserschutz, Publ. No. 645, Zurich 1977. (In German)

NASSAU, K., "Stormwater Overflow Basins; Construction, Operation and Cost Aspects," Gwf-Wasser/Abwasser No. 2, 1978. (In German)

UMVELT UND FLUIDTECHNIK GMBH, Bad Mergenlheim, Germany, Product Information.

6

Storage in Sewer Networks

6.1 GENERAL

Some of the existing combined wastewater-stormwater sewers are large enough to handle runoff from relatively large intensity storms without a surcharge in the system. As an example, a sewer designed for a five-year storm is expected to reach, or exceed, its capacity on the average once every five years. For storms that produce less runoff than the design storm and may account for more than 95% of all of the rainstorms, the combined sewer has excess capacity. This excess can be used to temporarily detain storm runoff.

To utilize this excess capacity for detention, real-time control (RTC) of the system is required. This is done through the use of flow regulators, rainfall measurement, and flow sensors in combination with the predictions of runoff as the storm is occurring. Torno et. al. (1985) compiled several papers that discuss the state-of-the-art technology of real time control in combined storm sewers. This is an excellent reference that should be studied by anyone interested in this topic.

6.2 VARIOUS FLOW AND STORAGE REGULATORS

Utilization of available storage volume in a sewer requires flow regulators inside a storm sewer. In-line regulators permit controlled storage of stormwater in the sewer system and may be

- fixed type,
- movable type, or
- patented, special-purpose type.

The *fixed type* regulators include installations that result in a permanent increase in depth or pressure level in the pipe. Examples of this would be a raised spillway crest or a constricted section of the sewer. This is feasible only where storm sewer surcharging is acceptable and will not cause the storm flows to surface above ground or back up into basements.

Movable type of regulators encompass a wide variety of devices that can vary the release rate and the actual volume being stored on an as-needed basis. The regulator is often a remote controlled valve, gate, inflatable weir, etc. that controls the water level or pressure in the sewer. When combined with rainfall sensing and runoff forecasting, movable type regulators can optimize the storage in the sewer network, and insure adequate capacity during larger storms.

The greatest advances that are expected in combined stormwater sewer management technology are predicted by Schilling (1985) to occur in the area of real time control. The advent of inexpensive computerized controls, linked to a network with a central control station in combination with weather forecasting and radar, will offer the potential for flow optimization in the entire network. This is not an easy task, since storm rainfall distribution over an area and the movement of each storm is not always possible to predict. Also, the equipment that is required is complex and, as a result, subject to occasional failures, even under the best maintenance environments.

In recent years, we have seen the emergence of *special control devices*. Some of these are patented, while others were developed by public agencies. These include devices such as the Steinscrew and the Hydrobrake system. These two are completely self-regulating and can be used in separate storm sewers and combined storm sewers. The technical configuration of the aforementioned various flow regulating devices is discussed in Chapter 11.

6.3 CHANGING THE FLOW ROUTE IN SEWERS

Most sewer systems in existence were designed to carry away stormwater as quickly as possible. This approach can occasionally lead to a "collision" of peak flows at the confluences of various subbasins. If the original design did not anticipate this, then some of the downstream portions of the system may be overloaded.

In some cases, it is possible to balance out the flow peaks by changing the flow routes. This is especially the case if real time control to divert the flows is used. As an example, one can transfer water from one subbasin to another in a fashion that puts the hydrograph peaks out of phase. To accomplish this, it is necessary to install cross-connections between the subbasins, which may or may not be cost-effective.

When planning a new storm sewer system, the travel time of each branch can be optimized to avoid collision of peaks. This is possible through varying the layout and flow lengths of the pipe system. However, detailed storm runoff routing modeling is needed to provide the details of flow in various parts of the system for such a design.

6.4 SOME PRACTICAL OBSERVATIONS

Combined sewer networks in densely urbanized areas generally are the result of many years of growth and expansion. The excess volume that may have been available when the system was new may no longer be available. As the urbanized area expands, the sewer system is modified in response to flow increases and public input (see Figure 6.1).

Because combined sewer systems are sensitive to changes in runoff conditions, especially to the density of urbanization, the use of pipes for detention storage is often not possible. Also, the use of choked sections that back up stormwater in a sewer can cause local flooding. Therefore, when considering the use of storm sewers for detention, detailed and thorough analysis of the system capacity must be performed. Every feasible scenario of the temporal and spatial distribution of rainfall needs to be examined using distributed routing models before deciding if, and how, pipe storage will be utilized.

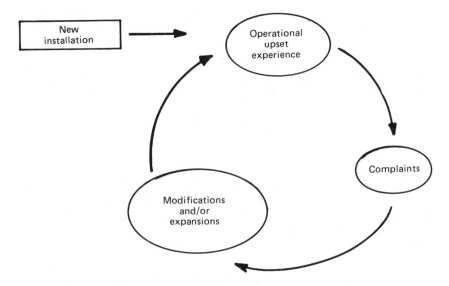

Figure 6.1 Operational experience influence on system modification.

REFERENCES

SCHILLING, W., "Urban Runoff Quality Management by Real-Time Control," *Urban Runoff Pollution*, Springer-Verlag, Berlin, 1986.

TORNO, H., MARSALEK, J., AND DESBORDES, M., *Urban Runoff Pollution*, Springer-Verlag, Berlin, 1986.

7

Pipe Packages

7.1 BASIC CONFIGURATION

Pipe packages is a term describing a detention storage facility consisting of one or more buried large-diameter pipes. These pipes are placed in parallel rows, and each pipe is connected to a common inlet chamber and an outlet chamber. Usually, but not always, pipe packages are connected in series to the sewer system. As illustrated in Figure 7.1, the connection of the package to the sewer takes place at the two end points, namely, inlet and outlet chambers.

The size of a pipe package is determined by the storage volume requirements and by the physical space availability at the installation site. The package does not need to be installed in a straight line along its entire length. It can change direction anywhere along its length to fit the site limitations. A typical pipe package is equipped with a flow regulator that is installed in the outlet chamber and an overflow spillway located at either the inlet or the outlet chamber.

This chapter describes the following aspects of a pipe package installation:

- pipes forming the package,
- inlet chamber,
- outlet chamber,
- spillway,

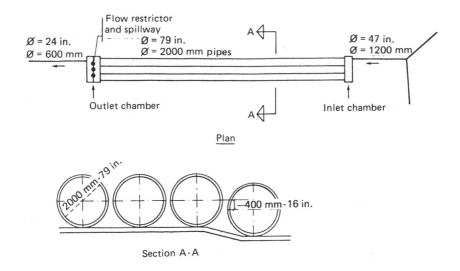

Figure 7.1   Basic layout of a pipe package storage.

- access openings, and
- operation and maintenance.

7.2 PIPES FORMING THE PIPE PACKAGE

The size of the pipes used in a package can vary considerably. However, to facilitate inspection and cleaning, it is recommended that, as a minimum, 54-inch (1400-mm) diameter pipes be used. For similar reasons, the pipes should be laid at a minimum slope of 2% to avoid standing pockets of water, which can occur due to lack of precision during construction.

Although sediments will settle out inside pipe packages, this same deposition can be reduced by installing one of the pipes somewhat lower than the others; see Figure 7.1. Confining the low flows to one pipe will help the system to become self-cleansing. To keep the other pipes from filling during low flows, the elevation difference between the low flow pipe and other pipes needs to be set to keep the low flows confined only to the low flow pipe.

Despite the fact that one pipe is set lower to carry the low flows, deposition of sediments and sludge will still occur. These deposits can be cleansed by maintenance personnel by diverting the dry weather flows manually to one pipe at a time. This is done by inserting gates in front of other pipes into frames that were installed for this purpose during construction. Although this system may be somewhat complex, it can facilitate the cleaning of pipe packages in combined sewer systems. This may not be possible in separate storm sewers unless there is a significant dry weather flow in the sewer.

7.3 INLET CHAMBER

At the upstream end, the pipe package is connected to the network through the inlet chamber (see Figure 7.2). This chamber can be constructed of reinforced concrete, or it can be assembled using large pipe fittings. Whichever way it is built, it needs to be large enough to permit comfortable access to all of the pipes by the maintenance personnel and their equipment.

7.4 OUTLET CHAMBER

At the downstream end the pipe package is connected to the storm sewer system through an outlet chamber. This chamber can also be built using reinforced concrete or assembled using large pipe fittings. The flow leaves the outlet chamber through one of the following types of flow regulators:

- a fixed orifice,
- a fixed outlet nozzle,
- a small outlet pipe,
- adjustable gates, or
- special (i.e., patented) flow regulators.

7.5 SPILLWAYS

To prevent water from surfacing at manholes or in upstream basements, emergency overflow spillways need to be installed either at the inlet or the outlet chamber. When runoff from larger storms exceeds the storage capacity of the pipe package, the excess can then be safely spilled, untreated, to the receiving waters.

If possible, locate the spillway at the inlet chamber. This type of an arrangement is illustrated in Figure 7.3, where the water has to back up into the inlet chamber before the spillway operates. As a result, the storage capacity in the pipe package is utilized fully. When locating the spillway inside the inlet chamber, be sure that water cannot back up into the upstream system and cause damages or other problems.

Figure 7.4 illustrates a spillway located in the outlet chamber. There is less risk of causing upstream flooding; however, as illustrated in the figure, it is possible that the storage capacity may not be fully utilized. Also, there is a greater risk in this configuration that the bottom deposits in the pipes will be resuspended and spilled, untreated, into the receiving waters.

Figure 7.2   Three 63-inch pipes at inlet chamber.

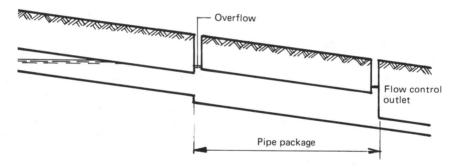

Figure 7.3   Pipe package with spillway at inlet chamber. (*After ATV, 1978.*)

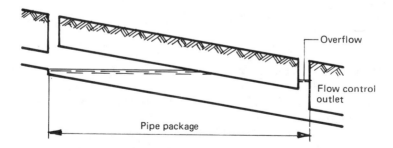

Figure 7.4   Pipe package with spillway at outlet chamber. (*After ATV, 1978.*)

7.6 ACCESS OPENINGS

Normal cleaning and maintenance of a pipe package requires that access openings, (i.e., manholes) be provided. Such openings at the inlet and at the outlet chambers are required for

- entry of personnel to the chamber,
- transport of equipment and materials,
- ventilation, and
- light shafts.

When pipe packages have more than three parallel pipes, it is recommended that two openings be installed in each chamber.

Experience in Europe and in the United States reveals that normal cleaning equipment can service approximately 80 to 100 linear feet (25 to 30 m) from the opening. As a result, pipe packages exceeding 200 feet (60 m) in length need additional access openings along each of the pipes in the package.

7.7 OPERATION AND MAINTENANCE

Like any other storage facility, pipe packages need regular maintenance. To insure this, a formal maintenance schedule should be prepared which also provides for routine inspection. Each time the detention facility is visited, it should be inspected for

- clogged outlets and obstructed inlets,
- excessive deposits,
- corrosion of metal parts,
- deterioration of concrete, and
- any other damage or visible problems.

The outlet can experience momentary clogging by large objects such as lumber, cans, balls, plastic sheets, etc. This type of problem can be significantly reduced by providing at least two outlet openings at two different levels in the outlet chamber.

Clogging at the outlet can also be caused by buildup of sludge, sediments, and debris. Regular inspection and the removal of accumulated deposits and debris is the most effective way to deal with such problems.

REFERENCES

ATV, *Guidelines for Design and Configuration of Storm Water Relief Facilities in Mixed Water Channels,* Arbeitsblatt A 128, 2nd edition, 1978. (In German)

MLYNAREK, L., "Stormwater Impoundment Channels of Asbestos Cement Pipes," Korespondenz Abwasser No. 4, 1975. (In German)

RANDOLPH, R., BORDERS, J., AND HELM, R., "Pipe Storage for Equalization of Backwash Discharges to Sanitary Sewers," *Journal of Water Pollution Control Federation,* No. 8, 1980.

8

Tunnel Storage

A conveyance tunnel for storm or combined sewage must, for technical reasons, be designed much larger than required to handle the design flow. As a result, tunnels often have significant excess volume that can be used for storage. Since the inflow into a tunnel usually takes place through drill holes or drop shafts, it is also possible to use large surcharge depths in tunnel systems. This chapter describes various tunnel storage configurations and also provides a brief description of the technical configuration for each of the arrangements.

8.1 CLASSIFICATION BY FUNCTION

Tunnel storage can be classified into three functional categories:

- detention,
- off-line storage, and
- sedimentation.

8.1.1 Detention Tunnels

Detention tunnels are used frequently in Sweden to convey wastewater flows to treatment plants. A detention tunnel is a conveyance tunnel that also detains stormwater or wastewater behind some form of a flow restrictor.

Often, the flow restrictor is designed to pass the dry weather flows undetained. At the same time, it is the configuration and the size of the flow restrictor that defines how detention takes place. It is safe to assume that a detention tunnel will have a continuous dry weather flow, as can be seen in Figure 8.1, and this low flow has to be accounted for in the design of the outlet.

8.1.2 Off-line Storage Tunnels

Off-line storage tunnels are used in several cities in Europe and in the United States. An example of this is the case where an overloaded combined sewer is relieved by diverting excess flows to a tunnel that is off-line to the main flow in the sewer. This type of installation differs from the one described in Section 8.1.1 in that it has no dry weather flow except for groundwater seepage.

Water stored in an off-line tunnel does not interact with the flow in the sewer network until it is routed back into the network. Typically, stored water is emptied from the tunnel using pumps after the flow in the sewer has subsided. A schematic representation of this type of an installation is shown in Figure 8.2.

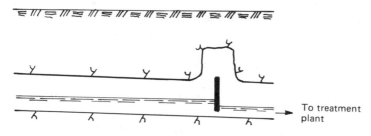

Figure 8.1   Detention tunnel.

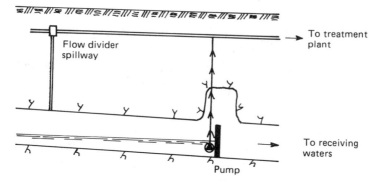

Figure 8.2   Off-line storage tunnel.

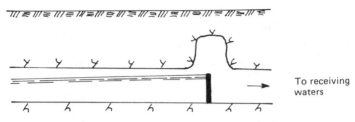

Figure 8.3   Tunnel as a sedimentation basin.

8.1.3 Sedimentation Tunnels

Tunnels can also be used as sedimentation basins. This is achieved by detaining the water in the tunnel so that settling of sediments can occur. The outlet of a sedimentation tunnel is usually equipped with a small orifice and an overflow weir so that all significant flows will be released over the weir. This type of an arrangement is illustrated in Figure 8.3.

8.2 DETENTION TUNNELS

Detention tunnels are in essence very low velocity conveyance conduits that provide detention by backing up water inside a large boring behind some type of a flow regulator. For the most part, detention tunnels are used to regulate or equalize storm flows in a combined sewer system.

8.2.1 Configuration of Flow Regulators

One common feature of flow regulators in detention tunnels is to permit dry weather flows to pass through unobstructed. Only when a desired flow rate is reached, the flow is held back by the regulator and detention occurs. The following are some examples of flow regulation in tunnels for which design details are discussed in Part 2 of this book:

1. *Restricted Outlet.* The most common flow regulator is a restricted outlet, such as an orifice, a nozzle, a gate, or a valve.
2. *Reduced Pipe.* A pipe having a smaller diameter than the tunnel.
3. *Pumps.* The most positive control can be achieved using only pumps to empty the tunnel.

8.2.2 Spillways

To avoid excessive surcharge depths, or to permit outflow when the flow restrictor clogs, a spillway or an emergency outlet has to be provided. The spilled water can either be returned to the tunnel downstream of the regulator or it can be routed to the receiving waters untreated. This decision will depend on local site conditions and tunnel configuration.

8.2.3 Example: Flow Regulator with Fixed Gates

A flow regulating structure with fixed gates was installed inside one branch of a combined sewage tunnel network in Gothenborg, Sweden. Flow restriction is provided by two rectangular manually controlled gates. Each 40-inch by 40-inch (1-m by 1-m) gate is installed in a concrete wall that is approximately two-thirds the height of the tunnel (see Figure 8.4).

The frequently occurring low flows are not impeded by these gates and detain only the larger flows. When the headwater behind the gates exceeds the height of the concrete wall, water spills over the wall and continues downstream. Sludge deposits upstream of the gates have been small and have not been a problem so far.

8.2.4 Example: Regulation with Moving Gates

The inflow into the Kappala sewage treatment plant, which is located outside of Stockholm, Sweden, is regulated with movable gates. These gates, illustrated in Figure 8.5, were installed in 1973 in a tunnel immediately upstream of the plant and equalize the hydraulic load to the plant during storms.

The opening is controlled automatically in accordance with a preset operating routine. This routine takes into account the maximum flow into the treatment plant and the expected duration of peak inflows into the tunnel. The latter is estimated during each storm. Flow regulation usually occurs for only short periods (e.g., less than one day). On the other hand, during snow melt flows can be detained for five to seven days.

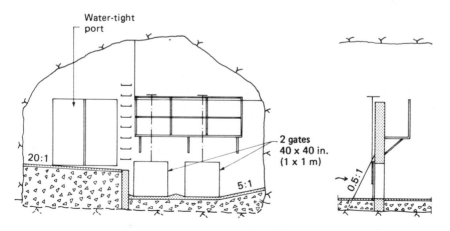

Figure 8.4   Flow regulator with fixed gates.

Figure 8.5   Flow regulating gate at the Kappala treatment plant.

Except for initial start-up problems, experience so far has been generally positive. One of the initial problems was the grit deposited in the tunnel overloading the plant's grit chambers when the gates were opened. This was solved by opening the gates more frequently to flush the grit accumulations.

During the first stage of testing, only 2.2 miles (3.5 km) of tunnel was used for detention. At that time, the available detention volume was 530,000 cubic feet (15,000 m³). Since 1980, up to 6.2 miles (10 km) of tunnel has been used for detention, providing a volume of 1,400,000 cubic feet (32 acre feet; 40,000 m³).

8.2.5 Example: Regulation with Pumps

At the Akeshov treatment plant in Stockholm, a pumping station with three centrifugal pumps lifts the water from a deep-lying tunnel system. The pumping height is approximately 100 feet (30 m), as shown in Figure 8.6. The tunnel is used as a detention facility to achieve a more uniform flow into the plant. Problems have been reported with the clogging of the suction lines of the pumps. This is understandable, since the water does not go through coarse separation of solids before pumping.

8.2.6 Example: Regulation with Reduced Pipes

A tunnel system that collects and transports combined drainage and wastewater in Gothenborg, Sweden crosses a major river. The river is crossed by a three-pipe inverted siphon. Each pipe is about 48 inches (1,200 mm) in diameter, and only two are connected at this time. The transition from the

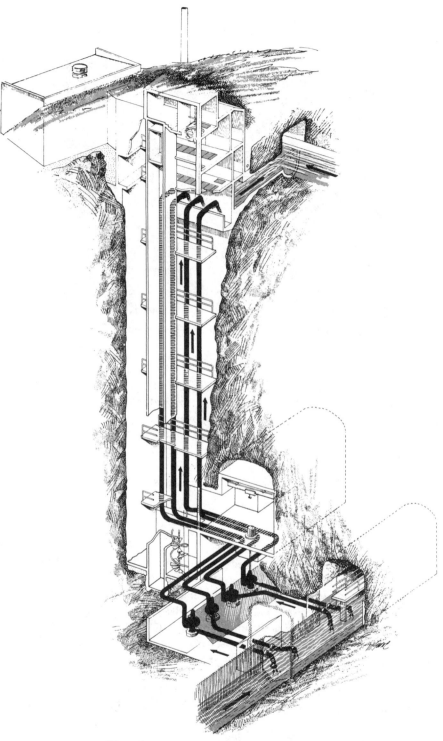

Figure 8.6 Pumping station at the Akeshov plant.

Figure 8.7   Tunnel-to-siphon transition in Gothenborg.

tunnel into a siphon occurs at a concrete wall, which is illustrated in Figure 8.7.

The siphon has significantly less flow capacity than the tunnel; thereby it acts as a flow restrictor. During high flows, the water backs up behind the siphon into the tunnel. An emergency spillway is located upstream of the siphon transition and provides relief when exceptionally high runoff occurs.

Initially, only one pipe in the siphon was connected to the tunnel. At that time, excessive sediment deposition was occurring in the tunnel. This deposition problem practically disappeared when the second siphon pipe was connected.

8.3 OFF-LINE STORAGE TUNNELS

Off-line storage refers to detention that occurs intermittently when a part of the flow in a collection system is diverted to a tunnel for temporary storage. Storage occurs only when the sewer system needs to be relieved. This means that, as a general rule, there is no base flow in these types of tunnels.

The water stored in an off-line storage tunnel has to be eventually returned to the sewer system and in most cases, this is done through the use of pumping. An exception is a system in very steep terrain where it could be drained by gravity.

The configuration of such a tunnel can vary from site to site. However, the following common elements can be found in many of the existing systems:

- a vertical drop shaft for the inflow;
- arrangements for emptying of the stored water;

- arrangements for ventilation; and
- provisions for the cleaning and removal of sediments.

8.3.1 Vertical Drop Shafts

Water is generally diverted to a tunnel through a number of points along the tunnel's length. These are customarily designed as vertical drop shafts. These shafts have to be designed to safely handle the maximum design inflow that may occur.

Occasionally, a vertical drop shaft can be designed to be used also for purposes other than inflow of water. These other uses can include descent openings for personnel, working pits, emergency evacuation points, air relief vents, etc.

Because of their deep and vertical configuration, the water flowing into the tunnel will have high kinetic energy at the bottom of the shaft. Because this high energy can cause structural damage to the tunnel and/or scour the rock out at the bottom of the shaft, some form of bottom reinforcement is needed at each drop shaft.

8.3.2 Draining the Tunnel

Because off-line tunnels tend to be located deep under the surface, they are usually drained through the use of pumps. The pumps and other appurtenances constitute the flow regulating structure, which can include:

- pumps for transferring water from the tunnel to the sewer system;
- a spillway to relieve excess inflow when full;
- pipes and pumps for decanting water from the tunnel to the receiving waters; and
- control equipment.

For a tunnel to act as a storage facility, the water has to be backed up by some form of a flow restriction at the downstream end. This can take a form of a concrete wall having a height to be determined by the following factors:

- slope of the tunnel;
- maximum allowable water level in the tunnel;
- magnitude of the inflow;
- capacity of the emptying facilities; and
- capacity of the spillway.

Tunnels used for temporary storage will also act as settling basins. As a result, if they store stormwater only, it is possible to decant the clarified water directly into receiving waters. Obviously, that is not the case with combined sewer systems.

Water stored in a temporary storage tunnel is usually transferred to the sewer network by pumping. Pump capacity and control is chosen in a way that the total system capacity is optimized. Following is a description of an optimizing procedure for the pumping of pollutants from an off-line tunnel to a treatment plant, as presented by Isgard in 1977.

Assuming that for a given pollutant the concentration C in a treatment plant's effluent, when treating combined sewage flows, can be expressed as a function of the inflow rate q into the plant, then

$$C = f(q) \tag{8.1}$$

Letting C_o be the effluent concentration when the plant effluent rate is q_o, the mass of the pollutant released during time T is

$$C_o \cdot q_o \cdot T \tag{8.2}$$

The volume of the stored water, V_s, to be pumped from the tunnel, is assumed to have concentration C_s of the pollutant, which corresponds to a mass of the pollutant equal to $C_s V_s$. If the stored water is pumped into the treatment plant over time T, the inflow into the plant will increase by

$$q_s = \frac{V_s}{T} \tag{8.3}$$

As a result, the total inflow into the plant during time T will be $(q_o + q_s)$ and the concentration of the pollutant in the effluent will increase to $(C_o + C_l)$. The mass of the pollutant leaving the plant over time T can be expressed as

$$(C_o + C_1) \cdot (q_o + q_s) \cdot T \tag{8.4}$$

In order to obtain any benefit at all from the storage (i.e., flow equalization), the following condition has to be met:

$$(C_o + C_1) \cdot (q_0 + q_s) \cdot T \le (C_o \cdot q_o \cdot T + C_s \cdot V_s) \tag{8.5}$$

If the preceding condition is not satisfied, it can be argued that instead of storing the water in storage tunnel, it is better to release it untreated directly to the receiving waters. This is because the total mass of the pollutants entering the receiving waters is not reduced by treatment and storage. Equation 8.5 can be rewritten as follows:

$$C_1 \cdot (q_o + q_s) \le q_s \cdot (C_s - C_o) \tag{8.6}$$

Let

$$C_2 = (C_s - C_o) \tag{8.7}$$

then,

$$\frac{C_1}{C_2} \le \frac{q_s}{q_o + q_s} \tag{8.8}$$

If it can be shown empirically that

$$C_1 = C_o \cdot \left(\frac{q_s}{q_o}\right)^2 \tag{8.9}$$

and

$$C_s = K \cdot C_o \tag{8.10}$$

one obtains

$$q_s \leq q_o \left(\sqrt{K - 0.75} - 0.5\right) \tag{8.11}$$

By determining the analytic expressions for C_1 and C_s for different pollutants, it is at least theoretically possible to optimize the pumping rate from the storage facility. Since different pollutants will have different treatment rates, it is not possible to find a solution for Equation 8.11 that will work for all pollutants needing treatment. It should work, however, for the constituents of greatest concern.

When the inflow into a plant drops below a certain rate, the concentration of the pollutant in the effluent should remain practically constant. This is usually the dry weather design capacity of the plant, and it is best to utilize this capacity by emptying the storage during dry weather low flow periods. Unfortunately, this is not always practical, since storms can follow each other within short periods of time. As a result, storage facilities need to be emptied as soon as possible, taking into consideration the treatment plant's capacity to deal with the added hydraulic load.

8.3.3 Ventilation

When the tunnel is filling, air will be displaced corresponding to the volume of water entering the tunnel. In order to permit this air to be displaced and not be trapped, the tunnel has to be equipped with air vent openings. These openings have to be sized to accommodate the maximum permissible air velocity through the ventilation shaft, which normally should not exceed 33 feet per second (10 m/s). Since the tunnel usually fills faster than it empties, the vent is sized to accommodate the air flow during this phase of the operation.

In addition to providing vents for air relief, it is also necessary to provide air ventilation to all underground control and equipment rooms. These rooms need fresh air for the personnel and for the equipment that may be located within them. It is also recommended that these rooms be heated and well lighted to provide a safe and comfortable working environment.

8.3.4 Cleaning Off-line Tunnels

To keep the odors and corrosive gases under control, off-line tunnels have to be cleaned to remove sludge deposits that accumulate within them. If self-cleaning cannot be realized, the tunnel needs to be constructed with a hard bottom to accommodate mechanical cleaning equipment. Cleaning of tunnels can be very expensive; thus it is best to design the tunnels large enough to require infrequent cleaning (i.e., 5- to 15-year intervals). Also, due to the inherent hazard of the tunnel environment to humans, mechanical cleaning is preferred over manual cleaning. Section 8.4 describes the mass and composition of the sludge deposits that can be expected inside storage tunnels.

8.3.5 Example: Off-line CSO Storage Tunnel

An example of an off-line tunnel used for temporary detention of stormwater and combined sewer overflows is the Alvsjo-Malaren tunnel in Stockholm, Sweden. This installation is illustrated in Figure 8.8. It is 3 miles (5 km) in length and extends from the fairgrounds in Alvsjo to Lake Malaren in the vicinity of a sewage treatment plant. The tunnel receives combined sewer overflows (CSO) from an area served by combined sewers and from another area served by a separate urban storm sewer system. Approximately 1,000 feet (300 m) from the downstream end of the tunnel is the flow regulating control system, which is located entirely underground.

An emergency spillway structure backs up the water in the tunnel and keeps it from flowing into the lake. When the surcharge level in the tunnel is greater than the spillway, water begins to overflow into the lake. The spillway

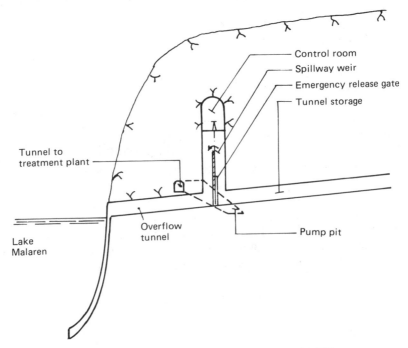

Figure 8.8 Alvsjo-Malaren tunnel. (*After Isgard, 1977.*)

structure is also equipped with an outlet gate, which opens automatically during unusually large storms when the spillway overflow cannot handle the hydraulic load by itself. The decision when to open the auxiliary gates is based on how fast the water rises in the upstream end of the tunnel.

During typical wet weather operation, the tunnel is emptied into the sewer system for conveyance to the treatment plant. The tunnel can be drained to a certain level by gravity, and the rate of outflow is controlled by flow regulating valves. The remainder of the water has to be emptied by pumping. It is also possible to decant the cleaner surface water and to release it directly into Lake Malaren.

A picture of the control room for this installation is shown in Figure 8.9. Among other things, the picture shows the upper part of the emergency release gate. Note that all control equipment is enclosed in a small heated and ventilated building. The pressure pipes from the submersible pumps can be seen in Figure 8.10. They are also located close to the emergency outlet gate.

8.3.6 Example: Storage of Stormwater

After extensive drainage and water quality studies, it was decided that the urban stormwater runoff from a new subdivision of Jarvafeltet in Stockholm, Sweden should be temporarily stored in a tunnel system. Because of the elevations, the tunnel had to be emptied by pumping. This installation, in addition to detention, was to act as a sedimentation tunnel.

The main body of the tunnel is about 4.3 miles (7 km) long. It has seven tributary branches having a combined length of 2.5 miles (4 km), and four

Figure 8.9   Alvsjo-Malaren tunnel control room.

Figure 8.10   Alvsjo-Malaren tunnel pressure pipes.

transport tunnels with a total length of 0.6 mile (1 km). In total, the system has 3.9 miles (6.3 km) of tunnel with a cross-section area of 183 square feet (17 m²), and 3.5 miles (5.7 km) of tunnel with an area of 269 square feet (25 m²). This corresponds to a total volume of almost 10 million cubic feet 220 acre feet (275,000 m³). Stormwater is conveyed to the tunnel system by 36 storm sewers or bore holes. Figure 8.11 shows a plan of the tunnel system.

The tunnel is emptied into the river Igelbacken through the Eggeby pumping station. The station has four pumps with a total capacity of 18 cubic feet per second (500 l/s) plus one reserve pump. This pumping station is illustrated in Figure 8.12.

Because the tunnel will also function as a sedimentation basin, its bottom was paved with asphalt. This was done to prepare it for mechanical cleaning of deposited sediments and sludge. Operational experience to date indicates that it will have to be cleaned at 5- to 10-year intervals.

8.4 TUNNELS AS SEDIMENTATION BASINS

Tunnels used as sedimentation basins, like conventional sedimentation basins, are normally kept full of water in between storm events. When new water enters the tunnel, it displaces the water stored in the tunnel. The amount of cleansing the water receives is a function of the quality of the influent, the holding time in the tunnel, the velocity of flow in the tunnel, particle size distribution, and many other factors. Due to the oxygen-depleting nature of

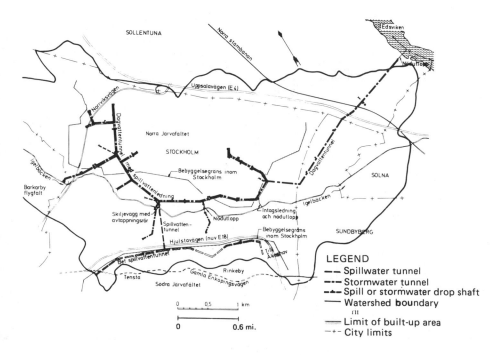

Figure 8.11   Tunnel plan for an area in Stockholm.

the deposits from combined sewage–stormwater and the difficulties associated with these deposits, sedimentation tunnels should be used preferably for separate stormwater systems.

For the most part, sedimentation tunnels are self-regulating. Although the physical layout and arrangement of facilities may vary between sites, some of the common elements found in most sites include:

- drop shafts for stormwater inflow;
- ventilation and air relief shafts along its length;
- spillway weir that acts as the main flow regulator;
- pump(s) or gravity pipes for emptying of the tunnel for cleaning and maintenance; and
- tunnel floor suitable for mechanical cleaning.

8.4.1 Sedimentation

A yearlong study of the sedimentation efficiencies in a stormwater sedimentation tunnel was conducted in Sweden by the Stockholm Water and Sewage Works between September 1976 and September 1977. The water quantities entering and leaving the tunnel were recorded and water samples

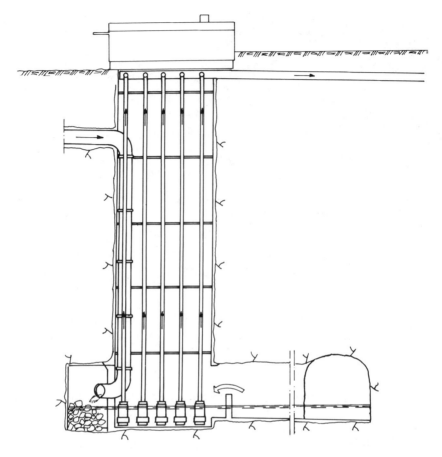

Figure 8.12 Diagram of the Eggeby pumping station. (After Stockholm Water and Sewage Works.)

were taken and analyzed. It was discovered that groundwater accounted for 25% of all the water entering the tunnel during the year. Since it was not feasible to readily measure the water quality of this groundwater, calculations of pollutant removal rates were made for the following two possible scenarios:

1. The pollutants in the groundwater were assumed to be zero.
2. The pollutant concentrations in the groundwater were assumed to be equal to those found in the stormwater.

The results of this study are summarized in Table 8.1. The low number in the range corresponds to the assumption that the pollutants in the groundwater are zero. The high numbers correspond to the assumption that groundwater pollutant concentrations equal those found in the stormwater. This table also

TABLE 8.1 Separation of Pollutants in a Settling Tunnel

Constituent	Percent Removal	
	Tunnel	Laboratory
Dry residual solids	(-12)–13	11
Annealing solids	(-7)–18	—
Suspended solids	73–80	69–81
Ammonia as N	59–70	—
Nitrate and nitrite as N	0–23	—
Total nitrogen	6–29	7
Phosphate as P	55–64	—
Total phosphorus as P	50–63	48
Chemical Oxygen Demand (COD)	20–40	57–64

After Stockholm Water and Sewage Works, 1978.

contains results of laboratory settling studies using the same stormwater. The laboratory studies used seven days as the sedimentation period, which corresponded to the average holding time in the tunnel.

The negative separations reported for the dry residual and the annealing solids resulted because of the assumption that the concentrations of pollutants in the groundwater were zero. The laboratory tests showed that the true reduction of these constituents was nèar the upper limit of the removal range measured in the tunnel.

The study also showed that stormwater was clarified for the most part during the first day of detention. When the concentration of the suspended solids decreased to 10 to 20 milligrams per liter in the water, further sedimentation became extremely slow. Similar results were observed in the laboratory tests of the stormwater samples. Very similar observations were also reported a few years later by Randall et. al. (1982) for stormwater detention pond studies in the United States.

In addition to the reported results from the aforementioned Swedish study, estimates were also made of removals for some of the other constituents found in stormwater. However, due to the limited data obtained during these tests, the conclusions should be treated as preliminary. Parallel laboratory tests of these additional constituents showed that it took four to seven days of detention to achieve the reported results. These tentative findings are summarized in Table 8.2.

8.4.2 Sludge Deposits

As part of the aforementioned investigation, the rate of sediment (sludge) deposition was also investigated. Based on calculated estimates, the layer of deposits inside the tunnel increased in depth between 6 and 13 millimeters per year (i.e., 0.25 to 0.50 inches per year). This study also predicted that deposition of bottom deposits will not be uniform throughout the tunnel and will vary according to the location in the tunnel.

Table 8.3 summarizes the chemical analysis of the deposits collected in two stormwater tunnels in Sweden. For comparison, the table also shows the analytical results of digested wastewater treatment plant sludge. It can be seen that stormwater deposits, except for lead, manganese, and cobalt have concentrations for all pollutants that are less than are found in digested wastewater treatment plant sludge.

TABLE 8.2 Separation of Metals in a Settling Tunnel
Based on Limited Data

	Percent Removal	
Constituent	Tunnel	Laboratory
Lead	76–82	62–98
Cadmium	74–82	—
Copper	16–36	57–82
Zinc	48–60	50–55
Thermostable coliforms	96–97	99
Fat and oil	97–98	—
BOD$_5$	58–68	32–73
Turbidity	34–65	42–98

After Stockholm Water and Sewage Works, 1978.

TABLE 8.3 Analysis of Stormwater Deposits in Two Tunnels

Constituent	Jarva Tunnel	Sollentuna Tunnel	Digested Sludge
Dry substance—%	31	32	—
Fat and oil—mg/(kg DW)	14,000	—	—
Hydrocarbons—mg/(kg DW)	8,000	21,000	—
Arsenic—mg/(kg DW)	7	—	—
Lead—mg/(kg DW)	420	580	100–300
Iron—mg/(kg DW)	42,000	48,000	—
Cadmium—mg/(kg DW)	3.7	5	5–15
Cobalt—mg/(kg DW)	36	24	8–20
Copper—mg/(kg DW)	120	150	500–1,500
Chromium—mg/(kg DW)	49	63	50–200
Mercury—mg/(kg DW)	0.036	0.22	4–8
Manganese—mg/(kg DW)	1,300	750	200–500
Nickel—mg/(kg DW)	52	49	25–100
Zinc—mg/(kg DW)	1,100	890	1,000–3,000
Phosphorus—mg/(kg DW)	5.4	—	—

According to Stockholm Water and Sewage Works.

Note: DW stands for dry weight.

8.4.3 Groundwater Lowering and Terrain Subsidence

It is not possible to prevent groundwater from seeping into tunnels. The rate of the seepage is a function of the groundwater depth, the extent of rock fractures, and the extent of the measures taken to seal off the seepage. Seepage into tunnels can lower the groundwater table and, as a result, cause general subsidence of the surface.

It is possible to control groundwater lowering by keeping the tunnel under a hydrostatic pressure. Obviously, this is not practical for detention tunnels. On the other hand, it is possible to do so with sedimentation tunnels by raising the outlet so that the tunnel is under constant internal pressure.

8.4.4 Example: Tunnel as a Sedimentation Basin

In 1970, a stormwater tunnel was built in Sollentuna, a community located north of Stockholm, Sweden. The tunnel is approximately 1 mile (1.5 km) in length, has a 75-square-foot (7-m²) cross-sectional area, is sloped at 0.5%, and is not sealed against groundwater infiltration. Since there was a risk of subsidence in a clay layer in the region, it was decided to keep the tunnel constantly under water pressure.

At the downstream end of the tunnel is an outlet and a spillway designed to keep the tunnel under positive pressure. The system is illustrated in Figure 8.13. The outlet was equipped with a gate that can be opened to prevent the water from rising too high. However, the gate is only to be used in the event of an extremely heavy inflow into the tunnel.

This tunnel functions only as a sedimentation basin for stormwater runoff. As a result, it has to be cleaned out whenever the sediment accumulation in the tunnel becomes excessive. The tunnel has to be drained to be cleaned so that the settled sludge can be mechanically removed. The tunnel was emptied for cleaning in 1977 after six years of operation. A layer of sediments was found to be 20 inches (0.5 m) deep at the upstream end and 10 inches (0.25 m) deep at the downstream end. As a result, cleaning was not considered necessary at that time. The tunnel was emptied again in 1979. The increase in sediment deposits, since it was inspected last, was judged insignificant.

8.5 HYDRAULICS OF TUNNEL STORAGE

Tunnel storage involves some special and sometimes unique hydraulic operational problems. Many of these were studied by the Department of Hydraulics Engineering at the Royal Institute of Technology in Stockholm, Sweden and addressed the following:

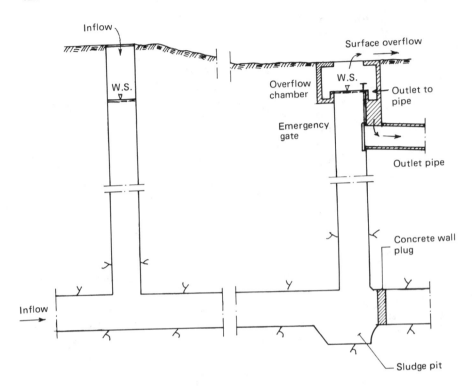

Figure 8.13   Sedimentation tunnel in Sollentuna, Sweden.

- hydraulic flow capacity,
- filling and emptying of tunnels,
- self-cleaning,
- air entrapment, and
- unsteady flow.

For a complete description of the study and its findings, refer to Bergh and Cederwall (1979).

8.5.1 Hydraulic Flow Capacity

The hydraulic flow capacity of a stormwater storage tunnel can be calculated using one of the empirical flow equations for steady uniform flow. The most widely used equation for this is Manning's formula:

$$Q = \frac{K_u}{n} A \cdot R^{2/3} \cdot S^{1/2} \tag{8.12}$$

in which Q = flow rate in cubic feet per second (m³/s),
$\quad K_u = 1.49$ for U.S. standard units, (1.0 for SI units),
$\quad A$ = cross-section area of tunnel in square feet (m²),
$\quad R$ = hydraulics radius of tunnel in feet (m),
$\quad S$ = longitudinal slope in feet per foot (m/m), and
$\quad n$ = Manning's roughness coefficient.

For circular sections, the flow capacity is greatest when the tunnel is 90% full. One should not design the tunnel at this theoretical maximum capacity depth. Instead, it is safer to design the tunnel to be at capacity when it is running full.

Stormwater storage tunnels are often designed to be lined, at least in part, with concrete and to have a V-shaped bottom similar to the one illustrated in Figure 8.14. Manning's coefficient n for this type of a section is a composite of the coefficient for rock and for concrete portions of the cross-section. The composite Manning's n can be estimated with the aid of the following formula:

$$\left[\frac{n_c^{3/2} \cdot P_c + n_r^{3/2} \cdot P_r}{P_c + P_r} \right]^{2/3} \tag{8.13}$$

in which n = Manning's composite roughness coefficient,
$\quad n_c$ = Manning's coefficient for concrete,
$\quad n_r$ = Manning's coefficient for rock,
$\quad P_c$ = wetted perimeter for concrete, and
$\quad P_r$ = wetted perimeter for rock.

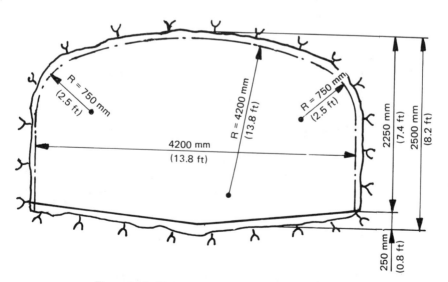

Figure 8.14 Typical stormwater storage tunnel section.

For tunnels having cross-section areas between 50 and 160 square feet (5 to 15 m²), the Manning's n for rock can be set at 0.030. For the concrete liner in the tunnel, the Manning's n can be set at 0.013.

8.5.2 Filling and Emptying a Tunnel

The design of a storage tunnel has to account for the way a tunnel fills with stormwater and how it is emptied. If the filling and emptying process is not adequately accounted for, stormwater can surcharge the system or cause waters to back up into areas being protected from flooding.

As an example, the hydraulic response of a tunnel equipped with an emergency outlet gate, similar to the one illustrated in Figure 8.8, was simulated using a computer. The results of how the water surface reacted during a storm are illustrated in Figure 8.15, which shows the water level variations in the tunnel after the emergency gate is opened. The gate was opened when the water level at the upstream end of the tunnel rose to a level twelve meters above the outlet.

Although the water level in some parts of the tunnel dropped rather quickly, the level at the inlet continued to rise. This time delay in the response has to be recognized both in the design and in the operation of the tunnel. Therefore, extensive dynamic computer modeling of such facilities is recommended when preparing the final design.

8.5.3 Self-Cleansing

When water flows, a shear stress occurs between the water and any surface it touches. This is universally true, including for flow in tunnels. In the

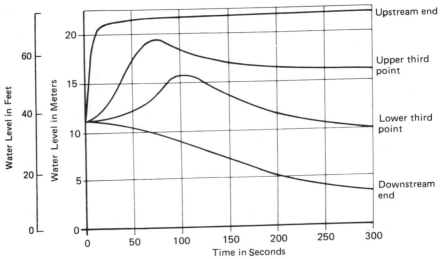

Figure 8.15   Water levels after downstream gate is opened.

case of uniform flow, the shear stress on the wetted perimeter of a tunnel can be calculated using the following formula:

$$T_{ave} = K_u \cdot \gamma \cdot R \cdot S \qquad (8.14)$$

in which T_{ave} = average shear stress on wetted perimeter in pounds per square foot (N/m²),

K_u = 1.0 for U.S. standard units (9.81 m/s² for SI units),

γ = density of water in pounds per cubic foot (kg/m³),

R = hydraulic radius in feet (m), and

S = slope of tunnel in feet per foot (m/m).

This shear force also acts on the materials that settled on the bottom of a tunnel. For these particles to be moved by the flow, a critical shear stress has to be exceeded. A tunnel can be considered self-cleansing if the average shear stress, T_{ave}, along the bottom of the tunnel is greater than the critical shear stress.

Lysne (1976), guided by the results obtained by a number of different researchers, proposed that the critical shear stress is 0.085 pound per square foot (4 N/m²) for stormwater sewers and 0.04 pound per square foot (2 N/m²) for sanitary sewers. The values are probably applicable in tunnels if self-cleansing of the tunnel is to be achieved. On the other hand, sedimentation tunnels need to be designed with a shear stress that is significantly less than 0.04 pound per square foot (2 N/m²).

8.5.4 Air Venting

Air that is trapped in a tunnel reduces both the available storage volume and the flow capacity of a tunnel. Also, compressed air can have a considerable amount of energy. For instance, 1,300 cubic yards (1000 m³) of air compressed under 80 feet (25 m) of water, if released suddenly, can produce the same explosive force as 110 pounds (50 kg) of dynamite.

Evacuation of compressed air that has been compressed inside of a tunnel can result in strong pressure waves in the tunnel and in the bore hole shaft (see Figure 8.16). As a result, water can surge out of the shaft in a form of a geyser. Such a phenomenon was observed at the Sollentuna tunnel north of Stockholm, Sweden. When this happened, a manhole lid weighing 110 pounds (490 N) was thrown almost 3 feet (1 m) into the air by a jet of water that eventually reached a height of 25 feet (8 m).

Air can enter the tunnel in the following ways:

• air entering with the stormwater;
• mixing of air into water at points of entry into the tunnel;
• mixing of air at hydraulic jumps inside the tunnel; and
• mixing of air in conjunction with pumping.

The best remedy is to prevent air from entering the tunnel, but this is virtually an impossible task. As a result, it is necessary to remove air from the tunnel by installing air traps at strategic locations inside the tunnel. Air can be trapped by installing vented enlarged sections and by venting it at other points inside the tunnel, such as at bends. The water can slow down at these locations and air can rise to the surface, thus escaping through the vent shafts (see Figure 8.17).

As mentioned earlier, rapid air evacuation can create shock waves. To avoid this, each evacuation shaft can be equipped with a sleeve that projects down into the tunnel having a series of air metering holes located near the ceiling of the tunnel. Air is thus released in a controlled fashion through the vent shaft (see Figure 8.18).

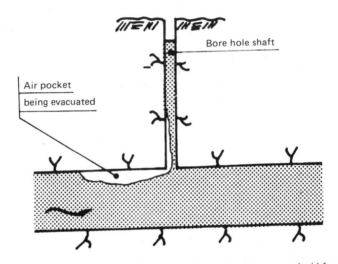

Figure 8.16 Air evacuation from a completely filled tunnel. (After Bergh and Cederwall, 1978.)

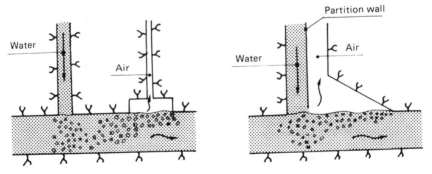

Figure 8.17 Evacuation of air through air traps. (After Bergh and Cederwall, 1978.)

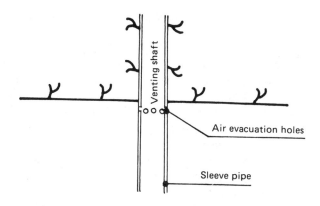

Figure 8.18   Air evacuation through venting in a sleeve pipe. (After Bergh and Cederwall, 1978.)

8.5.5 Unsteady Flow

As the tunnel fills or empties, it creates unsteady flow inside the tunnel. This is observed when gates are opened or closed, or when sudden inflow of stormwater occurs. As a result, the analysis of flow in tunnels cannot be performed using only steady flow equations. Unsteady flow is more properly described with partial differential equations, which can be solved using numerical methods.

Using computers to solve partial differential equations is a common practice these days. However, such numerical solutions can become unstable, and when these instabilities occur, the solutions can predict unreasonable water levels and flow fluctuations. We urge that the user always evaluate all numerical solutions for reasonableness before accepting the results.

REFERENCES

APWA, *Feasibility of Utility Tunnels in Urban Areas,* Special Report No. 39, 1971.

APWA, *Proceedings of the Conference on Engineering Utility Tunnels in Urban Areas,* Special Report No. 41, 1971.

BERGH, H., AND CEDERWALL, K., "Hydraulic Operating Problems in Storm Water Tunnels," KTH, Vattenbyggnad, Stockholm, 1978. (In Swedish)

FLOOD CONTROL COORDINATING COMMITTEE, *Development of a Flood and Pollution Control for Chicagoland Area,* Summary of Technical Reports, August, 1972.

ISGARD, E., "Undergrond Storage in Sewerage Systems," Rock Store, Proceedings of the First International Symposium, Vol. 1, Stockholm, 1977.

LYNAM, B., NEIL, F., AND DALTON, F., "Rock Tunnel Contracts Being Awarded for the Metropolitan Sanitary District of Greater Chicago Tunnel and Reservoir Plan (TARP)," Tunneling Technology Newsletter No. 17, March, 1977.

LYSNE, D. K., "Self-Cleaning in Runoff Pipes," PRA Report No. 9, 1976. (In Norwegian)

PARTHUM, "Building for the Future, The Boston Deep Tunnel Plan," *WPCF Journal*, April, 1970.

RANDALL, C. W., ELLIS, K., GRIZZARD, T. J., AND KNOCKE, W. R., "Urban Runoff Pollutant Removal by Sedimentation," *Proceedings of the Conference on Stormwater Detention Facilities*, American Society of Civil Engineers, New York, 1982.

STAHRE, P., "The Use of Tunnel Systems for Storage of Sewage Water," Rock Store, Proceedings of the International Symposium, Vol. 1, Stockholm, 1980.

STOCKHOLM WATER AND SEWAGE WORKS, Brochures, Drawings, etc.

STOCKHOLM WATER AND SEWAGE WORKS, *Studies of Stormwater Quality in the Jerva Drainage*, Internal Report, 1978. (In Swedish)

UNIVERSITY OF WISCONSIN, *Deep Tunnels in Hard Rock. A Solution to Combined Sewer Overflow and Flooding Problems*, College of Applied Science and Engineering, EPA Report 11020-02/71.

9

Storage at Sewage Treatment Plants

9.1 INTRODUCTION

The inflow into a sewage treatment plant can exhibit considerable variations over time. These variations can be significant in a smaller plant and can cause operational disturbances in the treatment process.

The variations in the flow can be balanced, to a certain degree, by installing some form of storage at the treatment plant. This storage can be in the form of:

- separate storage basins, or
- storage integrated into the plant itself.

9.2 EFFECTS OF FLOW VARIATION ON TREATMENT PROCESSES

9.2.1 General

The various treatment processes at a plant are not equally sensitive to the variations in the inflow. How sensitive each of the following treatment processes is to flow variations is discussed next:

- pretreatment,
- primary treatment,

- biological treatment, and
- chemical treatment.

9.2.2 Pretreatment

The pretreatment process consists of the screening out of coarse particles and the removal of sand and grit. None of the processes are especially sensitive to variations in flow or in the pollution load. Also, oversizing of these pretreatment facilities can be accomplished at a relatively small increment of added cost.

In new treatment plants, the pretreatment facilities should be installed ahead of any flow equalization storage. This assures reduced maintenance costs and means that the continuous operation of the basin is considerably simplified.

9.2.3 Primary Treatment

The primary treatment takes place in a treatment plant between the pretreatment and the biological or chemical treatment processes. Primary treatment consists of sedimentation and removal of the suspended solids in the wastewater. If this process is hydraulically overloaded, wastewater will pass through the primary tanks too fast for efficient settling to occur. As a result, the primary treatment process will not remove its full share of the pollutants and will pass them on to the subsequent treatment processes.

As with the pretreatment process, increasing the capacity of the primary treatment facilities is relatively inexpensive. Thus, it is good practice to provide sufficient primary treatment capacity to handle the anticipated maximum peak flows. Also, for some installations, flow equalization can be incorporated into the primary treatment tanks. This practice can provide a uniform stream of flow and pollutants to the downstream treatment processes.

9.2.4 Biological Treatment

Biological treatment usually occurs after the primary treatment process. It is normally accomplished in two steps. The first step transforms the organic matter carried by the waste water into microorganisms, while the second step removes these microorganisms from the water through settling. Because the growth of microorganisms is relatively slow, best treatment is obtained when the microorganisms are provided uniform living conditions (i.e., exposure to uniform flow and pollutant load).

Not all biological processes are affected equally by variations in flow. The sensitivity of treatment to inflow variations differs between the activated sludge process and the trickling filter and the rotating biological disk processes. The sensitivity of the biological process is said to depend, to a large extent, on the following factors:

1. the ability of microorganisms to break down organic matter;
2. the ability of microorganisms to form flock (i.e., sludge), which can readily settle out; and
3. the efficiency of the sludge settling unit.

In the activated sludge process, the ability of the organisms to break down organic matter is influenced by how much the rate of flow and pollutant load varies with time. Rapid variations cannot be accommodated efficiently. Variations in loading will also cause the development of sludge which will settle out very poorly.

Flow variations will also decrease the efficiency of the sludge settling units (i.e., clarifiers). As the flow rate reaches a critical level, a massive breaking off of the biological flock occurs and some, or all, of the sludge is flushed out of the clarifiers. If too much sludge is flushed out, the entire activated sludge process is disrupted for a long period of time.

In the trickling filter and the rotating biological disk processes, the microorganisms are normally under a heavier load than in the activated sludge process. Because the biological activity takes place on the surface of the filter or rotating disk media, variations in wastewater flow will have little effect on the ability of the flock to settle out in the clarifiers. With increasing flow, the efficiency of the biological process of the trickling filter and the rotating biological disk will decrease. There is, however, no critical flow level at which massive breaking off of the biological flocks occurs.

9.2.5 Chemical Treatment

The efficiency of chemical treatment, for the most part, is dependent on the following three factors:

1. precipitation of phosphates;
2. ability to form easily settlable flock; and
3. efficiency of the settling unit.

The efficiency of phosphate removal is only marginally affected by the flow rate or the quality of the wastewater. This assumes, however, that the chemical dosage is adjusted to the variation in the load. Nevertheless, the holding time in the flocculation basin is directly dependent on the inflow rate, and the ability to form flock is influenced by variations in flow.

The efficiency of the sedimentation basin to separate the chemical flock from the water is, however, directly affected by the flow rate through the basin. As with biological clarifiers, the vertical velocity of flow has to be less than the settling velocity of the flock for separation to occur. Generally, the chemical flock has greater settling velocities than the biological sludge, and the chemical settling basin can handle greater variations in flow. As the flow increases, the settling basin efficiency will decrease; however, even if massive loss of flock occurs, the total treatment process efficiency is not compromised for an extended period of time, as can happen in a biological process.

9.3 SEPARATE STORAGE BASINS

Flow equalization of inflow into a wastewater treatment plant can be accomplished with separate storage basins at the treatment plant. As illustrated in Figure 9.1, the basins can be connected either in-line or off-line to the main flow entering the plant. Regardless of the connection scheme, the storage basins are located between pretreatment and the primary treatment processes. This assures that most of the coarse floatables, sand, and grit are removed before the flow enters the storage basin. If, however, the basin has to be

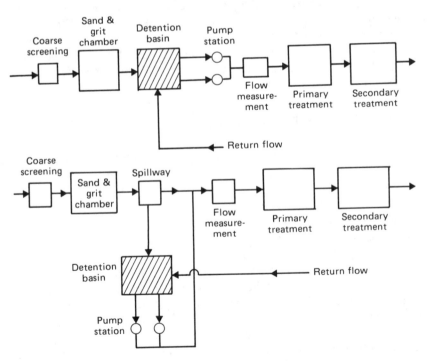

Figure 9.1 Flow equalization location in treatment plants. *(After EPA, 1974.)*

located ahead of the pretreatment unit, the basin needs to be equipped with equipment to remove sludge from its bottom.

9.3.1 In-line Basins

When the storage basin is connected in-line with the inflow, all the wastewater entering the treatment plant will flow through the basin. The flow out of the basin is then regulated through the use of either automated gates or pumps. The use of automated gates is only feasible when gravity flow into the subsequent treatment processes is possible.

Figure 9.2 shows a diagram of an in-line storage facility with a gravity driven outflow. The outflow is regulated by an automated gate valve that maintains a constant flow rate. Whenever the inflow rate exceeds the outflow rate, water is stored in the basin, and when the inflow rate is less than the outflow, the stored water is released. If the plant operators can predict the flow variations in advance, the outlet rate can be preset to balance out all of the flow peaks and valleys during the day.

Whenever unusually heavy flows occur, the storage volume will be exceeded. This will cause the basin to overflow, and the flow will continue downstream to the next treatment process. Because of the likelihood of this happening in a combined wastewater system, it is a good idea to provide an emergency overflow spillway.

For gravity flow to be feasible, the treatment plant site needs to have considerable vertical gradient. This is not possible at most sites, and supplemental pumping is required. Most plants utilize pumping as the primary means of controlling the flow rate into the treatment plant. Such an arrangement is illustrated in Figure 9.3. When the gradient through the plant is insufficient to permit gravity flow, it is necessary to provide emergency power and pump redundancy to ensure continuous operation of the system.

9.3.2 Off-line Storage Basins

Off-line storage basins are filled only when a preset rate of flow into the plant is exceeded (see Figure 9.4). The inflow to the storage facility is regu-

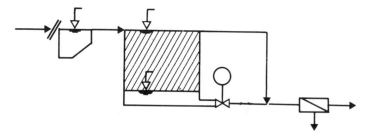

Figure 9.2   Storage in series with gravity outflow. *(After Nyseth, 1980.)*

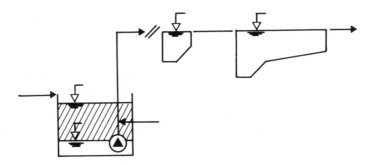

Figure 9.3   Storage in series with pumped outflow. *(After Nyseth, 1980.)*

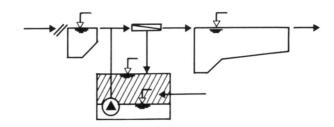

Figure 9.4   Storage in parallel to inflow to the plant. *(After Nyseth, 1980.)*

lated by a specially designed side channel spillway. The water that is stored in the basin is pumped to the main inflow stream when the inflow rate falls below a preset rate.

The off-line arrangement permits the dry weather wastewater to flow directly to the treatment processes. Since storage occurs only when flows spill into the basin, pumping requirements are less than for an in-line basin. Also, for the same reason, off-line basins are less prone to sludge accumulation than in-line basins.

9.3.3 Basin Configuration

The configuration of a separate storage basin is, for the most part, determined by site conditions. Among the factors affecting the configuration of a basin are

* storage volume needs,
* space availability, and
* vertical grade at the site.

Small- and medium-sized basins are often constructed out of structural concrete. Large basins, however, take the form of lined open ponds. Both were discussed earlier in Chapters 4 and 5.

A circular concrete detention tank is illustrated in Figure 9.5. It was under construction and was awaiting the installation of a rotating sludge scraper. In Figure 9.6, one can see an open concrete lined pond. The accumulated sludge in this pond is removed after the pond is drained using front end loaders and trucks.

For storage basins having long holding times, it may be necessary to

Figure 9.5   A 3 acre-foot (4,000 m³) tank under construction.

Figure 9.6   A 10 acre-foot (13,000 m³) open storage pond.

install mixing and aerating equipment. This equipment may be needed to prevent anaerobic conditions from developing inside the basin. See Metcalf and Eddy, Inc. (1979) or other wastewater treatment design texts for guidance in how to size such aerators.

9.4 INTEGRATED STORAGE

In some cases, it may be possible to incorporate the flow equalization storage into the basins used for primary treatment and aeration. This is feasible only when the variations in the flow are not very large. A detailed discussion on this topic can be found in Speece and La Grega (1976) and Spring (1977).

9.4.1 Flow Equalization in the Aeration Tanks

Flow equalization storage may be integrated into the aeration tanks of an activated sludge process. This is a possibility where the holding time in the aeration tanks is long and a relatively large portion of the basin volume can be used for detention. As Figure 9.7 illustrates, the water surface in the aeration tank will fluctuate with the flow.

Clearly, the biological processes will be affected by the variation in the water volume within the tank. To keep a stable biological system, the plant operators have to balance the hydraulic volume, pollutant load, the air supply, and the sludge mass being returned from the clarifiers. Careful monitoring of these parameters and of the average age of the sludge is necessary to maintain a stable biological treatment process, although it may be difficult with rapidly varying flow.

The main advantage of using aeration tanks for flow equalization is that the clarifier capacity is increased. However, as the sludge concentration entering the clarifiers increases, its hydraulic load has to be decreased to prevent solids from being flushed downstream. The main disadvantage of this approach is that the operation of the activated sludge process becomes significantly more complicated.

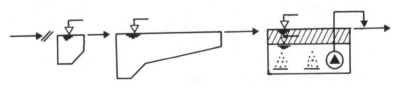

Figure 9.7   Flow equalization within an aeration tank.

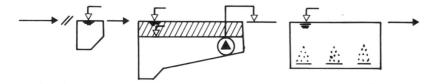

Figure 9.8   Flow equalization within a primary treatment tank.

9.4.2 Flow Equalization in Primary Treatment Tanks

Flow equalization can also be provided in the primary treatment tanks of the treatment plant. This is accomplished, as illustrated in Figure 9.8, by constructing the tanks with excess freeboard. The flow is regulated by pumping the tanks at a relatively constant rate.

The advantages of this concept include minimum land area requirements within a plant site and a relatively steady flow through the activated sludge process. It is possible, however, that the efficiency of the primary treatment process may be significantly reduced if very large inflow peaks are encountered.

REFERENCES

EPA, *Flow Equalization,* EPA Technology Transfer Seminar Publication, 1974.

FOESS, G., MEENAHAN, J., AND BLOUGH, D., "Evaluation of In-Line and Side-Line Flow Equalization Systems," *WPCF Journal,* January, 1977.

JUNKSGAARD, D., "Flow and Load Variations at Wastewater Treatment Plants," *WPCF Journal,* No. 8, 1980.

LA GREGA, M., AND KEENAN, J., "Effects of Equalizing Wastewater Flows," *WPCF Journal,* January, 1974.

METCALF & EDDY, INC., *Wastewater Engineering: Treatment Disposal and Reuse,* latest edition, McGraw-Hill.

NYSETH, I., "Use of Detention Basins at Sewage Treatment Plants," NTNF:s Utvalg for Drift av Renseanlegg, Prosjektrapport 23, 1980. (In Norwegian)

SPEECE, R., AND LA GREGA, M., "Flow Equalization by Use of Aeration Tank Volume," *WPCF Journal,* November, 1976.

SPRING, W., "Use of Free Capacities in the Pre-clarification by Recirculation of Storage," Kommunalwirtscaft H.9, 1977. (In German)

10

Other Types of Storage Facilities

10.1 INTRODUCTION

So far, only the more common types of storage facilities have been described. Naturally, there are other possibilities for storing stormwater or combined sewer overflows. Two examples of somewhat unconventional detention facilities are described here. In both cases, storage occurs within the receiving water body.

10.2 SUBMERGED CLOSED CONTAINERS

In the late 1960s, three full-scale tests were undertaken in the United States by the Environmental Protection Agency to collect and store combined sewer overflows in closed containers that are submerged in receiving waters. This technique was tested to see if such facilities could be installed in densely populated areas (see Figure 10.1). As a result of these tests, the following observations can be stated:

1. Submerged storage facilities are intended for the capture and storage of untreated combined sewer overflows that would otherwise enter the receiving waters.
2. These facilities are best suited in large, densely populated areas where open land near the receiving waters is not available.
3. This type of storage can be considered for areas such as harbors, indus-

Figure 10.1   Artist's rendering of a submerged storage. *(After Underwater Storage, Inc. and Silver Schwartz, Ltd., 1969.)*

trial complexes, waterfront business centers, swimming beaches, promenades, etc.

4. There are no major technical problems in anchoring closed containers to the bottom of the receiving waters.

5. Because the detention container is entirely submerged, it has virtually no adverse aesthetic impacts on the landscape.

We describe here three configurations tested by U.S. Environmental Protection Agency for the collection and storage of combined sewer overflows. All three facilities were submerged storage containers fabricated, in part or entirely, out of flexible membrane materials.

10.2.1 Technical Arrangements

Storage of water in submerged closed containers will routinely require the following equipment:

- diversion chamber in the trunk sewer,
- flow measuring instrumentation,
- pretreatment of the water to be stored,
- a storage container,
- connecting pipes,
- pumps for emptying the container, and
- control equipment.

Figure 10.2 shows a diagram of how the various parts of the installation may be arranged. As can be seen, only the storage unit itself and the pipes are located in the receiving waters. All other equipment is contained in a building located on land.

When the flow in the trunk sewer has reached a predetermined rate, the excess flow is diverted to the submerged storage container. Before the flow enters the storage container, it first passes through a pretreatment chamber. Here the large particles are screened out and much of the silt and grit are removed from the flow. Just downstream of the pretreatment chamber, the pipes are equipped with valves to shut off flow to the storage unit. This is needed to permit the isolation of the unit for cleaning and repair.

Wastewater is stored in the storage container until the trunk sewer has sufficient capacity to accept additonal flow. The decision when to pump the stored water is made on the basis of information being transmitted by flow measuring equipment inside the sewers. The pumping equipment is located on land and not in the submerged storage units, which permits easy access for maintenance and repairs. The inlet pipe to the storage unit can also serve as the suction pipe for the pumps.

10.2.2 The Storage Unit

Table 10.1 summarizes some of the characteristics of the three EPA test installations built in the late 1960s. In all three, the storage units were fabri-

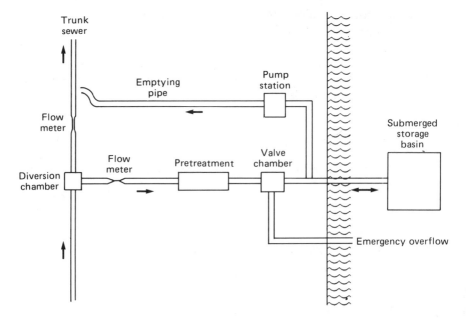

Figure 10.2   Arrangement of equipment for a submerged storage installation.

TABLE 10.1 Comparison of Three Submerged Storage Basins

Item	Location of the Installation		
	Washington, D.C.	Cambridge, Md.	Sandusky, Ohio
Storage volume	Two 100,000-gal (380-m³) units	One 200,000-gal (760-m³) unit	Two 100,000-gal (380-m³) units
Configuration	Rubber membrane anchored in steel cradle	Epoxy treated steel tank with rubber membrane top	Rubber membrane with steel frame inside and rigid bottom
Catchment area	30 acres (12 ha)	15 acres (6 ha)	20 acres (8 ha)
Distance to shoreline	115 ft (35 m)	1,300 ft (400 m)	On shoreline
Testing period	1969	1969	1968–1969

cated, at least in part, using nylon-reinforced synthetic rubber membranes. As far as it is known, no other submerged storage basins have been constructed to date for the purpose of storing combined sewer overflows.

Despite pretreatment, suspended solids accumulate in these storage containers. Since the deposits can clog pipes and valves, it was found necessary to install some form of agitation in the storage containers. During the testing by EPA, the following were used to maintain the solids in suspension:

- circulation pumping of the stored water,
- blowing compressed air into the storage containers, and
- rinsing of the containers with high-pressure water.

At the installation illustrated in Figure 10.3, the storage container was flushed with water as it was emptied. To facilitate sludge removal, this storage unit was equipped with a pit at the inlet/outlet point within the unit.

Air and other gases that accumulate inside a storage container are evacuated using one-way air-relief valves installed at the top of each container. Since the container is submerged in a receiving water body, the valve permits the release of gases from the container while at the same time preventing the liquids from escaping. This valve also should not permit water from the outside to enter the storage container.

10.2.3 Operation and Maintenance Experience

A common feature of all three test facilities was that they were in operation for a relatively short period of time. Certain difficulties arose with continuous operation of all test units, which included:

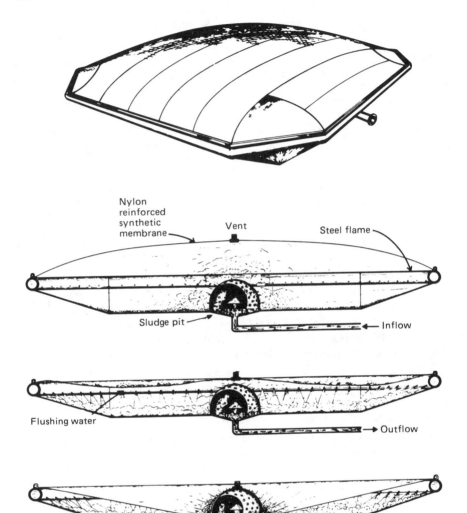

Figure 10.3   A sketch of the installation at Sandusky, Ohio. *(After Karl R. Rohrer, Inc., 1971.)*

- sediment deposits in the storage unit;
- damage to the rubber membrane from outside causes;
- failures of air-relief valves;
- anchoring of the storage containers to the bottom;
- clogging of the inlet/outlet pipes; and
- malfunctions of the land-based mechanical equipment.

It is only fair to mention, however, that most of these problems can be attributed to lack of experience at the time of testing with this type of technology. It is not unusual to experience "shakedown" problems whenever a new system goes on-line. It is likely that many of the aforementioned "problems" were solved since the tests were conducted in the late 1960s.

We discussed earlier in this book the importance of public perception in the design and installation of detention facilities. This point was driven home at one of the test sites when extremely strong negative public reaction forced a premature end of the test and the dismantling of the installation. The lesson learned from this experience is that it is important to consider more than purely technical issues when locating and designing detention facilities.

10.3 IN-LAKE FLOATING BASINS

In late 1970s, another unconventional storage/treatment facility was developed in Sweden to treat separate stormwater and combined sewer overflows. This technique was originally developed to reclaim heavily polluted lakes that had a limited number of annual exchanges of water. The storage unit consists of linear floats anchored to the bottom by plastic curtains, is always filled with water, and has an open connection to the lake.

10.3.1 Layout and Operation

The storage unit is made of floating docks that serve as the linear floats. The docks are held in place by steel pilings driven into the bottom of the lake and form a frame to which are attached plastic membrane curtains. The curtains are anchored to the bottom by concrete weights or chains, as illustrated in Figure 10.4.

The storage unit is divided into several flow-through basins that are con-

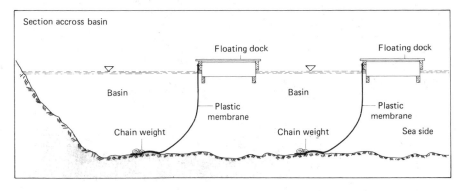

Figure 10.4   Cross-section of in-lake floating basins. *(By Soderlund, 1982.)*

nected in series. Water passes from one basin to the next through openings in the plastic curtain. An example plan of such a facility is shown in Figure 10.5. When stormwater runoff is flowing into the lake, it first enters basin A, from which water is pumped continuously to a treatment plant. During very heavy runoff, the inflow exceeds pump capacity and runoff enters the next downstream basin, B. If heavy runoff continues, all cells, namely A through E, will be filled with runoff and will enter the lake.

As the runoff passes through each storage cell, it displaces the lake water. While displacing lake water, some mixing of the lake's water with the runoff occurs. When storm runoff subsides and the inflow drops below the pump capacity, water then flows back into cell A, where it is pumped to the treatment plant. During dry weather, the treatment continues and lake

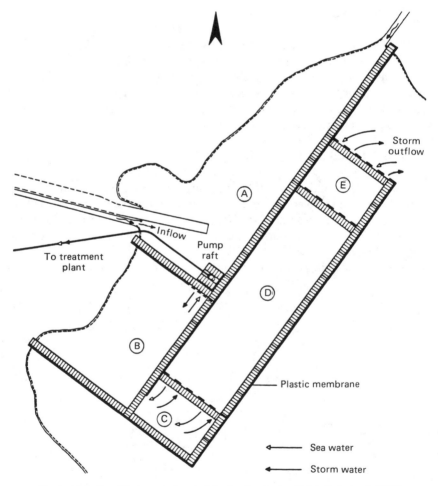

Figure 10.5   Possible layout of an in-lake floating basin. (After Soderlund, 1982).

TABLE 10.2 Study Findings of Three In-lake Storage Units

	Location of the Installation (Lake)		
Item	Trehorningen Huddinge	Ronningesjon Taby	Flaten Stockholm
Basin area	29,000 ft² (2700 m²)	15,000 ft² (1400 m²)	60,000 ft² (5600 m²)
Volume	175,000 ft³ (5000 m³)	81,000 ft³ (2300 m³)	530,000 ft³ (15000 m³)
No. of cells	15	5	2
Treatment	Chemical precipitation	Chemical precipitation and partial filtration	—
Capacity	8,500 ft³/hr (240 m³/hr)	2,500 ft³/hr (40 m³/hr)	—
Year installed	1978	1980	1980

water is drawn into the treatment plant. This process was designed to remove the phosphorus from the lake and help arrest the eutrophication process.

10.3.2 Field Experience

Through 1980, three in-lake storage facilities were built near Stockholm, Sweden. Their characteristics are summarized in Table 10.2. As part of the evaluation of this technology, flow mixing patterns were studied in detail at the basin installed in Lake Trehoningen. A complete report of the findings was prepared by Anderson (1980). Some of his key findings are summarized briefly here.

Using radioactive tracers, leakage was found to occur between separation curtains. The degree of leakage depended on the location along the curtains separating adjacent basins. When leakage occurred, some of the inflow short-circuited the treatment process.

Anderson (1980) reported that the most common points of leakage were at the corners, where two or more curtains joined. This was attributed, in part, to the pressure gradients found between "kitty-corner" storage cells. It was observed that the curtains bulged in the direction of flow and caused gaps to open between the curtains at the corners. Cementing and better sealing at the joints should help reduce this type of short circuiting.

During very high runoff, Anderson (1980) observed that the pressure differential between cells was sufficiently large to lift the curtains off the bottom. When that happened, some of the water flowed under the curtains and short-circuited the storage facility. After the curtains had been lifted off the bottom, they were found to catch on the anchors and would not drop down to seal against the bottom. This resulted in a recommendation to modify the anchoring system.

Anderson (1980) also reported that wind can also set up disturbances in the storage cells. A relatively moderate wind was found to set the water into rotational motion within the installation. However, it is possible to arrange the cells in a way that minimizes the effects of such wind disturbances.

REFERENCES

ANDERSON, L., "Detention Basins in Lake Trehorning-Huddinge Municipality, Study of Water Exchange," KTH Avdelningen for Vattenvardsteknik, Stockholm, 1980. (In Swedish)

KARL R. ROHRER ASSOCIATES, INC., *Underwater Storage of Combined Sewer Overflows,* USEPA Report No. 11022 ECVO9/71, NTIS No. PB 208 346, September, 1971.

MELPAR: AN AMERICAN STANDARD COMPANY, *Combined Sewer Temporary Underwater Storage Facility,* USEPA Report No. 11022 DPP 10/70, NTIS No. PB 197 669, October, 1970.

SODERLUND, H., *Flow Balancing Methods for Stormwater and Combined Sewer Overflows,* Swedish Council for Building Research, Publication D17, 1982. (In Swedish)

UNDERWATER STORAGE INC., AND SILVER, SCHWARTZ, LTD., *Control of Pollution by Underwater Storage,* USEPA Report No. 11020 DWF12/69, NTIS No. PB 191 217.

Overview of Flow Regulation

11.1 INTRODUCTION

Detention of stormwater or combined wastewater–stormwater flows is provided by a storage volume that is released by some type of flow regulating
device. It is the flow regulator that determines how efficiently the storage
volume is being utilized. Obviously, the flow regulator has to be in balance
with the available storage volume for the range of runoff events it was
designed to control.

The outlet structure or device, what we call here the *flow regulating
structure,* is an important component of the total detention storage facility. It
not only controls the release rate, but determines the maximum storage depth
and volume at the detention site. The flow regulating structure often is called
on to perform what may appear to be conflicting tasks, such as limit the flow
rates, be free of clogging, be relatively maintenance free, be designed to
provide safety to the public and, in some cases, be aesthetically appealing.

In Part 2 we deal primarily with the hydraulic function of flow regulation,
which can be accomplished in a number of different ways. The chapters of
Part 2 describe some of the conventional and some of the less conventional
ways to provide flow regulation. As an introduction, some of the fundamental
principles behind flow regulation are first examined.

11.2 FLOW REQUIREMENTS

The primary purpose for detention is to reduce the peak flow of runoff and equalize the rate of flow downstream. A rough estimate of the required storage volume can be made by assuming that the outflow rate is constant. However, a constant outflow rate cannot be easily achieved and most hydraulic structures have flow rates that vary with the depth of water. Obviously, the required storage volume for flow equalization is determined, to a large extent, by the outflow characteristics and the inflow hydrograph, as illustrated in Figure 11.1.

The specific configuration and details of an outlet structure will vary from site to site. However, for the more typical installations, the design of the operational outlet will try to do the following:

- Provide a maximum release flow rate for a single or multiple levels of design storm events.
- Minimize the storage volume by providing outlets to reach the maximum release rate early in the storm (see Figure 11.2).
- Permit flow-through of dry weather flows without backing up into the storage basin.
- Provide adequate trash racks to prevent clogging of the outlet.
- Where possible, provide the installation of simple, reliable, and operator-free equipment for regulating outflow.
- Provide good maintenance and inspection access, even when there is water in the storage basin.
- Allow for safety of the public and the maintenance and operating personnel.

11.3 LOCATION OF THE FLOW REGULATOR

The location of the flow regulating structure will depend on how the storage basin is connected to the storm conveyance system. If the storage is connected

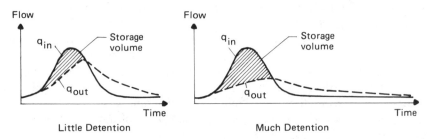

Figure 11.1   Storage volume needs vs. rate of outflow.

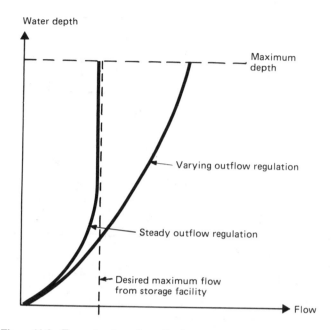

Water depth

Figure 11.2   Example of steady outflow and variable outflow regulation.

in-line (i.e., in series), the flow regulation takes place at the downstream end of the storage facility (see Figure 11.3). In this type of an arrangement, the flow regulator often is a flow restrictor located at, or near, the bottom of the storage basin. In some cases, where the topography does not permit emptying of the storage basin by gravity, pumping is used to regulate the flow rate.

When the storage facility is connected off-line (i.e., parallel) to the conveyance system, flow regulation is accomplished by limiting the rate of flow that bypasses the storage basin. The excess flow is diverted to the storage facility. Figure 11.4 shows two examples of how this system can be arranged. Other examples of how detention storage can be connected to the stormwater conveyance system can be found in Section 5.2.

In practice, the diversion to storage in a parallel connected system occurs through a side-channel spillway. The bypass flow is regulated by some form of a hydraulic constriction just downstream of the diversion, as illustrated in Figure 11.4. Off-line storage normally requires a separate outlet to totally drain the impoundment, as depicted by the dashed line on the upper illustra-

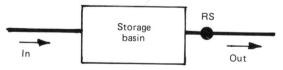

Figure 11.3   Location of a flow regulating structure in an in-line connected storage.

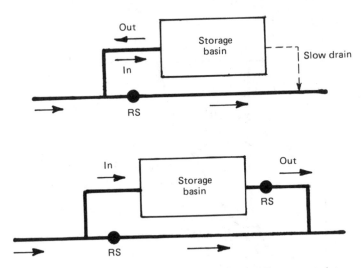

Figure 11.4   Location of a flow regulating structure in an off-line connected storage system.

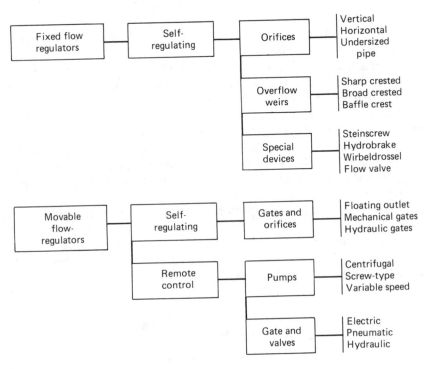

Figure 11.5   Various types of outflow control devices.

tion in Figure 11.4. In some cases, the site topography will require the water to be pumped out of the storage basin. It may also be necessary to provide a separate flow regulating structure (i.e. RS on Figure 11.4) at the outlet of the storage basin.

11.4 FIXED AND MOVABLE FLOW REGULATORS

The release rate from a storage facility can be controlled with either a fixed or a movable flow regulating structure. Fixed regulators are permanently attached to the basin structure and have a constant outlet cross-section during the entire detention cycle. Fixed regulators include orifices, nozzles, weirs, and special, sometimes patented, devices. Except for some of the special flow regulating devices, the flow rate through a fixed regulator will vary with the hydraulic head.

Movable regulators are characterized by an outlet that varies in size or elevation during the detention cycle. This family of regulating devices include gates, valves, floating orifices, floating weirs, and pumps. All of these devices require some form of control equipment. Movable flow regulators can be self-regulating or they can be designed for remote control. Figure 11.5 depicts some of the methods used to regulate flows.

REFERENCES

LAGER, J. A., AND SMITH, W. G., "Urban Stormwater Management and Technology: An Assessment," U.S. EPA Report No. EPA-670/2-74-040, (NTIS No. PB 240 687).

12

Types of Flow Regulators

Flow regulators can range from a simple fixed orifice to a complex, remotely controlled, automated mechanically operated gate or valve. Although the discussion in this chapter describes many of the conventional and some of the less conventional flow regulators, it is not intended to describe every type of regulator that is available or that can be used.

12.1 FIXED REGULATORS

As stated earlier, fixed regulators have a flow control section that does not change in area or elevation during the detention cycle. Once constructed, modification of the control requires physical modification to the outlet. No special control equipment is needed, and these type of regulators are relatively inexpensive to build and operate. As was listed in Figure 11.5, fixed regulators include weirs, orifices, choked pipes, and special devices.

12.1.1 Vertically Arranged Orifice or Nozzle

The simplest flow regulating structure is an orifice or a nozzle installed into the side of a storage basin. The trickle flows flow through the opening unimpeded, while the larger flows are backed up (see Figure 12.1). When the outlet is small in comparison to the depth of water, the discharge through the orifice, or a nozzle, can be calculated using the following formula:

$$Q = C_d \cdot A \sqrt{2g \cdot (h - a)} \qquad (12.1)$$

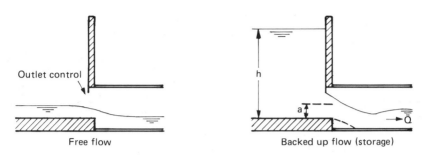

Figure 12.1   Outflow through a vertical orifice.

in which Q = discharge rate through the outlet,
C_d = discharge coefficient,
A = area of the orifice or nozzle,
g = acceleration of gravity,
h = water depth at outlet, and
a = one-half the height of the outlet opening (see Figure 12.1).

The preceding equation assumes that there is no back pressure from downstream (i.e., the outlet is not submerged). If the outlet is submerged, this equation can still be used. Just use the difference in the water surfaces between both sides of the orifice as the depth h in the equation.

The discharge coefficient, C_d, can vary significantly with the shape and the type of the orifice. A summary of the most commonly used orifice shapes is presented in Figure 12.2. As a result, it is important to pay careful attention to the details of the orifice shape during construction to ensure that the completed facility will operate as designed.

It is sometimes necessary to estimate the time it takes to drain a known stored volume through an orifice. This is to ensure that the pond is emptied either sufficiently fast or slow after the storm ends. We start this calculation with the fact that the time needed to drain down an increment of depth dh is

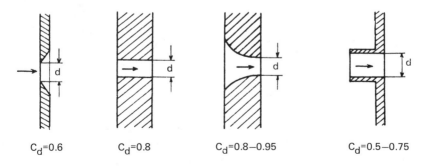

Figure 12.2   Discharge coefficient C_d for different outlets.

equal to the volume $A_R dh$ divided by the discharge Q. Integrating this between water depths h_1 and h_2, we get:

$$t = \int_o^t dt = -\int_{h_1}^{h_2} \left(\frac{A_R}{Q}\right) dh \qquad (12.2)$$

Substituting Equation 12.1 for Q yields a relationship for calculating the emptying time of the storage volume,

$$t = -\frac{1}{C_d A \sqrt{2g}} \int_{h_1}^{h_2} \left(\frac{A_R}{\sqrt{h}}\right) dh \qquad (12.3)$$

When the area of the reservoir, A_R, can be described as a mathematical function of the water depth, h, then this equation can be solved. For the special case where the surface area is a constant (i.e., vertical walls), Equation 12.3 is reduced to

$$t = \frac{2A_R}{C_d \cdot A \cdot \sqrt{2g}} \cdot (\sqrt{h_1} - \sqrt{h_2}) \qquad (12.4)$$

The opening of the outlet can be round, square, rectangular, or any other convenient shape. It can be a preset gate or a plate attached to a headwall located in front of the outlet pipe. The orifice in the latter case is cut into a plate which is then installed so that it can be easily removed for maintenance or replacement.

Outlets with openings of less than 6 inches (150 mm) are very susceptible to clogging. The chances of clogging can be significantly reduced by installing trash racks having a net opening that is more than 20 times the opening of the outlet. Larger outlets also need trash racks, but the ratio of the net area of the rack to the outlet area does not need to be as large.

When the size of the orifice is relatively large when compared to the water depth, orifice equations (e.g., Equations 12.1 through 12.4) are not accurate. When water depth above the invert of the orifice is less than two to three times the height of the orifice, more accurate results are possible using inlet control nomographs for culverts published by the Federal Highway Administration (1963) and by using the improved culvert inlet design procedures, which are also published by the Federal Highway Administration (1972). Nomographs for calculating the discharge of circular and rectangular culverts operating under inlet control conditions are reproduced here as Figures 12.3 and 12.4.

12.1.2 Horizontally Arranged Orifice

In some cases, the flow regulating orifice has to be installed in the bottom of the storage basin similar to a bathtub drain (see Figure 12.5). When the depth, h, is relatively large when compared to the orifice opening, its flow capacity can be calculated using the formula:

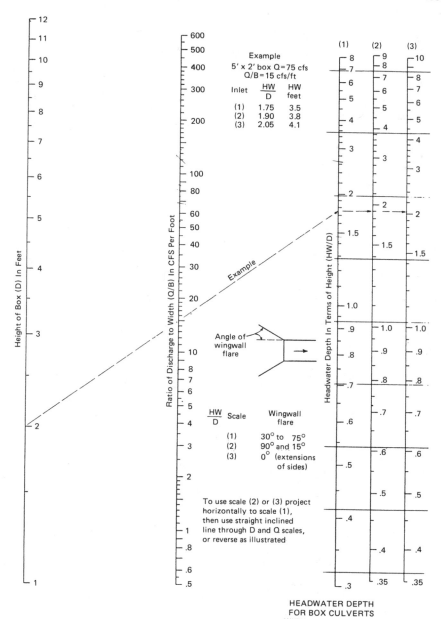

HEADWATER DEPTH
FOR BOX CULVERTS
WITH INLET CONTROL

BUREAU OF PUBLIC ROADS JAN. 1963

Figure 12.3 Nomograph for rectangular culvert capacity operating under inlet control. *(After Federal Highway Administration, 1974.)*

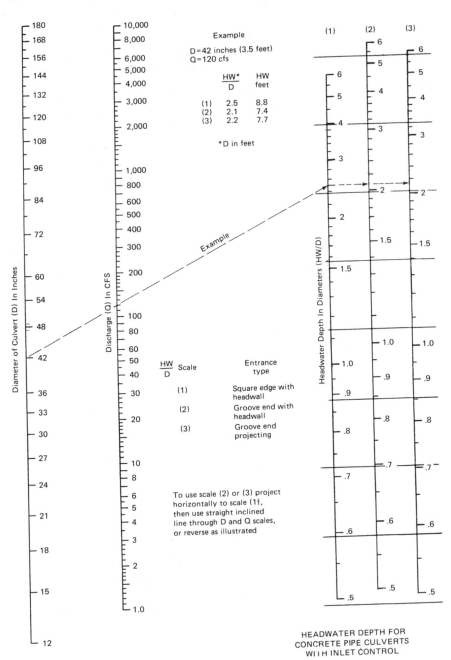

Example

D = 42 inches (3.5 feet)
Q = 120 cfs

	$\frac{HW^*}{D}$	HW feet
(1)	2.5	8.8
(2)	2.1	7.4
(3)	2.2	7.7

*D in feet

$\frac{HW}{D}$ Scale	Entrance type
(1)	Square edge with headwall
(2)	Groove end with headwall
(3)	Groove end projecting

To use scale (2) or (3) project
horizontally to scale (1),
then use straight inclined
line through D and Q scales,
or reverse as illustrated

HEADWATER DEPTH FOR
CONCRETE PIPE CULVERTS
WITH INLET CONTROL

BUREAU OF PUBLIC ROADS JAN. 1963

Figure 12.4 Nomograph for circular culvert capacity operating under inlet control.
(After Federal Highway Administration, 1974.)

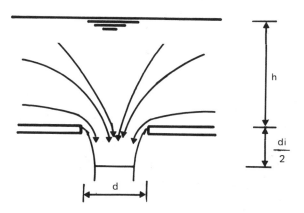

Figure 12.5 Flow through a horizontal orifice.

$$Q = C_d \cdot A \cdot \sqrt{2g \cdot \left(h - \frac{d}{2}\right)}$$ (12.5)

in which Q = discharge rate through the outlet,
C_d = discharge coefficient,
A = area of the orifice or nozzle,
g = acceleration of gravity,
h = water depth at outlet, and
d = diameter of the outlet opening.

The discharge coefficients for a horizontally arranged orifice are the same as for the vertically arranged orifice, and representative values for both types can be found in Figure 12.2. Equation 12.5 will not give accurate results whenever the water depth above the horizontal orifice is less than three times the diameters of the orifice. At smaller depths, severe vortex action develops which is not accounted for in Equation 12.5.

12.1.3 Flow Restricting Pipe

There are at least two reasons why a flow restricting pipe may be used as an outlet. One is that it is difficult to modify the hydraulic capacity of an outlet pipe, unlike a flow restricting orifice which can be easily removed. Flow control orifices being removed by owners, or as an act of vandalism, has been reported by Prommersberger (1984) and others. The hydraulic characteristics of a flow restricting outlet pipe are much more difficult to modify. As illustrated in Figure 12.6, the net flow restricting effect of the pipe is mostly a function of the pipe length and pipe roughness characteristics.

A pipe outlet may also be used to provide greater flow reduction while using a larger diameter outlet. If the pipe is set at a slope that is less than the

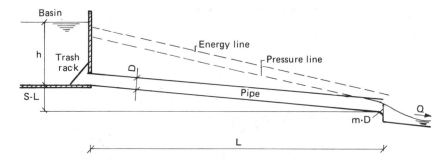

Figure 12.6   Flow regulation with an outlet pipe.

hydraulic friction slope, outlet capacity can be reduced without the use of a small diameter orifice. It is important, however, to maintain a minimum velocity of 2 to 3 feet per second (0.6 to 0.9 m/s) in the pipe in order to keep the silt carried by the water from settling out within the pipe.

If we assume that the pipe is flowing full and the discharge end of the pipe is not submerged, the outlet capacity can be calculated using basic hydraulic principles. If we begin with the continuity equation:

$$Q = A \cdot v \tag{12.6}$$

and calculate losses at the outlet using

$$H_t = K_L \cdot \frac{v^2}{2g} \tag{12.7}$$

combining these two equations yields:

$$Q = A \cdot \sqrt{2g \cdot \frac{H_t}{K_L}} \tag{12.8}$$

in which Q = outlet capacity,
   v = flow velocity when pipe is full,
   A = area of outlet pipe,
   g = acceleration of gravity,
   H_t = total hydraulic losses in a pipe outlet, and
   K_L = sum of loss factors for the outlet.

From Figure 12.6 we observe that,

$$H_t = h + S \cdot L - m \cdot D \tag{12.9}$$

Thus, Equation 12.9 can be substituted into Equation 12.8 and rewritten as

$$Q = A \cdot \sqrt{2g \cdot \frac{h + S \cdot L - m \cdot D}{K_L}} \tag{12.10}$$

in which h = depth of water above outlet pipe's invert,
   D = diameter of outlet pipe,
   S = slope of outlet pipe,
   L = length of outlet pipe, and
   m = ratio of water depth to pipe diameter at the outlet end of the pipe.

How to calculate outlet capacities for medium sized dams is explained in much detail by the U.S. Bureau of Reclamation (1973). However, some of the most commonly used procedures are repeated here. The sum of the loss factors will depend on the characteristics of the outlet. For example, it may contain

$$K_L = k_t + k_e + k_f + k_b + k_o \qquad (12.11)$$

in which k_t = trash rack loss factor,
   k_e = entrance loss factor,
   k_f = friction loss factor,
   k_b = bend loss factor, and
   k_o = outlet loss factor.

Trash Rack Loss Factor.   According to Creager and Justin (1950), the loss factor at a trash rack can be approximated using the following equation:

$$k_t = 1.45 - 0.45\left(\frac{a_n}{a_g}\right) - \left(\frac{a_n}{a_g}\right)^2 \qquad (12.12)$$

in which a_n = net open area between the rack bars, and
   a_g = gross area of the rack and supports.

When estimating the maximum potential losses at the rack, assume that 50% of the rack area is blocked. Also calculate the maximum outlet capacity assuming no blockage. Always calculate the minimum and maximum outlet capacities to ensure that the installation will function adequately under both possible operating scenarios in the field.

Entrance Loss Factor.   By taking the orifice equation, rearranging its terms, and recognizing that the depth term in the equation is actually the sum of the velocity head and the head loss, we find that

$$k_e = \frac{1}{C_d^2} - 1 \qquad (12.13)$$

in which C_d = orifice discharge coefficient.

Friction Loss Factor.   The pipe friction loss factor for a pipe flowing full is expressed as

$$k_f = f\frac{L}{D} \qquad (12.14)$$

in which f = Darcy-Weisbach friction loss coefficient, which, under certain simplifying assumptions, can be expressed as a function of Manning's n, namely,

$$f = 185 \frac{n^2}{D^{1/3}} \qquad (12.15)$$

Bend Loss Factor.   Bend losses in a closed conduit are a function of bend radius, pipe diameter, and the deflection angle at the bend. The bend loss factor was studied by a number of investigators. Unfortunately, it was found to vary between different studies. However, for 90 degree bends having a radius at least twice the pipe diameter, a value of $k_b = 0.2$ appears to be a reasonable average using data from all of the studies. For bends having other than 90 degree bends, the bend loss factor can be calculated using the following equation:

$$k_b = K \cdot k_{90} \qquad (12.16)$$

in which K = coefficient taken from Table 12.1, and
    k_{90} = loss factor for 90 degree bend.

Outlet Loss Factor.   Virtually no recovery of velocity head occurs where the pipe freely discharges into the atmosphere or is submerged under water. As a result, unless a specially shaped flared outlet is provided, it is safe to assume that $k_o = 1.0$.

In calculating the pipe outlet capacity, it is generally assumed that the pressure line at the outlet end of the pipe is at the center of the pipe (i.e., $m = 0.5$). In certain cases, this assumption may not be valid. Li and Patterson (1956) developed Figure 12.7 to help estimate a correct value of m. First, find pipe capacity using Equation 12.10, assuming that $m = 0.5$. Then find a new value of m from Figure 12.7 using the calculated velocity. Recalculate the pipe outlet capacity using Equation 12.10 with the new value of m. One recalculation is sufficient to obtain an accurate answer.

TABLE 12.1   Factors for Other
Than 90° Bend Losses

Angle of Bend in Degrees	Adjustment Factor
00	0.00
20	0.37
40	0.63
60	0.82
80	0.90
100	1.05
120	1.13

After U.S. Bureau of Reclamation, 1973

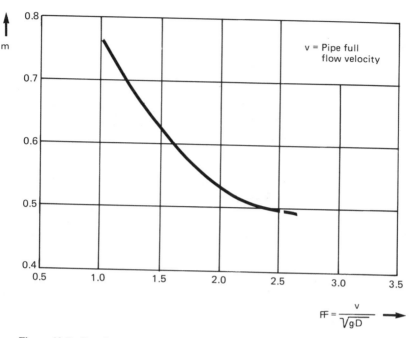

Figure 12.7 Froude Number vs. m at the pipe outlet. *(After Li and Patterson, 1956.)*

As stated, the outlet capacity is calculated assuming the pipe is flowing full. Figure 12.8 was also developed by Li and Patterson (1956) to help determine if the pipe is, in fact, entirely full. Although this figure is based on model tests using plastic pipe, it should provide reasonable basis for checking the flow condition in pipes manufactured of different materials.

12.1.4 Weirs

Weirs are often used as primary overflow control devices. They can provide the first level of emergency overflow, or actually be a part of the outflow regulating system. Weirs can come in many different shapes and sizes, and it is relatively easy to calculate the capacity of the more standard weir types. On the other hand, complicated compound weir configurations often do not have laboratory tested coefficients of discharge. As a result, calculations of their capacity may not be accurate. Fortunately, experimental data for many of the less standard shapes have been published by King and Brater (1963) and others.

Sharp-crested Weir.   The flow over a sharp-crested weir having no end contractions can be calculated using the following equation:

$$Q = C \cdot L \cdot h^{3/2}$$

(12.17)

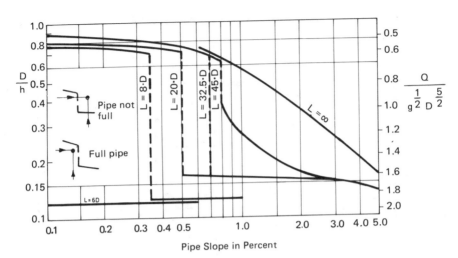

Pipe Slope in Percent

Figure 12.8 Length upstream of outlet needed to assure full pipe flow. (*After Li and Patterson, 1956.*)

in which Q = discharge over the weir in cubic feet per second (m³/s),
  C = discharge coefficient,
  L = effective length of the weir crest in feet (m) (see Equation 12.19), and
  h = head above the weir crest feet (m).

The measurement of a representative head h for a sharp-crested weir is made at a distance of approximately $2.5 \cdot h$ upstream of the weir crest. Also, according to the weir equation originally proposed by Rehbock (1929), the discharge coefficient for a sharp-crested weir can be calculated using

$$C = K_u\left(3.27 + 0.4\,\frac{h}{P}\right) \qquad (12.18)$$

in which P = height of weir crest above the channel bottom (see Figure 12.9), and
  K_u = 1.0 for U.S. standard units (0.55 for SI units).

This equation gives accurate results if the weir nape is fully aerated and is not submerged. If the nape is not aerated, a partial vacuum develops under the nape and the flow over the weir increases. The flow also becomes very unstable and undulating. Such a condition is not desirable; therefore provisions for aerating the weir have to be made.

In most detention applications, the weir crest does not extend completely across the channel. Therefore, the length needs to be corrected for flow

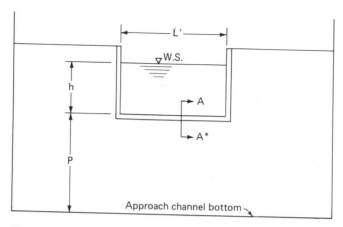

*See figure 12.10 for Section A-A

Figure 12.9   Sharp-crested weir.

contractions at each end of a sharp-crested weir. The effective weir length is calculated using

$$L = L' - 0.1\, n \cdot h \qquad (12.19)$$

in which L = effective length of the weir crest in feet (m),
L' = measured length of the weir crest in feet (m),
n = number of end contractions, and
h = head of water above the crest.

   Triangular Sharp-crested Weir.   A triangular sharp-crested weir should be considered whenever the weir needs also to control low flows. As can be seen in Figure 12.10, the water surface crest over this weir varies with depth. As a result, weir capacity is sensitive to the water depth at low flows. The discharge over a triangular sharp-crested weir is given by

$$Q = C_t \cdot h^{5/2} \cdot \tan\left(\frac{\alpha}{2}\right) \qquad (12.20)$$

in which C_t = discharge coefficient for a triangular weir,
α = weir notch angle in degrees, and
h = head above weir notch bottom.

   The head h is measured from the bottom of the notch to the water surface elevation at a distance of $2.5h$ upstream of the weir. Table 12.2 lists values of the discharge coefficient for the triangular weir and is based on the work reported by Lenz (1943) for a free, nonsubmerged nape downstream of the weir.

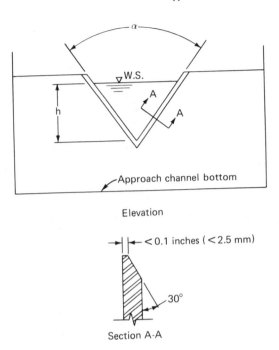

Elevation

Section A-A

Figure 12.10   Triangular sharp-crested weir.

Submergence of a Sharp-crested Weir.   So far, we have described sharp-crested weirs that had a free, nonsubmerged nape on the downstream side. When the tailwater rises to above the weir crest, the discharge calculations for the nonsubmerged case have to be corrected for submergence. Villemonte (1947) suggested the following equation for this purpose:

$$\frac{Q_s}{Q} = \left[1.0 - \left(\frac{h_s}{h}\right)^n\right]^{0.385} \tag{12.21}$$

TABLE 12.2   Discharge Coefficients for a Triangular Sharp-crested Weir for U.S. Standard Units (for SI Units)

Depth h in Feet	COEFFICIENT C, FOR NOTCH ANGLE		
	45°	60°	90°
0.2 (0.06)	2.66 (1.47)	2.62 (1.45)	2.57 (1.42)
0.4 (0.12)	2.57 (1.42)	2.53 (1.40)	2.51 (1.39)
0.6 (0.18)	2.53 (1.40)	2.51 (1.39)	2.49 (1.37)
0.8 (0.24)	2.52 (1.39)	2.50 (1.38)	2.48 (1.37)

After Lenz, 1943

in which Q = discharge calculated for a nonsubmerged weir equation,
$\quad Q_s$ = discharge for a submerged weir,
$\quad h$ = head upstream of the weir,
$\quad h_s$ = tailwater depth above the weir crest, and
$\quad n$ = the exponent in the sharp-crested weir equation (i.e., $\frac{3}{2}$ for rectangular and $\frac{5}{2}$ for triangular).

Theoretically, the preceding equation can be used to correct for submergence of any shape of a sharp-crested weir. All that is needed is to use the appropriate value for the exponent n. According to Villemonte, this equation has an accuracy of 5%.

Broad-crested Weirs.   Broad-crested weirs (see Figure 12.11) are commonly used in stormwater storage facilities as overflow devices or spillways. The discharge over a broad-crested weir is given by the equation

$$Q = C \cdot L \cdot H_t^{3/2} \tag{12.22}$$

in which Q = discharge in cubic feet per second (m^3/s),
$\quad C$ = coefficient of discharge,
$\quad L$ = effective length of the weir crest in feet (m),
$\quad H_t = (h + V^2/2g)$, total head above the weir crest in feet (m),
$\quad V$ = approach velocity at $3 \cdot h$ upstream of crest in feet per second (m/s), (usually taken at $V = 0$ for detention overflow), and
$\quad g$ = acceleration of gravity, 32.2 feet per second (9.8 m/s)

The discharge coefficient C for a broad-crested weir has been determined experimentally to range between 2.67 to 3.05 (corresponding to 1.47 to 1.68 SI units). A value of $C = 3.0$ (corresponding to 1.66 SI units) is often used for the design of detention overflow structures and spillways.

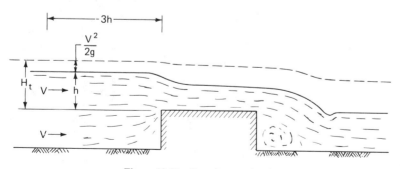

Figure 12.11 Broad-crested weir.

12.1.5 Compound and Nonstandard Flow Regulators

All the flow regulators described so far are often combined in a variety of ways to fashion compound outflow vs. stage control systems that provide the desired discharge and flood routing characteristics. Such compounding of outlet controls can be illustrated with the aid of Figure 12.12. First, a small orifice is installed to control the most frequently occurring events, such as 2-year floods, or to control release of the water quality design volume. This small orifice releases the routing volume of a smaller storm very slowly.

During larger storms, such as 10- and 100-year floods, the water spill over the riser and is initially controlled by a sharp-crested weir, which is the riser structure's top. As the water continues to rise, the top of the riser begins to function as a horizontal orifice. However, much more reliable flow regulation can be achieved for larger floods by designing the outlet pipe to provide *pipe control.* In such an arrangement the weir length is oversized to ensure that it will not choke off the flow before the outlet pipe control is activated. During very large storms the water may rise until it overflows through the emergency spillway, which is often designed as a broad-crested weir.

To account for the various flow regulating elements, the designer must develop a stage–discharge chart for each of them. These individual stage–discharge relationships are then composited into a single flow regulating stage–discharge curve similar to the one in Figure 12.13. Note that at various stages different flow regulating elements control the release rate.

Sometimes, however, the outlet is composited from familiar elements in

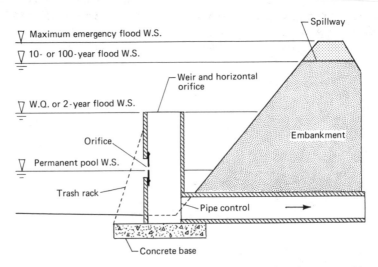

Figure 12.12   An outlet structure using various flow regulating elements, and its stage–discharge curve.

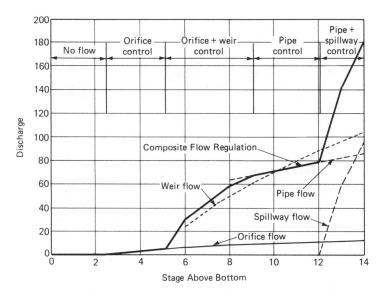

Figure 12.13 Compositing a flow regulating stage–discharge chart for a compound outlet.

an atypical fashion. An example of such an outlet is shown in Figure 12.14. It has a vertical slit-type orifice with an overflow at the top and a grated inlet behind the slit. As the water rises, more of the slit orifice is inundated, resulting in a variable-flow control area. This outlet had functioned for some time with very little maintenance when the photograph was taken. From that perspective it is a success. However, because of its unusual configuration, it is virtually impossible to accurately quantify its stage–discharge characteristics. If accurate outflow characteristics are important, it is suggested that the designer incorporate the previously described "classic" flow regulating elements into the outlet. The standard shapes or special outlets described later can be designed to look attractive and even to have an architectural flair.

12.1.6 Special Flow Regulators

During the 1970s, a number of flow regulating devices were introduced with the intent of providing flow equalization. The most prominent of these are:

- Steinscrew,
- hydrobrake,
- wirbeldrossel, and
- flow valve.

Figure 12.14 An atypical composite flow regulating outlet. (*Courtesy of Urban Drainage and Flood Control District, Denver, Colo.*)

All of these were designed to provide a more constant rate of outflow with varying water depth than is possible with an orifice or a flow restricting pipe outlet. Because of their unique configurations and designs, these special flow regulating devices are described in detail in Chapter 13.

12.2 MOVABLE FLOW REGULATORS

Movable flow regulators are classified into:

- self-regulating, and
- remote controlled.

Self-regulating flow regulators have an opening controlled by the water level in the storage basin or immediately downstream of the storage basin. The control is generally accomplished by the use of floats. No additional outside energy is required except for what is produced by the variations in the water level.

Remote controlled regulators are much more complex. Besides the equipment at the outlet itself, some form of electrical or pneumatic control equipment is needed. Its purpose is to give signals to the outlet structure to increase or decrease the release rate. Although remote controlled flow regulation can be expensive, it can be very effective in balancing the outflow rate against available sewer capacity downstream.

12.2.1 Flow Regulating Strategies

It is possible to "control" the release rate from the storage basin using only the water level upstream of the outlet. In this case, the flow downstream of the outlet is not monitored to see if the desired flow rate is being achieved. This approach can result in erroneous control signals and improper flow releases downstream.

As an example, if an outlet is partially clogged or silted in, the water level will rise in the storage basin. The control equipment interprets this water rise as an increasing release rate at the outlet. To keep the release rate constant, the control equipment throttles the outlet, further closing off the outlet. Obviously, the correct action should have been to open the outlet and flush out the clogging materials, or if it remains clogged, to signal the operator that there is a problem.

A much more effective flow control is possible by sensing the flow or water level downstream of the outlet. This permits direct interpretation of what is actually being released from the storage facility. By comparing the measured release rate with the desired flow rate, it is then possible to control the outlet to ensure that the downstream system capacity is being properly utilized.

In summary, for reasons of operational reliability, the release rate from a storage basin is best regulated using flow data obtained downstream of the outlet. One should avoid controlling movable flow regulators using only the water level inside of a storage basin.

12.2.2 Movable Gate with Mechanical Level Control

One type of movable self-regulating gate is controlled by the water level immediately downstream of the outlet. It consists of a stilling basin immediately downstream of the outlet and a float controlled flap gate. When the water level (i.e., the release rate) drops, the weighted float drops and opens the gate. When the water rises, the opposite occurs. This sequence can be set to provide a relatively constant release rate from a storage basin.

Experience has shown that operation can be impaired by the accumulation of sand, grit, and sludge in the float chamber. The valve eventually can be blocked from opening fully and the release rate diminished. This type of an installation requires considerable maintenance unless it is used in a sediment-free water.

12.2.3 Floating Outlet

A floating outlet is another type of a self-regulating movable flow regulator. The release from the storage facility occurs over an outlet that rises and falls with the water level in the storage basin. This permits the water depth at the outlet itself to be relatively constant, resulting in a uniform release rate.

An example of a floating outlet manufactured in England is illustrated in Figure 12.15. This outlet is equipped with a surface skimmer that keeps the floatables from being flushed downstream or from clogging the outlet itself. Since the water is skimmed off the top of the storage basin, much of the suspended solid load is trapped inside the basin. The device illustrated in this figure is manufactured with outlet pipes ranging between 3 and 15 inches

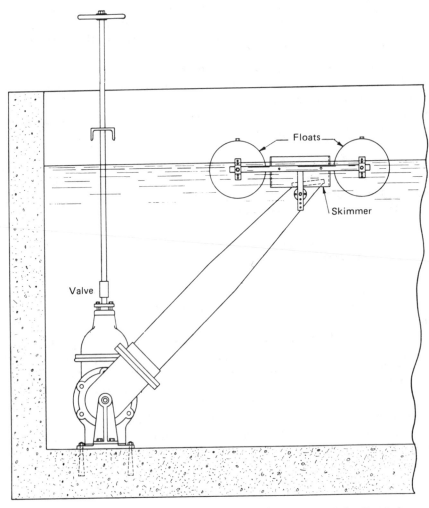

Figure 12.15   A floating outlet with a shut-off valve. *(Adams-Hydraulics, Ltd., York, England.)*

(80 and 375 mm) in diameter and capacities of up to 2,500 gallons per minute (160 l/s).

12.2.4 Remote Controlled Gates

Remote controlled gates vary from site to site, and their specific details depend on the conditions found at each location. With the advent of microprocessors and recent improvements in telemetering, the last 10 years have seen very significant advances in the technology of flow regulation. It is now feasible to simultaneously control the release rates at a number of storage facilities for the purpose of optimizing total system capacity.

The basic principles for remotely controlled flow regulators are briefly described here. The reader is referred to papers by Shilling (1986) and others to learn more about the full potential of modern technology for this purpose. A remote controlled flow regulation system will typically consist of

- flow or water level sensing equipment,
- adjustable flow regulating gates, and
- a data processing unit.

Flow Measurement.   The release from a storage basin is measured at a specially designed measuring section downstream of the outlet. Figure 12.16 shows one example of how flow sensing downstream of the storage basin can be arranged.

Adjustable Gates.   Gates can be operated using electrical, hydraulic, or pneumatic controls. To improve operational reliability, gates should be installed in a separate access chamber located downstream of the storage basin. The automatic flow control gate is typically installed in a flow-through pipe located inside the vault. To permit the removal of the control gate for maintenance, it is recommended that a bypass pipe, equipped with a manually operated valve, also be installed (see Figure 12.16). To reduce the risk of clogging at the outlet, a free opening at least a 10 inches (250 mm) in diameter is suggested.

Experience in Europe and in the United States (Schilling, 1986) clearly dictates that the control gate access vault be kept dry and dehumidified. Control and mechanical equipment deteriorate much more rapidly when the vault is humid and is subjected to inundation by wastewater. Good access, which is kept dry and free of humidity, is a cost-effective investment when one considers the consequences of equipment failures.

Control Processor.   Flow measurements or water levels at the monitoring section are transmitted to the processor unit. Here, data are transformed into signals for setting the opening of the control gate. When the measured rate exceeds the desired flow rate the gate opening is reduced, and when the

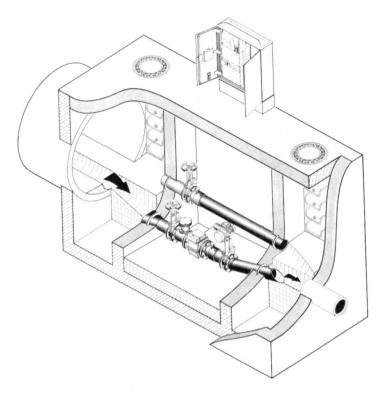

Figure 12.16 Flow measuring downstream of a storage basin. *(Umvelt und Fluidtehnik GmbH, Bad Mergentheim, Germany.)*

flow rate is less than desired the gate is opened more. This form of regulation is referred to as a "feedback system."

Figure 12.17 illustrates the operation of a feedback system. The water level at a section downstream of the gate was used to control the opening of the control gate. When the water at the control section rises above h_{max} the processor tells the gate to close. The gate opening is reduced in small increments until the water level drops below h_{max}. Similarly, when the water level drops below h_{min} the gate is told to open more. Whenever the water level is between h_{max} and h_{min}, the gate opening is not changed.

During a large storm the release rate from the storage facility can rise very rapidly and exceed level $h_{max-max}$ at the control section. When this happens, the processor instructs the gate to close rapidly and brings the surcharge under control. Typically, the control system is designed not to fully close the gate. This minimum gate opening should be set to permit a desired release rate when the basin is full.

An automatic flow regulating system can be as simple as the one just described, or it can be made very sophisticated through the use of micro-

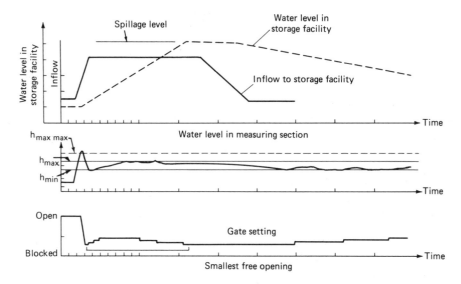

Figure 12.17   Example of feedback regulation of flow releases. *(After Jedelhauser, 1978.)*

processors, computer modeling, and telemetering. Such a system can be designed to "anticipate" the flow rate entering the storage basin and the release rate at the outlet by also providing flow measurements at the basin inlet, or by measuring the rainfall in the watershed. The latter requires simulation of the runoff process and is less reliable than inflow measurements. On the other hand, if the system needs more lead time to anticipate the control action it must take, such as may be needed for a storage basin located within an undersized sewer system, the use of rainfall and runoff simulation, along with monitoring for flow verification may need to be an integral part of the control processor.

12.2.5 Flow Regulation With Pumps

Whenever the site topography does not permit draining of the storage basin by gravity, use of pumps is the only remaining option. The control processor is then used to operate pumps instead of gates. Because of the electrical and mechanical nature of pumps, the potential for electrical and mechanical failures is ever present and should be anticipated in design. Problems may include pump failure, electric power interruptions, clogging, and processor failures. Such problems can be handled by providing redundancy of equipment and by providing emergency power generation. With off-line storage facilities, operational reliability of pumps is further reduced by the intermittent nature of water storage in the basin.

The most common types of pumps used in flow regulation are:

- centrifugal pumps,
- eccentric screw pumps,
- screw pumps, and
- variable speed pumps.

Centrifugal Pumps. Centrifugal pumps generally are an excellent choice for the emptying of either in-line and off-line storage basins because of their reliability and relatively low maintenance needs. A uniform flow rate can be achieved by providing a depressed wet well which can maintain a relatively stable submergence on the pump impellers. Also, the outflow can be kept constant by a flow regulator that "throttles." The latter will result in the pump operating at less than its maximum efficiency.

Eccentric Screw Pumps. Continuously operating eccentric screw pumps will maintain a constant discharge rate, regardless of the water level in the storage basin. The disadvantage of this type of a pump is its relatively high cost and that the rotor is susceptible to wear. Due to their design, eccentric screw pumps have a tendency to clog more easily than centrifugal pumps.

Screw Pumps. Screw pumps will maintain a constant discharge as long as there is enough water in the storage basin. In other words, screw pumps are hydraulically self-regulating. Their capacity is set by the slope of the screw trough, the rate of rotation, and the size of the screws. Although they are quite expensive, screw pumps offer operational advantages over other types of pumps used for this purpose. They are practically free from clogging, require a minimum of control equipment, and are usually very reliable to operate.

Variable Speed Pumps. These pumps offer probably the greatest potential for flow control. The pump speed can be varied to increase or decrease the discharge rate to whatever the control processor demands. Because of their sophistication, variable speed pumps can be quite expensive to install and maintain. These pumps can be operated in combination with fixed speed pumps to maintain uniform flow.

12.3 FLOW REGULATORS FOR WATER QUALITY ENHANCEMENT

12.3.1 Goals of Separate Stormwater Water Quality Regulators

Flow control devices used to regulate the outflow of stormwater for the purpose of improving its quality must provide a minimum detention time during which this volume is allowed to empty. The reasons for the emptying times used in design of water quality detention facilities are discussed in Chapters 22–25. Suffice it to say here that for retention ponds the surcharge water quality capture volume is released over 6 to 12 hours, while for extended detention basins the emptying time is between 24 and 48 hours. The resultant outlet size can be very small when the detention facility serves a small tributary watershed. A simple fact is that small water quality outlets tend to clog easily. Therefore, the design of water quality flow regulators has to incorporate features that reduce clogging.

12.3.2 Perforated Riser Outlets

Perforated risers are often used as water quality outlets in separate stormwater retention ponds and extended detention basins. This type of outlet is a vertical pipe with uniform-sized holes drilled throughout its length. A perforated steel plate embedded as a face in a concrete outlet structure will perform identically to a perforated pipe.

Risers in Retention Ponds. Figure 4.10 illustrates a perforated riser attached to a large concrete overflow structure located within a retention pond. A similar riser, except that it is a stand-alone riser, is shown in Figure 12.18. In both examples the small perforations are protected from being clogged with floating debris by a porous surface skimmer. Such a skimmer can be fabricated using stiff steel mesh, well screen material, or some other porous heavy-duty sheet steel stock with openings smaller than the perforations in the riser. For guidance in the design of such trash racks see Section 4.3.5.

Risers in Extended Detention Basins. Figure 12.19 shows a vertical riser similar to the one in Figure 4.10, except that it is located within an extended detention basin. In this installation the perforations are protected from clogging by a 1.5- to 3.0-inch (3.8- to 7.6-cm) mound of gravel. However, some of the perforations may be partly blocked by individual stones in the gravel pack. This can be compensated for by increasing the perforated area by approximately 10%.

Since a perforated riser regulates the flow rate through the use of many small orifices, the design calculations can be somewhat cumbersome. They can be significantly simplified, however, if one is willing to accept a small degree of standardization. Figure 12.20 was developed for Douglas County, Colorado (UDFCD, 1986), to assist in the sizing of perforated risers. The charts in this figure permit the designer to quickly select the area of one row of perforations needed to drain a water quality capture volume in either 12 or 40 hours. These charts can be used only for a perforated vertical riser, or a perforated plate, with a 4-inch (10.16-cm) spacing between vertical rows of perforations and otherwise conform to the standards in Figure 12.21.

A Design Example. Given an extended detention basin (i.e., a dry basin) with a water quality capture volume of 2.0 acre feet (2470 m^3) at a depth

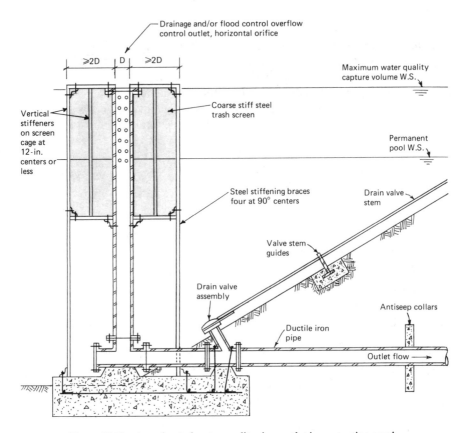

Figure 12.18 A perforated water quality riser outlet in a retention pond.

of 4.0 feet (1.22 m), find the area of each row of peforations needed to drain
the basin in approximately 40 hours. First, on the water quality ordinate of the
chart for a dry basin with a 40-hour drain time in Figure 12.20, find the
2.0-acre-feed (2,470-m³) value. Next, move horizontally until the 4.0-depth
(1.22-m) line is intercepted. Finally, move vertically to the abscissa to find that
an area of 2.0 square inches (12.9 cm²) is needed for each row of peforations.

Next, configure the riser with the aid of Figure 12.21. From this figure
we ascertain that we need a little more than 10 perforations per row with a
diameter of ½ inch to provide the needed area. Since the riser will be packed
in gravel, we will compensate for potential blockage of the holes by the stones
by increasing the number of holes to 11 per row. Figure 12.21 also suggests
that a pipe 6 inches or larger in diameter can be used for this number of
perforations. Thus, the installed riser should have a total of 12 rows of ½ inch
perforations with 11 holes drilled in each row, each row being separated
4 inches (10.2 cm) vertically from the next.

W.S.
▽
≂

10-year or 100-year detention volume elevation for flood control

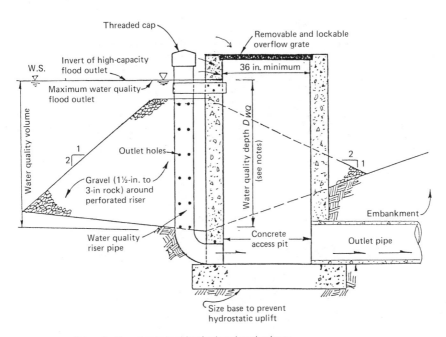

Note: 1. Riser pipe to be galvanized steel or aluminum.
        2. Design must provide for permanent access to the outlet
           structure at all times.
        3. Required water quality volume determines D_{WQ} minimum.

Figure 12.19   A perforated water quality riser outlet in a detention pond. (*After UDFCD, 1986.*)

12.3.3 Other Outlet Configurations

A perforated outlet is only one type of flow regulator that can be used in controlling the releases from separate stormwater quality enhancement detention facilities. Typically, the round and rectangular orifices described in this chapter can be used in combination with trash racks and surface skimmers when controlling larger volumes. Under such circumstances these types of flow regulators can be made sufficiently large to minimize clogging problems.

As the size of the flow regulator decreases, the clogging potential increases. The use of some of the special flow regulators described in Chapter 13 can sometimes help. Some of these can have lower flow rates for the same flow opening than can be obtained with an orifice. The larger the opening, the less likely it is to become clogged.

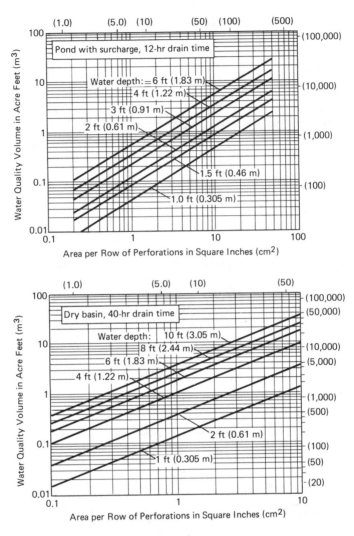

Figure 12.20 Perforated riser sizing charts. (*After UDFCD, 1986.*)

For very small detention volumes, the designer can consider using graded gravel or sand filter with known conductivity rates to provide the desired flow regulation. Unfortunately, infiltration surfaces in such installations tend to plug with time and need regular maintenance to stay in operation. Despite the high maintenance needs of filters, they offer one of the few options in the design of flow regulators for very small tributary areas.

(a) Riser pipe limitations

Minimum number of holes per outlet structure: 8
Maximum number of holes per outlet structure: none
Minimum hole size: 1/8 In. diameter
Maximum hole size: 1 in. diameter

Spacing between rows is a constant 4 in.

(b) Perforated column limitations

Maximum number of perforated columns

Riser diameter (in.)	Hole diameter			
	1/4 in.	1/2 in.	3/4 in.	1 in.
4	8	8	6	4
6	12	12	9	6
8	16	16	12	8
10	20	20	14	10
12	24	24	18	12

(c) Riser pipe definition sketch

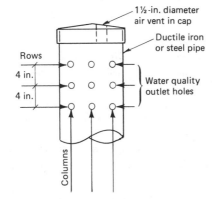

1½-in. diameter
air vent in cap

Ductile iron
or steel pipe

Rows

4 in.

4 in.

Water quality
outlet holes

Columns

Conversion factors:
1 in. = 25.4 mm
1 in.^{2} = 6.45 cm^2

(d) Areas of circular drain holes

Diameter (in.)	Area (in.^{2})
1/8	0.013
1/4	0.049
3/8	0.110
1/2	0.196
5/8	0.307
3/4	0.442
7/8	0.601
1	0.785

Figure 12.21   Standardized perforated riser for use with the sizing charts in Figure 12.20. (*After UDFCD, 1986.*)

REFERENCES

ADAMS-HYDRAULICS LTD, York, Great Britain, Product Brochures.

CHOW, VEN TE, *Open Channel Flow,* McGraw-Hill, New York, 1959.

CREAGER, W. P., AND JUSTIN, J. D., *Hydroelectric Handbook,* 2nd edition, John Wiley and Sons, Inc., New York, 1950.

EPA, *Urban Stormwater Management Technology: An Assessment*, Environmental Protection Agency, May, 1979.

FEDERAL HIGHWAY ADMINISTRATION, "Hydraulic Charts for the Selection of Highway Culverts," *Hydraulic Engineering Circular No. 5*, U.S. Department of Transportation, Washington, D.C., reprinted 1974.

FEDERAL HIGHWAY ADMINISTRATION, "Hydraulic Design of Improved Inlets for Culverts," *Hydraulic Engineering Circular No. 13*, U.S. Department of Transportation, Washington, D.C., 1972.

FAHRNER, H., "Planning of Rain Basin Discharge Controls Using Automatic Throttle Discs," Abwasser No. 5, 1979. (In German)

JEDELHAUSER, H., "Outflow Control for Storm Water Settling Basins by Means of Pneumatic Slide Valves," Osterreichische Abwasser-Rundschau No. 2, 1978. (In German)

KING, H. W., AND BRATER, E. F., "Handbook of Hydraulics," McGraw-Hill, New York, 1963.

KORAL, J., AND SAATCI, A. C., "Storm Overflow and Detention Basins," 2nd edition, Zurich, 1976. (In German)

LENZ, A. T., "Viscosity and Surface Tension Effects on V-notch Weirs," *Transactions of the American Society of Civil Engineers*, vol. 69, New York, 1943.

LI, W. H., AND PATTERSON, C., "Free Outlets and Self-Priming Action of Culverts," *Journal of Hydraulics Division*, ASCE, HY 3, 1956.

PROMMERSBERGER, B., "Implementation of Stormwater Detention Policies in the Denver Metro Area," *Flood Hazard News*, Urban Drainage and Flood Control District, Denver, Colo., December, 1984.

REHBOCK, T., "Discussion on Precise Weir Measurements by Earnest W. Schoder and Kenneth B. Turner," *Transactions, American Society of Civil Engineers*, Vol. 93, pp. 1143–1162, 1929.

SCHILLING, W., "Urban Runoff Quality Management by Real-Time Control," *Urban Runoff Pollution*, NATO ASI Series G: Ecological Sciences, Vol. 10, Springer-Verlag, Berlin, 1986.

U.S. BUREAU OF RECLAMATION, *Design of Small Dams*, pp. 469–85, United States Government Printing Office, Washington, D.C., 1973.

UDFCD, *Douglas County Storm Drainage Design and Technical Criteria*, prepared by WRC Engineers, Inc., under a contract to Urban Drainage and Flood Control District, Denver, Colo., January 1986.

VILLEMONTE, J. R., "Submerged-weir Discharge Studies," *Engineering News-Record*, p. 866, December, 1947.

13

Special Flow Regulators

In recent years, we have seen the development and marketing of flow regulators designed to provide a more uniform release rate under a varying depth. Here we describe four special regulators that have received considerable attention. These are not the only ones worth considering, but they are the ones we are most familiar with. Each of the following is a self-regulating unit requiring no mechanical control:

- Steinscrew,
- hydrobrake,
- wirbeldrossel, and
- flow valve.

13.1 STEINSCREW

The Steinscrew was developed in Sweden in the 1970s. It was designed to regulate wastewater flow rates in combined sewer pipes. The detention, as originally intended, occurs in the pipe itself, and no additional storage facility is needed. As a result, it is recommended that the Steinscrew be installed in pipes 36 inches (800 mm) or larger in diameter to provide the flow balancing volumes. There is no upper limit on the pipe size for which it would work, and it could be used in storage tunnels.

13.1.1 Technical Configuration

Steinscrew consists of a screw-shaped plate that is twisted into a 270°
spiral and attached to the pipe as illustrated in Figure 13.1. The device occupies 90 percent of the pipe's diameter with a gap left between its longitudinal
side and the crown of the pipe. The other longitudinal side is attached with
stainless steel bolts to the bottom of the pipe.

The screw-shaped plate is equipped with two obliquely directed wings
and form four triangular overflow sections between the plates and the wings,
see Figure 13.2. In the bottom of the screw there is a circular opening to pass
base flows. This base flow opening is made sufficiently large to permit self
cleansing of the pipe's invert. Typically, the length of the Steinscrew is approximately three times the diameter of the pipe.

The Steinscrew is manufactured from a steel plate which is carefully
shaped into the desired form. After welding and grinding, it is galvanized and
epoxy-coated to protect it against corrosion. This treatment has proved to be
sufficient protection in most installations.

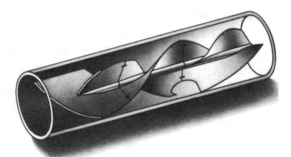

Figure 13.1   "Steinscrew" flow regulator. (After Janson and Bendixen, 1975)

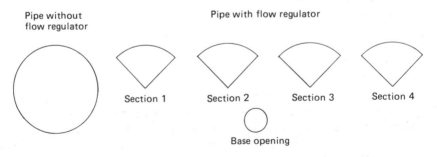

Pipe without
flow regulator

Pipe with flow regulator

Section 1   Section 2   Section 3   Section 4

Base opening

Figure 13.2   Flow conveyance sections of the "Steinscrew". (After Janson and
Bendixen, 1975)

13.1.2 Function

Whenever the flow exceeds the capacity of the low flow opening, water backs up into the pipe or into a tunnel. The amount of detention that takes place depends on pipe diameter and slope. Figure 13.3 can assist in estimating how much detention volume is available upstream of the Steinscrew when the pipe is 75% full just upstream of the regulator. It is recommended that the system be designed to operate so as not to exceed the 75% depth during the design rainstorm. More depth of storage in the pipe will cause the system to surcharge frequently, which is an unacceptable design condition.

As long as the water depth in the pipe is less than one-half pipe diameter,

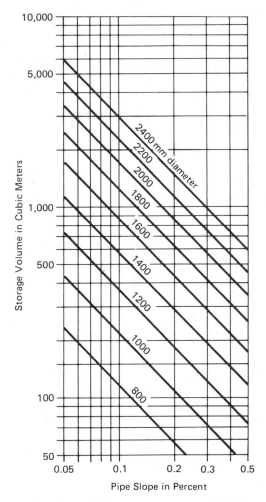

Figure 13.3   Storage volume in a pipe upstream of a Steinscrew.

all of the flow passes through the base opening. When the water rises further, it starts to spill through the triangular overflow sections, as illustrated in Figure 13.2. As the water continues to rise, the flow conveyance area rapidly increases until the flow capacity of the Steinscrew is almost equal to the capacity of the unobstructed pipe. See Figure 13.4 for the relationship between the water level and the flow capacity of this device. This device can be most useful when several regulators are installed in series. The simulated effect of such a series installation is shown in Figure 13.5.

13.1.3 Operational Aspects

When the Steinscrew was developed, the goal was to have a device that would be simple to build and simple to install. It was hoped that the device would be self-cleansing and would require no more maintenance than a sewer pipe. By providing the inlet side with smooth oblique edges, most of the clogging problems appear to have been prevented. Debris that strikes the edge of the plate is moved by the flow along the edge until it passes through the space between the crown of the pipe and the regulator.

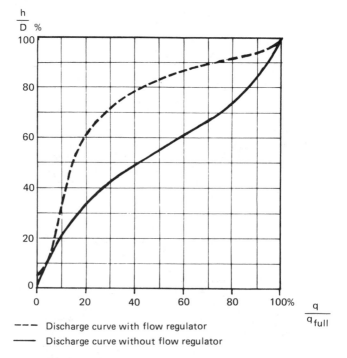

$\frac{h}{D}$ %

--- Discharge curve with flow regulator
—— Discharge curve without flow regulator

$\frac{q}{q_{full}}$

Figure 13.4   Discharge characteristics of the Steinscrew. (After Janson, Bendixen, and Harlaut, 1976.)

The regulator was tested by introducing trash and debris, some of it being pieces of wood up to $4\frac{1}{2}$ feet (1.4 m) in length, into the water. Field (1978) reported that all debris passed through the regulators without difficulty.

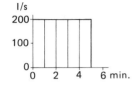

Pump capacity = 200 liters/second (4.5 mgd)
Pumping time = 5 minutes

Note: 100 l/s = 2.25 mgd

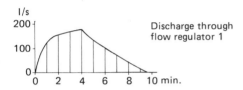

Discharge through flow regulator 1

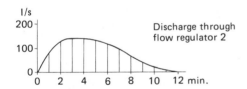

Discharge through flow regulator 2

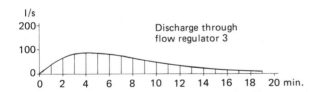

Discharge through flow regulator 3

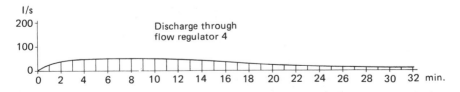

Discharge through flow regulator 4

Figure 13.5   Performance of four regulators in series. (After Janson, Bendixen, and Harlaut, 1976.)

13.1.4 Hydraulics

A method was developed by Schnyder and Bergerons to calculate the hydraulics of the Steinscrew. This method requires that the following be known:

- free water area in the upstream pipe,
- the discharge curve of the regulator in use, and
- inflow hydrograph.

The method is described by Janson, Bendixen, and Harlaut (1976). Anyone wanting to use this device should study this reference. Since the calculations are very tedious, computer modeling is suggested.

13.2 HYDROBRAKE

In the 1960s, a flow regulator called hydrobrake was developed in Denmark. This is a self-regulating device that is normally used as a flow controlling outlet at a storage facility. It does not matter if this storage occurs in a pipe, an underground storage vault, a surface detention basin, etc. The rate of discharge through the hydrobrake is, in part, a function of the pressure head upstream of the device.

13.2.1 Technical Configuration

The hydrobrake consists of an eccentric cylinder housing with an inlet opening located on the side. As depicted in Figure 13.6, the flow enters the hydrobrake tangentially to the outlet pipe. An outlet pipe is installed normal to the housing cylinder. This pipe is inserted into the basin's outlet (see Figure

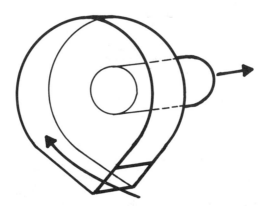

Figure 13.6 Illustration of a hydrobrake. (After Hydro-Brake Systems Inc., Portland, Maine.)

13.7) using a standard O-ring to seal the annular space between the basin's outlet and the pipe. Normally, no additional anchoring is needed to hold this device in place.

The hydrobrake is manufactured from stainless steel and it can be fabricated to fit any outlet dimension. However, for very large installations it may have to be delivered in several parts and assembled at the site. It is available in two configurations illustrated in Figure 13.8. The one to the left in the figure is

Figure 13.7   Installation of a hydrobrake. (After Hydro-Brake Systems Inc., Portland, Maine.)

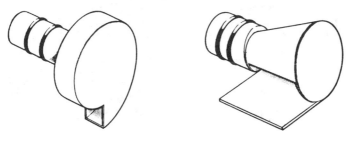

Figure 13.8   Two types of the hydrobrake. (After Hydro-Brake Systems Inc., Portland, Maine.)

a standard hydrobrake. The one on the right is designed to operate under large base flow conditions.

13.2.2 Function

As the storage basin fills, the water pressure sets the water inside the hydrobrake housing into helical motion. This causes the discharge to be significantly less than through a similar sized orifice. The available hydrostatic head upstream of the device is transformed into kinetic energy, which is only partially utilized as motion in the direction of the outlet. As can be seen in Figure 13.9, the greatest velocity component is perpendicular to the outlet.

The discharge through a hydrobrake depends on the design type and the size of the outlet. The discharge characteristics for a standard hydrobrake and an orifice, all with a 150 millimeter (approx. 6-inch) diameter outlet, are shown in Figure 13.10. Compared to an orifice, the hydrobrake has the following advantages:

1. A larger opening can be used for the same discharge rate. This can significantly reduce the risk of clogging the flow regulator.
2. The discharge varies much less with the water depth in the storage basin. As a result, a more constant release rate is obtained.

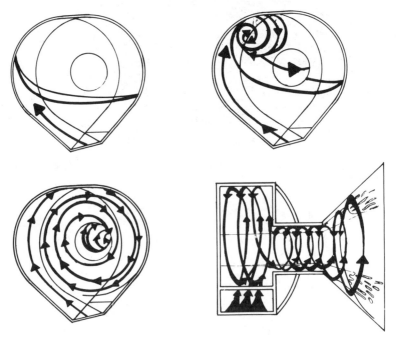

Figure 13.9 Filling of a standard hydrobrake. (After Hydro-Brake Systems Inc., Portland, Maine.)

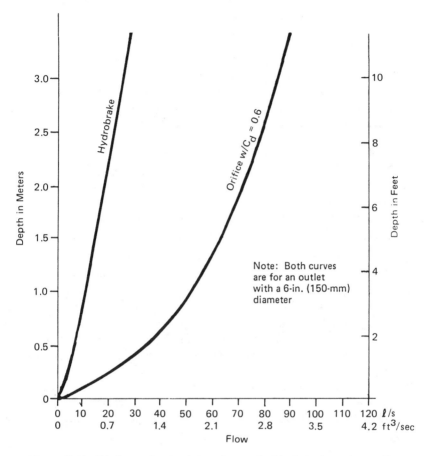

Figure 13.10   Discharge characteristics of a standard hydrobrake and an orifice with the same opening. (After Hydro-Brake Systems Inc., Portland, Maine.)

13.2.3 Hydraulics

The discharge capacity of the hydrobrake device can be calculated using the following empirical formula suggested by Hydro-Brake Systems Inc.:

$$Q = C_d \cdot A \cdot \sqrt{2g \cdot \left(h - \frac{D}{2}\right)} \tag{13.1}$$

in which Q = discharge rate,
$\quad\ C_d$ = discharge coefficient,
$\quad\ A$ = area of inlet or outlet opening, whichever is less,
$\quad\ D$ = diameter of the outlet opening,
$\quad\ h$ = water depth above invert of outlet opening, and
$\quad\ g$ = acceleration of gravity.

Discharge coefficients can be obtained from Hydro-Brake and can vary from 0.13 to 0.3 depending on the model used.

13.2.4 Operational Aspects

The hydrobrake device has been used primarily in the United States, Canada, and Scandinavia. The Danish inventor has in recent years made significant improvements to this device. The modified device is called the Mosbak regulator. The experience has been favorable, and no unusual operational problems have been encountered. There appears, however, to be some flow instability in the device when the water depth upstream of the device is relatively small. This, by itself, should not be of significant concern, since it occurs during low flows.

The only reported maintenance need was the emptying of the sedimentation pit that is usually installed just upstream of the outlet. Also, larger objects that could not pass through this device had to be removed. This must, however, be considered normal for any type of outlet.

13.3 WIRBELDROSSEL

The wirbeldrossel (i.e., turbulent throttle) was developed at the University of Stuttgart in Germany in mid-1970s and has many similarities to the hydrobrake. As a result, the following description explains how the wirbeldrossel differs from the hydrobrake. It appears, however, that the two devices were developed totally independent of each other.

13.3.1 Technical Configuration

The wirbeldrossel has a symmetrical cylinder housing with an inlet pipe connecting tangentially to the cylinder. The outlet is a circular opening in the bottom surface of the cylinder. The opening of the outlet can be adjusted using manufactured rings of various sizes. On the opposite side from the outlet is an air supply pipe (see Figure 13.11).

This device is installed with the outlet pipe being vertical, and the device is always located in a separate chamber downstream of the storage basin. As a result, it is accessible for inspection and maintenance when the storage basin is filled (see Figure 13.12).

A modified version of the wirbeldrossel was also developed and was called wirbelvalve. This device is similar to the original wirbeldrossel, except that its rotation chamber is slanted and has a cone-shaped bottom, as illustrated in Figure 13.13. The wirbelvalve has the advantage that it requires less vertical height between the basin outlet and the downstream sewer.

The wirbeldrossel and the wirbelvalve are fabricated using welded steel plate. Corrosion protection is provided by hot-dipped galvanizing and coating

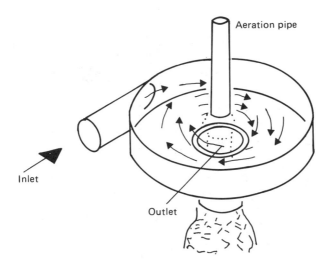

Aeration pipe

Inlet

Outlet

Figure 13.11   An illustration of the wirbeldrossel. (After Brombach, Umvelt und Fluidtechnik GmbH Bad Mergentheim, Germany.)

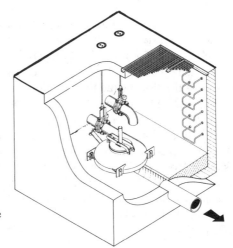

Figure 13.12   Typical installation of the Wirbeldrossel. (Umwelt und Fluidtechnik GmbH, Germany.)

all surfaces with epoxy. Both are manufactured in standardized sizes, with inlet pipes ranging between 50- and 500-millimeters (approximately 2- to 20-inches) in diameter.

13.3.2 Function

The wirbeldrossel and the wirbelvalve are similar in their function. The flow enters the chamber tangentially, creating a rotational velocity which is proportional to the water depth upstream of the device. Due to the centripetal

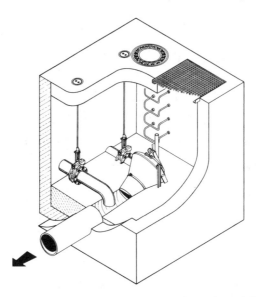

Figure 13.13 An illustration of the wirbelvalve. (Umwelt und Fluidtechnik Gmbh, Germany.)

acceleration, a pocket of air develops at the axis of rotation. This reduces the net flow area inside of the chamber, thus limiting the flow. To insure adequate air supply, an aeration pipe is connected to the axis of rotation, as shown in Figure 13.11. This aeration pipe virtually eliminates cavitation within the device, and the flow inside the cylinder has very little turbulence.

Figure 13.14 compares the capacity of a wirbeldrossel and an orifice. The capacity of the device as shown in this figure was measured at a field installation. It had a 200-millimeter (7.8-inch) inlet and a 150-millimeter (5.9-inch) outlet. Due to site conditions, the capacity of this installation was affected by backwater from downstream. Without this backwater, the flow through this device would have been reduced even further. For comparison, Figure 13.14 also contains the discharge curve for an 150-millimeter (5.9-inch) diameter orifice, which shows that the orifice has considerably larger and more variable flow capacity.

13.3.3 Operational Aspects

Because the flow inside the housing has little turbulence, even fairly large particles in the water can pass through this device without difficulty. At the University of Stuttgart's Institut für Wasserbau (1976), this device was tested for clogging by introducing various debris into the flow. The wirbeldrossel passed through sand, gravel, long rags, etc. without any problems. As far as it is known, this device has been used mainly in West Germany and Switzerland. The reported experience at existing installations has been very good.

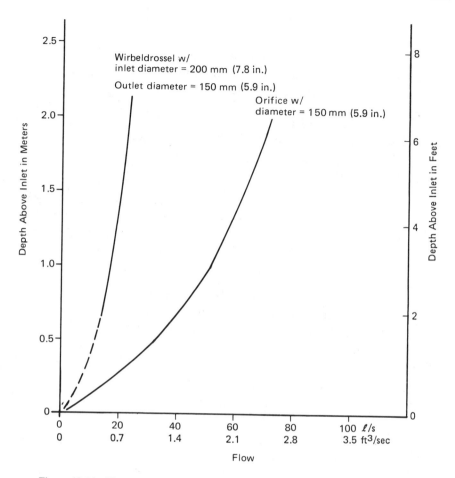

Figure 13.14   Flow capacity of wirbeldrossel vs. an orifice. (After Quadt and Brombach, 1978.)

13.4 FLOW VALVE

In the late 1970s, the, so called *flow valve* was developed in Sweden to maintain a constant release rate from a storage basin. The flow valve is a self-regulating device, and it utilizes the pressure head in the storage basin to throttle the flow. Although this device can be designed to operate in a variety of outlet conditions, we describe its installation inside a vertical inlet pipe intended to control the inflow into an overloaded sewer. By installing it at a storm sewer inlet, the inlet chamber and the street above it are used as temporary storage basins.

13.4.1 Technical Configuration

The flow valve was designed for easy installation into a circular manhole (see Figure 13.15) It is attached to the walls of the manhole, and the annular space is sealed using a rubber O-ring. The flow valve consists of a vertical central pipe surrounded by an air-filled pressure chamber, as illustrated in Figure 13.16. The top of this pressure chamber and its connection to the central pipe are made of flexible rubber fabric supported by steel housing.

13.4.2 Function

As the flow valve comes under pressure from above, the pressure is transmitted through the pressure chamber to the central pipe. The upper part of the rubber membrane is pressed in and causes the air inside the chamber to push out the rubber membrane inside the central pipe. As this occurs, the cross-section of the flow opening is reduced and the flow is throttled to maintain a constant discharge, regardless of the water depth upstream.

Figure 13.17 shows a comparison between the flow valve and an orifice. It can be seen here that as the flow increases, the flow through this device remains relatively constant. In fact, a small decrease in flow is observed with increasing depth of water upstream. The laboratory tests of this device did not, however, study it to see how it performs with trash and debris in the water.

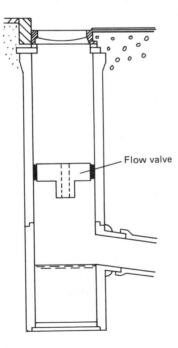

Flow valve

Figure 13.15 Flow valve installed inside a manhole. (After Bendixen and Stahre, 1983.)

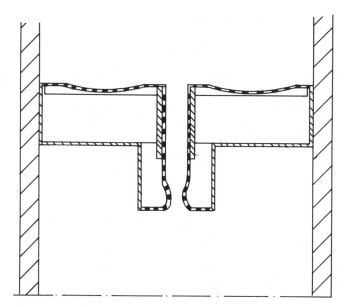

Figure 13.16   Diagram of a flow valve. (After Bendixen and Stahre, 1983.)

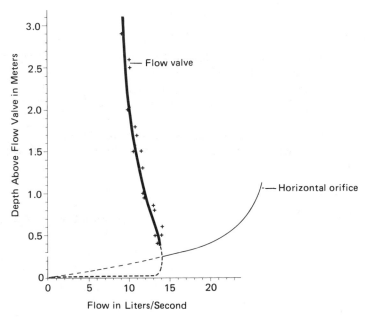

Figure 13.17   Discharge curve of the flow valve. (After Bendixen and Stahre, 1983.)

REFERENCES

Steinscrew:

FIELD, R., "Trip Report," United States Environmental Protection Agency, October, 1978.

JANSON, L. E., AND BENDIXEN, S., "New Methods for Detaining Flow Variations in Gravity Flow Lines," Stadsbyggnad No. 6, 1975. (In Swedish)

JANSON, L. E., BENDIXEN, S., AND HARLAUT, A., "Equalization of Flow Variations in a Combined Sewer," *Journal of the Environmental Engineering Division,* ASCE, December, 1976.

Hydrobrake:

BROWN, R., "Controlling Storm Water Runoff," *APWA Reporter,* May, 1978.

HYDRO-STORM SEWER CORPORATION, Miscellaneous product information from brochures, etc.

LAGER, J., SMITH W., AND TCHOBANOGOLOUS, G., "Catchbasin Technology Overview and Assessment," Environmental Protection Agency, Cincinnati Ohio, Contract 68-03-0274, 1974.

MEAGAARD, C., "A New Approach Should End Basement Floodings," *CIVIC,* April, 1979.

THEIL, P., "High Level of Flood Protection at Low Cost," APWA International Public Works Congress in Boston, October, 1978.

Wirbeldrossel:

INSTITUT FUR WASSEREAU DER UNIVERSITAT STUTTGART, "Prospect Sheet on the Wirbeldrossel," Ausgabe Bro, July, 1976. (In German)

QUADT, K. S., AND BROMBACH, H., "Operational Experiences with the Wirbeldrossel in Storm Water Overflow Basins," Korrespondenz Abwasser, No. 1, 1978. (In German)

UMWELT UND FLUIDTECHNIK GMBH, Bad Mergentheim, West Germany, Reference List on Wirbeldrossel, miscellaneous product information from brochures, catalogs, etc. (In German)

Flow Valve:

BENDIXEN, S., AND STAHRE, P., "Self-regulating Valve for Constant Flow," Vatten No. 2, 1983. (In Swedish)

14

Flow Regulation
in Larger Systems

So far, we have discussed the control of flow from one basin only. However, the engineer is often faced with the possibility of a system of several storage facilities located within a separate stormwater or combined sewer network. In such cases, it is necessary to control the release rates from many storage facilities simultaneously.

The goal of controlling the storage and releases at multiple sites in a combined sewer system is to minimize the possibility of surcharged sewers while keeping the overflows to the receiving waters to a minimum. To accomplish this, the flows and water levels must be monitored simultaneously at several locations within the network. Along with this data, information about the status of various control devices in the system is transmitted to a central surveillance center. Here, the operators with the aid of computers make adjustments to control settings throughout the system. This process permits a much more efficient operation of the entire system than would otherwise be possible.

14.1 BACKGROUND

Since the late 1960s, much attention has been focused on upgrading the performance of combined sewer systems in the United States and Western Europe. The upgrading usually consists of the following two actions:

- conversion of combined sewer systems into separate sewer systems; and

- improving the capabilities of combined sewer systems by the installation of storage facilities within the system.

Unfortunately, separating a combined sewer system into two separate wastewater and storm sewer systems can be extremely expensive and can rarely be justified. It is cost-effective only in select, densely populated areas. Also, separation of sewers was found only to marginally improve the water quality of the receiving waters over what can be done to reduce overflows through adding storage and system controls. As a result, it is possible and more cost-effective to improve the function of the existing combined sewer systems by adding detention storage to the system.

There is no standard method for upgrading combined sewer systems. Each case is unique and has to be studied for its own possibilities. Often, the resultant upgrade of the system includes a variety of actions and measures. Schilling (1986), however, after studying a large number of upgraded combined sewer systems, found certain similarities. Very often, the upgraded systems included:

1. rainfall, flow, and water level sensors;
2. pumps, inflatable weirs, and mechanical gates as flow regulators;
3. telephone lines for data and control telemetry;
4. distributed digital control systems linked to dual central minicomputers.

Table 14.1 lists several locations that utilize coordinated real time flow control as part of the system. Through the assistance of a central computer, these systems will automatically

- open or close gates and valves,
- raise or lower overflow weir crests, and
- turn pumps on or off.

Figures 14.1 and 14.2 illustrate two examples of coordinated flow regulating structures used in larger systems. The first one, located in Seattle, Washington uses available volume in an existing combined sewer. Here the flow is normally routed to a trunk sewer which then conveys it to the treatment plant. As the flow increases, and the control system determines a need, the control gate throttles the flow to the trunk sewer and causes the excess water to be stored. Should the flow exceed storage capacity, it then overflows into the receiving waters. The second system, located in Minneapolis-St. Paul, although utilizing different equipment has almost an identical operational scenario.

TABLE 14.1   Several Realtime Flow Control Sewer Systems in the U.S.

Location	Description
Chicago	Detention in tunnels. Regulation with preset overflows and remote controlled pumps to feed treatment plants. Monitoring of water levels and overflows.
Cleveland	Detention in sewer network. Monitoring of precipitation, flow, and water quality.
Detroit	Detention in sewer network and storage basins. Regulation with remote controlled gates, pumps, and inflatable rubber cushions. Monitoring of precipitation and flow.
Minneapolis-St. Paul	Detention in sewer network. Regulation with remote controlled gates and inflatable rubber cushions. Monitoring of precipitation, flow, and water quality.
San Francisco	Detention in sewer network, tunnels, and storage basins. Monitoring of precipitation and flow.
Seattle	Detention in sewer network. Regulation with remote controlled gates and pumps. Monitoring of precipitation, flow, and water quality.

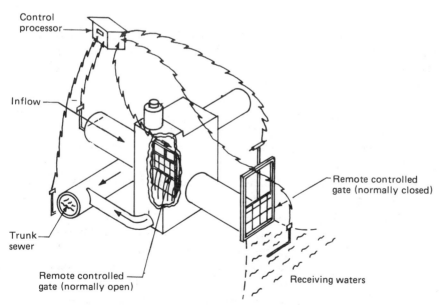

Figure 14.1   Flow regulating structure in Seattle. (After Leiser, 1974.)

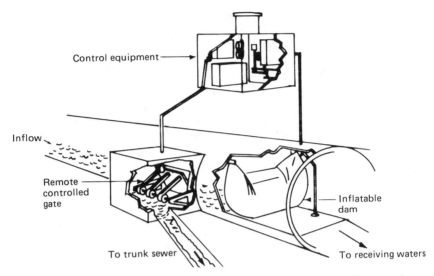

Figure 14.2 Regulating structure in Minneapolis-St. Paul. (After Anderson and Callery, 1974.)

14.2 DESIGN CONSIDERATIONS FOR A REGULATING SYSTEM

Usually the primary goal is to improve water quality by optimizing the use of existing sewer networks. The objectives include the reduction of overflows to the receiving waters and the equalization of flow to the treatment plant. These tasks require considerable sophistication in that:

- All flow regulators in the sewer network need to receive continuous control signals during the entire storage and detention cycle.
- The signals from each site have to transmit information about storage and flow at each of the many flow regulators within a catchment.
- The control of each regulator must also consider how all of the regulators work together as a system.
- The processing of all data received at the control center and its transformation into control signals has to occur almost instantaneously.
- The runoff hydrograph needs to be anticipated to optimize the storage resources. This has to be done with simple models, as there is not enough time for complete simulation of all dynamic conditions.
- The computer hardware and software need to accommodate growth and changes in equipment, sewer network, treatment plant capacity, population growth, and treatment technology.

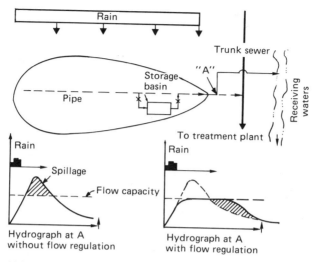

Figure 14.3   Regulation of flow in a catchment within a larger sewer network. (After Grigg and Labadie, 1974.)

In Figure 14.3, the operation of a single catchment is illustrated. The inflow into the storage basin depends on the character of the drainage area, the sewer network, and the temporal and spatial distribution of the precipitation. Flow regulation is determined by how the inflow is to be distributed between storage, spillage, and transport downstream (see Figure 14.4). This cannot be decided without understanding downstream system capacities, existing and projected flow conditions, and how the flows from other subbasins will interact.

Large sewer networks consist of smaller networks serving individual catchments (see Figure 14.5). Here, several smaller networks are connected to a trunk sewer, which conveys flow to a treatment plant. By knowing the conditions within each catchment, it is possible to coordinate various regulators in a manner that optimizes the performance of the entire system. Of course, optimization will be determined by the goals and objectives of the system. In this example, the goals could include

- The flow to the treatment plant is to be kept uniform.
- Wastewater from certain areas is to receive priority transport to the treatment plant.
- Spillage of untreated wastewater is to be minimized.
- Spillage is to occur only at certain locations.

Coordinated flow regulation cannot be achieved using only information about flows and volumes. Effective flow regulation also requires the collection

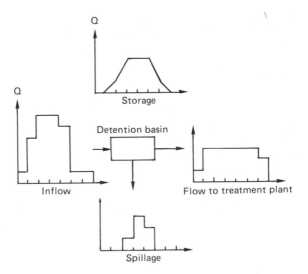

Figure 14.4 Inflow allocation between storage, spillage, and transport downstream. (After Bruce and Bradford, 1977.)

of precipitation data throughout the watershed and the prediction of how much runoff may occur, where it will occur, and how it will be distributed over time. In some cases, it may even be necessary to predict rainfall in advance of actual measurement. Obviously, such systems are expensive and difficult to design, install, and operate, and as a result their use to date has been limited to larger cities.

14.3 EXAMPLE: BREMEN, GERMANY, CONTROL SYSTEM

A computer control system for the sewer network of the city of Bremen, Germany was installed in the late 1970s. One such installation was in a watershed having an area of 1,550 acres (628 ha) located on the west bank of the river Weser. The older city within this watershed had combined sewers, while the newer fringe zones had separated sewer systems. The stated goal for this project was to control storm runoff such that:

- Backing up of stormwater within the sewer network would be eliminated.
- Spillage of untreated combined sewage into receiving waters would be significantly reduced.
- Operational reliability would be improved.
- Energy costs would be reduced.

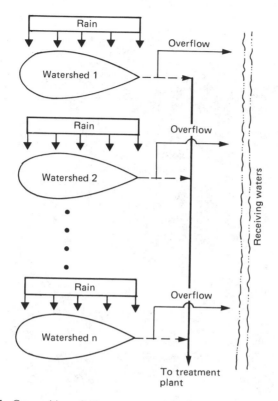

Figure 14.5 Composition of a larger sewer network. (After Grigg and Labadie, 1974.)

- The operational environment for personnel would be improved through automation.
- The use of existing treatment facilities would be optimized.

Martin et. al. (1978) described this system in detail. Following is a brief description of some of the components of the Bremen system.

14.3.1 The West Bank Pumping Station

The West Bank pumping station shown in Figure 14.6 is the main control center of the Bremen system. Data from three rain gauges, 19 pumping stations, and 17 water level meters are received and processed at this location. The central computer then sends control signals to all the pumping stations and storage facilities within the watershed.

The West Bank pumping station is equipped with trash racks and grit chambers that remove the coarse particles from the flow before it is pumped to

Figure 14.6 West Bank pumping station and control building in Bremen, West Germany.

the treatment plant. The station's maximum pumping capacity is rated at 88 cubic feet per second (2.5 m³/s), which is four times the dry weather flow. When inflow exceeds this capacity, the excess water is transferred to storage basins having a total capacity of 353,000 cubic feet (10,000 m³). This storage capacity was later doubled to improve treatment efficiencies at the downstream wastewater treatment plants.

Combined wastewater is routed to the storage basins by three screw pumps having a total capacity of 320 cubic feet per second (9 m³/s). The storage basins, in turn, are emptied into the pumping station by gravity after the storm flows subside. When the storage basins are full and the incoming flow still exceeds the pumping capacity of the station, the excess water overflows into the Weser River.

14.3.2 The Krimpel Pumping Station

This pumping station is the second largest pumping station in the system. It has a pumping capacity of 25 cubic feet per second (0.7 m³/s). Like the West Bank station, it also has a storage capacity of 353,000 cubic feet (10,000 m³) (see Figure 14.7). This station was designed to handle a one-year rainstorm, and the station is expected to have, on the average, a spill once a year.

14.3.3 Measuring Equipment

The equipment for data collection within this system is varied and complex, and we touch only briefly on some of the equipment in use. For example, the rain gauges, which telemeter data to the West Bank pumping station, were especially developed for this project. The commercial gauges available when this system was designed (i.e., early 1970s) were judged by the designers to be unreliable and incompatible with the central processing system. Since then, many new products have been introduced into the market that probably could do the job without modification.

As mentioned earlier, the water level is measured at 17 locations within the watershed. Six of these locations measure a differential in water levels, thereby providing data for the estimate of flow rates. The other gauges report water levels at overflows and storage basins. In almost all cases, pressure transducers were installed in conventional manholes, as illustrated in Figure 14.8.

Figure 14.7   Storage basin at Krimpel pumping station in Bremen, West Germany.

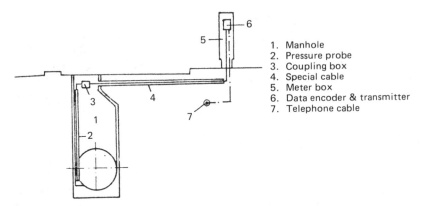

1. Manhole
2. Pressure probe
3. Coupling box
4. Special cable
5. Meter box
6. Data encoder & transmitter
7. Telephone cable

Figure 14.8 Water level measurement installation in Bremen. (After Martin et. al., 1978.)

14.4 EXAMPLE: REAL TIME CONTROL IN MALMÖ, SWEDEN

In the late 1980s a *real-time control* (RTC) system was implemented for part of the sewer system in the city of Malmö, Sweden. The area in question is the Turbinen watershed in central Malmö, which has a total drainage area of 6,670 acres (27 km²).

The sewer network in the Turbinen watershed is of a combined type. At the downstream end of the system there is a large dry weather pumping station, which has a total capacity of 88 cubic feet per second (2.5 m³/s). When this capacity is exceeded, combined sewage water is released from the system through three major CSO outfalls to a sensitive canal system surrounding the oldest parts of the city. During heavy rainstorms the pollution load on the canal system is considerable. Heavy rainstorms also cause severe problems with basement floodings in the lower parts of the watershed.

In the early 1980s the city prepared a 10-year upgrading plan with the aim of controlling both basement floodings and CSO. In the first phase of this plan (1982–86) most of the effort was directed towards the construction of storage facilities and other traditional upgrading measures (see Larsson and Persson, 1984). In the second phase of the plan (1987–91) the aim was to utilize the potential benefits of real-time operation of the available storage volumes in the sewer system. For this purpose a monitoring and control system was implemented. By the end of 1991 the RTC installations in the Turbinen watershed included five rain gauges, eight level sensors, and four movable gates with local control.

14.4.1 Operating Strategies

One of the most important parts of the RTC activities in Malmö has been the specification and development of a hydraulic simulator that describes the effects of different operation strategies. Development of the simulator was based on the Danish MOUSE model (see Section 19.5). With the help of the simulator the effects of different alternative operation strategies can be compared as regards CSO as well as basement floodings.

In Malmö a large number of different operation strategies of varying complexity have been tested. They can be divided into the following two main groups:

• local level control, with the existing RTC facilities; and
• global control with an extended network of sensors, where the optimal set points are determined by the known runoff situation and by prediction of runoff over the nearest future periods.

The strategies of local level control provide increased protection against basement floodings. The other group of operation strategies will permit more effective utilization of the available volume in the system and, in this way, reduce the frequency of CSO.

The operation strategies were tested for both 1 year of continuous precipitation data and several extreme events based on rainfall statistics. When the alternative operation strategies were tested, a need for more sensors and regulators was identified.

Figure 14.9 is a schematic layout of the RTC system that, with the help of computer simulation, was found to be "optimal." Of special interest is the location of regulators and sensors and the connections between them. The optimal system has the same number of sensors as the existing system, but the number of regulators was increased to two movable weirs and five movable gates. As shown, the operation strategies are global in that a specific regulator can be controlled by several sensors located in different parts of the system. The effects of this optimal RTC were evaluated by testing several types of operation and control strategies, at which time the optimal strategy for each event was chosen.

14.4.2 Evaluation of the Effects of RTC

The canal system in Malmö is especially sensitive to CSO during summer. Table 14.2 shows a comparison of CSO volumes for the whole year and for the summer (June, July, and August) for different degrees of RTC. The table shows that RTC in the Turbinen watershed gives the greatest reduction in CSO during the summer.

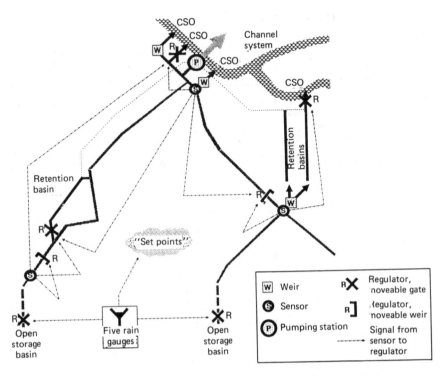

Figure 14.9 Sketch of the optimal RTC system for the Turbinen watershed in Malmö, Sweden.

TABLE 14.2 Relative CSO Volume Compared with the Situation Before Upgrading

	Whole Year	Summer
Before upgrading	19,400,000 ft³ (550,000 m³)	3,700,000 ft³ (150,000 m³)
After upgrading with control of the available storage volumes	90%	80%
Optimal RTC system with global control and more regulators	65%	25%

According to Table 14.2, CSO volumes during the most sensitive part of the year can be reduced by 55% with the optimal RTC implementation (i.e., from 80% to 25%). An alternative for achieving the same reduction in overflows is to build storage basins without RTC near the Turbinen pumping station having a volume of 424,000 cubic feet (12,000 m³).

A comparison of costs for the upgraded optimal RTC system with construction costs for the storage basins favors the use of RTC. The storage basins are 5 to 10 times more expensive than the RTC alternative. In addition, simulations with extreme rainfall events show that flooding in the Turbinen watershed can also be reduced through the use of RTC. It was determined that the optimal RTC system with global control can reduce flooding damages resulting from storms with return periods of less than 2 years to storms with a return period of approximately 5 years.

REFERENCES

ANDERSON, J., AND CALLERY, R., "Remote Control of Combined Sewer Overflows," *Journal of WPCF*, No. 11, November, 1974.

BRUCE AND BRADFORD, "Optimal Storage Control in a Combined Sewer System," *Journal of the Water Resources Planning and Management Division*, WR1, May, 1977.

FAHRNER, H., "Planning of Storm Basin Discharge Control Using the 'Automatic' Throttle Plate," Abwassertechnik No. 5, 1979. (In German)

FLOOD CONTROL COORDINATING COMMITTEE, *Development of a Flood and Pollution Control for Chicagoland Area*, Summary Reports, August, 1972.

GRIGG, N., LABADIE, J., SMITH G., HILL, D., AND BRADFORD, B., "Metropolitan Water Intelligence Systems," *Completion Report, Phase II*, Department of Civil Engineering, Colorado State University, June, 1973.

GRIGG, N., AND LABADIE, J., "Computing the Big Picture," *Water and Wastewater Engineering*, May, 1975.

GRIGG, N., LABADIE, J., AND WENZEL, H., "Metropolitan Water Intelligence Systems," *Completion Report Phase III*, Department of Civil Engineering, Colorado State University, July, 1974.

LABADIE, J., GRIGG, N., AND BRADFORD, B., "Automatic Control of Large-Scale Combined Sewer Systems," *Journal of Environmental Engineering*, EEI, February, 1975.

LAGER, J., "Control of Dry Weather Pollution," *Water and Wastewater Engineering*, September, 1974.

LARGER, J., SMITH, W., LYNARD, W., FINN, R., AND FINNERMORE, J., "Urban Stormwater Management and Technology," *Update and Users's Guide*, EPA-600/8-77-014, July, 1977.

LARSSON, J., and PERSSON, B. L., "Combined Sewer Analysis for the City of Malmö," *Proceedings of the Third International Conference on Urban Storm Drainage*, Gothenburg, Sweden, June, 1984.

LEISER, C.P., "Computer Management of a Combined Sewer System," EPA-679.274-022, July, 1974.

MARTIN, G., MECKELBURG, H. J., VOUGT, D., AND WINTER, J., "Central Data Recording Systems for Controlling the Municipal Sewer Net of the City of Bremen," Korrespondenz Abwasser No. 3 1978. (In German)

MUNICIPALITY OF METROPOLITAN SEATTLE, "Maximizing Storage in Combined Sewer Systems," EPA 11022 ELK 12/71.

PARTHUM, "Building for the Future, the Boston Deep-Tunnel Plan," *Journal WPCF,* April, 1970.

SCHILLING, W., "Urban Runoff Quality Management by Real-Time Control," *Urban Runoff Pollution,* Springer-Verlag, Berlin, 1986. (In English)

TROTTA, P., LABADIE J., AND GRIGG, N., "Automatic Control Strategies for Urban Stormwater," *Journal of Hydraulics Division,* HY 12, December, 1977.

WESTON, R., "Combined Sewer Overflow Abatement Alternatives," EPA 11024 EXF 08/70, Washington, D.C., 1971.

15

Basic Principles

15.1 GENERAL

The term *storage facility* is used here to describe various types of facilities for the retardation of separate stormwater or combined stormwater–wastewater. The technical configuration of these facilities is subordinate to their intended function, of which there are three basic types:

- infiltration and percolation facilities,
- detention facilities, and
- retention facilities.

15.2 INFILTRATION AND PERCOLATION FACILITIES

As described in Part 1, the storage volume for an infiltration facility is over the infiltrating surface. The storage volume in a percolation basin consists of the pore volume of the stone filling. These storage facilities are emptied either through percolation to the underlying layers of soil or through specially designed underdrain pipes. They can also be equipped with an overflow outlet to drain off the excess water (see Figure 15.1).

The geohydrologic conditions at the site have to be known and understood in order to design infiltration and percolation facilities. Data on soil permeability and porosity, groundwater level and its fluctuations with seasons, soil profiles, etc. are needed for proper design.

15.3 DETENTION FACILITIES

Detention facilities store water for a relatively short period of time and, unless they are used for stormwater quality enhancement, they are primarily used to reduce the peak rate of flow downstream. When the detention facility is connected in-line with the conveyance system, as shown in Figure 15.2, all flows entering the basin are metered through the outlet and are temporarily stored within the basin. When the volume of water exceeds the available storage volume, the excess water is released via an emergency spillway.

If a detention basin is connected off-line to the conveyance system, all initial stormwater flows and dry weather flows bypass the basin. Flow enters the basin only after a preset rate is exceeded, at which point the flows exceeding the preset rate are diverted into the pond. As a result, only the "peak" portion of the hydrograph is stored in the pond.

Obviously, detention facilities cannot be sized to handle all possible storm scenarios, and often a single or a set of several design storm frequencies is selected for sizing purposes. Chapters 18 and 19 discuss the design principles for the sizing of detention facilities.

15.4 RETENTION FACILITIES

Retention facilities trap the water for an indefinite period of time. As a result, they are often used as sedimentation basins to remove some of the pollutants from the stormwater. The degree of pollutant removal is a function of

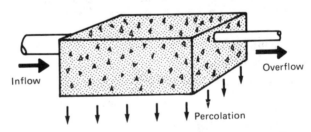

Figure 15.1 Schematic of a percolation facility with an overflow.

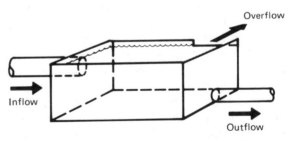

Figure 15.2 An in-line detention facility with a spillway.

- quality of inflow, and
- holding time in the storage basin.

Unlike infiltration/percolation or detention facilities, retention facilities do not typically have an operational bottom outlet. It is a good idea, however, to provide a bottom drain, as shown in Figure 15.3, for maintenance purposes. In operation, a retention basin is constantly full of water. A detailed discussion of how to size a retention facility for water quality enhancement appears in Part 4 of this book.

15.5 REGIONAL APPROACH TO ON-SITE DETENTION

Although much work has been done on the sizing and the effectiveness of individual detention basins using various design frequency scenarios, very little has been reported on how a random system of individually sized detention basins affect the flow regime along the drainageways. McCuen (1974) reported a computer model study of the Gray Haven Watershed using basin information reported by Tucker (1969). The study modeled 17 subbasins and two scenarios of detention storage. The first scenario used 12 ponds (total storage was not reported by McCuen), and the second used 17 ponds with 22,000 cubic feet (623 m^3) of total storage. The watershed had an area of 23.3 acres (9.4 ha) and had 52% impervious surface. McCuen suggested on the basis of the model study

(1) That the "individual-site" approach to stormwater detention may actually create flooding problems rather than reduce the hydrologic impact of urbanization; and (2) that a regional approach to urban stormwater management may be more effective than the "individual-site" approach.

Hart and Burges (1976) investigated a hypothetical 2,000-acre (809-ha) watershed by modeling three subbasins with three individually sized detention facilities. They concluded the following:

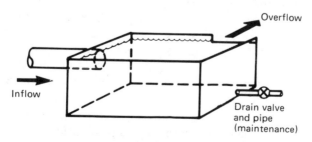

Figure 15.3 A retention facility with a spillway.

Restricting the outflow from a retention facility to a level less than the undeveloped rate could achieve a composite peak flow rate that would equal the pre-urbanized flow but would run at a much greater duration at that rate. The increased flow duration would have potentially undesirable effects on the channel system.

In 1981–1982 Urbonas and Glidden (1983) studied the potential effectiveness of various detention policies. They modeled a 7.85 square-mile (20.3 km²) watershed in the Denver area under preurbanization and posturbanization conditions. The kinematic model had 56 subbasins and 52 channel segments. After determining the "historic" and fully developed runoff at various points in the watershed, the model was modified to incorporate 28 individually sized detention basins. Computer runs were made using the 2-, 10- and 100-year design storms and three recorded storms.

Next, using the results of these runs, Urbonas and Glidden tested several empirical on-site detention sizing equations for the study watershed. These equations were limited to the sizing of detention basins to limit peak runoff from the upstream watershed to the historic 10- and 100-year runoff peaks. The storage–discharge characteristics of the previously modeled 28 detention basins were modified to conform with these empirical equations and the system response was again tested. They concluded the following:

1. The peak flows along the drainageways can be controlled by random on-site detention to almost the "historic" levels only for the large intensity storms such as the 10- and the 100-year design storm.
2. The control of runoff peaks from these large storms is limited to the design frequency used to design the detention basins. The peak flows from other frequency storms are either not controlled, or controlled only marginally. In other words, a system of on-site ponds designed to control the 10-year flood, if fully and properly implemented, has the potential of controlling the peaks along the urban drainageways resulting from the 10-year storm. It will not do the same for lesser or larger storms.

   Detention basins designed to control both the 10- and 100-year peaks performed better in controlling a range of larger runoff events than basins designed to control only a single runoff frequency.
3. A system of detention basins designed to control more frequent storms, such as the 2-year or lesser storm, are effective in controlling peaks from the frequently occuring storms only immediately downstream of each storage facility. Control of frequently occuring runoff peaks along the downstream drainageways becomes ineffective as the number of detention basins increases.
4. It appears feasible to develop simple empirical on-site detention sizing equations for a given watershed and possibly for an entire metropolitan area. The simulations by Urbonas and Glidden showed that a system of

on-site detention basins designed using the simplified equations can be as effective as a system of basins designed individually.

The authors believe that a system of detention basins sized using uniform volume and release requirements can, in fact, be more effective in controlling peaks along the drainageways than a system of random designs. The latter suffers from the fact that each detention basin design can vary in size and discharge characteristics due to the approach, assumptions and expertise of each designer.

REFERENCES

McCUEN, R. H.,"A Regional Approach to Urban Stormwater Detention," *Geophysical Research Letters,* 74–128, pp. 321–22, November, 1974.

TUCKER, L. S.,"Availability of Rainfall-Runoff Data for Sewered Drainage Catchments," ASCE Urban Water Resources Research Program Technical Memorandum No. 8., New York, 1969.

URBONAS, B. R., GLIDDEN, M. W.,"Potential Effects of Detention Policies," Proceedings of the Second Southwest Regional Symposium on Urban Stormwater Management, Texas A & M University, November 1983.

16

Precipitation Data Needs
for Estimating Storage Volumes

16.1 GENERAL

When an engineer designs a storm sewer or an open channel, the main concern is the rate of rainfall runoff (i.e., peak flow) the conveyance facility needs to handle. Flows from storms with less rainfall intensity than designed for are safely conveyed within the facility without backing up water into streets, parking lots, basements, etc. The volume of runoff is only of secondary interest.

Storage facilities are used in storm drainage systems to either extend system capacities, to provide flow equalization, or to provide water quality enhancement. Design of storage, however, requires knowledge of rainfall and runoff volumes. Rainfall intensity, by itself, is not sufficient information. As a result, rainfall information that is adequate for the sizing of storm sewers is not adequate for the sizing of storage facilities.

We now discuss various types of precipitation data that may be considered or acquired for the design of storage facilities. We have classified the data into the following groups:

- intensity–duration–frequency data;
- standardized design storms;
- chronologic rainfall records;
- snow melt; and
- chronologic series of flow records.

The first two groups currently form the basis for most drainage and water quality design in the United States and Europe. Although often criticized by some, they are well entrenched into engineering practice, offer fast results, and are relatively simple to use.

As the designs become more complex and system-operations-oriented, it becomes necessary to shift to the use of chronologic rainfall records. Unfortunately, these may not be available to many communities. Data from other, hopefully meteorologically similar, sites has to be borrowed whenever local records are inadequate, thereby reducing confidence in the data's applicability at the design site.

Also, the analysis or operation of large systems require not only the knowledge of how precipitation varies with time, but also how it is distributed over the watershed at any given time. Precipitation data of this complexity is practically nonexistent and, therefore, storm runoff storage and conveyance system designs are often based on less than complete information. This fact should not deter the engineer from doing his or her job, however. Generalized information, although not as complete as we often would like to have, can serve as an adequate basis for design. What's important is that we recognize the limitations of the information and use it to the best of our abilities.

16.2 INTENSITY–DURATION–FREQUENCY DATA

The use of rainfall intensity–duration–frequency data became a part of the storm sewer design practice when the Rational Formula was introduced. Although the Rational Formula is used primarily for the sizing of storm sewers, it is currently also being used for the design of detention, retention, infiltration, and percolation facilities. The Rational Formula assumes that the effective rainfall intensity over the entire catch-basin is equal to the intensity found at the time of concentration. Figure 16.1 illustrates this principle for a five-year storm.

Most of the rainfall data for the development of the intensity–duration–frequency (i.e., I-D-F) curves in the United States are collected by the U.S. Weather Service, primarily at its first-order stations. However, the users of these data need to understand that each data set is representative only of the rainfall characteristics at the gauging site.

The I-D-F curves are constructed by searching the records of all storms for the most intense periods of rainfall. Rainfall depths are then ranked and tabulated by duration, as shown in Table 16.1. The tabular values are then converted to I–D–F graphs. Another example of a set of I-D-F values, for a storm having a much longer duration, are listed in Table 16.2. As can be seen by these two examples, rainfall I–D–F information can be radically different, depending on the local hydrologic conditions and the purpose for which this information will be used.

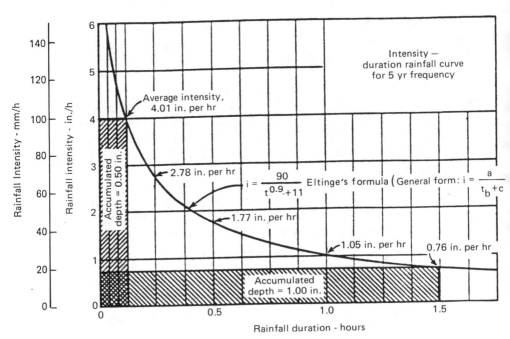

Figure 16.1   Intensity–duration curve for a five-year storm.

TABLE 16.1   Intensity–Duration–Frequency; Chicago, Ill.

	RETURN PERIOD IN YEARS		MAXIMUM DEPTH IN INCHES AND STORM NUMBER FOR STATED DURATION			
Rank	Annual	Exceedance	5-min.	10-min.	15-min.	25-min.
1	36.0	35.0	.61(7)	1.11(7)	1.29(7)	1.64(7)
2	18.0	17.5	.58(8)	.96(5)	1.22(5)	1.58(4)
3	12.0	11.7	.55(6)	.94(6)	1.16(6)	1.49(3)
4	9.0	8.8	.53(1)	.92(8)	1.16(4)	1.45(2)
5	7.2	7.0	.51(5)	.88(4)	1.15(8)	1.45(8)
6	6.0	5.8	.50(4)	.80(3)	1.12(3)	1.39(5)

Storm Number	Storm's Date
(1)	June 29, 1920
(2)	July 7, 1921
(3)	August 11, 1923
(4)	June 20, 1928
(5)	August 11, 1931
(6)	June 26, 1932
(7)	September 13, 1936
(8)	July 6, 1943

TABLE 16.2 Intensity–Duration–Frequency, Stockholm, Sweden

Return Period in Years	MAXIMUM DEPTH IN INCHES (mm) FOR STORMS OF FOLLOWING DURATION in DAYS			
	0.5	1.0	2.0	4.0
0.25	0.51 (13)	0.62 (16)	0.76 (19)	0.92 (23)
0.50	0.68 (17)	0.83 (21)	1.01 (26)	1.22 (31)
1.00	0.87 (22)	1.06 (27)	1.28 (32)	1.56 (40)
2.00	1.09 (28)	1.32 (34)	1.60 (41)	1.94 (49)
5.00	1.46 (37)	1.78 (45)	2.16 (55)	2.62 (67)
10.00	1.86 (47)	2.28 (58)	2.75 (70)	3.33 (85)

Examination of Table 16.1 reveals that the six rankings of I–D–F values for four durations of rainfall came from eight different storms. For example, the fourth ranked event had its 5-minute rain depth from storm (1), its 10-minute depth from storm (8), its 15-minute depth from storm (4), and its 20-minute depth from storm (2). This approach of normalizing rainfall data maximizes the depth at each duration. It does not consider if the successive rainfall depths are from the same storm, or even from the same type of storms. Nevertheless, despite this apparent inconsistency in the construction of I–D–F curves, this technique permits engineers to come up with reasonable rainfall values for estimating storage volumes.

16.3 STANDARDIZED DESIGN STORMS

Another popular approach for sizing storage facilities is to use standardized design storms. In practice, design storms are developed in a variety of ways. Some are derived using the I–D–F information, while others are derived using other available rainfall data. A design storm, in theory, is expected to be representative of many recorded rainstorms and may also be expected to reflect the intensity, volume, and duration of a storm having a given recurrence frequency (i.e., 5-year, 50-year, etc.).

When a standardized design storm is used to design a storage facility, it is assumed that the facility will operate at capacity, on the average, at the same recurrence frequency as the design storm. This assumption presupposes many things.

First, it assumes that the design storm has a rainfall volume equivalent to a real storm having the same statistical recurrence frequency. Second, it assumes that the temporal distribution of rainfall within the storm is representative of a storm occurring in nature. Third, it assumes that the storage facility is empty and ready to accept all of the runoff when the design storm occurs. Namely, the storage basin is not partially full from runoff that may have occurred only a few hours or a few days prior to this storm. Fourth, the design storm is uniformly distributed over the entire watershed. This is probably a reasonable assumption for small watersheds, but is not appropriate for the larger watersheds.

Standardized design storms are used extensively in practice. In fact, for practical reasons their use may be the only readily available alternative at many locations. Nevertheless, the use of standardized design storms for the design of storage facilities has been criticized by many investigators (Marsalek, 1978; Marsalek et.al., 1986; McPherson, 1976, 1977; Walesh, 1979; Wenzel, 1978). Most of the criticism centers around the argument that the use of design storms cannot adequately reproduce the runoff volume frequency distribution (see Figure 16.2). Although this criticism appears to have merit, often the lack of local rainfall data still mandates that the storage facilities be designed using standardized design storms. We now describe some of the design storms being used in the United States and in Europe.

16.3.1 Block Rainstorm

The simplest form of standardized design storm is the so-called *block rainstorm*. As is seen in Figure 16.3, a block rainstorm has a constant intensity during the entire event. The intensity of the block rainstorm, for different durations and recurrence frequencies of rain, can be obtained directly from the I–D–F curves, as illustrated in Figure 16.4. It is clear that the development of the block rainstorm has its roots in the Rational Method.

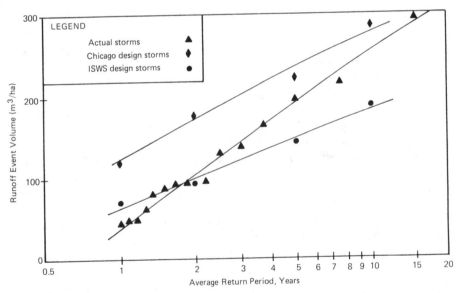

Figure 16.2 Runoff volumes resulting from actual and two design storms. (After Marsalek, 1978.)

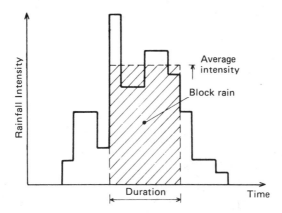

Figure 16.3   Definition of the block rainstorm as a design storm.

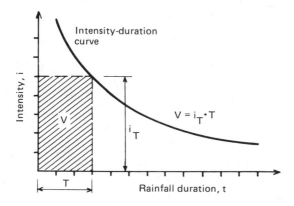

Figure 16.4   Derivation of the block rainstorm using the I–D–F curve.

As illustrated in Figure 16.3, the block rainstorm represents only the average of the most intense portion of an actual storm. The rain that falls before or after this period is not included. The use of the block rainstorm may have merit in the sizing of storm sewers, but its use is of questionable validity in the sizing of storage facilities. It is expected that the use of the block rainstorm will result in too small of a storage volume.

16.3.2 Sifalda and Arnell Rainstorms

A modification to the block rainstorm was suggested by Sifalda (1973). The modification includes a trapezoidal rainfall pattern before and after the block rainstorm, as illustrated in Figure 16.5.

Arnell (1978), after comparing rainfall duration–volume statistics, con-

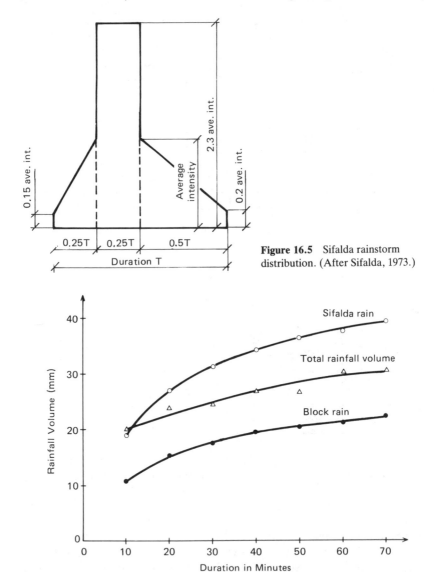

Figure 16.5 Sifalda rainstorm distribution. (After Sifalda, 1973.)

Figure 16.6 Duration–volumes of Block and Sifalda rainstorms. (After Arnell, 1978.)

cluded that the Sifalda rainfall tended to overstate the rainfall volume. (His findings are shown in Figure 16.6.) By modifying the Sifalda rainstorm, Arnell succeeded in constructing a design rainstorm that, at least for Sweden, appears to be consistent with duration–volume statistics. Arnell's storm is illustrated in Figure 16.7. This approach appears to have achieved volumetric

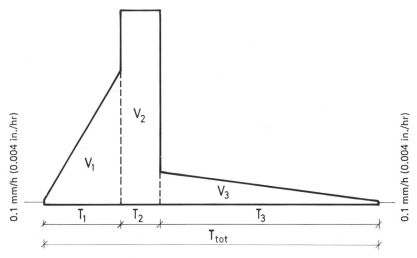

Figure 16.7   Arnell rainstorm distribution. (After Arnell, 1982.)

consistency; however, it has not been tested against the probabilities of storage basin performance using a continuous rainfall record.

16.3.3 Chicago and the ISWS Design Rainstorms

Keifer and Hsien Chu (1957) described the development of the now well-established Chicago design rainstorm. This method has been widely used in North America because it is simple to derive using standard I–D–F information. Its simplicity is also its major shortcoming; namely, it is merely a redistribution of the I–D–F.

The developers of the Chicago rainstorm attempted to incorporate some of the features found in actual rainstorms. The storm takes into account the maximum rainfall intensities of individual storms, the average antecedent rainfall before the peak intensity, and the relative timing of the peak. To develop the Chicago design rainstorm, one needs to study a number of recorded storms to determine the value of t_r such that

$$t_r = \frac{t_p}{T} \tag{16.1}$$

in which t_r = ratio of time from start of storm to peak intensity to total duration of the storm (average of recorded storms),

t_p = time from start of storm to peak intensity, and
T = total duration of the storm.

The hyetograph is then constructed using the following formula:

$$i_{av} = \frac{a}{t_d^b + c} \tag{16.2}$$

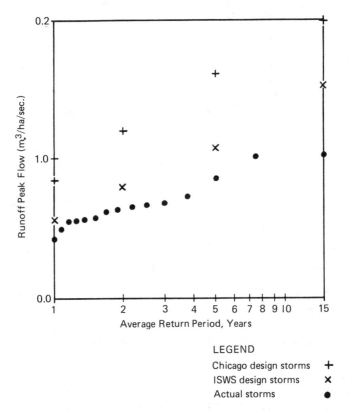

Figure 16.8 Comparison of runoff peaks for Chicago and ISWS design storms vs. recorded storms. (After Marsalek, 1978.)

in which i_{av} = average rainfall intensity over duration t_d,

  t_d = duration of storm for the average intensity, and

a, b, c = constants used to fit the data.

After studying numerous recorded rainstorms in Illinois, Huff (1967) suggested an alternate method for developing design storms in Illinois. This technique was later incorporated by Terstriep and Stall (1974) into the Illinois Urban Area Simulator (i.e., ILLUDAS), after which it became known as the Illinois State Water Survey (i.e., ISWS) design storm. In this procedure, the one-hour rainfall depths are distributed into a hyetograph of desired duration using a normalized relationship developed from Illinois data. Marsalek (1978) compared these two procedures, and his findings for the prediction of runoff peaks are presented in Figure 16.8. The actual rainfall patterns are compared in Figure 16.9.

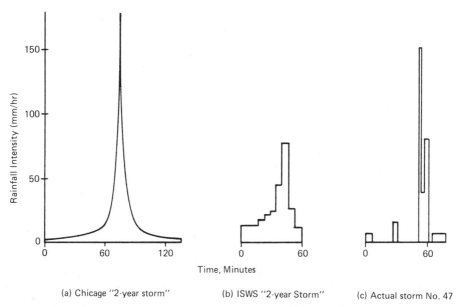

(a) Chicage "2-year storm"   (b) ISWS "2-year Storm"   (c) Actual storm No. 47

Figure 16.9   Comparing Chicago, ISWS, and actual hyetographs. (After Marsalek, 1978.)

16.3.4 Colorado Urban Design Storms.

As part of an effort to update the Colorado Urban Hydrograph Procedure for the Denver area, Urbonas (1979) developed a regional set of normalized design storm distributions. These design storms were based on a runoff
and rainfall data base within the semi-arid region of Denver. For watersheds
of 5 square miles (13 km²) or less, a Colorado Urban Design Storm hyetograph
can be obtained for recurrence frequencies of 2, 5, 10, 50, or 100 years by
distributing the one-hour depth. This is done using a given multiplier for each
of the five-minute increments within the two-hour storm. The distribution
multipliers for each reoccurrence storm are given in Table 16.3, which was
taken from the *Urban Storm Drainage Criteria Manual* (1969). Good comparisons of the calculated peak runoff rates were found when tested against
simulation results obtained using long-term series of recorded rainfall records
(see Figure 16.10).

16.4 CHRONOLOGIC RAINFALL RECORDS

Since the occurrence of precipitation is a stochastic process, the occurrence of
the resultant runoff is also a stochastic process. Besides precipitation, runoff is
affected by the watershed characteristics and the configuration of the con-

TABLE 16.3. Design Storm Distribution of 1-hour NOAA Atlas Depth for Denver, Colorado Area

Time Minutes	PERCENT OF 1-HOUR NOAA RAINFALL ATLAS DEPTH				
	2-year	5-year	10-year	50-year	100-year
5	2.0	2.0	2.0	1.3	1.0
10	4.0	3.7	3.7	3.5	3.0
15	8.4	8.7	8.2	5.0	4.6
20	16.0	15.3	15.0	8.0	8.0
25	25.0	25.0	25.0	15.0	14.0
30	14.0	13.0	12.0	25.0	25.0
35	6.3	5.8	5.6	12.0	14.0
40	5.0	4.4	4.3	8.0	8.0
45	3.0	3.6	3.8	5.0	6.2
50	3.0	3.6	3.2	5.0	5.0
55	3.0	3.0	3.2	3.2	4.0
60	3.0	3.0	3.2	3.2	4.0
65	3.0	3.0	3.2	3.2	4.0
70	2.0	3.0	3.2	2.4	2.0
75	2.0	2.5	3.2	2.4	2.0
80	2.0	2.2	2.5	1.8	1.2
85	2.0	2.2	1.9	1.8	1.2
90	2.0	2.2	1.9	1.4	1.2
95	2.0	2.2	1.9	1.4	1.2
100	2.0	1.5	1.9	1.4	1.2
105	2.0	1.5	1.9	1.4	1.2
110	2.0	1.5	1.9	1.4	1.2
115	1.0	1.5	1.7	1.4	1.2
120	1.0	1.3	1.3	1.4	1.2
Totals	115.7	115.7	115.7	115.6	115.6

After *Urban Storm Drainage Criteria Manual*

veyance and storage system. As a result, the statistical distribution for rain-storms may not be the same as for the resultant runoff.

If a chronologic record of rainfall is used to size storage facilities, it first needs to be transformed into a record of runoff. This can be done with the aid of computer runoff simulation models, and the results can then be statistically analyzed. The assumption that the runoff and the rainfall, as is the case with design storms, have the same statistical properties no longer is an issue when using the chronological record. This is an advantage, since the conveyance system and storage within this system can strongly influence the runoff process.

Unfortunately, the cost of simulating a continuous long period of runoff under different system configurations is time-consuming and, as a result, expensive. This type of analysis can be justified only for large systems, where the numbers of combined wastewater–stormwater overflows are limited by an

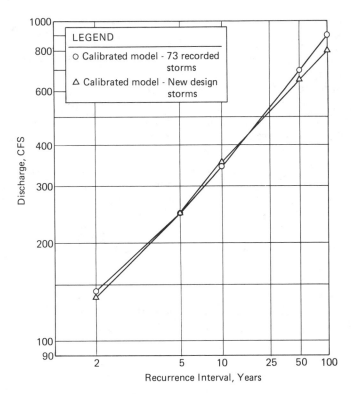

Figure 16.10   Runoff estimates using Colorado design storms vs. recorded storms. (After Urbonas, 1979.)

NPEDS permit, and where real time operations are to be used in combined sewer systems.

Walesh (July, 1979) proposed an alternative to continuous long-term simulation. He suggested that a chronologic rainfall record be analyzed to develop an annual series of peak flows and runoff volumes for a select variety of small watersheds. With the aid of this information, several representative storms that array around the desired T-year recurrence period are selected. The selected storms, along with their antecedent rainfall, can then be used in the design or evaluation of storm sewers, channels, and detention storage facilities. Thus, instead of simulating the runoff for, say, all storms in a 20-, 40- or 60-year period, one needs to only simulate maybe 30 to 50 storms in order to develop T-year recurrence period distribution of runoff peaks or volumes.

16.5 SNOW MELT

Stormwater detention storage facilities are typically designed to handle the runoff from rainstorms. However, with the advent of water quality concerns for urban runoff, it may, in some cases, be necessary also to account for snow melt. Unlike the intensity–duration–frequency data for rainfall, there is no equivalent methodology for estimating runoff due to snow melt. There are, however, procedures available for estimating the rates of snow melt that are based on local experiences.

In order to calculate the rate of runoff from snow melt, one must first be able to determine the intensity of snow melt. Snow melting in spring usually occurs slowly at first, accelerating as the snow becomes water-soaked and the albedo of the snow is reduced. In Figure 16.11 we see the intensity increasing as the seasons shift from winter to spring in the month of April. As the warm weather advances, the intensity of the snow melt and runoff increases. At the same time this is happening, the amount of snow in the fields decreases. Eventually, the mass of the snow shrinks such that, despite increasing snow melt rates, the resultant runoff begins also to decrease.

Theoretically, the snow melt intensity could reach about 0.29 inches per hour (7 mm/hr). In practice, however, the maximum intensity rarely exceeds one-half of this rate. When calculated for a whole day, heavy snow melt can produce 0.82 to 1.1 inches (20 to 30 mm) of water.

Because the ground is usually frozen, one would expect most of the snow melt to run off. However, it has been found that much of the snow melt actually infiltrates through the frozen ground. As in unfrozen ground, the

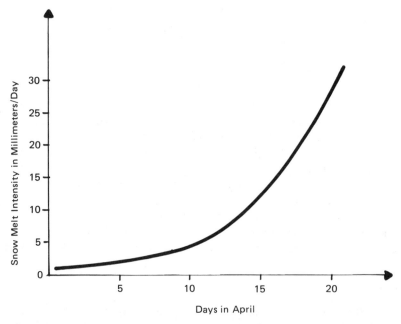

Figure 16.11   Snow melt rate in Sweden in an open field. (After Bengtsson et. al., 1980.)

infiltration rate decreases as the soil becomes saturated. What often happens is that when the snow melt rate is the highest, the ground is saturated and most of the water becomes surface runoff.

Snow melt generally does not control the size of conveyance facilities for stormwater systems. Nor does snow melt control the sizing of conveyance or treatment facilities for combined systems. It is usually the summer thunderstorms which govern the sizing of the conveyance, treatment, and storage facilities in urban areas. Prolonged periods of snow melt can, however, produce very large quantities of runoff. But due to the slow rates of runoff, the only type of facilities it may affect are percolation and infiltration basins. These can take a long time to empty, and prolonged large inflows can overtax them. As a result, it is always wise to limit such facilities to the control of runoff from small tracts of land.

16.6 CHRONOLOGIC SERIES OF MEASURED FLOW DATA

The most direct method for sizing a detention storage facilities uses a chronologic series of actually measured flows at the storage site. Unfortunately, such data is very rare and, when available, is mostly limited to measurements at wastewater treatment plants. As a result, for practical reasons this technique is generally used for the design of storage at, or near, treatment plants in combined sewer systems.

Flow variations in a combined sewer can be categorized into the following groups:

- cyclic diurnal variations due to the daily rhythm of human activity;
- temporary shock loads due to releases from industry, swimming pools, water treatment plants, etc.;
- temporary shock loads due to discontinuities in operation of the upstream system (e.g., pumps, storage releases, etc.);
- temporary shock loads due to runoff from rainstorms;
- seasonal variations due to discontinuities in the use of water by schools, restaurants, hotels, industry, etc.; and
- cyclic variations in groundwater infiltration.

These types of variations in flow can act together and be additive. This concept is illustrated in Figure 16.12, where the runoff from a rainstorm is superimposed on the cyclic daily dry weather flow variations.

16.6.1 Daily Variations in Wastewater Flow

Dry weather flow of wastewater in a sewer has a characteristic diurnal variation which is dependent, among other things, on the size of the tributary area and its characteristics, such as the population density, industry, etc. As the tributary watershed increases, the variations in flow decrease. Conversely, the flow variations are most pronounced in sewers serving small tributary watersheds. Daily inflow can be intensified by temporary shock loads from industry, discontinuities in operation of pumping stations, etc.

Diurnal dry weather flow variations can be equalized with relatively moderate detention volumes. The EPA (1947) reported that flow equalization of the diurnal wastewater flow variations can be accomplished with a storage volume of 10% to 20% of the average one-day inflow. Of course, local conditions of flow, infiltration, etc. can significantly affect these storage requirements.

16.6.2 Shock Loads Due to Rainfall

In combined sewer systems, rainfall runoff significantly increases the flow in the sewers (see Figure 16.12). The magnitude of the flow increase is a function of many factors, including:

● type and age of the sewer system,
● layout of the system,

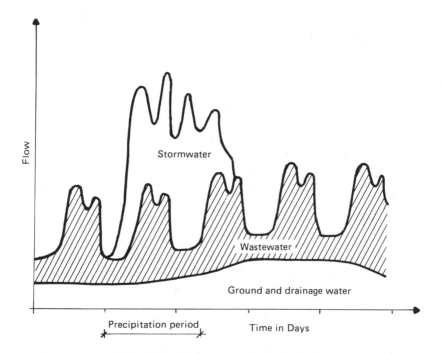

Figure 16.12   Various types of variation in flow.

- intensity and duration of rainfall, and
- land uses in the tributary basin.

Increases in flow in separate wastewater systems also occur during rainstorms due to inadvertent inflow. However, the increases in the peak flow are not nearly as pronounced as in combined sewer systems.

Large storage volumes are needed to provide flow equalization for rainfall-induced shock loads. For practical reasons, it is not possible to achieve complete flow equalization or to control the flows resulting from larger storms.

16.6.3 Variations Due to Snow Melt

Snow melt will also cause an increase in flow in combined sewers and storm sewers. The duration of snow melt can vary from a few hours to several weeks. The intensity and duration of snow melt within the sewer system will depend on the following:

- the climate,
- the amount of snow pack,
- the type of conveyance system, and
- temperature conditions.

The increase in flow within the sewers will continue after all the snow has melted. This is due to infiltration of the snow melt into the ground, which will in part seep into the sewer system.

Because snow melt can occur over a long period of time and produce large runoff volumes, it is unrealistic to build flow equalization storage for this runoff. Thus, in combined sewer systems, this flow increase is handled by providing additional hydraulic capacity at treatment plants.

16.6.4 Variations Due to Groundwater Seepage

Groundwater will seep into any sewer system as long as it in part, or totally, inundates any sewer pipe, manhole, inlet, etc. The infiltration rate will vary with the depth of groundwater and the condition and age of the sewer system. The older and more deteriorated systems have loser pipe joints, imperfect seals at manholes, and at other structures which act as conduits between the groundwater and the sewer pipes. Seepage rates fluctuate very slowly, and these slow variations cannot be effectively balanced through detention. It is suggested that measures be taken to reduce infiltration and exfiltration through restorative maintenance whenever it becomes a problem.

REFERENCES

ABRAHAM, C., LYONS, T. C., AND SCHULZE, K.W., "Selection of a Design Storm for Use with Simulation Models," *National Symposium on Urban Hydrology, Hydraulics and Sediment Control*, Lexington Ky., 1976.

ARNELL, V., "Rainfall Data for Design of Detention Basins," Seminar on Detention Basins in Sweden, 1978. (In Swedish)

ARNELL, V., "Rainfall Data for the Design of Sewer Pipe Systems," Chalmers University of Technology, Report Series A:8, Sweden, 1982.

BENGTSSON, L., JOHNSSON, A., MALMQUIST, P-A., SARNER, E., AND HALLGREN, J., "Snow in Urban Areas," Swedish Council for Building Research, Report R 27, 1980. (In Swedish)

EPA, *Flow Equalization*, EPA Technology Transfer Seminar Publication, 1974.

GEIGER, W., AND DORSCH, H., "Quality-quantity Simulation (QQS), Detailed Continuous Planning Model for Urban Runoff Control," Volume I, EPA Grant No. R 805100, 1980.

HUFF, F. A., "Time Distribution of Heavy Rainfall Storms," *Water Resources Research*, Vol. 3, No. 4, 1967.

KEIFER, C. J., AND HSIEN CHU, H., "Synthetic Storm Pattern for Drainage Design," *Journal of the Hydraulics Division*, Vol. 83, ASCE, August, 1957.

MARSALEK, J., "Research on the Design Storm Concept," *ASCE Urban Water Resources Research Program, Technical Memorandum No. 33*, ASCE, New York, 1978.

MARSALEK, J., URBONAS, B., ROSSMILLER, R., AND WENZEL, H., (i.e., UWRRC Design Storm Task Committee), "Design Storms for Urban Drainage," *Proceedings, Water Forum '86*, ASCE, August, 1986.

MCPHERSON, M. B., "Urban Hydrology: New Concepts in Hydrology for Urban Areas," Northwest Bridge Engineering Seminar, Olympia, Wash., October, 1976.

MCPHERSON, M. B., "The Design Storm Concept," *Urban Runoff Control Planning*, ASCE Urban Water Resources Research Council, ASCE, June, 1977.

SIFALDA, V., "Development of a Design Rain for Assigning Dimensions to Sewer Nets," Gwf, Wasser/Abwasser No. 9, 1973. (In German)

TERSTRIEP, M. B., AND STALL, J. B., *The Illinois Urban Drainage Area Simulator, ILLUDAS*, Bulletin 58, Illinois Water Survey, Urbana, 1974.

THORNDAL, U., "Precipitation Hydrographs," Stads- og Havneingsnioren No. 7, Copenhagen, 1971. (In Danish)

URBAN STORM DRAINAGE CRITERIA MANUAL, Urban Drainage and Flood Control District, Denver, Colo., 1984 edition.

URBONAS, B., "Reliability of Design Storms in Modeling," *Proceedings of the International Symposium on Urban Storm Runoff*, University of Kentucky, July, 1979.

WALESH, S. G., "Statistically-Based Use of Event Models," *Proceedings of the International Symposium on Urban Storm Runoff*, University of Kentucky, July, 1979.

WALESH, S. G., "Summary—Seminar on the Design Storm Concept," *Proceedings, Stormwater Management Model (SWMM) Users Group Meeting*, May, 1979, EPA 600/9-79-026, June, 1979.

WENZEL, H. G., JR., "Rainfall Data for Sewer Design," *Section III of Storm Sewer Design*, Dept. of Civil Engineering, University of Illinois-Urbana-Champaign, 1978.

17

Calculation Methods
for Infiltration
and Percolation Facilities

17.1 GENERAL

The design of infiltration and percolation facilities is similar to the design of other types of detention facilities. The goal is to design the facility so that it will contain the design inflow without overflowing. At infiltration facilities, water is infiltrated into the ground from the surface. If the flow to the infiltration surface exceeds its infiltrating capacity, excess water is stored on the surface. At percolation facilities, the water is conveyed to a percolation pit from where it percolates out into the ground. In a percolation basin, the effective pore volume serves as the storage volume.

As a general note, infiltration and percolation facilities will work best for very small runoff basins such as individual lots. It cannot be overemphasized that they need to be designed conservatively, using low hydraulic unit loading rates on the infiltration/percolation surfaces. These facilities need to "rest" between runoff events to "heal" and rejuvenate the pores in the receiving soils. If the loading rates do not permit this, the soil's pores seal and the infiltration capacity of the site may be lost, possibly forever. In addition, time will be needed for the groundwater mound that develops under a local disposal facility to drain away. Even in sandy soils with a pore ratio of 0.25, each centimeter of surface water becomes 4 centimeters in the ground. Thus, if the unit loading rate is too high, the groundwater dome will rise to the surface and the infiltration facility will fail.

The installation and use of infiltration and percolation facilities was described in Chapter 2, which introduced the concept of local disposal facilities, explained some of the different concepts in arranging such facilities, and discussed their suitability under various soil and groundwater conditions. It is suggested that the reader review Chapter 2 before proceeding to use the principles described in the remainder of this chapter.

17.2 DESIGN FLOW

The volume of runoff reaching an infiltration or a percolation facility depends on several factors. These include the tributary basin size, the degree of development in the basin (i.e., amount of impervious surface), and the characteristics of rainfall and snow melt in the area. We begin by discussing the suggested techniques for estimating rainfall and snow melt runoff for the design of infiltration and percolation facilities.

17.2.1 Stormwater Runoff

Since infiltration and percolation facilities are mainly used for small runoff basins, runoff calculations can be based on the Rational Formula; thus, in Metric units:

$$Q_T = C \cdot \frac{I_T}{1,000} \cdot A \qquad (17.1)$$

in which Q_T = runoff rate for a T-year storm, cubic meters/second,
    C = runoff coefficient, nondimensional,
    I_T = rainfall intensity for a T-year storm at a storm duration t, in liters/second/hectare, and
    A = area of the tributary watershed, in hectares.

By multiplying the average runoff rate, Q_T, by the design storm duration, t, we obtain the cumulative volume over the storm duration, namely

$$V_T = 3,600 \cdot C \cdot \frac{I_T}{1,000} \cdot t \cdot A \qquad (17.2)$$

in which V_T = total runoff volume at time t for a T-year storm in cubic meters, and
    t = storm duration in hours.

Thus, the volume calculations can be performed using the intensity-duration–frequency curves for any design storm having a T-year return period. By deciding on the design storm duration, the volume of rainfall (i.e., block rain = $I_T t$) can be calculated, the simplification being justified for small urban watersheds. This procedure is illustrated in Figure 17.1 for three storm durations.

Block rain represents only the average intensity of the most intense por-

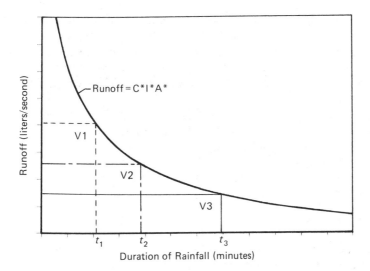

Figure 17.1 Derivation of block rain inflow hydrographs.

tion of the rainstorm. The rain that falls before and after this period is not included in the I–D–F curve and consequently is not reflected in the block rain calculations. Since the sizing of an infiltration or a percolation basin depends mostly on volume of runoff, it is necessary to somehow account for that part of the rainstorm not included in block rain.

Sjoberg and Martensson (1982) studied how the runoff from block rainfall differed from the results obtained using continuous simulation with chronological rainfall records. Assuming the latter provided more accurate runoff estimates, they concluded that by increasing block rainfall volume by 25%, the runoff volume estimates with Rational Formula can be quite accurate. This modification does not affect the simplicity of the calculations. Thus, the volume of runoff reaching an infiltration or a percolation facility can be estimated using Equation 17.3, which is a slightly modified version of Equation 17.2:

$$V_T = 1.25 \left(3{,}600 \cdot C \cdot \frac{I_T}{1{,}000} \cdot t \cdot A \right) \tag{17.3}$$

in which all of the terms have been defined earlier.

When sizing infiltration and percolation facilities, it is practical to assume that all runoff occurs only from the impervious surfaces having runoff coefficients between 0.85 and 0.95. It is not uncommon to design infiltration and percolation facilities for the average runoff volume from all the storms that occur over a period of years. The average runoff event is considerably smaller than the runoff from a two-year design storm. This is because the storm data include *all* runoff-producing events and not only the most intense storms of each year, which is the case for typical I–D–F curves. For example, in the Denver area the average runoff producing storm has 0.44 inch

(11.2 mm) of precipitation. The two-year design storm, on the other hand, has approximately 1.10 inch (27.9 mm) of rainfall. Because the average runoff events are relatively small, facilities sized to handle them will be loaded to full capacity much more frequently. As a result, they will be stressed and the infiltration and percolation surfaces may not have a chance to sufficiently rest between storms.

The choice of the recurrence frequency and storm duration is often dictated by local or state government rules, regulations, or criteria. Nevertheless, for most stormwater drainage disposal situations it is recommended that the design for these types of facilities be based on a 2-year storm totally infiltrated into the ground within 36 hours. This will ensure a longer life for the infiltration and percolation facilities.

17.2.2 Snow Melt

In certain parts of the United States and Europe, snow melt can govern the sizing of infiltration and percolation facilities. This is especially the case when the basins have a relatively small amount of impervious surface compared to the pervious surface. Under such conditions, the runoff from snow melt may produce prolonged and larger volumes of runoff than rainfall.

Under extreme conditions, actual snow melt intensities could reach as much as 0.15 inch (3.8 mm) of water per hour. However, more typical runoff rates from melting snow appear to be considerably less than this rate.

Unlike rainfall on unfrozen and unsaturated soils, snow melt will contribute to surface runoff from the pervious surfaces. However, it is not possible to generalize how much runoff can be expected under the varying climatic conditions throughout the United States and Europe. To insure acceptable operation, check the design of an infiltration or percolation facility against the runoff from melting snow. We suggest that this be done using the following minimum snow melt rates:

Minimum Snow Melt Rates for Design

IMPERVIOUS SURFACES		PERVIOUS SURFACES	
English Units	Metric Units	English Units	Metric Units
0.04 ft³/s/ac	2.8 l/s/ha	0.02 ft³/s/ac	1.4 l/s/ha

17.3 SELECTING AND SIZING INFILTRATION SURFACES

17.3.1 Site Selection for Infiltration

Many factors affect the suitability of a site as an infiltration facility for the disposal of stormwater. Among these, the following are most important:

- depth to groundwater;
- depth to bedrock;
- surface soil type;
- underlying soil type;
- vegetation cover of the infiltrating surface;
- the uses of the infiltrating surfaces; and
- the ratio of tributary impervious surface to the infiltrating surface.

There are several conditions that will rule out a site as a candidate for an infiltration facility. **If the following conditions are discovered or likely, disposal of stormwater by infiltration is not recommended:**

- seasonal high groundwater is less than 4 feet (1.2 m) below the infiltrating surface.
- bedrock is within 4 feet (1.2 m) of the infiltrating surface.
- the infiltrating surface is on fill (unless the fill is clean sand or gravel).
- the surface and underlaying soils are classified by the Soil Conservation Service as Hydrologic Group D, or the saturated infiltration rate is less than 0.3 inch per hour (7.6 mm/h) as reported by SCS soil surveys.

If the preceding conditions do not rule out the site, the site should be evaluated using a method developed by the Swedish Association for Water and Sewer Works (1983). This procedure is based on evaluating a series of site conditions and assigning points for each one of them. If a site gets less than 20 points, it should not be considered for infiltration. On the other hand, a site with more than 30 points is considered to be excellent. Sites receiving 20 to 30 points are considered good candidates for an infiltration facility. Figure 17.2 was prepared to summarize this process and to assist the reader in evaluating infiltration sites.

The points to be assigned for each of the site characteristics are tabulated in Table 17.1. Points are assigned for each site condition and are then added to determine the total points for the site. This evaluation system should only be used for preliminary screening of potential sites. It is not intended as a substitute for good engineering and site-specific testing, evaluation, and design.

17.3.2 Sizing an Infiltration Facility

When the site has been judged to be an acceptable candidate for an infiltration basin, the next step is to find the required surface area and storage volume for the facility. Table 17.1 indicates that the infiltration surface area should not be smaller than one-half of the tributary impervious surface. This requirement sets the lower limit for the size of the infiltration surface. However, not all of this area needs to be where ponding eventually occurs. Credit

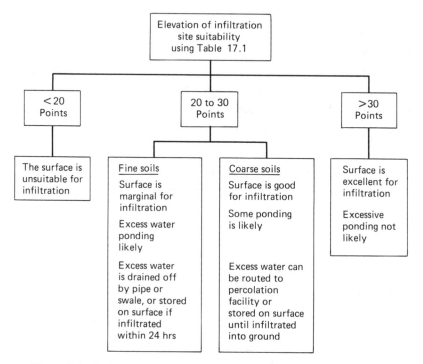

Figure 17.2 Evaluation of infiltration site for suitability. (After Swedish Association for Water and Sewage Works, 1983.)

for loss of runoff can be taken when the impervious surfaces are made to sheet-flow over lawns before the water reaches the ponding surfaces. As a result, practical considerations dictate that the ponding part of the infiltration area be set at no less than one-fourth of the impervious surface area. There is no upper limit, and the size of the infiltration surface will be constrained only by the available right-of-way.

The size of the infiltration surface will also be governed by the release rate, namely the infiltration rate for the water stored on the infiltration surface. The exact value of the infiltration rate is one of the most difficult parameters to determine. Among the factors influencing infiltration rates are:

- the structure of the ground surface,
- the type and condition of the vegetation zone,
- soil moisture,
- the nature of the underlying soils, including permeability, and
- the depth to groundwater.

It is not possible to generalize about infiltration rates. Table 17.2 contains data that illustrate their diversity among various soil groups. Clearly, the

TABLE 17.1   Point System for Evaluating Infiltration Sites

1. Ratio between tributary connected impervious area (A_{IMP}) and the infiltration area (A_{INF}):
   - $A_{INF} > 2\,A_{IMP}$ 20 points
   - $A_{IMP} \le A_{INF} \le 2\,A_{IMP}$ 10 points
   - $0.5\,A_{IMP} \le A_{INF} < A_{IMP}$ 5 points

   Pervious surfaces smaller than $0.5\,A_{IMP}$ should not be used for infiltration.

2. Nature of surface soil layer:
   - Coarse soils with low ratio of organic material   7 points
   - Normal humus soil   5 points
   - Fine-grained soils with high ratio of organic material   0 points

3. Underlaying soils:
   - If the underlaying soils are coarser than surface soil, assign the same
     number of points as for the surface soil layer assigned under item 2.
   - If the underlaying soils are finer grained than the surface soils,
     use the following points:
     - Gravel, sand, or glacial till with gravel or sand   7 points
     - Silty sand or loam   5 points
     - Fine silt or clay   0 points

4. Slope (S) of the infiltration surface:
   - $S < 7\%$ 5 points
   - $7 \le S \le 20\%$ 3 points
   - $S > 20\%$ 0 points

5. Vegetation cover:
   - Healthy, natural vegetation cover   5 points
   - Lawn—well-established   3 points
   - Lawn—new   0 points
   - No vegetation—bare ground   −5 points

6. Degree of traffic on infiltration surface:
   - Little foot traffic   5 points
   - Average foot traffic (park, lawn)   3 points
   - Much foot traffic (playing fields)   0 points

only practical recommendation we can make is to perform several infiltration tests at each site and then to use the lowest measured rates in the design of an infiltration facility.

When the inflow envelope curve (see Equation 17.3) and the infiltration rate are known, the storage volume can be calculated graphically. As illustrated in Figure 17.3, the required storage volume is found by measuring the largest vertical difference between the inflow envelope function, $V(t)$, and the cumulative infiltration function $F(t)$. Note that this graphical procedure can easily be programmed on any commonly available spreadsheet. This calculating procedure is virtually identical to the one described later in Section 18.2, except that the exfiltration rate is used as the outflow, and to the example given in Section 20.2.2

TABLE 17.2 Typical Infiltration Rates

	Infiltration Rate	
SCS Group and Type	Inches per Hour	Millimeters per hour
A. Sand	8.0	200
A. Loamy sand	2.0	50
B. Sandy loam	1.0	25
B. Loam	0.5	12.7
C. Silt loam	0.25*	6.3*
C. Sandy clay loam	0.15	3.8
D. Clay loam and silty clay loam	<0.09	<2.3
D. Clays	<0.05	<1.3

*Minimum rate; soils with lesser rates should not be considered as candidates for infiltration facilities.

This figure has two distinct regions. For storms having runoff duration equal to or less than t_b, all of the runoff cannot infiltrate into the ground. When the duration of rain is greater than t_b, infiltration capacity exceeds the inflow volume and the stored water is infiltrated into the ground.

These hydrologic calculations tell us how much runoff is not infiltrated into the ground for a given I–D–F condition. This excess either runs off or is stored on the infiltration surface. As an alternative, the infiltration area can be increased so that the runoff envelope curve $V(t)$ never exceeds the cumulative infiltration line $F(t)$. The designer may wish to try several infiltration area sizes until a satisfactory balance is achieved between storage volume and the size of

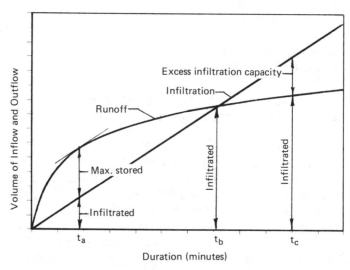

Figure 17.3   Sizing storage volume at an infiltration facility using runoff envelope.

the infiltration surface. Do not hesitate to oversize the area if more grassed surface area is available at the site than is required for a minimum design. Take full advantage of the site to reduce hydraulic loading rates on the infiltration surfaces, thereby increasing longevity and reducing the period of wet site conditions.

17.4 SELECTING AND SIZING PERCOLATION BASINS

17.4.1 Site Selection for Percolation Basins

The factors affecting the suitability of a site for percolation are similar to those affecting infiltration facilities, namely:

- depth to groundwater;
- depth to bedrock;
- soil type adjacent to and below the percolation bed; and
- ratio of tributary impervious surface to the percolation surface area.

As with infiltration, there are site conditions that can rule out a site as a viable candidate. **If the following conditions are discovered or are likely to occur at the site, disposal of stormwater by percolation is not recommended:**

- Seasonal high groundwater is less than 4 feet (1.2 m) below the bottom of percolation bed.
- Bedrock is within 4 feet (1.2 m) of the bottom of the percolation bed.
- Percolation bed is located on fill unless the fill is clean sand of gravel.
- The adjacent and underlying soils are classified by the Soil Conservation Service as Hydrologic Group C or D, or the field tested saturated hydraulic conductivity of the soils is less than 2×10^{-5} meter per second (6.6×10^{-5} foot per second).

When these do not rule out the site, we again suggest that the percolation facility be designed using a method developed by the Swedish Association for Water and Sewer Works (1983). Since this procedure comes from Europe, all equations are in metric units.

17.4.2 Darcy's Law

The rate at which water percolates into the ground can be estimated with the aid of Darcy's Law, namely:

$$U = k \cdot I \qquad (17.4)$$

in which U = flow velocity in meters per second,
   k = hydraulic conductivity in meters per second, and
   I = hydraulic gradient in meters per meter.

To be precise, Darcy's Law applies to groundwater flow in saturated soils. However, we try to locate percolation facilities with their bottoms at least 4 feet (1.2 m) above the seasonal high ground-water table. It is nevertheless safe to assume that the soil will be saturated when the facility is operating and that, because the bottom of the percolation field is above normal ground-water, the hydraulic gradient k = 1.0 meters/meter.

It is not possible to generalize what hydraulic conductivity should be used and we recommend that percolation tests be performed at each individual site. Table 17.3 contains published ranges of hydraulic conductivity for various types of soils. As you can see, the value of conductivity for any soil type can vary by as much as four orders of magnitude, which further reinforces the need for site-specific data.

When performing field hydraulic conductivity tests, unless there is good reason, the lowest conductivity test value is the one that should be used. Remember that the soils will tend to gradually clog with time, and the available conductivity will decrease. For this reason, it is recommended that the field conductivity test values are reduced by a safety factor of 2 to 3 when designing any percolation facility. Keep in mind that once a percolation facility fails, it will be very expensive or impossible to rebuild. Therefore, a conservative design philosophy is recommended. Designing a system that has a chance of failing in a few years is considered to be poor engineering practice.

17.4.3 Effective Porosity of Percolation Media

The effective porosity of the porous fill media inside of the percolation pit of trench determines the volume that is available for storage of water. Table 17.4 lists representable values for some of the most commonly used materials.

TABLE 17.3   Hydraulic Conductivity of Several Soil Types

Soil Type	Hydraulic Conductivity (Meters per Second)
Gravel	10^{-3}–10^{-1}
Sand	10^{-5}–10^{-2}
Silt	10^{-9}–10^{-5}
Clay (saturated)	$<10^{-9}$
Till	10^{-10}–10^{-6}

TABLE 17.4   Effective Porosity of Typical Stone Materials

Material	Effective Porosity (Percent)
Blasted rock	30
Uniform sized gravel	40
Graded gravel (¾-inch minus)	30
Sand	25
Pit run gravel	15–25

17.4.4 Effective Percolation Area

It is recommended by the Swedish Association for Water and Sewer Works that the bottom of a percolation pit or trench is considered impervious. The reason for this is that the bottom seals quickly by the accumulation of sediments. It is a good idea to anticipate this by assuming that all water will percolate into the ground only through the vertical sides of the basin or trench.

17.4.5 Calculating the Needed Storage Volume

The outflow rate from a percolation facility can be estimated using Darcy's Law. The water depth in the basin will vary during the filling and emptying process. To approximate the average release rate, the water depth can be arbitrarily set at one-half of the maximum depth. This means that the effective percolation area will be equal to one-half the area of the sides of the basin. With a hydraulic gradient equal to 1.0, Darcy's Law gives the following expression for the outflow from the basin:

$$V_{out}(t) = k \cdot 1.0 \cdot \frac{A_{perc}}{2} \cdot 3{,}600 \cdot t \qquad (17.5)$$

in which $V_{out}(t)$ = volume of water percolated into the ground, in cubic meters,

k = hydraulic conductivity of soil, in meters per second,

A_{perc} = total area of the sides of the percolation facility, in square meters, and

t = percolation time, in hours.

The volume of water stored, V, in the facility is the maximum difference between $V_{in}(t)$ and $V_{out}(t)$, which can be expressed as follows:

$$V = \max[V_{in}(t) - V_{out}(t)] \qquad (17.6)$$

or

$$V = \max\left[t \cdot 3{,}600 \cdot \frac{I_t}{1{,}000} \cdot C \cdot A \cdot 1.25 - k \cdot \frac{A_{perc}}{2} \cdot 3{,}600 \cdot t\right] \qquad (17.7)$$

in which A = area of the tributary impervious surfaces in hectares,
C = runoff coefficient for the impervious surfaces, and
I_t = average rainfall intensity over time t, in liters/second/hectare.

If both sides of Equation 17.7 are divided by $(C \cdot A)$, we get,

$$\frac{V}{C \cdot A} = \max\left[1.25 \cdot t \cdot 3.6 \cdot I_t - k \cdot \frac{A_{perc}}{2} \cdot 3,600 \cdot \frac{t}{(C \cdot A)} \right] \qquad (17.8)$$

and if in Equation 17.8 the following substitutions are made:

$$D = \frac{V}{C \cdot A} \qquad (17.9)$$

$$E = \frac{1,000 \cdot k \cdot \dfrac{A_{perc}}{2}}{C \cdot A} \qquad (17.10)$$

we get:

$$D = \max[4.5 \cdot I_t \cdot t - 3.6 \cdot E \cdot t] \qquad (17.11)$$

In this expression, the parameter D represents the specific percolation volume, which is the storage volume expressed in cubic meters per hectare of connected impervious area. The parameter E represents the specific outflow from the basin expressed as liters per second and hectare of connected impervious area.

As a first step, an envelope curve of the specific inflow, V_{in}, has to be constructed. This is done by graphing the expression $(4.5 \cdot I_t \cdot t)$ for different values of t. The values of I_t are taken from the intensity–duration–frequency (I–D–F) curve used for the region or location. An example of this is illustrated in Figure 17.4.

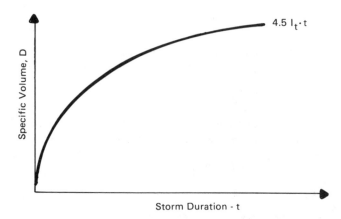

Storm Duration - t

Figure 17.4   Envelope curve of specific inflow V_{in} to a percolation facility.

Various specific outflow rates, V_{out}, can now be superimposed on the same diagram as straight lines. The specific storage volumes, D, for different specific outflow rates can be obtained graphically as the maximum vertical distance between the envelope curve and the outflow line (see Figure 17.5). The corresponding values of D are plotted against the values of E, as shown in Figure 17.6. Figure 17.6 shows a curve for a single recurrence design rainstorm

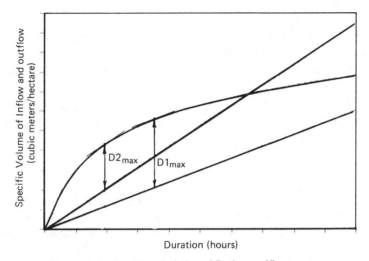

Figure 17.5   Graphic calculation of D, the specific storage.

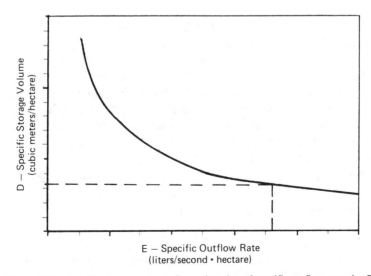

Figure 17.6   Specific storage volume D as a function of specific outflow capacity E.

frequency. If desired, this same process can now be repeated for other recurrence rainfall frequencies. The actual sizing of a percolation facility can now be performed using a simple trial-and-error procedure described next.

17.4.6 Step-by-Step Calculating Procedure

In practice, percolation facilities can be dimensioned using the following step-by-step procedure:

1. Construct a design curve similar to Figure 17.6, where the specific storage volume D is plotted as a function of the specific outlet capacity E.
2. Estimate the area of the impervious surfaces hydrologically connected to the percolation facility.
3. Calculate the specific outflow capacity E for the percolation facility in question. This is done using Equation 17.10, namely,

$$E = \frac{1,000 \cdot k \cdot \dfrac{A_{perc}}{2}}{C \cdot A}$$

In this expression, the value of A is the tributary area, C its runoff coefficient, and k the hydraulic conductivity of the soil are known. As we suggested earlier, k values measured in the field should be first multiplied by a factor of 0.3 to 0.5 as a safety factor. Thus, after the k value is determined, one has to estimate the total area of the sides of a percolation facility (A_{perc}) to calculate E. This area is expressed as

$$A_{perc} = 2 \cdot (a + b) \cdot h \qquad (17.12)$$

in which a = length, b = width, and h = height of the stone filled trench. The value of h must be chosen after considering local conditions and keeping in mind that the entire percolation facility must lie above the highest seasonal groundwater level. Since the outflow is expected to take place only through the sides, the design should strive to maximize the area of the sides and not the bottom. The practical consequence of this is that most efficient percolation facilities are relatively long and narrow.

As a practical matter, the width b and the height h are normally set between 3 and 7 feet (1.0 and 2.1 m).

4. When the value of the parameter E has been calculated, the specific storage volume D is found on the D vs. E curve (see Figure 17.6).
5. The necessary storage volume is calculated using:

$$V_{storage} = D \cdot (A \cdot C) \qquad (17.13)$$

6. If the effective porosity of the stone filling in the trench is n, the total volume of the basin will be:

$$V_{basin} = \frac{V_{storage}}{n}$$ (17.14)

7. The calculated total basin volume, V_{basin}, is then compared to the volume found using the assumed $(a \cdot b \cdot h)$ dimensions.
   If V_{basin} is less than $(a \cdot b \cdot h)$, the assumed basin was undersized and the calculations are repeated with larger values of a, b, or h. If V_{basin} is greater than $(a \cdot b \cdot h)$, then the assumed basin is oversized and the calculations can be repeated with smaller values for a, b, or h until a reasonable agreement is achieved between the assumed basin volume and the one calculated as required to do the job.

17.4.7 Checking Snow Melt Condition

All percolation facilities should be checked to be sure that they will not be overloaded by melting snow. During prolonged snow melt periods, the facility may operate near full depth. Because of the prolonged runoff period, the water depth can be assumed to be at full height of the trench or basin. Thus, the area of the percolation facility, namely the area of the sides of the trench or basin, under snow melt conditions may be calculated using:

$$A_{perc} = 2 \cdot (a + b) \cdot h$$ (17.15)

The designer must now check to see if the percolation facility sized to dispose of rainfall runoff can handle the runoff from melting snow. Unlike rainfall, runoff from melting snow is expected to occur from both the impervious and pervious surfaces. As a result, the following condition has to be satisfied:

$$(A_{perc} \cdot k \cdot I \cdot 1{,}000) > (S_{perv} \cdot A_{perv} + S_{imperv} \cdot A_{imperv})$$ (17.16)

in which S_{perv} = design snow melt runoff rate from the pervious surfaces, and S_{imperv} = design snow melt runoff rate from the impervious surfaces.

The preceding expression can also be written as:

$$[h \cdot 2 \cdot (a + b) \cdot k \cdot 1{,}000] > (S_{perv} \cdot A_{perv} + S_{imperv} \cdot A_{imperv})$$ (17.17)

When the snow melt rates from pervious and impervious surfaces are equal, the preceding equation becomes:

$$[h \cdot 2 \cdot (a + b) \cdot k \cdot 1{,}000] > S \cdot (A_{perv} + A_{imperv})$$ (17.18)

17.4.8 Auxiliary Outlet Pipe

Sometimes, even when all of the selection criteria are met, it may still not be practical to construct the required storage volume for a percolation facility. This can occur when the soils do not have sufficient hydraulic conductivity to empty the facility in a reasonable amount of time using only perco-lation. In some of these situations, it may be possible to install an auxiliary outlet pipe. This pipe collects the water from the percolation basin and re-leases it slowly through an orifice or a flow throttling valve. The following rule-of-thumb guidelines can be used to evaluate the need for an auxiliary pipe:

1. Whenever the soils have a hydraulic conductivity that is less than 2×10^{-5} meter per second (6.5×10^{-5} foot per second), the percolation rate is considered zero and the site declared unsuitable.

   If, however, a percolation facility is installed despite this recom-mendation, it should be designed assuming that the entire outflow will occur through the auxiliary outlet pipe. Normally, such an installation is unjustified, and we suggest that the designer investigate an alternative type of a detention facility, such as pipe packages, underground tanks, surface basins, etc.

2. When soils have hydraulic conductivity greater than 5×10^{-4} meter per second (1.5×10^{-3} foot per second), it is safe to assume that all emptying takes place through percolation into surrounding soils.

3. An auxiliary outlet pipe may be feasible in soils with hydraulic conduc-tivity between 2×10^{-5} and 5×10^{-4} meter per second. (6.5×10^{-5} and 1.5×10^{-3} foot per second). Such a pipe can provide a margin of safety and insure that the facility drains in a reasonable amount of time.

4. The auxiliary outlet pipe should always be equipped with a flow restric-tor. This restrictor is designed to provide a total outlet rate (i.e., perco-lation through soil and auxiliary outlet) equivalent to a basin having a percolation rate of 5×10^{-4} meter per second (1.5×10^{-3} foot per second).

If, however, the percolation basin is being provided primarily to improve stormwater runoff quality, the emptying pipe would not produce the desired results. With water quality, the goal is to trap and infiltrate into the ground as much of the runoff as possible. As a result, the auxiliary emptying pipe should be located near the top of the percolation pit and act as an uncontrolled emergency overflow. The water trapped below this pipe may eventually perco-late into the ground and receives filtering as it flows through the soils. Such a system for disposal of runoff to improve water quality should never be used when soil permeability k is less than 4×10^{-5} meter per second (1.5×10^{-3} foot per second), and should be seriously questioned whenever k is less than 10^{-4} meter per second (3.3×10^{-4} foot per second).

17.5 INFILTRATING ROADSIDE DITCHES AND SWALES

17.5.1 Introduction

Infiltrating roadside swales, sometimes referred to as borrow ditches, have been in use for a very long time. The use of roadside ditches is a common practice in the design of county or rural roads, and they are particularly suited to flat terrain. When they are located over permeable soils with their bottoms sufficiently above the top of the groundwater table, bedrock, or other impermeable strata, they often function as elongated infiltration basins. Along rural roads the ratio of impermeable to permeable surface is low and, as a result, ditches and swales have often been observed to operate without problems for extended periods of time.

Infiltrating ditches and swales can be designed as free-flowing ditches with a positive longitudinal slope, causing water movement along the swale. If site conditions permit, roadside ditches can be designed to be nonflowing, with all the surface runoff being disposed of through infiltration. Whenever the longitudinal slope is too steep or the effective surface area is too small to permit total surface infiltration, percolation trenches similar to the one in Figure 2.5b can be installed intermittently along the ditch.

According to Whalen and Callum (1988), when the soils underlying a free-flowing ditch or swale are porous and have a high infiltration rate, removal efficiencies for some of the pollutants commonly found in stormwater can exceed 80%. More typically, however, pollutant removal efficiency is probably lower than that. The uncertainty of infiltration stormwater and the removal of pollutants can be substantially reduced by designing infiltration ditches and swales with either a zero longitudinal grade or with berms across them that create a series of small, elongated infiltrating ponds (see Figure 17.7). As in other infiltration facilities, the seasonal high groundwater level and bedrock, or other impermeable soil layer, must be at least 4 feet (1.2 m) below the bottom of the infiltrating swale.

17.5.2 Sizing of Free-Flowing Ditches and Swales

The design of grass-lined ditches and swales to carry flow uses standard open-channel equations such as Manning's equation. Wanielista (1986) suggests that once the flow carrying capacity Q is established, the length of a ditch or swale needed to infiltrate the design flow rate can be found using Equation 17.19:

$$L = \frac{10{,}000 K_u (V/H)\,(Q^{5/8} \cdot S^{3/16})}{(n^{3/8} \cdot i)} \qquad (17.19)$$

in which L = length of infiltration swale in feet (m),
K_u = 1.0 U.S. standard unit (77.3 SI units),
V = vertical distance of side slope,
H = horizontal distance of side slopes, plus bottom width,
Q = average flow rate in cubic feet per second (m³/s),
S = longitudinal slope of swale or filter strip,
n = Manning's coefficient, and
i = saturated infiltration rate in inches per hour (cm/h) from Table 17.2 or measured at the site.

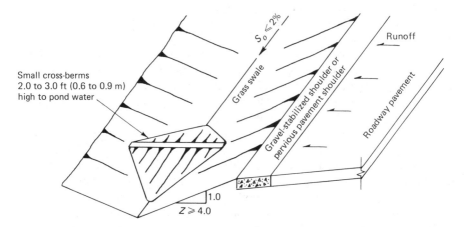

* Berms may be constructed from rocks 2 to 6 in. (5 to 15 cm) in size, using compacted erosion-resistant soils with a small drain through them, or low concrete or stacked timber sections.
* Space berms so that the top of the downstream berm is at the same elevation as the toe of the upstream berm.
* Whenever the longitudinal slope of the roadway is greater than 2%, limit the longitudinal slope of the adjacent swale S_o to 2% through the use of small, less than 2.0 ft (0.6 m), grade control check structures.

Figure 17.7   Infiltration swale with a cross-berm.

It is often not possible to provide a free-flowing ditch of sufficient length to infiltrate all the design flow. To facilitate infiltration the longitudinal grade should be set as flat as practicable, but never steeper than 0.02 foot per foot (m/m). Flatter longitudinal grades can be achieved in steeper terrain with the use of low [i.e., less than 2-foot (0.6-m)] check structures installed along the ditch. In addition, side slopes should be $4H : 1V$ or flatter ($6H : 1V$, $8H : 1V$, $10H : 1V$, etc.) to maximize the area in contact with the flowing water. Whenever the swale has a flat bottom (i.e., is trapezoidal in shape), add one-half of the bottom width to the value of H used in Equation 17.19 to account for the increase in horizontal distance in the channel's cross-section.
   Examination of Equation 17.19 reveals that as the longitudinal slope of the ditch approaches zero, the length L of the swale needed to infiltrate the

flow also appears to approach zero. This is not the case, however, since as the longitudinal slope approaches zero, the flow rate in a swale also approaches zero. Thus, the swale's flow capacity is always in balance with its infiltrating capacity as presented by Equation 17.19, provided that Manning's equation is used to calculate the flow capacity. Nevertheless, one must be cautious when using Equation 17.19, and a somewhat modified approach is suggested next for slow-moving swales.

17.5.3 Nonflowing and Slow-Moving Ditches and Swales

As for any other infiltration basin, it is recommended that the 2-year runoff volume be used when sizing nonflowing or very slow-moving infiltration ditches and swales. This runoff volume should then be disposed of by surface infiltration through the bottom and sides of the swale within a 36-hour period.

The length and width of nonflowing ditches can be determined using the simple mass balance procedure illustrated in Figure 17.3 and described in Section 17.3.2, Section 18.2 and Section 20.2.2. The designer simply adjusts the infiltrating surface area until the runoff from a 2-year storm is infiltrated into the ground within a 36-hour period. Because of the sloping sides of a ditch or a swale, the surface area available for infiltration will vary with time as the available volume is filled and emptied. The following steps are suggested for simplifying the design process of a nonflowing infiltration swale:

1. Assume that the effective bottom area available for infiltration is the area wetted by one-half of the runoff volume from a 2- to 6- hour 2-year storm.

2. Using the infiltration rate appropriate for the soils on which the swale is located, compute the average infiltration rate for the surface area found in step 1.

3. Using the design storm's depth–duration relationship and the infiltration rate found in step 2, use the mass balance procedure described in Sections 17.3.2, 18.2 and 20.2.2 to check if the swale will infiltrate the runoff from a design storm within 36 hours. If not, resize the swale and repeat steps 1 through 3.

4. If it is not possible to provide a swale large enough to infiltrate all the runoff water into the ground within 36 hours, provide a supplemental outflow structure to ensure that the swale will be emptied out within a 36-hour period using the combined outflow rate of infiltration and of the supplemental outlet.

For slow-moving swales and ditches, the sizing procedure is identical to that for nonflowing ditches, with one exeception. The rate at which the water leaves the swale through surface flow along the swale is added to the infiltration rate. Since ditch-full flow occurs only a small portion of the time, it is suggested that less than the full ditch flow rate be added to the infiltration rate. Again, a simplifying assumption is suggested—for this purpose use the flow rate that occurs when the ditch is one-third to one-half full.

17.6 DESIGN EXAMPLES

17.6.1 Evaluation of an Infiltration Site

An infiltration site is connected to a 100 square meters roof. The infiltration surface is a 210 square meter lawn with a slope of 10%. The topsoil and the underlaying soils are composed mostly of coarse silt. Check to see if the lawn is a good candidate for infiltration.

The site is first evaluated using the point system listed in Table 17.1. The results are as follows:

1. The ratio between the impervious surface and the infiltration surface areas is

$$A_{inf} = 2.1 \, A_{imp}$$

   This gives the site *20 points*.
2. The topsoil is coarse silt. This gives the site *5 points*.
3. The underlaying soil is coarse silt. This gives the site *5 points*.
4. The slope of the infiltration surface is 0.10 ft/ft. This gives the site *3 points*.
5. The infiltration surface is a new established lawn. This gives the site *0 points*.
6. It is expected the lawn will have normal foot traffic. This gives the site *3 points*.
7. The total is *36 points* for this site evaluation. According to the guidelines shown in Figure 17.2, the site can be used for infiltration. Surface runoff from this site is not likely to occur, except during larger than usual storms.

17.6.2 Sizing of a Percolation Facility

In this example, runoff from a roof with an area of 800 square meters (assume the runoff coefficient C = 1.0) and a lawn of another 800 square meters is led to a percolation facility. Find the length of the percolation trench using the following design parameters and other constraints:

Tributary area:

$$A_{imp} = 800 \text{ m}^2 \qquad\qquad A_{perv} = 800 \text{ m}^2$$

Percolation facility:
Maximum height of stone filled trench = 0.8 m.
Maximum width of stone filled trench = 1.0 m.
Porosity of stone filling: $n = 0.4$
Minimum depth to seasonal groundwater = 2 m.
Hydraulic conductivity of soil: $k = 4 \times 10^{-5}$ m/s.

Design rainfall:
Two-year storm.

The calculation procedure is as follows:

1. Construct a design curve as shown in Figure 17.8 using the I–D–F curve for the two-year storm.
2. The native soils have a hydraulic conductivity of 4×10^{-5} m/s. To compensate for the uncertainties of the soils investigation, a safety factor is applied to this value. This assures that the percolation rate is not overstated and the facility is not underdesigned. Thus, the design hydraulic conductivity used in this example is $0.5 \times 4 \times 10^{-5} = 2 \times 10^{-5}$ meter per second.

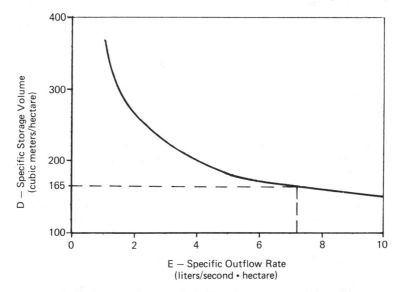

Figure 17.8   Design curve for example facility using a two-year design storm I–D–F.

3. For the first trial, assume the length of the percolation trench is 35 meters. The value for E is calculated using Equation 17.10:

$$E = \left[2 \cdot \left(35 + 1.0\right) \cdot \frac{0.8}{2.0} \right] \cdot 2 \times 10^{-5} \cdot \frac{1,000}{0.08}$$

$$= 7.2 \text{ liters per second hectare}$$

4. Using Figure 17.8, we see that when $E = 7.2$, $D = 165$ cubic meters per hectare.

5. Since the impervious area tributary to the percolation trench is 0.08 hectares, the needed storage volume is found using Equation 17.11:

$$V_{storage} = 0.08 \cdot 165 = 13.2 \text{ cubic meters}$$

6. Given that the effective porosity of the stone fill media is 0.4, the total trench or basin volume is found using Equation 17.14:

$$V_{basin} = \frac{13.2}{0.4} = 33 \ m^3$$

7. The assumed total trench volume in step 3 was $V_{basin\text{-}assumed} = (35 \cdot 1.0 \cdot 0.8) = 28$ cubic meters, which is less than the calculated volume of 33 cubic meters.

We see that the assumed length of the trench does not provide sufficient basin volume. Therefore, the calculations are repeated starting with step 3 assuming a trench length of 40 meters. This time we get:
Calculated:

$$V_{basin} = 30 \text{ cubic meters}$$

vs.
Assumed:

$$V_{basin} = 32 \text{ cubic meters}$$

The second assumption resulted in slightly more volume than needed. However, this oversizing is relatively small, and the 40-meter-long trench is chosen for final design.

As a final step, the design is tested to see if it is adequate under snow melt conditions. Using the design snow melt rates recommended in Section 17.2.2, check to see if the limitations set forth by Equation 17.16 are satisfied, namely:

$$A_{perc} \cdot k \cdot 1 \cdot 1,000 = 2 \cdot 0.8 \cdot (40 + 1.0) \cdot 2 \times 10^{-5} \cdot 1,000 = 1.312$$

$$S_{perv} \cdot A_{perv} + S_{imperv} \cdot A_{imperv} = 1.4 \cdot 0.08 + 2.8 \cdot 0.08 = 0.336$$

Since $1.312 > 0.336$, the snow melt condition does not govern, and the original design is considered acceptable for final design.

REFERENCES

SJOBERG, A., AND MARTENSSON, N. "Analysis of the Envelope Method for Dimensioning Percolation Facilities," Chalmers University of Technology, 1982. (In Swedish)

SWEDISH WATER AND SEWAGE WORKS ASSOCIATION, *Local Disposal of Storm Water*, Publication VAV P46, 1983. (In Swedish)

WANIELISTA, M. P., "Best Management Practices Overview," *Urban Runoff Quality—Impact and Quality Enhancement Technology*, American Society of Civil Engineers New York, 1986.

WHALEN, P. J., and CALLUM, M. G., *An Assessment of Urban Land Use/Stormwater Relationships and Treatment Efficiencies of Selected Stormwater Management Systems*, South Florida Water Management District, Technical Publication 88-0, 1988.

18

Calculation Methods for Detention Facilities

18.1 GENERAL

As the name implies, a detention facility temporarily detains stormwater runoff. They are used primarily to reduce the peak rate of flow in the downstream conveyance system so that its capacity is not exceeded. Sometimes, and more particularly now than in the past, detention is used to remove sediments in the runoff and, as a result, improve water quality. Typically, detention facilities are designed to have sufficient volume to control the peak rate of flow during a given design storm.

Detention storage volume is estimated by calculating the differences between the inflow and outflow hydrographs as illustrated in Figure 18.1. The basic equation for these calculations is

$$V = \int_o^{t_o} (Q_{in} - Q_{out}) \, dt \qquad (18.1)$$

in which V = required stage volume,

t = time from beginning of storage,

t_o = time when the outflow hydrograph intersects the recession limb of the inflow hydrograph,

Q_{in} = inflow rate, and

Q_{out} = outflow rate.

The design inflow into a detention facility is usually defined by the design storm which is used to calculate an inflow hydrograph. If however, the

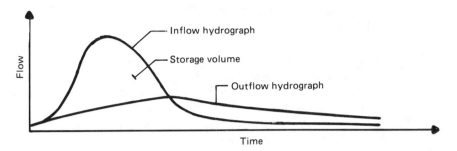

Figure 18.1 Determination of storage volume.

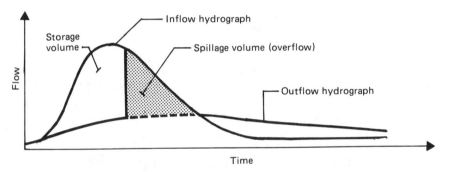

Figure 18.2 Hydrographs when the storage capacity is exceeded.

storage basin experiences a hydrograph that is larger than it was designed to store, the excess water spills over the embankment or a spillway. The idealized shapes of the inflow and the outflow hydrographs under such a scenario are illustrated in Figure 18.2.

The volume of a detention storage basin can be calculated in many different ways. The following are some of the categories of methods that are used to calculate detention storage volumes:

- calculations without considering time of concentration,
- calculations considering time of concentration,
- time–area method,
- rain point diagram method,
- summation curve method, and
- detailed flow routing methods.

18.2 CALCULATIONS WITHOUT CONSIDERING TIME OF CONCENTRATION

The first step in this procedure is to calculate the cumulative runoff volume for a range of storm durations. This is done using Equation 18.2. The storm duration is increased incrementally, and the volume for each duration is calculated, as shown in Figure 18.3. This results in the transformation of an I–D–F curve into a volume–duration curve, i.e., a runoff envelope diagram similar in shape to the one in Figure 18.4.

$$V_{in} = C \cdot I \cdot A \cdot t \tag{18.2}$$

in which V_{in} = cumulative runoff volume in cubic feet (m³),
  C = runoff coefficient,
  I = storm's intensity taken from the I–D–F curve at time t in inches per hour (l/s/ha)
  A = tributary area in acres (ha²), and
  t = duration in seconds.

If it is assumed that the detention basin empties at a constant rate, the cumulative volume leaving the basin can be estimated using Equation 18.3:

$$V_{out} = k_o \cdot Q_{out} \cdot t \tag{18.3}$$

in which V_{out} = cumulative volume of outflow in cubic feet (m³),
  Q_{out} = maximum outflow rate in cubic feet per second (m³/s),
  k_o = outflow adjustment factor from Figure 18.4, and
  t = duration in seconds.

The required detention volume is then found by taking the difference between Equations 18.2 and 18.3 until the maximum difference is found.

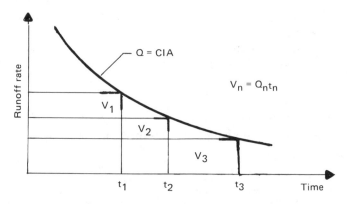

Figure 18.3 Calculating runoff volumes V for various rain durations t.

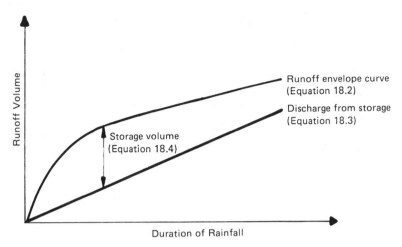

Figure 18.4   Finding the storage volume using the runoff envelope diagram.

Equation 18.4 describes this process of finding the desired storage volume V, which is illustrated graphically in Figure 18.4.

$$V = \max(V_{in} - V_{out}) \qquad (18.4)$$

As stated earlier, this procedure assumes a constant outflow rate Q_{out} which normally is taken to be the rate of outflow when the detention basin is full and the outlet is under maximum head. Obviously, with the exception of the special flow regulators discussed in Chapters 12 and 13, this is not true for all depths of water storage. For most conventional outlets the outflow rate varies with the depth of water as the basin fills and empties. This apparent shortcoming in Equation 18.3 is compensated for by an outflow adjustment factor k_o.

A study comparing the calculated storage volumes found using detailed single-event hydrograph procedures and those found using Equations 18.3 through 18.5 was conducted by Urbonas and Guo in 1990. The findings led to the development of Figure 18.5 (Guo, 1991), relating the outlet adjustment factor (k_o) to the ratio of the peak inflow rate ($Q_{peak-in}$) and the design peakoutflow rate (Q_{out}). The peak design outflow rate Q_{out} used with Figure 18.5 is the outflow rate when the detention basin is full. The peak inflow rate $Q_{peak-in}$ is found using the values of C and A for the tributary watershed and of the rainfall intensity I at the watershed's time of concentration in the Rational Formula.

This calculating procedure can be easily automated using a personal computer and any commercially available spreadsheet. The use of a graphical procedure then becomes secondary and is relegated to the role of display only. The results of using such a spreadsheet can be found in Table 20.3.

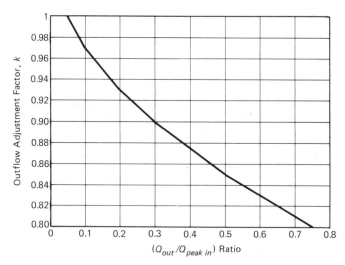

Figure 18.5 Outflow adjustment factor vs. (design outflow rate)/(peak inflow rate). (After Guo, 1991.)

The preceding example was for a single recurrence frequency storm. If one wants to calculate volumes for other frequencies, the calculations have to be repeated and a runoff envelope diagram constructed for each design frequency.

According to the DRCOG (1961), this procedure tends to overestimate the runoff and storage volume for larger urban watersheds. They recommend that the Rational Method and all procedures related to it be limited to watersheds having an area that is less than 160 acres (65 ha).

18.3 CALCULATIONS CONSIDERING TIME OF CONCENTRATION

The aforementioned method calculates the storage volume without considering the time of concentration of the watershed. Now we describe a technique that uses the Rational Method and considers the time of concentration. This technique and its many variations were described by Lautrich (1956), Annen and Londong (1960), Malpricht (1962), Pecher (1970), Kao (1975), and APWA (1974, 1981).

The required storage volume is determined by finding the maximum difference between the areas under the trapezoidal inflow hydrographs and the desired basin release discharge rate K. This procedure is illustrated graphically in Figure 18.6. When the storm duration is equal to the time of concentration T_1, the storage volume is V_1 and is based on a triangular hydrograph that is symmetrical around T_1. When the duration is less than T_1, the volume is

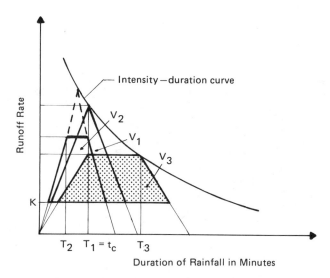

Figure 18.6   Storage volume calculation using Rational Method considering the time of concentration.

V_2 and is constructed by truncating the top of the triangle at a level where the recession limb intersects the time of concentration T_1. When the duration is greater than T_1, the volume is found under the trapezoid V_3. This trapezoid is constructed by drawing a horizontal line back from the value on I–D–F curve found at duration T_3 to T_1. The rising limb of the V_3 hydrograph is then a straight line connecting $T = O$ and the top of the trapezoid, and the falling limb is merely a mirror image of the rising limb.

A complete, step-by-step example of how the required volume is found, using metric units, is illustrated in Figure 18.7.

18.4 TIME–AREA METHOD

The time–area method was developed when computers were not as readily available as they are today. It is a method that has been incorporated into some of the common computer models such as British Road Research Model (BRRL) and Illinois Urban Drainage Area Simulator (ILLUDAS). It was developed to generate a more realistic runoff hydrograph than what is possible using the two Rational Formula procedures just described. In light of the available software on the market, it is not practical to use manually the time–area method. The method is described here because it is incorporated into some of the computer models on the market and also provides an example of one technique that can be used to construct a runoff hydrograph.

The time–area method received its name from the fact that the tributary watershed is subdivided into areas having similar flow times to the outlet.

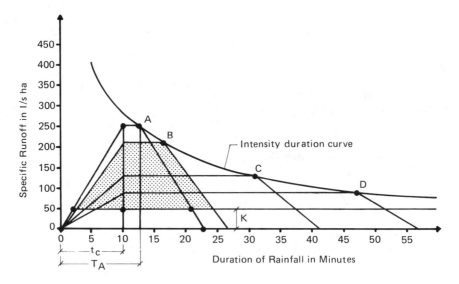

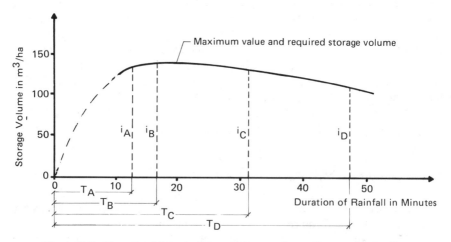

Figure 18.7 Example of the calculation of storage volume when considering time of concentration. (After Koral and Saatci, 1976.)

Using these subareas, a time–area curve is constructed using the following simplifying assumptions:

- each subarea remains constant throughout a storm;
- the time–area curve for each subarea is linear;
- the time of concentration is independent of the rainfall intensity; and

• the surface and pipe flow velocity remains constant throughout the storm.

The procedure for constructing a time–area curve for a large irregular watershed is illustrated in Figure 18.8. The drainage area is first divided into a number of subwatersheds. For each subwatersheds, a time–area curve is plotted with its starting point lagged by the time it takes water to flow from the bottom of the subbasin to the bottom of the watershed. All of the subbasin

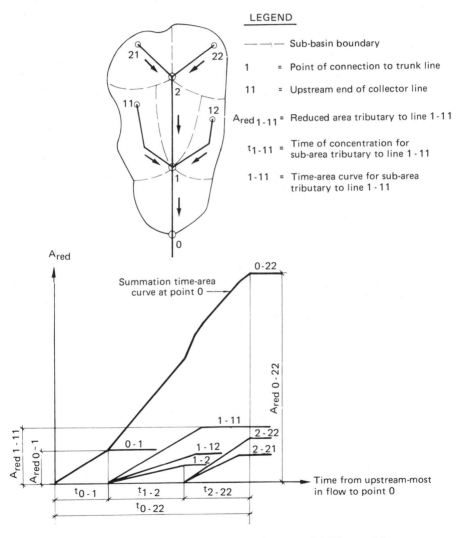

Figure 18.8 Constructing a time–area curve. (After Swedish Water and Sewage Works Association, 1976.)

time–area curves are then added to obtain the cumulative time–area curve for the entire watershed.

The flow rate at the bottom of the watershed for any storm duration can be found by multiplying the tributary area and the rainfall intensity at that duration by the runoff coefficient. You may have noticed that this technique sounds similar to the Rational Formula. In fact it is, since it uses block rainfall.

The design rain is assumed to begin at time zero of the time–area curve and has a duration equal to the time of concentration for the watershed. Obviously, after the rain stops, the effective tributary area of the watershed begins to shrink as the surface water is drained off. This method assumes that the runoff velocity after the rain stops remains the same as when the rain is falling. Thus, the time–area curve for the diminishing tributary area phase of the storm is the same as for the increasing tributary area phase of the storm. A runoff hydrograph for any block storm with a duration greater than the time of concentration can be found using the procedure illustrated in Figure 18.9:

1. Plot a parallel time–area curve that is shifted to the right a distance equal to the storm duration.
2. Subtract the ordinates of the shifted time–area curve (i.e., decreasing area phase) from the ordinates of the increasing time–area phase curve.

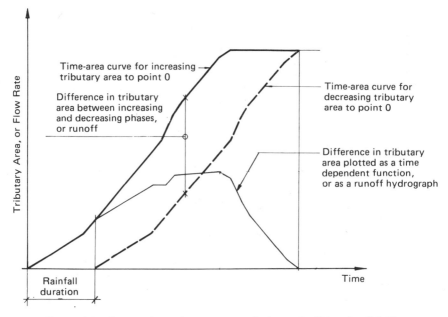

Figure 18.9 Constructing a time–area curve hydrograph. (After Swedish Water and Sewage Works Association, 1976.)

3. Multiply the difference in ordinates at each duration by the average rain intensity of the block design storm duration.

4. Multiply the values obtained in step 3 by the runoff coefficient for the watershed.

When the time–area method is used to size a detention facility, it is necessary to develop several runoff hydrographs for different storm durations. All of them are then analyzed to determine which will give the greatest storage volume. See Figure 18.10 for a graphic illustration of this process. The volume of storage is determined by measuring (i.e., numerically integrating) the area between the inflow hydrograph and the design release rate. However, note that the height scale in Figure 18.10, when converted to a flow hydrograph, will vary for each storm duration when it is multiplied by the block rainfall intensity. Figure 18.10 is, in fact, a representation of composite time–area curves for various storm durations before they are multiplied by rainfall intensity and the runoff coefficient.

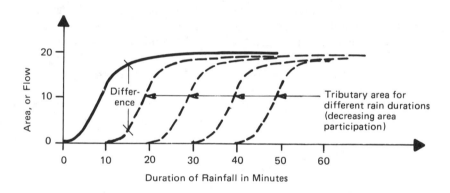

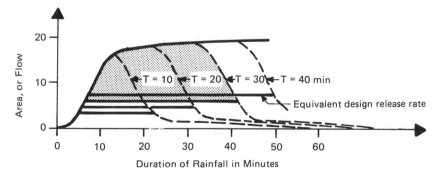

Figure 18.10 Constructing a time–area hydrograph for various storm durations. (After Swedish Association for Water and Sewer Works, 1976.)

18.5 RAIN POINT DIAGRAM METHOD

The methods described so far were based on the intensity–duration–frequency rainfall data. Although the intensity–duration data were originally intended for the calculation of peak runoff rates using Rational Formula, it is now commonly used to calculate storage volumes. This shift in the use of Rational Formula has been questioned by many and, as a result, the design of detention facilities using it has not always been accepted as accurate.

A method for estimating runoff volumes based on other types of rainfall data was suggested by van den Herik (1976). Van den Herik chose to base the calculations solely on the amount of total rainfall depth and the duration of recorded rainstorms. The method described next includes modifications suggested by Pecher (1978, 1980) which tailor it for the sizing of detention facilities.

18.5.1 Rain Point Diagram

This procedure requires the preparation of a rain point diagram by plotting total rainfall volume, the dependent variable, against the rainstorm duration, the independent variable for each recorded rainstorm (see Figure 18.11). To do this, it is first necessary to differentiate between individual rainstorm events in the data base.

Originally, van den Herik (1976) and Pecher (1978, 1980) suggested that individual storms be defined as separate events when the end of one storm is separated from the beginning of the next by at least one hour. Subsequent to this, Urbonas and Stahre, based on their own experience, developed modifica-

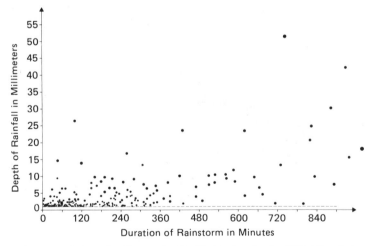

Figure 18.11   Rain point diagram for Stockholm, Sweden for 1978–79 period and 60 minutes between storms.

tions to these recommendations which will be discussed later in this chapter. Note that the rain point method ignores the temporal distribution of the rainfall intensity within a storm.

18.5.2 Estimating Rainfall Abstraction

When using the rain point diagram method for estimating storage volumes, it is also necessary to estimate rainfall abstractions that are likely to occur during all storms. In its simplest form, this can be done considering only the following:

- Runoff from unpaved surfaces can be assumed to be virtually zero. This assumption is reasonable for most rainstorms. It may not be accurate for storms that have large rainfall volumes or very high intensities.
- Initial losses are due to the wetting of pavement and entrapment in depression storage. These can range, according to Pecher (1969), from 0.02 inch (0.5 mm) for steep areas to 0.06 inch (1.5 mm) for flat areas. Viessman et al. (1977) reported depression storage on pavement to range from 0.02 inch (0.5 mm) for very steep areas to 0.135 inch (3.5 mm) for very flat areas.
- Evaporation losses. These can vary significantly between regions due to climatic conditions. For Holland, Pecher (1969) estimated evaporation losses from impervious surfaces at 0.01 to 0.02 inch per hour (1.0 to 1.6 l/ha-s) Similar rates can be expected for many of the northeast coastal regions of the United States. Higher rates can be expected in southern regions and in the semi-arid regions of the western and southwestern United States.

18.5.3 Developing Abstractions and Discharge Envelope

Combining all of the rainfall abstractions and the storage facility discharge rates results in a diagram as shown in Figure 18.12. This diagram contains envelopes of volumes that should not require storage. Thus, by superimposing this diagram on top of the rain point diagram, it is possible to determine the numbers of rainstorms that will be stored in a storage basin of a known volume. All the points above the storage envelope represent storms that will exceed the facility's capacity and cause it to be overtopped.

18.5.4 Determining Storage Volume

As noted, the adequacy of any storage volume can be evaluated by superimposing the rainfall–abstractions–discharge envelope diagram onto the rain point diagram. The process of sizing the required storage volume can be

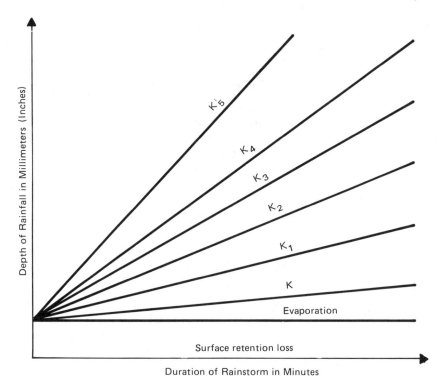

Figure 18.12 Rainfall abstractions and discharge envelope. (After Pecher, 1978.)

expedited by plotting the rainfall–abstractions–discharge envelope on a transparent overlay. This can be laid over the rain point diagram so that it can be parallel-shifted and various storage and/or release scenarios can be tested.

Shifting the overlay to the left a distance equal to the watershed's time of concentration (i.e., t_c) accounts for the watershed's time of concentration. Next, the overlay is parallel-shifted upward a distance corresponding to the storage volume of the detention facility (i.e., V) plus the surface retention loss.

An example of this procedure is illustrated in Figure 18.13. Using this procedure, various combinations of storage V and storage release discharge rates K can be quickly evaluated. All the points above the selected K line represent the storms that exceed the storage volume and result in an overflow condition. This analysis provides an indication of how runoff obtained using a long-term record of rainstorms interacts with the proposed design. Estimates of how frequently a given detention facility can be expected to be overloaded provides the designer information on how well local criteria or project goals are going to be met.

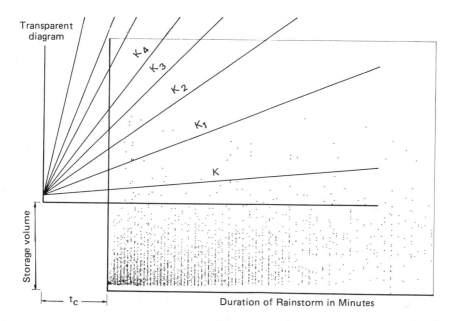

Figure 18.13 Example of volume determination using rain point diagram. (After Pecher, 1978.)

18.5.5 Summary and Suggested Update of Method

The foregoing method appears to have many advantages over traditional, Rational Formula-based methods for sizing of storage volumes. The main advantage is that actual rainfall data is used in the region instead of intensity–duration information, the latter being only a representation of rainfall and not actual storms as they may have occurred. However, the rain point diagram method has certain deficiencies and limitations as well.

For the rain point diagram to have a degree of reliability, it needs a continuous rainfall record of at least 15 to 20 years. This period is probably adequate only when designing storage for smaller than 10-year runoff events. Design for control of a 100-year runoff event will require in excess of 100 years of continuous data, while a 10-year event may be adequately estimated using 20 or more years of data. As a result, this method should be most reliable for the design of detention facilities for the control of frequently occurring rainstorms. These smaller storm events are of prime interest in the design of water quality treatment facilities.

The other major shortfall of this method is the arbitrary nature of separating rainfall data into discrete storm events. It does not take into account the effect of several successive rainstorms. As a result, the tendency will be to underestimate the storage volume for detention basins with low release rates, since the volume is not likely to be emptied between successive events. To compensate for this potential problem, the authors recommend the following when separating storms for the rain point diagram:

1. Determine the desired release rate K_i from the storage prior to the rainfall data analysis.
2. Using the desired release rate, determine the time it will take for a full basin to be completely drained (T_D).
3. Determine the time of concentration for the watershed (T_c).
4. Separate storms using no less than 1-hour, $\frac{1}{2} T_D$, or T_c, whichever is the largest, as the separation interval between individual storms.

The preceding accounts for the rate of runoff from the watershed in relation to rate the water is released from the storage pond. For most small urban watersheds, the time of concentration is very small (i.e., approximately 10 minutes) and will not govern the storm separation period.

This procedure is only a partial remedy and a simplification for a very complex stochastic process. It should not be viewed as rectifying all shortcomings; however, it should reduce the probability of an undersized detention facility. The rain point diagram method with the preceding modification should result in reasonable storage volume estimates without performing continuous simulation modeling. This method will be used in Section 23.5 to describe a procedure for optimizing and sizing water quality capture volumes for treating urban stormwater.

18.6 CUMULATIVE CURVE METHOD

18.6.1 Introduction

In some situations, the designer's goal is to equalize the daily variations in dry weather flow in a sewer system. These may occur because of the natural variations in dry weather flow or may be caused by short-term wastewater loads from an industry. Flow equalization volume in such cases is determined using the cumulative mass curve method. Cumulative mass curves are based on inflow measurements.

When developing cumulative mass curves, be aware that flow can vary within a given day, from day to day, from week to week, from month to month, and even over much longer periods of time. As a result, the designer has to decide over what period of time flow equalization has to be provided. This decision is typically based on flow observations over an extended period of time. As a minimum, one year's data has to be available before a reasonable flow equalization volume can be estimated. Even then, it is advisable to provide a safety factor in the final design.

An example of daily inflow variations is illustrated in Figure 18.14. In addition to flow, this figure also shows the measured variations in biochemical oxygen demand (BOD). We describe the steps needed to estimate an appropriate flow equalization volume necessary to balance the flows over a one-day period.

18.6.2 Construction of a Cumulative Curve

The inflow hydrograph for the desired equalization period is transformed into a cumulative curve by

1. subdividing the entire flow equalization time period into uniform time increments, such as one-hour increments;
2. calculating the volume of inflow for each time step; and
3. accumulating all the incremental volumes over time.

The resultant cumulative volume table is then plotted against time, resulting in a cumulative mass curve similar to the one illustrated in Figure 18.15. This curve is based on the flow data shown in Figure 18.14.

The slope of the straight line connecting the beginning and end points of the cumulative mass curve represents the average flow rate over the period. The portions of the curve with a greater slope than the connecting line represent periods when the flow rate is greater than average. Similarly, portions of the curve with lesser slope than the connecting line represent periods of less than average inflow rate.

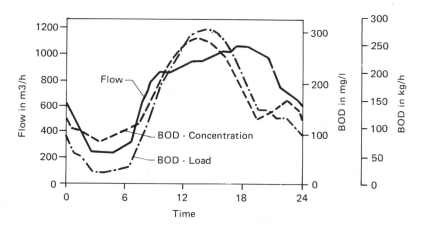

Figure 18.14 Example of daily flow variation at a wastewater treatment plant. (After EPA, 1974.)

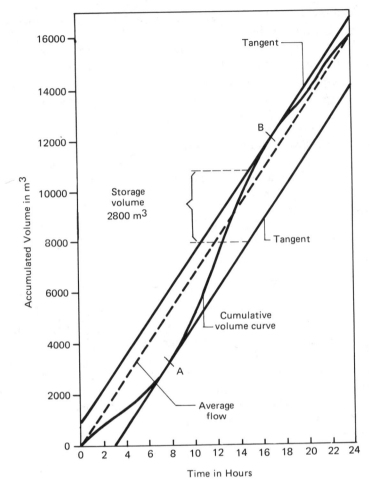

Figure 18.15 Storage volume determination using cumulative curve. (After EPA, 1974.)

18.6.3 Determination of Storage Volume

The flow equalization volume is found using the cumulative mass curve as follows:

1. Draw tangents to the curve parallel to the line representing the average flow (see Figure 18.15).
2. At the lower point of tangency A, the average flow rate begins to be exceeded and storage begins to fill.
3. The inflow is greater than the outflow until the upper point of tangency is reached at B.

4. The vertical distance between the two tangent lines is the required minimum design storage volume.

5. In practice, the design volume is set somewhat larger than determined in step 4 to provide a safety margin against unforeseen flow variations.

18.7 DETAILED CALCULATION METHODS

Detailed calculation methods encompass a family of computer rainfall runoff simulation models that have become readily available to any engineer in recent years. These models can simulate runoff, with or without water quality, on the basis of watershed characteristics, conveyance system characteristics, and recorded rainfall. If recorded rainfall is not readily available, the models can also be used with design storms. Although these models perform a large number of hydraulics calculations each second, their reliability and accuracy depends entirely on calibration against recorded simultaneous rainfall and runoff data.

There is a large number of models on the market, most of which will run on a personal computer. Any of them can be used to design and or analyze stormwater detention. However, we limit our discussion to the following three:

- Illinois Urban Drainage Area Simulator (ILLUDAS),
- EPA Storm Water Management Model (SWMM), and
- Urban Drainage Storm Water Model Version 2 (UDSWM2-PC).

These models were selected for description because all three are in public domain, are well-documented, and are supported by governmental agencies. Also, all three are very inexpensive to acquire.

These models are designed to simulate the entire runoff process, on the surface and inside storm sewers. Stormwater detention simulation routines are only a small part of each of the computer models. The performance of the three is described in greater detail in Chapter 19.

The main advantage of the detailed calculation methods is that the design no longer has to be based on block rainfall or the I–D–F curves. Any conceivable rainstorm distribution can be used, or the runoff from an entire chronologic series of recorded rainstorms can be studied. Pecher (1980), after studying several locations in Germany, reported significant differences in detention sizing results when using continuous simulation instead of I–D–F-based block rain design storms.

The results of the studies by Pecher in Germany show that

- traditional design methods underestimate storage volumes for facilities with small specific outlet capacities; and

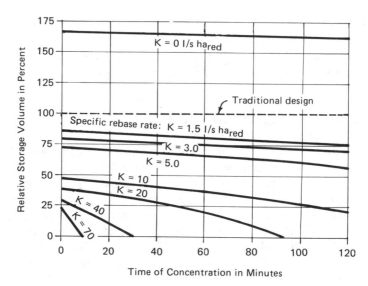

Figure 18.16 Comparison of storage volume calculated using continuous simulation and "traditional" methods. (After Pecher, 1980.)

- these same methods overestimate the storage volume for facilities with large specific outlet capacities.

Underestimates in detention volumes for facilities with low release rates K are attributed to successive storms arriving before the storage basin is completely drained. On the other hand, the overestimating of volume for facilities that empty rapidly is attributed to the fact that design storms rarely represent storms that actually occur in nature. They are biased toward overestimating average intensities because of the fact that they are a composite of the most severe portions of many storms. It was also observed that the overestimating of storage volumes increased with increasing tributary area and specific release rate from the storage basin.

Some of Pecher's (1980) findings are presented in graphical form in Figure 18.16. In this figure, the storage volume obtained using traditional methods based on the Rational Formula was set equal to 100%. As can be seen, the variation in storage volume was found to be very significant. This is a compelling argument for similar investigations in the United States. Although it may be premature to draw general conclusions, Pecher's studies indicate that we may be in fact building thousands of detention basins that may either be wasteful or inadequate in size.

REFERENCES

ANNEN, G., AND LONDONG, D., "Comparative Contributions to Dimension-Determining Procedures for Detention Basins," Technisch-Wissenchaftlicht Mitteilungen der Emschergenossenschaft und des Lippeverbandes, No. 3, 1960. (In German)

APWA, *Practices in Detention in Urban Stormwater Runoff,* Special Report No. 43, American Public Works Association, Chicago, Ill., 1974.

APWA, *Urban Stormwater Management,* Special Report No. 49, American Public Works Association, Chicago, Ill., 1981.

DRCOG, *Urban Storm Drainage Criteria Manual,* Denver Regional Council of Governments (Currently being published by the Urban Drainage and Flood Control District), Denver, Colo., 1961.

EPA, *Flow Equalization,* Technology Transfer Seminar Proceedings, May, 1974.

FAA, *Airport Drainage,* Federal Aviation Agency, Washington, D.C., 1961, revised 1966.

GUO, C. Y. *User's Manual for HYDRO POND,* A Personal Computer Software Program for Reservoir Routing and Outlet Structure Design, University of Colorado at Denver, 1991.

HERIK, A. G. VON DEN, "Water Pollution by Storm Overflow From Mixed Sewer Systems," Berichte der ATV, No. 28, Bonn, 1976. (In German)

KAO, T. Y., "Hydraulic Design of Stormwater Detention Basin," Mini Course No. 3, National Symposium on Urban Hydrology and Sediment Control, University of Kentucky, July, 1973.

KELLY, H. "Designing Detention Basins for Small Land Developments," *Water and Sewer Works,* October, 1977.

KOOT, A. C. J., "Storage and Runoff Capacity of Mixed Water Sewers and Their Effects on Drainage and Clarification Plants," *Netherlands Calculation Methods,* Berichte der ATV, No. 23, Bonn, 1969. (In German)

KORAL, J., AND SAATCI, A.C., *Rain Overflow and Rain Detention Basins,* 2nd edition, Zurich, 1976. (In German)

KROPF, A., AND GEISER, A., "Detention Basins and Storm Water Clarification Installations," Schweizerische Bauzeitung No. 18, 1957. (In German)

LAUTRICH, R., "Graphic Determination of Storage Volume for Flood Containers, Seepage and Rain Equalization Basins and the Limiting Values of the Retardation," Wasser und Boden No. 8, 1956. (In German)

MACINNES, C., MIDDLETON, A., AND ADAMOWSKI, K., "Stochastic Design of Flow Equalization Basins," *Journal of the Environmental Division,* ASCE, December, 1978.

MALPRICHT, E., "Planning and Construction of Storm Water Detention Basins," Berichte der ATV, No. 15, Landesgruppentagungen, 1962. (In Swedish)

METCALF & EDDY, INC., *Wastewater Engineering, Treatment, Disposal, Reuse,* 2nd edition, McGraw-Hill, 1979.

ORDON C., "Volume of Storm Water Retention Basins," *Journal of the Environmental Division,* ASCE, October, 1974.

OUANO, E. A., "Developing a Methodology for Design of Equalization Basins," *Water and Sewer Works,* November, 1977.

PECHER, R., "The Runoff Coefficient and its Dependence on Rain Duration," Berichte aus dem Institut fur Wasserwirtschaft und Gesundheitsingenieurwesen, No. 2, TU Munich, 1969. (In German)

PECHER, R., "Design of Storm Water Retention Basins," NORDFORSK Report, Seminar on Detention Basin, Marsta 7–8 November, 1978. (In Swedish)

PECHER, R., "Dimensions of Storm Water Detention Basins According to Modern Rain Evaluation," Koncept 1979. (In German)

PECHER, R., "Extensive Storm Evaluation for Designing Storm Water Detention Basins," Abwassertechnik No. 1, 1980. (In German)

STAHRE, P., "Superficial Calculations of Storage Volumes," Royal Institute of Technology, Stockholm, Sweden, 1979. (In Swedish)

SWEDISH WATER AND SEWER WORKS ASSOCIATION, *Calculation of Detention Basins,* Publication P31, 1976. (In Swedish)

SWEDISH WATER AND SEWER WORKS ASSOCIATION, *Calculation of Sewer Networks,* Publication P28, 1976. (In Swedish)

VIESSMAN, W., JR., KNAPP, J., AND LEWIS, G. L., *Introduction to Hydrology,* 2nd edition, Harper & Row, p. 69, 1977.

YRJANAINEN, G., AND WARREN, A., "A Simple Method of Retention Basin Design," *Water and Sewer Works,* December, 1973.

19

Overview of Several Computer Models

19.1 GENERAL

Since the advent of the personal computer (i.e., PC), there has been an explosion of computer model use in water resources engineering. Today, there is a wide variety of stormwater system design models, most of them at very inexpensive prices. Because of this variety in available models, we limit our discussion to three models which we have personally used.

All three models are in public domain and are associated with a government agency. Unlike most of the software offered by private vendors, the source code for these three models can be obtained from each of the sponsoring agencies, examined, and modified by the user. We do not discourage the use of proprietary models, since many of them are excellent. We are not in the position however, to explain how proprietary models perform their calculations, or if they in fact have been adequately tested under a wide range of design conditions.

Computer models provide the ability to mathematically describe the performance of the entire stormwater system in much greater detail than was possible using hand calculations. This should not be misinterpreted that answers obtained using computer models are more accurate. In fact, it is too easy to have the model do the work without questioning the validity of the results. Computer models are only as good as the user and his or her experience. They cannot think for the user.

We suggest that you become totally familiar with the models you wish to use. Once you start using any model, always inspect its output very carefully to insure that the model, in fact, is giving representative results. As a rule, always calibrate your model either against field data or, lacking data, against a regionally accepted calculation technique. At least in the latter case, the results will be consistent for the location in which you are working.

The fact that computer models are now common should not exclude from your consideration other methods of calculation. Very often, it is sufficient to use simple hand calculations to estimate flows or to size a detention facility. This is particularly true for small urban watersheds. Unless sufficient rainfall and runoff data are available, single detention facilities can often be sized accurately using simple hand calculations. Remember, design storms do not give you an exact representation of what happens in nature, and processing them through a sophisticated model will not improve the accuracy of the results. Models do, however, give you an edge in comparing the effects of system performance as various proposed system components are tested for relative performance.

19.2 ILLUDAS

ILLUDAS stands for Illinois Urban Drainage Area Simulator. It has an option for the sizing of storm sewers given the basin runoff characteristics, design rainstorm, and the layout of the sewer network. If the sewer sizes are already known, such as in an existing system, the program will calculate the flows within the entire sewer network.

The model was first developed during the 1960s at the Road Research Laboratory in England and was referred to as the RRL method. It was further developed and enhanced by the Illinois State Water Survey and, since it was in public domain, it was made available to anyone by the state of Illinois upon request. In recent years, this model was converted to a PC version by two individuals working for the Illinois Water Survey and is being distributed as a proprietary model outside of Illinois.

ILLUDAS includes routines for estimating detention storage volumes. One of these routines is a simplification of the flood routing process occurring at a stormwater detention facility. This simplified routing option in ILLUDAS should only be considered for preliminary presizing of volumes before serious and more detailed studies are initiated. We refer to this preliminary routing procedure whenever ILLUDAS is discussed. For more information on the model and its capabilities, contact the Illinois State Water Survey.

19.2.1 Calculation Principles

ILLUDAS calculates flows within any sewer network using the normal depth technique. Like most other computer models, it does not account for backwater effects occurring in the sewer system. As a result, the flow capacity

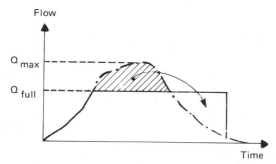

Figure 19.1   Illustration of storage calculation in ILLUDAS. (After Terstriep, 1974.)

in a sewer pipe is reached when it is flowing full. If the flow entering the sewer exceeds the pipe-full capacity, the excess is accounted for by "storing" it at the upstream end of the sewer until the pipe flow decreases and capacity becomes available to "empty" the "storage." Note that we put quotes around "storage" and "empty" to emphasize that these processes are, in fact, only mathematical and are used to account for the mass balance in the system. Storage and emptying may not be actually taking place physically in the drainage system. The excess flow may instead be flowing overland in streets, yards, parking lots, etc.

The principle of storage and emptying in ILLUDAS is illustrated as a hydrograph in Figure 19.1. ILLUDAS reports the accumulated excess water in the output printouts. As a result, the user may compare the computed results against system constraints or desired results.

19.2.2 Detention Calculations

When designing a new stormwater sewer system using ILLUDAS, it is possible to incorporate detention facilities at any location within the sewer network. New detention facilities can be sized in two ways:

Available Storage Volume is Specified.   ILLUDAS will size a circular outlet pipe from the facility. The longitudinal slope and Manning's roughness for the outlet pipe must be given. The pipe is sized, using pipe-full flow to achieve exactly the stated available storage volume using the design runoff hydrograph.

Maximum Allowable Outflow Rate is Specified.   The model calculates the detention volume using the specified maximum outflow rate. In this option, the maximum release rate can be specified either as a numeric value or the characteristic of the outlet pipe, namely pipe geometry, slope, and Manning's roughness coefficient.

Existing sewer networks may be analyzed either to determine the adequacy of existing detention facilities or to learn how much additional storage volume is needed. If the discharge exceeds the capacity of the outlet pipe, ILLUDAS calculates the required storage volume, which can be compared to the available volume. As an alternative, the available storage volume can be used as the limiting factor and the required outlet pipe size can be estimated. All flows are determined using normal depth calculations and do not account for surcharge of the outlet. As a result, the general tendency for this type of an algorithm is to underestimate the required volume or the size of the required outlet pipe. In effect, this algorithm simulates an off-line storage basin.

19.2.3 Summary

Detention design using ILLUDAS is performed using certain simplifying assumptions. Of these, the most significant is that the outflow from the detention facility is held constant during the entire detention process, namely, during filling and emptying. This simplification limits the use of ILLUDAS to preliminary systems planning. Figure 19.2 illustrates a hypothetical installation that approximates the detention model used by ILLUDAS.

19.3 SWMM

SWMM stands for Storm Water Management Model. It was developed and is being distributed under the sponsorship of the U.S. Environmental Protection Agency. It appears to be the most comprehensive urban stormwater network analysis model in practical application today. It was originally introduced in 1971 and has been updated several times since. Version III was released in 1981, which for the first time provided a continuous simulation option for this model. As a result, Version III and IV and subsequent updates can be run as single event models or as continuous simulation models. Practical consider-

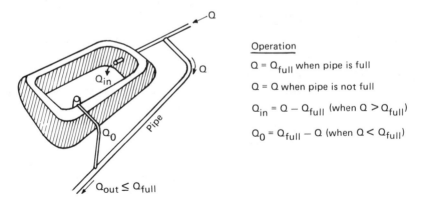

Operation

$Q = Q_{full}$ when pipe is full

$Q = Q$ when pipe is not full

$Q_{in} = Q - Q_{full}$ (when $Q > Q_{full}$)

$Q_0 = Q_{full} - Q$ (when $Q < Q_{full}$)

Figure 19.2 Example of a hypothetical detention as modeled by ILLUDAS. (After Terstriep, 1974.)

ations of time or rainfall data availability may require the use of a longer integration time increment when using the continuous simulation option. The model is available through the University of Florida in Gainesville, where it is maintained and supported under a contract with EPA, or from the EPA office in Athens, Georgia.

Since its original release, SWMM was modified for specific applications, or for proprietary marketing by many different organizations. One version of it was modified for the province of Ottawa, Canada and was released as OTSWM. Another version was released as a proprietary PC compatible version by a professor at University of Hamilton in Canada. Currently, this version continues being marketed by the same group, but it is no longer associated with the University of Hamilton.

The Runoff Block of SWMM was also extensively modified by the Missouri Division of the Army Corps of Engineers. This version became known as the MRD Version of SWMM. The MRD Runoff Block has many of the flow routing options normally found in the Transport Block of the EPA version and also has some features not found in the EPA version of the Runoff Block. The MRD model offers a single package with many of the options frequently used in urban stormwater hydrology. In its current version, it is not recommended as a model to be used for estimating the runoff and transport of urban runoff pollutants. If storm runoff water quality needs to be modeled, the EPA version appears to be more appropriate. A modified version of the MRD SWMM is available from the Urban Drainage and Flood Control District (UDFCD) in Denver, Colorado as the UDSWM2-PC model.

The following discussion is limited to the EPA Version III SWMM program package. The UDSWM2-PC version is further described in section 19.4. Other versions are not described further here, and the reader may wish to contact the institutions we have mentioned or others offering their own versions for further information.

19.3.1 General Description of SWMM

The SWMM program consists of the following six blocks (see Figure 19.3)

- runoff,
- transport,
- extended transport (EXTRAN),
- storage/treatment,
- receiving water, and
- executive.

All of these blocks are not used simultaneously. Only the blocks best suited for a specific task are used at any given time. Output from one block can

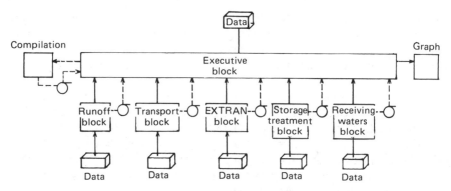

Figure 19.3   SWMM program blocks.

be used as input for another. This provides SWMM great flexibility and a staged approach toward modeling complex systems. Because of its extensive capabilities, the model obviously is very complex and is not one to be used casually. Effective use of SWMM is only possible after some training and after some experience has been gained by the user. For more details about this model, refer to the support manuals and publications for the Storm Water Management Model (1971, 1975–77, 1981, 1988), and subsequent updates.

Runoff Block.   The Runoff Block is used to estimate stormwater runoff from various subwatersheds, and its output can be used as input to the transport, EXTRAN, storage/treatment, or receiving blocks. Initial storm runoff calculations are based on sheet flow kinematic wave principle for the water that is not lost due to infiltration and surface retention. Any temporal and spatial distribution of rainfall can be used as input. Version III and subsequent updates permit continuous simulation of a chronologic series of rainfall and dry weather flow. Sheet flow, including the simulated pollutant load, is intercepted by trapezoidal gutters and circular pipes, which are then combined with flow and pollutants in other gutters and pipes. All flows and pollutants are eventually routed to specified discharge points. It is not necessary, however, to simulate pollutant runoff in order to use the runoff block.

Transport Block.   The Transport Block simulates the flow and pollutant transport in the major sewers of the system. Input data for the Transport Block consists of the output from the Runoff Block. This block can also simulate detention facilities at any point in the system. The calculations are based on the normal depth and continuity principle, which means they do not account for backwater effects or surcharge. If the inflow into any sewer segment exceeds its pipe full capacity, the excess is temporarily stored at the upstream end of the pipe segment. This algorithm is identical to the one we described for ILLUDAS and has a tendency to underestimate needed detention volumes.

Extended Transport Block (EXTRAN). By replacing the Transport Block by EXTRAN, it is possible to account for backwater effects in the flow conveyance system. The pressure gradient can go up to the ground surface at the nodes of the model. When the incoming flows surcharge the system so that it reaches the surface, the excess flows are not returned to the system. As a result, continuity is not maintained when a sewer system is surcharged excessively. EXTRAN also provides for the simulation of certain standard facilities such as overflows, pumping stations, detention facilities, etc.

Storage/Treatment Block. This block permits for simplified simulation of a single treatment plant in the system. The plant, however, has to be located at the downstream end of the sewer network. The treatment plant can include a single detention storage basin.

Receiving Water Block. The Receiving Water Block was designed to simulate the hydraulics and the fate of pollutants in the receiving bodies of water such as rivers, lakes, estuaries, etc. We do not discuss this block any further.

Executive Block. This block has the task of coordinating the information and transferring data between all of the other blocks in SWMM.

19.3.2 Detention Calculations in Transport Block

The Transport Block in SWMM III can be used to approximate in-line and off-line detention storage in the sewer system. At most, two storage basins can be simulated by this block (see Figure 19.4). If there are more than two

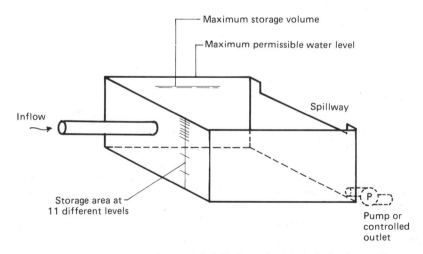

Figure 19.4 Detention facility as defined in Transport Block. (After Storm Water Mangement Model, 1971.)

basins, the system has to be broken up into smaller subsystems which can be simulated sequentially using the results of the upper network as input into the lower sewer network. The input data needed for storage calculations will include the following:

- Type of outlet structure. The choices provided by the model include bottom orifice outlet, constant rate pump, and a spillway.
- Depth–area relationship for up to 11 different water levels. This may be simplified in the case of a storage basin having the shape of an inverted circular truncated cone, in which case the user inputs only the bottom area and the slope of the walls.
- The maximum water level.
- The water level and the discharge rate at the start of the simulation.

The following three equations are used to describe the discharge through each type of outlet:

$$Q = A \cdot K_1 \cdot H^{1/2} \qquad \text{bottom orifice outlet} \qquad (19.1)$$

$$Q = L \cdot K_2 \cdot (H - h)^{3/2} \qquad \text{spillway} \qquad (19.2)$$

$$Q = K_3 \qquad \text{constant rate pump} \qquad (19.3)$$

in which Q = discharge rate,
H = depth of water above basin bottom,
A = area of the orifice outlet,
K_1 = constant dependent on orifice configuration,
L = length of spillway,
K_2 = constant dependent on spillway configuration,
h = height of spillway crest above basin bottom, and
K_3 = constant pump capacity.

When the pump option is used, it is also necessary to input the levels at which the pump is turned on and off.

If the water level in the storage basin during simulation rises above the maximum permissible level, the excess is not routed through the storage basin. Instead, it is accounted as excess volume in the printout of the simulation. This way, the modeler is aware of how much the basin may have been overloaded.

The pollutants in the system can also be routed through the storage basin. The program can estimate the removal of the settleable pollutants within the storage basin. This simulation can be performed, at the user's option, using plug flow or total mixed flow assumptions.

As a result, the program provides the modeler with a simulated hydrograph and a pollutograph after they are routed through the detention basin. Also, for each time step, the output provides the water depth and storage volume. The program does not provide a hydrograph of the water that may exceed the storage capacity of the facility and may spill as uncontrolled overflow.

19.3.3 Detention Calculations in Storage/Treatment Block

The SWMM program permits simulation of a treatment plant located at the downstream end of the system. Simulation of the following treatment plant components and processes is possible:

- gratings,
- swirl concentrator,
- sand trap,
- flotation,
- strainer,
- sedimentation,
- filtration,
- biological treatment, and
- chlorination.

The modeler excludes those treatment steps which are not applicable and provides the necessary basic parameters for the processes to be used. A storage facility can be located in-line or off-line to the sewer pipe entering the plant (see Figure 19.5). It is possible to use other connection schemes of detention and treatment plant than those shown in this figure. For example, when the storage is connected off-line, it is possible to route or pump the water from the storage basin to the plant.

Simulation of detention in this block is done using the same mathematic equations as used in the transport block described earlier. The only difference is that in the Storage/Treatment Block, the user has to specify the treatment efficiency for pollutant removal in the detention storage facility.

19.3.4 Detention Calculations in the EXTRAN Block

In the EXTRAN Block, the sewer network is represented by a series of links which are connected to each other at nodes. The modeler provides geometry, roughness, and invert elevations for each pipe. The user also has to provide the ground surface elevation at each node (i.e., manhole). Detention is simulated simply by providing the geometry of a pipe that best describes the storage vs. volume relationship of the installation. If the storage facility has an unusual shape, its characteristics can be approximated using any combination of pipes connected in parallel and series. The pipe sections that are supplied

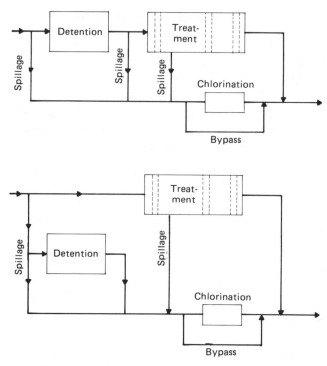

Figure 19.5 Treatment processes simulated by Storage/Treatment Block of SWMM.

by the program are illustrated in Figure 19.6. The user may, however, describe additional pipes having any desired geometry.

It is possible to simplify the initial testing of a potential detention storage site without going into great geometric detail of the facility. This is done by defining node storage basins. All that is needed is to input the water surface area available at the node in question. EXTRAN assumes that the surface area remains constant as the water rises and falls and calculates the volume being stored at the node.

The outflow from a storage basin in EXTRAN is described by either giving the dimensions of the outlet pipe or one of the following flow regulating elements:

- overflows,
- outlet orifices,
- pumps, and
- high-water gates.

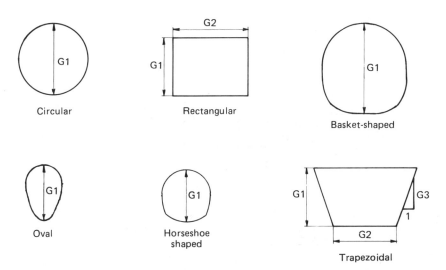

Figure 19.6 Standard pipe sections provided in EXTRAN Block. (After Storm Water Management Model, 1975–77.)

When these regulation elements are used to describe the discharge characteristics between two nodes, the user has to enter their hydraulic characteristics, e.g., discharge coefficients, spillway lengths, pumping rates, etc. An example of how a detention basin can be simulated using links, nodes, and flow regulating elements is illustrated in Figure 19.7.

The output from the EXTRAN block can provide for each time step the flow velocities in all the pipes and the water levels at all the nodes in the sewer network. At each of the detention sites, the inflow hydrograph, the outflow hydrograph, and the water levels are interdependent and are calculated simultaneously for each time step. This block is not simple to use, since all the component parts of the sewer system have to be described in detail and the calculations tend to become unstable if the element lengths are too short. It is a powerful tool for the analysis of an existing system and for the testing of proposed designs. It is not, however, the block that one would use for the general screening of many alternatives during planning.

19.3.5 Summary of SWMM Model Description

Detention calculations can be performed by the SWMM program in the following blocks:

- Transport Block,
- Extended Transport Block (EXTRAN), and
- Storage/Treatment Block.

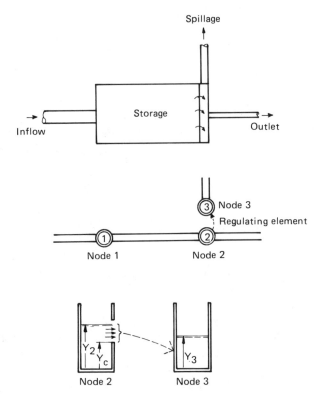

Figure 19.7 Example of how detention can be described using links, nodes, and flow regulators in EXTRAN Block. (After Storm Water Management Model, 1975–77.)

The same mathematical equations are used in detention calculations in the Transport Block and the Storage/Treatment Block. The latter block only permits the simulation of detention at a treatment facility. Backwater effects are not considered in the Transport Block. If backwater effects are of significant concern, the Transport Block can be replaced by EXTRAN, which accounts for water surface levels in the entire system.

Using SWMM, one can simulate most of the urban storm runoff and routing processes. It is a comprehensive and a powerful model and can be an extremely valuable tool in experienced hands. However, the model is complicated and imposes many requirements on the user. It is not a model of choice for casual investigation of what detention requirements may be needed at a single site. It is the model of choice for analyzing the performance of complete storm sewer systems, which may include detention facilities within such systems.

19.4 UDSWM2-PC

As mentioned earlier, the Runoff Block of SWMM was modified by the Missouri Division of the Army Corps of Engineers, which version was further modified to run on a PC for the Urban Drainage and Flood Control District (UDFCD) in Denver, Colorado by the Boyle Engineering Company. In rewriting it for the UDFCD, the surface runoff calculations from tributary subbasins were decoupled from the gutter, pipe, detention, and other flow routing calculations. As a result, the user needs to generate the subbasin runoff hydrographs only once and then use them as input in subsequent runs. Various flow routing options can thus be studied at considerable savings in computer run time.

The user may also choose to generate storm runoff hydrographs using the UDFCD's Colorado Urban Hydrograph Procedure (CUHP) program. The output hydrographs from the CUHP program are then read by UDSWM2-PC, which routes these hydrographs through the conveyance system, detention facilities, diversions, etc.

This program has many of the routing options normally found in the Transport Block of SWMM. It also has some features not found in the Transport Block. Like the MRD Version of the Runoff Block, UDSWM-PC provides the following flow routing elements:

1. trapezoidal channels;
2. circular pipes;
3. direct flow links (i.e., no flow routing);
4. trapezoidal channels with an overflow channel;
5. circular pipes with an overflow channel;
6. detention facilities (based on Storage vs. Outflow rating table);
7. diversion facilities (based on Flow in Main Flow Element vs. Diverted Flow rating table); and
8. out-of-basin inflow hydrographs (based on Time vs. Flow table).

Also, like the MRD version of the Runoff Block, UDSWM-PC offers a single program block with many of the options frequently used in urban storm-water hydrology. In its current version, it has no capability to estimate the runoff and transport of urban runoff pollutants. If storm runoff water quality needs to be modeled, the EPA version of SWMM, despite its shortcomings in simulating pollutant loads, is the model of choice at this time. A feature was recently added to the new version of UDSWM that can automatically design the size of circular storm sewers.

19.4.1 Detention Calculations in UDSWM-PC

Detention calculations can be performed in two ways using UDSWM2-PC. The first option is an informal one and is similar to what we described for ILLUDAS. The user can obtain preliminary detention volume requirements by merely specifying a circular pipe of known flow capacity. The model will route the flows through the pipe until its pipe-full capacity is reached. Any excess flow is then held back in storage until the flows decrease and capacity in the pipe again becomes available to carry off the stored excess. The volume held back this way is reported along with the flow hydrograph and as the maximum volume stored in a summary table. Backwater effects and surcharge in the pipes are not considered in the calculations. As with ILLUDAS, the informal option produces estimated volumes that tend to be on the low side.

The second and formal detention option of UDSWM2-PC permits the user to define the outflow vs. storage characteristics for up to 25 detention facilities. The outflow vs. storage input data are used by the program only after the outlet pipe capacity is exceeded. In other words, the program will satisfy the normal depth capacity of the pipe element first before utilizing the outflow vs. storage tables provided by the user. This option permits an experienced user considerable flexibility in testing storage scenarios.

To simulate a surcharged outlet, the user enters the storage–outflow table and the characteristics for a very small pipe element that virtually has no flow capacity to satisfy. To approximate an off-line detention facility, the user specifies the pipe size equal to the bypass pipe and then enters the volume–outflow table for the flows that exceed its pipe full capacity. UDSWM2-PC is a single event model and will handle one storm event a time. Continuous modeling is not a currently available option.

The formal detention option calculates the storage in the basin using a Modified Puls flood routing procedure. The time increment used is the user-specified time increment of integration for all flow routing calculations in the model. The output consists of a printout that lists all the storage and discharge values throughout the run and the maximum discharge rate and volume stored throughout the storm. Full hydrograph values are printed only for the user-specified flow routing elements. A summary table of peak discharge rates and volumes stored, along with their respective times of occurrence, are printed for all routing elements within the model.

19.4.2 Summary

UDSWM2-PC is a modified version of the SWMM Runoff Block that will run on a PC. The modifications allow the user a variety of flow routing options, including detention facilities. Detention calculations can either be performed informally in a manner similar to how ILLUDAS handles them, or formally using the Modified Puls flood routing procedure. In the latter case, the user can specify up to 25 separate detention facilities anywhere in the flow routing network.

19.5 MOUSE

MOUSE stands for *M*odeling *O*f *U*rban *SE*wers. It was developed jointly by the Danish Hydraulic Institute, the Department of Environmental Engineering at the Technical University of Denmark, and two private Danish companies. In Europe, MOUSE is one of the most widely used tools for the analysis of urban drainage problems, and it is also extensively used in Australia and New Zealand.

The first version of the integrated MOUSE package for PCs was released in 1985. Today it is also available for application on UNIX workstations. MOUSE is based on more than 10 years' experience with a mainframe modeling system, and several hundred copies have been sold in more than 20 countries.

The Danish Hydraulic Institute is responsible for the continuous ongoing development, marketing, and distribution of MOUSE. It is a proprietary software package, and users are offered regular updates reflecting feedback from the large user group.

19.5.1 General Description of MOUSE

The MOUSE system contains a number of modules of varying sophistication allowing for description of overland flows, inflows and infiltration, pipe flows, and pollution loads. Simplified as well as generalized equations have been included in the system, permitting the user to select the most appropriate method for a specific task. The facilities available to the user are:

- An interactive menu-based system for data manipulation and program execution;
- A database for catchment and pipe system data;
- A time series and a rain database;
- Routines for tabulated and graphical presentation of input and output data;
- Computational modules comprising generalized hydrological modeling, generalized pipe flow modeling, and pollution load modeling.

An outline of the system is shown in Figure 19.8. The individual components and the computational modules will be described below. For a more detailed

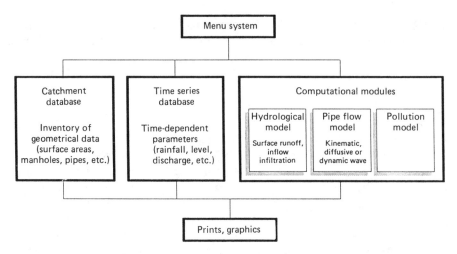

Figure 19.8 Overview of the MOUSE system.

description the reader is referred to Lindberg et al. (1986) and to Danish Hydraulic Institute (1992).

Menu system. All communication between the user and the MOUSE system takes place interactively through a number of screen menus. Input and output data are presented in tabular form on a printer or graphically on a screen or a plotter.

Use of the system requires no knowledge of programming or operating systems. The menus guide the user through the application. Input data are entered into standard forms on the screen and checked by the system for consistency and correct order of magnitude. A user manual is integrated into the system and Help menus can be displayed on the screen when required.

Catchment and pipe database. The layout and geometry of the catchment and pipe system is described in 12 standard forms, e.g., for manholes, pipes, etc. The database also contains files describing the composition of the sewage water. Sub data sets for calculation and plotting are retrieved automatically by the computational modules and the print–plot modules.

Time series and rain databases. The time series database includes all time-dependent parameters such as rainfall, water level, and discharge data. The system can handle measured as well as simulated data. This facilitates a direct comparison of measured and computed data and makes it possible to use output from one simulation as input to the next. A special feature for the generation of diurnal dry weather flow (weekdays and weekends) is included.

A special rain database is provided for the processing of historical rain data as well as synthetic rain data. Synthetic rains are described by means of

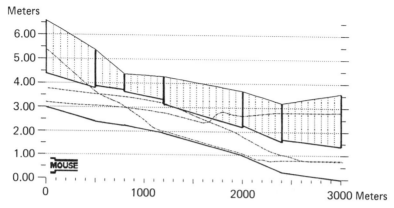

Figure 19.9 Longitudinal profile of a pipe showing simulated water levels.

intensity–duration–frequency formulas or tables. Single rainstorms and continuous time series are retrieved automatically by the computational and the print-plot modules.

Prints and graphics. Input data as well as output data may be presented either in tabular form (screen, printer, or textfile) or in graphic form (screen, printer, or plotter). Layouts of the pipe system and longitudinal profiles can be retrieved from the catchment and pipe database. Time series as well as longitudinal profiles can be retrieved from the output data set. An example of a longitudinal profile showing water levels in a surcharged pipe is shown in Figure 19.9.

19.5.2 Hydrological Model

When examining the real flow conditions in a sewer system, one often encounters discharges somewhat larger than expected from the connected impervious areas. This phenomenon is referred to here as *indirect runoff* and can be explained by infiltration inflow from the surrounding soils among other factors. According to Gustafsson et al. (1991), indirect runoff depends on the actual rainfall and also to a large extent on the preceding rain events—the so-called hydrological history.

The hydrological model (MOUSE-NAM) includes simulation of both direct surface runoff and indirect runoff. Each catchment is described by its total area, the distribution of the area between the direct and the indirect runoff components (DRC and IRC), and the relevant hydrological parameters. The principal model structure is shown in Figure 19.10.

The input time series consists of precipitation, potential evaporation, and temperature. The two latter parameters are optional. The model allows for continuous simulation of a long time series, and a hot-start feature is included.

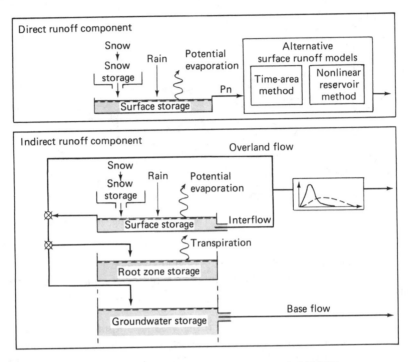

Figure 19.10   Hydrological model concept in MOUSE.

Direct runoff component.   Two methods available for calculation of the direct surface runoff.

- The time–area method. Calculation of the discharge is based on individual time–area curves for the different catchment areas (standard or user-specified time–area curves).
- The nonlinear reservoir method. Calculation of the discharge is based on Manning's formula:

$$Q = \text{area} \cdot K \cdot \text{depth}^{5/3}$$

in which $K = \text{Manning} \cdot \text{slope}^{1/2}/\text{length}$.

The lumped K-factor, which includes three physically based parameters, makes the calibration process easier.

Indirect runoff component.   The calculations are based on the NAM model from the MIKE 11 system, a river modeling package developed by the Danish Hydraulic Institute (see Danish Hydraulic Institute, 1990). The technique in the NAM model is based on a deterministic description, where individual hydrological processes are lumped together in a conceptual approach. It

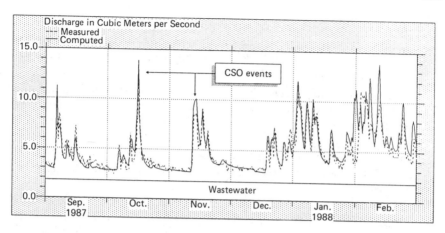

Figure 19.11   The result of continuous simulation of inflow to a wastewater treatment plant.

is an imitation of the land phase of the hydrological cycle. There are four types of water storage: snow, surface, root zone, and groundwater. Some of the input parameters are related to the corresponding physical data, but the final model calibration must be based on a comparison with historical recorded discharges, covering some years with daily mean values and some months with high resolution (minutes and hours).

An example of a comparison between model results and measured inflow to a treatment plant is shown in Figure 19.11. The simulated results show the runoff from a single catchment of 77 square miles (200 km²) and five rain gauges.

19.5.3 Pipe Flow Model

The pipe flow model (MOUSE-PIPE) is the internationally recognized tool for simulation of the entire runoff process through pipes, manholes, and hydraulic structures on the basis of St. Venants' equations. The model is well suited for analyzing the hydraulic performance of complex looped sewer systems including overflows, storage basins, and pumping stations. The extent and the recurrence intervals of floodings can be mapped, critical bottlenecks can be identified, and pipes and storage basins can be sized to reduce surcharges to an acceptable level. The pipe model is also widely used for modeling open-channel networks and tunnel systems. It provides for three different hydraulic descriptions:

- *Kinematic wave approach.* The pipe flow is calculated based on the principle of a balance between friction and gravity forces. This simplification implies that the kinematic wave approach cannot simulate backwater effects.

- *Diffuse wave approach.* In addition to friction and gravity forces, the hydrostatic gradient is included in this description. This allows the user to take downstream boundaries into account and thus simulate backward effects as well as pressurized flow.
- *Dynamic wave approach.* Using the full-momentum equation, including acceleration forces, the user is able to simulate even very fast transients in the system.

Depending on the type of problem, the user can choose the most appropriate hydraulic description. All three approaches can simulate branches as well as looped systems.

The pipe flow model accommodates free surface flows in pipes, as well as pressurized flows and flooding and storage on the surface. Flow distributions in looped systems are computed accurately. Head losses at manhole inlets and outlets, as well as in various flow control structures (valves, weirs, pumps, etc.) are taken into account. Combinations of supercritical and subcritical flows, with associated hydraulic jumps, can be simulated with dynamic and diffuse wave formulations. The model also allows the user to step back in time and resimulate the network with changed conditions (a hot start).

19.5.4 Pollution Transport Model

The pollution transport model (MOUSE-SAMBA) is used for the analysis of pollution loads in connection with combined sewer overflows and inlets to wastewater treatment plants. The basic idea behind this model is to facilitate the calculation of large sewer networks with long time series of historical rainfall data as input. To achieve this, a simple runoff and flow model is used. A time–area formulation is combined with simplified routing routines for surface runoff and pipe flow.

The results from the model simulations are presented as extreme statistics and as yearly loads. The yearly load is important when judging discharges of pollutants that have an accumulated effect, such as nitrogen and phosphorus. The extreme statistics are of special interest when judging discharges of pollutants that have an acute effect, such as bio (BOD) and bacterial pollution.

19.5.5 Add-on Modules

Although MOUSE is an integrated package with a number of items useful to design engineers, some features have been encapsulated in fully compatible add-on modules. The more important add-on modules are:

MIMI. This module is used for the design of new pipes. The design is based on the Rational Method and can be executed for the entire system or for selected profiles on an interactive spreadsheet.

MOUSE-CAD. This module serves as an interface to AutoCAD. Catchment and pipe data can be digitized in AutoCAD and transferred to MOUSE (DXF format). Similarly, results from MOUSE can be converted to DXF format for display in AutoCAD.

AMM. This module is used for handling distributed rainfall and for the simulation of moveable weirs and gates. As rainfall by nature varies in time and space, it is essential to have a certain resolution in both dimensions, not only in time. This is especially the case for large sewer networks. The AMM module makes it possible to simulate both time and area distributed rainfall patterns. In the basic version of MOUSE, flow can be controlled by pumps and a dedicated flow control feature not related to the physical operation of a structure. For more general use, in the AMM module these features have been extended to include the operation of moveable weirs and sluice gates based on the level and velocity or flow in arbitrary nodes. A more flexible operation of pumps is also provided.

19.5.6 Development of New Features

MOUSE for RTC applications. As a result of increased concern for the environment, real time control of combined sewer systems is becoming more and more common. Implementation of RTC can sometimes be cost-effective when compared to more traditional upgrading measures. This trend creates a need for reliable tools for analysis if the potential use of and the effect of RTC.

For the assessment of long-term effects, continuous modeling is required. However, simulating long-term periods (several years) with a dynamic model and small time steps (10 seconds) is still not practical. The continuous model is therefore a combination of a new steady-state option and the well-proven dynamic model. Based on the actual flow conditions, the continuous model automatically switches back and forth between steady state and dynamic resolution.

The continuous model, including the extended flow control possibilities, is an efficient tool for evaluating the potential of RTC. Further, it can be used in assessing optimal operation strategies and as a training tool by system operators. Other features included in the RTC package are:

- A module for communication with sensors such as level, discharge, and precipitation meters;
- Updating features (data assimilation) in the hydrodynamic model;
- An optimizing module for the current evaluation of the optimal operation strategy; and
- A rainfall forecast system.

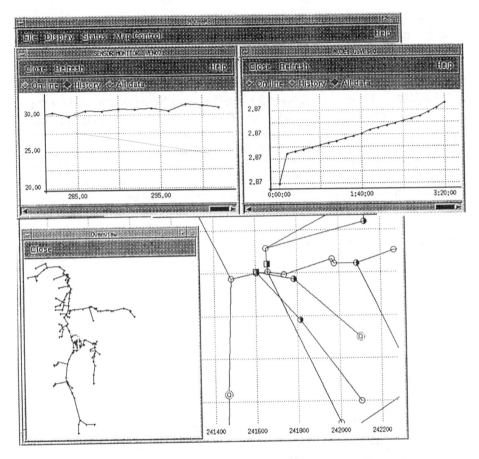

Figure 19.12   Monitor display of a real-time forecast in the on-line mode.

When installed in an on-line environment, the above features provide the capability to produce "complete" flow pattern for a sewer system with the actual operation strategy or to forecast with different strategies. The calculations are based on the output from a few on-line rain gauges and water level and discharge sensors.

Figure 19.12 shows a monitor display from a prototype on-line project where the operator has simultaneously updated windows showing both measurements and the forecasted runoff picture predicted with the model.

Sediment transport model.   Ideally, the increased risk for sedimentation and flushing caused by changed flow conditions in sewers should be accounted for the RTC model. For the purpose of describing the effects of sedimentation in sewers, in terms of changed hydraulic capacity and transportation of pollutants from the source to the wastewater treatment plant, a special tool (MOUSE-ST) has been developed.

MOUSE-ST consists of an implicit geomorphic model for the simulation of uniform noncohesive sediment scour and deposition. The quantitative process is well described by the hydrodynamic model in MOUSE. When sediment deposits influence the performance of the sewer system, the MOUSE-ST model may be applied. Some of the main tasks MOUSE-ST can be used to study include:

- Prediction of the reduction in hydraulic capacity due to sediment depositions;
- Prediction of where sediment will deposit in the sewer system;
- Prediction of the effect of flushing on sediment deposits; and
- Prediction of pollution transport by noncohesive sediment.

Further features which will be included in MOUSE-ST are:

- A transport dispersion model for the simulation of dissolved pollutants carried by the flow;
- A cohesive sediment transport model; and
- A formulation of the transport of graded sediment.

REFERENCES

DANISH HYDRAULIC INSTITUTE, *NAM—Documentation and User's Guide*, 1990.

DANISH HYDRAULIC INSTITUTE, *MOUSE—Technical Reference and User's Guide*, Version 3.1, 1992.

GUSTAFSSON, L. G., LINDBERG, S., OLSSON, R., "Modeling of the Indirect Runoff Component in Urban Areas," *Proceedings of the International Conference on Urban Drainage and New Technologies*, Dubrovnik, June 17–21, 1991.

LINDBERG, S., JÖRGENSON, T. W., and WILLEMOES, T., "MOUSE—Modelling of Urban Storm Sewer Systems," *Proceedings of the International Symposium on Comparison of Urban Drainage Models With Real Catchment Data*, Dubrovnik, April 8–11, 1986.

STORMWATER MANAGEMENT MODEL, *SWMM User's Manual*, Volumes I–IV, EPA 11024 Doc 07-10/71, 1971.

STORMWATER MANAGEMENT MODEL, *SWMM User's Manual Version II*, EPA 670/Z-75-017, 1975. Supplemented 1976 and 1977.

STORMWATER MANAGEMENT MODEL, *SWMM User's Manual Version III*, EPA Project No. CR-805664, 1981.

TERSTRIEP, M. L., AND STALL, J. B., "The Illinois Urban Drainage Area Simulator, ILLUDAS," Illinois State Water Survey, Bulletin 58, 1974.

Urban Drainage Stormwater Management Model—PC Version (UDSWM2) Users Manual, Urban Drainage and Flood Control District, Denver, Colo., 1985.

20

Examples of Detention Basin Sizing

20.1 GENERAL

So far, we have described various methods to calculate detention basin volumes. These included the use of different design rainfall information and procedures to calculate storage volumes. It is up to the designer or planner to select the detention sizing methodology. In some cases, rough estimates of volumes and release rates are sufficient. In others, detailed system analysis is needed. We can arbitrarily subdivide the various sizing or analysis procedures into two general categories, namely:

- superficial sizing methods, and
- detailed calculation methods.

Superficial methods are of value during the initial planning phase of a project when rough estimates of volumes, land areas, and costs are needed. These methods, for the sake of jurisdictional consistency, are sometimes mandated by local authorities for final design as well. During the planning phase, it is not practical to use detailed procedures. At that time, the designer wants to assess many sites and facilities, and sizing calculations during this phase do not need to be very refined.

Detailed methods are reserved for the preliminary and final design phase. By the time the detailed methods are used, detention site locations have been identified and each of the facilities is designed or analyzed much more precisely. Detailed methods may also be used to evaluate the performance of entire stormwater collection, transport, and detention systems to improve the overall system performance.

20.2 EXAMPLES OF CALCULATIONS

Two examples are presented to illustrate the variability that is possible using various design procedures. The first example is based on experience in Sweden. The second is based on experience in the Denver metropolitan area of the United States. Both are simple single detention basin sizing examples which do not analyze the performance of an entire drainageway system.

20.2.1 Example from Sweden

In this example, a detention basin needs to be designed to limit the runoff from a 116-acre (51.3-ha) residential watershed to 10.6 cubic feet per second (300 l/s) during a 1-year storm. The watershed has 47 acres (20.8 ha) of impervious area; i.e., the watershed has 40.5% impervious surface. The time of concentration was estimated to be 12 minutes.

As a first step, the detention volume was estimated using one of the superficial methods and block rain. To get an idea of how the results may vary due to the calculation method, calculations were first performed using a method that does not consider the time of concentration (see Figure 18.4). They were then repeated using a method that considers the time of concentration (see Figure 18.6). The results from both cases were then compared to the results obtained using the preliminary sizing option of ILLUDAS and block rain as input and are summarized in Table 20.1.

As can be seen, the calculated volumes are sensitive to the method of calculation. Both of the superficial methods appear to overestimate the storage volume when compared to ILLUDAS. However, we pointed out earlier that the calculating algorithm used in these runs of ILLUDAS has a tendency to underestimate detention volumes.

In Chapter 18, we mentioned that the block rain represents only a part of the total volume of a rainstorm. This is because it assumes that there is no rain-

TABLE 20.1 Comparison of Volumes Calculated Using Superficial Rational Formula-Based Methods and ILLUDAS in Cubic Feet (m³)

| | RECURRENCE FREQUENCY (years) | | |
CALCULATION METHOD	0.5	1.0	2.0
Without time of concentration	34,900 (988)	48,700 (1,380)	67,200 (1,903)
With time of concentration	29,400 (832)	42,600 (1,206)	60,950 (1,726)
ILLUDAS	24,500 (693)	38,100 (1,079)	55,500 (1,571)

TABLE 20.2   Comparison of Volumes Calculated Using Three Different
Design Storms and ILLUDAS in Cubic Feet (m³)

	RECURRENCE FREQUENCY (years)		
CALCULATION METHOD	0.5	1.0	2.0
ILLUDAS with Sifalda rain	38,600 (1,092)	57,500 (1,627)	81,500 (2,308)
ILLUDAS with Arnell rain	34,300 (970)	66,000 (1,870)	89,500 (2,535)
ILLUDAS with block rain	24,500 (693)	38,100 (1,079)	55,500 (1,571)

fall before or after the central block rain. Sifalda and Arnell tried to compensate for this apparent shortfall through modifying the block rain (see Figures 16.5 and 16.7). These same calculations were repeated using ILLUDAS and the Sifalda and Arnell design rainfall patterns, and the findings are compared in Table 20.2.

As can be seen from Table 20.2, the choice of design rainfall pattern can have as much, or even more, effect on the results than the choice of calculation method. The smallest volume resulted from the use of block rain, probably because it had the least total rainfall in the storm. The other two storm patterns were larger because of the so-called adjustments to make them more "representative" of real storms. At this time, there is no basis for judging which of the design storm patterns is most accurate in calculating storage volumes. Factors such as the detention period, the time of concentration of the watershed, and the duration of the design rainfall need to be considered before deciding which of these three storm patterns are most appropriate.

In all the calculations presented so far in Tables 20.1 and 20.2, the outflow rate from the storage basin was assumed to be constant at 10.6 cubic feet per second (300 l/s) (see Figure 20.1). In most detention facilities, the outflow rate will vary with the water depth. To illustrate how this variable outflow rate affects volume calculations, a more precise flow routing algorithm was used. This was done with the aid of KTH-UTMAG (Anderson and Stahre, 1981) computer model developed in Sweden. The same inflow hydrograph used in the ILLUDAS calculations and illustrated in Figure 20.1 was also used with the KTH-UTMAG model.

First, the storage volume obtained under the constant outflow rate assumption, namely 38,100 cubic feet (1,079 m³), shown in Figure 20.1, was fixed. It was also assumed that the storage basin was rectangular in shape with vertical walls. The outlet was assumed to be a vertical circular orifice. The inflow hydrograph was then routed through the basin and an outflow hydrograph was calculated. The results are graphed in Figure 20.2, where we see that the actual peak outflow from a 38,100-cubic foot (1,079 m³) basin is 17.6 cubit feet per second (500 l/s).

For the detention basin to maintain the 10.6-cubic-foot-per-second (300 l/s) maximum outflow rate, the volume has to be larger. Next, the KTH

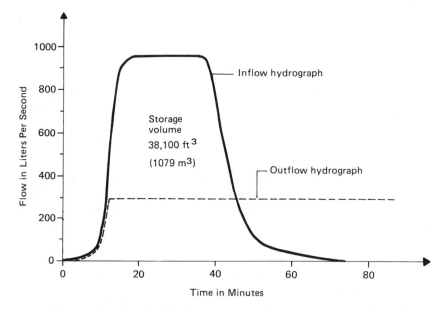

Figure 20.1   Results of ILLUDAS storage calculations under a constant 10.6 cubic feet per second (300 l/s) outflow rate.

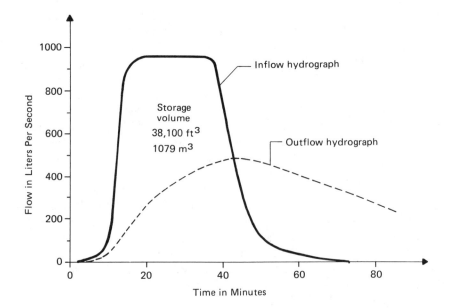

Figure 20.2   Results of detention basin calculations assuming a fixed volume shown in Figure 20.

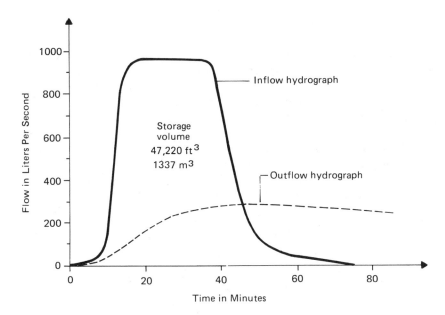

Figure 20.3   Results of detention basin calculations assuming a maximum release rate of 10.6 cubic feet per second (300 l/s).

model was used to find the detention basin volume needed to maintain the maximum outflow rate at 10.6 cubic feet per second (300 l/s). The results of these calculations are shown in Figure 20.3. We see that the volume needs to be 25% larger than calculated previously to maintain the 10.6 cubic feet per second (300 l/s) release rate.

Obviously, the basin size is affected by how accurately the outflow vs. depth function is simulated. The lesson to be gained from these examples is that use of the ILLUDAS model did not improve the accuracy of the calculations. In fact, both of the "superficial" methods estimated the final volume closer than ILLUDAS. This is not to say that ILLUDAS or similar models (i.e., Transport Block of SWMM, informal storage calculation procedure of UDSWM2–PC, or other similar procedures) should not be used. On the contrary, they are valuable tools during early planning as long as the user realizes that the estimates of storage volumes obtained using them will probably have to be adjusted upwards.

Another lesson from all this is to *know the algorithm that is used in the model you are using.* Blind faith in computer "black box" models has very little room in good engineering practice. Only through understanding of the various flow routing processes and the algorithms used to simulate them can the engineer be in position to judge which tools to use under various conditions.

20.2.2 Example from the United States

In this second example, a detention basin has to limit the runoff from a 100-year storm to 1 cubic foot per second per acre (70 l/s/ha). The tributary watershed is a 100-acre (40.5-ha) residential development with 40% of its surface covered by pavement and rooftop. The watershed has a length to width ratio of two, a time of concentration of 32 minutes, a runoff coefficient of 0.68 during a 100-year storm, and an outlet adjustment factor $K_o = 0.88$.

As we did for the first examples, the detention volume was first estimated using the Rational Formula storage calculation method without consideration for the time of concentration. The calculations for this method are tabulated in Table 20.3.

Next, the storage volume was determined using the computer program

TABLE 20.3 Modified Rational Method for Detention Storage Calculations
Project Title: Example Problem for Denver Area

Basin size, A:		100 acres		
Percent impervious:		49%		
Runoff coefficient, C:		0.68		
Design frequency:		100–year		
One-hour rainfall:		2.6 inches		
Design discharge, Q:		100 cubic feet per second		
Outflow factor, K_o:		0.88		

Storm Duration (min)	Rainfall Intensity (in./hr)	Runoff Volume (ft^3)	Outflow Volume (ft^3)	Storage Volume (ft^3)	Storage Volume (acre ft)
(1)	(2)	$(3) = -60 \cdot (1)$ $\cdot (2) \cdot A \cdot C$	$(4) =$ $60 \cdot (1) \cdot Q$	$(5) =$ $(3)-(4)$	$(6) =$ $(5)/43,560$
5.0	8.82	181,403	26,400	155,003	3.56
10.0	7.03	289,383	52,800	236,583	5.43
15.0	5.90	364,244	79,200	285,044	6.54
20.0	5.11	420,819	105,600	315,219	7.24
25.0	4.53	465,999	132,000	333,999	7.67
30.0	4.08	503,483	158,400	345,083	7.92
35.0	3.72	535,458	184,800	350,658	8.05
40.0	3.42	563,316	211,200	352,116	8.08*
45.0	3.18	587,990	237,600	350,390	8.04
50.0	2.97	610,135	264,000	346,135	7.95
60.0	2.63	648,615	316,800	331,815	7.62
70.0	2.37	681,321	369,600	311,721	7.16
80.0	2.16	709,803	422,400	287,403	6.60
90.0	1.99	735,064	475,200	259,864	5.97

* Required storage = 8.08 acre feet (9,970 m³).
Conversions: 1.0 in. = 25.4 mm; 1.0 ft³ = 0.0283 m³; 1.0 acre-ft. = 1,234 m³; 1.0 acre = 0.405 ha.

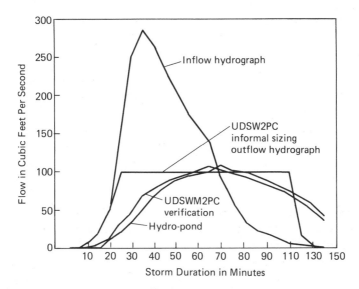

Figure 20.4 Comparison of hydrograph routing using UDSWM2–PC and HYDRO POND for an example in Denver.

HYDRO POND (Guo, 1991) a PC program developed at the University of Colorado at Denver to help design detention storage ponds. The inflow hydrograph for this example was generated using the Colorado Urban Hydrograph Procedure (CUHP) and its 100-year design storm. The use of the CUHP is of no particular significance here, and any other hydrograph generating method would have served as well for this example. It was used to keep the entire example consistent with the methods employed in the Denver region.

The results obtained using the modified rational method and HYDRO POND were then compared to the results obtained using the informal and formal flow routing process in UDSWM2–PC described in Chapter 19. The outlet hydrographs generated by UDSWM2–PC and HYDRO POND are shown in Figure 20.4.

Note that the informal process in UDSWM2–PC produces a similar outlet hydrograph shown earlier for ILLUDAS. Also note that the outflow hydrograph for the formal routing process in UDSWM2–PC and from HYDRO POND are almost identical. There appears to be approximately a 10-minute time shift between the two, but the shape, peak outflow, and the storage volume are identical. The results of all four calculations are summarized in Table 20.4.

Again, we see that the storage volume requirements vary with the method of calculation. In this example, the informal routing process, which approximates an off-line storage basin, gave the lowest volume. Specifically, it estimated a volume that was almost 20% lower than the two "exact" storage

TABLE 20.4   Volumes Calculated Using Rational Formula Method, UDSWM2–PC, HYDRO-POND, and CUHP Design Storm

Calculation Method	100-YEARS RECURRENCE FREQUENCY	
	Volume in Acre Feet (m³)	Peak Flow in Cubic Feet per second (l/s)
Modified rational method	8.08 (9,970)	100 (2,830)
HYDRO-POND	8.21 (10,130)	106 (3,000)
UDSWM2–PC formal routing process	8.21 (10,130)	106 (3,000)
UDSWM2–PC informal storage sizing	6.7 (8,260)	100 (2,830)

routing calculation methods. The superficial Rational Formula-based method estimated a volume that was within 2% of the volume found using the "exact" calculating methodology.

Based on the examples from Sweden and Denver, it is tempting to conclude that the so-called "superficial" detention sizing methods may in fact be superior to the Transport Block of SWMM and the informal options of UDSWM2–PC and ILLUDAS, or to other models using similar algorithms. However, such a conclusion would be irresponsible. Before it can be reached, sufficient local studies need to be performed to determine which simplified procedures give the best preliminary results.

REFERENCES

ANDERSON, J., AND STAHRE, P., "KTH-UTMAG, Calculation Routine for Detention Facilities," KTH, Vattenvardsteknik, Rationella Avloppssystem, Medelande 17, 1981. (In Swedish)

GUO, C. Y., *User's Manual for HYDRO POND, A Personal Computer Software Program for Reservoir Routing and Outlet Structure Design*, University of Colorado at Denver, 1991.

21

Stormwater Pollutants

21.1 INTRODUCTION

In Part 4, we discuss the emerging technology of using stormwater detention for the removal of pollutants found in separate urban stormwater runoff. Although many different constituents can be found in urban runoff, to avoid being overwhelmed it helps to focus primarily on certain pollutants that can be used as representative indicators of others. Because of this, the EPA (1983) adopted for their Nationwide Urban Runoff Program the following constituents as " . . . standard pollutants characterizing urban runoff":

TSS	Total suspended solids
BOD	Biochemical oxygen demand
COD	Chemical oxygen demand
TP	Total phosphorus (as P)
SP	Soluble phosphorus (as P)
TKN	Total Kjeldahl nitrogen (as N)
$NO_{2\&3}$	Nitrite & nitrate (as N)
Cu	Total copper
Pb	Total lead
Zn	Total zinc

A number of other constituents were evaluated by the EPA before selecting the foregoing list. The EPA explains this selection as follows:

The list includes pollutants of general interest which are usually examined in both point and nonpoint source studies and includes representatives of important categories of pollutants—namely *solids, oxygen consuming constituents, nutrients,* and *heavy metals.* [emphasis added]

21.1.1 National Urban Runoff Program

Although there were many studies of separate urban stormwater runoff quality, none was as extensive or included more sites than the U.S. Environmental Protection Agency's National Urban Runoff Program (i.e., NURP). This program collected data during 1981 and 1982 which was analyzed and summarized in the final NURP report by EPA (1983). The final report, along with its technical appendices, provides much insight into urban stormwater runoff quality. It discusses the potential water quality standards violations in receiving waters and suggests the best management practices for reducing pollutant concentrations in stormwater runoff.

The final acceptable data base for this project came from 81 sites located in 22 different cities throughout the United States. It included more than 2,300 separate storm events. However, since all pollutants were not measured at all sites, the numbers of samples for individual pollutants were somewhat less than that. For the most part, the data consisted of the flow weighted average concentration, namely, the event mean concentration of each pollutant for each runoff event. In some cities, however, discrete samples were collected throughout the runoff event to characterize how the concentrations varied during any given event. These were then also flow weight composited to determine the Event Mean Concentration (i.e., EMC) for all storms.

21.1.2 Generalized NURP Findings

Before looking at the data summaries reported in the final NURP report, it helps to understand what the initial statistical analysis of the data revealed. Since the original NURP report was published, data analysis has continued and, as a result, there were follow-up activities by EPA and the United States Geological Survey to further refine the initial findings. It may be that some of the conclusions reported in the NURP report may yet be modified. However, it is unlikely that the broad observations reported in the final NURP report regarding data variability will be modified significantly. Briefly, EPA (1983) reported the following in its final NURP report:

- The EMCs at each test site were found to exhibit log-normal statistical distribution.
- The site median of the EMCs from all the test sites were found to also exhibit a log-normal statistical distribution. Figure 21.1 illustrates this for total copper (i.e. C_u).

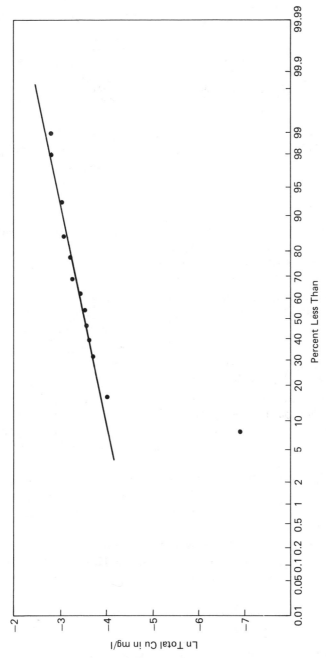

Figure 21.1 Log-normal distribution of total copper data collected under NURP. (After EPA, 1983.)

TABLE 21.1   Water Quality Characteristics of Urban Runoff

Constituent	EMC Coef. of Var. Event to Event	URBAN SITE MEDIAN EMC IN MG/L	
		Median Site	90th Percentile
TSS	1.0–2.0	100.000	300.000
BOD	0.5–1.0	9.000	15.000
COD	0.5–1.0	65.000	450.000
TP	0.5–1.0	0.330	0.700
SP	0.5–1.0	0.120	0.210
TKN	0.5–1.0	1.500	3.300
NO_{2+3}	0.5–1.0	0.680	1.750
Cu	0.5–1.0	0.034	0.093
Pb	0.5–1.0	0.140	0.350
Zn	0.5–1.0	0.160	0.500

After EPA, 1983

- For TSS, 90% of the individual storm EMCs were found to vary over a range of three to five times the site median EMC. Apparently, the variation in EMCs between storms can be significant, but not out of the ordinary for random data such as this.

- For constituents other than TSS, 90% of EMCs were found to be two to three times the site median EMC.

- Although some cities exhibited higher or lower EMC values than the national median EMC for one or more constituents, no clear geographical patterns were revealed. The national median EMC values of urban pollutants are listed in Table 21.1.

- Land use categories (i.e., residential, mixed, commercial, industrial and open/nonurban) do not provide a statistically significant basis for predicting differences in EMCs. Although not considered as significant by NURP, differences were observed and reported in the final report (see Table 21.2).

- Fecal coliform EMCs varied from 300 to 281,000 organisms per 100 ml during warm weather and from 20 to 3,300 organisms per 100 ml during cold weather. One cold weather sample, however, reported 330,000 organisms per 100 ml, which appears not to be representative and may have been the result of sample contamination.

- No corrolation was found between EMCs and runoff volumes, indicating that EMCs and runoff volumes are, for the most part, independent of each other.

- Runoff volume coefficient exhibited a logarithmic correlation to total basin imperviousness.

The NURP Final Report states that there are little, if any, statistically significant differences in constituent EMCs between geographic regions, be-

TABLE 21.2   Median EMC for All NURP Sites by Land Use Category

Constituent (mg/l)	RESIDENTIAL		MIXED		COMMERCIAL		OPEN/ NONURBAN	
	Median	CV	Median	CV	Median	CV	Median	CV
BOD	10.000	0.41	7.800	0.52	9.300	0.31	—	—
COD	73.000	0.55	65.000	0.58	57.000	0.39	40.000	0.78
TSS	101.000	0.96	67.000	1.10	69.000	0.85	70.000	2.90
Pb	0.144	0.75	0.114	1.40	0.104	0.68	0.030	1.50
Cu	0.033	0.99	0.027	1.30	0.029	0.81	—	—
Zn	0.135	0.84	0.154	0.78	0.226	1.10	0.195	0.66
TKN	1.900	0.73	1.290	0.50	1.180	0.43	0.965	1.00
NO_{2+3}	0.736	0.83	0.558	0.67	0.572	0.48	0.543	0.91
TP	0.383	0.69	0.263	0.75	0.201	0.67	0.121	1.70
SP	0.143	0.46	0.056	0.75	0.080	0.71	0.026	2.10

Note: CV stands for coefficient of variance.
After EPA, 1983

tween various cities, or between storm events at a given site. The results appear to be relatively uniform across the United States. However, the data reveals wide ranges in EMCs of all constituents. This finding tends to support the need for local data before making what may be far-reaching and expensive water quality management decisions.

21.2 SUSPENDED SOLIDS IN STORMWATER

We begin by discussing primarily total suspended solids (TSS) in stormwater, their characteristics, and the technology for their removal. It was the belief that the removal of TSS from stormwater would also be accompanied by a proportionate removal of other pollutants. This assumption was shown not to always be the case. Nevertheless, most pollutants appear to have a strong affinity to suspended solids, and the removal of TSS will very often remove many of the other pollutants found in urban stormwater.

Apparent exceptions to the assumption that the removal of TSS will also remove other pollutants are dissolved solids, nitrites and nitrates ($NO_{2\&3}$), and soluble phosphorus (SP). Dry detention basins, namely, basins that drain fully between storm events and have no permanent pool of water, have consistently exhibited very poor dissolved $NO_{2\&3}$ and SP removal efficiencies. Because the reductions in the $NO_{2\&3}$ and SP EMCs are difficult to achieve, facilities designed for their removal should provide significant reductions in the EMCs of other pollutants. Detention storage basins that have a permanent pool appear to provide the best efficiencies in reducing dissolved $NO_{2\&3}$ and SP concentrations.

21.2.1 Factors Affecting Settlement of TSS

As noted, stormwater quality appears to vary from one location to the next. Of significance are the type and quantities of pollutants found in stormwater and to what degree these pollutants may be associated with sediments. It is, therefore, a good idea to sample and analyze the stormwater that is to be treated in water quality enhancement basins. Among others, the following factors seem to be of significance in describing the settling characteristics of TSS and associated pollutants:

- pollutant load in the stormwater by type;
- the percentages of settleable pollutants;
- particle size distribution;
- distribution of the solids by their settling velocities;
- distribution of pollutants by settling velocities;
- particle volume distribution of the solids; and
- the density of the settleable pollutants.

21.2.2 First Flush vs. No First Flush

Pollutants enter stormwater in many ways, among which are the following:

- Pollutants are absorbed as the raindrops pass through the atmosphere.
- Pollutants are washed off the paved and unpaved surfaces by stormwater runoff.
- Pollutants that have accumulated since the last storm in sewers, ditches, and channels are picked up by the new stormwater. This source can be also aggravated by illegal wastewater connections to the stormwater conveyance system.

Some studies show that the pollutant concentrations are largest early in the runoff process. This is explained by speculating that the paved surfaces are most polluted before rain begins. As rainfall continues, the surface pollutant accumulation is depleted and pollutants are diluted by the larger flows in the transport system. Also, it is speculated that the so-called first flush also depends on the intensity and the duration of rainfall.

Studies at other sites have not found an identifiable first flush. At those sites, the pollutant concentration seems to have no relation to the duration of rainfall. This was the case in the Denver Urban Runoff Evaluation Project by DRCOG (1982). Some speculated that because Denver is in a semi-arid climate, the runoff never left first flush. This point of view is not supported by the data, since some of the storm events were in excess of 1.5 inches and had sufficient duration to clearly show if there was a strong first flush. Also, the EPA (1983) reported a nonexistent negative statistical correlation between EMCs and runoff volumes (i.e., $r^2 = 0.3$). If first flush was uniformly present, a much stronger negative correlation should have been found.

As a result of the conflicting findings, it is not appropriate to assume that by merely capturing the first flush most of the pollutants will be captured. In fact, lacking local data, it is safer to assume that there is no first flush. If local investigations do find a significant first flush, then it is necessary to define its volume and duration. It has been suggested that a strong first flush is present when 20% of the runoff contains 80% of the pollutants. This is not a truism, and the definition will vary between communities and investigators. Nevertheless, its quantification can significantly simplify the definition of the volume of runoff that has to be captured and treated.

21.2.3 Initial TSS Concentrations vs. TSS Removal

Stockholm's Water and Sewer Works (1978), namely their water works department, found that the rate of sedimentation is dependent on the initial concentration of TSS in stormwater. Figure 21.2 compares data of incoming TSS concentrations against the percent reduction in TSS in stormwater collected at a sedimentation tunnel near Stockholm. A clear trend supporting a correlation between incoming TSS concentrations and its removal can be seen in this figure. The same study also revealed that this installation could not reduce the TSS concentrations to lower than 10 to 20 milligrams per liter.

In contrast, recent laboratory settling studies in the United States by Randall et al. (1982) showed that even very small initial TSS concentrations in stormwater can be reduced further. Of course, these findings were for nondynamic conditions in laboratory settling tubes (see Table 21.3) and not for dynamic field conditions. The findings by Randall et al. support the Swedish findings that the amount of sediment removed through settling increases with increasing initial concentration of TSS.

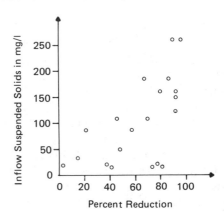

Figure 21.2   Percent reduction in TSS vs. the TSS concentrations in the inflow. (After Stockholm's Water and Sewer Works, 1978.)

TABLE 21.3   Time to Remove 60% of TSS at 4-foot Depth

Initial TSS, mg/l:	15	35	38	100	155	215	721
Settling time, hours:	38	24	8	5	1.0	1.5	0.5

After Randall et al., 1982

21.2.4 Easily Settling Pollutants

Currently, there is an interest to quantify the TSS in stormwater for the purpose of designing sedimentation facilities. Since many of the pollutants are attached to the solids, the removal of TSS will also remove many of the other pollutants. Unfortunately, as reported by Sartor and Boyd (1977), most of the pollutants are attached to the smaller size fractions of the TSS and are difficult to settle out. That is particularly a problem in the dynamic and turbulent environment found in a detention basin as it first fills with water and then is drained. Turbulence and wave action can maintain fine particles in suspension and even resuspend them from the bottom of the basin.

The settling ability of pollutants via the removal of TSS from stormwater involves the removal of different sized and density particles. The heavier particles will obviously settle out earlier than the lighter ones. As a result, there is a fraction of TSS that can be easily removed by simply holding the water for a short period of time in a forebay, which we call a *coarse pollutant chamber*. Such a chamber should be designed to detain the water for approximately five minutes during an average runoff event.

Particle weight by itself is not a total indicator of whether or not a particle will settle out rapidly. The proclivity of any individual particle to settle easily is also determined by the particle's effective density; namely, weight divided by total volume. As a result, some large particles may be difficult to remove through settling if their effective density is very low.

21.2.5 Particle Size Distribution of TSS

Laboratory particle size distribution and settling tests of urban pollutants were conducted by the EPA (1983, 1986), Grizzard, et al. (1986), Randall et al. (1982), Rinella and McKenzie (1982), and Whipple and Hunter (1981). In addition, Peter Stahre studied particle size distribution in Sweden. Stahre used a light blocking instrument developed by Wiksell (1976) which can measure 15 different TSS size intervals ranging from 2 to 500 microns (μm). All of the samples analyzed had first undergone a coarse separation using five minutes of sedimentation.

Stahre's findings are shown as a bar graph in Figure 21.3. As can be seen in this figure, the number of particles is greatest in the 10 to 20 μm range, while the numbers for particles larger than 40 μm are less than 10 particles per milliliter. Because of their small numbers, they do not appear on this graph.

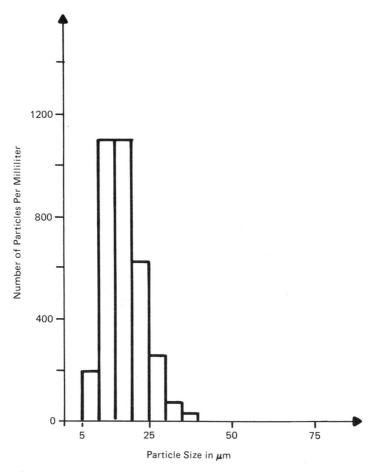

Figure 21.3 Sample of particle size distribution found in studies of stormwater by Stahre in Sweden.

A similar study, but using different instrumentation, was performed by Rinella and McKenzie (1982) of the U.S. Geological Survey in Portland, Oregon. They, on the other hand, did not use coarse separation of sediments before performing particle size analysis. We have summarized the results of their analysis of the February 12, 1981 Fanno Creek sample in Table 21.4. It can be seen that only 30% of all TSS by weight was found to have particles larger than 31 μm in diameter.

A similar study in Virginia by Randall et al. (1982) found that 80% of particles by weight were less than 25 μm, 89% were less than 35 μm, and 93% were less than 45 μm in size. The common theme among the three investigators supports the findings of Sartor and Boyd (1977) that most suspended pollutants in stormwater are associated with relatively small particles.

TABLE 21.4   TSS Distribution by Size of Particles in February 12, 1981
Sample of Fanno Creek

Particle Size (Microns)	TSS Load mg/l	Percent Finer than Given Size	Percent Increment of Sample
All sizes	832	100	100
<62	701	84	16
<31	584	70	14
<15	391	47	23
<8	262	31	16
<4	222	27	4

After Rinella and McKenzie, 1982

A word of caution about the data reported in this book. All of the data are representative only of the sampling sites from which they were taken. They may or may not be representative of other urban sites. Although we believe that the data reported here provide reasonable trends found in urban runoff, they should not be construed as applicable for any specific site you may study. We suggest that local data be collected for design and planning purposes.

21.2.6 Particle Volume Distribution

To help understand the makeup of the TSS in stormwater, we also discuss the distribution of volumes and surface areas by size of particles. A microscopic study of stormwater samples revealed that for the most part, particles in stormwater can be considered to be spherical in shape. This means that one can simply transform the particle size distribution into particle volume distribution. Figure 21.4 contains a bar graph of such transformation based on the same data used in the development of Figure 21.3.

An examination of Figure 21.4 reveals that very little volume of TSS is found in particles that are less than 5 microns in diameter. On the other hand, the 10 to 35 μm sized particles account for 90% of the TSS volume in this sample. Also of note is the fact that the volume of particles larger than 40 μm in diameter represent a significant fraction of the total TSS load. You may recall that this fraction did not even appear in Figure 21.3. This indicates that a relatively small number of particles can, in fact, represent a relatively significant load by volume and weight of the total TSS measured in stormwater.

As discussed earlier, some sites exhibit a first flush in pollutant loads. At those locations, the particle size and volume distribution can vary significantly throughout the storm. How the TSS volume distribution varied with time during one stormwater runoff event in Sweden is illustrated as a bar graph in Figure 21.5. This point is further illustrated in Figure 21.6 as a line graph of the total TSS volume vs. time from beginning of storm. From both of these figures, it is evident that the total particle volume in milliliters per liter de-

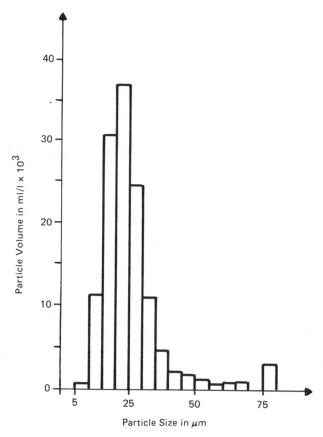

Figure 21.4   Sample of particle volume distribution found in studies of stormwater by Stahre in Sweden.

creased 75% in just 20 minutes. Such a finding at any location can significantly aid in the design of water quality detention facilities.

21.2.7 Particle Area Distribution

Knowledge of the distribution of particle volumes can indicate the weight of each particle size in TSS. Studies by Randall et al. (1982) revealed that the settling of pollutants occurs in two ways. First, the coarser particles settle out as discrete individual particles. The smaller particles, on the other hand, tend to agglomerate with time into larger particles, and their settling rate then accelerates. As a result, simple settling estimates may not reveal the actual mechanism of removal. The process can be multistepped and time-dependent. In other words, the removal of TSS and attached pollutants may in

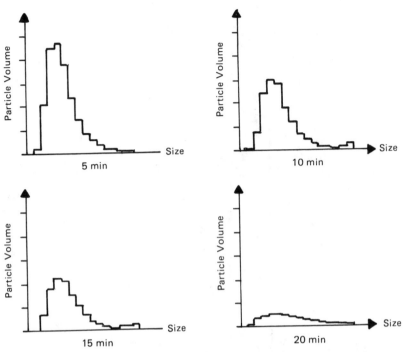

Figure 21.5   Sample particle volume distribution variation with time from start of runoff, according to Stahre.

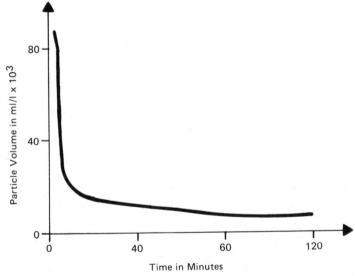

Figure 21.6   Sample of particle volume variation with time from start of runoff, according to Stahre.

fact occur in steps, and the smaller particles may not be removed if the residence time in the detention facility is insufficient for flocculation to take place.

Knowledge of how the total surface area of the particulates varies with particle size can help us appreciate how other pollutants that attach to TSS may be removed. It is the available surface area that is used by ionic forms of other pollutants to bond to the particles. Also, agglomeration of smaller particles into larger ones is probably a function of the surface area available for the bonding to occur. A study by Grizzard et al. (1986) indicated that the majority of particle surface area was found in particles having a diameter of less than 50 to 60 microns (see Figure 21.7). These findings are based on the particle size distribution reported by Randall et al. (1982) and discussed near the end of Section 21.2.5.

21.2.8 Density of Stormwater Pollutants

To calculate the settling velocity for a particle with a known size, it is necessary to know the density of that particle. There are other, more direct, ways of finding the particle settling velocity than by measuring particle sizes and their densities. These more direct techniques are described later, but for now we discuss particle density to help explain the basic principles of sedimentation in storage basins.

Density data is scarce and is often contradictory. Oscanyan (1975) re-

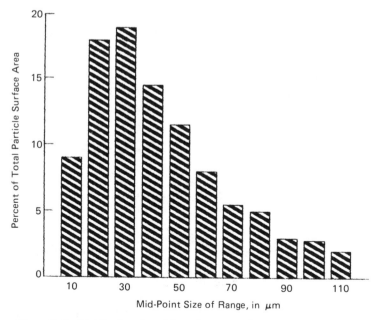

Figure 21.7   Distribution of particle surface areas. (After Grizzard, 1986.)

ported 165 pounds per cubic foot (2,650 kg/m³) per cubic meter as the operative particle density. Obviously, this value is based on the specific gravity of solid rock materials and it is assumed that no pores are present within the TSS particles. Bondurant et al. (1975) reported TSS particle densities of 69 to 81 pounds per cubic foot (1,100 to 1,300 kg/m³).

Peter Stahre performed a number of studies to determine the particle densities of TSS in stormwater samples collected in Sweden. His findings suggest that particle densities, among other things, depend on

- particle size,
- the pH of the water, and
- the content of heavy metals in the water.

Exactly how the density depends on these factors has not been clarified. It was found that it helps to describe the variations in densities if the particles are separated into two groups. The first is made up of particles having densities of 62 to 72 pounds per cubic foot (1,000 to 1,160 kg/m³) (light particles) and the second of particles having densities greater than 72 pounds per cubic foot (1,160 kg/m³). For the latter, it was assumed that the average density of particles is 81 pounds per cubic foot (1,300 kg/m³). For comparison, water has a density of 62 pounds per cubic foot (1,000 kg/m³) at a temperature of 20°C.

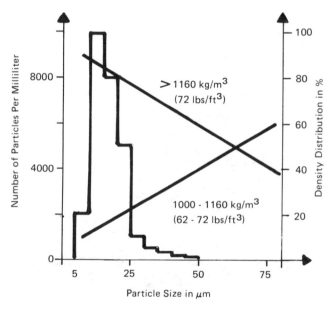

Figure 21.8 Sample TSS density distribution by particle size, according to Stahre.

Figure 21.8 illustrates how the density distribution varies with particle size for the two density groups. We see that the proportion of heavier density particles declines with increasing particle size. At the same time, the proportion of lighter density particles increases with particle size. Also, some of the results suggested that the decrease for the heavier particles is less pronounced at lower pH, which may be related to dissolved metals in the water.

21.2.9 Particle Settling Velocity Distribution

As mentioned earlier, settling velocity tests for samples of urban stormwater runoff were reported by EPA (1986), Rinella and McKenzie (1982), Randall et al. (1982), and Whipple and Hunter (1981). The most extensive set of data used for this purpose was in support of the EPA (1986) document. It was based on 50 different runoff samples from seven different sites, which among others included the data gathered under NURP and the results reported by Whipple and Hunter (1981).

The data was found to vary as much between runoff events at the same site as between different sites. As a result, all data were combined and presented as typical for urban stormwater (see Figure 21.9). Based on this data and Figure 21.9, Table 21.5 was presented by the EPA (1986) which groups all the settling velocities as five distinct size fractions. While these "typical" results can suffice for initial planning estimates, it may be wise to obtain site-specific settling velocity data for final design.

Site-specific settling velocity measurements are not difficult to perform. The equipment for such measurements was suggested by Whipple (1981), Rinella and McKenzie (1982), and others. It is briefly described, along with the suggested procedure, in the 1986 EPA publication on detention basins. It basically consists of a vertical clear plastic settling cylinder approximately 6 inches (15 cm) in diameter and 6 feet (1.8 m) high (see Figure 21.10). Usually, four sampling ports are installed in its side at 1-foot (30-cm) intervals measured from the top.

The tube is filled with stormwater runoff sample and small samples are withdrawn from the ports at preset time intervals. These are usually taken at 0.5, 1, 2, 4, 8, 12, 24, and 48 hours, and the samples are analyzed for TSS and/or other constituents. The constituent concentrations are then compared against the initial, fully-mixed sample, and the concentrations and the percent removal, port depth h, and time t are recorded. The settling velocity is simply the ratio of port depth and time (i.e., h/t). Thus, each percent removal measurement is plotted as the percent with a settling velocity equal to or less than the indicated value vs. settling velocity (see Figure 21.9). Figure 21.10 illustrates the equipment and the calculating procedure as it was presented in the EPA's 1986 publication titled *Methodology for Analysis of Detention Basins for Urban Runoff Quality*.

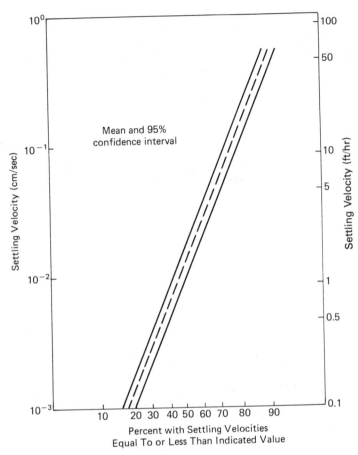

Figure 21.9 Probability distribution of particle settling velocities in urban runoff. (After EPA, 1986.)

TABLE 21.5 TSS Settling Velocity Distribution Feet for Five Size Fractions

Size Fraction	% of TSS in Urban Runoff	Average Settling Velocity	
		Feet per Hour	Centimeters per Second
1	0–20	0.03	0.25×10^{-3}
2	20–40	0.30	2.54×10^{-3}
3	40–60	1.50	12.7×10^{-3}
4	60–80	7.00	59.3×10^{-3}
5	80–100	65.00	550×10^{-3}

After EPA, 1986

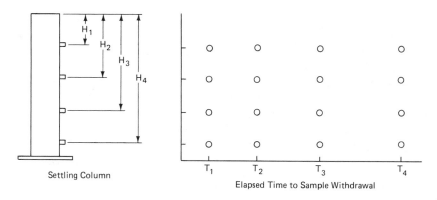

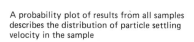

O = Data Point - Record % removed based on observed vs. initial concentration

Settling velocity (V_S) for that removal fraction is determined from the corresponding sample depth (h) and time (t)
$V_S = H/T$

Observed % removed reflects the fraction with velocities equal or greater than computed V_S

A probability plot of results from all samples describes the distribution of particle settling velocity in the sample

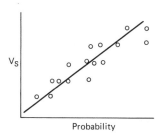

Figure 21.10   Particle settling velocity measurement equipment and procedure. (After EPA, 1986.)

REFERENCES

BONDURANT, J. A., BROCKWAY, C. E., AND BROWN, M. J., "Some Aspects of Sedimentation Pond Design," *National Symposium on Urban Hydrology and Sediment Control,* University of Kentucky, 1975.

DRCOG, *Denver Urban Runoff Evaluation Program, Final Report,* Denver Regional Council of Governments, Denver, Colo., 1982.

EPA, *Results of the Nationwide Urban Runoff Program,* Final Report, U.S. Environmental Agency, NTIS Accession No. PB84-185552, December, 1983.

EPA, *Methodology for Analysis of Detention Basins for Control of Urban Runoff Quality,* U.S. Environmental Agency, EPA440/5-87-001, September, 1986.

GRIZZARD, T. J., RANDALL, C. W., WEAND, B. L., AND ELLIS, K. L., "Effectiveness of Extended Detention Ponds," *Urban Runoff Quality—Impacts and Quality Enhancement Technology,* Proceedings of an Engineering Foundation Conference, ASCE, 1986.

OSCANYAN, P., "Design of Sediment Basins for Construction Sites," *National Symposium on Urban Hydrology and Sediment Controls,* University of Kentucky, 1975.

RANDALL, C. W., ELLIS, K., GRIZZARD, T. J., AND KNOCKE, W. R., "Urban Runoff Pollutant Removal by Sedimentation," *Stormwater Detention Facilities,* Proceedings of an Engineering Foundation Conference, ASCE, 1982.

RINELLA J. F., AND MCKENZIE, S. W., "Determining the Settling of Suspended Chemicals," *Stormwater Detention Facilities,* Proceedings of an Engineering Foundation Conference, ASCE, 1982.

SARTOR, J. D., AND BOYD, G. B., "Water Pollutant Aspects of Street Surface Contaminants," U.S. Environmental Protection Agency, EPA-600/2-77-047, 1977.

STOCKHOLM'S WATER AND SEWER WORKS, *Stormwater Studies at Jarvafaltet,* 1978. (In Swedish)

WHIPPLE, W. JR., AND HUNTER, J. V., "Settling Ability of Urban Pollution," *Water Pollution Control Federation Journal,* Vol. 53(12), pp. 1726–31, December, 1981.

WIKSELL, H. "Development of an Instrument for Measuring Particle Size Distribution in Water and Sewerage Engineering," *Vatten* No. 1, 1976. (In Swedish)

22

Fundamentals of Sedimentation

22.1 INTRODUCTION

Sedimentation occurs when particles have a greater density than the surrounding liquid. Under laboratory quiescent conditions, it is possible to settle out very small particles; the smallest practical settling size in the field is around 10 micrometers (Metcalf & Eddy, 1979). The smallest particles have been observed sometimes to become electrically charged, which can further interfere with their ability to settle out. The fact is that we do not know if there is a particle size limit for separation by settling in water. If there is a lower limit, it probably is site-specific.

We briefly describe the following basic relationships that are often used to quantify the sedimentation process:

- Newton's formula,
- Stokes' law, and
- Hazen's surface load theory.

22.2 Newton's and Stokes' Sedimentation Laws

For spherical particles falling through a liquid, Newton suggested the following formula to define their maximum fall velocity:

$$v_s = \sqrt{\frac{4}{3} \cdot \frac{d \cdot g \cdot (r_p - r_v)}{C_D \cdot r_v}} \qquad (22.1)$$

in which v_s = fall velocity of the particle,
d = diameter of the particle,
r_p = density of the particle,
r_v = density of the fluid,
g = acceleration of gravity, and
C_D = drag coefficient of the particle.

The drag coefficient C_D will depend on whether the flow around the particle is laminar or turbulent and is a function of the Reynolds Number (Re) (see Figure 22.1). For Reynolds Numbers between 0.3 and 10,000, the drag coefficient can be approximated using the following equation:

$$C_D = \frac{24}{Re} + \frac{3}{\sqrt{Re}} + 0.34 \qquad (22.2)$$

For Reynolds Numbers smaller than 0.3, one can neglect the last two terms of the preceding equation, and the drag coefficient can be approximated using

$$C_D = \frac{24}{Re} \qquad (22.3)$$

By substituting the following equation into the preceding expression

$$Re = \frac{v_s \cdot d \cdot r_v}{\mu} \qquad (22.4)$$

and combining it with Newton's Formula for particle fall velocity, one obtains Stokes' law:

$$v_s = d^2 \cdot g \cdot \frac{(r_p - r_v)}{18 \cdot \mu} \qquad (22.5)$$

in which μ = dynamic viscosity of the fluid.

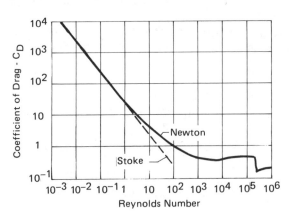

Figure 22.1 Drag coefficient C_D vs. Reynolds Number for spherical particles. (After McCabe and Smith, 1976.)

The fall velocity is directly proportional to the square of the particle diameter and the difference in the densities between the particle and the fluid. In water, Stokes' law is applicable to particles having an equivalent spherical diameter of up to 100 microns.

If the dynamic viscosity of the water and the density of the particles are known, the fall velocity can be calculated as a function of particle diameter. Figure 22.2 shows the results of such a calculation assuming the fluid is water at 15°C. As can be seen, the particle's density has a significant effect on the fall velocity. For example, a decrease in density from 2,000 to 1,500 kilograms per cubic meter, i.e., a decrease in specific gravity from 2.00 to 1.50, will reduce the particle's fall velocity by approximately one-half.

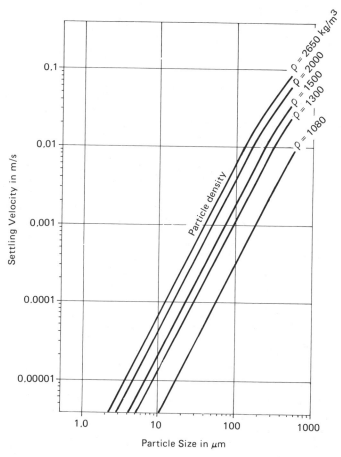

Figure 22.2 Theoretical fall velocity of spherical particles in water at a temperature of 15°C.

22.3 HAZEN'S SURFACE LOAD THEORY

Hazen's surface load theory assumes that for a particle to be permanently removed from the water column, it must reach the bottom of a basin before the water carrying it leaves the basin. Consider a long rectangular basin of length L, width W, and depth D. The surface area A of the basin is then

$$A = W \cdot L \qquad (22.6)$$

and the volume V is

$$V = A \cdot D \qquad (22.7)$$

Further, assume that fluid passing through the basin at a flow rate of Q is uniformly distributed over the cross-section $W \cdot H$ and that all the particles which have time to sink to the bottom will be permanently removed from the fluid. The descent height is the largest for particles entering the basin at the water surface (i.e., D, the depth of the basin).

The time T for the flow to pass through the basin can be given by

$$T = \frac{V}{Q} = \frac{(A \cdot D)}{Q} \qquad (22.8)$$

For a particle to settle to the bottom as it passes through the basin, its average descent velocity has to be at least

$$v_s = \frac{D}{T} = \frac{Q}{A} \qquad (22.9)$$

It can thus be stated that the sedimentation effect of a basin can be expressed by the ratio between Q and A, which is sometimes referred to as the surface load. Equation 22.9 states that the surface load is equal to the descent rate of the smallest particle that can just be separated in the basin.

This surface load theory presupposes that the flow through the basin is uniform and laminar. Unfortunately, these are not the conditions found in practice. A field installation can experience multilayered flow, turbulence, eddies, circulation currents, diffusion at inlets and outlets, etc. (see Figure 22.3). Some investigators speculate that under turbulent conditions no more than 60% of the removal predicted using Hazen theory is achieved. In design, correction factors are used to compensate for this observed difference between theory and actual performance.

According to the preceding equations, depth has nothing to do with sediment removal in a basin. However, because of turbulence, diffusion, and local velocities, sediments can be resuspended from the bottom. To reduce the chances of resuspension, it is recommended that the average basin depth be no less than 3.5 feet (1.07 m). It is suggested, however, that sedimentation basins be between 5 and 12 feet (1.5 and 3.5 m) deep.

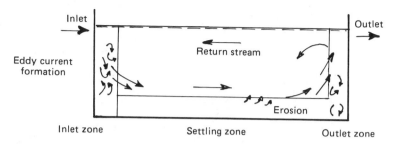

Inlet →   Outlet →

Eddy current formation   Return stream ←   Erosion

Inlet zone   Settling zone   Outlet zone

Figure 22.3   Examples of flow disturbances in a basin.

22.4 SEDIMENTATION IN STORMWATER UNDER QUIESCENT CONDITIONS

Until the early 1980s, very few studies dealt with the separation of pollutants from stormwater by sedimentation. One of these is further commented on here; namely, the work by Peter Stahre in Sweden. Since then, studies by Rinella and McKenzie (1983), Randall et al. (1982), and Whipple and Hunter (1981) have produced significant new information about the settling characteristics of TSS and associated pollutants. Nevertheless, the literature on this topic is still very limited.

22.4.1 Stahre's Findings

A more comprehensive study of sedimentation properties of TSS in stormwater was conducted by Stahre. He investigated how particle size distribution and particle volume varies with time. Using a pipette, Stahre sampled water in a settling tube at various times after settling was permitted to begin. During the first hour, samples were taken at 5-minute intervals. After that, additional samples were taken at 90 and 120 minutes. Each sample was analyzed for particle size distribution, and the particle volume distribution by particle size was calculated.

Figures 22.4 and 22.5 depict Stahre's findings of particle numbers and volumes for each size fraction in the water column as a function of sedimentation time. Both figures show results only for particles smaller than 25 microns.

As can be seen in Figure 22.4, the number of particles in the 5 to 10 micron size appears to increase rapidly during the first hour and continues to increase for a total of 90 minutes from the start of the test. After that, the number of particles appears to decrease. Something similar was observed for the 10 to 15 micron size fraction, except the numbers increased only very slightly for the first 15 minutes.

An explanation for this apparently unusual finding was offered by Stahre. He speculated that the equipment that counted the particles may have

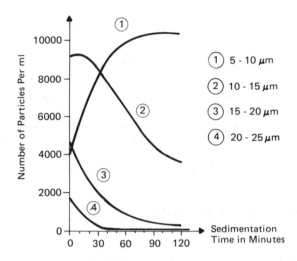

Figure 22.4   Number of particles in water column as a function of sedimentation time.

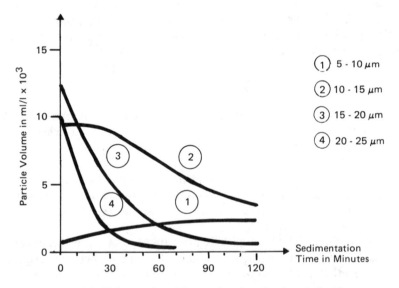

Figure 22.5   Volumes of particles as a function of sedimentation time.

mistaken small air bubbles in the water for particles. He did not, however, explain what may have caused the small air bubbles to appear early in the test. Regardless, because the 5 to 10 micron particles are very small, they contribute very little to the volume estimates of the suspended solids in the water column (see Figure 22.5).

By compositing all of the size fractions into a single volume of suspended solids, Stahre obtained a very smooth, exponentially decaying curve. This is shown in Figure 22.6, where the effect of sedimentation time is related to the total volume of suspended solid particles remaining in the water column.

22.4.2 Randall's Findings

Randall et al. (1982) reported results of laboratory settling tube tests of seven urban stormwater runoff samples. They found that the TSS concentration after 48 hours of sedimentation leveled off to between 5 and 10 milligrams per liter (see Figures 22.7 and 22.8). This is similar to the findings reported for sedimentation tunnels in Sweden, where the TSS concentrations bottomed out at 10 milligrams per liter. Although the settling tube tests appear to have somewhat lower final concentrations, both sets of results indicate a practical bottom limit of approximately 10 milligrams per liter in the removal of TSS by sedimentation.

The Randall et al. findings confirm another observation in Sweden, namely the percentage of TSS removed increased as the initial TSS concentration increased. Stahre and Urbonas plotted Randall's data as percent TSS

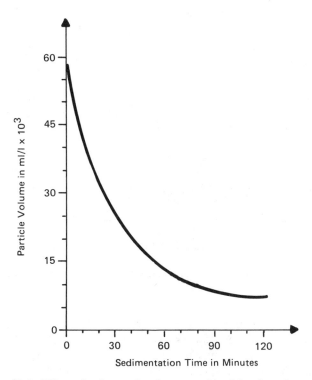

Figure 22.6   Effects of sedimentation time on total particle volume in stormwater.

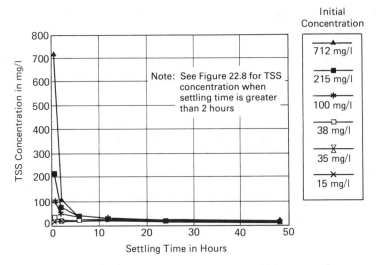

Figure 22.7 Effects of time of sedimentation on TSS concentrations. (After Randall et al., 1982.)

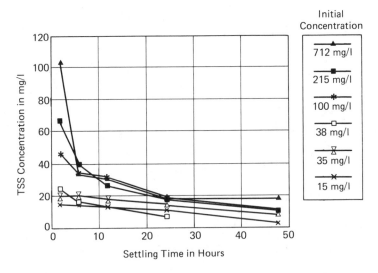

Figure 22.8 Effects of time of sedimentation, 2 to 48 hours, on TSS concentrations. (After Randall et al., 1982.)

removed vs. initial concentration (see Figure 22.9). This graph clearly indicates that the TSS removal efficiencies are very poor when initial concentrations are around 10 milligrams per liter. The removal efficiencies increase rapidly as the initial concentration increases to about 100 milligrams per liter, after which the removal efficiency begins to level off.

In addition to TSS, Randall's group also conducted settling characteristics tests in settling tubes for several other constituents found in the same stormwater samples. None of the other constituents exhibited the same consistency or uniformity in removal efficiencies found for TSS. However, it was clear that sedimentation was able to reduce their concentrations in water. Figures 22.10 through 22.14 contain graphs showing percent removal vs. sedimentation time for several of the constituents.

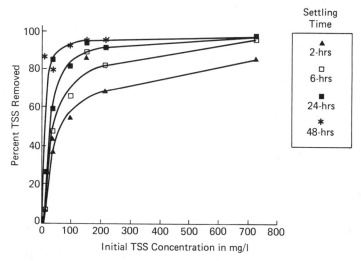

Figure 22.9   Effects of initial TSS concentration on removal rates. (After Randall et al., 1982.)

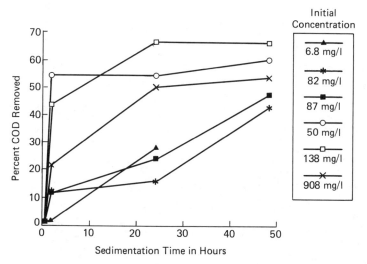

Figure 22.10   Percent COD removed vs. sedimentation time. (After Randall et al., 1982.)

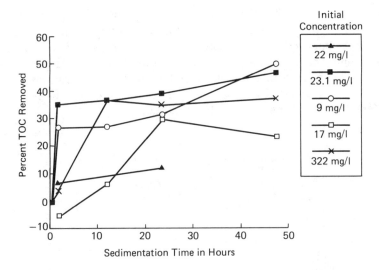

Figure 22.11 Percent TOC removed vs. sedimentation time. (After Randall et al., 1982.)

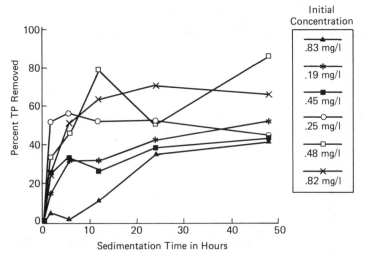

Figure 22.12 Percent TP removed vs. sedimentation time. (After Randall et al., 1982.)

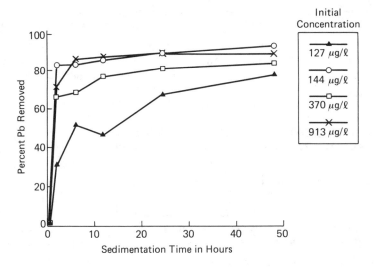

Figure 22.13   Percent Pb removed vs. sedimentation time. (After Randall et al., 1982.)

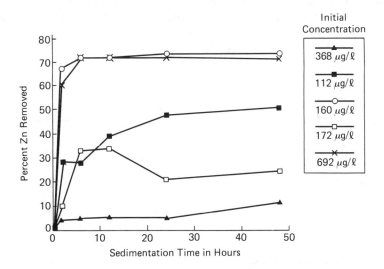

Figure 22.14   Percent Zn removed vs. sedimentation time. (After Randall et al., 1982.)

After 48 hours of sedimentation, COD removal was observed to range between 40% and 65%, TOC between 20% and 50%, TP between 40% and 80%, Pb between 75% and 95%, and Zn between 10% and 70%. All of these ranges can be viewed as possible maximum removal rates in detention ponds which, because of their dynamic flow conditions, are not likely to be as efficient.

22.5 SEDIMENTATION UNDER FLOW-THROUGH CONDITIONS

22.5.1 Kuo's Findings

Sedimentation in stormwater detention basins does not occur under static conditions. Typically, sedimentation basins are designed for chronological flow-through. Unfortunately, very few experiments of sedimentation under these conditions have been performed, with Kuo (1976) being one of the few to have actually conducted such tests. He reported his results from tests conducted in a flow-through setup depicted in Figure 22.15.

In the first set of tests, Kuo held the basin length constant at 19.7 feet (6 m) and the depth was varied between 3.3 and 13.1 feet (1 and 4 m). The tests were performed using water carrying sediment having particle sizes of 55, 126, and 290 microns. Kuo's findings for the first set of these tests were plotted as the ratio of basin length over depth (i.e., L/D) vs. percent sediment removed for different particle sizes (see Figure 22.16). These figures indicate

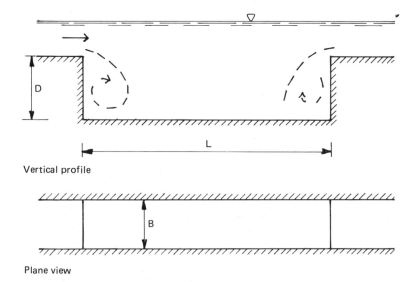

Vertical profile

Plane view

Figure 22.15   Test basin for flow-through separation of TSS. (After Kuo, 1976.)

that the sediment removal efficiency is independent of basin depth, which supports the surface load theory derived by Hazen.

In the next set of experiments, Kuo held the basin depth constant at 2.4 meters and varied the length between 19.7 and 98.4 feet (6 and 30 m). Again, the basin L/D vs. percent sediment removed were plotted for different particle sizes (see Figure 22.17). As indicated in the figure, TSS removal improved with basin length. The improvement was most apparent for the larger sized particles.

Next, Kuo held the basin depth and basin length constant and varied the flow through rate between 39.9 and 120 feet per second (1.13 and 3.40 m³/s). Figure 22.18 contains a plot of these results, showing that sedimentation improved as the flow rate, and the resultant surface loading, decreased.

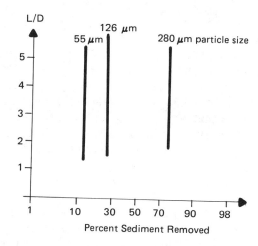

Figure 22.16 Sediment removal as affected by basin depth for $L = 19.7$ feet (6 m). (After Kuo, 1976.)

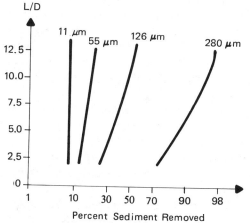

Figure 22.17 Sediment removal as affected by basin length for $D = 7.9$ feet (2.4 m). (After Kuo, 1976.)

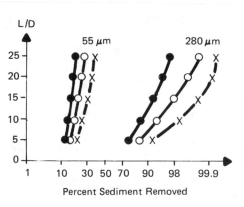

Figure 22.18 Sediment removal as affected by flow-through rate. (After Kuo, 1976.)

Again, the differences were most significant for the largest particles. Nevertheless, Kuo's findings appear to support the original surface loading theory proposed by Hazen. We have to stress that these tests were performed under controlled laboratory conditions. In the field, the flows vary with time, there is a possibility of particle resuspension, and density and temperature currents are likely. As a result, we caution in using these findings and suggest that a safety factor be applied to compensate for unpredictable field conditions.

22.5.2 Grizzard's Findings

Grizzard et al. (1986) reported the results of a study comparing the laboratory settling tube test results against the pollutant removal rates at a prototype field installation. The facility being studied received runoff from a townhouse complex of 34.4 acres (13.9 ha) having 19.2% impervious cover. The extended detention basin was expected to drain completely between storms and was designed with a brim full water quality detention volume of 38,000 cubic feet (1076 m³). This is equivalent to 0.3 inches (7.6 mm) of runoff from the entire site or 1.55 inches (39.4 mm) of runoff from the impervious surfaces only.

The outlet was sized to drain the total water quality detention volume in 40 hours. As a result, the average drawdown time for all storm events during the test period was expected to be approximately 24 hours. Due to unanticipated leakage at the outlet, the test basin emptied in approximately 10 hours when full, and the more frequent storm events drained in approximately six hours.

The stormwater samples were compared to the laboratory settling tube results described in section 22.4.2. Grizzard found that for many of the pollutants, the prototype extended detention basin with a six-hour drawdown period had removal efficiencies comparable to those found in settling tubes after approximately two hours. There were several exceptions to this. One was for total phosphorous (TP). The removal rate for TP in the field was 6 hours, compared to the one-half hour removal rate in the settling tube. In other words, the basin performed very poorly in removing TP when compared to settling tube tests.

Another exception was the results for the removals of Pb and Zn, for which the field removal rate was equivalent to the settling tube test results after 24 hours of settling. Thus, for at least these particular tests, the pond out-performed the settling tube results in removing Pb and Zn.

It is worth noting that the lesser removal efficiencies in the pond for TP are consistent with findings by others for the removal of TP in dry ponds. Outside of this, the observed trends in an extended detention dry pond compared favorably with the settling tube results. Thus, by applying a safety factor to tube settling results, an extended detention pond outlet design could be based on settling tube test findings.

REFERENCES

GRIZZARD, T. J., RANDALL, C. W., WEAND, B. L., AND ELLIS, K. L., "Effectiveness of Extended Detention Ponds," *Urban Runoff Quality—Impacts and Quality Enhancement Technology,* Proceedings of an Engineering Foundation Conference, ASCE, 1986.

KUO, C. Y., "Sedimentation Routing in an In-Stream Settling Basin," *Proceedings of the National Symposium on Urban Hydrology, Hydraulics and Sediment Control,* University of Kentucky, 1976.

LISPER, P., *Pollution in Storm Water and Its Variations,* Dissertation, CTH, Sweden, 1974. (In Swedish)

MCCABE, W. L., AND SMITH, J. C., "Unit Operations of Chemical Engineering," 3rd edition, McGraw-Hill, 1979.

METCALF & EDDY, INC., *Wastewater Engineering, Treatment, Disposal, and Reuse,* 2nd edition, McGraw-Hill, 1976.

RANDALL, C. W., ELLIS, K., GRIZZARD, T. J., AND KNOCKE, W. R., "Urban Runoff Pollutant Removal by Sedimentation," *Proceedings of the Conference on Stormwater Detention Facilities,* ASCE, 1982.

RINELLA, J. F., AND MCKENZIE, S. W., *Methods for Relating Suspended-Chemical Concentrations to Suspended-Sediment Particle Size Classes in Storm-Water Runoff,* U.S. Geological Survey Water-Resources Investigation 82-39, Portland, Oreg., 1983.

WHIPPLE, W., AND HUNTER, J. V., "Settleability of Urban Runoff Pollution," *Journal Water Pollution Control Federation,* Vol. 53, No. 12, 1981, pp. 1726–31.

23

Design of Water Quality Basins
for Stormwater

23.1 INTRODUCTION

It is clear that the design of stormwater quality enhancement basins is an emerging technology. We attempted to provide in this book some of the technical basis for the removal of pollutants by sedimentation, which appears to be the primary water cleansing mechanism. Apparently, there are other water quality mechanisms at work also. As an example, in properly sized basins with a permanent pool of water, there is evidence of biological activity at work in the removal of nutrients (Randall, 1982).

The engineering profession is only beginning to learn about this technology, and the best we can offer here is what we have learned so far. More important, we caution you not to rely fully on any technique presented here or in any other publication to date. As in any emerging technology, there are many questions to be answered before we can design stormwater quality enhancement basins with complete confidence in how they will perform in the field. Also, we are dealing with random processes for which we can, at best, design only for a certain range of probable events. Larger storm events will happen. It is only a question of how often and when.

We discuss several design approaches, ranging from very technical to totally empirical and rule of thumb. We do not pass judgment on which of these basin sizing methods will give the best results. That will depend on the designer and on the water quality goals. All of the sizing methods are for the removal of the fine sediments and the constituents associated with fine sediments. In addition, we suggest a procedure for how to remove coarse sediments.

23.2 SIZING OF BASINS USING SURFACE LOAD THEORY

23.2.1 Basic Relationships

Separation of sediments from the water column occurs within the body of a detention pond. You may recall that according to the surface load theory, water depth in a pond should have no role in this separation process. We know, however, that this theory is only valid under uniform, steady, laminar flow conditions, which are not found in stormwater detention ponds.

To help us estimate sedimentation under turbulent flow conditions, we turn to the works of Dobbin (1944) and Camp (1946). They derived an analytical expression for sedimentation under turbulent flow conditions. Figure 23.1 is based on their work and shows how three nondimensional parameters relate, namely:

$$\frac{V_s}{\dfrac{Q}{A}}, \frac{V_s H}{2\epsilon}, \text{ and } E \qquad (23.1)$$

in which V_s = settling velocity of a particle,
Q/A = surface load,
H = water depth in the basin,
ϵ = diffusion coefficient, and
E = sedimentation effectiveness (i.e., the fraction of sediment removed).

With the help of Figure 23.1, it is possible to estimate the sedimentation effectiveness for various particle sizes. Examining this graph, we see that sedimentation is influenced by the flow conditions in the basin. Small values of $V_s H/2\epsilon$ correspond to turbulent flow and large values represent laminar flow conditions. As the value for this parameter increases, sedimentation effectiveness E approaches the value

$$E = \frac{V_s}{\dfrac{Q}{A}} \qquad (23.2)$$

which is in full agreement with Hazen's surface load theory. Now, if we assume that the velocity distribution in the basin is parabolic, the diffusion coefficient, according to Camp (1946) can be expressed as

$$\epsilon = 0.075 H \cdot \sqrt{\frac{\tau}{\rho}} \qquad (23.3)$$

in which H = water depth,
τ = critical shear stress, and
ρ = water density.

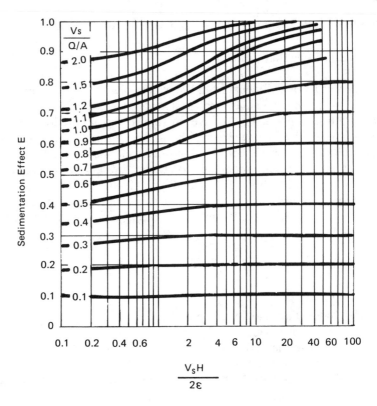

Figure 23.1 Diagram for estimating sedimentation. (After Camp, 1946.)

The value of critical shear stress is determined by the size and density of the smallest particle that will not be moved by water flowing through the basin. Figure 23.2 relates the values of critical shear stress for silicon particles to particle size and the purity of the water. This figure represents the recommendations by U.S. Bureau of Reclamation (1973) for non-eroding shear stress in channels. Notice that the critical shear stress stops declining when the particle sizes become small. This is attributed to cohesive forces between the smallest particles. Thus, if we use the critical shear stress values found at the extreme left of Figure 23.1, we should be working in a fairly conservative and stable range.

If the settling velocities, V_s, are known for all particles in the stormwater passing through a pond, we can estimate the sedimentation effectiveness of each size group with the aid of Figure 23.1. This can be done for any known or desired design surface loading (i.e., Q/A). Figure 23.3 presents the results of such calculations under the assumption that the parameter $V_s H/2\epsilon$ is equal to 0.1 (i.e., turbulent flow) and that only gravitational and tractive forces are at work during sedimentation. This assumption is questionable for particles

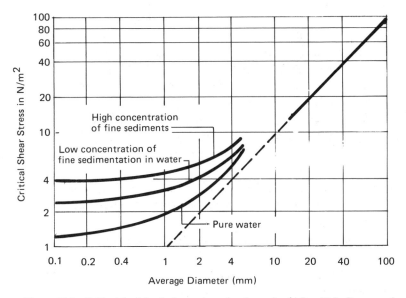

Figure 23.2 Critical bed load shear stress in channels. (After U.S. Bureau of Reclamation, 1973.)

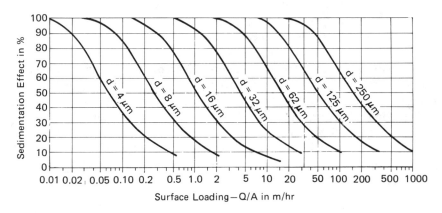

Figure 23.3 Sedimentation as a function of surface load for various particle sizes.

smaller than 5 to 10 microns in diameter, because electrostatic forces can influence their settling rates.

23.2.2 Suggested Pond Sizing Procedure

The preceding information can be put together into a procedure which can be used to size water quality enhancement ponds. The following suggested procedure has a physical basis and a theoretical foundation:

1. Determine the particle size and particle volume distribution associated with the pollutants in your stormwater samples.

2. Decide on the basis of the sediment data how much of the various particle sizes will need to be removed to achieve the desired water quality. Keep in mind that in some cases sedimentation alone may not achieve your goals.

3. Using Figure 23.3, make a preliminary estimate of the maximum allowable hydraulic surface loading rate.

4. With the aid of Figure 22.2, estimate the settling velocities for all representative particle sizes.

5. Using the information developed in steps 1 through 4, with the aid of Figure 23.1, calculate the sedimentation effectiveness for all of the representative particle sizes.

6. Composite the total sedimentation effectiveness using the results from step 5.

7. If the composite total sedimentation effectiveness is too small, repeat the calculations using a lower hydraulic surface loading rate than assumed in step 3.

8. After you are satisfied with the adequacy of the hydraulic surface loading rate, determine the surface area of the pond and its configuration. The hydraulic surface loading rate used can be based on the average flow-through rate in the storage basin.

The preceding calculating procedure is far from being fully developed. It is a procedure that can easily be converted into a computer algorithm and, with proper data and calibration, it could provide sound pollutant removal estimates in sedimentation ponds. How accurate these estimates will turn out to be is yet to be tested. We suspect that if the pond is properly configured geometrically, has good energy dissipation at the inlet, and the sediment/pollutant relationships for the stormwater are well-defined and the model is calibrated, this procedure should produce very good results.

23.3 SIZING OF PONDS USING 1986 EPA RECOMMENDATIONS

In 1986, the Environmental Protection Agency published a suggested methodology for the analysis of detention basins for the control of urban runoff pollution. This document, according to EPA (1986), provides analysis methodology to " . . . guide planning level evaluation and design decisions. . . . " for the sizing of detention ponds. The procedure is an adaptation of probabilistic methodology originally formulated by DiToro and Small (1979) under partial funding by the EPA and reported in a Hydroscience, Inc, (1979) report to the

EPA. The actual methodology in the 1986 EPA publication was the work of Eugene D. Driscoll, with technical consultation from Dominic M. DiToro. All of these efforts were undertaken with Dennis Athayde of EPA as the Project Officer.

23.3.1 Relationships for Dynamic Conditions

The EPA (1986) methodology combines probabilistic techniques for the analysis of rainfall and runoff with the sedimentation theory for removal of sediments under quiescent and dynamic conditions. The approach used to estimate sediment removal under dynamic conditions is very similar to what was described in section 23.2 and is based on a similar sedimentation removal equation found in Fair and Geyer (1954), namely:

$$R_d = 1.0 - \left[1.0 + \frac{1}{n} \cdot \frac{V_s}{\dfrac{Q}{A}} \right]^{-n} \tag{23.4}$$

in which R_d = fraction of the initial solids removed under dynamic conditions,
V_s = settling velocity of particles in feet per hour,
Q = peak flow-through rate in cubic feet per second,
A = surface area of detention pond in square feet, and
n = turbulence or short circuiting constant that is used to indicate the settling performance of the pond. Suggested values of n by Fair and Geyer (1954):

$n = 1$, poor performance,
$n = 3$, good performance,
$n > 5$, very good performance, and
n = infinity, ideal performance.

When n approaches infinity, Equation 23.4 reduces to the following, and familiar, exponential decay form:

$$R_d = 1.0 - e^{-kt} \tag{23.5}$$

in which $k = v_s/h$, a sedimentation rate coefficient,
h = average depth of the basin in feet,
$t = V/Q$, residence time, and
V = volume of basin in cubic feet.

Solving Equations 23.4 and 23.5 and plotting the results gives us a graph that looks very much like the one in Figure 23.1. Reducing these calculations further to a range of particle settling velocities and surface loading rates (i.e., flow-through rates) most probable under urban runoff conditions results in a graph shown in Figures 23.4(a) and 23.4(b). Figure 23.4(a) is the exact solution of Equation 23.4(b), assuming $n = 3$ (i.e., good removal conditions), and

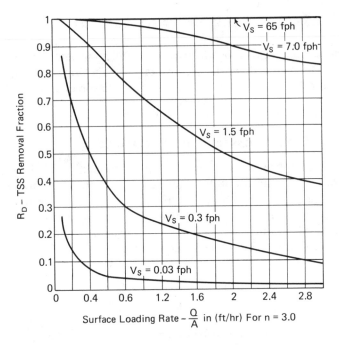

Figure 23.4(a) Loading rate vs. removal by sedimentation ($n = 3$).

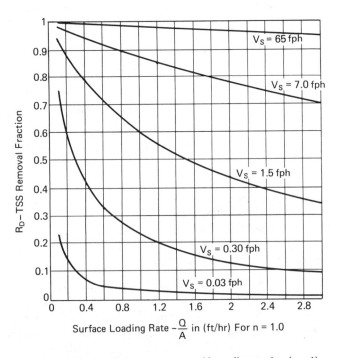

Figure 23.4(b) Loading rate vs. removal by sedimentation ($n = 1$).

Figure 23.4(b) is the exact solution assuming $n = 1$ (i.e., poor conditions). The latter of the two may be the more appropriate solution under dynamic field conditions of variable inflow and depth.

The removal under dynamic conditions varies with storm intensity. As a result, estimates made for average seasonal or annual conditions have to be corrected to estimate the actual fraction of TSS removed over an extended period of time.

Long-term average removal is estimated with the aid of Equation 23.6. It accounts for the variations in hourly storm depths, and its graphic solution is presented in Figure 23.5. While the estimates made using average rainfall intensities and volumes according to EPA (1986) are not exact, they may be useful for planning level purposes. A more exact estimate of long-term removal rates can probably be obtained using similar principles with a chronological continuous model.

$$R_L = Z \cdot \left[\frac{r}{r - \ln\left(\frac{R_M}{Z}\right)} \right]^{(r+1)} \tag{23.6}$$

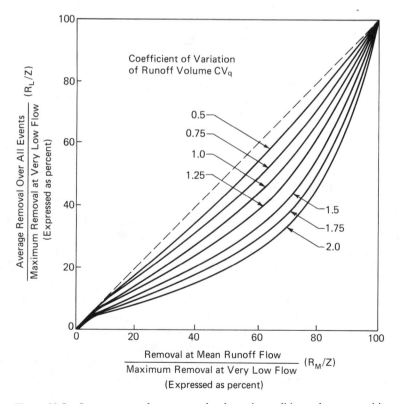

Figure 23.5 Long-term performance under dynamic conditions when removal is sensitive to flow rate. (After EPA, 1986.)

in which R_L = long-term dynamic removal fraction,

R_M = mean storm dynamic removal fraction,

$r = 1/CV_Q^2$,

CV_Q = coefficient of variation of runoff flow rates, and

Z = maximum fraction removed at very low flow rates.

When using Equation 23.6 or Figure 23.5, the value for Z can be assumed to be 80% to 100% for all fractions. An exception to this would be where the smallest sizes of sediments are electrostatically charged (i.e., clays), in which cases 10% to 50% would be more appropriate to use for the sediment fractions having 0.3 and 0.03 feet per hour settling velocities.

23.3.2 Relationships for Quiescent Conditions

Surface storm runoff occurs only during a fraction of the time in any given year. As a result, a significant amount of runoff is trapped and retained inside a pond where sedimentation continues between storms under quiescent conditions. How large the pond volume is relative to storm runoff volume determines the TSS removal effectiveness under quiescent conditions. The removal of TSS under quiescent conditions can be approximated by:

$$R_Q = V_S \cdot A_B \qquad (23.7)$$

in which R_Q = solids removal rate, quiescent conditions,

V_S = settling velocity of a particle, ft/hr, and

A_B = pond surface area, ft^2.

When and for how long the quiescent periods occur is a random process. Although estimates of TSS removal can be made using long-term averages, these estimates need to be adjusted to reflect this random process. Such adjustments can be made with the aid of Figure 23.6.

To calculate the TSS removal using Figure 23.5, it is first necessary to find the ratio of *effective storage volume* to *mean runoff volume. Effective storage volume* is not the same as the total pond volume and is dependent on how and when rainstorms occur in relation to the quiescent periods.

The *effective storage volume* vs. *mean basin volume* ratio can be estimated using Figure 23.7. Its use, however, requires that we know the watershed's *mean runoff volume,* which can be found by using the nearest National Weather Service hourly precipitation records and processing them through a rainfall runoff model. Once we have all the necessary data, we enter the graph in Figure 23.7 with a value for the *storage basin volume* to *mean runoff volume* ratio and with a value for *volume of TSS removed under quiescent conditions* to *runoff volume* ratio as given by the following expression:

$$E = \frac{U_M \cdot R_Q}{V_R} \qquad (23.8)$$

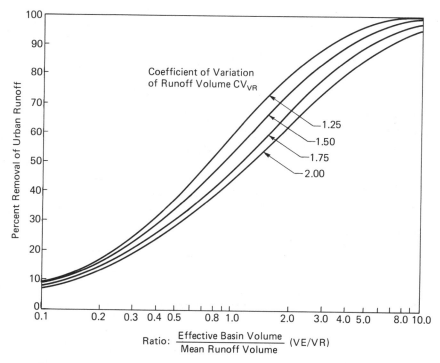

Figure 23.6   Average long-term performance of a detention pond under quiescent conditions. (After EPA, 1986.)

in which E = removal ratio under quiescent conditions,
U_M = mean interval between storms, hours, and
V_R = mean storm runoff volume for study period, ft^3.

The procedure and the examples published by EPA (1986) utilize rainstorm intensities and volumes averaged over a long data collection period. The use of monthly rainfall/runoff statistics and month-to-month analysis for an extended period of time should result in different TSS removal performance conclusions. Although long-term averages and variance statistics can be used for a quick and easy evaluation of how various facilities may remove TSS over an extended period of time, personal computers make it just as easy to perform analysis on a chronological series of data. This type of analysis should provide a better understanding of what to expect at any given site.

23.3.3 Relationships for Combined Conditions

The relationships described so far can be used to estimate the removal to TSS under dynamic or quiescent conditions. Now let's combine both as suggested by EPA (1986) to estimate the total TSS removal by a detention pond.

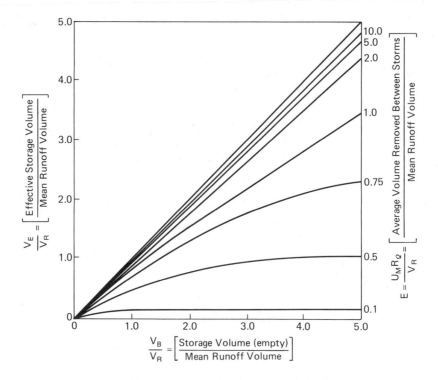

Figure 23.7 Effect of previous storms on long-term performance under quiescent conditions. (After EPA, 1986.)

If we define the fraction of time the pond is expected to operate under dynamic conditions as

$$f_D = \frac{D}{U_M} \tag{23.9}$$

then the fraction of time under quiescent conditions is

$$f_Q = (1.0 - f_D) \tag{23.10}$$

in which D = mean storm duration, and
U_M = mean interval between storm mid-points.

The TSS entering the pond first undergoes removal under dynamic conditions. For large ponds, this can occur more than one time since runoff from other storms is likely to occur before the inflow from an earlier storm fully drains from the pond. For a single dynamic removal period the removal efficiency is a function of the overflow rate divided by the effective pond surface area (i.e., loading rate).

The quiescent removal process operates on that fraction of inflow that remains in the pond after storm runoff ceases and the storm surcharge is emptied. The settling process continues on that fraction of TSS that was not removed during the dynamic conditions. The combined total fraction removed under both processes can be expressed as

$$f_T = 1.0 - F_D \cdot F_Q \qquad (23.11)$$

in which f_T = total TSS fraction removed,

F_D = fraction *not* removed under dynamic conditions, and

F_Q = fraction *not* removed under quiescent conditions.

23.3.4 Example 1: Long-term Average TSS Removal

Given: A 100-acre (40.5-ha) single-family residential development in Arkansas has a runoff coefficient $C_v = 0.25$. A pond is built to intercept all runoff and has the following dimensions:

Surface area: $A_B = 12,000$ square feet (1115 m²)
Average depth: $h_B = 4$ feet (1.2 m)
Storage volume: $V_B = 48,000$ cubic feet (1360 m³)

The rainfall statistics, as reported by the EPA (1986), are as follows:

	Units	COEFFICIENT OF VARIANCE	
		Mean	CV
Volume (V)	inch	0.75	1.54
Intensity (I)	in/hr	0.122	1.35
Duration (D)	hr	8.7	1.29
Interval between storms (U_m)	hr	136.	1.06

For this example, we assume that the particle settling velocities are the same as given in Table 21.5.

Required: Estimate the potential long-term removal rate of TSS from stormwater by the given detention pond.

Solution:

1. Calculate the mean storm runoff parameters:

Flow rate: $Q_R = I \cdot C_v \cdot A = \dfrac{0.122 \cdot 0.25 \cdot 100 \cdot 43{,}560}{12}$

$= 11{,}100$ cubic feet/hour

Volume: $V_R = V \cdot C_v \cdot A = \dfrac{0.75 \cdot 0.25 \cdot 43{,}560}{12}$

$= 68{,}100$ cubic feet

Assume that the runoff has the same statistical distribution as rainfall, namely,

$$CV_Q = 1.09 \quad \text{and} \quad CV_v = 1.10$$

2. Calculate removal under dynamic conditions:
The average loading rate during the mean storm is

$$Q_R/A_s = \frac{(11,100 \text{ ft}^3/\text{hr})}{(12,000 \text{ ft}^2)}$$

$$= 0.925 \text{ ft/hr}$$

Each size fraction of TSS will have its own settling velocity for which the removal by sedimentation, R_D, is calculated using Equation 23.4 assuming $n = 1$ (i.e., poor removal conditions), or Figure 23.4(b).

Next, we need to find a value for Z (i.e., TSS removal at very low loading rates). This can be very subjective; however, assuming $Z = 1.0$ introduces very little error.

Using $Z = 1.0$ and R_D and the removal of TSS at the mean runoff flow rate calculated with the aid of Figure 23.4(b), we next calculate the long-term average removal for each size fraction with the aid of Figure 23.5 at $CV_Q = 1.09$.

The results for long-term dynamic removal are:

Size Fraction	V_S (ft/hr)	R_D (Fig. 23.4)	Fraction Removed (Fig. 23.5)
1	0.03	.03	.03
2	0.3	.27	.21
3	1.5	.66	.53
4	7.0	.89	.82
5	65	.99	.99
	Total average fraction removed = 0.52		
	Fraction not removed $F_D = 1.0 - 0.52 = 0.48$		

3. Calculate removal under quiescent conditions:

Ratio of pond volume to mean runoff volume:

$$\frac{V_B}{V_R} = \frac{48,000}{68,100} = 0.70$$

We find the long-term removal efficiency under quiescent conditions with the aid of Figure 23.6, which relates the percent of TSS removal to the ratio of *effective basin volume/mean runoff volume* (i.e., V_E/V_R) and the coefficient of variation in runoff volume, $CV_v = 1.10$ defined in step 1.

The V_E/V_R ratio is not the same as the V_B/V_R calculated previously;

instead, it is found using Figure 23.7. To do this, we need to first calculate E using Equation 23.8, namely:

$$E = \frac{U_M \cdot R_Q}{V_R} \quad \text{or} \quad E = \frac{U_M \cdot (A_B \cdot V_S)}{V_R}$$

in which E = removal ratio under quiescent conditions,
$R_Q = A_B \cdot V_S$, solids removal rate, ft³,
V_R = volume of runoff, ft³,
A_B = pond surface area, ft²,
V_S = particle settling velocity, ft/hr, and
U_M = mean interval between storms, hr.

Thus, using all of the foregoing, we calculate the removal of each particle size fraction separately and find the total average fraction removed under quiescent conditions.

This yields the following results:

Size Fract.	V_S (f/s)	$A_B \cdot V_S$ (ft³)	E	V_E/V_R (Fig. 23.7)	% Removed (Fig. 23.6)
1	0.03	360	0.7	0.45	47
2	0.3	3,600	7.2	0.70	57
3	1.5	18,000	36.2	0.75	58
4	7	84,000	169	0.75	58
5	65	780,000	1570	0.75	58

Total average removed = 47

Fraction not removed $F_Q = \dfrac{100 - 47}{100} = 0.53$

4. Calculate removal under combined conditions:

The combined total average long-term TSS removal is calculated using the values for F_D and F_Q calculated previously and Equation 23.11, namely:

$$f_T = (1 - F_D \cdot F_Q) = (1 - 0.48 \cdot 0.53) = 0.75$$

The combined total annual removal breaks down as follows:

Size Fract.	V_S (f/s)	% Dynamic Removal	% Quiescent Removal	% Combined Removal
1	0.03	3	35	66
2	0.3	21	48	51
3	1.5	53	51	77
4	7	82	51	91
5	65	99	51	100
Average:		52	47	77

You will notice that the quiescent removal rates for size fractions 3, 4, and 5 are less than for dynamic removal. Because of the basin size, the statistical distribution of storms, and the intervals between storms, most of the removal process took place during the dynamic periods for these two fractions. In other words, quiescent removal hardly came into play.

5. All of these calculations assume that all TSS removal occurs because of sedimentation. These calculations do not account for any resuspension of sediments by inflow or wave action, remobilization of pollutants by chemical or biological processes in the pond, or the removal of pollutants by biological processes.

23.3.5 Example 2: Long-term Average Phosphorus Removal

Given: Use the same site, rainfall, runoff, and detention pond as described in the preceding example. This time we are given the following data concerning total phosphorus (i.e., TP) found in stormwater:

Total phosphorus: 0.71 milligrams per liter
Dissolved phosphorus: 0.32 milligrams per liter
Suspended phosphorus: 0.39 milligrams per liter

The suspended fraction has the following settling velocity distribution:

Size Fraction	V_S (ft/hr)	% of Mass in Urban Runoff
1	0.15	0–20
2	1.3	20–40
3	6.3	40–60
4	26	60–80
5	115	80–100

Required: The long-term removal rate of TP by the pond.

Solution:

1. Use the same storm runoff parameters found in Example 1, namely:

Flow rate: $Q_R = 11,100$ cubic feet per hour
               $CV_Q = 1.09$

Volume: $V_R = 68,100$ cubic feet
            $CV_v = 1.10$

2. Calculate removal under dynamic conditions:

From Example 1, we have $Q_R/A_B = 0.925$ ft/hr.

Again we assume $Z = 1.0$, and using Figure 23.4a we calculate the removal rate under dynamic conditions for each of the size fractions. Also, the long-term average removal for each size fraction is found with the aid of Figure 23.5 at $CV_Q = 1.09$. The results are summarized in the following table:

Size Fraction	V_s (ft/hr)	R_D (Fig. 23.4)	Fraction Removed (Fig. 23.5)
1	0.15	0.15	0.11
2	1.3	0.50	0.38
3	6.3	0.85	0.76
4	26	0.95	0.91
5	115	1.00	1.00

Average fraction removed = 0.63
Fraction not removed $F_D = 1.0 - 0.63 = 0.37$

3. Calculate removal under quiescent conditions:

From Example 1 we know that $V_B/V_R = 0.70$, $CV_V = 1.10$, and $U_M = 136$ hours. We can now calculate the new values for E using

$$E = \frac{U_M \cdot (A_B \cdot V_S)}{V_R}$$

and Figures 23.6 and 23.7. The results are as follows:

Size Fract.	V_S (f/s)	$A_B \cdot V_S$ (ft^3)	E	V_E/V_R (Fig. 23.7)	% Removed (Fig. 23.6)
1	0.15	1,800	3.6	0.65	44
2	1.3	15,600	31	0.75	51
3	6.3	75,600	151	0.75	51
4	26	312,000	624	0.75	51
5	115	1,380,000	2760	0.75	51

Total average removed = 50

Fraction not removed $F_Q = \dfrac{100 - 50}{100} = 0.50$

4. Calculate removal under combined conditions:

The combined total average long-term removal of suspended phosphorus (SP) is calculated using the values for F_D and F_Q calculated in steps 2 and 3 and Equation 23.10, namely:

$$f_{SP} = (1 - F_D \cdot F_Q) = (1 - 0.37 \cdot 0.50) = 0.82$$

The combined total SP removal breaks down as follows:

Size Fract.	V_s (f/s)	% Dynamic Removal	% Quiescent Removal	% Combined Removal
1	0.15	11	44	50
2	1.30	38	51	70
3	6.30	76	51	88
4	26.00	91	51	96
5	115.00	100	51	100
Total averages:		63	50	81

The removal of total phosphorus is then found by compositing the dissolved phosphorus and the remaining suspended phosphorus. Thus, the average long-term TP concentration in the water leaving the pond is

$$TP = DP + (1 - f_{SP}) \cdot SP$$
$$= 0.32 + (1 - 0.81) \cdot 0.39 = 0.39 \text{ mg/l}$$

Thus, the long-term removal rate for TP is

$$F_{TP} = 100 \cdot \frac{0.71 - 0.39}{0.71}, \text{ or } 45\%$$

5. Note that despite an 81% removal rate for the suspended fraction, the removal of total phosphorus was less than 50%. This is because we assumed that no removal of the dissolved fraction takes place due to sedimentation. Also, as in the first example, these calculations do not account for any resuspension of sediments by inflow or wave action, remobilization of phosphorus by chemical or biological processes in the pond, or removal of dissolved phosphorus by biological processes.

23.3.6 Modification of the 1986 EPA Procedure

First, the technique just described is the same as that recommended in EPA (1986). It assumes that average hourly rainfall intensities can be used to adequately describe the sedimentation process and the long-term performance of detention basins. This is not always the case. This assumption may be reasonable for storms that are of low intensity and last a long time, but not in the case of thunderstorms. Thunderstorms can have very intense rainfall rates and can be much shorter in duration than 1 hour. As a result, the average inflow rate throughout a thunderstorm can be much greater than estimated using hourly averages.

When working with hourly precipitation rates, we suggest that the designer at least double the average hourly surface loading rate (i.e., Q/A) in performing the TSS removal calculations described in Sections 23.3 through 23.3.5. Use of this "safety factor" is recommended until this methodology is refined through field observation. Until then, a designer is better off erring on the safe side.

Second, EPA (1986) originally presented the results of a long-term rainfall statistical analysis for several regions of the United States. Because the results reported in 1986 were based on all precipitation events and not only on those expected to produce surface runoff, the design averages recommended by EPA were low. Subsequently, Driscoll, et al. (1989) published, under a contract with the U.S. Environmental Protection Agency, a new set of rainfall distribution charts for the United States based on storms with precipitation totals of 0.10 inch (2.5 mm) or more. Figure 23.8 presents the distribution of the average storm depth across the United States using only storms with 0.10 inch (2.5 mm) or more water depth. This incipient runoff-producing precipitation value for an urban area is supported by field data reported by Manaker and Urbonas (1990) and others.

Driscoll et al. (1989) also developed average values and statistical coefficients of variation CV for annual number of storms, storm duration, intensity, volume, and storm separation. These averages and their coefficients of variation are summarized in Table 23.1 for the 15 rain zones of the Unites States shown in Figure 23.9.

Although it is possible to estimate removal rates in the United States using the rainfall averages and other statistics reported in Table 23.1, it is recommended that the designer analyze local rainfall data whenever they are available. In 1987, after investigating several rainfall databases in the United

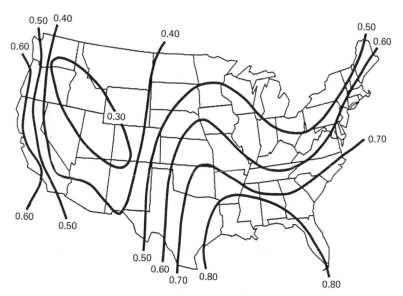

Figure 23.8   Average storm rainfall depths in the United States. (After Driscoll et al., 1989)

TABLE 23.1 Typical Values of Individual Storm Event Statistics for 15 Zones of the United States

Rain Zone	Annual No. of Storms		Duration (hours)		Intensity (in./hr)		Volume (inches)		Storm Separation (hours)	
	Avg.	CV	Avg.	CV	Avg.	CV	Avg.	CV	Avg.	CV
Northeast	70	0.13	11.2	0.81	0.067	1.23	0.50	0.95	126	0.94
Northeast, coastal	63	0.12	11.7	0.77	0.071	1.05	0.66	1.03	140	0.87
Mid-Atlantic	62	0.13	10.1	0.84	0.092	1.20	0.64	1.01	143	0.97
Central	68	0.14	9.2	0.85	0.097	1.09	0.62	1.00	133	0.99
North Central	55	0.16	9.5	0.83	0.087	1.20	0.55	1.01	167	1.17
Southeast	65	0.15	8.7	0.92	0.122	1.09	0.75	1.10	136	1.03
East Gulf	68	0.17	6.4	1.05	0.178	1.03	0.80	1.19	130	1.25
East Texas	41	0.22	8.0	0.97	0.137	1.08	0.76	1.18	213	1.28
West Texas	30	0.27	7.4	0.98	0.121	1.13	0.57	1.07	302	1.53
Southwest	20	0.30	7.8	0.88	0.079	1.16	0.37	0.88	473	1.46
West, inland	14	0.38	9.4	0.75	0.055	1.06	0.36	0.87	786	1.54
Pacific Southwest	19	0.36	11.6	0.78	0.054	0.76	0.54	0.98	476	2.09
Northwest, inland	31	0.23	10.4	0.82	0.057	1.20	0.37	0.93	304	1.43
Pacific Central	32	0.25	13.7	0.80	0.048	0.85	0.58	1.05	265	2.00
Pacific Northwest	71	0.15	15.9	0.80	0.035	0.73	0.50	1.09	123	1.50

(After Driscoll et al., 1989.)

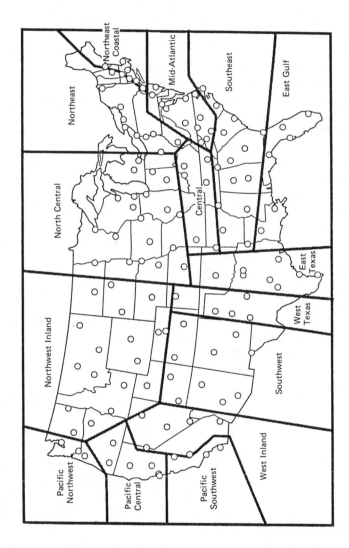

Figure 23.9   Fifteen rain zones of the United States. (After Driscoll et al., 1989)

States, Urbonas concluded that it was best to define individual storms on the basis of 6 hours of separation between the end of one storm and the beginning of another. At the same time Driscoll, et al. (1989) was analyzing a large number of rainfall data records in the United States and came to the same conclusion. Therefore, it is suggested that hourly (or 15-minute) rainfall data be separated into individual storm depths using a 6-hour storm separation period. These data then need to be filtered to retain only storms with precipitation total exceeding the incipient runoff value (i.e., 0.10 inch or 2.5 mm). The resultant storm depth population can be processed through a continuous rainfall abstractions model. Statistical analysis of the resultant runoff volumes can provide the needed runoff volume averages, CV_v, CF_Q, durations, and periods between runoff events.

Third, more representative results are likely if continuous chronological runoff modeling and sedimentation removal are used. This can be done by transforming the hourly, or 15-minute, rainfall record into a runoff record using a simple rainfall runoff model. The resultant runoff can then be processed through a chronological series of sediment removal calculations for the dynamic and quiescent conditions, and a more representative picture of sediment removal efficiencies can be developed. Such a model should be simple to develop using any of the commercially available personal computer programming languages or even a spreadsheet.

Obviously, the investigator will need a way to estimate loads of total suspended solids in each runoff event. If local data or other better information is lacking, use of the event mean concentrations for TSS listed in Table 21.1 and the distribution of sediment settling velocities presented in Figure 21.9 should provide a rational basis for planning purposes and for comparison of the effectiveness of alternative designs.

23.4 SIZING DRY BASINS

The design of dry detention basins for water quality is much less scientific than for the design of ponds. Although sedimentation is still the primary pollutant removal mechanism, the calculation of how much occurs has to be based mostly on empirical findings. Unlike a pond with a permanent pool of water, the dry basin fills during the storm and empties completely through an outlet at the bottom of the basin. As a result, surface load theory does not apply throughout the entire filling and emptying cycle. The water surface area changes throughout the storm, and the settling particles flow out through the outlet at the bottom instead of being trapped below the overflow. Also, no part of the runoff remains in the pond after it empties for sedimentation to take place under quiescent conditions.

Despite all of these apparent disadvantages, extended detention water quality basins can provide good removal rates for total suspended solids, lead, and zinc and fair removals for total organic carbon and chemical oxygen demand. Grizzard et al. (1986), Metropolitan Washington Council of Governments (1983), and Occoquan Watershed Monitoring Laboratory (1986) reported similar findings for the removal efficiencies of extended detention basins. From their findings, certain conclusions can be made concerning how to size these basins.

According to the results reported by Grizzard et al. (1986), the average storm runoff volume needs to be detained 24 hours in the extended detention basin to achieve equivalent total suspended solids removed after 6 hours in a settling tube. They suggested that the water quality basin volume be larger than the volume of runoff from an average rainstorm and that the outlet be designed so that the basin's full volume is drained in approximately 40 hours.

When designing an extended detention basin, the water quality basin volume should be no less than the average runoff event during a year (note that this is not the runoff from the average rainstorm). We concur with Grizzard et al. (1986) and recommend that the basin be designed to drain its full water quality volume in no less than 40 hours. In summary, the recommended design parameters for an extended detention basin are as follows:

- Basin volume: somewhat larger than average runoff event; and
- Outlet: size outlet to drain the full basin volume in no less than 40 hours.

23.4.1 Possible Long-term Pollutant Removals

Based on field studies by EPA (1981), Grizzard et al. (1986), Occoquan Watershed Monitoring Laboratory (1986), and Whipple and Hunter (1981), it appears that a properly designed extended detention basin can be expected to achieve the following long-term removal rates:

TSS: 50% to 70%
TP: 10% to 20%
Nitrogen: 10% to 20%
Organic matter: 20% to 40%
Lead: 75% to 90%
Zinc: 30% to 60%
Hydrocarbons: 50% to 70%
Bacteria: 50% to 90%

For planning purposes, it is recommended that the middle of these ranges be used until local data are available to draw better conclusions.

23.4.2 Example: Sizing Extended Detention Basins

Given: The same 100-acre (40.5 5-ha) single family residential development in Arkansas as used in the examples for sizing of ponds with a permanent water pool. The area has a runoff coefficient $C_v = 0.25$. The rainfall statistics, as reported by Driscoll (1989), are as follows:

	Units	Annual Mean	CV
Volume (V)	inches	0.75	1.10
Intensity (I)	in/hr	0.122	1.09

Required: Size an extended detention pond that will remove 50% to 60% of total suspended solids, 40% to 50% of zinc, and 70% lead found in stormwater runoff.

Solution:

1. Calculate the mean runoff event parameters:
   The average runoff volume is estimated at 68,100 cubic feet (1928 m³):

$$V_R = V\,C_v\,A = \frac{0.75 \cdot 0.25 \cdot 100 \cdot 43,560}{12}$$

$$= 68,100 \text{ cubic feet}$$

2. Thus, the required basin volume:

$$V_B = V_R = 68,100 \text{ cubic feet}$$

3. The outlet for this basin will be a perforated riser. It will overflow only when the volume in step 2 is exceeded. The perforations will be sized to drain the full volume of the pond in approximately 40 hours. They will also ensure that the lower one-half of the volume drains in approximately 24 hours. This will ensure that the smaller storms will be detained sufficiently to provide pollutant removal.

23.5 OPTIMIZATION OF STORMWATER QUALITY CAPTURE VOLUME

23.5.1 Introduction

The size of a runoff event to be captured by a detention basin, or as a surcharge above a detention pond, is critical in the design of stormwater quality detention basins. If the design runoff event is too small, the effectiveness will be reduced because too many storms will exceed the capacity of the facility. If, on the other hand, the design event is too large and the detention basin has an outlet that drains the total capture volume within a reasonable time (i.e., in 40 hours or less), the smaller runoff events will empty too fast for adequate settling out of pollutants. As a result, the larger basin often will not provide the needed retention time for the predominant number of small runoff events.

A balance is needed between the size of the captured volume and water quality treatment effectiveness. Recall that Grizzard et al. (1986) found that dry basins provide good levels of treatment when they are sized to have an average emptying, or drain, time of approximately 24 hours. This equates to a 40-hour emptying time for a water quality detention basin filled to its brim (i.e., a brim-full basin).

Also recall that earlier we described an EPA (1986) methodology for estimating the sediment removal efficiencies of facilities with surcharge storage above a permanent pool (i.e., wet ponds). Urbonas used this technique to analyze the effectiveness of wet ponds in Denver designed to have a brim-full surcharge volume equal to 0.5 inch (13 mm) of runoff from tributary impervious surfaces. This analysis indicated that such facilities could remove 80% of the annual suspended solid load.

However, aside from these and similar rule-of-thumb sizing techniques, some of which have been incorporated as local stormwater management criteria, no generalized approach for the sizing of stormwater quality capture volumes has gained general acceptance. While the EPA (1986) method permits an estimate of the potential efficiency of a given detention facility, the designer still has to find a reasonable detention basin size using a trial-and-error approach. In response to this problem, Urbonas et al. (1990) devised a simple method that uses hourly rainfall records. This sizing procedure is described next.

23.5.2 Optimization of Stormwater Runoff Capture Volume Using a Runoff Volume Pond Diagram

Section 18.5 described a rainfall data-based method developed by von den Herik (1976) and subsequently modified by Pecher (1978, 1979). It permits the sizing of detention facilities through the use of a rain point diagram. Urbonas et al. (1990) used a simplification of this methodology and simply transformed the rain point diagram into a runoff volume point diagram by multiplying the individual rainstorm depths on the rain point diagram by the runoff coefficient of the tributary watershed.

The runoff volume point diagram takes into account all runoff events found in the record without setting up a continuous model. To start with, the engineer has to aggregate the incremental hourly or 15-minute rainfall data into storm totals. Separate storms are defined by the specific period of time from the end of one rainstorm to the beginning of the next. Very small storms that are not likely to produce runoff are removed from the record, and storm precipitation totals for the remaining storms are then converted to runoff depths (i.e., volumes) by multiplying the total precipitation depth by the watershed runoff coefficient C.

To illustrate the use of the runoff volume point diagram, a plot of 1,084 storms is shown in Figure 23.10, where individual storm runoff depths are plotted against storm duration. Note that this figure is similar to Figure 18.12, although there are two differences. First, the effects of time of concentration are ignored because its short duration in an urban basin has little effect on the final results. Second, all the points on Figure 23.10 represent only precipitation depths for events larger than the surface retention loss that have been multiplied by the watershed runoff coefficient C.

The runoff capture envelope is the straight line shown in Figure 23.10. This envelope is based on a brim-full volume of the detention facility and on an outflow rate computed using the time it takes to empty out this brim-full volume. To illustrate this point, the runoff capture envelope in Figure 23.10 is based on a detention basin with a brim-full capacity of 0.3 watershed inch (7.6 mm) and an outflow rate that empties this volume in 12 hours. This emptying time is sometimes called the *drawdown time*.

All the points above the capture volume envelope line represent storms that exceed the available storage volume of the detention basin. Obviously, plotting and counting all the points for a long record of rainstorms is a very tedious job. However, this procedure is easy to program on a personal com-

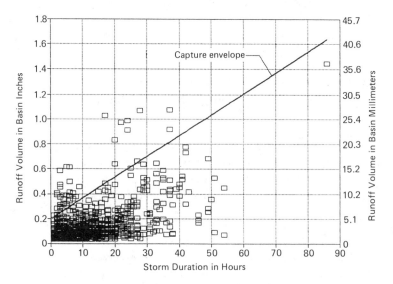

Figure 23.10   Runoff volume point diagram and capture volume envelope.

puter. Once the individual rainfall increments are aggregated into separate individual storms, the procedure can even be set up on a simple spreadsheet. While the procedure is a simplification of a continuous modeling process, the results are very similar to those obtained using continuous simulation and should be as accurate when one takes into account the broad range of the confidence limits typically observed in any hydrological analysis (ASCE, 1984).

One problem is that the runoff volume point diagram procedure does not account for the effects of several successive rainstorms. Therefore, this method may have a tendency to underestimate the capture effectiveness of detention basins with very small release flow rates. The runoff captured during one storm may not be fully drained before the next storm occurs. This can be compensated for when performing this analysis.

To compensate for storms that are closely spaced, it is suggested that the modifications recommended for the rain point diagram procedure in Section 18.5.5 be used. In particular, it is recommended that when aggregating the recorded individual rainfall depths into individual storm totals, a storm separation interval equal to one-half the emptying time for the brim-full volume be used.

Urbonas et al. (1990) tested the sensitivity of the storm separation period used to define what constitutes a new storm. They found virtually no difference in the capture volume effectiveness when using a storm separation period equal to the time it takes to empty the brim-full volume compared to the results found when using a separation period equal to one-half the time needed to empty the brim-full volume. This reinforces the recommendations made in Section 18.5.5. Nevertheless, it is recommended that sensitivity tests be performed for each rain gauge record to ensure that these recommendations are valid in the hydrologic region being studied.

Capture Volume Optimization.   After all the incremental precipitation depths in a rain gauge record are aggregated into a record of individual storm precipitation totals, the runoff volume for each storm is estimated using the Rational Method as expressed by Equation 23.12:

$$V_r = C \cdot P_t \qquad (23.12)$$

in which V_r = total runoff volume for a storm in watershed inches (mm),
$\quad C$ = runoff coefficient, and
$\quad P_t$ = total precipitation over the watershed for each storm in inches (mm).

For any given detention basin with a brim-full volume of V_r that empties in time T_e, the average release rate q is defined by Equation 23.13:

$$q = \frac{V_r}{T_e} \qquad (23.13)$$

Then, the runoff volume the basin can capture during any storm V_m can be estimated using Equation 23.14:

$$V_m = V_r + q \cdot T_d \qquad (23.14)$$

in which T_d = storm duration.

The term $q \cdot T_d$ in Equation 23.14 is the storage volume that the basin can capture because it is being emptied at the release rate q. As a result, the total runoff volume captured and dynamically treated for the removal of suspended solids by the basin is equal to V_r, the storm runoff volume when V_r is less than V_m; otherwise, it is equal to V_m. As a simplifying assumption, whenever the storm runoff exceeds V_m, the overflow is presumed to receive no water quality treatment, which is often not completely accurate since some treatment continues to occur in an in-line reservoir even after it is overtopped. This assumption permits us to add up all the runoff volumes from individual storms captured for the period of record being studied. This total volume we define as V_t. Thus, the volume capture ratio for the study period is defined as

$$R_v = \frac{V_t}{V_{tr}} \qquad (23.15)$$

in which R_v = volume capture ratio for period of record,
V_t = total volume captured during this period, and
V_{tr} = total runoff volume during this period.

Similarly, we can define the runoff event capture ratio as

$$R_e = \frac{N_f}{N} \qquad (23.16)$$

in which R_e = runoff event capture ratio for the period,
N_f = number of runoff events less than or equal to V_m in volume, and
N = total number of runoff events.

For any set of runoff events based on rain gauge records, there is a detention volume that will capture all the runoff events within this period. For practical reasons this volume P_m is defined as being equal to the 99.9% probability runoff event for the period of record. P_m can then be used to normalize all detention volumes being tested using the equation

$$P_r = \frac{P}{P_m} \qquad (23.17)$$

in which P_r = relative detention volume normalized to P_m,
P = detention volume being tested, and
P_m = 99.9% probability runoff storm volume.

First, it is necessary to find (i.e., plot) the normalized distribution of the runoff volume ratio or event capture ratio—R_v or R_e—as a function of the normalized pond size. This can be done with the aid of the runoff volume point diagram method by incrementally increasing the relative pond size and then calculating the relative runoff event or volume capture ratio.

This is best illustrated using an example. An analysis of the Denver rain gauge recorded between 1948 and 1984 reveals that the 99.9% probability runoff-producing storm had 3.04 inches (77.2 mm) of water. For comparison, this was 6.9 times the precipitation of an average runoff-producing storm for the same period of record. This value of P_m was then used to normalize all the individual storm precipitation totals in the period of record. In this case the individual storms were defined by a 6-hour period of separation. Figure 23.11 summarizes the results of this analysis for a detention pond designed to capture the runoff from a watershed with a runoff coefficient of $C = 0.5$ and a pond outlet capable of emptying its brim-full capture volume in 12 hours.

The optimized capture volume occurs where the 1 : 1 slope is tangent to the runoff event capture function. Before this point is reached, the capture rate increases faster than the capture volume size. After this point is reached, increases in the capture rate become less than corresponding increases in the capture volume size. In other words, an increasingly diminishing number of storms are captured totally once the optimization point is passed. In the example in Figure 23.11, the optimized point occurs when the relative capture volume is equal to 0.18. At this point approximately 82% of the entire runoff that has occurred during the study period is captured in total. This relative capture volume is then converted to the actual runoff volume using a re-arranged form of Equation 23.17:

$$P = P_r \cdot P_m$$
$$= (0.18)(0.5 \cdot 3.04)$$
$$= 0.27 \text{ watershed inch (6.86 m)}$$

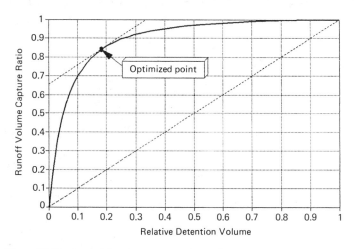

Figure 23.11   Optimizing the capture volume. (After Urbonas et al., 1990.)

in which 0.5 is the watershed runoff coefficient and $P_m = 3.04$ inches (77.2 mm), the depth of rain during the 99.9% probability storm.

23.5.3 Case Study

The hourly precipitation data recorded at the Denver rain gauge were analyzed using several storm separation periods. A summary of rainfall characteristics for all storms that exceeded a total of 0.1 inch (2.54 mm) is given in Table 23.2. A 0.1-inch (2.54-mm) precipitation depth was used to screen the record and to eliminate very small storms. According to field investigations by Manaker and Urbonas (1989) and by others, these small storms are likely to produce very little or no runoff. Manaker (1989) found that approximately 0.08 to 0.12 inch (2.03 to 3.05 mm) of rainfall depth was needed to cause incipient runoff to take place in an urban watershed located within the Denver metropolitan area.

Table 23.2 clearly shows that the precipitation totals exhibit a skewed distribution. Note that more than two-thirds of the storms have less precipitation than the average runoff-producing storm. It is also clear that the average runoff-producing storm is a relatively large event. The same observation was reported for a number of different rainfall zones. According to EPA (1986), storm depths exhibit a lognormal statistical distribution, the average depth for runoff-producing storms being larger than the median storm event, i.e., the 50th percentile event.

Once the precipitation distribution is known, it is possible to relate the optimized capture volume as a function of the tributary watershed runoff coefficient. Remember that the optimized point occurs when additional storage volume results in a diminishing number of storms or storm runoff volume being captured in total. Figure 23.12 relates the optimized capture volume to the watershed runoff coefficient for the example being discussed here. Sepa-

TABLE 23.2   Denver Rain Gauge Hourly Data Summary for 1948–84 Period and Storms Larger Than 0.1 Inches (2.54 mm)

Separation Between Storms (hr)	Number of Storms	Average Depth (in.)	Average Depth (mm)	Average Storm Duration (hr)	Average Time Between Storms (hr)	Percent of Storms Smaller Than Average
3	1091	0.42	10.7	9	275	71.7
6	1084	0.44	11.2	11	275	70.7
12	1056	0.46	11.7	14	280	70.8
24	983	0.51	12.9	23	392	69.8
48	876	0.58	14.7	43	310	70.0

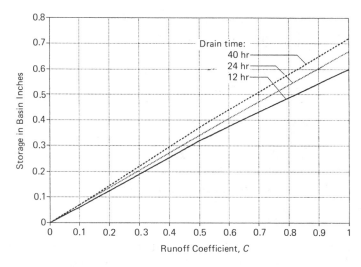

Figure 23.12   Optimized capture volume for water quality, Denver rain gauge 1948–84 period. (After Urbonas et al., 1990.)

rate curves are illustrated for urban basins having brim-full emptying times of 12, 24, and 40 hours.

For this example, the storage volume based on the capture volume ratio exceeds 80% of all runoff volumes, and the storage volume based on the storm event capture ratio exceeds 86% of all runoff events. The storm event capture ratio should have the greatest impact on the ecosystem of the receiving waters. It is the frequency of the shock loads that has the most effect on the aquatic life in the receiving streams. Thus, capturing and mitigating the impacts of the most frequently occurring runoff events should produce the greatest benefit.

On the other hand, examination of the precipitation records in many cities in United States and Europe clearly indicates that the volume capture ratio is affected by few very large storms. Since during large runoff events catastrophic flooding is likely, the primary concern is safety, minimizing property damage, and avoiding loss of life. Nevertheless, even during storm events that exceed the design capture volume, treatment through settling of solids in in-line basins and ponds continues to take place, but at somewhat reduced efficiency.

23.5.4 Sensitivity of the Procedure

Capture Volume.   The designer must understand how sensitive the event capture ratio is to changes in the capture volume (i.e., the design brim-full volume). This helps in selecting a cost-effective volume for these water quality enhancement facilities. To illustrate this point, a sensitivity analysis was performed for the case study described above using the following steps:

- A tributary urban watershed was assumed to have a runoff coefficient of $C = 1.0$, which should produce the greatest possible runoff response to rainfall.

- An optimized volume was found using the above-mentioned methodology for a detention basin with an emptying time of 12 hours for its brim-full surcharge volume.

- The capture volume of the basin was increased and decreased in small increments, and the results were divided by the "optimized volume" and its "optimum volume capture rate"; i.e., the results were normalized around the "optimum capture volume point."

- Figure 23.13 was then plotted to summarize the findings, which typify the trend for all such similar tests made using the Denver precipitation gauge data.

Examination of Figure 23.13 reveals that the optimum capture volume must be doubled—increased from 1.0 to 2.0 on the abscissa—to capture an additional 10% of the runoff volume in the record. Reducing the capture volume by 25% results in only an 8% reduction in the runoff volume not totally captured by the smaller detention basin. Keep in mind that capturing less than the entire volume of a runoff event still provides for the removal of a considerable amount of suspended solids from the water as it passes through the pond. As a result, suspended solids continue to settle out when overtopping occurs, but at reduced efficiency.

Removal of Suspended Sediments.   The sensitivity of sediment removal was also tested. Sediment settling data provided in EPA (1986) was used to see

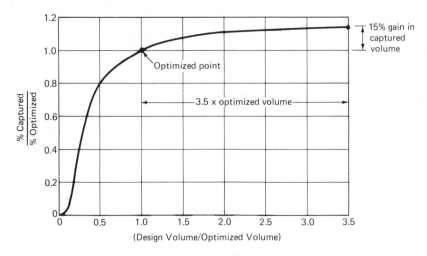

Figure 23.13 Results of a sensitivity analysis for the Denver rain gauge. (After Urbonas et al., 1990.)

how annual sediment removal was affected by varying the capture volume. The procedure described in Section 23.3 was used to estimate both the dynamic and the quiescent removal rates of each capture volume. The following table is a summary of these findings.

Ratio of Capture Volume to Optimized Volume	Percent of TSS Removed Annually
0.70	86
1.00	88
2.0	90

One can conclude from these tests that suspended solids removal is rather insensitive to the capture volume. It is clear that doubling of the optimized capture volume results in very little additional removal of suspended solids annually. It also appears that a capture volume somewhat less than the optimized volume can be very effective in removing total suspended solids. Clearly, this hypothesis needs further testing. It does imply, however, that very effective detention ponds could be constructed having less than the optimized volume. Such smaller basins may be more cost-effective.

While the above discussion focused on the removal of total suspended solids, the removal of dissolved nutrients such as phosphorus and nitrates requires an entirely different analysis. Nutrient removal from the water column is difficult and requires either chemical precipitation or biological uptake. The residence time for stormwater for biological uptake within the permanent water pool of a wet pond is considerable. Increasing the capture volume above this pool has little effect on the removal efficiencies of these compounds. Similarly, dry detention basins exhibit only a marginal removal capability for dissolved nutrients since their primary removal mechanism is sedimentation (Grizzard, et al., 1986; Schueler, 1987; Roesner, et al., 1989).

23.5.5 Conclusions

It is possible to develop simplified design guidelines for the sizing of optimized stormwater quality facilities for removing settleable pollutants. Such guidelines can be developed using local rain gauge records. The procedure uses a runoff volume point diagram method to approximate a continuous simulation process in combination with an optimization routine.

23.6 RECOMMENDED BASIN CONFIGURATIONS

How water quality (i.e., sedimentation) detention pounds or basins are sized and confured is important in how effectively they will remove pollutants. This was discussed throughout the entire book. However, it is worth going over the key elements again. We again describe the basic elements of good design for both wet ponds and dry detention basins. We also recomment that a coars pollutant removal basin or forebay be provided for both types of basins.

23.6.1 Removal of Coarse Materials

There are operational advantages in removing coarse material as they enter the storage basin. A forebay near the basin inlet can be built for this purpose. Another approach is to install a separate coarse materials separating facility just ahead of the storage basin. The forebay, or a separate basin, could be lined with concrete or soil cement to facilitate cleaning.

A coarse pollutant basin needs to be sufficiently deep to prevent frequent resuspension of deposited sediments. Also, it needs to have a storage volume sufficient to detain the seasonal average inflow rate for about 5 minutes and a water surface area that provides surface load of approximately 50 feet per hour for a seasonal average hourly inflow rate.

The average runoff rate is expected to be $Q = 0.25 \cdot 100 \cdot 0.122 \cdot 43,560/12 = 11,000$ cubic feet per hour, $(310 \text{ m}^3/\text{h})$. Under these conditions, the forebay should have a surface area sized as follows:

$$A = \frac{Q}{V_S}$$

or,

$$A = \frac{11,000}{50} = 220 \text{ square feet } (20.5 \text{ m}^2)$$

and its volume should be no less than

$$V = (11,000 \text{ ft}^3/\text{hr}) \cdot \frac{5 \text{ min}}{60 \text{ min/hr}} = 915 \text{ ft}^3$$

Thus, a basin 4.5 feet (1.4 m) deep with a surface area 11 feet (3.4 m) wide and 20 feet (6.1 m) long should provide an adequate forebay. All the larger particles should settle out at this location and, as a result, the effective service life of the remaining pond should be extended.

Much of the coarse fraction of the sediment load is not reported in water quality data, since it is carried near the bottom of the drainageway where it is not sampled. Yet, this fraction can account for a large percentage of the solids entering a pond. When these solids settle out inside a pond, they reduce its volume. Thus, cleaning of the forebays when solids accumulate within them is an important part of operating water quality enhancement facilities.

Another feature of a forebay is the installation of a surface skimmer, such as a floating boom between the forebay and the pond, or a fixed skimming baffle. A skimmer will keep most of the floating trash from entering the pond itself and will confine floating debris to the area where it can be removed more easily.

23.6.2 Wet Ponds

In designing a wet pond, namely a basin with a permanent pool of water, the following features are recommended:

- Extend the flow length as much as possible between the inlet and the outlet.
- Minimize the hydraulic surface loading during regularly occurring rainstorms.
- Prevent short circuiting of flow.
- Provide sufficient volume in the permanent pool to capture as much runoff as possible for quiescent sediment removal between storms.
- Enhance conditions for biological treatment between storms.

Let's examine these elements with the aid of Figures 23.14 and 23.15. First, the pond has and elongated shape. Its length to width ratio, if we ignore the forebay area, is equal to three. This provides a fairly long flow path before the water exits at the outlet.

Second, the pond expands gradually from the outlet toward the inlet, insuring that there are no "dead zones." Namely, water entering the pond gradually spreads out and uniformly displaces the water already present in the pond (tries to achieve plug flow).

Third, a baffle is located at the outlet of the forebay. The baffle can be built out of redwood, cedar, or other decay-resistant wood or material and is designed to break up any jets of flow that may have not fully diffused on entering the pond. This type of a device is the best insurance against short-circuiting.

Fourth, size the permanent pool volume in accordance with the recommendations and the procedures described in Section 23.3. To insure that this volume is available for many years of sediment deposition, add approximately 25% more for sediment accumulation.

Fifth, design the outlet so that the average runoff event is captured in a surcharge volume above the permanent pool. This surcharge then is drained off in approximately 12 hours. During larger storms, the excess volume can be allowed to overflow freely at the outlet or at the spillway. This combination of permanent pool and surcharge volume should provide a cost-effective configuration, especially if the water quality pond is a part of a larger basin used to regulate runoff from larger storms such as the 2-, 5-, 10-, or 100-year events.

Sixth, maintain the average pond depth between 4 and 8 feet (1.2 and 2.4 m). Also, provide a 10- to 20-foot (3- to 6-m) wide shallow bench along the shores for safety and to encourage bottom vegetation to develop. It is expected that this vegetation will enhance the biologic treatment characteristics of the pond. When the shoreline has mature bottom vegetation, the pond will also have a more "natural" appearance.

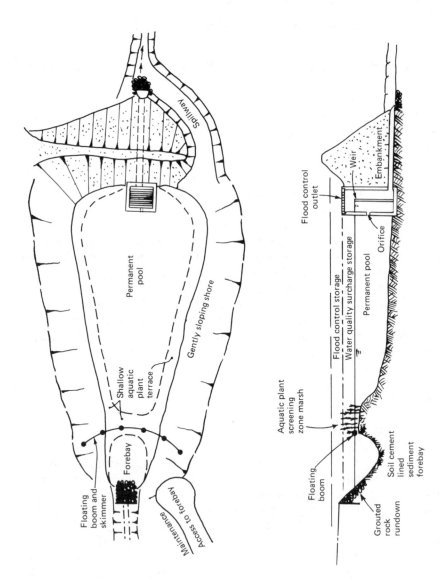

Figure 23.14 Example 1 of a wet pond—primarily stormwater management use.

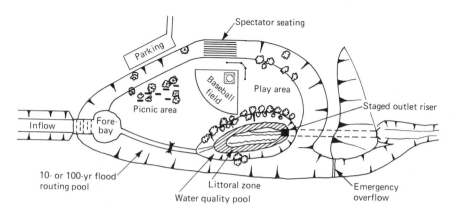

Figure 23.15   Example 2 of a wet pond —multiobjective use.

23.6.3 Dry Basins

The configuration of a dry detention basin is, in many respects, similar to what was described for wet ponds. It does, however, need additional features to enhance its use, its aesthetics, and its maintainability. In configuring a dry pond, try to provide the following:

• Extend the flow length between the inlet and the outlet.
• Minimize short circuiting during the filling phase.
• Provide sufficient volume to capture as much runoff as possible for sedimentation to be effective before water leaves the pond.
• Extend its use and aesthetics during periods between storms.
• Provide features to enhance ease of routine maintenance.

Let's examine these with the aid of Figures 23.16(a) and 16(b). First, the dry basin also has an elongated shape. Its length to width ratio, if we ignore the forebay area, is similar to a wet pond, but this feature is not quite as critical as in a wet pond.

Second, short circuiting is reduced by an outlet that drains very slowly and is packed in coarse gravel. Also, the fill and drain volume (i.e., similar to surcharge volume in a wet pond) needs to be somewhat larger than for a wet pond to trap a wider range of storms.

Third, the basin volume is zoned vertically. The lower level is provided for frequent inundation. It is intended to limit the extent of the muddy or marshy bottom so that the rest of the bottom can be used for passive recreation and can be maintained more easily. If base flows permit, establishing a

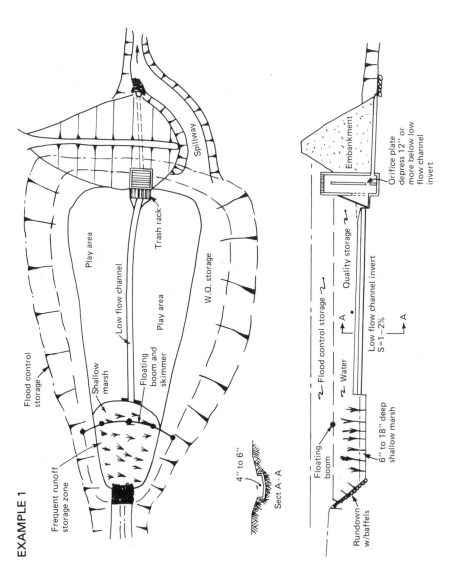

Figure 23.16 Two examples of basic configuration of a dry basin.

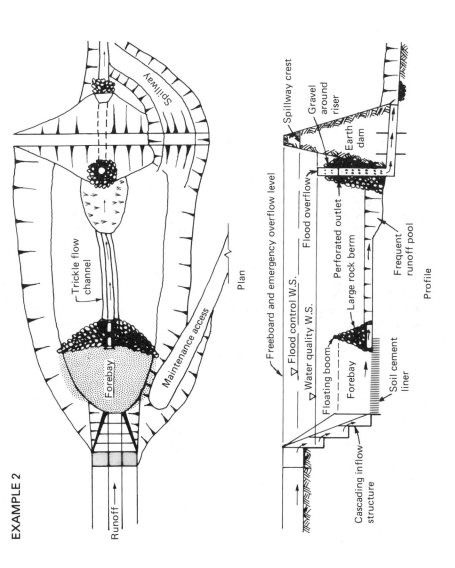

EXAMPLE 2

marsh bottom in the lower zone should also help reduce resuspension of sediment during the filling phase.

Fourth, a trickle flow, or a low flow channel, between the inlet and the lower zone will greatly enhance the recreational usability of the upper zone and its maintenance.

REFERENCES

BROWN, C., "Sediment Transportation," *Engineering Hydraulics*, Hunter Rouse, ed., New York, 1950.

CAMP, T. R., "Sedimentation and Design of Settling Tanks," *Transactions of the American Society of Civil Engineers*, Paper No. 2285, pp. 895–958, ASCE, 1946.

DRISCOLL, E. D., PALHEGYI, G. E., STRECKER, E. W., AND SHELLEY, P. E., *Analysis of Storm Event Characteristics for Selected Rainfall Gauges Throughout the United States*, a report by Woodward-Clyde Consultants prepared for and funded by U.S. Environmental Protection Agency, Washington, D.C., November, 1989.

DOBBIN, E., "Effect of Turbulence on Sedimentation," *Transactions of the American Society of Civil Engineers*, Paper No. 2218, pp. 629–78, ASCE, 1944.

EPA, *Methodology for Analysis of Detention Basins for Control of Urban Runoff Quality*, U.S. Environmental Protection Agency, EPA440/5-87-001, September, 1986.

EPA, *Results of the Nationwide Urban Runoff Program, Final Report*, U.S. Environmental Protection Agency, NTIS No. PB84-185545, Washington, D.C., 1983.

GRIZZARD, T. L., RANDALL, C. W., WEAND, B. L., AND ELLIS, K. L., "Effectiveness of Extended Detention Ponds," *Urban Runoff Quality*, American Society of Civil Engineers, 1986.

MAKER, P. W., AND URBONAS, B. R., "Incipient Runoff Value of Rainfall in the Denver Region," *Flood Hazard News*, Urban Drainage and Flood Control District, Denver, December, 1989.

METROPOLITAN WASHINGTON COUNCIL OF GOVERNMENTS, *Urban Runoff in the Washington Area—Final Report, Washington, D.C. Area Urban Runoff Project*, 1983.

OCCOQUAN WATERSHED MONITORING LABORATORY, *Final Contract Report: Washington Area NURP Project*, Prepared for the Metropolitan Washington Council of Governments, 1986.

PECHTER, R., "Design of Storm Water Retention Basins," *NORDSFRSK Report, Seminar on Detention Basin*, Marsta, November 7–8, 1978. (In Swedish)

PECHTER, R., "Dimension of Storm Water Retention Basins According to Modern Rain Evaluation," *Koncept*, 1978. (in German)

RANDALL, C. W., "Stormwater Detention Ponds for Water Quality Control," *Stormwater Detention Facilities—Planning Design Operation and Maintenance*, Proceedings of an Engineering Foundation Conference, ASCE, 1982.

ROESNER, L. A., URBONAS, B., AND SONNEN, M. A., Ed., *Current Practices in the Design of Urban Runoff Quality Facilities*, Proceedings of an Engineering Foundation Conference, ASCE, New York, 1989.

SCHUELER, T. A., *Controlling Urban Runoff,* Metropolitan Washington Council of Governments, Washington D.C., July, 1987.

URBONAS, B., AND ROESNER, L. A., Eds., *Urban Runoff Quality—Impacts and Quality Enhancement Technology,* Proceedings of an Engineering Foundation Conference, ASCE, New York, 1986.

URBONAS, B. GUO, C. Y., AND TUCKER, L. S. "Optimization of Stormwater Quality Capture Volume," *Urban Stormwater Quality Enhancement,* Proceedings of an Engineering Foundation Conference, ASCE, New York, 1990.

U.S. BUREAU OF RECLAMATION, *Design of Small Dams,* 1973.

VON DEN HERIK, A. G., "Water Pollution by Storm Overflow From Mixed Sewer Systems," *Berichte der ATV,* No. 28, Bonn, 1976. (In German)

WHIPPLE, W., AND HUNTER, J. V., "Settleability of Urban Runoff Pollution," *Journal Water Pollution Control Federation,* pp. 1726–32, 1981.

24

Design of Wetland Detention Basins and Channels

24.1 INTRODUCTION

A wetland behaves similarly to a conventional detention basin. It routes the flows that enter by storing part of the inflow volume as a surcharge above its dry weather surface. This dry weather surface can be a shallow ponding area, a mangrove swamp, a reed bed on top of a nearly saturated soil layer, a cattail marsh, a peat bog, or any other form of wetland that can be found or constructed. Wetland beds are often typified by zero or almost-zero grades and sluggish flow characteristics. As a result, the incoming flow is slowed down, causing temporary detention to take place. The degree of storage and detention residence time are a function of its size, nature, and geometry in relation to the inflow hydrograph volume and the hydrograph's temporal distribution.

Wetlands can be used to manage stormwater peak flow rates and to enhance stormwater quality, not unlike conventional detention ponds and basins. In fact, some of the detention basins that originally were built to modulate peak flow rates have, over time, developed wetland growth in their bottoms. Such growth in an urban detention basin was often considered a nuisance. Foul odors, mosquitoes, and an undesirable appearance are the most common complaints, which on occasion have resulted in removal of the accumulated silts and vegetation from the basin's bottom. The accumulation of sediments, followed by their removal and the removal of wetland growth from such detention basins enhances the quality of stormwater, often without the owner knowing that such an improvement in water quality is occurring.

The use of wetlands in recent years has gained recognition and popularity as one of the best management practices for improving stormwater quality. Many states within the United States, and some European countries, now recommend the use of wetlands for this purpose. Much is claimed as to their ability to remove nitrogen and phosphorus compounds, as well as metals, organics, and suspended solids.

Many of the claims that wetlands remove nutrients from water originated from tests performed on facilities designed to treat municipal wastewater, where the inflow concentrations of nutrients are about an order of magnitude higher than those found in separate urban stormwater runoff. On the other hand, the few data available for stormwater do not paint a clear picture. Until much more field-based research is completed, the use of wetlands to remove nutrients must be approached very cautiously. While data on the removal of nutrients from stormwater show mixed results, the removal of metals and suspended solids by wetlands appears to be very good, at least equaling, and sometimes exceeding, the removal efficiency of extended detention basins and water quality ponds.

This chapter summarizes much of what is known about the pollutant removal efficiency of wetlands. In addition, procedures are suggested for the design of wetland basins and wetland channels. The latter can be used as post-treatment facilities downstream of traditional extended detention basins and ponds. Since extended contact time with the biological treatment media found in wetlands is extremely important to their ability to remove dissolved pollutants, the combination of extended detention ponds and downstream wetland bottom channels offers the possibility of a combined treatment efficiency that is better than either element may be able to provide by itself.

The use of wetlands for stormwater quality enhancement is currently evolving. Much of what we know about their design will probably change as more is learned about how wetland systems behave under various geographic, climatic, and meteorologic conditions around the world. Nevertheless, the suggestions offered in the following pages are based on the latest information available. They should provide a glimpse into current practices and what one may expect to achieve when using this stormwater best management technology.

24.2 WETLAND DETENTION BASINS

24.2.1 Pollutant Removal Characteristics

The use of wetlands was suggested for the removal of nutrients from urban stormwater in the mid-1980s. It was felt intuitively that wetlands could use these nutrients in their growth and thereby reduce concentrations in the water column. Studies by Kadlec and Hammer (1980), Nichols (1983), Watson et al. (1989), and others showed that wetlands could be used effectively for wastewater treatment, provided nutrient loading rates were not excessive. However, according to these same investigators, there is an apparent deterioration in the nutrient removal efficiency of a wetland with time.

Goldstein (1988) observed that the efficiency of nutrient uptake from agricultural runoff in a Florida wetland decreased as the annual unit loading rate increased and as the wetland aged over a 3-year period. Nitrogen removal was classified by Goldstein as "poor," while phosphorus removals ranged from 25% to 50% as long as the loading rates were less than 88 pounds per acre per year (100 kg/ha/year). These findings were not dissimilar to those reported for the treatment of municipal wastewater. Apparently, the aging of wetland vegetation, and possibly other processes, tends to decrease its ability to remove phosphorus and other nutrients. The implication is that wetland plant harvesting and, possibly, frequent sediment removal from wetland wastewater treatment systems (i.e., mucking out) may be needed if removal of phosphorus is the goal.

Strecker et al. (1990) summarized the performance of several wetlands in the United States that were used for the treatment of urban stormwater. Their report indicates that wetlands can be very effective in removing suspended solids and total lead. Average removal efficiencies for suspended solids at the listed sites ranged between 40% and 96%, with the average for all sites being 87%. An average site's removal rates for lead ranged between 20% and 94%, with the average for all sites being 85%. However, the data for lead were for inflow concentrations no longer found in urban stormwater runoff in the United States. Data obtained in 1989 and 1990 indicate lead concentrations in stormwater are about 10 to 40 micrograms per liter, which is equal to one-fifth or less of the concentrations measured in the United States in 1978 and 1979 (see Table 21.1). These reductions in the concentration of lead in stormwater can be attributed to decreased use of leaded gasoline. Therefore, the high removal rates for lead reported by Strecker et al. (1990) and others using pre-1989 data are unlikely to be occurring with the much lower lead concentrations found in stormwater after 1989. Preliminary data obtained in 1989 and 1990 in Denver at a single stormwater detention pond seem to substantiate this opinion.

The efficiency of wetlands in removing nutrients found in stormwater appears to vary between different sites (e.g., -4% to 62% for NH_3 and -4% to 90% for total phosphorus). This was substantiated by Harper et al. (1988), who concluded:

Wetland systems appear better suited for removing heavy metals than nutrients, suggesting that wetlands may be particularly effective in treating highway runoff where heavy metals are primary pollutants. Systems designed for removal of nutrients should avoid long detention times and stagnant conditions; both can decrease oxidation reduction potential and pH and reduce the efficiency of phosphorous removal.

From all the data evaluated to date, the picture is far from being clear. It appears that the removal of nitrogen by wetlands is not effective, while removal of phosphorus varies with design, loading rates, site conditions such as soils [especially the availability of extractable aluminum in soil (Richardson, 1985)], type of wetland, and climate. The removal of most metals appears to be good to excellent. However, some metals such as zinc and copper exhibit wide variations in removal rates between sites, ranging from net export during storms to removals exceeding 80%. When the performance data are compared (see Table 25.2), it is difficult to conclude that wetlands outperform retention ponds and extended detention basins in removing most pollutants. Nevertheless, wetland basins do offer another detention alternative that has a potential for improving the removal of pollutants from stormwater.

24.2.2 Capture Volume and Size of Wetland Basins

Capture Volume.   The storage volume in a wetland is the available surcharge volume above its dry weather surface, which may be the surface of a shallow pond, wet soils of a reed marsh, or one of the many other types of wetland surfaces. When designing a wetland, the flow regulator at the outlet must be sized in balance with the design volume. Section 23.5 describes one method for optimizing a water quality detention volume. The optimized volume (i.e., the 80th to 90th percentile storm runoff volume), or other capture volume, above a wetland should be based on emptying times of 20 to 40 hours. Although the actual runoff volume to be captured will vary from one meteorologic region to another, it appears that a volume equal to approximately 0.5 inch (13 mm) of runoff from the impervious surfaces tributary to the wetland will capture about 80% to 90% of all runoff events in many cities in United States, Canada and, possibly, Europe (Urbonas et al., 1990; Roesner, 1991; Urbonas and Roesner, 1992).

The above recommendations for sizing the capture volume are those of the authors. Many local jurisdictions and authorities have evolved their own, which may be just as valid. As an example of local criteria, the state of Maryland (1987) requires the capture volume to be equal to the runoff from a 1-year runoff event which is to be released over a 24-hour period.

Surface Area.   Some authorities (e.g., EPA, 1986, 1988) suggest sizing a wetland surface area without regard for its capture volume. These sizing criteria are often stated strictly as a percentage of the tributary watershed surface area. Most common recommendations range from 1.5% to 3.0% of the tributary watershed area.

A fixed surface area recommendation may not be appropriate, since the volume of runoff from storms having less than 1 inch (25.4 mm) of precipitation is proportional to the amount of impervious area in the tributary watershed.

The fact is that a tributary watershed with a more impervious cover produces more surface runoff than a watershed with a less impervious area. As a result, wetlands sized using a fixed percentage of the tributary watershed tend to disproportionately burden less intense land uses.

As an example, a watershed with a low-density residential development that has a very small directly connected impervious area has to provide as much wetland area as a watershed with a commercial development that is totally covered with pavement. In the first case there is very little surface runoff, while in the second case most of the precipitation falling on the paved surfaces becomes surface runoff.

Base Flow Needs for Sustaining a Wetland.   Last, the wetland surface area must be kept wet during extended periods of no precipitation. Stated another way, a wetland needs sufficient base flow to sustain itself as a wetland. If there is no base flow, or if it is less than the evapotranspiration losses, this best management practice is not recommended.

The designer must know what the dry weather base flow will be and then use it to calculate a water budget for the wetland over an extended period of time. This involves defining statistics for the length of time between runoff-producing precipitation events and comparing them with the evapotranspiration rates on a month-to-month basis and the expected infiltration losses. As an alternative, a simple water budget continuous model can be set up using 1-hour or daily precipitation data. Simulated runoff volumes are then compared with the expected base flow, exfiltration, and evapotranspiration, using continuous data for temperature, wind, and relative humidity.

When designing a wetland basin using water budget calculations, size the wetland to ensure that the inflow is greater than all the projected losses. This will ensure that the salinity of the permanent water pool does not become excessive. Increased concentrations of dissolved solids and metals are flushed out with the first runoff event that follows an extended dry period. If the runoff event has little dilution volume, the flushed-out water may contain toxic or near-toxic concentrations of metals or other constituents. As a result, under extreme conditions a wetland or a detention pond could cause the very problems it is supposed to be solving.

24.2.3 Shape and Depth of Wetland Basins

Wetland Basin Shapes.   Figure 24.1 shows three idealized wetland basins designed to enhance stormwater quality. All three have a shallow permanent pool. Like conventional detention basins and ponds, wetlands should be shaped to optimize the contact of the inflow with the wetland basin surface. The three idealized wetland layouts in Figure 24.1 have an elongated shape. The idea shape is an oval, with the outlet and inlet at opposite ends. If an oval shape is not possible, use any other elongated shape that separates the inlet

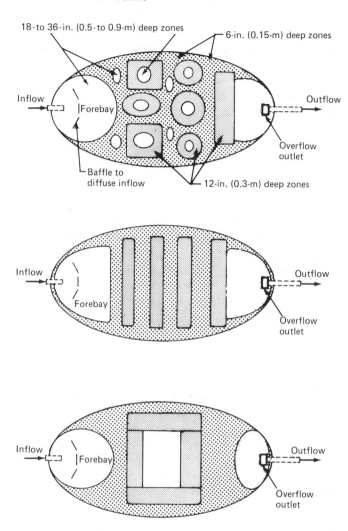

NOTE: Longitudinal Slope Between Inlet and Outlet Should Be Zero or Near-Zero.

Figure 24.1 Three idealized wetland basin layouts.

and outlet as much as possible. It is suggested that the length-to-width ratio of the wetland surface be no less than 3 (i.e., $L/W \geq 3$). The primary goal is to increase the contact time of the inflow with the wetland surfaces and to ensure that the inflow does not short-circuit the facility. An elongated basin shape helps to achieve these goals.

The three examples in Figure 24.1 display a forebay. This forebay helps settle out the largest sediment particles before the flow passes over the areas covered with emergent vegetation. It also helps to spread the inflow uniformly over the entire wetland. Such a forebay needs to be cleaned on a regular basis. Cleaning of a properly designed forebay described in Section 23.5.1 can be accomplished at much less cost than cleaning out the entire wetland. If the forebay is regularly cleaned, the wetland will function for a significantly longer period before it will have to be totally dredged.

The forebay should also have a baffle near the inlet as illustrated in Figure 24.1. Such a baffle must be designed to break up the inflow jet and facilitate spreading of the inflow over the entire surface area of the wetland. This spreading out of the flow maximizes its ability to remove suspended solids from stormwater and to maximize the contact time between stormwater and the biological treatment surfaces of wetland vegetation and bottom detritus.

An overflow outlet, not dissimilar to a riser used in a conventional pond, is placed within a deepened portion near the outlet end of the basin. This deepened basin helps keep the outflow zone free of emergent vegetation and makes the outlet less likely to clog. Wetlands serving small tributary watersheds should have very small outlets in order to ensure that the drain time of the design capture volume is no less than 20 hours. However, designing small outlets that do not clog is difficult, if not impossible. Thus, small wetland outlets need regular inspection and maintenance to ensure that they continue to operate as designed.

Variable Depth.   The bottom of the wetland should have a variable depth between the inlet and the outlet. Although the depths are shallow compared to those of a conventional detention pond, they should vary throughout the facility to promote diversity of ecological systems and of biological and physical treatment processes. In the three layouts in Figure 24.1 the depth varies in a number of ways throughout the wetland. The goal in shaping the bottom is to prevent the development of preferred flow routes within the wetland as sediments accumulate on its bottom with time. Thus, any pattern that provides transverse barriers to the direction of flow between the inlet and the outlet helps achieve this goal.

Dry Weather Depths in a Wetland.   If the depth of the water in a wetland during dry weather periods is too shallow, or virtually nonexistent, the wetland can become a nuisance. Excessive mosquito breeding and a boggy appearance will result in complaints from the neighbors. It is suggested that the permanent pool be designed to have a depth varying between 6 and 36 inches (0.15 and 0.9 m). This should provide the conditions needed to breed mosquito predators, thereby controlling the mosquito population to a large extent. On the other hand, depths less than 12 inches (0.3 m) are needed to promote growth of many of the emergent vegetation species found in wetlands such as bull rush, cattail, etc.

A well-designed urban wetland should have a shallow permanent pool of water that varies in depth. Variations in depth provide zones for emergent vegetation and zones where predator species can thrive. It is suggested that

40% to 70% of the wetland have depths of less than 12 inches (0.3 m), with the balance ranging in depth between 18 and 36 inches (0.5 and 0.9 m). Of the 40% to 70% that is less than 12 inches (0.3 m) in depth, about one-third to one-half should be about 6 inches (0.15 m) in depth. As a general rule, the water depth should not be uniform over large portions of the wetland. Instead, the bottom should be rough and undulating so that the depth varies throughout. Table 24.1 summarizes the above recommendations on how to proportion a wetland area by depth.

Wet Weather Surcharge Depths.   During storm events the water rises above the dry weather water surface. Therefore, wetland plants must be protected from long periods of excessive inundation. The maximum depth of inundation of wetland plants should play a role in determining the surface area of a wetland and not an arbitrary surface area rule of thumb.

Practically all wetland species can survive periods of inundation as long as these periods are not too long. It is hard to say what maximum period the surcharge volume should be designed for. Since it is normally designed to drain in approximately 20 hours, it does not mean that the capture volume zone will always empty out in this time because a series of closely spaced storms can keep it filled for longer periods.

A maximum depth of inundation during the wet weather period should be set to ensure that a large percentage of the plants will survive and continue to function. There is virtually no guidance on what this depth should be. To some extent, the surcharge depth depends on the wetland plant species to be used, as some species grow very tall. As a general rule, surcharge depths for a design capture volume of 1 to 2 feet (0.3 to 0.6 m) should be relatively safe once the emergent vegetation has become established.

It is important to remember that a wetland designed for stormwater treatment will provide a rather harsh environment for emergent vegetation. Only the most hardy species can be expected to thrive. Species such as cattail should do well with the above-stated maximum surcharge depth.

An example of how to size the area of a wetland should illustrate the process. Let's design a wetland basin to capture and treat urban stormwater runoff from 0.5 inch (0.15 m) of runoff from all impervious surfaces in the

TABLE 24.1   Dry Weather Depth Distribution
in a Wetland

Depth		Percent of Wetland Surface
Inches	Meters	
<12	<0.3	50 to 70*
18 to 36	0.5 to 0.9	30 to 50

* One-third to one-half of the depth zone less than 12 inches (0.3 m) should be only 6 inches deep.

tributary watershed. Also, we will limit the surcharge depth at this capture volume to 1.5 feet (0.46 m). Fifty percent of the watershed's surface area is impervious.

The resultant wetland basin will have a surface area equal to 1.4% of the tributary watershed total area. This percentage is calculated as follows:

Wetland area as a percentage of the tributary watershed area

$$= \{[0.5 \text{ in.} \cdot (50/100)/12 \text{ in./ft})]/1.5 \text{ ft}\} \cdot 100 = 1.4\%$$

On the other hand, if the same tributary watershed is a commercial area with 100% of its surface impervious, the wetland area needed for the same surcharge depth constraints will be 2.8% of the tributary watershed area.

Alternative Designs. Different types of wetland treat stormwater differently. The designer should consider the use of meadow wetland consisting primarily of meadow-type wetland grasses. Meadow wetlands only occasionally have standing water. Another form of wetland is the boggy type consisting of practically no permanent pool and reed-type emergent vegetation.

Both of these two types of wetlands are prone to breeding mosquitoes and may in fact be undesirable in an urban setting. Regardless of which type (or even a series of different types) is eventually selected, it is always a good idea to precede wetland basin installations with a detention pond, a detention basin, or an adequately sized forebay. Upstream detention can equalize the flow through the wetland and remove most of the sediment load from the stormwater, while the forebay helps to remove the heaviest sediments before stormwater is applied to the wetland's surface.

Wetlands Following Detention Facilities. When a wetland follows an extended detention basin or a retention pond, very little surcharge volume is required, and there is no need for a forebay. In such an arrangement, the surface area of the wetland cannot be sized using the surcharge depth procedure described earlier. Instead, in current practice one must revert to a simple design based on a percentage of the tributary watershed. Since surface runoff is somewhat proportional to watershed imperviousness, it is suggested that whenever a wetland is designed to follow an extended detention basin or a pond, the surface area of the wetland be sized to be at least 1.5% to 3.0% of the directly connected impervious area within the tributary watershed.

24.3 WETLANDS CHANNELS

24.3.1 General

A wetland bottom channel can provide some level of water quality treatment for urban base flows, releases of upstream water quality ponds and extended detention basins, and smaller runoff events even when upstream detention is not present. The effectiveness of pollutant removal within a flowing channel bed with wetland vegetation has not yet been quantified, but is likely that a wetland bottom channel helps to somewhat enhance the quality of urban runoff before it enters the receiving waters.

A wetland bottom channel is one of many artificial channel possibilities for urban areas. A properly designed channel can serve as part of a major drainage system. It often costs less, provides residual capacity in excess of its design capacity whenever flows are larger than designed for (a feature not available in a storm sewer), and offers a degree of flow routing storage not available in fast-flowing storm sewers or concrete-lined channels.

The disadvantages of wetland open channels, when compared to storm sewers, include greater right-of-way needs within an urban area and higher maintenance costs. In addition, a wetland channel bottom is boggy and can become overgrown, providing a habitat for mosquitoes. It is not practical to mow the bottom of such a channel, and it is very difficult to control the density of the vegetation. This abundant bottom vegetation traps sediments, eventually resulting in a reduced flood carrying capacity. Depending on the sediment loads carried by the flow, the wetland bottom of the channel will eventually need to be dredged to restore its capacity. On the other hand, careful land use planning and sound design can minimize the disadvantages and increase the benefits.

Grass-lined and wetland bottom artificial channels offer the greatest potential for achieving a variety of urban objectives. An ideal grass-lined channel or wetland bottom channel resembles a slough, a brook, or a creek shaped by nature over a long period of time. The benefits of such a channel include:

- Flow velocities are usually relatively low, sometimes resulting in longer concentration times and lower downstream peak flows.
- Channel and overbank storage decreases peak flows downstream.
- It is reasonably safe for local residents and children if flow velocities are kept low and the bank side slopes are no steeper than $3H:1V(4H:1V$ or flatter recommended).
- The channel provides a green belt that can support urban wildlife and recreation activities, adding significant social and environmental benefits.

24.3.2 Channel Design

Open channels, including grass-lined and wetland bottom channels are often designed on the assumption that they will carry a uniform flow at normal depths. But owing to ignored conditions, flow depths vary throughout the reach and may differ from uniform flow depth. The engineer must be aware that uniform flow computations provide only an approximation of what may actually be taking place within any reach of an open channel.

The rate of flow at any given depth can be computed using several commonly used equations. One of the most popular is Manning's formula, Equation 24.1:

$$Q = \frac{K_u}{n} A \cdot R^{2/3} \cdot S_o^{1/2} \qquad (24.1)$$

in which Q = discharge in cubic feet per second (m³/s),
K_u = 1.49 for U.S. standard units (1.0 for SI units),
n = Manning's roughness coefficient,
A = area in square feet (m²),
R = hydraulic radius A/P in feet (m),
P = wetted perimeter in feet (m), and
S_o = channel bottom slope in feet per foot (m/m).

On the other hand, the normal depth for any given flow cannot be found directly using Equation 24.1 or any other commonly used equation. It can be found using Equation 24.1 with the aid of nomographs, by trial-and-error calculations, or with the use of one of many commercially available software packages for the design of open channels. Chow (1959) provides a nomograph-based procedure for finding normal depth of flow, which the reader is encouraged to review.

Since a wetland bottom channel is a special case of a grass-lined channel, the design procedure for a wetland bottom channel suggested here first requires that a stable grass-lined channel be designed. This is then followed by a set of modifications that convert a grass-lined channel design into a wetland bottom channel design.

The design of channels with wetland bottoms is an iterative process. In order to simplify the design procedure, assumptions must be made concerning how the flow depth in a channel interacts with the wetland vegetation and how this vegetation affects the channel's flow roughness. The recommended design procedure accounts for two flow roughness conditions. To ensure vertical channel stability, the longitudinal slope of the channel is found first assuming there is no wetland vegetation on the bottom (i.e., the "new channel" condition). To ensure adequate flow capacity after the wetland vegetation matures and some siltation occurs, the channel's cross-section is modified using the roughness coefficients expected to occur under "mature channel" conditions. Specifically, the suggested design parameters are as follows:

Design Flow.   It is suggested that a wetland bottom channel be designed to carry a 2-year peak runoff from the upstream watershed.

This recommendation has to be modified if the wetland bottom channel is preceded by a stormwater detention facility that reduces the 2-year runoff peak and prolongs the period of its runoff in the channel. Although the 2-year flow downstream of a detention facility may be less than for an uncontrolled watershed, the wetland bottom channel initial section and longitudinal slope are best when set using the undetained 2-year flow. This slope will ensure that the channel will have few or no erosion problems. At the same time, the channel's cross-section may have to be designed for a larger flood than the 2-year flood if an upstream detention significantly reduces the flow rate. A wetland bottom width of 6 feet (1.8 m) is probably a reasonable practical lower limit under such flow-modified circumstances.

Channel Cross-Section.   The channel cross-section can be of almost any type suitable to the site. Often the shape is chosen to suit open space, recreational needs, or a wildlife habitat, and/or to create other community benefits. The only requirement is that at the 2-year peak flow rate the depth be uniform over the channel's bottom and that the bottom width be at least eight times the 2-year flow depth. Typically, the following guidelines should result in a functioning artificial wetland bottom channel:

- Side slopes. Protect the banks within the 2-year low flow channel section from being undermined by flowing water. When bank protection is provided, such as riprap, the protected side slopes should be between $2.5H{:}1V$ and $3H{:}1V$. Above the 2-year flood level, vegetation alone can normally protect the banks against erosion. The side slopes of the overflow channel should be made as flat as possible, but no steeper than $4H{:}1V$.

- Depth. Maintain the flow depth of the 2-year flood between 3.0 feet (0.9 m) and 6.0 feet (1.8 m).

- Maximum design velocity and Froude number. Initially size the cross-section of the channel not to exceed the recommendations in Table 24.2 for the new channel condition. For a newly built channel, flow velocity and Froude number for the 2-year flood must be limited to relatively mild, nonscouring levels. It is likely that for the first 2 years after the channel is constructed, its wetland vegetation will be immature and not fully established.

- Bottom width. Set the bottom width initially to satisfy the hydraulic capacity, recognizing the limitations of velocity, depth, and Froude number recommended for the new channel condition. After the channel's longitudinal slope is set, enlarge the bottom width to convey the design flow using the channel roughness coefficient (Manning's n) for the mature channel condition [with (bottom width) ≥ 8.0].

- Freeboard. There is no practical reason to provide a freeboard for a 2-year flood channel (i.e., a low flow channel) designed using the mature channel condition. On the other hand, it is suggested that at least 1 foot (0.3 m) of freeboard be provided above a 100-year design water surface for the mature channel condition. If the flood conveyance system will have less than a 100-year flood capacity, provide at least 1 foot (0.3 m) of freeboard between the 100-year flood profile of the residual floodplain and any human-occupied structure built within or adjacent to the floodplain.

Longitudinal Channel Slope. Set the longitudinal channel slope using Manning's roughness coefficient for the new channel condition, i.e., the condition before the wetland vegetation and the channel roughness factor that it produces become established. Solve Equation 24.1 using the uncontrolled (i.e., no upstream detention influences, or ignoring those influences) 2-year flow for the slope. Limit the maximum 2-year flow velocity to the one recommended in Table 24.2. The charts in Figure 24.2 were developed to help estimate the longitudinal slope for new trapezoidal grass-lined channels flowing at a velocity of 2.5 feet per second (0.76 m/s) and of 4.0 feet per second (1.22 m/s). The new channel slope can be maintained through the use of grade control checks and drop structures.

TABLE 24.2 Suggested Maximum Uncontrolled 2-Year Flow Velocities for New Wetland Channels

	Erosion-Resistant Soils*	Erodible Soils
Two-year flood velocity	4.0 ft/s (1.22 m/s)	2.5 ft/s (0.61 m/s)
Maximum Froude number	0.5	0.3

* Erosion-resistant soils are defined as consolidated cohesive soils.

Roughness Coefficient. To determine the longitudinal slope and the initial cross-section area of the channel, use Manning's n for the new channel condition. To design the final channel cross-section and freeboard to meet local regulatory floodplain management levels (typically a 100-year flood in the United States), use the mature channel condition. It is suggested that the following Manning's n for the design of wetland bottom channels be used:

1. Newly built grass-lined channel:
   Two-year flood capacity, $n \leq 0.030$
2. Mature wetland channel:
   Wetland channel (see Figure 24.3)
   Grass-lined banks above the wetland bottom zone, $n = 0.035$
   Composite Manning's n of the channel using Equation 24.2.

$$n_c = \frac{n_o \cdot p_o + n_w \cdot p_w}{p_o + p_w}$$

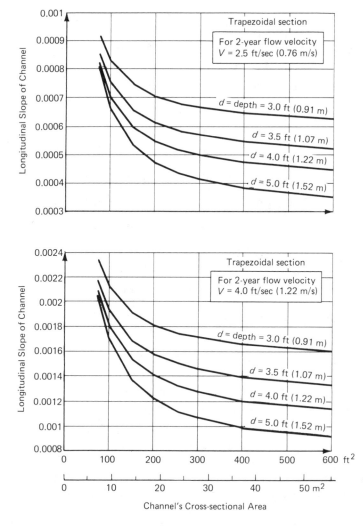

Figure 24.2   New channel ($n = 0.030$) slope-estimating charts for an uncontrolled 2-year peak flow with $V = 2.5$ feet per second (0.76 m/s) and 4.0 feet per second (1.22 m/s).

in which n_c = Manning's n for the composite channel,

n_o = Manning's n for areas above the wetland area,

n_w = Manning's n for the wetland area,

p_o = wetted perimeter above the wetland area, and

p_w = wetted perimeter of the wetland zone, equal to $B_w + k_u$,

where k_u = 10 feet (3 m).

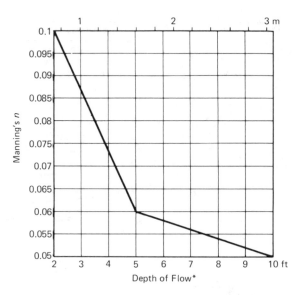

*Use normal flow depth, ignoring all backwater effects.

Figure 24.3   Suggested Manning's *n* roughness factors for wetland bottom channels. (After Urban Drainage and Flood Control District, 1991.)

The charts in Figure 24.4 were developed to help estimate the flow capacity of wetland bottom channels. They permit one to estimate the flow capacity of a channel with depths between 3 and 5 feet (0.91 and 1.52 m) and a longitudinal channel slope between 0.0002 and 0.003 while using the composite Manning's roughness coefficients suggested earlier.

Vegetation.   The grassed areas above the wetland bottom zone need to be planted with native turf-forming grasses. The wetland portions of the channel should be revegetated using wetland species common to the locality. Where possible, use species such as cattail, wetland reed grasses, etc., which are more tolerant to occasional high water flows. The services of a local horticulturist specializing in wetland vegetation can help with identification of the species, seed mixes, and application methods that will work best for local site conditions.

24.3.3 Design Examples of a Wetland Bottom Channel

This example illustrates the basic steps needed to design a wetland bottom channel. The goal is to have a channel that will be stable immediately after it is built, yet will have sufficient capacity for the 0.5 probability flood (i.e., the 2-year flood) after its wetland vegetation matures. In this example the design is for a composite channel having a 2-year low flow channel (wetland

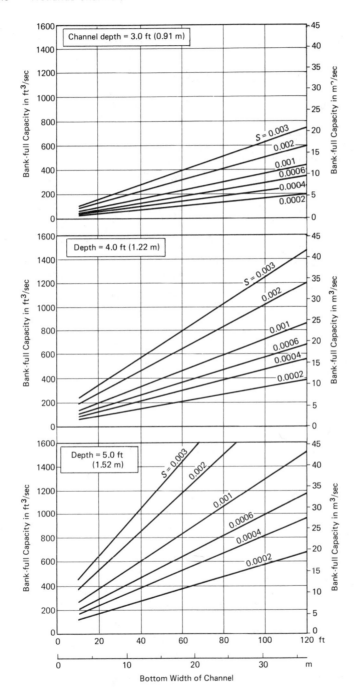

Figure 24.4   Wetland channel bank-full capacity.

channel) which, in combination with the major channel, has the capacity to carry a 100-year flood. The wetland bottom is confined to a stabilized low flow section.

To start with we are given the following design requirements:

Projected 2-year flow after urbanization: 250 cubic feet per second (7.1 m³/s)

Projected 100-year flow: 1000 feet per second (28.3 m³/s)

Erosion-resistant soils

Desired channel shape: see Figure 24.5

1. Determine the preliminary cross-section for a new grass-lined low flow channel.
    a. picking a new channel 2-year flow velocity of 2.5 feet per second (0.76 m/s) from Table 24.2 for erosion-resistant soils and a depth of 5.0 feet (1.52 m), estimate the cross-sectional area of the low flow channel:

$$A = \frac{Q}{v} = \frac{250 \text{ ft}^3/\text{s}}{2.5 \text{ ft/s}}$$

$$= 100 \text{ ft}^2 \ (9.3 \text{ m}^2)$$

    b. Find the corresponding bottom width:

$$B = \frac{A - zd^2}{d} = \frac{100 - 3(25)}{5}$$

$$= 5 \text{ ft } (1.52 \text{ m})$$

2. Determine the longitudinal slope of the low flow channel.

$$S = \frac{n^2 \cdot Q^2}{K_u^2 \cdot R^{4/3} \cdot A^2} \tag{24.3}$$

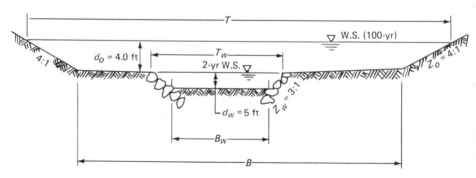

Figure 24.5 Example of a wetland bottom channel within a 100-year flood control channel.

in which all variables are the same as in Equation 24.1 and $n = 0.030$, $Q = 250$ cubic feet per second (7.1 m³/s), $WP = 36.6$ feet (11.2 m), $A = 100$ square feet (9.3 m²), and $R = A/WP = 2.73$ feet (0.832 m).

$$S = 0.00067 \text{ ft/ft (m/m)}$$

Figure 24.2 may be used as an aid in estimating the needed slope.

3. Estimate the bottom width of the low-flow wetland bottom channel.

    Figure 24.4 indicates that a 5-foot (1.52-m) deep wetland bottom channel with a longitudinal slope of 0.00067 and a bottom width of 14 feet (4.3 m) will convey a little over 250 cubic feet per second (7.1 m³/s). Before proceeding further, check the capacity of this low flow channel and adjust the bottom width if the use of Figure 24.5 missed the mark.

4. Find the composite Manning's n_w for the low-flow wetland bottom channel.

    Using the wetland Manning's n from Figure 24.3 for a 5-foot (2.26 m) flow depth ($n = 0.060$), find the composite Manning's roughness coefficient for the entire low flow channel using Equation 24.2:

$$n_w = (0.035 \cdot 21.6 + 0.06 \cdot 24.0)/45.6 = 0.048$$

Using this n_w we find that the channel will convey 228 cubic feet per second (6.46 m³/s), which is somewhat less than the desired 250 cubic feet per second (7.08 m³/s), but is close enough for the purpose of this example. Also in this example no attempt was made to achieve a minimum bottom width-to-depth ratio of eight, a limitation that should be adhered to.

5. Using the geometry and Manning's n for the low flow section developed using steps 1 through 4, design a flood overflow channel, in combination with the low flow channel, to carry the entire 100-year flow of 1000 cubic feet per second (28.3 m³/s):

    Using the composite n_w for the wetland low flow channel found in step 4 and setting the depth of the main channel (sometimes referred to as the overflow channel) outside the low flow section to 4 feet (1.52 m), incrementally increase the bottom width B until the desired flow capacity is found using the longitudinal slope of 0.00067 determined in step 2. To do this, first revisit Manning's equation for each part of the composite channel:

Wetland low-flow channel portion:

$$\text{Area:} \quad A_w = (B_w + z_w \cdot d_w) \cdot d_w = [14 + (3.0 \cdot 5.0)] \cdot 5.0$$

$$= 145 \text{ ft}^2 \text{ (13.5 m}^2\text{)}$$

Top width: $T_w = B_w + 2 \cdot z_w \cdot d_w = 14 + 2 \cdot 3.0 \cdot 5.0$

$$= 44 \text{ ft } (13.4 \text{ m})$$

Wetted perimeter: $P_w = B_w + 2 \cdot [d_w^2(1 + z_w^2)]^{1/2}$

$$= 14 + 2 \cdot [25 \cdot (1 + 9)]^{1/2}$$

$$= 45.6 \text{ ft } (13.9 \text{ m})$$

Manning's n for a wetland channel at $d_t = 9.0$ feet (2.7 m). From Figure 24.4, $n_w = 0.052$. For the areas outside the wetland zone, $n_{ow} = 0.035$. The composite Manning's n_{wc} for the wetland channel at a flow depth of 9.0 feet (2.7 m) is

$$n_{wc} = [n_w(B_w + k_u) + n_{ow}(P_{ow} - (B_{ow} + k_u))]/P_w$$

$$= [0.052 \cdot (14.0 + 10.0) + 0.035(45.6 - 24.0)]/45.6$$

$$= 0.044$$

Overbank channel portion:

Area: $A_o = (B + z_o \cdot d_o) \cdot d_o = (B + 4 \cdot 3.5) \cdot 3.5 \text{ ft}$

$$= [(B + 4 \cdot 1.07) \cdot 1.07 \text{ m}]$$

Top width: $T = B + 2 \cdot z_o \cdot d_o = B + 2 \cdot 4.0 \cdot 3.5$

$$= B + 28 \text{ ft } (B + 8.53 \text{ m})$$

Wetted perimeter: $P_o = B - T_w + 2 \cdot [d_o^2(1 + z_o^2)]^{1/2}$

$$= B - 44 + 2 \cdot [12.25 \cdot (1 + 16)]^{1/2}$$

$$= B - 15.1 \text{ ft } (B - 4.61 \text{ m})$$

Manning's n for the overflow grass-lined channel:

$$n_o = 0.035$$

Composite total channel capacity:

Area: $A_t = A_w + A_o = 145 \text{ ft}^2 + (B + 4 \cdot 3.5) \cdot 3.5 \text{ ft}$

$$= [13.5 \text{ m}^2 + (B + 4 \cdot 1.07) \cdot 1.07 \text{ m}]$$

Top width: $T = $ same as for overflow section

Wetted perimeter: $P_t = P_w + P_o$

Manning's n for the composite channel:

$$n_c = \frac{n_{wc} \cdot P_w + n_o \cdot P_o}{P_t}$$

Using these relationships, incrementally increase B and solve for the flow:

$$B = 44 \text{ ft } (13.4 \text{ m}) \quad Q = 918 \text{ ft}^3/\text{sec } (26.0 \text{ m}^3/\text{s})$$
$$= 50 \text{ ft } (15.2 \text{ m}) \quad = 971 \text{ ft}^3/\text{sec } (26.0 \text{ m}^3/\text{s})$$
$$= 54 \text{ ft } (16.8 \text{ m}) \quad = 1006 \text{ ft}^3/\text{sec } (26.0 \text{ m}^3/\text{s})$$

This leads to the conclusion that the bottom width of the overflow channel must be approximately 54 feet (16.5 m). Adding 1 foot (0.3 m) of freeboard results in a top width of 73 feet (22.3 m). Providing for a 12-foot (3.77-m) wide maintenance access bench on one side of the channel requires a right-of-way width of 85 feet (26 m) to be reserved for this channel. The exact right of way will probably be greater because drop structures will need more right of way than the channel and because site grading needs will most likely expand the above-calculated minimum right-of-way limits.

REFERENCES

CAMP DRESSER AND MCKEE, INC., *An Assessment of Stormwater Management Programs*, Florida Department of Environmental Regulations, December, 1985.

CHOW, VEN TE, *Open Channel Flow*, McGraw-Hill, New York, 1959.

EPA, *Results of Nationwide Urban Runoff Evaluation Program, Final Report*, U.S. Environmental Agency, NTIS PB84-185552, December, 1983.

EPA, *Methodology for Analysis of Detention Basins for Control of Urban Runoff Quality*, U.S. Environmental Protection Agency, EPA440/5-87-001, September, 1986.

EPA, *Lake and Reservoir Restoration Guidance Manual*, U.S. Environmental Protection Agency, 440/5-88-002, February, 1988.

EPA, *Wetland Identification and Delineation Manual*, U.S. Environmental Protection Agency, Vols. I and II, April, 1988.

GOLDSTEIN, A. L., "Utilization of Wetlands as BMPs for the Reduction of Nitrogen and Phosphorous in Agricultural Runoff from South Florida Watershed," *Annual International Symposium on Lake and Watershed Management*, St. Louis, 1988.

HARPER, H. H., WANIELISTA, M. P., BAKER D. M., FRIES, B. M., AND LIVINGSTON, E. H., "Treatment Efficiencies for Residential Stormwater Runoff in a Hardwood Wetland," *Annual International Symposium on Lake and Watershed Management*, St. Louis, 1988.

KEDLEC, R. H., AND HAMMER, D. E., "Wetland Utilization for Management of Community Wastewater," *1979 Operations Summary, Houghton Lake Wetland Treatment Project*, NTIS PB80-170061, February, 1980.

MARYLAND DEPARTMENT OF NATURAL RESOURCES, *Guidelines for Construction of Wetland Stormwater Basins*, March, 1987.

NICHOLS, D. S., "Capacity of Natural Wetlands to Remove Nutrients from Wastewater," *Journal of the Water Pollution Control Federation*, 1983.

ROESNER, L. A., BURGESS, E. H., AND ALDRICH, J. A., "The Hydrology of Urban Runoff Quality Management," *Proceedings of Water Resources Planning and Management Conference,* American Society of Civil Engineers, New Orleans, May, 1991.

ROESNER, L. A., URBONAS, B., AND SONNEN, M. B., Eds., *Proceedings of an Engineering Foundation Conference on Current Practices and Design Criteria for Urban Runoff Quality Control,* American Society of Civil Engineers, New York, July, 1988.

SCHUELER, T., *Controlling Urban Runoff: A Practical Manual for Planning and Design of Urban BMP's,* Metropolitan Washington Council of Governments, July, 1987.

SOIL CONSERVATION SERVICE, *Handbook of Channel Design for Soil and Water Conservation,* U.S. Department of Agriculture, Washington, D.C., March, 1947, revised June, 1954.

STRECKER, E. W., PALHEGYI, G. E., AND DRISCOLL, E. D., "The Use of Wetlands for Control of Urban Runoff Pollution in the U.S.A.," *Proceedings of the Fifth International Conference on Urban Storm Drainage,* Osaka, Japan, July, 1990.

URBAN DRAINAGE AND FLOOD CONTROL DISTRICT, *Urban Storm Drainage Criteria Manual,* Denver Regional Council of Governments, Denver, 1969, revised by UDFCD, 1991.

URBONAS, B., AND ROESNER L. A., Eds., *Proceedings of an Engineering Foundation Conference on Urban Runoff Quality—Impact and Quality Enhancement Technology,* American Society of Civil Engineers, June, 1986.

URBONAS, B., GUO, C. Y., AND TUCKER, L. S., "Optimization of Stormwater Quality Capture Volume," *Proceedings of the Engineering Foundation Conference on Urban Stormwater Quality Enhancement—Source Control, Retrofitting and Combined Sewer Technology,* Davos, Switzerland, October, 1989, American Society of Civil Engineers, 1990.

URBONAS B. R., AND ROESNER, L. A., "Hydrologic Design for Urban Drainage and Flood Control," in D. R. Maidment, Ed., *The McGraw Hill Handbook of Hydrology,* Chap. 28, McGraw-Hill, New York (in press).

USGS, *Constituent-Load Changes in Urban Storwater Runoff Routed Through a Detention Pond-Wetland System in Central Florida,* Water Resources Investigation Report 85-4310, U.S. Geological Survey, Tallahassee, Fla., 1986.

WATSON, T. J., REED, S. C., KADLEC, R. C., KNIGHT, R. L., AND WHITEHOUSE, A. E. "Performance Expectation and Loading Rates for Constructed Wetlands," *Constructed Wetlands for Wastewater Treatment: Municipal, Industrial and Agricultural,* Lewis Publishers, Chelsea, Mich., 1989.

25

Best Management Practices
for Stormwater Quality

25.1 INTRODUCTION

The technical literature and the not-so-technical literature suggest a number
of methods for reducing the pollutant load found in urban stormwater runoff.
Because these techniques do not depend on mechanical treatment, such as a
secondary wastewater treatment plant or a physical-chemical treatment plant
consisting of chemical flocculation followed by settling and filtering, they have
been labeled best management practices. Many BMPs rely on good housekeeping and public education, while others rely on structural facilities providing
passive treatment. Unfortunately, the entire field of BMPs has limited data
supporting the design practices in use today. This is not to say that BMPs are
not effective. They can and are effective when properly designed, constructed,
operated, and maintained.

Some BMPs probably perform as described in the literature, while others
may not do as well as claimed. The fact is that the reliability of BMPs has not
yet been well established, even at the locations where most of the performance
data come from. This point was mentioned by Roesner et al. (1988) in a
literature review concerning the field performance of various BMPs:

> Among all these [BMP] devices the most promising and best understood are
> detention and extended detention basins and ponds. Less reliable in terms of
> predicting performance, but showing promise, are sand filter beds, wetlands,
> infiltration basins, and percolation basins. All of the latter appear to be in their
> infancy and lack the necessary long-term field testing that would provide data for
> the development of sound design practices.

Obviously, meteorologic conditions vary throughout the United States, Canada, Europe, and every other continent in the world. As a result, adopting and using BMPs as a general practice needs to be approached with local conditions in mind. The authors have evaluated a number of commonly suggested best management practices for potential effectiveness and will describe each BMP and its ability to remove pollutants from stormwater. However, it is still suggested that local field testing, evaluation of findings, and development of design guidelines be conducted before any of the BMPs are adopted for use.

25.1.1 Areas Undergoing Land Use Change vs. Developed Areas

The use of best management practices can be grouped into two categories. One set of BMPs, primarily structural in nature, can be considered for areas undergoing land use changes, namely, the development of new land and the redevelopment of urbanized areas. Some of these are relatively easy to incorporate into new site plans but are probably impractical for use in areas that are already fully developed.

The amount of land area a given BMP requires often dictates how it fits into an existing development. *Retrofitting* land-intensive BMPs is not practical in developed urban areas since land values are high and the relocation of residences or businesses may be required. Therefore, clear evidence of adverse impacts must be present before land-intensive BMPs are considered for use in such areas. On the other hand, the use of *nonstructural BMPs,* e.g., good housekeeping practices, can reduce the pollutant loads being flushed into receiving waters.

In cases where clear public health concerns or severe receiving water impacts are evident, retrofitting of structural BMPs requiring the least amount of land can be considered. A number of structural, as well as nonstructural, approaches for retrofitting into an urban area were described by a number of investigators in the 1989 Engineering Foundation Conference Proceedings edited by Torno (1990). Some of them are described in this chapter as well.

25.1.2 Construction Phase vs. Long-Term Needs

There are two phases of urbanization. One phase consists of a temporary, relatively short-lived period when the land is disturbed or when construction is taking place. At that time vegetation is stripped off the land, and soils are moved to prepare the site for the new development. New streets, utilities, and buildings or other man-made structures are then constructed or reconstructed. Of primary concern during this phase are the erosion of soil by stormwater runoff and proper disposal of construction waste such as concrete delivery truck wash water, unused asphalt, old timber and plaster, wiring, piping, and roofing materials. The second phase involves the control of stormwater pollutant runoff from developed areas after construction activities end. This phase lasts as long as the constructed facilities are in place. The main concerns are control of continued erosion and reduction of pollutants being flushed into the receiving systems by stormwater after the construction period is over. Unless properly provided for through the use of stabilization techniques and structures, soil erosion can continue after the construction period is over, especially in open waterways. Ongoing maintenance activities will need to deal with this erosion until it is fully arrested with time.

The use of nonstructural BMPs will be needed after the land is urbanized. These nonstructural practices must become part of each community's daily activities if the reduction of stormwater pollutants is in fact the stated goal. In addition, ongoing maintenance of all structural BMPs must become a very important part of the postconstruction phase. This maintenance will be needed to keep various structural BMPs installed during the construction phase operating for many years after they are built.

25.1.3 Stormwater Quality Hydrology

Section 23.5 described a method suggested by Urbonas et al. (1990) for sizing water quality basins by optimizing stormwater quality capture volumes. The resultant volumes are significantly less than one would expect for traditional flood control or drainage detention facilities. While traditional drainage and flood control detention basins are designed to control large, infrequent storms, stormwater quality enhancement facilities should be designed to treat smaller, frequently occurring events. These are typically smaller than a 1-year storm, capturing the 50th to 90th percentile runoff event. Attempts to capture larger storms quickly produce diminishing returns and, in passive treatment facilities such as detention basins, result in very little additional incremental removal of the suspended solids and accompanying pollutants from stormwater.

Roesner et al. (1991) came to the same conclusion after studies more extensive than those reported by Urbonas et al. (1989). Roesner's studies included continuous modeling using calibrated runoff models in six cities in different meteorologic regions of United States. The reason for the use of small precipitation events to design stormwater quality facilities can be seen by examining Figure 25.1. It shows that for a watershed in Cincinatti, Ohio, having a runoff coefficient of 0.5, almost 95% of the runoff events can be totally captured with a storage volume of 0.5 watershed inch (12.7 mm), resulting in only four runoff events a year, on average, exceeding this capture volume.

It is also seen in Figure 25.1 that increasing the detention volume beyond

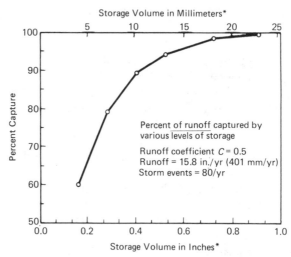

Figure 25.1 Runoff capture volume rates in Cincinnati, Ohio. (After Roesner et al., 1991.)

this point has very little effect on the number of storms being captured. Similarly, Urbonas et al. (1990) showed that for the Denver, Colorado, area a watershed with a 0.5 runoff coefficient needs a storage volume of only 0.37 watershed inch (9.4 mm) to totally capture 87% of runoff events. Despite the vastly different climates in Cincinnati and Denver, a similar detention volume can capture about the same percentage of runoff events at both locations.

25.1.4 Objectives in the Use of BMPs

When developing a stormwater quality management program that includes water quality best management practices, the following five basic objectives should be kept in mind:

- *Prevention.* Prevention of pollutant deposition in urban areas should be the primary objective. This may also be the most cost-effective. This practice is based on the principle that good housekeeping measures exercised by the residents of a municipality reduce the amount of pollutants being deposited on the urban landscape and eventually entering the urban stormwater system. Obviously, for this objective to be met, citizens must be aware of the problem they may be causing and be willing to actively participate in finding and implementing solutions.
- *Control pollutants at their source.* Meeting this objective requires the use of nonstructural practices and structural facilities, both of which reduce or prevent pollutants from coming into contact with precipitation and

surface runoff, thereby minimizing the migration of pollutants off-site. A very important part of this objective are local ordinances, land development practices, and criteria and enforcement programs aimed at minimizing the migration of pollutants form individual sites.

- *Source disposal and treatment of runoff.* The argument for pursuing this objective is the observation that urbanization results in major increases in surface runoff. Whenever site conditions permit, preventing or reducing surface runoff also reduces the volume and the rate of runoff to be handled by downstream stormwater facilities. When some of the pollutants can be removed from stormwater near the point of precipitation, the demand on downstream passive treatment facilities is lessened. Thus, whenever site conditions permit, on-site infiltration and percolation can reduce the volume of surface runoff, while on-site detention, retention, or filtration can reduce the pollutants transported by stormwater downstream.

- *Follow-up treatment.* Prevention, controlling pollutants at the source, and source disposal and treatment depend on the participation of many individuals. Some of these practices depend on the owner's ability and willingness to keep on-site facilities in good operating condition. This cannot always be ensured. Therefore, it is advisable to also intercept stormwater runoff downstream of all source and on-site controls to provide final follow-up treatment. The resultant series of best management practices, starting with source control and ending with follow-up treatment devices, was labeled the "treatment train" by Livingston et al. (1988), a concept that provides the most opportunities to enhance stormwater quality. In this way, one does not totally rely on a single best management practice. Figure 25.2 illustrates this concept.

25.2 NON-STRUCTURAL BEST MANAGEMENT PRACTICES

25.2.1 Period of Land Use Change

There are opportunities for the installation of structural BMPs in areas undergoing land use changes that do not exist in areas that are fully developed. The best time to require such BMPs is when land is being annexed to a municipality or when land use zoning is being negotiated between a land developer and local authorities. Failing that, the next best time is during the platting process when subdivision agreements between the city, or the county, and the landowner are being prepared. The most difficult time is when a building permit is being requested for a tract of subdivided land. At that time a city, county, or other local authority may have contractual obligations regarding how the landowner can use each parcel of land.

However, the use of structural BMPs is not the entire answer to controlling urban runoff quality. Nonstructural BMPs are an essential part of any

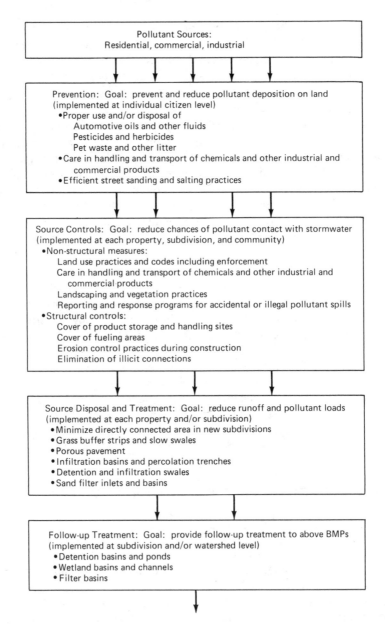

Figure 25.2 BMPs in series, maximizing the opportunity for water quality enhancement.

stormwater quality management program for areas undergoing land use changes. On the list of nonstructural BMPs are local approval procedures that pursue long-term water quality goals and technical criteria and enforcement programs ensuring that the required BMPs are appropriately implemented. More specifically, these nonstructural practices include the following.

Building and Site Development Codes.   Local land use authorities must adopt building and site development codes that provide for stormwater quality control. This is an essential part of any successful stormwater quality management program. Without such municipal laws the staff has no legal basis or technical guidelines for requiring structural measures when land uses are being modified. Such codes and regulations need to spell out the following:

- Goals and objectives of the stormwater management program,
- Responsibility within local government for implementation,
- How appeals for variances and conflicts will be handled,
- Enforcement procedures and penalties for violations,
- Responsibility for operation and maintenance of BMPs, and
- Program funding sources and commitments.

Site Disturbance Permits.   Whenever building, site grading, or general construction is to take place, each local land use authority should require the landowner or his agent to obtain a site disturbance permit. This permit must spell out, among other provisions, the responsibility for the control of erosion at the construction site and limit any sediment movement off the site. The following four types of site disturbance permits, or some modified form of them, can be used to meet the erosion control needs of a local land use authority:

- *Building permit.* In addition to the traditional requirements associated with the building of structures, a building permit can also list conditions for controlling the water quality of storm runoff from the building site. This permit can impose requirements for drainage facilities, maximum land slopes, landscaping, on-site detention or local disposal (where applicable), site erosion control, separate water quality control facilities (if any), etc. Such permit conditions provide the local building inspector(s) with a list of items required for compliance.
- *Grading permit.* A grading permit is intended to control all site grading, excavation, and fill operations that take place in advance of or independent of any building of structures. The objective of a grading permit is to control soil erosion by requiring approved erosion control practices or the preparation of an erosion control plan that would be normally submitted with the application.

- *Construction Permits.* A construction permit is similar to a building permit, except that it involves more than a single structure on a single lot. It covers the construction of all facilities and structures for a subdivision, commercial development, or industrial site. This type of permit spells out specific site development requirements, including erosion control, drainage, and stormwater quality facilities.
- *General Permits for Small Sites.* A general permit, often developed by a state or a local land use authority, can cover erosion control regulations for small sites without creating an excessive administrative burden. In-fill construction on single lots, or construction on limited acreage, can be covered by such a permit. This removes the need to process individual site development permit applications for small sites. Instead, the builder files a notice of intent with the city, the county, or the state 1 to 7 days before construction begins. A general permit outlines the minimum soil erosion control practices to be used during construction and provides for their enforcement.

Use of Grassed Areas.   The use of grassed areas for the removal of pollutants has been suggested by Maryland (1985) and other states in the United States, and by several of the contributing authors in DeGroot (1982), Urbonas (1986), and Roesner (1988). Grass-covered areas alone have a somewhat limited effect on stormwater quality. They can, however, be very effective when used in combination with other BMPs. Grassed surfaces, as discussed here, include grass swales, grass buffer strips, and landscaping practices in conjunction with buildings, streets, and parking lots, all of which are described in Section 2.3.

Grassed buffer strips help to remove coarse sediment from stormwater, especially during less intense rainstorms. They have little effect on the removal of dissolved pollutants and pollutants attached to very fine sediment. Chapter 21 described how smaller particulates and dissolved pollutants comprise a significant part of the pollutants found in stormwater. While only marginally effective in the removal of pollutants associated with very fine sediment, grass buffer strips are relatively inexpensive and can remove significant percentages of coarser sediment and other debris found in urban runoff. In addition, grassed areas are efficient traps for pollutants that fall to the ground during dry weather periods.

Specific guidelines in local subdivision regulations and criteria for the use of grassed areas must list the types of vegetation to be used, limits on land slopes, soil preparation needs, adequacy of soils, and maximum permissible flow velocities over vegetated areas. Maintenance guidance for vegetated areas must include mowing, watering, weed and pest control, and the repair or replacement of damaged areas.

Trapped sediment accumulates between the surfaces of grasses, and this can become bothersome in areas adjacent to paved surfaces draining onto the grass. As the sediment accumulates, the surface of the turf rises with time, eventually interfering with drainage of the paved area. When this happens, the turf adjacent to the pavement must be removed, the grade lowered, and new turf installed.

Street and Parking Lot Drainage Design Standards.   The policy of using *curb and gutter* along streets and within parking lots in areas undergoing development or redevelopment should be examined by local land use authorities. Where it is possible, *roadside swales* or *borrow ditches* should be used instead of curb and gutter. Runoff can be detained in the swale at each driveway, thereby slowing down the flow and reducing the rate of runoff in the downstream system. In many cases it may be possible to spread the runoff from parking lots across grass buffer strips, which takes advantage of the benefits described above for grassed areas.

The use of roadside swales instead of curb and gutter is not a technique that can be used everywhere. Site constraints, such as steep slopes, extremely erodible soils, and limited right of way mandate the use of curb and gutter. Nevertheless, a reduction in the use of curb and gutter, along with stabilized roadway shoulders, deserves consideration. Also, where site conditions permit, standards using automobile wheel stops and concrete pavement edging instead of curb and gutter can be developed.

Land Use Density Controls.   According to data collected by EPA (1983), stormwater runoff volume and, as a result, stormwater pollutant loads increase in proportion to the amount of impervious surface in the watershed. The zoning of land for different land use densities plays a major role in the generation of pollutant loads. The control of land use densities through zoning practices is another nonstructural activity. However, the privilege of making land use decisions is jealously guarded by cities, counties, and other land use control authorities. As a result, stormwater quantity and quality management practices suggested by others are not popular with these individuals.

The following two options should be considered when land use density controls are being contemplated:

- *Zoning incentives.* These include incentives to land developers to set aside more open space, such as reduced vehicle parking ratios, greater building heights, clustering of buildings, and building density trades. All these incentives are aimed at increasing open space and reducing the amount of directly connected impervious surface area within a new development.

- *Alternative land uses.* Land use control authorities may want to reexamine their long-term comprehensive land use plans. Closer scrutiny of the existing land use zoning in a community can reveal imbalances toward high use densities. Although downzoning is a politically difficult task, it can sometimes be justified for reasons other than stormwater management. Stormwater managers can then help elected officials by providing sound reasons for such zoning actions.

25.2.2 Post Land-Use Change and Fully Developed Areas

As stated earlier, structural best management practices are often not practical and are very expensive to retrofit into developed urban areas. On the other hand, nonstructural BMPs, e.g., good housekeeping practices, require little initial capital. They do, however, require operational funding to keep them viable from one year to the next.

Nonstructural BMPs can reduce the pollutant loads being flushed from developed areas into receiving waters. The same can be said for older urban centers and recently completed developments that incorporate the latest in structural BMPs. The degree to which good housekeeping practices can reduce pollutant loads is virtually impossible to quantify. At best, intuition tells us that some of these practices should have a positive effect and simply make good environmental sense.

Nonstructural BMPs for the post–land use change period and for developed areas fall into the following activity groups:

- Public education;
- Measures to prevent and reduce pollutant deposition on land;
- Street sweeping, leaf pickup, and deicing programs;
- Elimination of illicit discharges;
- Enforcement of private facility operation and maintenance; and
- Retrofit of structural BMPs in areas of major concern.

Public Education. The goal of public education is to prevent inappropriate use and disposal by the public of substances that can pollute surface runoff. Preventing the deposition of pollutants on land and their eventual transport by stormwater to receiving waters can be the most cost-effective in limiting the amount of pollutants in stormwater. Obviously, the general population has to be interested in solving the problems it is causing and willing to actively participate in preventing and reducing pollutant deposits on the urban landscapes.

Public education is the first step in getting the general population involved. First, it is necessary to raise public awareness by describing the basic water quality problems caused by citizens through their daily activities that can deposit pollutants on the urban landscape. Next, it is necessary to explain how pesticides, animal droppings, old crankcase oil, antifreeze, and many household chemicals and by-products deposited on the urban landscape find their way to the receiving waters. Finally, the public must be shown how the materials they use or dispose of improperly affect the water quality and the aquatic habitat of a multitude of species in streams, lakes, and rivers.

In addition to explaining the problem, a public information program must provide information about the following:

- How each resident can help;
- Efficient use of fertilizers;
- Proper use and disposal of pesticides and herbicides;
- Proper disposal of old paints and solvents;
- Proper disposal of unused soaps and detergents;
- Proper disposal of various household chemicals and caustics;
- Proper disposal of used automotive oils, solvents, and antifreeze;
- Proper disposal of litter; and
- The need to pick up and properly dispose of pet droppings.

Preventing and Reducing Pollutant Deposition.   Several good housekeeping activities can be employed by all citizens. One of these is the control of pet waste. Animal feces and urine, much of it consisting of the droppings of pets living in urban areas, constitute a significant source of fecal coliform and fecal streptococci bacteria, biological oxygen demand, and nutrients. Owners should be aware that their pets' droppings, especially when left on paved areas, pollute streams, lakes, rivers, coastal bays, and estuaries. Public education programs need to be backed up by local government animal control activities.

Another set of good housekeeping practices includes the collection and disposal of household chemicals and automotive maintenance products. The collection and proper disposal of unwanted household pesticides and herbicides; automotive products such as crankcase oil, antifreeze, and solvents; soaps and detergents; disinfectants such as chlorine bleach and chlorine products used for pool and spa maintenance; and old paint, paint thinner, and cleaning products; has a potential for reducing the amount of these substances reaching receiving waters. Most communities do not have an active program for collecting and disposing of these materials, and individuals sometimes discard them through community trash collection programs. At other times individuals merely flush such products down a storm drain or a street gutter or dump them onto the urban landscape.

A public education program, along with strong ordinances and formal collection and disposal programs for such materials will minimize the incidence of improper disposal. This requires establishment of an infrastructure for the collection and disposal of these products and an ongoing educational program to inform residents of its availability.

Street Sweeping, Leaf Pickup, and Deicing Programs.   Studies made by Robert Pitt for EPA revealed that street sweeping, even using vacuum-type sweepers, has only a marginal water quality benefit. Street sweeping picks up mostly coarse sediment and litter, but it apparently does poorly in removing fine sediment and potentially dissolvable pollutants from paved surfaces. EPA (1983) concluded that sweeping streets every 2 days, using vacuum-type sweepers, has a potential for reducing the amount of toxic pollutants reaching receiving waters by only 2% to 5%.

Street sweeping requires the commitment of significant municipal resources for the purchase of street sweeping equipment and the cost of its operation, storage, maintenance, insurance, support administration, and eventual replacement. Therefore, intense use of this BMP during the spring and summer months is of questionable effectiveness. There is no sound technical reason why this practice could not be limited to one sweeping a month during the spring and summer months. This should pick up litter, trash, and debris, mostly for aesthetic reasons.

In the fall, a single street sweeping scheduled to coincide with a community leaf pickup program has a potential for reducing the volume of organic matter, in the form of fallen leaves, being washed off paved areas into the receiving water system. Unfortunately, no data are available to support this hypothesis. The argument rests on the premise that leaf litter on paved surfaces will find its way to the receiving waters quicker and in greater quantities than the same litter on a forest floor or in a meadow. This improved wash-off mechanism is the result of increased surface runoff from paved surfaces and the hydraulic efficiency of stormwater conveyance systems.

In the winter months, when roadway sanding and salting are used to maintain traffic flow in cities, street sweeping following snow melt picks up at least part of the previously applied sand and deicing products. EPA (1983) data show that it is unlikely that the salt concentrations in melting snow are toxic to aquatic life. However, the transport of fine sediments from street sanding can silt over aquatic habitats.

Elimination of Illicit Discharges.   Illicit discharges into a separate municipal storm sewer system fall into three categories:

- Illicit connection of wastewater lines to a storm sewer,
- Wastewater sewer surcharge relief connections to storm sewers, and
- Illegal dumping of pollutants into streets, gutters, or storm inlets.

The first two categories occur primarily when a storm sewer line is mistaken for a sanitary sewer at the time a service connection is made. Most of these connections are inadvertent, and regularly scheduled training of city inspectors should help prevent new ones from being made.

It is likely that a significant number of *illicit connections* exist throughout the United States because of poorly controlled practices in the past. An example of this was reported by Hubbard and Sample (1989) in Michigan. Field investigations revealed a large number of industrial and residential wastewater connections to storm sewers, some of which were discharging significant amounts of toxic pollutants. An aggressive program was set up to search out and reconnect illicit wastewater connections to sanitary sewers. An improvement in the quality of the receiving waters was observed as the effort eliminated large number of illicit connections.

Improvement in receiving water quality as a result of eliminating illicit connections depends on local conditions. The volume and nature of wastewater discharging via separate storm sewers is diluted as this discharge enters receiving waters. The net improvement in the quality of the receiving waters depends on how much these discharges are diluted. If the dilution ratio is very high, the impact will be imperceptible. If, on the other hand, the dilution ratio is low, the impact will be very noticeable and eliminating illicit connections can result in profound improvements in the quality of the receiving body of water.

Untreated wastewater also poses a potential public health problem. Thus, despite the extent to which improvement will occur in the receiving water body, finding and elimination illicit wastewater connections should be of high priority. While finding illicit connections is not an easy task, it is much more difficult to trace down unknown *wastewater surge relief connections.* Since surge relief lines operate only during storm events, the flows are diluted and masked by stormwater. Even sampling and testing often yields inconclusive results. Thus, unless there is a set of original design plans or "as-constructed" plans, finding sanitary sewer relief connections will require a well thought-out plan of attack, lots of patience, and considerable luck.

The last category, *illegal dumping of pollutants,* especially hazardous ones, is most difficult to control since it often occurs surreptitiously. Unless local authorities are made aware of such practices, it is virtually impossible to stop these criminal activities while they are occurring. Most municipalities have hazardous waste spill response teams that respond to spills as soon as they are reported. Although public education and cooperation can help, catching someone in the act of illegal dumping remains a matter of chance. As with all criminal activities, it is not likely that illegal dumping can be totally eliminated, only reduced. Thus, strong control ordinances that include aggressive law enforcement, severe fines and jail sentences, public education and citizen cooperation are some of the means of minimizing these types of activities. Another is to make the disposal of more hazardous pollutants much more convenient and less expensive to eliminate the incentive for illegal dumping.

Enforcement of Operation and Maintenance of Privately Owned Facilities. At the time land is developed, an agreement is drawn up between the land developer and the land use control entity—a city, a county, or another local authority. This agreement often lists the homeowners' responsibilities for the maintenance of common facilities. Privately owned on-site stormwater structural BMPs fall into this category. However, privately owned structural BMP facilities often fall into disrepair and lose their original effectiveness unless local authorities enforce the subdivision agreements requiring the maintenance of stormwater facilities. This is not a politically pleasant task to perform, however. If on-site controls are to provide the water quality enhancement for which they were originally designed, proper maintenance and operation have to be carried out. In the United States the recently enacted federal stormwater discharge laws are likely to increase such enforcement action by cities and counties.

Retrofitting of Structural BMPs in Areas of Major Concern.   This practice should be reserved for areas where there is clear evidence that a serious impact on the receiving waters will be significantly reduced. The cost of retrofitting structural BMPs in urbanized areas must be evaluated against how effective their installation will be, because retrofitting structural BMPs into existing urban areas is very expensive.

Retrofitting of storage devices is sometimes used to reduce the number of combined sewer overflows because of public health concerns associated with untreated sewage. However, it is difficult to justify the cost of stormwater quality controls in already urbanized areas with separate storm sewer systems. Because of the limited available right of way in urbanized areas, the only practices often available are underground storage tanks, storage inlets, flow-retarding storm drainage inlets, and sedimentation tunnels. All these have been described earlier in this book, but not all of them by themselves improve water quality.

25.3 STRUCTURAL BEST MANAGEMENT PRACTICES

25.3.1 Control of Runoff and Pollutants at the Source

The concept of providing various best management practices in series, as illustrated earlier in Figure 25.2, relies on both structural and nonstructural BMPs. Various structural BMPs will be discussed next in order of how they fit into the treatment train, starting upstream and then moving downstream within an urban watershed. Keep in mind that stormwater runoff quality enhancement begins with avoidance and prevention of pollutant deposition onto the urban landscape and its contact with stormwater. Structural BMPs back up any of the good housekeeping measures, if any, being practiced within a community.

Minimize Directly Connected Impervious Area.   First in the series of structural BMPs is the reduction of directly connected impervious areas. This is feasible mostly in new growth areas, since it requires a nontraditional layout of urban streets, parking lots, and buildings. Figure 25.3 illustrates the basic

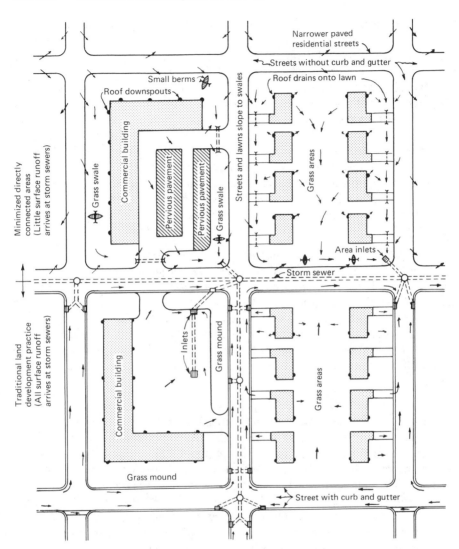

Figure 25.3   Contrast between traditional land development and one that minimizes a directly connected impervious area.

differences between a traditional approach to land development and one that minimizes impervious surface areas with a direct hydraulic connection to the stormwater collection system. While the traditional approach to drainage maximizes the efficiency of surface runoff, minimizing the directly connected impervious area maximizes the inefficiency of draining off runoff once it leaves impervious surfaces.

Minimizing a directly connected impervious area in an urbanized watershed reduces stormwater runoff volume by slowing it down as it progresses from the headwaters of a watershed to the receiving waters. In the process, the opportunity for infiltration is increased. This slowing of surface flow by grassed surfaces allows some of the suspended solids, and other pollutants as well, to be trapped in the grasses before the surface runoff reaches the hydraulically efficient conveyance parts of an urban drainage system. Thus, whenever feasible, the reduction of directly connected impervious surfaces should improve the water quality of urban stormwater runoff reaching the receiving waters.

Keeping the directly connected impervious area to a minimum is especially effective during small rainfall events and when the runoff consists of melted snow. As previously stated, smaller runoff events impact receiving waters most frequently because the runoff from small storms comprises a very large percentage of events pulsing through these waters.

Infiltration Practices in General. Infiltration practices generally fall into four groups: (1) swales and filter strips, (2) porous pavement and modular pavement, (3) percolation trenches, and (4) infiltration basins. Since most of the infiltrated water ultimately becomes part of the groundwater flow, care must be taken when these practices are used near water wells or when gasoline stations, chemical storage areas, or other industrial or potentially contaminating commercial activities, such as fertilizer handling and retailing, are drained by infiltration practices. Each of the four infiltration practices will be discussed next.

Grass Swales and Filter Strips. Various configurations of swales and roadside ditches are illustrated in Figures 2.5, and 17.7. Also, Section 17.5 describes the design of infiltrating swales. Even when total infiltration of a design storm via a ditch or a swale is not possible, a ditch can be designed to slow the rate of flow, thereby encouraging settling out of sediment near its source. The degree to which a swale or a ditch removes pollutants is not easy to quantify, but the slower the flow, the more effectively the pollutants are removed from stormwater. The ultimate in the slowing down of runoff occurs when the swale is designed as a series of linear detention basins as illustrated in Figure 17.7. For this type of design, sediment removal rates can be estimated using the surface loading theory procedures described in Chapter 23.

Grass Filter Strips. Grass filter strips were only briefly mentioned in Section 2.3.3. Grass filter strips are feasible only where turf-forming grasses are present. In arid and semi-arid areas native grass filter strips may not provide sufficient grass cover to perform the cleansing sometimes found in more rainfall-abundant regions. Nevertheless, this practice can be employed even in relatively dry regions if the grass strips are maintained in a healthy state through irrigation.

An example of using a grass filter strip is a grass turf strip surrounding an area inlet. This strip removes at least a portion of the suspended sediment present in stormwater, thus improving the water quality before it leaves the site. Typically, a minimum of a 10- to 20-foot (3- to 6-m) wide strip between the edge of the pavement and the inlet (see Fig. 2–9b) can provide significant pollutant removal during smaller storm events. Eventually sediment builds up in the grasses, most noticeably next to the pavement's edge, and the turf rises with time above the adjacent pavement. Runoff from the pavement is then impeded, and the turf must be stripped off, the grade lowered, and new turf installed.

Porous Pavement. Porous pavement, in the form of modular pavement blocks with large perforations, can be used effectively for parking lots and in remote parking areas near office buildings, shopping centers and other commercial buildings, factories, sporting event complexes, churches, etc. This best management practice is described in detail in Section 2.3.7. *Modular perforated concrete block porous pavement* has been in use since the mid-1970s and has been described by Day et al. (1981), Goforth et al. (1984), Smith (1984), Pratt (1990), and others.

Although modular perforated concrete block paving surfaces are more expensive to install than conventional paving, they offer a method of reducing the amount of directly connected impervious area. They can be used along residential streets, as highway shoulders, in residential driveways, in high-density residential neighborhood parking areas, and in commercial development parking areas. Where land costs are very high, little opportunity exists to minimize directly connected impervious areas through the use of grassed areas. In these instances, perforated modular paving blocks provide such an opportunity.

Figures 2.12 and 2.13 in Section 2.3.7 illustrate the use of modular perforated concrete block paving. Note that the modular concrete blocks are placed within cells constructed of poured-in-place concrete walls that also cut off horizontal flow within the permeable rock media. Without such concrete cutoff barriers, stormwater will flow along the porous rock media. The water moves horizontally in the porous media until it surfaces at the bottom of the slope and will not infiltrate into the soils as intended.

The maintenance of modular paving block surfaces should be less than the maintenance of *poured-in-place porous concrete or asphalt*. The surface of perforated modular pavement is less likely to seal. When it does, the paving blocks can be lifted up, the sand in the annular spaces and immediately under them removed and disposed of, and the removed sand and the paving blocks replaced. If the surface filter layer is designed to remove fine sediments, the underlying porous media and the soil on which it is placed should not seal for many years. A standard bricklayer's mortar sand mix should filter out all the coarse and medium-sized particles normally found in stormwater, passing through only the very fine silt and clay particles.

Examples of early failures of porous paving have been reported by Hoagland et al. (1987) and others. Most were due to excessive surface deposition of sediments originating from poorly controlled construction sites, sanding of paved surfaces to improve traction during winter months, and excessive deposits by wind. Pratt (1990), however, found that if excessive sediment deposits on the surface are controlled, modular paved surfaces can function for at least 15 years. He also estimated that the underlying base materials may not fill for as long as 100 years. The latter obviously is a speculated projection, since none of the data examined remotely approached that number of years.

Percolation Trenches.   Percolation trenches are described in Chapter 2. Site selection and design procedures for these types of devices are discussed in Section 17.4. Percolation trenches are normally designed to serve very small tributary areas, typically 5 acres (2 ha) or less of paved surface. However, under carefully controlled conditions, where meteorology, site geology, and groundwater conditions permit, infiltration trenches can be designed to serve larger areas. The limiting constraint is the rate at which the groundwater under the trench drains away. When too large an area is drained into a percolation trench, a groundwater mound can rise and inundate the trench. The services of a groundwater hydrologist, along with a three-dimensional groundwater flow analysis, will help to ensure that such failures do not occur.

As explained in Section 2.3.5, the clogging of infiltration trenches can be a problem. Once clogged, they stop functioning. As a result, grass buffer strips and/or surface filters should be a part of each installation. Follow-up maintenance of buffer strips and surface filters is also necessary. When percolation trenches function properly, they can be effective in reducing the volume of runoff and, therefore, the amount of pollutants carried off-site to the receiving waters.

Infiltration Basins.   Infiltration basins are also described in Chapter 2, while their site selection and design procedures are described in Section 17.3. Infiltration basins are also normally designed to serve very small tributary areas, typically not exceeding 5 to 10 acres (2 to 4 ha) of paved surface. As for infiltration trenches, the limiting constraint is the buildup of groundwater under the basin. Three-dimensional groundwater flow analysis should help ensure that failures of infiltration basins do not occur because of groundwater surfacing into the basin.

An infiltration basin is a detention basin that captures surface runoff and outlets this runoff by infiltrating it into the ground. Clogging of infiltrating surfaces eventually occurs. When clogged, the basin can be rehabilitated by removing the sediment layer that has accumulated on the infiltrating surfaces and then reestablishing vegetation on the restored bottom. Follow-up maintenance of infiltration basins must be a part of each installation. When infiltration basins function properly, they can be effective in reducing the volume of runoff and the amount of pollutants carried off-site to the receiving waters.

Filter Basins and Filter Inlets.   The use of sand filters for the reduction of pollutants found in stormwater runoff from a commercial site in Tampa,

Florida, was reported by Wanielista et al. (1981), and for a site in Austin, Texas, by Veenhuis et al. (1988). Wanielista tested a filter that followed a small detention basin. Veenhuis, on the other hand, tested a filter bed at the edge of a shopping center that did not have a separate detention basin upstream to pretreat storm runoff.

The filter bed monitored by Veenhuis in Austin, Texas, was installed in the early 1980s. This particular installation had to have the surface layer cleaned out on a relatively frequent basis, about once a year, as it tended to clog it rather quickly. In addition, it was relatively expensive to install ($16,000 per acre of impervious watershed served).

After considering the experience gained at a single installation in Maryland, Shaver (1992) modified the design procedures developed in Austin, Texas, and suggested a design for a sand filter stormwater inlet. The details of this design, shown in Figure 25.4, are based on the rainfall and runoff conditions in the state of Delaware (1991). This device consists of an area inlet where stormwater enters a sedimentation chamber. After initial pretreatment in this chamber, the stormwater overflows into an adjacent filter chamber filled with sand. The water passes through the sand filter before being discharged into a storm sewer system, into a posttreatment device, or directly into receiving waters. Many of the suspended pollutants are removed from the stormwater by the filter inlet. This is probably not the case for most dissolved constituents.

Shaver (1992) reported on the Delaware (1991) regulations, which require sand filter inlets to be designed using the hydraulic per acre (per hectare) of tributary watershed loading rates and filter volumes summarized in Table 25.1. The hydraulic unit loading rate used in these criteria was based on Delaware meteorology and 1 inch (2.54 cm) of runoff being drained over a 24-hour period.

This filter inlet design was intended primarily for use in commercial

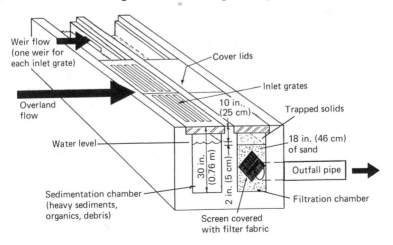

Figure 25.4   Sand filter stormwater inlet. (After Shaver, 1992.)

TABLE 25.1 Delaware Design Standards for a Sand Filter Inlet

Design Parameter	U.S. Standard	SI Standard
Inflow rate	0.04 gpm/ft^2	0.0027 l/s/m^2
Maximum surcharge	1.0 ft	0.3 m
Trap chamber volume	540 ft^3/acre	37.8 m^3/ha
Filter chamber volume	540 ft^3/acre	37.8 m^3/ha
Filter surface area	360 ft^2/acre	83 m^2/ha
	(equal to 0.83% of tributary area)	

After Shaver (1992).

parking lots. Each inlet is limited to receiving runoff from no more than 5 acres (1.6 ha) of watershed. According to Shaver (1992), one such installation in Maryland operated for 6 years before maintenance was needed. Maintenance for this type of installation includes cleaning out the sediment trap chamber and removing and replacing the top 6 inches (15 cm) of the sand filter.

The very low level of maintenance reported by Shaver implies that it may be possible to reduce the size of this filter inlet if greater maintenance frequency is accepted. For example, using the Delaware criteria, a 5-acre (2.0 ha) watershed will need an inlet almost 1200 feet (366 m) in length to satisfy the requirement for 360 square feet (33.4 m^2) of filter surface area per acre of watershed. This length results if the filter chamber is only 18 inches (0.46 m) wide. Such an installation is estimated to cost approximately $250,000 to construct, which extrapolates to a cost of $1 million for a 20-acre (8-ha) commercial development.

The owner or developer may want to investigate trading off increased maintenance, say once a year, for a reduced filter size. However, a reduction in the size of the filter inlet should not be made at the expense of creating frequent drainage problems caused by inadequate capacity during design storms. As an example, cleaning out the sediment chamber and removing and replacing the top 6 inches (15 cm) of the sand filter are estimated to cost $1.00 to $1.50 per linear foot ($3.30/m to $5.00/m) of inlet length. Assuming that a 200-foot (61-m) long inlet will require annual restorative maintenance and that an inlet six times as long will require the same maintenance once every 6 years, the present worth of both installations over a 6-year period, using a 4.0% discount rate, compare as follows:

Cost Item	Inlet Length 200 ft (61 m)	Inlet Length 1,200 ft (366 m)
Initial construction cost	$45,000	$250,000
Present worth of maintenance for 6 years	1,570	1,420
Total present worth	$46,570	$251,420

Clearly, the economics in this case favors the smaller installation, provided good surface drainage is not compromised. Even if the cost of maintenance is transferred from a private owner to a local public body, the difference
in the projected maintenance cost is not sufficient to favor the larger installation. From the private owner's perspective, it makes more sense to pay the local
public body a single maintenance fee of $12,000. This fee should offset the
estimated $300 annual maintenance cost and cover the cost of inflation in the
future. However, until field data are available to substantiate that a smaller
filter will work without creating a drainage problem for the owner, Delaware's
sizing criteria is recommended for the design of these facilities.

25.3.2 Follow-up Detention
Storage—Systemization

Unlike the systemization of storage basins for combined sewer systems
described in Section 5.2, the use of stormwater detention, or other types of
facilities, for water quality enhancement in separate stormwater systems
should not bypass base flows or the runoff from small storms. The goal of
separate stormwater systems is to capture and treat the runoff from all base
flows and all smaller storms. If possible, they should be designed to also
provide at least some level of water quality enhancement for the runoff from
larger storms.

Capture of the so-called first flush for separate stormwater systems is not
emphasized in this book. The first-flush phenomenon discussed in Section
21.2.2 is mostly attributed to combined sewer systems. Because of the different
nature of separate stormwater systems, unless a water quality treatment system
exists downstream of the detention basin, an off-line system is not a viable
alternative. Such a system typically bypasses all base flows and the runoff from
smaller events without providing any water quality enhancement. On the other
hand, if a detention basin is followed by a wetland basin or a water quality
detention basin or pond, any of the off-line arrangements described in Section
5.2 can be considered to help reduce the peaks of larger runoff hydrographs
and equalize the flows arriving at the water quality treatment facility.

Three types of separated stormwater quality interception arrangements
are described. All three are in-line systems and assume that there is no
posttreatment downstream. One is a multipurpose system where water quality
and flood control functions are combined. The second is intended for the
capture and water quality enhancement of the runoff from smaller storm events
only. The third arrangement uses two basins with separate water quality and
flood control functions. Each system has its advantages and disadvantages.
Although these arrangements are generally considered to apply to stormwater
detention basins and ponds, the water quality component can also be a wetland
basin or a filter basin, provided it has sufficient surface storage capacity to
entrap at least the runoff from the smaller storms being designed for.

Figure 25.5 shows an arrangement for a multipurpose detention pond or

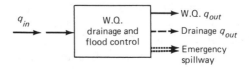

Advantages of multipurpose in-line storage are as follows:

- One installation handles water quality and drainage or flood control
- One inflow structure arrangement
- Requires the least amount of land area to combine water quality and flood control
- Much flexibility in design
- Continues to remove floatable and suspended solids, at somewhat reduced efficiency, even when quality volume is exceeded
- Single spillway.

Disadvantages are:

- Water quality basin or pond may conflict with multiuses, such as recreational fishing
- Water in the permanent pool within a multiuse facility may be less attractive than expected by residents
- Potential exists for resuspension of sediment deposits during a large storm
- Some floatable trash may not be removed, especially during large storms
- Will likely require some form of emergency spillway.

Figure 25.5 Multipurpose in-line detention facility.

basin designed to address both water quality improvement and flood control. Layouts of these types of detention facilities are shown in Section 23.6. The pond or basin is connected in series with the stormwater runoff system and intercepts all runoff, small and large. The outlet works and the stormwater storage volume are both designed to capture and release inflow in stages that vary with water depth. Initially, the runoff from smaller storms is captured within the lower part of the installation and is released, depending on whether there is a permanent pond or not, within 12 or 40 hours. If the runoff volume and its rate exceed the storage of the lower water quality basin, stormwater is detained above this volume and released at rates consistent with the flood control and drainage system goals and objectives.

Figure 25.6 shows an arrangement for a detention pond or basin designed to address only water quality improvement. This facility is connected in-line with the stormwater runoff system by an inflow device that first directs all runoff to the detention facility. The *filling phase* continues until the water depth rises and backs up into the inflow device. The *bypass phase* begins at the point where the stormwater bypasses the water quality detention basin. The water

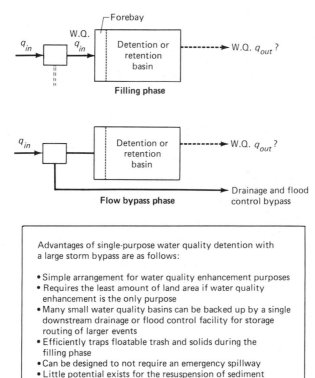

Figure 25.6   Single-purpose water quality detention facility with a bypass during larger storms.

intercepted by the detention facility is either released slowly or infiltrated into the ground. During the bypass phase no flood storage routing occurs, and all stormwater is conveyed downstream without water quality treatment or change in its flow rate.

Figure 25.7 shows an arrangement for a combined system consisting of two separate basins designed to independently address water quality and drainage and flood control. During the *filling phase* all stormwater enters the water quality basin of the pond until the water depth rises and backs up into the inflow control device. At that time the *bypass phase* begins, and stormwater

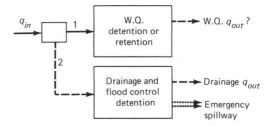

Advantages of a compound water quality and drainage and
flood control system are as follows:

• Handles water quality improvement and drainage and flood
  control very well
• Offers the most flexibility in design
• Traps floatable and suspended solids in the water quality
  basin very well during the filling phase
• Little potential exists for the resuspension of sediment deposits
  in the water quality basin during the bypass phase
• Can be designed to remove some of the floatables and larger
  suspended solids during the bypass phase
• Can be designed to function with one emergency spillway.

Disadvantages are:

• Requires the most land area to construct
• Has a more complicated inflow and bypass structure arrangement
• Requires some form of emergency spillway
• Less efficient than a multipurpose in-line system in removing
  suspended solids during larger storms.

Figure 25.7   Combination of water quality and drainage and flood control facilities
in a single installation.

is conveyed to the drainage and flood control basin. The water intercepted by
the water quality basin is released slowly or infiltrated into the ground. During
the bypass phase, flood storage routing occurs in the second basin.

The arrangements in Figures 25.6 and 25.7 require a flow divider inflow
structure. This flow divider directs all base flows and the runoff from smaller
storms into a water quality basin or pond during the filling phase and bypasses
all flow once the water quality basin is full. Figure 25.8 illustrates such an
installation where stormwater is delivered by an open channel or a swale. The
water is first diverted into the water quality basin via a rundown chute. As the
inflow fills the basin and the water level rises above the overflow crest, flows
bypass the water quality basin and very little new stormwater enters it.

The inflow divider structure shown in Figure 25.9 can be used when
stormwater is contained in a storm sewer. Initially, stormwater enters the
manhole and is directed inside the manhole to the water quality basin. As the
basin fills and the water level rises above the invert of the bypass pipe, incoming

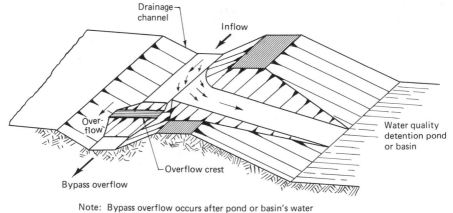

Note: Bypass overflow occurs after pond or basin's water
      surface rises above overflow crest.

Figure 25.8   Bypass overflow channel inlet.

stormwater begins to bypass the water quality basin. Very little new stormwater enters the water quality basin or pond after that.

25.3.3 Follow-up Water Quality Detention Basins (Dry)

Detention basins (i.e., dry basins) are the most common type of detention used in the United States, Canada, Australia, and other countries. As discussed in Chapter 21, approximately 80% of the pollutants associated with suspended solids are attached to particles less than 60 micrometers in size, namely, fine silts and clays. Long detention periods are needed to settle out these smaller particulates. As a result, dry basins are typically designed to empty their *brim-full volume* in 24 to 48 hours with no more than 50% of this brim-full volume being released during the first one-quarter to one-third of the emptying period. Even this extended detention period does not remove all the suspended solids entering the basin, nor does it remove any of the dissolved pollutants. Because of the long emptying period for dry water quality detention basins, they are referred to as *extended detention basins*.

Section 23.6.3 contains illustrations of typical extended detention basin configurations which, along with the recommendations for trash racks in Section 4.3.5 and for the design of outlet flow regulators described in Chapter 14, comprise one technical basis for their design. In these illustrations, the water quality basin is located within a larger stormwater management and flood control basin. Since Section 23.6 deals with the geometric layout of extended water quality detention basins and Sections 23.4 and 23.5 discuss how such basins should be sized, the topics covered in those three sections will not be

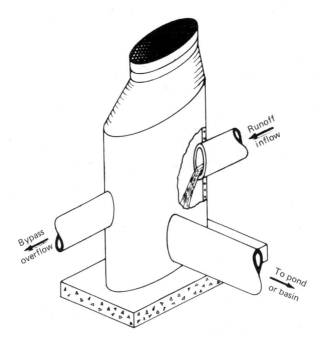

Figure 25.9   Bypass overflow manhole inlet.

repeated here. Here we will elaborate on some of the features and concerns that must be considered when designing extended detention basins.

In the two configurations illustrated in Section 23.6.3, i.e., Figure 23.16, stormwater entering the lower part of the basin is impounded and released slowly through a water quality outlet. In one case, the water quality volume is released through an orifice, while in the other it is released through a perforated riser outlet. A trash rack in front of the orifice in one of these installations and coarse aggregate packing around the perforated riser in the other screens out leaves, paper, plastic bags, and other debris. This prevents the outlet from being plugged. When the lower part of the basin—the water quality volume portion—is full, water then begins to spill over an overflow structure. In Figure 23.16(a) this overflow occurs over a weir, and in Figure 23.16(b) it occurs over the top of a perforated riser pipe. During very large storms, water can also spill over the emergency spillway.

Although outlet controls should be designed to drain the basin as slowly as possible, excessive periods of bottom inundation will kill off grasses and other vegetation in the water quality basin. To reduce the chances of vegetation dying off, the brim-full emptying time should not exceed 24 to 36 hours. When drainage through bottom exfiltration is a possibility or is desired, the bottom of the basin must be located at least 4 feet above the annual high-water table.

25.3.4 Follow-up Water Quality Retention Ponds

Some of the treatment processes that may be at work in retention ponds are siltation, chemical flocculation, agglomeration of smaller particles into larger ones, ion exchange, adsorption, biological uptake and remobilization, remobilization of solids into the water column through solution or chemical processes, and physical resuspension of particulates during rapid inflow of stormwater and wave action between storm runoff events. In the main body of the pond, pollutants are removed by settling, and nutrients are removed by phytoplankton growth in the water column. Shallow marsh plants found around the perimeter of the pond also remove nutrients. However, algae growth and the decay of dead aquatic plants can remobilize some previously removed nutrients back into the water column.

Hartigan (1989) suggested a design for the permanent pool for a retention pond that is based on an eutrophication model for removing dissolved phosphorus and other nutrients from stormwater. According to him, the permanent pool of a detention pond needs two to seven times more volume than the temporary storage volume used in an extended detention basin. Although the permanent pool can be located below the water quality outlet level, it will require considerably more land than an extended detention basin or a pond designed using sedimentation theory.

Investigations in the Washington, D.C., area by Schueler (1992) indicate that large permanent pools can act as heat sinks. In these pools the larger retention pond water temperature can rise significantly above the temperature of many receiving waters. Schueler concluded that large extended ponds in the Washington, D.C., area should not be used when they discharge to receiving waters that support trout.

Data collected at two sites near Denver, Colorado, by the Cherry Creek Basin Water Quality Authority suggest that nutrient remobilization in the form of algae growth and dissolution of a particulate phosphates into the water column can occur between storms. The net effect was that the annual removal rates of nutrients were significantly lower than originally anticipated. It is possible that a eutrophication model may not account for all the nutrient cycle processes occurring in a pond under various site and climatic conditions.

Water depth in the permanent pool of a water quality pond should be sufficiently deep to minimize daylight penetration to the bottom of the pond. This should reduce bottom weed growth. On the other hand, the pool should be shallow enough to permit mixing and aeration of the water by wind. Without mixing, the bottom of the pond can become depleted of oxygen, and the sediments anoxic. A shift to an anoxic state will mobilize nutrients and metals back into the water column, which defeats the purpose of constructing a water quality pond in the first place. To reduce the chances for anoxic conditions in a pond, the water depths of the permanent pool should be between 3.5 and 12 feet (1.1 and 3.7 m).

Figures 23.14 and 23.15 in Section 23.6.2 illustrate two of the many possible configurations for water quality ponds which, along with the recommendations for trash racks in Section 4.3.5 and for the design of outlet flow regulators described in Chapter 14, comprise one technical basis for their design. These ponds are often located within a larger flood control basin, but they can be designed as single-purpose ponds also. Stormwater entering the installation first passes through a forebay equipped with a floatable surface-skimming boom. The forebay removes coarse sediments, and the floating boom at its downstream end skims off some of the floatable material before stormwater enters the main body of the water quality pond.

The outlet in Figure 23.14 and 23.15 in Section 23.6.2 is staged to first release the water quality inflow volume over a 6- to 12-hour period. When the inflow causes the water quality capture volume to be exceeded, water then flows over a weir, the top of a perforated riser, another outlet pipe, or an emergency spillway. A balanced pond ecology is provided in the permanent pool by a littoral zone that covers 25% to 50% of the permanent pond's surface area. Outlets should be protected from clogging by trash racks, surface skimmers, and other devices.

In arid and semi-arid areas, a detention pond with a permanent pool may not always be feasible. The base flow needed to maintain a permanent pool may be lacking for ponds serving smaller tributary watersheds. Thus, where a paucity of precipitation or little base flow is the rule, a water budget analysis should be performed. Before a water quality detention pond is selected, this analysis should show that there is more than sufficient inflow water to make up for all the water lost by the permanent pool through exfiltration and evapotranspiration. Otherwise, the pond will dry out and become an unattractive hole in the ground, producing undesirable odors, breeding mosquitoes, and becoming an unwanted part of an urban community.

25.3.6 Follow-up Treatment—Wetlands

Chapter 24 discussed the design and use of wetlands for stormwater quality enhancement. *Wetland basins* are an emerging technique and provide another structural best management practice for stormwater quality enhancement. Wetland basins can be used either as source controls or as follow-up treatment devices. They are, in essence, just another form of a detention pond which can be designed to serve as the primary treatment facility or as a treatment facility that follows an extended detention basin or a retention pond. Wetlands, when properly designed, constructed, and maintained, can be effective tools in the removal of stormwater pollutants, including many nutrients. However, what constitutes "proper" design and maintenance for the removal of nutrients has not yet been determined. We do know, however, that sustained removal of nutrients requires occasional wetland harvesting and mucking out.

25.3.7 Follow-up Treatment—Filters

Unlike on-site filter inlets or basins, follow-up sand filter basins can serve tributary areas in excess of 100 acres (40.5 ha). Urbonas and Ruzzo (1986) suggested a postdetention filter design to serve larger subregional tributary watersheds of 10 to 200 acres (4 to 81 ha). Figure 25.10 shows some of the details based on that concept that were adopted by the city of Aurora, Colorado (1987).-

In the procedures adopted by Aurora, the sand filter surface area is sized using Equation 25.1:

$$A_f = \frac{Q_{\max}}{q_f} \qquad (25.1)$$

in which A_f = surface area of filter in square feet (m²),

$Q_{\max}$ = maximum release rate from upstream detention basin in cubic feet per second (m³/s),

q_f = permissible surface loading rate on the filter, 0.09 gallon per minute per square foot in U.S. standard units (0.12 l/s/m² in SI units). This release rate may be doubled if a retention pond is used instead of an extended detention basin.

Unless there are unusual structural requirements, a filter sufficient to serve the first 0.5 inch (13 mm) of runoff from 100 acres (40.5 ha) of a single-family residential neighborhood having 40% of its area as impervious cover should cost $30,000 to $50,000 to construct. This cost estimate is based on a unit loading rate of 0.09 gallon per minute per square foot (0.06 l/s/m²) of filter area and the filter being installed downstream of a detention basin that meters out the brim-full volume through a water quality outlet in a 36-hour period.

The filter surface loading rates suggested for use with Equation 25.1 are for filters located downstream of extended detention basins or downstream of water quality detention ponds. In such arrangements the upstream detention facility removes a considerable fraction of the suspended solids from stormwater. Under normal runoff conditions the filter is expected to function for at least 5 to 6 years before the top layers of sand have to be removed and replaced. Higher unit loading rates would most likely require more frequent maintenance.

Although not recommended by the authors, if a designer wants to use the filter shown in Figure 25.10 without an extended detention basin or a retention pond upstream of it, the unit hydraulic loading rate should be less than 0.09 or 0.18 gallon per minute per square foot (0.12 l/s/m²) of filter area. The inlet structure to the filter bed should also be different, designed to uniformly spread out the inflow hydrograph over the filter bed, since it will not be modulated by an upstream detention facility. In addition, sufficient detention volume must be provided on top of the filter to buffer the variable stormwater runoff.

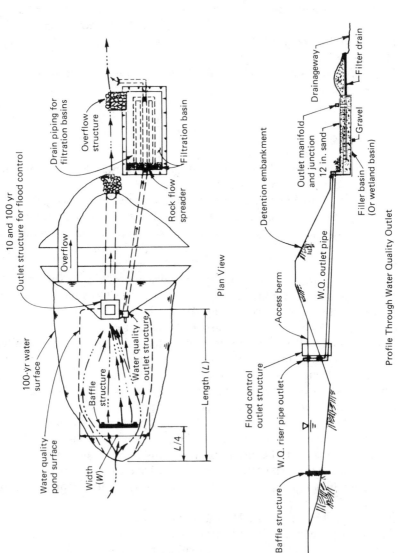

Figure 25.10 Sand filter design downstream of a detention pond. (After UDFCD, 1986.)

A design procedure similar to the one suggested in Chapter 17 for infiltration basins can be used to size the needed surcharge storage volume above the filter's surface.

As a tradeoff to using significantly lower hydraulic loading rates, a filter bed without an upstream pond needs much more frequent maintenance to keep it operating. The top 3 to 6 inches (7 to 15 cm) of the sand filter bed must be removed and replaced whenever its flow-through capacity diminishes to a point where it backs up water too frequently. This could be once a month, once a year, or some other frequency, depending on the unit hydraulic rates used in the design, the number of storms occurring at the site, and the type of sediment being carried by stormwater. The exact maintenance schedule is very difficult to predict accurately in advance.

25.4 EFFECTIVENESS ASSESSMENT OF BMPs

25.4.1 Effectiveness of Nonstructural Best Management Practices

Public Education and Citizen Involvement Programs.   Public education is the necessary first step in developing awareness and in changing the habits of the public as to how it handles and disposes of various household products, some of which find their way into surface runoff. It is not enough to make an individual aware of the problem he or she may be contributing to. Only if the individual has a deep sense of guilt or environmental responsibility, or can see an advantage in changing the way he or she uses and disposes of fertilizers, pesticides, herbicides, crankcase oil, antifreeze, etc., will he or she modify individual activities. To what degree and in what numbers such changes will occur as a result of public education has yet to be determined.

A good example of a successful public education education program is the antismoking campaign in the United States. Despite its success and the clear health benefits of not smoking, many individuals continue to smoke. Another successful citizen participation program is the aluminum can recycling effort in many parts of the United States. After more than 10 years of recycling, participation by 40% of community households is considered to be a major success—despite the fact that people are paid cash for recycling aluminum cans.

Obviously, the more aggressive the public education process, the more people will be reached. Public education will probably need to be supplemented by community programs to facilitate disposal of unwanted household products. Convenience, and some form of enforcement action should increase participation. However, it will probably require 5, 10, or even 20 years to effect a significant change in the current habits of everyone. "Significant" has yet to be defined, but a noticeable change in 25% of the households will probably be considered excellent in the next 5 to 10 years. The sooner public education begins, the quicker will be the return in the form of reduced pollutant deposits on the urban landscape.

Street Sweeping, Leaf Pickup, and Deicing Programs.   Street sweeping was demonstrated by EPA (1983) to have very little effect in improving stormwater quality. However, strategically scheduled sweepings in the fall and winter months can reduce the loads of leaf litter and street deicing products reaching receiving waters. Although the concentration of chlorides in melting snow were shown by EPA (1983) to be well below chronic levels that affect aquatic life, sediments from street sanding can impact aquatic habitats. Street sweeping picks up some of the coarser particles, while leaving behind fine sediment and clay particles that seem to cling to pavement surfaces. On the whole, street sweeping at this time appears to be not a cost-effective best management practice for improving stormwater quality.

Local Government Rules and Regulations.   While local government rules and regulations alone cannot improve stormwater quality, their vigorous implementation and enforcement can. Thus, well-drafted ordinances, rules, and criteria, and their enforcement by local governments, provide the basis for an effective stormwater management program. Implementing them costs money, but significantly less than what it costs to retrofit structural BMPs at a later date. Thus, developing sound building and site development codes, site disturbance permits, stormwater drainage design standards, land use density controls, enforcement of agreements for the operation and maintenance of private stormwater facilities, and other regulatory programs to reduce pollutant loads from developing areas is one of the more important nonstructural BMPs a city, a county, or another local government can undertake.

Elimination of Illicit Discharges.   Since the volume and nature of wastewater discharging via separate storm sewers are diluted by the flows in the receiving waters, the degree of improvement in the quality of the receiving waters depends on the extent to which illicit discharges are diluted. Where the dilution ratio is relatively low, eliminating illicit connections can result in a clear improvement in the water quality of the receiving body of water. Since untreated wastewater discharged through illicit connections can be a public health problem, finding and disconnecting illicit wastewater connections is justified by more than just a need to enhance the quality of the receiving waters.

Although illegal dumping of pollutants is very difficult to control because of its covert nature, it can cause massive environmental damage when toxicants are dumped into a storm sewer system. It is not likely that illegal dumping can be totally eliminated. However, efforts to reduce it are needed and will be as effective as the community's commitment toward achieving this goal. Like any municipal activity, passing and implementing strong control ordinances, law enforcement, public education, and citizen cooperation cost money. However, the disproportionate environmental impacts that illegal dumping can create make such programs an essential part of stormwater management activities.

25.4.2 Effectiveness of Structural Best Management Practices

Minimize Directly Connected Impervious Area.   Whenever feasible, this method is probably one of the most effective structural stormwater best management practices a municipality can implement for developing and redeveloping areas. Although it is not possible to provide a simple percentage of how much pollutant load is reduced through its use, it reduces the peak flow rate of storm runoff, its volume, and the pollutants it carries. The degree to which this occurs depends on the exact way in which this practice is implemented at each site and the site conditions themselves. Under an ideal application of this practice at an ideal site, surface runoff from storms with less than 0.5 inch (13 mm) of precipitation can be virtually eliminated. This practice can often be accomplished at no greater cost, and sometimes at less cost, than traditional land development practices.

Grass Swales.   Removal rates for suspended solids by grass swales exceeding 80% have been suggested by Whalen and Callum (1988). This may be possible where the soils underlying the swales have high infiltration rates and the swales are designed to have flow velocities of less than 0.5 feet per second (0.15 m/s). In cases where flow velocities are not very slow, pollutant removal efficiencies are not likely to be this high. Nevertheless, this best management practice can be effective when properly used on terrains with land slopes of less than 3.0%. On steep terrains it is difficult to keep longitudinal grades sufficiently flat and the swale sufficiently wide to keep flow velocities low.

Grass Filter Strips.   Grass filter strips can remove some of the sand and silt carried by stormwater, provided the flow over them is kept relatively shallow and slow moving. The less impervious the area that is a tributary to a grass filter strip, the more effective it is in removing suspended particles. Removal rates for suspended solids of 5% to 25% are suggested when stormwater flows slowly as a shallow sheet flow over a grass filter strip.

By themselves, grass filter strips provide only limited water quality enhancement. They are, however, an essential part of reducing a directly connected impervious area. They are also an important part of a treatment train acting in combination with other structural best management practices such as infiltration, percolation, wetlands, and detention.

Porous Pavement.   Field data of the performance of porous pavement are lacking, and most of the claims for its effectiveness are based on computer simulation. These estimates are probably reasonable, provided porous pavement remains porous. Estimates of the effectiveness of this practice in removing various pollutants must consider the possibility of porous pavement plugging, an eventuality already experienced by many of the installations set up in the early 1980s in the eastern United States. Where site conditions permit the use of porous pavement, using perforated modular concrete blocks has resulted in a lower failure rate. When sealing does occur, modular block pavement can be rehabilitated without destroying the entire installation. Estimates for the removal of pollutants from stormwater surface runoff by porous pavement range from 0% to as much as 95%, depending on the functional reliability of the installation.

Percolation Trenches.   When site conditions permit their use and function as designed, percolation trenches are estimated to remove up to 99% of several constituents in stormwater, including suspended solids. These estimates are supported by data showing that a properly functioning percolation trench can capture all runoff from 75% to 95% of storms. These estimates do not consider the possibility of some pollutants dissolving in groundwater and eventually surfacing in the receiving waters. However, data available so far indicate that groundwater quality does not degrade noticeably because of the infiltration of stormwater from residential and many types of commercial developments.

Infiltration Basins.   Infiltration basins appear to have a history of failure more frequently than percolation trenches installed in the eastern United States. This is attributed to design practices that use excessive hydraulic surface loading rates and apply too much water depth over basin surfaces. Estimates of their ability to remove pollutants range form 0% to as high as 70% to 99%, depending on the constituent. The more conservative design approach suggested in Chapter 17 should improve the reliability of this practice where site conditions permit the use of infiltration basins.

Sand Filter Basins and Filter Inlets.   The average removal efficiencies reported by Veenhuis (1988) for sand filters in Austin, Texas, were between 60% and 80% for suspended solids, biochemical oxygen demand, total phosphorus, total organic carbon, chemical oxygen demand, and dissolved zinc. On the other hand, the dissolved solids concentration in the filter effluent increased an average of 13% over the inflow concentrations. Also, average concentrations of total nitrite plus nitrate ($NO_2 + NO_3$) and nitrogen (N) were about 110% greater in the outflow than in the inflow during storm events. Sand filter basins can be an effective structural best management practice when land area is at a premium. Filter beds, and especially filter inlets, can be expensive to construct and can require considerable maintenance to keep them in operating condition.

Extended Detention Basins.   The design and use of extended detention basins for water quality enhancement has a good foundation in field and laboratory data. Removal rates range from 10% to 75%, depending on the constituent and the geometry of the installation, to as high as 20% to 90%, also depending on the constituent being measured. For some of the more soluble pollutants, namely, total phosphorus, total nitrogen, and zinc, this practice appears to provide a more consistently predictable performance than retention ponds and wetlands, even though the upper range of the removal rates for these constituents is probably higher in retention ponds and wetlands. Also, for similarly sized extended detention basins, removal rates for total suspended solids, lead, and other less soluble constituents are somewhat less those for retention ponds and wetlands.

Retention Ponds.   Retention ponds, sometimes called detention ponds or wet ponds, capture and detain new stormwater above their permanent water surfaces. In addition, as they fill, new stormwater displaces some, or all, of the water in the permanent pool. This displacement can occur as plug flow, but more often the new stormwater entering the pond mixes with the water in the permanent pool. This mixing process is more likely to occur when stormwater enters the pond in a rapid fashion. It cannot always be assumed that the relatively clean water in the permanent pool will be discharged first.

Hartigan (1989), EPA (1986), Northern Virginia Planning District Commission (1983), and others report that retention ponds can be somewhat more effective than extended detention basins in removing pollutants from stormwater. This can be especially true, but not always, for total phosphorus, total nitrogen, and some dissolved metals. While Hartigan (1989) states that properly designed detention ponds should remove 40% to 60% of phosphorus instead of the 20% to 30% expected for dry detention basins and 30% to 40% of total nitrogen instead of the 20% to 30% expected of extended detention basins, other studies show somewhat lower annual removal rates. Like extended detention basins, retention ponds can be designed with a reasonable degree of reliability, knowing the removal ranges to expect for a variety of constituents.

Wetland Basins.   Although wetlands provide another form of stormwater quality enhancement practice, they do not appear to remove pollutants better than detention basins or retention ponds. The often-cited claims that they are more effective in removing nutrients from stormwater are not conclusively substantiated by field data. Such claims may be based on data from wetlands being used to treat wastewater. The inflow concentrations of nutrients in wastewater systems are much higher than in stormwater. Untreated stormwater has concentrations of phosphates equivalent to those found in effluent from wetlands treating wastewater.

At this time this technology suffers from a lack of prolonged field studies, especially on how wetlands respond to stormwater input over a number of years. Such studies are badly needed to develop reliable design techniques and also to predict accurately how various wetland designs will remove a variety of pollutants from stormwater, especially nutrients, under different climatic conditions. Some of the data available to date indicate that wetlands may be

TABLE 25.2   Pollutant Removal Efficiencies of BMPs

Type of Practice	TSS	Total P	Total N	Zinc	Lead	BOD	Bacteria
Porous pavement[1]	85–95	65	75–85	98	80	80	n/a
Infiltration[1]	0–99	0–75	0–70	0–99	0–99	0–90	75–98
Percolation trench[1]	99	65–75	60–70	95–99	n/a	90	98
Retention ponds[2]	91	0–79	0–80	0–71	9–95	0–69	n/a
Extended detention[3]	50–70	10–20	10–20	30–60	75–90	—	50–90
Wetland[4]	40–94	(−4)–90	21	(−29)–82	27–94	18	n/a
Sand filters[5]	60–80	60–80	(−110)–0	10–80	60–80	60–80	n/a

After Colorado Stormwater Task Force, 1990.

[1] Schueler (1987). Estimates based on assumed removal efficiencies and modeling.

[2] EPA (1983). Based on NURP data without regard to design.

[3] EPA (1986), Grizzard et al. (1986), Whipple and Hunter (1981). Based on field and laboratory data.

[4] USGS (1986) for all constituents except Total P, based on average performance from 13 sampled runoff events in Orlando, Fla.; Lakatos and McNemer (1987) for Total P only, summary of field data from 8 study sites in the eastern United States. Strecker et al. (1990) for all except for Total N and BOD, summary of field data at 10 sites in the United States.

[5] Veenhuis et al. (1989), based on field data from Austin, Texas.

somewhat more effective in removing some dissolved metals, such as copper, lead, and zinc in urban surface runoff, than extended detention basins or retention ponds.

Summary.   Table 25.2 summarizes the removal efficiencies of several structural best management practices currently in use in the United States. Some of these estimates, as discussed above, are based on computer simulations, while others are based on field data and laboratory studies. All the practices listed, when properly used and designed recognizing local climate and site conditions, show promise in their ability to remove pollutants from stormwater. However, outside of retention ponds and extended detention basins, all the practices could benefit from prolonged field studies. Such studies must be well conceived and should include construction of the best management practices with the intent of collecting data.

Five years of data should be a minimum goal. Data on water quality, sediment accumulation, and maintenance costs, and other pertinent information, would then permit more reliable predictions of how each structural best management practice performs. Just as important, such data could be used to improve on the design of such facilities and could reveal how, or if, initial construction costs could be traded off against the larger maintenance needs of each type of facility.

REFERENCES

ATHAYDE, D., "Nationwide Urban Runoff Program," *APWA Reporter,* Chicago, 1984.

AURORA UTILITIES DEPARTMENT, *Rules and Regulations for Water Quality of Surface Drainage Best Management Practices,* WRC Engineers, Inc., Aurora, Colo., 1987.

COLORADO STORMWATER TASK FORCE—TECHNICAL COMMITTEE, *BMP Practices Assessment for the Development of Colorado's Stormwater Management Program,* Final Report to Colorado Water Quality Control Division, Denver, 1990.

DAVIES, P. E., "Toxicology and Chemistry in Urban Runoff," *Urban Runoff Quality—Impacts and Quality Enhancement Technology,* American Society of Civil Engineers, New York, 1986.

DAY, G. E., SMITH, D. R., AND BOWERS, J., *Runoff and Pollution Abatement Characteristics of Concrete Grid Pavements,* Bulletin 135, Virginia Water Resources Research Center, Blacksburg, Va., 1981.

DEBO, T. N., "Detention Ordinances—Solving or Causing Problems," *Stormwater Detention Facilities,* American Society of Civil Engineers, New York, 1982.

DELAWARE, STATE OF, *Sediment and Stormwater Management Regulations,* Department of Natural Resources and Environmental Control, State of Delaware, Dover, Del., 1991.

Design of Roadside Drainage Channels, U.S. Dept. of Commerce, Bureau of Public Roads, Washington D.C., 1967.

DRISCOLL, E. D., "Performance of Detention Basins for Control of Urban Runoff," *1983 International Symposium on Urban Hydrology, Hydraulics and Sediment Control,* University of Kentucky, Lexington, 1983.

DRIVER, N., AND TASKER, G. D., *Techniques for Estimation of Storm-Runoff Loads, Volumes, and Selected Constituent Concentrations,* USGS Open File Report 88–191, USGS, Denver, 1988.

EPA, *Results of the Nationwide Urban Runoff Program, Final Report,* U.S. Environmental Protection Agency, NTIS PB84-18552, Washington D.C., 1983.

EPA, *Methodology for Analysis of Detention Basins for Control of Urban Runoff Quality,* U.S. Environmental Protection Agency, EPA440/5-87-001, Washington D.C., September, 1986.

FAIRFAX COUNTY, *Preliminary Design Manual for BMP Facilities,* Department of Environmental Management, Fairfax County, Va., 1980.

FLORIDA CONCRETE PRODUCTS ASSOCIATION, *Pervious Pavement Manual,* Orlando Fla., 1988.

GOFORTH, G. F., DINIZ, E. V., AND RAUHUT, J. B., *Stormwater Hydrological Characteristics of Porous and Conventional Paving Systems,* Report PB84–123 728, Municipal Environmental Research Laboratory, Environmental Protection Agency, Cincinnati, Ohio, 1984.

GRIZZARD, T. J., RANDALL, C. W., WEAND, B. L., AND ELLIS, K. L., "Effectiveness of

Extended Detention Ponds," *Urban Runoff Quality—Impact and Quality Enhancement Technology,* American Society of Civil Engineers, New York, 1986.

HAMLIN, H., AND BAUTISTA, J., "On-the-spot Tests Check Gutter Capacity," *The American City,* April, 1965.

HARTIGAN, J. P., "Basis for Design of Wet Detention Basin BMP's," *Design of Urban Runoff Quality Controls,* American Society of Civil Engineers, New York, 1989.

HEISE, P., "Infiltration Systems," *Proceedings of a Seminar in Surface Water Technology,* Fagernes, 1977. (In Danish)

HOAGLAND, W., NIEMCZYNOWICZ, J., AND WAHLMAN, T., "The Unit Superstructure During the Construction Period," *Science and Total Environment,* 1987.

HUBBARD, T. P., AND SAMPLE, T. E., "Source Tracing of Toxicants in Storm Drains," *Design of Urban Runoff Quality Controls,* American Society of Civil Engineers, New York, 1989.

LAKATOS, D. F., AND MCNEMER, L. J., "Wetlands and Stormwater Pollution Management," *Wetland Hydrology, Proceedings of National Wetland Symposium,* Chicago, 1987.

LAWRENCE, A. I., AND GOYEN, A. G., "Improving Urban Stormwater Quality—An Australian Strategy," *Proceedings of the 4th International Conference on Urban Storm Drainage,* Lausanne, Switzerland, 1987.

LIVINGSTON, E. H., "Use of Wetlands for Urban Stormwater Management," *Design of Urban Runoff Quality Controls,* American Society of Civil Engineers, New York, 1989.

LIVINGSTON, E. H., et al., *The Florida Development Manual: A Guide to Sound Land and Water Management,* Department of Environmental Regulation, Tallahassee Fla., June, 1988.

Local Disposal of Storm Water—Design Manual, Swedish Association of Water and Sewage Works, Publication VAV, 1983, (In Swedish)

MURRAY, J., SCHMIDT, S. D., AND SPENCER, D. R., "Nonpoint Pollution: First Step in Control," *Design of Urban Runoff Quality Controls,* American Society of Civil Engineers, New York, 1989.

NORTHERN VIRGINIA DISTRICT PLANNING COMMISSION, *Washington Metropolitan Area Urban Runoff Demonstration Project,* Annapolis Md., April, 1983.

OSCAYAN, P., "Design of Sediment Basins for Control of Construction Sites," *Proceedings of a National Symposium on Urban Hydrology and Sediment Control,* University of Kentucky, 1975.

PRATT, C. J., "Permeable Pavement for Stormwater Quality Enhancement," *Urban Stormwater Quality Enhancement,* American Society of Civil Engineers, New York, 1990.

RANDALL, C. W., ELLIS, K., GRIZZARD, T. J., AND KNOCKE W. R., "Urban Runoff Pollutant Removal by Sedimentation," *Stormwater Detention Facilities,* American Society of Civil Engineers, New York, 1982.

ROESNER, L. A., BURGESS, E. H., AND ALDRICH, J. A., "The Hydrology of Urban Runoff Quality Management," *Proceedings of a Water Resources Planning and Management Conference,* American Society of Civil Engineers, New Orleans, May, 1991.

ROESNER, L. A., URBONAS, B. R., AND SONNEN, M. B., Eds., *Design of Urban Runoff Quality Controls,* Proceedings of an Engineering Foundation Conference on Current Practice and Design Criteria for Urban Quality Control, American Society of Civil Engineers, New York, 1989.

SCHUELER, T. R., *Controlling Urban Runoff: A Practical Manual for Planning and Designing Urban Best Management Practices,* Metropolitan Washington Water Resources Planning Board, Washington, D.C., 1987.

SCHUELER, T. R., AND GALLI, J., "The Environmental Impact of Stormwater Ponds," *Proceedings of an Engineering Foundation Conference on Effects of Urban Runoff on Receiving Systems, August 1991, Crested Butte, Colorado,* American Society of Civil Engineers, New York, 1992.

SHAVER, E., "Sand Filter Design for Water Quality Treatment," *Proceedings of an Engineering Foundation Conference on Effects of Urban Runoff on Receiving Systems, August 1991, Crested Butte, Colorado,* American Society of Civil Engineers, New York, 1992.

SMITH, D. R., "Evaluation of Concrete Grid Pavements in the United States," *Proceedings of the Second Conference on Concrete Block Paving,* Delft, Australia, 1984.

STRECKER, E. W., PALHEGYI, G. E., AND DRISCOLL, E. D., "The Use of Wetlands for Control of Urban Runoff Pollution in the U.S.A.," *Proceedings of the Fifth International Conference on Urban Storm Drainage,* Osaka, Japan, July, 1990.

TORNO, H. C., Ed., *Urban Stormwater Quality Enhancement,* Proceedings of an Engineering Foundation Conference in Davos, Switzerland, October 1989, American Society of Civil Engineers, New York, 1990.

TORNO, H. C., MARSALEK, J., AND DESBORES, M., Eds., *Urban Runoff Pollution,* Proceedings of a NATO Advanced Research Workshop, Springer-Verlag, Berlin, 1986.

USGS, *Constituent-Load Changes in Urban Stormwater Runoff Routed Through a Detention Pond—Wetland System in Central Florida,* Water Resources Investigations 85-4310, U.S. Geological Survey, Tallahassee, Fla., 1986.

URBONAS, B. R., GUO, C. Y., AND TUCKER, L. S., "Optimization of Stormwater Quality Capture Volume," *Urban Stormwater Quality Enhancement,* American Society of Civil Engineers, New York, 1990.

URBONAS, B. R., AND ROESNER, L. A., Eds., *Urban Runoff Quality—Impact and Quality Enhancement Technology,* Proceedings of an Engineering Foundation Conference, American Society of Civil Engineers, New York, 1986.

URBONAS, B. R., AND RUZZO, W., "Standardization of Detention Pond Design for Phosphorus Removal," in Torno, H. C., Marsalek, J., and Desbores, M., Eds., *Urban Runoff Pollution,* NATO ASI Series Vol. G10, Springer-Verlag, Berlin 1986.

VEENHUIS, J. E., PARISH, J. H., AND JENNINGS, M. E., "Monitoring and Design of Stormwater Control Basin," *Design of Urban Runoff Quality Controls,* American Society of Civil Engineers, New York, 1989.

WANIELISTA, M. P., "Best Management Practices Overview," *Urban Runoff Quality—Impact and Quality Enhancement Technology,* American Society of Civil Engineers, New York, 1986.

WANIELISTA, M. P., YOUSEF, Y. A., HARPER, H. H., AND CASSAGNOL, C. L., "Detention With Effluent Filtration for Stormwater Management," *Proceedings of the 2nd International Conference on Urban Storm Drainage,* Urbana Ill., 1981.

WARD, A., HAAN, T., AND TAPP, J., *The Deposits Sedimentation Pond Design Manual,* Institute for Mining and Mineral Resources, University of Kentucky, Lexington, 1979.

WATER RESOURCES ADMINISTRATION, *Guidelines for Constructing Wetland Stormwater Basins,* Maryland Department of Natural Resources, Annapolis Md., March, 1987.

WHALEN, P. J., AND CALLUM, M. G., *An Assessment of Urban Land Use: Stormwater Runoff Quality Relationships and Treatment Efficiencies of Selected Stormwater Management Systems,* South Florida Water Management District, Technical Publication 88-9, 1988.

WHIPPLE, W., AND HUNTER, J. V., "Settleability of Urban Runoff Pollution," *Journal of the Water Pollution Control Federation,* Vol. 53, 1981.

WIEGAND, C., SCHUELER, T., CHITTENDEN, W., AND JELLICK, D., "Cost of Urban Quality Controls," *Design of Urban Runoff Quality Controls,* American Society of Civil Engineers, New York, 1989.

Appendix A
Common Conversion Factors
Used in Book

To Convert	Into	Multiply By
acre feet	cubic meters	1234
acres	hectares	0.4047
cubic feet	cubic meters	0.02832
cubic feet	liters	28.32
cubic feet/acre	cubic meters/hetare	0.070
cubic feet/second	cubic meters/second	0.02832
cubic inches	milliliters	16.39
cubic yards	cubic meters	0.7646
feet	centimeters	30.48
feet	meters	0.3048
feet/second	meters/second	0.3048
foot-pounds (force)	joules	1.356
gallons/minute/square foot	liters/second/square meter	0.679
gallons	cubic centimeters	3,785.0
gallons	cubic meters	3.785×10^{-3}
gallons	liters	3.785
gallons/minute	liters/second	0.0631
inches	centimeters	2.54
inches	millimeters	25.4
miles	kilometers	1.609
million gallons/day	liters/second	43.86
pounds force	newtons	4.448
pounds/square inch (psi)	pascals (N/m^3)	6897
square feet	square meters	0.0929

Index